Charles Bartlett's daughter Paula in 1911

I Shall Not Be Away Long

The First World War Letters of Lt Col Charles Bartlett

Presented by ANDREW TATHAM

Foreword by WILLIAM BOYD

Arvo Veritas

A donation from the proceeds of this book will be made in aid of the Royal National Institute of Blind People (RNIB) in honour of Charles Bartlett★ who made such efforts on the behalf of blind people.

A donation from the proceeds of *'A Group Photograph - Before, Now & In-Between'* will be going to the International Tree Foundation in honour of Donald Stileman★, Man of the Trees.

First published by Arvo Veritas in 2020
www.arvoveritas.co.uk

Letters of Lt Col Charles Frederick Napier Bartlett
© The Estate of Lt Col Charles Frederick Napier Bartlett

Foreword © William Boyd

Picture credits, see p.461

Research, editing, lay-out, unquoted text and notes,
and most present-day photographs by Andrew Tatham

All enquiries to andrew@groupphoto.co.uk

British Library Cataloguing-in-Publication Data
A catalogue record for this book is
available from the British Library

ISBN 978-0-9935302-2-7

Printed and bound by Healeys, Ipswich

www.ishallnotbeawaylong.co.uk

www.groupphoto.co.uk

To Gay, granddaughter of Charles & Margaret Bartlett.

Her generosity in sharing these letters
has made so many things possible.

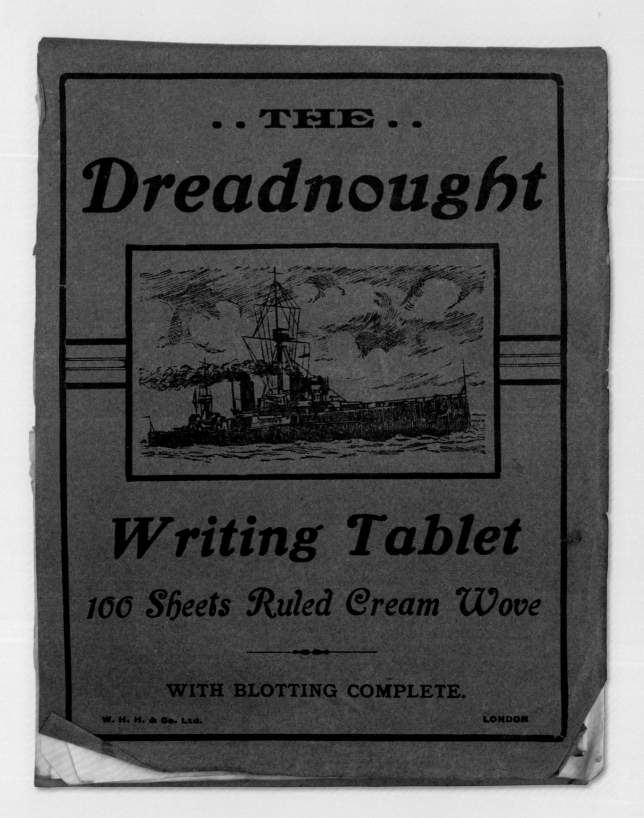

A pad of writing paper of the type requested by Charles Bartlett in his letter of 29th June 1916.

Contents

List of Maps

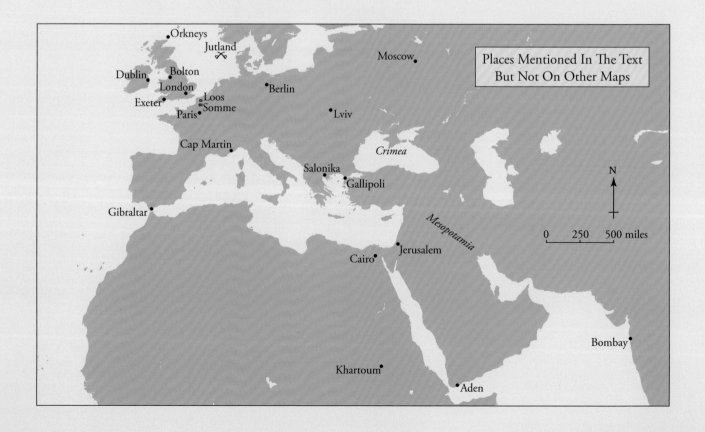

Foreword by William Boyd

Lt Colonel Charles Bartlett, the author of these revelatory and compelling letters, is a figure that could easily come from a novel by Evelyn Waugh or J.G.Farrell. Bourgeois, privileged, raffish, lazy, self-indulgent, hedonistic, with a wispy fair moustache and a weak chin, his attitude to life appears utterly typical of his class. However, no-one can prefigure where the most telling witnesses to history will spring from and Charles Frederick Napier Bartlett is exemplary in this regard.

Born in 1878 – four years after Winston Churchill, to place him in a context we can grasp – Charles Bartlett's world was, like Churchill's, entirely Late Victorian with all the rigid value systems that were implied by the classification. Bartlett was 22 years old when Queen Victoria died. The British Empire was in its pomp; half of the map of the world was imperial red; the Englishman, and his peculiar ethos, reigned supreme, unchallenged. Modestly educated at public school (Rugby), with a substantial trust fund due on his 21st birthday, Bartlett went straight into the army, that professional safety-net for the not-very-bright sons of the well-heeled. In his case it was to the Royal Berkshire Regiment where he was commissioned as a 2nd Lieutenant in 1900.

Bartlett left his regiment for unspecified reasons in 1906 (possibly as a result of some financial improprieties), and then, to his family's quiet shock, married a very young actress, Peggy Bethel – the recipient of almost all of these letters. When war broke out in 1914 he was 36 years old, and he re-joined his former regiment. He was elderly to be returning as a junior officer – most of his peers were in their early 20s – and because of his previous military experience he was quickly promoted to higher ranks. Moreover, his life and times had already shaped him, irrevocably, as his letters demonstrate. He is, in a way, a classic throwback, and all the more fascinating for it.

Once the war was underway, and once the couple were separated, letter writing on an almost daily basis – at both ends of the correspondence – sustained husband and wife. One forgets how, in that era of super-efficient postal services, letters were almost like emails. Even on the front-line Bartlett complains when his wife's letters don't arrive promptly.

These letters home, as they steadily accumulate, provide a wealth of astonishing detail and paint a guileless but superbly textured picture of the mundane realities in the life of an officer in the British Army as the war progresses. Bartlett's letters to Peggy detail the minutiae of army life, all the material that doesn't make it into official histories. One is reminded – and one needs reminding – that most soldiers in any war throughout history, even the privileged officer class, quickly become reluctant Stoics as their lives become a constant search for modest comforts – warmth, dryness, victuals, alcohol, safety from harm. The same subjects – the same gripes – appear again and again. The weather, the billets, the tedium, the deplorable state of French WCs, food, drink, health and discomforts dominate. Because Bartlett is writing home to his young wife the language is at times almost clichéd – *'we're giving the Bosche absolute hell'* – and the sentiments, though fondly expressed – *'My darling*

wife' – are familiar and worn with over-use. And then a letter of the 27th September 1915 draws you up short.

Bartlett's battalion takes part in the Battle of Loos, whose first day is second only to the Somme's in its grim casualty count. *'Our officers fared as follows,'* he writes, tersely. *'Brakspear wounded in knee / Oldman wounded / Hanna missing believed dead reported seriously wounded / Tosetti wounded, not seriously / Paramore missing no hope / Cassells dead / Berlein dead / Peacock dead / Glen missing'* and so on for another nine names. What makes it so chilling is that many of these people have already figured in Bartlett's letters home as he detailed anecdotes and grumbles to Peggy about life in the battalion. The jolt of this grim reality is palpable and, for the reader, the tenor of the letters home changes thereafter, despite the humdrum realities of life after the battle – food, billets, discomfort, ill-health – coming to the fore once again. We become all too aware of the desperate, fatal subtext of the First World War; it thrums as a kind of baleful basso profundo drumroll under the banter and the reportage – *'a ghastly business too awful to describe,'* Bartlett says.

The letters continue as the war continues. Bartlett is promoted to Lt Colonel and becomes the CO of the battalion and his responsibilities increase dramatically. The Royal Berkshires participate in the Battle of the Somme in 1916 and more casualties are recorded. Despite his shortcomings as an individual Bartlett seems to have measured up as a soldier. However, the sentimental verities of Charles and Peggy's married life come under strain and the resolution of their problems adds a poignant and all-too-human undertone to the reports from the front line. The letters home cease in March 1917 when Bartlett is sent to the Côte d'Azur to convalesce after a period of ill health. He never returned to active service. He died of pneumonia in Putney, London, in December 1940.

Of course, these letters were never intended for posterity – and thereby lies their appeal. The voice, the attitudes, the feelings, the anecdotes, the remorseless toll of warfare reverberate in them with an absolute authenticity. But they only achieve their full resonance as a result of Andrew Tatham's extraordinary research into the background and context and his copious and fascinating annotation to the throwaway remarks and references. Lt Colonel Bartlett's life is illuminated and referenced in a way he could never possibly have imagined and we are all the richer for it.

This is not only a beautiful-looking book, generously and wonderfully illustrated, it is also a remarkable human document, as rich in detail and commentary on the human condition as a long novel. Tens of thousands of books have been written about the First World War and who would have thought that, over a hundred years since it ended, there was anything more to say. But *'I Shall Not Be Away Long'* fully earns its place in the Pantheon of literature about the Great War. We come away from it amused, moved, informed, baffled, shocked, saddened and, with a bit of luck, wiser. It is a classic of its kind.

William Boyd, London, May 2020

THE OFFICERS OF THE 8ᵀᴴ BATTALION ROYAL BERKSHIRE REGIMENT – SANDHILL CAMP, WILTSHIRE – MAY 1915

TOP ROW: 1 Harold COHEN, **2** George Bertrand COOTE, **3** Cecil Stedman CLOAKE, **4** Brian Dudley BRIGG, **5** Thomas Edward ALLEN, **6** Alfred Percival DOBSON, **7** Frank Mariner SUMPSTER, **8** Geoffrey Heslop BLACK, **9** Cyril Arthur WILLIAMSON, **10** Harold Charles Linford KEABLE, **11** Harold Vivian WOODFORD, **12** Mervyn Phippen PUGH, **13** William Howe BISSLEY

SECOND ROW: 1 William Franklin George JOSEPH, **2** Richard Stephen Pierrepont POYNTZ, **3** Clifford SALMAN, **4** Thomas Bernard LAWRENCE, **5** Charles Randolph WATSON, **6** Henry Cyril THORNE, **7** Donald Fenwick STILEMAN, **8** Thomas Gordon PEACOCK, **9** William George HOBBS, **10** Louis Arthur KLEMANTASKI, **11** Frederic Clifford GARDENNER, **12** Douglas Eric FOOT, **13** Gordon Fraser MARSH, **14** Thomas Gerald ROBINSON, **15** Morice Bell THOMPSON

THIRD ROW: 1 Leslie Herman BERLEIN, **2** George Henry HEWITT, **3** Charles Gordon PARAMORE, **4** Lionel Huddlestone EDWARDS, **5** Charles Frederick Napier BARTLETT, **6** William Crawford WALTON, **7** Ronald William BRAKSPEAR, **8** Douglas TOSETTI, **9** Douglas Murray HANNA, **10** Wilfred Southey Deare OLDMAN, **11** James BARROW *(Those with coloured names are enlarged below & feature strongly in the letters)*

BOTTOM ROW: 1 Wilfrid Lawson CLARKE, **2** Aubyn Redmond ROUSE, **3** Basil Perrin HICKS, **4** David Corse GLEN, **5** Edward Sidney Beaumont TAVENER, **6** Cyril SPARTALI, **7** Hugh Kennedy CASSELS

Introduction

In the hundred years since the First World War many voices have been heard in poems, letters, diaries and interviews and it may seem that there could be nothing new in terms of first-hand accounts that might shed a different light on that time. Often what has remained and been valued are the writings and recollections of a few who are known for their earnestness or insight or military knowledge with their writing done removed from the action and with a wider audience in mind or a particular axe to grind. Rarer is the candid voice of someone with a live-for-today spirit who is reacting almost uncensored to events as they are happening, and with no view to posterity. That is what you get in the letters of Lieutenant Colonel Charles Bartlett, and not only that but his social and military rank as well as his sociable nature means that you get to meet all manner of other interesting characters from all walks of life along the way. Before I tell you a bit about the letters themselves, let me describe how I first came to be interested in Charles Bartlett and what led me to find his letters.

In March 1994, after a visit to the Imperial War Museum, I started to research my own family's First World War history. I knew that my great-grandfather had been some kind of general and after going up into my parents' loft and reading his letters, I wanted to find out more. I returned to the Imperial War Museum, this time to the Reading Room where his Battalion's Regimental History was laid out ready for me. On turning the pages, I came upon the group photograph opposite. It is a portrait of the officers of the 8th Battalion, Royal Berkshire Regiment, and sitting in the centre is my great-grandfather, Colonel William Crawford Walton, their commanding officer. I had had an idea for artwork based on a First World War group photograph and the short version of what happened next is that I decided that this photograph would be the one on which I would centre my research and creation – and only 21 years later the resulting artwork formed the basis of an exhibition at In Flanders Fields Museum in Ypres and

the book *'A Group Photograph – Before, Now & In-Between'*.

In the process of this project, I contacted the families of all 46 men in the picture. I hoped that I would find some interesting pictures and artefacts but never dreamed of the extraordinary richness of the material that came my way. For the most part these amazing heirlooms had only been seen by their families and passed down through the

generations or hidden in attics and brought out for the first time in many years as the result of my enquiries. One of the greatest of these treasures was associated with the man highlighted in the photograph opposite. Seated at my great-grandfather's right hand, he was the Battalion second-in-command and his name was Charles Frederick Napier Bartlett. His family had taken a lot of finding.

Initially all I had to start my search were the names of the men as listed underneath the photograph but, though there were a few errors of initials and spelling, it didn't take me too long to identify them in Army records. I soon found that Charles Bartlett had been born in 1878 and had been an officer in the regular Army before the war, one of only two from the group photograph with that experience (the other being my great-grandfather). Even so he had still only

been a Lieutenant when he left in 1906 after 6 years' service and here he was in 1915 at the age of 37 as a Major & second-in-command of a Battalion of 1000 men. Not only that but he also went on to take over the command of the Battalion during both the Battle of Loos and the Battle of the Somme. He left the front for the last time in March 1917 after which time he only served at home. Military records took me to when he finally left the Army in 1921. I would have to look elsewhere for the rest of his life story.

At this time right at the beginning of my project I was extremely lucky still to be able to interview a primary source very close at hand. My Gran had been a 14-year-old girl when she visited her father's Battalion at their training camp during the summer of 1915 (in the picture I later found of that visit, *(left)*, she is in the centre and Charles Bartlett has his arms round her and her sister). She was now 94 and living in an old people's home. She would often forget things which had happened only minutes before but there was a lot that was etched into her long-term memory which was reachable with the right prompts. I read out the names of the men in the photograph and several of them brought a response of *'oh, yes'* and then some snippets of detail. One of these was Major Bartlett and she warmly remembered him as *'friendly and kind'*, that he was married to a *'famousish singer'* and that he had had *'wife trouble'*. I had so much on my mind at the time that I didn't think to ask her more about that but it's amazing that a 14-year-old from that era would have had such an insight, and, as you will see, it proved to be the case (though when you've read this book you'll realise that it would also be fair to say that his wife had husband trouble).

So Charles Bartlett had started to come alive to me as a person – I knew his full name and age, that he was married and had survived until at least 1921, but I was still a long way from being able to connect him to his family and the wider world, particularly considering that at that time the Internet and online genealogy databases did not exist. There were no computerised indexes of births, marriages and deaths or of wills or of the ten-yearly censuses of the British population. It was a case of having to trawl through huge numbers of paper indexes and documents in archives.

A search of the annual probate indexes up to when he would have been 100 did not turn up a will for him, but along the way I spotted some other Bartletts who had the third name Napier and on reading their wills I found Charles mentioned as their brother. Things were starting to come together but my efforts to find any of the next generations were stymied by a lack of addresses and the fact that searching for current contact details was then only possible via a visit to the library and a manual search of the 110 phone books that covered the UK.

Luckily I was making better progress with the searches for many of the other men in the group photograph, and it was when visiting my first contact with the families that I got my next major lead for Charles Bartlett. John Cloake had the notebook containing hand-written First World War memoirs of his father Cecil (third from left in the top row of the group photograph). Right at the end were two letters from Charles Bartlett making arrangements for a reunion dinner in 1937. Prompted by that, I then made a search of the death indexes (I had been putting this off because it was so laborious – with an index for each quarter of each year, searching for 60 years after the First World War could involve pulling out 240 heavy indexes – and the search could be for nought if they had died abroad, as was the case on a few occasions). His death was in the index for the first quarter of 1941 and feeling that my luck was in, I decided to look for his marriage, which I found in the second quarter of 1908. When I received the certificates a week later, there were two particularly interesting pieces of information. Firstly, at his marriage in 1908 he was 30 whilst his wife was 19, and secondly, when he died in December 1940, the wife who reported his death was not the woman he had married in 1908.

By now we were in 1998 and the next big thing was the public release of the service records of First World War army officers. These turned out to be of huge value to my search as many of them contained details of the men's families, but in the case of Charles Bartlett I was disappointed to find that his record no longer existed. In the end though, my persistence would be rewarded when I wasn't quite expecting it.

In late 1999 I was invited to South Africa by the family of one of the other men in the group photograph and in preparation for my trip I remembered that a nephew of Charles Bartlett had been listed in a will with an address in Johannesburg in 1956, and crucially that he too had Napier as his third name. After my cousin picked me up at the airport, I mentioned this to her – that I was looking for Bartletts and that all the men had the third name Napier – and she said, *'Well, I live on Napier Road – that's got to be a good sign'* and when we got into her house almost the first thing she did was hand me the phone book. There among the Bartletts were two with three initials, third initial "N". Normally I wrote to people to introduce myself and my project rather than just ringing out of the blue, but with the schedule of my trip there just wasn't time for that so I picked one of the numbers and rang it. Very soon I found myself sitting down for a lunch of ostrich neck stew with two great-nephews of Charles Bartlett. Yes, their father was the nephew mentioned in the will, and yes, their third names were Napier but not only did they know nothing about their great uncle Charles, they had never heard of him. Their mother was still alive and might know something so after lunch we went to meet her.

It turned out that she had heard of Charles and not in a good way. She told me a story connected to a piece of family silver. She showed me a large biscuit box in the shape of a drum with drumsticks on top of its hinged lid, and the story was that Charles, at the time being a bit broke, had secretly pawned it. Charles's brother was furious when he found out and managed to buy it back but Charles's reputation as the black sheep of the family was sealed.

She also showed me the large family bible that commemorated the marriage of Charles's parents and listed all of their children along with their birth and death dates. Charles was listed but there were no details of any offspring for him. I thought the trail was going cold again only for them to point me to Aunt Kit who was living in an old people's home in Shropshire and who would surely know something to help me.

So when I got back to England, I did get in touch with Aunt Kit and after a hesitant start as I established my bona fides, she told me that her uncle Charles's only daughter had died a few years before but that she had had three children. She wasn't in touch with them now but crucially she gave me the married name of Charles's daughter and that was enough for me with

one final push in the archives to at last find a descendant of Charles Bartlett.

By this time the electoral register and phone book had been computerised so I was soon able to write to Charles's granddaughter, and then, bingo, I was speaking to her. In amongst telling me some family stories, she mentioned that she had a few of his letters from the war but that I probably wouldn't be interested as it was day-to-day stuff like *'thank you for the grouse'*. I had a feeling that I would be interested but even so I was bowled over when on visiting her she opened a large biscuit tin and I saw bundles and bundles of letters. There were 341 written from when he first arrived in France in August 1915 until he left in March 1917. Incredibly generously, she allowed me to borrow them and then after three days spent photocopying, and scarcely believing my luck, I settled down to read.

They really are the most extraordinary collection of spontaneous jottings and give a window on his world on so many levels. There are the relationships with his wife, his family and friends, and his brother officers and soldiers as they all deal with the ever-changing abnormality of the war. There is the everyday routine of the Army in France as well as the chaos of battle and the contrast of all that with life on the home front. He is senior enough to have a bigger picture of events but still he is right at the sharp end, living through the conditions of the front line and reporting incidents as they occur. He believes in his cause but is not po-faced about it and is keen on saving his own skin and enjoying the pleasures of life. Being of the moneyed sports and social set, he is not a fan of the intellectual, but he is able to put his thoughts clearly into words. Though by default he cultivates a certain bluffness, and tends to be playful and kind, he can let out his feelings and appear angry, brutal, depressed or frightened. He likes a good gossip and he was of high enough rank to get away with writing the truth of things that is often missing from the letters of others writing with greater attention from the Army censors. Surprises abound, not just in the letters but in the incredible stories I have uncovered of the people he mentions along the way. Those include big stars known from his and his wife's work in the theatre and show no-one was immune from the effects of the war.

The very first sentence of his opening letter provides the title for this book: *'I shall not be away long'*. That he was so wrong about that becomes abundantly clear and should serve as a warning to us all.

Life before the Letters

Many of the details of Charles Bartlett's early life, family and friends come out in the course of reading the letters but some introduction is necessary to set the scene before we start.

Charles Frederick Napier Bartlett was born into huge wealth and privilege. Arriving in the world on Friday 12th April 1878, he was the seventh of eight children. His father, John Edward Bartlett, was a Buckinghamshire banker who upheld the Victorian patrician tradition. That meant not only owning land and creating wealth as a partner in banks in Buckingham and Aylesbury as well as being Chairman of the Board of the Bucks & Oxon Union Bank – but also giving generously of his time and money to local institutions and societies, including acting as treasurer to both the local hospital and Board of Health, and sitting on numerous committees for the County as well as for the Visitors of the County Lunatic Asylum (which was in the local village of Stone). As if that was not enough he had been an active justice of the peace since qualifying as a magistrate in 1849 at the age of 25. He was highly connected within the fabric of Buckinghamshire society (being friendly with Baron de Rothschild who lived nearby) and would go on to be High Sheriff and a Deputy Lieutenant of the County. I have not found a photograph of John Edward Bartlett but the local Methodist Chapel has his name carved into its foundation stone, *(left)*, and that seems to make a fitting portrait of a man who was so central to his local community. His were high ideals to follow and though they would provide the building blocks to Charles's outlook on life, he would find it difficult to fully live up to his father's example.

Disaster struck in 1888. Firstly in January Charles's sister Edith died aged 18 after suffering for a year with liver cancer. Soon after that blow, the health of Charles's father started to fail and despite seeking a cure in Bournemouth and then at the spa in Buxton, he died of prostate cancer in August. He was 64 and Charles was left fatherless at the age of 10. I don't know who took over as the father figure in Charles's life but in among the few items of early Bartlett family memorabilia is the photograph to the *left*. The uniform rules it out from being Charles's father but I wonder if this was an uncle or cousin who might have inclined Charles towards his later choice of a military career.

In his father's will, Charles was left £10,000 as well as his father's lands in Shropshire. In all, the value was later estimated at being over £15,000 which in today's terms would make him well over a millionaire. Being only ten, the money was held in trust until his 21st birthday. He continued in school, though it looks like the decision was taken to bring him closer to home. His first school, Hazelhurst, was 70 miles away in Frant on the Sussex-Kent border, whereas in the 1891 census he was just 16 miles from home at Lockers Park School near Hemel Hempstead. No pupil records remain to tell of Charles's days at either school.

Peverel Court, (opposite), was the home of the Bartlett family from soon after it was built in 1864 through to 1902. It is set in extensive grounds near the village of Stone two miles from Aylesbury. Of rather a rambling construction, it is more a series of interconnected buildings than being to a single overarching design. Still, there was enough room for this large family and their guests and at least eight live-in servants. Very little has changed in the look of the house from their time there except that a large new wing has appeared in the grounds to extend it in its current use as an old people's residential care home called Bartlett's. The extensive lawn is still used for croquet and it has the sort of panoramic view looking out high above the valley towards the Chilterns that makes you feel as if you command all that you survey.

Charles Bartlett's first known letter, to an unnamed uncle:

My dear Uncle

    I have a sweet little pot of musk. My holidays begin in 4 days. How is Grannie? will you tell her that Vic is longing to see her. We are going to have a Jersey cow. We had a game of cricket last night. Miss Eding got 6 runs and I got 11. I have painted 5 pictures and a half. When you come you shall hear me play my new duet.

With love and kisses,

    I remain,

      your loving nephew,

        Charlie

Charlie <u>can</u> do better than this, but Miss E did not let him make a copy first, it is <u>all</u> his <u>own</u> composition.

Even after Charles went to Rugby in the winter of 1892, he didn't do much to trouble the school historians. The only traces I saw of him in the school magazine *The Meteor* were in November 1894 with the report of his promotion from Private to Lance Corporal in the Rugby School Rifle Volunteer Corps, and in the summer of 1895, soon before he left, when his performance in some house cricket matches was noted (in one he took a catch and scored 37 out of 172, being caught and bowled by Cartwright

minor, and in another he scored 33 out of his house's total of 72). He also appears in a number of school group photographs *(above)* where you can see him growing from coy uncertainty into a self-confidence bordering on arrogance.

On leaving Rugby, he followed his brother Edward into the 3rd Battalion of the Oxfordshire Light Infantry, often then still known by its old name of the Royal Buckinghamshire (King's Own) Militia. The Militia was part-time but included periods of full-time

training and it was seen as a backdoor route to a regular Army commission for those not bright enough to beat the tough competition for places at the Army's officer training establishments. He was first commissioned as a militia 2nd Lieutenant in July 1895, but resigned the next month (having just turned 17, he was underage). In March 1899, the month before coming into his inheritance on his 21st birthday, he was commissioned with them again (as *opposite*, fresh-faced amongst a lot of much older soldiers).

Charles Bartlett received his regular commission as a 2nd Lieutenant in the Royal Berkshire Regiment on 21st April 1900 and the photographs *opposite* are from his army career, during which he served in Gibraltar, Woking, Dublin, Egypt and Khartoum (note the Royal Berkshires' policeman-like helmet with top spike at top right).

The *above* group shows the officers of 1st Battalion Royal Berkshire Regiment at Inkerman Barracks, Woking, Surrey. It was probably taken on their arrival there in April 1903, as the commanding officer Lt Col Carter left the battalion that month. In the key below for each officer there is: their age in this photograph, their age at death, highest known rank, any notes including the cause of their death if they died younger than 50. Those with surnames underlined appear elsewhere in this book.

TOP ROW: ❶ Lt Arthur Mervyn <u>HOLDSWORTH</u> (27, 40, Lt Col, ✝ 7th July 1916, *died of wounds during the Battle of the Somme with 2nd Royal Berkshires*), ❷ Lt Charles Frederick Napier <u>BARTLETT</u> (25, 62, Lt Col), ❸ Capt Edward Henry BLUNT (38, 78, Capt, *severely wounded in January 1900 during the Boer War; in the 1911 census his wife omitted herself as a means of suffragette protest, but included a 'rather deaf' 12½-year-old 'stud dog' called 'King of the Brownies' & two cats called Francis & Gertrude*), ❹ Capt & Adjutant William Redmond Prendergast KEMMIS-BETTY (34, 65, Lt Col), ❺ Capt Alexander Scott TURNER (34, 70, Maj, *captured 21 days after the outbreak of the war and held prisoner for over 4 years*).

2ND ROW: ❶ Capt Arthur Gabell MACDONALD (28, 70, Lt Col), ❷ Lt Richard Prentice HARVEY (29, 41, Maj, ✝ 9th May 1915 *died of wounds during the Battle of Aubers Ridge with 2nd Royal Berkshires, leaving a widow and 4 little girls; his family's company made the sherry Harvey's Bristol Cream*), ❸ Lt Cecil PIERCE (25, 73, Col), ❹ Lt Frederick John GOSSET (29, 49, Maj, *when on sick leave in 1918 he got in trouble for drinking 12 whiskeys and 8 bottles of beer, and using filthy language and telling coarse stories in front of the waitresses at his depot; died of kidney disease and pneumonia*), ❺ Capt Arthur Stephen CAVE (37, 80, Maj), ❻ Capt Robert Bruce SWINTON (38, 39, Capt, *died of Bright's disease & heart failure*).

3RD ROW: ❶ Capt Charles MOORE (37, 45, Maj, *died of a haemorrhage due to a duodenal ulcer*), ❷ Maj William Kerr McCLINTOCK (44, 81, Brig-Gen), ❸ Lt Col Francis Charles <u>CARTER</u> (44, 72, Brig-Gen), ❹ Maj Ramsay Gordon <u>CHASE</u> (41, 72, Lt Col).

FRONT ROW: ❶ Capt George Holme <u>ARBUTHNOT</u> **(standing)** (38, 87, Lt Col), ❷ Lt & Quartermaster James Harry REDSTONE (38, 77, Maj & QM), ❸ 2Lt Guy William HOPTON (21, 33, Capt, *son of a general*, ✝ 28th July 1915, *shot dead at Ploegstreet with 5th Royal Berkshires, leaving a widow*), ❹ Lt Thomas Edward CAREW-HUNT (28, 76, Maj), ❺ 2Lt Percy Edmond Lindredge ELGEE (28, 82, Maj), ❻ 2Lt Alexander James <u>FRASER</u> (22, 81, Maj), ❼ 2Lt Henry Michael Lannoy HUNTER (20, 23, Lt, *died of pneumonia in Dublin*), ❽ Maj John Henry Willes SOUTHEY **(standing)** (41, 69, Maj).

On 21st February 1906, Charles Bartlett resigned his commission and left the Army. With no written evidence it is left for us to guess why that might have been. In his six years in the Army he'd reached the rank of Lieutenant and travelled a bit but not seen any active service. Maybe he was bored and wanted to seek other opportunities, but there are hints that something had gone wrong. His name is not in the lists of ex-officers returning for Regimental dinners, which strikes me as odd given how social and clubbable a man he was, and he lived in London so distance wasn't a factor. So what might have gone wrong?

When you look at him in the Royal Berkshire Regiment group photographs, he often exhibits a rather different air to his brother officers. Not only is he sitting on the ground at the front due to his junior rank, but he is usually lounging in a very laid back and unmilitary way. Still, that would not be sufficient grounds for him leaving and possibly we have to go back to an event that happened at around the time he first joined the Royal Berkshires. In June 1900 he had gone to court to sue some money lenders for fraud. Just before coming into his inheritance at the age of 21 he was short of ready cash so found the money lenders through their ads in the papers and took out loans using his inherited property as collateral. Some of the rates of interest were up to 300% and as he tried to juggle the repayments of both interest and hefty enabling fees he got drawn into other financial schemes that he did not fully understand and somehow he ended up losing his entire inheritance then valued at over £18,000. Luckily for him, before his QC had even finished his opening statement in court, news came that the defendants had decided to settle out of court. The judge insisted on reading the settlement and concluded it to be proper and just recompense and practically an admission of fraud on the part of the defendants.

The Army took a dim view of officers getting into financial difficulties so if Charles had got into a further mess with money he might have been asked to leave. It's also possible his wandering eye for the ladies might have got him into trouble.

Of course I may be seeing trouble where there was none, but whatever the reason for his leaving, he was now back to being a civilian. Evidence is pretty thin as to how he spent his time in the period leading up to the war but the next significant event in his life was his marriage in 1908.

Whilst his brothers' very grand society weddings with their hundreds of guests had been extensively reported in the local press, when Charles got married there was only a standard notice in the Marriages

column of the Morning Post. Also worthy of note is that though his parents were listed, those of his bride were not.

Margaret Robinson, *(above)*, came from a very different background to Charles's. She had been born in Bolton in Lancashire in 1888 and whilst her father Bethell Robinson had started his working career as an office clerk, he had made his name as a footballer for Preston North End right at the start of their history as a club (for more detail see p.404). After his retirement from football, he moved down to Chiswick in London but things turned bad in 1900

when his wife died from a blood clot after going into premature labour and he was left with five children under 18, including Margaret aged 11.

Despite the trauma of losing her mother, Margaret managed to make her way in the world by using her talent for the theatre. She and her sister Dolly had minor parts in the fairy play *'Blue Bell in Fairyland'* in 1902 when she was 15 – and she went on to have her first big break in 1905 and in rather a strange way. As reported in a story about her in *The Sketch* in 1909 (under her stage name of 'Peggy Bethel'), an audition was arranged with a composer and *'she was given an appointment for eleven o'clock one morning. Naturally, she kept it punctually, only to be told that she could not be seen, and must return at twelve o'clock. At twelve she again presented herself, and was told to go away until one o'clock. She waited for the composer from one till half-past, when a messenger arrived to say she would be seen at three. Then she really got annoyed for she had tickets for a matinée which she did not wish to miss. She decided, however, to keep the appointment, and at three she went back to the theatre, and was shown on to the stage, where she waited until half-past. It was very cold, and she was growing more and more impatient, so she turned to another girl who was also waiting and said rhetorically, 'When is this awful man coming?' 'The awful man is here,' a voice replied at her elbow. She turned and saw the composer, who, with dramatic opportuneness, had that moment arrived and was standing by her. Instead of being angry, as many men would have been at being spoken of in that way by a girl who was still on the threshold of the stage-door, so to speak, the composer was very kind, and did what he could to soothe Miss Bethel's feelings. She was much too upset, however, to sing, so without her doing so the composer gave her an engagement. That he has never had occasion to regret the unusual way of doing business is evident, for during the four years which have elapsed since that day Miss Bethel has never 'rested,' except when she had to take an enforced rest through being ill with appendicitis.'*

Above left: Margaret (third from left and known as 'Peggy', born 1888) as the smallest of her siblings, with, on the left, Bethell (born 1885) and Martha ('Dolly', born 1887), and, on the right, Elizabeth ('Betty', born 1882). A sister, Constance ('Connie'), would follow in 1893.

Below: Peggy and Dolly at about the time they appeared in *'Blue Bell in Fairyland'*.

Above right: Peggy from a newspaper cutting in 1907 when she appeared in a junior version of *'Miss Hook of Holland'* at the Prince of Wales's Theatre, playing Mina, a role she would reprise as an adult.

That the ——
able prices ——
management ——
sixpenny ga——
male voices,——
"Mountains
right, which wa
, this actor w
public knows
it to mention
person of Mi
hat experience
g may render
covery and mu
ism is silenced
hich Mr. Cu
ore ack be pl
ter ma
convict than
his k's
h t. bt-
n. ng
hel, es-
mat
ad d et
g dr-
ne, li-
ry ng
ere s
pr
fifteen

part, while for Miss Peggy Bethel, age not stated, but
I should think about sweet seventeen or so, who took
Miss Gracie Leigh's place for the afternoon, I desire
to place it on record that here is a genuine little discovery, full of talent, brightness, and charm, and if I
was sending the piece on the road Miss Bethel is the
lady I would secure for the part of Mina.

Miss Peggy Bethel, who appears as
"Suzanne" in "The Girl in the Taxi," at
the Opera House at Blackpool this week, is
a charming young actress-vocalist. She is
not powerful as a vocalist but there is a
delicacy of quality in her voice which is
delightful. Her admirable restraint and un-
affectedness readily wins the appreciation
of her audience. On Monday night, she was
the recipient of two handsome bouquets.

performance given by these clever young people was so
himself gr—d, that it might well be repeated for charity, or some
art and busi—wood cause.
Mr. Ruben——

FOUR HUNDREDTH PERFORMANCE.

Three ——
lustre of ——
as merril ——
comedy h ——
seems to ——
the drolle ——
able Mr. ——
than in ——
does mak ——
when dis ——
to form ——
items las ——
dian Mas ——
Miss Peggy Bethel, who played the part of Mina, in the absence of Miss
Gracie Leigh, in a style that was not mere slavish understudy, but revealed
quite considerable powers of independent and very clever interpretation. She
was excellent in the skirt song and dance. Miss Isabel Jay is still a lovely Sally
Hook, and Mr. Maurice Farkoa as the bandmaster continues to win enthu——

ments of a born prima donna in Miss Isabel Jay's
part of Sally Hook herself. There was Miss Peggy
Bethel, whose really rich humour in Miss Gracie
Leigh's part, as Mina, of the petticoats, was only
enhanced by her dimpled frankness and grace.
Then there were Miss Nancy Rich and Miss

No. 17. SONG.—MINA.

"A PINK PETTY FROM PETER."

1.

I've been spoilt such a lot—
It's *my* fault?—No, I'm sure that it's not!
It's the men won't leave me alone—
Worry me like a bone;
All day presents I get,
As if I hadn't got enough yet!
  Why, there's one more come with a note—
  It's a *new* petticoat!

  Oh, lor! dearie, oh, lor!
    What on earth shall I do
  If I get any more?

REFRAIN.

I've a little pink petty from Peter,
  And a little blue petty from John;
    And I've one, green and yellow,
    From some other fellow,
  And one that I haven't got on.
I've one made of lovely red flannel,
  That came from an Amsterdam store—
    But the point that I'm at,
    Is that *underneath* that—
  Well, I haven't got on any more!

2.

I don't know what to think—
It's enough to make any one drink!
Fancy wearing all that I've got
When the weather is hot!
When you think of the old
Ladies shivering out in the cold—
  Well, I call it positive mean,
  Me—wearing fifteen!

  Oh, lor! dearie, oh, lor!
    I shall look like a tent
  If I wear any more!

The stars of yesterday's performance were Miss
Master Arthur Bailey as Simon Slinks, Miss
Peggy Bethel in Miss Leigh's part, and Miss
Maggie Jarvis as the prima donna.

Margaret's stage name 'Peggy Bethel' came from taking her father's first name as her surname (and giving in to the fact that the press never managed to spell his name with a second 'L' by dropping it herself). She appeared in a number of shows by the big name composer of the era, Paul Rubens, and given his renowned antipathy to early starts, it seems likely that he was the *'awful man'* from her first audition, and indeed he became a supporter and friend.

In the main, Peggy had minor roles that might involve a few lines and singing and dancing in the ensemble sections of the production, but in two shows she was valued enough to also be the understudy to two stars of the day: for Gracie Leigh as 'Mina' in Paul Rubens' *'Miss Hook of Holland'*, and for Yvonne Arnaud as 'Suzanne' in *'The Girl in the Taxi'* (an English version of a German operetta that caused some outrage for its Continental immorality). Both shows ran for hundreds of performances and Peggy was called upon to take those lead roles in the absences of the stars, as well as when the productions went on tour. You can see how successful she was in the reviews **opposite**. She scored a particular hit with her turn as Mina singing *'A Pink Petty from Peter'* (**opposite, top left**, and words, **below**).

Charles must have counted himself lucky to make such a catch. When they married at St Saviour's Church, Paddington, on 6th May 1908, he was 30 and she was just 19 – see how young she looks in the pictures **on this page** with her dark-haired sister Dolly and Charles and an unknown man. I'm not sure how Charles met her, but he was soon describing himself as a private secretary in the theatre – though whether that had started before and they met through work, or he had seen her performing and their relationship led to his involvement in the theatre is unclear. I have not found the name of his boss, though it seems likely that whoever it was is the man referred to in Charles's letters with the common theatre business epithet of *'the Guvnor'*.

REFRAIN.

I've a little pink petty from Peter,
    And a little blue petty from John,
        And I've one, green and yellow,
        From some other fellow,
    And one that I haven't got on.
I've one made of lovely red flannel,
    That came from an Amsterdam store ;
        If I meet a *new* friend,
        Where on earth will it end?
    I shall never get in at the door !

3

What do English girls do?
For I hear that they wear very few !
When they do gymnastics, or run,
Then, sometimes, they wear none.
I should not have the face—
England must be a curious place ;
    Would that Milo make money, too,
    If she wore what *I* do?

Oh, lor ! dearie, oh, lor !
    I shall say something wrong
    If I say any more !

REFRAIN.

I've a little pink petty from Peter,
    And a little blue petty from John ;
        And I've one, green and yellow,
        From some other fellow,
    And one that I haven't got on.
I've one made of lovely red flannel,
    That came from an Amsterdam store—
        When I think of the strings,
        And the hundreds of things—
    Oh ! it's not safe to dance any more.

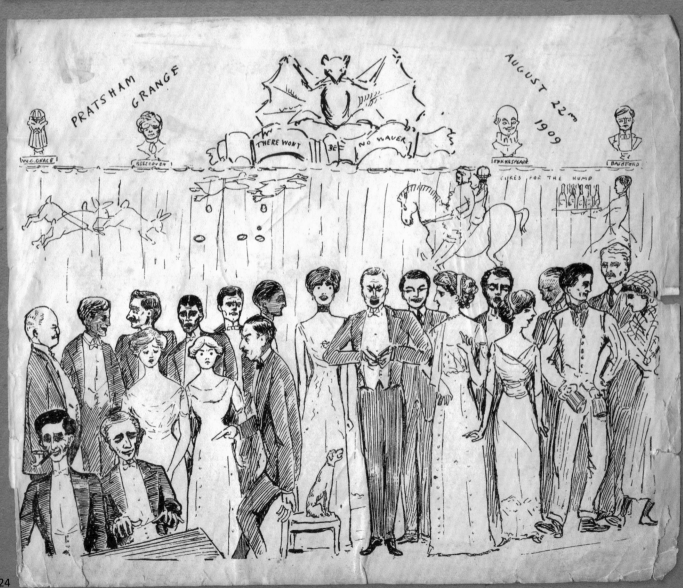

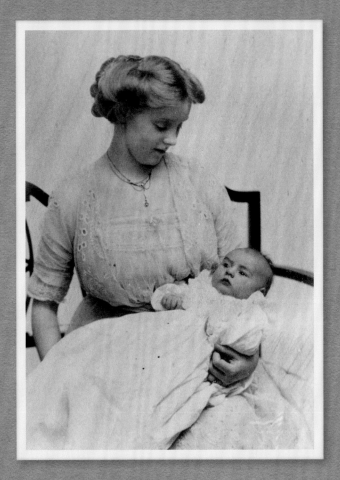

Opposite page: In August 1909, Charles and Margaret attended a country house party at Pratsham Grange, near Holmbury St Mary in Surrey. A stellar fellow guest was Paul Rubens — he can be seen at front left of both photographs (in dark jacket and white trousers, as is Charles on the right) and he is smoking a cigar at the piano on the bottom left edge of the cartoon. Margaret is seated in the front centre of the top left photo and also appears on the left of the cartoon, looking daggers as a result of something that Charles (with his finger pointing across her) has said to the woman with the demurely downcast eyes.

After their marriage Charles and Margaret moved in to apartment Nº 9 in the very swanky Stanley Mansions in Chelsea and it was there in 1910 that their only child Paula was born (her name being in honour of Paul Rubens). Margaret went back to work, even going on tour as far afield as Leeds and the Isle of Man in 1913. That same year Charles became secretary to Arthur Pearson, the newspaper magnate and champion of the blind who we will meet later.

The pictures on *this page & next* show Paula as the centre of attention (although in one hilarious photo she doesn't look very happy about it whilst Charles has his back turned in the distance ignoring both her and the photographer). The possibility of a war looks like it couldn't be further from their minds.

When war was declared on 4th August 1914 Charles did not rush to rejoin the Army. He was now 36 and maybe thought he was too old, certainly if he was to go back at his old rank of Lieutenant. He did however go straight into working for the National Relief Fund. This was set up by the Prince of Wales (later King Edward VIII but then aged 20). The aim was to provide assistance to those on the home front: the families of serving men and those suffering from the war's effect on their livelihood. Within one week, it had raised £1 million. After 7 weeks working from the Prince of Wales's wing of St James's Palace, Charles resigned. The Prince's treasurer wrote him a letter which ended, *'His Royal Highness wished me to convey to you his warmest thanks for your kindness and assistance, and to wish you all good luck in your new vocation.'*

Charles's new vocation was his old vocation, the Army. In another hint that there might have been some kind of cloud over his leaving the Royal Berkshires in 1906, he first joined the Territorial unit in the area of his childhood home, the Buckinghamshire Battalion of the Oxfordshire & Buckinghamshire Light Infantry. He was commissioned as a Captain with them on 30th September. Officers with regular experience were in short supply and he was soon poached back by the Royal Berkshires. In fact the very

next day he was appointed as Adjutant to the newly formed 8th Battalion of the Royal Berkshire Regiment. The general story of their formation and training is in my first book but there are some specific details about Charles Bartlett's involvement that should be mentioned here.

From their camp at Boyton Park near Codford in Wiltshire, one of their first jobs was to recruit officers and men for the Battalion. An early officer candidate to make the journey down from London to be interviewed was Cecil Cloake. After a brief inspection by Colonel Walton and Captain Bartlett he returned home on the train and was soon being given an allowance to buy uniform and equipment – and in early November he was back in the camp with all his kit as a shiny new 2nd Lieutenant.

The picture, **below**, was taken to mark an officers *v* sergeants football match. Cecil Cloake is in a scarf sitting in the centre. He is at the feet of Charles Bartlett and Colonel Walton (wearing his cap rather skewiff). Behind them are the tents of the camp and at this time things were far from shiny. The tents were surrounded by thick mud from the nearly continuous rain, and with very little in the way of uniforms and equipment, morale amongst the men was very low. In fact just a few days after Cecil's arrival, the men refused to go on parade.

As Cecil noted, *'Little did they realise that this was open mutiny in time of war!'* The consequences of that could have been execution by firing squad but Charles took a more pragmatic approach and *'mounted his beautiful charger, "Punch", and arraigned the assembled men; promising that in a short time they would be moved, by train, to billets in Reading.'* This defused the situation and indeed within a week they were striking camp and entraining for Reading which then became the base for the majority of their training.

Very soon after, Charles was promoted to Major and Second-in-Command of the Battalion (so from leaving the Army 9 years before as a platoon commander in charge of 50 men, he was now one injury to the Commanding Officer away from being in command of 1000 men). The Battalion was in uniform seven days a week with the only respite from training being church parade on Sunday mornings followed sometimes by a few hours' relaxation, which Charles would enjoy in the company of the other majors and captains in a private room in the White Hart Hotel.

In May the Battalion moved to a purpose-built camp on Salisbury Plain where my Group Photograph was taken, and then on 7th August 1915 they embarked on the train that was to take them to war.

Left: McIlroy's department store on Oxford Road in Reading. Whilst the men were billeted in various halls around the town, the officers made themselves at home in the hotel above the store. McIlroy's was the most extraordinary sight. It opened in 1903 and with its turret and decorative features as well as its vast expanse of plate glass windows it became known as 'Reading's Crystal Palace'. In its heyday it employed 1000 staff. Somewhere in amongst the architectural exuberance above the shop was Charles's room.

Below: Charles in a portrait taken in a studio, possibly to mark his promotion to Major.

Left: Looking west from the other end of McIlroy's, the **White Hart Hotel** is first on the left at N° 1, Oxford Road. In addition to being Charles's favoured watering hole it was the Battalion's Headquarters.

Above left: In the door to one of the huts in Sandhill Camp on Salisbury Plain, Charles stands alongside Douglas Tosetti who looks like he's been doing some washing up.

Above right: A private glances at the camera with an unimpressed air as Major Bartlett sits astride his horse, Punch, and observes some live firing on the ranges.

Right: Some of the men of the 8th Royal Berkshires in a practice trench on Salisbury Plain.

Major Charles Bartlett flanked by Colonel William Walton *(left)* and Captain Lionel Edwards *(right)*.

Margaret Bartlett (signed *'Peggy'* – it was her stage name and how she was
known in her family, but Charles never calls her that in the letters).

Notes on the Presentation of the Letters

Before we go to the letters, it will help you if I tell you something about them as a whole and how I've chosen to present them.

Most of the letters are from Charles Bartlett to his wife Margaret. Very few of Margaret's letters still exist. Even if he had been sentimental enough to keep them it would have been difficult to preserve them given the conditions at the front.

The total number of letters is more than the 341 that I usually quote. '341' came from adding up the sequences of numbers that Margaret wrote on the envelopes, but there are a few of those numbered letters missing (as marked in the sequence) and then the number has been increased by the inclusion of other items: letters to or from other people that were with his letters or which I have found during my research, and military reports and newspaper articles.

Every word that I have found written by him is included except for some items that appear in the Battalion's war diary (and for completists, that can be downloaded from the National Archives website for £3.50, with reference WO 95/1265/1). The war diary has helped with the letter notes but obviously it has more detail than I could include here and, again, completists might find a parallel reading of interest. There is surprisingly little repetition in all these items, but where there is, it often gives an insight as to how he presented himself to different people.

I would have loved to have included images of all the pages of the letters but the resulting book would have been unfeasibly huge. However, all the different shapes, sizes, colours and types of paper along with the changes in his handwriting style are a key part of transporting you back to that time, so I have included scans of all the letters, with the transcriptions having show-through from the originals underneath. For some letters on small pieces of paper, I have left them for you to read in his original handwriting. Most were written in pencil so as not to run in the rain and even after all these years I have found them easy to read.

Each letter has an item number. I've put them into one continuous sequence though originally they were marked in batches separated by his periods of leave. I don't know when that numbering was done and In some cases I have changed the sequence when it was obvious to me that the letters were written in a different order. The postal service was amazingly quick considering the conditions and the volume of letters (up to 12 million a week were delivered to soldiers at the front), but it could be a bit erratic, and some letters overtook each other. His own dating can't be relied upon (indeed sometimes the errors give an idea of his mental state) and I have included various other clues: postmarks, envelope addresses and forwarding details. The items are fitted into a calendar of days, with some days including more than one letter, and letterless days not being included.

I've tried to preserve the original format of the letters in the transcriptions. He's not one for consistency in dating or topping and tailing his letters, and I've shown all the variations, as well his own spellings and punctuation. He is a good writer and speller but he has certain idiosyncrasies that I thought important to keep. If there's anything I thought might be unclear I have tried to clarify it in a note and have done likewise if there's something that I think might not be known to a general reader (my apologies to First World War buffs who might occasionally get more explanation than they need). Most place names associated with Charles Bartlett or mentioned by him can be found on the maps listed on p.8, especially those inside the front and back covers of this book.

To try and avoid you having to turn to the back of the book, as much as possible the notes are presented on the page next to the item to which they refer. I have tried to let the letters speak for themselves and with the notes I have aimed to only include comments or other bits of material that give further context or enhance the view.

Many of the notes are about the over 300 people who are mentioned along the way. The index lists them all even if I haven't been able to fully identify them. **(IMPORTANT: if you need a reminder of who someone is at any point, look in the index for their biographical mentions).** Except for a few major characters most people only appear once or twice in the notes, usually when they are first mentioned or when something particularly significant happens to them. In the space available it is only generally possible to give a hint of each life so I have picked details that give an idea of the variety of human experience and show the impact of the war on them and their families. Some repetition from my previous work has been inevitable but I have tried to avoid it:

★ means the man named is in my original group photograph & more details about him can be found in my first book.

Some of the people Charles mentions are very famous and further detail is widely available on them elsewhere. Most, however, are not so well-known and there were some cases where I just felt I could not leave out the stories that I had uncovered, either because I felt the person deserved to be better remembered or because their stories were so extraordinary:

➔ means there is more detail about the person in the Additional Stories section **(IMPORTANT: these are designed to be read in line with the main text – go to the page number by the arrow, and after reading the named story there is the page number to take you back to your place in the main text).**

The first mention of any person includes their age at that time, and throughout the book you will see symbols like this:

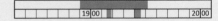

This is a life grid. One appears with the main note or photograph for each person where space allows (and if not then their dates appear with their listing in the names index). The grey bar shows their life span on top of a date grid going from 1830 on the left to 2010 on the right in 10-year steps, with the spans of the two World Wars shown in red. In this example you can see the person lived from just after 1890 through both World Wars before dying soon after 1950. The idea is that you can get a quick indication of their place in history, particularly in comparison to other life grids on the same page. One thing we all share is our presence on Earth for a period not of our choosing.

Ranks & Structure of the British Army

These notes and tables are intended to give you a basic primer on the British Army particularly with respect to Charles Bartlett's position with his foot soldiers in an infantry battalion in his time during the First World War.

Commissioned Officers and Non-Commissioned Officers (NCOs)

Officers ranked from Field-Marshal down to the subalterns (Lieutenants & 2nd Lieutenants). They held the King's Commission and were akin to Management in industry. They were supposed to do the high level planning and provide overall leadership. The Non-Commissioned Officers were like the foremen (sergeant-majors & sergeants) and skilled workers (corporals) who got the actual nitty-gritty of soldiering to happen with the lowly privates.

'Regiment' v 'Battalion'

A Regiment is an organisation within the Army that has a particular cap badge and traditions and provides administrative support and reinforcements for a number of Battalions, whereas a Battalion is a unit of set size within the fighting structure of the Army. It's probably clearer to use Charles's experience as an example. His Regiment was the Royal Berkshire Regiment, with its depot at Brock Barracks in Reading. During the First World War, the Royal Berkshire Regiment had 8 battalions that served overseas (as well as reserve and training battalions at home). Each of these battalions at full strength had about 1000 men. Charles Bartlett served with the 8th Battalion of the Royal Berkshire Regiment, which fought as part of 1st Brigade (which included 3 other battalions of different regiments), whereas the other Royal Berkshire Regiment battalions served in completely different Brigades and could even be serving in other countries entirely. Admittedly there can be some confusion, because sometimes Charles refers to his Battalion as 'the Regiment', for example when talking about the Regimental Headquarters, but this is just him being old-fashioned and usually if he's talking about what's going on locally it should be apparent that by 'Regiment' he means 'Battalion'. So that's clear, then.

Rank	Unit commanded	Approximate number of men in the unit
Field-Marshal *FM*	Army Group	2,000,000
General *Gen*	Army	300,000
Lieutenant-General *Lt-Gen*	Corps	60,000
Major-General *Maj-Gen*	Division	12,000
Brigadier-General *Brig-Gen*	Brigade	3,500
Colonel *Col* or **Lieutenant-Colonel** *Lt Col* = commanding officer, CO	Battalion	1,000
Major *Maj* or **Captain** *Capt*	Company	200
Lieutenant *Lt* or **2nd Lieutenant** *2Lt*	Platoon	50
Corporal *Cpl* or **Lance Corporal** *L/Cpl*	Section	12
Private *Pte*	None	0

Unit	Subunits included	Unit Headquarters includes
Division	3 infantry brigades, artillery, engineers, cavalry, supplies, medical	Chief of Staff *(Lt Col)*
Infantry Brigade	4 infantry battalions	Brigade Major *(Maj or Capt) running the staff*
Battalion	4 infantry companies, Machine gun section	Second-in-command *(Maj)* Adjutant *(Adjt, in charge of admin & discipline) (Capt or Lt)* Quartermaster *(QM, in charge of supplies & equipment) (Capt or Lt)* Transport Officer *(Capt or Lt)* **Regimental Sergeant Major** *(most senior NCO, for regimental standards & discipline) RSM*
Company	4 platoons	Second-in-command *(Capt or Lt)* **Company Sergeant Major** *CSM* **Company Quartermaster Sergeant** *CQMS*
Platoon	4 sections	Second-in-command, **Sergeant** *Sgt*

BERKSHIRE BOYS OF THE BULLDOG BREED.

Another of the County's New Battalions.

The Regiment that Does Things.

"If anything has to be done it's always the Berkshires who do it, and they are well known by other regiments."—Corpl. H. MILES, 1st Batt. Royal Berkshire Regiment, in a letter to friends at Reading.

"The Gurkhas said that they would storm any position with the Berkshires in support. Not a man of the 1st Batt. has yet left his trench under shell fire. Few regiments can make this boast."—General Officer Commanding 6th Infantry Brigade.

Photo by] THE OFFICERS 6th BATT. ROYAL BERKSHIRE REGIMENT. [C. E. May.

How to End the War.

More men, and still more men, are necessary in order to end this life-and-death struggle.

This is what Lce.-Cpl. H. G. Davis, of the 2nd Batt. Royal Berkshire Regt., says in a letter home :—"If only all the young men would come forward and join the Army, the war would not be long in ending. There must be hundreds who—much to their shame—have not yet offered their services."

The late Lce.-Corpl. T. LAILEY, 1st Batt. Royal Berkshire Regiment, Shinfield.—Killed in action. Aged 21.

The late Pte. T. WILLOUGHBY, 1st Batt. Royal Berkshire Regt., 121, Oxford Road, Reading.—Killed in action. Aged 19.

The late Lce.-Corpl. F. PONTIN, 1st Batt. Royal Berkshire Regt., Windsor.—Killed in action.

The late Pte. THOMAS WELLS, 2nd Batt. Royal Berkshire Regiment, 19, Elm Park Road, Reading.—Killed in action. Aged 31.

Photo by] "A" CO. 8th BATT. ROYAL BERKSHIRE REGIMENT. [C. E. May.

Photo by] "B" CO. 8th BATT. ROYAL BERKSHIRE REGIMENT. [C. E. May.

If you are fit and free—go to the Recruiting :: Office. ::

See next week's "Reading . . . . Standard" for further . portraits. .

Pte. HARRY THATCHER, 1st Batt. Royal Berkshire Regiment.—Unfit—Wounded.

Pte. F. HAVELL, 2nd Batt. Royal Berkshire Regiment, Home Close Lodge, Peppard Rd., Emmer Green.—Ill with enteric fever.

Photo by] "C" CO. 8th BATT. ROYAL BERKSHIRE REGIMENT. [C. E. May.

The late Lce.-Corpl. CHAS. AUSTIN, 2nd Batt. Royal Berkshire Regiment, Cornwell Street, Maidenhead.—Died of wounds. Aged 20.

The late Pte. RALPH TODD, 2nd Batt. Royal Berkshire Regt., Easthampstead Road, Bracknell.—Killed in action.

Photo by] "D" CO. 8th BATT. ROYAL BERKSHIRE REGIMENT. [C. E. May.

The Letters

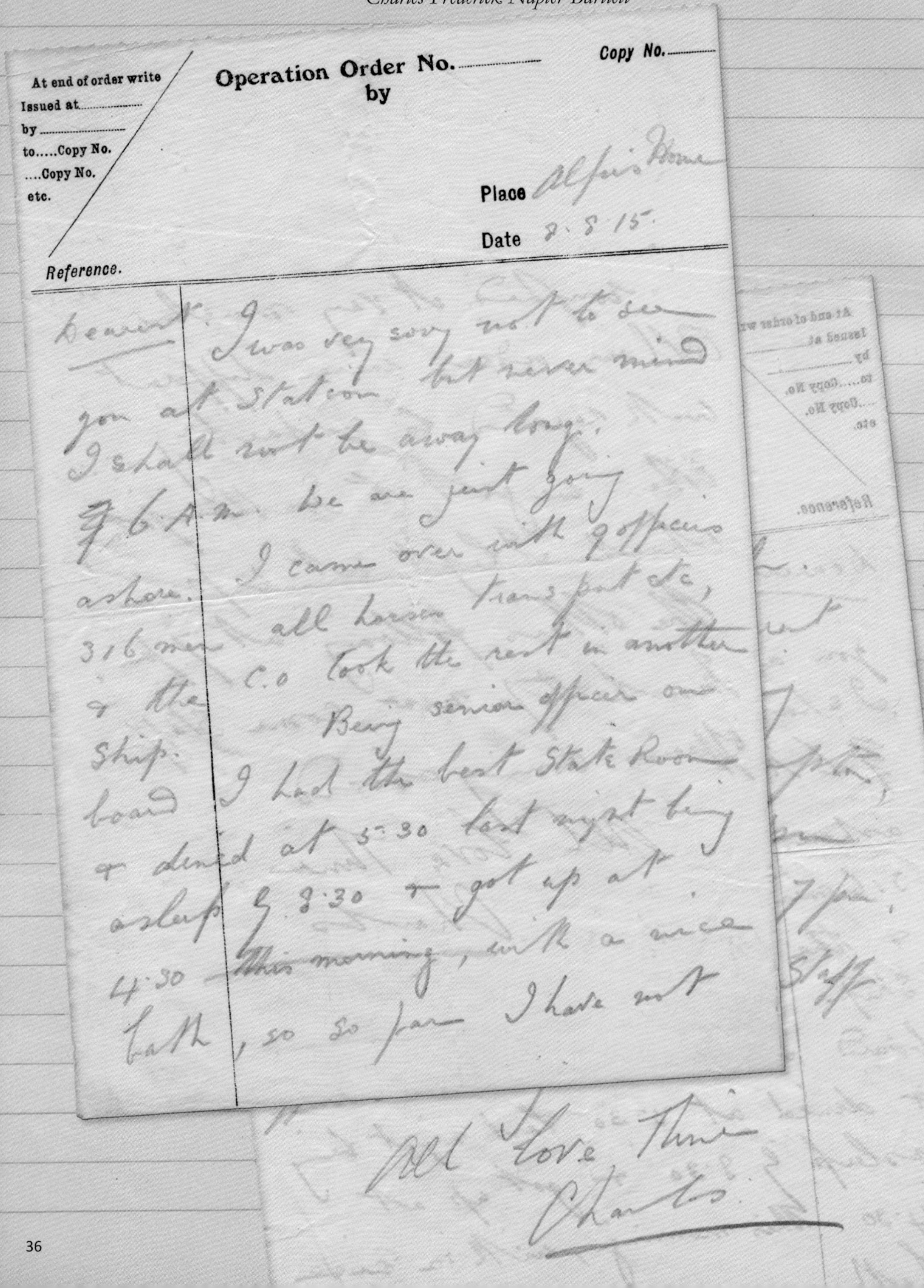

Operation Order No. .... Copy No. ....
by

At end of order write
Issued at ....
by ....
to .....Copy No.
.....Copy No.
etc.

Place Alfi's Home

Date 7.8.15.

Reference.

Dearest. I was very sorry not to see
you at station but never mind
I shall not be away long.
7 6 A.m. we are just going
ashore. I came over with 9 officers
316 men all horses transport etc,
& the C.O took the rest in another
Ship. Being senior officer on
board I had the best State Room
& dined at 5.30 last night being
asleep by 8.30 & got up at
4.30 this morning, with a nice
bath, so so far I have not

All Love Thine
Charles.

36

Place *Alfie's Home*[1]
Date *8.8.15*

DAY 1 SUN

8 AUG 1915

Item 1
Letter to Margaret

Envelope
161 Haverstock Hill
London

SOUTHAMPTON
2.30 PM
AUG 9 15

Dearest

I was very sorry not to see you at station but never mind I shall not be away long.

6 A.M. We are just going ashore. I came over with 9 officers 316 men all horses transport etc., & the C.O.[2] took the rest in another ship.[3] Being senior officer on board I had the best State Room & dined at 5:30 last night being asleep by 9:30 & got up at 4:30 this morning, with a nice bath, so so far I have not roughed it very much. All our orders were different with regard to embarking when we got to Southampton, which I left at 4 pm the others following at 7 pm. Must stop now, some staff officers coming aboard.

All love Thine[4]

Charles

Charles looks like he is showing off by writing this first letter on an Operation Order pad.

He had been in command of the first train taking the Battalion from Warminster and his wife arrived down on the line just as the train pulled off so she was not able to say goodbye.

'*I shall not be away long*' is such a loaded statement, especially viewed from the present day when we have a view of the whole war. Of course he is trying to allay his wife's fears as he goes off to fight, but he is also showing the confidence that then seemed to infect so many people. Another battalion's commanding officer said in his memoirs that at this time betting on the Stock Exchange was four to one on the war ending in the next month. Knowing what we do now, it seems astonishing that at this stage anyone can have thought that the war was not going to last long, or that they would have a good chance of surviving it. The Western Front had stagnated into lines of trenches and attempts to change that had shown little movement accompanied by huge numbers of casualties. They may not have known the precise numbers but the casualty lists occupied columns and columns in the newspapers. According to the Commonwealth War Graves Commission, the British Army had lost a total of 91,189 dead in all theatres by this day of the war. So in only one year the loss was just under half the 219,420 that it is estimated the British Army lost in the whole of the Napoleonic Wars from 1804-1815 (and that number included 193,851 who died from wounds, accidents and disease).

Before Charles went ashore he must have given this letter to someone on the ship who posted it in Southampton (as you can see on the first envelope on the front cover of this book).

1 Alfie = Charles's brother-in-law **Alfred Fraser**, aged 41. He had married Charles's youngest surviving sister, **Florrie** (now 47), at the Cathedral in Singapore in 1900, his job then being in North Borneo. By the time he joined up in August 1914 he had become a brewery manager in Northampton with three young daughters. Now a Captain in the Army Service Corps, the huge Base Supply Depot in Le Havre had been his home for 2 weeks when Charles's ship arrived there.

2 C.O. = commanding officer of a battalion, in this case **Colonel William C Walton★** (aged 50 and my great-grandfather).

3 The C.O. was on the packet & passenger ship *RMS Viper*, whereas Charles was on the cargo steamer *SS Inventor*, **(below)**.

4 '*Thine*' as a way of signing off has continued in his family even into the email era.

As Charles heads off on his adventure into the unknown, spare a thought for his wife. At the age of 26, Margaret was not only left at home with sole charge of their 5-year-old daughter and of their household and staff, but she also now had the unaccustomed role as a senior officer's wife, providing support for the families of those fighting at the front and acting as a hub to pass on any information she received from Charles, all whilst not knowing whether she would ever see her husband again.

DAY 2 MON
9 AUG 1915

Item 2
Letter to Margaret

Envelope
(missing)

The Badminton Club

Monday Morning

My Dearest Margaret

We are off at 1 mid day today, but where to no one knows. We are stopping in Alfie's camp at present. Cooper of Northampton is also here. Alfie is fed up with being here & wants to move up. We slept most of yesterday afternoon as we were not allowed out of camp or we should have gone into the town for a decent dinner. However we dined at 7 pm & sat talking until 11.30 pm.

My boots have not arrived yet. Will you go to Manfields[1] please & see about them. Capt. Oldman[2] has the other pair of boots & will send Manfield a cheque as soon as he can get at his cheque book.

The ground was infernally hard last night & I am very bruised in consequence, but Alfie has a beautiful mattress, it is an air one & can be used as a mackintosh sheet, they can be got at Wilkinsons the sword shop[3] in Pall Mall. Please send me out one. I am afraid you will have to pay for it, also order one for Ronald.[4] I enclose his cheque, I am afraid I have not a form.

That is all my news.

It is very hot here & someone has stolen my new mackintosh.

All love to you & Paula

Thine

Charles

P.S. Love to Renee & Billy[5]

---

1 **Manfields** were one of the first large-scale footwear manufacturers to open their own retail outlets (in the 1880s), with several branches in London by this time. The only branches that still exist are in the Netherlands and France.

2 **Wilfred Oldman** ★ (aged 36) was likely to have been fairly new to Charles, given that he had lived abroad for most of his adult life. Having arrived back from South Africa on Christmas Eve 1914, he applied for a commission on 30th December, became a Lieutenant on 11th January and then Captain on 18th February. There cannot have been many quicker appointments. No doubt his service as a sergeant in the Boer War counted in his favour, but it also might have helped that his uncle was in command of the Royal Berkshire Regiment's depot in Reading.

3 **Wilkinson Sword** is well-known these days for their razors, but it was for quality fighting blades that they made their name. In the time of machine-guns and high explosive artillery it's amazing that swords were still seen as relevant, but they also received a contract for two million bayonets during the war, and had already started showing the talent for diversification that would ensure their survival as a company.

4 **Ronald Brakspear** ★, 39, was a friend whom Charles had known for over 15 years. As young men they both served part-time in the militia before Charles joined the Regular Army. In the 1901 Census they are listed next to each other whilst staying at the Badminton Club (nothing to do with shuttlecocks – it was a gentleman's club with its premises at 100, Piccadilly, in London, *above left*). Charles had been Ronald's best man in 1903 (his wedding presents being a gold cigarette case and a gold chain purse) and their closeness is shown by the fact that Charles calls him Ronald (and later Ronnie) rather than by his surname as would have been the case with most of his contemporaries. After Colonel Walton, Charles and Ronald, being majors, were the next most senior officers in the Battalion.

5 I haven't been able to identify Renee & Billy but they are friends who may even have been staying with Margaret.

Item 3
Letter to Margaret

Envelope
161 Haverstock Hill
London

Wednesday   Aug 10th 1915   9.30 am

Dearest Margaret

      We were not left long in peace yesterday & ordered to be at the station at 2 pm. We left at 6 pm destination untold but were told we should reach it about midnight tonight or tomorrow morning. Officers are 6 in a second class carriage except the C.O. & Ronny & I who have a second class compartment to ourselves. The men are 40 in cattle trucks, & the whole lot including transport are on one train, quite the longest train I have ever seen. At 4.15 am we stopped for the men to have hot tea & rations served out, & were then told we should reach our destination about 11.30 or 12 <u>mid day</u> today and d-d[1] glad I shall be to get out of this infernal carriage for the flies & heat are awful. We had some way to march to the station yesterday, & one of the transport horses reared over backwards & broke his riders toe. Several men tried to fall out but I whipped them all on except two who fainted & I chucked them on a cart & got them to the station. Punch the silly ass played the fool shying at everything until he came down on the cobbles & got my right leg under him but no damage was done, & he went more quietly after that.

Oldman tells me he has written you & addressed it 161 Hampstead Hill.[2] Wherever we are going, we are going to relieve a Guards Batt[n] & I think we shall be spending the next day or two at the place I lunched at when I came out before & when I returned.

Bully Beef and Biscuits are not much in my line.[3]

When we had loaded our train yesterday Oldman & I went off to get some papers. We had our heads washed & found a nice little restaurant where we had an omlette & a bottle of DM 06;[4] we dont seem to be able to get away from it. Let Lilian and John[5] know where I am.

      All my love to Paula Renee & Billy

         Thine

         Charles

Haverstock Hill

1   d-d = 'damned' – this is as close as he gets to swearing (at least in writing).

2   It should have been Haverstock Hill (which is not far from Hampstead).

3   Bully Beef (from the French *boulli* 'boiled') was tinned corned beef and along with hardtack biscuits were the main field rations of the British Army. The biscuits *(left)* were manufactured at the Huntley and Palmers factory in Reading not far from the Regimental depot, with the result that the Royal Berkshires had become known as 'The Biscuit Boys'.

4   As you shall see, Charles was decidedly keen on champagne. 'DM' was 'Duc de Montebello', a very well-known champagne house at the time, with 1906 being a particularly celebrated vintage. In 1929 the Wall Street crash would put them into difficulties and they were taken over by another champagne house and pretty much forgotten.

5   **Lilian** (also known as 'Lil'), 48, and **John**, 41, were Charles's unmarried elder siblings.

Item 4
Letter to Margaret

Envelope
*161 Haverstock Hill
London*

FIELD POST OFFICE
11 AU
15

Wednesday

My Dearest Wife

    We arrived here yesterday where I thought we should about 12 midday after all. I had to remain at the Station[1] & see all the horses wagons etc unloaded, so did not get away until about 2, as the French Ry officials take hours to shunt a train. Then a 2½ mile walk from the station in a blinding thunderstorm and not a dry rag when we arrived here. It was 6 pm when we had got all the men into billets & got some tea which was the first food from 6 am except your chocolate which was most useful. I have a ripping bedroom, & a huge Bath but that is in the Boiler house of the Brewery. It is quite the biggest bath I have ever seen and our Quarter Masters Stores are in the next Barn, so I interviewed him[2] while I was bathing, & had one or two fowls for an audience as well. We shall stay here probably until Saturday, when we move up to take the place of a Guards Batt[n] in the First Army.[3]

Anyway I shall have a rough idea of the country. The men are in the most filthy Billets 40 or 50 in cow houses lofts etc, no rooms at all. I have not yet had a letter from you, but have hopes. Everyone is very well. I heard our 6th Batt[4] was badly cut about on Sunday & there seems to be some pretty fighting going on by the gun flashes etc we heard & saw last night. We are being inspected by some General from H.Q. tomorrow. Who it is I dont know.

    All love to you, Paula & the family

        Thine

          Charles

P.S. Please send on anything to Lil that will interest her.

---

1 They had arrived at St Omer after getting on the train at Le Havre.

2 The battalion's Quartermaster was in charge of its equipment and supplies. In this case he was Lt **James Barrow ★**, 47, *(right)*, the son of a railway labourer from Lancashire. You can see he is wearing 3 medal ribbons from his previous Army service, 2 from the Boer War along with the Long Service & Good Conduct Medal (he'd served for 25 years, retiring as a Sergeant Major in 1913). He was mentioned in dispatches in 1901, so it seems he had seen more action in Cape Colony than he would have expected as a Staff Sergeant in the Pay Corps.

3 The Guards battalions from different divisions were to be combined into a new Guards Division. 1st Coldstream Guards and 1st Scots Guards were leaving the 1st Brigade in 1st Division, to be replaced by 8th Royal Berkshires and 10th Gloucestershires.

4 'Our' 6th Battalion points to the 6th Battalion of the Royal Berkshire Regiment, but their war diary shows no fighting or casualties on Sunday 8th August 1915 – in fact they had only gone into the trenches for the first time on the night of 4th August and had sustained their first and only casualty so far on 5th August (one wounded by a shell). He's either referring to a different unit or this is an example of the rumour mill at work.

Thursday

Dearest

    No time for letter today. Generals inspection all the morning & a Route March this afternoon (d-d) hot too. The General very pleased with us, said we were very fit & well trained & said he would recommend us to take our place at the front at once. Quite good so I suppose we shall soon be having a dash.

        Best Love to All

            Your

              Charles

DAY 5 THU

12 AUG 1915

Item 5
Letter to Margaret

Envelope
161 Haverstock Hill London

7.30 am   *Friday*

Dearest Wife

    Just a line to thank you for your letter of last Saturday, which arrived late last night, but I hope the posts will quicken in future, now the G.P.O.[1] have found we are across. I will write a line tonight, but as we are parading at 8 there is no time now & the post will have gone by the time we are back.
Am having some trouble with the mens food, as it is now under company arrangements, & they dont[2] seem to understand it and from one Company to the last one it is about ¾ of a mile.

          In haste

          All love

          Thine

           Charles

P.S. I address this to Paula to please her.

DAY 6 FRI

13 AUG 1915

Item 6
Letter to Margaret

Envelope
(missing)

---

1 G.P.O. = General Post Office   **2** Charles often misses or misplaces apostrophes though few instances needed editing to be clearly understood on first reading. In particular he so consistently writes *'dont'* that it is almost a point of style & I'm going to leave it like that throughout.

Item 7
Letter to Margaret

Envelope
*161 Haverstock Hill
London*

FIELD POST OFFICE
14 AU
15

RAMC cap badge

Saturday

Dearest Margaret

We are still in the same spot & hope to remain until Monday. If you have a map & look for the place Noah lived in you wont be very far out.[1] Many thanks for your letter of Tuesday which reached me last night. I am afraid you had a rotten journey back to town. The Dr[2] is very worried as he has not yet heard from his wife I do hope by now you have been to see Mrs McGibbon. I was glad to hear such good news of General Carter.[3] We had a nice Route March yesterday, and only one man fainted, so they are improving. I have a splendid rule now & that is if a man falls out before he faints the other men in his company have to carry him, it is most effective. This morning all the men are doing physical drill & bathing and this afternoon we shall have another Route March. It is a good thing we have these few days here to get their feet hard & accustomed to the pavée roads, as of course they are carrying much more weight than they ever did in England. Each man has to carry altogether 61 lbs. Tomorrow we are playing the RAMC[4] at cricket. Last night Douglas Tosetti[5] sent me a note & said he had found a nice Restaurant, & would I dine with him Ronald & Hanna,[6] so off we went, but the ladies at our farm cook better, & the wine was nothing to write home about. The weather keeps gloriously fine here. I dont want any washing done at present, as I can get it done here very quickly in fact I have no dirty linen. I am looking forward to getting my easy boots.

There are a number of aeroplanes about today. Hendon[7] is nothing to it.

All Love to you Paula Lilian & all

Thine

Charles

---

1 They were in Arques (pronounced 'Ark'). Did he really think a German spy wouldn't know his Bible stories?

2 The Doctor was the Medical Officer of the 8th Royal Berkshires, **Peter McGibbon**, 41. A Canadian, he qualified from the University of Toronto in 1906. His wife of 5 years, **Mabel**, 32, had accompanied him over the Atlantic and was staying in London.

3 Brigadier-General **Francis Carter**, 56, had been Charles's first C.O. in the 1st Royal Berkshires up until 1903. He'd come of retirement in 1914 to command 24th Brigade, but after their first

big battle at Neuve Chapelle in March 1915 he fell ill and had to give up his command. The good news may have been that he was on the mend, but Charles had obviously not heard that the younger of Carter's two sons had been killed nine days before. ➔393

4 RAMC = Royal Army Medical Corps

5 **Douglas Tosetti★**, 38, was also a member of the Badminton Club and being a champagne merchant would have very much endeared him to Charles. At the very least they had people in common before the war, and soon became the firmest of friends.

6 **Douglas Hanna★**, 42, was another member of the Badminton Club, though they may not have met before the war as Hanna had lived in Ceylon for 21 years. A tea merchant, he would have stayed at the club during his periods of leave and also after he first arrived back in England to join up on 27th January 1915.

7 Hendon Aerodrome in north London was an important centre for the initial development of the aviation industry before the War, with displays and races seeing huge crowds attracted by the novelty of powered flight (it was after all only 12 years since the Wright brothers had flown for the first time).

Saturday

Dearest Margaret

Since writing this morning your letter has arrived. Many thanks for looking after all my things. Yes the Regimental censor stamp is 1996. Your letters take about 3 days to reach here. We move on early tomorrow morning where we know not, but are going into the 1st Army. Where am I? In the same place as Noah lived in. Yes, I have just written Frank a line. It was my best cane I sent you to take care of, please dont lose it.

Ronald has given me a very nice wrist watch.

In haste
All Love
your
Charles

Item 8
Letter to Margaret

Envelope
161 Haverstock Hill
London

FIELD POST OFFICE
14 AU 15

Monday

Dearest Margaret

Just a hurried line as we march off early again this morning, & move up to the Firing line this evening, and tomorrow we start occupying the trenches that is one company will go in with 3 companies of guards. I think we shall be in the 1st Brigade 1st Division 4th Corps of first army. We had a much longer march than we expected yesterday, and how we shall get the sorefooted ones the rest of the way I dont know. I will write fully tomorrow, but at the present we are being rushed so as to get a guards Batt^n away.

All love
Thine
Charles

DAY
9
MON
16 AUG 1915

Item 9
Letter to Margaret

Envelope
161 Haverstock Hill
London

FIELD POST OFFICE
16 AU 15

The 8th Royal Berkshires were going to piggy-back on other units to get experience of trench routine in the front line. They had arrived in Béthune via one night's stop in Ham-en-Artois. The sore feet cannot have been a surprise, going by this note in the Battalion's war diary on this day: *'About one dozen men suffered from sore feet due to new boots issued to whole battalion on the day previous to departure from Warminster'.*

Item 10
Letter to Margaret

Envelope
161 Haverstock Hill
London

FIELD POST OFFICE
16 AU
15

5 pm

Dearest Margaret

    At last we have arrived at our destination. We are at Bethune[1] only please dont put it on the envelope or the Brigade we are in, which is the 1st Brigade 1st Division 4th Army Corps of 1st Army. I will write you fully tomorrow morning, as we do not go into the trenches until 6 pm tomorrow night and then only for 2 days, & as the Batt[n] Headquarters are some 2 miles in rear of the fire trenches you need not worry about me.

By cheering them on & swearing & joking I managed to whip up the Batt so that we did not leave a single man on the road, but there were some terrible lame ducks & there are some awful sores on the feet. Au revoir or I miss the post.

        All love
        Thine
        Charles

1 This time there is no attempt at encoding their location (or his unit details!).

DAY
10
TUE
17 AUG 1915

Item 11
Letter to Margaret

Envelope
161 Haverstock Hill
London

FIELD POST OFFICE
17 AU
15

Tuesday

Dearest Margaret

    I have not much news since I wrote last night. It has rained heavily & we hear all the communication trenches are a foot or more deep in water and as my Cording[1] boots have not arrived I look like getting wet feet tomorrow. Each company goes to a different Regiment in the trenches tonight, & the Regimental H[d] Q[rs] are about 2 miles in rear. Tomorrow morning we are going to make a tour & see all the trenches returning at night to sleep in comfort at H.Q. This morning I rode about 3 miles to within a mile of the fire trenches, & saw our 1st Batt[n] or what is left of it.[2] They were in the reserve and only two officers who were with me in the Regiment are left. I only saw one of them Bird[3] by name, as Radford[4] was out on duty. We have had no letters for two days but hope to get some tonight. We look like having a very easy time for a bit as our Division is going to be sent for a rest, and we are sure to go with it. I believe the Division has not had more than 3 days rest since Dec last. The country I rode through this morning had been shelled to blazes, and there were some nice large holes where the Jack Johnsons[5] had fallen.

44

The Rain here is a caution,[6] the storms start with large drops of about a pint each, & then it rains more in 10 minutes than it does in a month at home. I must try & buy another mackintosh, mine having been stolen, & I hear there is a good store here. The post has just arrived 5 mailbags full, I hope to hear from you. If I have time I will answer any questions you may have asked.

All love to all

Thine

Charles

Just rec[d] nice long letter of Sat. morning. There being no questions I can give no answers. Money seems to crop up again. Je n'ai rien de tout.[7] My French has all come back to me.

HAMPSTEAD S.O.
8.45 PM
18 AU
15
N.W.

---

1 **Cordings** is a still existing clothing company that made its name in the 19th Century with waterproof products & clothing for explorers like Henry Morton Stanley. As proof of quality, one of their canvas and leather Newmarket boots stayed submerged in a glass tank full of water in their Piccadilly shop window for so many years that it became part of 'the knowledge' for London taxi drivers.

2 Our 1st Batt[n] = 1st Battalion Royal Berkshire Regiment, his old unit from before the war. They had been one of the first battalions to go out to France, embarking on 12th August 1914, and had been heavily involved since their first contact with the Germans near Mons on 25th August 1914.

3 Major **Lawrence Bird**, 31, had been a regular Captain in India in August 1914. He arrived in France in November, was wounded whilst out digging a trench in the open at 9 o'clock one night in February, was back in France in May, and became C.O. at the end of June after the previous C.O. was killed. At the Battle of Loos in September he would be wounded & earn the Distinguished Service Order (DSO), but survived to marry twice, get an OBE & reach the age of 76. His pre-war scarlet tunic is in the collection of the Regimental Museum.

4 Capt **Clive Radford**, 31, was also in India in 1914, as a regular Lieutenant. In June 1915 he had rescued men from a mine which had been filled with gas & then blown up by the Germans, & was awarded the DSO. He would be killed at the Battle of Loos, one week after his investiture at Buckingham Palace. ➜402

5 **Jack Johnson** = the British Army nickname for a type of heavy German shell that exploded with big clouds of black smoke. It was a tribute to one of the most famous men then on Earth. In 1908 Jack Johnson had become the first black heavyweight boxing world champion, and he beat all comers to keep his title for over 6 years. People packed out music halls all around the world to see 'The Galveston Giant' during his promotional tours.

His autobiography doesn't mention what he thought of being compared to a shell, but amazingly it does say that he was living in Haverstock Hill at the time of this mention in Charles's letter. He was in exile having skipped the US after being convicted on trumped up charges that were racially motivated (it didn't sit well with some folk that a black man kept beating the latest Great White Hope or that he enjoyed the company of white women, three of whom he married). He tells of being followed by a Zeppelin as he drove his white Benz through the streets of London, and it would be his love of driving fast that would kill him. Ironically, the pardon for his 1913 conviction would come from Donald Trump.

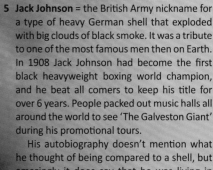

6 'a caution' = an amusing/surprising thing

7 'Je n'ai rien de tout' = I don't have any (!)

45

DAY
11
WED

18 AUG 1915

Item 12
Letter to Margaret

Envelope
161 Haverstock Hill
London

FIELD POST OFFICE
19 AU
15

Wednesday night

7 pm

My dearest Margaret

Yours of Sunday the 15th just arrived, and I was very pleased to get it. As you say I am to answer your question in your own way I say "Be Good", and not only that please dont write any more such nonsense on the subject. My views are very strong as far as that subject goes, & I shall never forgive you one slip. I will say no more.[1]

We have had a long tiring day leaving at 7.45 am & getting back at 7.15 pm nearly all the time walking about the trenches. Each of our companies are with a different Batt & each Batt[n] has nearly a mile frontage with two or three lines of trenches in it, so by the time one has waded through the lot one has covered some ground, and not only that the communication trench up to the fire trenches where the lads are was no less than 4700 yds long. However everything was very quiet & if it had not been for a few shells bursting about the place you would have thought we were back at Sandhill[2] practising. There was a nice air skirmish this evening, & I think we must have brought one down, we could see a German Plane being attacked by two of ours, & it dropped like a log within about 1000 ft & then righted itself & whether we actually got it in our lines I could not see, anyway it was badly hit, and in retaliation they sent a bomb aeroplane over Bethune & dropped a few but no damage was done.

Tomorrow we go back to B for 3 days, & then according to the latest orders we go into the trenches for a spell of 10 days which will just bore me stiff, as one can get no exercise, & I dont even get the excitement of having a shot. Although I was in the trenches all day I saw none of the senior officers, so can tell you nothing of how they feel about it.

I will try and remember the 23rd is your Birthday, & if my letter for the day does not reach you in time (for you have not told me how long they take) Here's wishing you all the very best of luck, may we spend the next one and many more together.

All to you Paula & all

Thine

Charles

1 This first paragraph is cryptic to say the least. One can only guess at what Margaret had to say but it is interesting in terms of what was later to transpire in their marriage.

2 Sandhill was the name of the camp just south of Warminster where they completed their training before shipping out. On the map it was in the area to the right of the track going up from the Farm to Sand Hill.

Item 13
Letter to Margaret

Envelope
*161 Haverstock Hill
London*

One of Leslie Berlein's
sleeve stars

Aug 19th 1915

Dearest Margaret

    For the love of heaven send me a fly whisp, fly papers, fly catchers, fly cages, and anything that will keep the blighters away. I have not been up into the trenches today, as I went back to Bethune to find some billets for the next 3 days. I have found quite a nice house but no sheets to the bed. The one I had intended to take for H^d Q^{rs} was the one Ronald had last time we were there, but the Germans dropped a bomb just outside it last night, & it blew all the windows in, so I think the subalterns[1] can go there instead. I hope that mattress will arrive soon, do hurry it up, as it will be most useful in the trenches. Have you seen Mrs McGibbon yet if not please go & call at once, as the little man is much worried,[2] she has moved from The Cecil so phone there & find her address.

We did not have a single casualty last night or the night before, so everyone is sure there are no Germans about. I am sending Punch to stay with the first Batt^n for a bit, as they have stabling, & he can come over for me each morning. I have a filthy headache today what from I dont know as I have given up drink so I suppose it is the lack of it.

This is a filthy village we are in,[3] & since I left Southampton I have not found a clean W.C.

Berlein[4] & Paramore[5] both pulled the stars off their sleeves without permission & put them on their shoulders instead.[6] Paramore sulked for 24 hours when I told him to replace them. It is now time to be packing up so no more until tomorrow.

    All Love to you & Paula

      Thine

       Charles

---

1 Subalterns = junior officers (2nd Lieutenants & Lieutenants).

2 Peter McGibbon's concern for his wife may have been related to the fact that only the year before they had lost their first child, a son who had lived for only six days.

3 They were in Sailly-la-Bourse.

4 **Leslie Berlein★**, 22, was a law-unto-himself Cambridge law graduate from South Africa.

5 **Gordon Paramore★**, 30, a painter studying at the Royal Academy, appeared to be under

no illusions as to what he was getting into. When appointed battalion bombing officer, he wrote to his sister saying *'Everybody in bombing parties gets wiped out, which is disappointing, but the game is sufficiently amusing to compensate for that'*.

6 At the beginning of the War, officers wore their badges of rank on the cuffs of their tunics. Not only were there stars and crowns but also a braided border enclosing them and rings looping around the sleeve. They were very easy to spot from a distance and that enabled German snipers to pick off the officers when they were out in the open lead-

ing their men during attacks. Charles Bartlett was a traditionalist who did things the way things were always done in the Regular Army. The innate belief was in the need to display courage in the face of the enemy, and the idea of moving the badges smacked of fear. At this time, reason had started to replace blind tradition in some units, with officers' badges of rank being dulled and moved to the top of the shoulders, but it was only officially sanctioned for active service in 1917 and then only became standard in British Army uniform three years after the war had ended, sadly too late for many.

DAY
13
FRI
20 AUG 1915

Item 14
Letter to Margaret

Envelope
*161 Haverstock Hill
London*

Friday morning

Dearest Wife

    I am sending a line for early post. We are back here until Sunday when we now go up into the reserve for 5 days. Our orders alter daily. I regret this morning I found no subalterns up at 7.15 or even 7.35 when breakfasts were issued. I did not know which 4 ought to have been on duty, but of course had to run them in & have caught the unfortunate Berlein Haynes[1] & Stileman,[2] also Birch[3] who is being returned to duty with his company as he is a hopeless failure with the transport. There is going to be a real rousing up this afternoon as I found 10 Sgts in bed & heaven knows how many men, & how one can expect them to do their job when the young officers dont I dont know. I am real sorry Leslie[4] was on duty today, but it is no use overlooking these matters.

Have got a real good Billet here with a bathroom & a decent W.C.

I am just off to see the Town Major[5] & get what cleaning materials I can out of him.

    All Love to you Paula & everyone

Thine

Charles

P.S. <u>Very</u> <u>Very</u> <u>Very</u> many happy returns of the day

---

POST ... TELEGRAPHS.

Handed in at	Office of Origin and Service Instructions		Words	Charges to pay	

11 LONGBRIDGE DEVERILL 10

THIS FORM MUST ACCOMPANY ANY ENQUIRY RESPECTING THIS TELEGRAM.

Received here at

TO LIEUT BERDEN PICCADILLY HOTEL LONDON

12 36. P.

EXPECTING YOU TOMORROW LOVE ✝ PEGGY

---

1 Lt **William Haynes**, 24, was an assistant in his father's ironmongery in Reading. A fine all-round sportsman, he held his school record for running the mile.

2 Lt **Donald Stileman**★ had celebrated his 21st birthday the day before (which may explain everyone's late rising!).

3 Lt **Cyril Gentry-Birch**, 22, was a clerk at Reading Town Hall who had married in June, with one of his brother officers, David Glen★, 21, as his best man.

4 Lt **Berlein**★ must have known Charles from before the war to be being called '**Leslie**' – and in fact in amongst his belongings there is a photo of Margaret signed '*Peggy 1915*' & labelled '*Leslie's friend Mrs (Major) Bartlett*' as well as this telegram to him which I think is her making arrangements for his pre-embarkation leave at the end of July.

5 Béthune, like every town, had a Major responsible for billeting & liaison with the civil authorities.

popular things according to those who use them. Yes Dear, I

Friday

My dearest Wife

Since I writing you this morning, I have rec[d] your letter including your photo, which I do not think much of.

I am very glad you have seen Mrs McGibbon as the little man is very upset, at her being so much upset.

The address you put is plenty as you will see by the time it takes. Your letter of Wednesday morning 18th reached me midday 20th, but would perhaps be one day longer if I was 6 miles further up in the trenches. I dont think the air mattress will be wasted, as they seem very popular things according to those who use them. Yes Dear I have my boots, & am wearing them this very moment, they are quite excellent, & when I have earned some money I hope to be able to repay you.

You seem to be having disturbing times with air raids,[1] it is surely safer this side. You will be glad to hear that it was not Berlein's turn for duty this morning so he did not catch it but Messrs Hobbs[2] Stileman & Haynes. Birch the silly ass lost his job, he was a mug when he had a nice soft one without hardly a chance of getting hit.[3] Well au revoir.

Many Many happy returns of the day. Your loving hubby

Charles

Item 15
Letter to Margaret

Envelope
*161 Haverstock Hill
London*

FIELD POST OFFICE
21 AU 15

---

1 On the night of 17th August, in the second air raid to reach London, a single Zeppelin had dropped bombs in Leyton and Leytonstone. In a period of 11 minutes of bombing they killed 10 people and injured 48.

2 **Tod Hobbs★**, 23, had qualified as a solicitor in December 1913 following on from his father who was the clerk of a police court, but going further back he was descended from a plumber, a house painter, a bootmaker, a carpenter, an optician and a map engraver.

3 Being transport officer would have meant being some way behind the trenches looking after the horses and wagons somewhere not visible to the Germans. It would have avoided being in the frontline or going over the top, but was still vulnerable to shellfire.

Saturday 21st

Dearest Darling

Just got your letter of the 19th. I have been down in the town but could find nothing you would appreciate as a birthday present even if it reached you, but once more I send you all my best wishes & I love you more than when we were married.

Yes I do read your letters all through & I much appreciate them & look forward to them. Patricia's letter[1] fetched up 2 days ago, as she gave it to her mother to post or rather enclose when she wrote to the C.O. & she forgot it for some days. Yesterday

DAY
14
SAT
21 AUG 1915

Item 16
Letter to Margaret

Envelope
*161 Haverstock Hill
London*

some officers of the 2nd Batt motored over to see me & the 1st Batt, which is in the trenches about 7 miles off. They had tea with the 1st Batt in the trenches, & while there those d-d Germans got an officer & 6 men with a shell.

Yes the watch Ronnie gave me is luminous & quite useful. I have just heard from Frank who says nothing at all of interest. Ask Renee to write me a letter we all screamed at the one she wrote "Dug".[2] We found some champagne last night to drink your health in, but just our luck there were only two bottles left.

All my love & many many happy returns. Love to Paula & all.

> Thine
> Charles

1 **Patricia Walton** (my grandmother, aged 14) was the C.O.'s daughter, and quite precocious to be writing to her father's second-in-command.

2 It may have be a misspelling but given their situation in the trenches 'Dug' was a very apt name for **Douglas Tosetti ★**, and it stuck.

DAY 15 SUN

22 AUG 1915

Item 17
Letter to Margaret

Envelope
161 Haverstock Hill
London

Sunday

My Dearest Wife

Not a letter from you today & not a letter from anyone. We have had quite a nice day German Aeroplanes being very busy, one got over us early this morning, & dropped a few bombs but not near us, and most of them failed to explode, one fell in our padre's garden[1] but did not go off. We move up to the firing line at 7 pm tonight but will be in the reserve for the next 5 days. Last night Ronald & I dined with the senior supply officer who produced some 06 Champagne, which we did real justice to. I told Douglas where we dined so we adjourned there at 11 am this morning and did in a couple and everyone said "Mrs Bartlett said if there is any champagne about trust the 8th Berkshires to find it". You will be glad your prophecy is being carried out.

Will you please send me a supply of Keatings[2] I have tried every shop in the place, & the powder we are served out with, well, the lice and fleas just grow fat as butter on it.

We are all fit. Best love to you & All

> Thine
> Charles

Many Many Many happy returns of the day

1 The Padre was **Arthur Longden**, 36, whose official rank was 'Temporary Chaplain to the Forces, 4th Class'. His letters to the bereaved would show there was nothing 4th Class in his compassion for others.

2 **Keating's** were famous for their insect powder sold with the motto '*Keating's Powder Kills with Ease, Bugs & Beetles, Moths & Fleas*' and they certainly made a killing during the war. ➜397

August 23rd 1915

Dearest Margaret

    We are thinking of you on this your twenty first birthday[1] & wishing you all the best of luck. We moved up here last evening, & now we are told to move somewhere else tomorrow. Oldman was out last night with a digging party up near the firing line, & all got back safely. There is a big fight going on on our right & a cricket match just behind us. Your letters arrive now pretty quickly but if you want to put more address you can now put 1st Division 4th Corps. Post two letters at the same time & see how it works. The Billets here are quaint. Ronald, Dug, Hannah and I live in two small rooms over the village shop, to get to which we climb over sandbags & up the most rickety staircase. We cannot have the windows open until we are in bed as we cannot show a light. Outside are dug outs where we dive into when shelling commences. Just as we were turning in we were told to "Stand By" & be ready to move at ½ hours notice, but that did not stop me from putting on my pyjamas, which reminds me I could do with a clean pair as I have not a change with me and have been wearing the same ever since we left. In this village there are very few houses that are not full of holes & the church is in pieces. The churchyard holds a lot of the 13th Hussars,[2] & several other Regiments.

All water here has to be boiled but we drank a lot before we discovered the fact. However no one seems any the worse.

I envy you being in London for one reason, & that is you have a decent lavatory & they dont know what that means here.

I hope you have seen more of Mrs McGibbon the little man is quite upset about her, & was awfully pleased you went to tea with her. I hope he will be able to get a day or two's leave when the Division goes back for rest, as his case is I think exceptional.

Well All Love old Lady or a rather older Lady.

           Love to Paula

           Thine

           Charles

DAY
16
MON

23 AUG 1915

Item 18
Letter to Margaret

Envelope
161 Haverstock Hill
London

FIELD POST OFFICE
23 AU
15

Tobaccanist's shop in
Noyelles-les-Vermelles

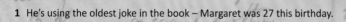

1 He's using the oldest joke in the book – Margaret was 27 this birthday.

2 What I think he means is that these units are camped in the churchyard. He is in Noyelles-les-Vermelles and according to the Commonwealth War Graves Commission, no members of the 13th Hussars are buried there.

Item 19
Letter to Margaret

Envelope
*161 Haverstock Hill
London*

August 24th 1915

Dearest Wife

Not much news this morning. There is an Aeroplane show on at the moment about 6 of them hovering over us, I wish to goodness they would go away, or they will draw fire.

I said so, two shells have just gone over our heads. Last night we had a lot of men out digging. Oldman's lot were under a fairly warm fire, but although there were casualties of other regiments working all round us we did not have a single one. I think we have been very lucky up to now, & go out of range for 4 days at 7.30 pm today. I do not go out with these working parties and it seems that all the trouble occurs then. We had 2 bottles of port last night Ronny, Dug, Oldman, Hannah & self and all solemnly drank your health out of tea cups.

I am president of the next Court Martial to assemble, I hope I dont have to sentence anyone to be shot.[1] Well Dearest I have no more news today, & I see the party arriving I have to hand over these filthy pigstyes to, so au revoir.

with all love   Thine
Charles

---

1 At this time, death was the penalty for crimes like murder but if you were serving in the British Army during a war you could also be shot for casting away arms, cowardice, leaving post without orders, sleeping when on sentry post, mutiny and sedition, striking a superior officer, disobedience in defiance of authority, and desertion or attempt to desert.

To be eligible to serve as president of a Court Martial (the equivalent of a judge in a civil court) an officer had to hold the rank of major or above, and it must have been the case that Charles's pre-war regular service gave him the knowledge and experience to take on the role.

There are a lot of mentions of Courts Martial in the letters that follow but my attempts to find out more about the cases in which Charles Bartlett was involved have been hampered by the fact that few records still exist. Documents recording courts martial proceedings were amongst the huge volume of paperwork stored by the War Office in a warehouse in Walworth, two miles directly south of St Paul's Cathedral in London. On the first night of the Blitz (7th September 1940) that warehouse was hit by German incendiaries & destroyed. From the original 1,400 tons of files in the store, only 300 tons of charred & water-damaged documents were saved.

People researching the First World War history of their ancestors will be familiar with these 'burnt documents' as they include what remains of the service records of wartime soldiers (only a third of all soldiers have any records left, and many of those are just scraps). Less well-known is the fact that a lot of records had already been systematically destroyed by the War Office in the 1930s.

A lot of this destruction was as part of a weeding process to lessen the space needed for storage (I have come across countless officers' service records which have a rubber stamp of *'KEPT'* followed by a list like *'1, 4, 5, 6, 7 destroyed in 1930'*) but it appears that the opportunity was taken to get rid of a lot of 'difficult' material too. Evidence of this can be seen in the war diaries of Army Divisions where sections relating to courts martial have been cut out with a blade, with *'weeded'* written above the resulting blank hole (I can't imagine the people who did this ever thought their work would be viewable worldwide at the touch of a button).

For most courts martial, the only thing that might remain is the barest of entries in a register of cases, and possibly a few remarks in a man's service record. The exceptions to this come from those 306 who were actually executed (out of the over 3000 who were sentenced to death).

From this meagre evidence, none of which has Charles Bartlett's name on it, I have managed to identify a number of the men who appeared before him at courts martial and I was able to answer the question of whether he sentenced anyone to be shot, as you shall see.

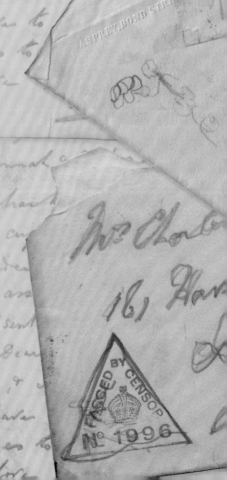

8ᵗʰ *R.B.R.*

August 25ᵗʰ 1915

4 pm

Dearest Margaret

This is the second day I have not heard from you but I expect it is because of the move. We arrived here[1] last night at 10 pm, & I was glad when we left the other place as there was a nice artillery duel going on, & of course all our lads would crowd out in the open when the shells were dropping about 200 yds in front of us, & it would not have surprised me at all if the Germans had lengthened out & dropped one amongst the lads. They will never learn to take care of themselves until a few of them have been shot. Here I have a nice billet, clean with a clean bed, & nice clean sheets, & the cleanest WC since I left home. The mens quarters are better, but far from satisfactory.

Last night I was recognised in the dark by two officers in the Camerons[2] I had not seen since I left Gib,[3] I suppose they spotted my back.

Here we are under two hours notice to move but dont expect to move for 5 or 6 days, but as you can imagine we never know.

We have not a good mess place[4] here, & I fear we shall live on the old stew which is so stringy it gets in my teeth.

I have written to Cox[5] to see how much I am overdrawn at the end of the month (I have not cashed more than a fiver since I left), & will send you all I can.

Tomorrow is washing day & the next a clean issue of underclothing for the men, which is the first. If a letter comes in from you later I will answer it.

All Love to All

Thine

Charles

DAY
18
WED

25 AUG 1915

Item 20
Letter to Margaret

Envelope
161 Haverstock Hill
London

FIELD POST OFFICE
25 AU
15

HAMPSTEAD S.O.
8.45 PM
26 AU
15
N.W.

On the envelope that contained this letter you can see evidence of Charles's 5-year-old daughter playing with a pencil, drawing on the back and tracing over the address.

1 They were now in Verquin.

2 Camerons = 1ˢᵗ Battⁿ Queen's Own Cameron Highlanders, another battalion in 1ˢᵗ Brigade.

3 Gib = Gibraltar – he was there in 1900-1902.

4 mess place = somewhere the officers could meet and eat, separate from the men.

5 Cox = **Cox & Co**, the bank that the majority of British Army officers had their accounts with. It had its origins in the 18ᵗʰ Century as a regimental agent responsible for pay and the marketing of officers' commissions. In 1914, its staff numbered 180 but by 1918 that had increased to 4,500 and their Charing Cross office was clearing 50,000 cheques a day. That expansion could not be sustained after the war, and despite merging with another bank in 1922, losses became so huge that they were forced to sell to Lloyds in 1923. The name continues today in Cox & Kings, a travel company based in Mumbai with a turnover of over £300m.

Item 21
Letter to Margaret

Envelope
161 Haverstock Hill
London

FIELD POST OFFICE
27 AU
15

Friday Aug 27th 1915

Dearest Margaret

    Of course I want a letter every day, I look forward to them although I had quite a bunch yesterday, which I suppose wont recur again.

Lilians letter I enclose, it apparently takes much longer to get a letter from Dinard[1] than from London.

I also heard from John, who had no news.

Mrs. Henderson[2] thanking me for tea sugar etc I sent her from Warminster.

Mrs. Walton[3] & Patricia about the tray. I did not get a letter off to you yesterday as I was delayed 2 solid hours at the Brigade, & the post had gone when I got back. Today we have an inspection by the new General who has come to command our Brigade, and we have formed what is called a Headquarters company of signallers, orderlies sanitary squad etc., which have been placed under my charge, so I shall have more to do.

Goodrich[4] must have been a bit wrong because unless Worlock[5] was the man who lunched at the same table in a Restaurant I have not yet lunched with that Regiment. I wrote to the Chief Constable about your camera, & asked him to reply direct to you, if he has not done so I should drop him a line & remind him.

The Coldstreams & Scotts Guards have left this Brigade as they are forming a Guards division.

Ronald is very well, and sends his love.

I shall certainly keep your photo, it is better than none. The D͏ʳ has got his leave, I wonder if you will see him, I am so glad he was able to get it.

Now I must close all Love Dearest to you Paula & all.

        Thine
        Charles

1 Dinard is a coastal resort in Brittany.

2 **Phyllis Henderson**, 33, was the third wife of Reading's Chief Constable, **John Henderson**, 54 (his first two wives had died aged 29 (from dysentery caught in Ceylon) & 41 (as a result of childbirth)). She was involved in the Berkshire Women Volunteers who ran a refreshment stall for servicemen at Reading station. A rector's daughter, she was also secretary of the Reading branch of 'Our Dumb Friends League', an animal charity that was the forerunner of The Blue Cross.

3 **Emmie Walton**, 46, daughter of a Professor of Ecclesiastical History at Glasgow University, was the C.O.'s wife, and had been presented with a large silver tray ★ by the officers of the battalion to mark their leaving for France.

4 **Louis Goodrich** was the stage name of Louis Goodrich Abbot-Anderson, 43, now serving as a 2nd Lieutenant in the Artists' Rifles. He'd been a farmer in British Columbia and a tea planter in Ceylon before becoming an actor, and had appeared with Charles's wife in *The Girl in the Taxi* at The Lyric in 1912 (though the picture, *(left)*, shows him with the original star of the show, Yvonne Arnaud). ➔**396**

5 **Frederick Worlock**, 28, was also an actor. His London stage debut was in a 1910 production of *Mrs Skeffington* in which he was very well reviewed, playing a cavalry captain. In real life he was now a 2nd Lieutenant in the London Scottish.

Sunday

My Dearest Margaret

      Something must have happened to the post as I rec[d] all three letters last night, written the 25th and 26th. Many thanks for same. I am awfully sorry you are having such trouble with the solicitors & I will help you all I can, but at the present moment I dont know if I have any money or not. However old Darling, you must make the best of things, you have all I have except my pay, & you know out of that I have to pay back £10 a month, so there is not much left, & I dont think we shall be any better off for sometime, with income tax 5/- in the pound.[1] However, cheer up, only dont complain in war time, it cant be helped that my income is £300 or £400 less than it ought to be,[2] and we must live accordingly. I was delighted to get Bobbys letter also Lilians, and it makes no difference in time how much address you put on but the Military Postal Authorities have issued a warning to say that if any more than the name of the Regt is put on the letters will be delayed. I have written you about your camera. Our General is a man called Reddie[3] & a charming fellow. Berlein is behaving quite nicely at present, he & Paramore dont seem quite so thick as they were.[4] Please thank Paula for her letter & Renee for her share of the letter, which made us smile somewhat. Last night Ronald Oldman Self Dug & Hannah rode into town & had a good dinner with Dover Soles & Roederer 06. We move back about Tuesday I think. The Germans seem to have superior aeroplanes now.[5] We have seen some fine ones the last day or two. I am enclosing you all the ready money I have, which you will have to pass through some account. Many thanks for the pyjamas fly net papers Keating's etc.

All my love Dearest & cheer up. Yours ever & ever

                Charles

Item 22
Letter to Margaret

Envelope
*161 Haverstock Hill
London*

FIELD POST OFFICE
29 AU
15

1 Income tax at 5 shillings in the pound = 25% (there were 20 shillings in a pound). His first inspection of the 8th Royal Berkshires was on his 42nd birthday. →**403**

2 An army Major was paid 17 shillings a day (£310 a year), so he was earning half of what he was pre-war. That said a Private then was earning only £20 a year. Today a Private's salary starts at £18,489, and a Major's at £50,417 (i.e. roughly a ratio of 1/3 not 1/16).

3 Brigadier-General **Anthony J Reddie**, was the commander of 1st Brigade. Though Scottish, his parent regiment was the South Wales Borderers. He spoke French, Urdu & Baluchi and had served in Egypt, Gibraltar, & India.

4 **Berlein ★**, *(right)*, and **Paramore ★**, (CGP), *(left)*, were great pals – *this picture and note* from their time in training along with Charles's comments are what remain of their friendship.

5 The new Fokker fighters could fire a machine gun through their propellers, giving the Germans a significant advantage. The 'Fokker Scourge' went on into early 1916.

Item 23
Letter to Margaret

Envelope
*The Old House,
Aylesbury*

*Forwarded to:
161 Haverstock Hill
London*

FIELD POST OFFICE
30 AU 15

AYLESBURY
2 PM
1 SP
15

> *Monday*
>
> *4 pm*
>
> **My Dearest Darling**
>
> Many thanks for your letter of Friday just rec^d. I could not write before today as I have been president of a Court Martial all day, only just back & the post is just going. Yesterday we motored with our supply officer to a Boxing Match about 12 miles off & the first person I ran into was "Kid" Kennedy who wished to be remembered to you.
>
> We move from here tomorrow where to you must find out. It is about 12 miles from here & is no nearer the firing line.[1]
>
> Yes I know where Scrub[2] is but dont see much chance of meeting him at present. I will write tomorrow, as tonight I am dining out with the London Scottish,[3] & the post is waiting for this.
>
> All Love Dearest to you & Paula also Tilly & family
>
> *Thine*
>
> *x Charles x*
>
> *x x x x   x x x x x*

This was the first of his letters to be signed off with lots of kisses, and this then became a regular feature. My guess is that reality might have been kicking in and he'd realised that things might not be forever. It would have been about this time that the battalion were first told that they would be taking part in the next Big Push. The previous morning the battalion had attended a church service on the lawn at the back of the Château of Verquin *(left)*. They were in beautiful surroundings and the Divisional Band played. I can imagine the atmosphere must have touched all who were there. He didn't mention it in his letters, maybe not wanting to worry Margaret.

1 His complicated underlining code spells out their next location, 'Ames'.

2 'Scrub' is the nickname for Charles's younger brother Alfred, and a not very complimentary one at that, given its implication of inferiority (as in scrubland rather than fine upstanding trees). Charles, being the 7th of 8 children, may have felt the need to exert any superiority he had, however meagre. **Alfred James Napier Bartlett**, 31, was a regular army captain, married with two infant daughters. At the start of the war, he was the adjutant of a Territorial (i.e. part-time) battalion of his regiment, the Oxfordshire and Buckinghamshire Light Infantry, and had arrived in France at the end of March 1915.

3 The London Scottish was the commonly used name for the 14th Battalion of the London Regiment, a Territorial unit originally founded for Scots living in London.

RÉPUBLIQUE FRANÇAISE
5 c POSTES

Châteaux des Environs de BÉTHUNE
31 — Château de VERQUIN

Edition F. R

August 30[1] 1915   6.30 a.m.

Dearest   x x x x x
Darling   *for you*

                 x x x x
                    for Paula

       As I told you last evening we are on the move again, it is a long march[2]
and it is going to be a very hot day.
We had quite a nice dinner with the London Scottish last night, & unlike us
they have some whisky left, & we are without a drop, which is a calamity I never
dreamt would occur. From accounts you seem to have been feeding yourselves well,
I wonder what grouse tastes like. We hope to be able to replenish our stores today
or tomorrow at the place I lunched at when out here before.
The inhabitants of this village are filthy no less than 3 pigs being killed in various
streets at the same time, one just under my window, & I was not feeling my best.
Also a cow had to have a love affair with a bull & that operation took place in the
middle of the village square.
Do you ever write to Paramore now, if so ask him about the pretty girl where he
is now billeted. She is quite the prettiest thing you could want to see, & he sleeps
alone there, I dont thinks its nice, & I notice the Billeting officer never arranges
anything like that for me.
We expect our D[r] back tomorrow. I wonder if you will have seen him.
Here we get Mondays papers at 6 on Tuesday morning and so on, which is not
bad, but there is not much in them. The fly net is quite a success thank you, & I
am very grateful for all you have sent. I cannot return Bathursts[3] letters as they
are packed in my case, but will do so tomorrow. Love to Tilly & All Love to you &
Paula.

                 Thine
                 Charles

DAY
24
TUE

31 AUG 1915

Item 24
Letter to Margaret

Envelope
The Old House,
Aylesbury

Forwarded to:
161 Haverstock Hill
London

FIELD POST OFFICE
31 AU
15

AYLESBURY
1 PM
2 SP
15

1 It's early in the morning and he puts on the previous day's date.

2 It was at least 13 miles on the roads from Verquin to Ames.

3 **Algernon Bathurst**, 52, was Charles's solicitor, with premises in Lincoln's
Inn Fields. He had power of attorney over the Bartletts' financial affairs
whilst Charles was away on active service. He would live to see another
World War, his brother Allen being killed whilst staying in a Knightsbridge
hotel during the worst night of the Blitz (10th-11th May 1941).

| Algernon: | | | 1900 | | 2000 |
| Allen: | | | 1900 | | 2000 |

57

Item 25
Letter to Margaret

Envelope
The Old House,
Aylesbury

Forwarded to:
161 Haverstock Hill
London

FIELD POST OFFICE
1 SP
15

AYLESBURY
11.30 AM
3 SP
15

Tuesday   Aug 31ˢᵗ 1915

Dearest Darling

We are off in 5 minutes & have just received your letter of Saturday. I have written every day and caught the post every day except one but of course letters may get hung up but you ought not to have been two days without. I am very sorry about Major Moyse, he really ought not to be "Lowsy" in England, & perhaps it was only a harvest bug, I shouldn't think it was excitement if he has sufficient left in him, he had better come out here, as men are still wanted. I hope to goodness Malcolm gets caught. It looks like real hard rain & has suddenly turned quite cold, so I expect we shall do a good march.

We have a lot of men down with Diarrheoa (dont know how to spell it) & I did not know how they were going to do the march, but we have just been told to find a working party of 60 who will follow us tonight in motor lorries, so I have given each one of them a cork & turned them into the working party, and the marching reputation of the regiment will be saved once more.

The Walton family[1] are staying at The Manor House Aylesbury, so I sent Patricia a line & told her to go & see you & Paula. No time for more.

> *All Love to All*
> *Thine*
> *Charles*
> *x x x x x x for you*
> *x x x x x for Paula*
> *x x x x for Tilly*
> *x x x for Elizabeth*
> *x x for the Babe*
> *x for the wild duck* ⓧⓧ
> ⓧⓧ *are they good to eat.*

[1] The Walton family as they were in 1912, from left to right: Billy, mother Emmie, father Colonel **William Walton★**, Sandy, Diana & Patricia.

Billy won cups for polo & horse racing & retired as a Lt Col in the Gurkhas. He once told his wife he was off to post a letter & disappeared for 2 days giving someone directions to Southampton.

Sandy, an aesthete & friend of writers, recorded a musical version of Edward Lear's *The Dong with a Luminous Nose*. He lived in Greece and died from injuries sustained in a mugging.

Diana was an accomplished painter and married a pioneering officer of the Tank Corps who had become the youngest DSO in the British Army during the Boer War.

Sept 1ˢᵗ 1915

2.30 pm

My Dearest Darling

Have just rec[d] your letter of Sunday. The march here was much longer than we thought, & we arrived in the dark last night & had a rare job settling in. Of course I have got the best billet & am staying with Ronald in the Mayors house, which is quite clean, & superior to anything I have struck yet. The C.O. is away this afternoon & I am having a merry time, as we had an inspection by a big bug of a General this morning, who said the mens clothes were dirty. They only have one suit to live & sleep in, no blankets at night, no straw, the roof full of holes so what the Devil or how the hell the poor devils are expected to keep them clean I cant think, however I am doing my best.[1] Also I am starting a portable coffee shop & tobacco shop for the men, which I hope will be successful. Thank goodness a bottle of whisky has turned up, not that I want to drink it, but one has to have something to take away the taste of the water.

Our men seem at last to be beginning to realize what discipline is and I should be very sorry to have some of the punishments I have heard of here.[2]

Not having a Battalion mess one sees little of some officers and I have seen very little of Berlein lately.

The men had a great reception in this village yesterday the natives supplying tea fruit etc gratis; no troops have been here for a long time.[3]

My legs are getting so thin I shall have to send my breeches home to be taken in, so when you get back, will you send the _thick_ pair made by Brass & Pike[4] to them & tell them where they lace up are to be made quite ¾ inch smaller below the knee & in comparison above. One pair of breeches are now worn quite through where I grip on the saddle, & can only be used in fine weather.

It is raining steadily this afternoon & thank goodness we are in comparative comfort. I am sending this to Aylesbury as you have not stated when you are leaving there. I am glad you are getting on with the frock, which I am sure will be a success.

Well, Dearest All Love to you & Paula, Tilly & her family

Thine always

Charles

X pour les deux

Item 26
Letter to Margaret

Envelope
*The Old House,
Aylesbury*

Forwarded to:
161 Haverstock Hill
London

FIELD POST OFFICE
2 SP
15

AYLESBURY
9 PM
3 SP
15

(Revised System of Squaring).

Allouagne   Verquin

1000 yards = 0.57 miles = 914 metres
(The British Army was still using imperial units)

1 The general was Major General **Richard C B Haking**, 53, who at this time was commander of 1ˢᵗ Division. This was not the only time that he would complain about a unit having dirt on their clothes, seemingly out of touch with the hard realities his men were dealing with. He was known as a 'thruster' and had already been involved in actions where his over-optimism had led to disproportionately heavy casualties amongst the troops under his command. Three days after this letter he was promoted to command XI Corps and

would acquire a reputation as a 'butcher' and an organiser of pointless 'stunts'. He was later awarded three knighthoods: GBE, KCB, KCMG, and lived to be 83.

| | | | | | | | 19|00 | | | | | | 20|00 |

2 Flogging was abolished in the Army in 1881 but in its place came 'Field Punishment N° 1' where men were tied to a gun wheel or fence post in a strained position for up to two hours a day. This practice was only stopped in 1923.

3 On the *above* map from amongst Leslie Berlein's belongings, you can just about see the dots where he marked the location of Ames, off the top edge of the printed grid. It was a long way behind the front line so hadn't seen British troops until this time when the Army was concentrating for the forthcoming battle. The front line was off to the right of this map, 7 miles to the east of Béthune.

4 **Brass & Pike** were tailors in the City of London (liquidated in 1952).

DAY
26
THU
2 SEP 1915

Item 27
Letter to Margaret

Envelope
The Old House,
Aylesbury

Forwarded to:
161 Haverstock Hill
London

FIELD POST OFFICE
2 SP
15

Thursday

Sept 2ⁿᵈ 1915

Dearest Darling

     No time for a letter today. We are back here "resting" which is a farce. I was up at 5.30 a.m. at the Brigade office 6.45 to 7.15 breakfast at 8 a.m., out with the C.O. from 8.30 to now 12.30, when we are snatching lunch & have to be off again at 1 pm, so you can see I have no time for a letter. Tonight I have night digging to superintend so leave here at 7.30 and get back at 1.30 am; a pretty good day's rest.
I will write again after tea but it will be too late for post.

       Au revoir

       All Love

       Thine

       Charles x

AYLESBURY
11.30 AM
4 SP
15

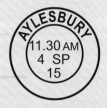

The battalion had now definitely been told that they were to prepare to go into action. **Colonel Walton★** ordered trenches to be dug so that they could be used for practising the attack.

Sept 2ⁿᵈ 1915

Dearest "Old Woman"

I have not heard from you today. I wrote you a hurried note while I was swallowing my lunch. We are very busy, in fact after I had got out into the country this afternoon with the Colonel I remembered I had to examine a lot of N.C.O.s[1] in Guard Duties etc. so had to gallop home for all I was worth. We are having mutton tonight, the first time, as an issue of rations, for 3 months. I happened to see it in the stores, so had a nice saddle cut for our dinner tonight. We have no luxuries in this place, but I have sent the transport cart 24 miles for some whisky tobacco etc.

Another post is just in & no letter from you. I am fed up, I do look forward to them, & I suppose it is because you have not heard from me as you say in your last letters, but I have written every day.

All All All Love Dearest to you & Paula

Thine

Charles

[1] N.C.O.s = non-commissioned officers, e.g. corporals & sergeants.

Item 28
Letter to Margaret

Envelope
The Old House, Aylesbury

Forwarded to:
161 Haverstock Hill London

This is a spare piece of paper from a court martial I have just done[1]

Sept 3ʳᵈ 1915

My darling Wife

Many thanks for your long letter of the 1ˢᵗ just arrived. I am afraid you will be short of letters again as I have been addressing them to Aylesbury for the last 3 days. I did not mention Ronald had killed a German, because I was not quite sure he had, but as it has now been entered in the Regimental records it must be true.[2] I am sure I told you about taking the Walton kids to Aylesbury which was the same Sunday as I went to see about poor old Teds funeral.[3] I should not worry about Hilda's remarks,[4] she is a typical officers wife, & they cant help it, and there is only one thing to be said for them, that they must be better than the new officers wives judging by the husbands. Am glad your camera has arrived. I dont think John Samuels would soldier for two thousand per year. Never mind grumbling about money, remember it is not money you grumble about but the lack of it.

DAY 27 FRI
3 SEP 1915

Item 29
Letter to Margaret

Envelope
161 Haverstock Hill London

I know I have got into debt since the war started & meant to in case I dont get another chance, but not very much has come out of my income, & I am repaying the £200 out of my pay, "so lets be fair". I dont mind your working, I know it only means temptation for you, & if you are earning £5 per week it costs you all that in new clothes etc. Certainly be independent that is why I am not touching my private income.

I will certainly speak to Berlein about his mother[5] & make him write to her, as I told you I have not seen much of the lad lately but whether it is lack of initiative or laziness I dont know, he wants more push in him. My tobacco and coffee bar opens tonight & already two other regiments have been round to enquire how I have managed to start such a thing. It has poured with rain all day, & we have two digging parties out and another from 7.30 to 12.30 tonight, so I expect we shall all be laid up. Personally I got thoroughly wet yesterday with the result I have a beautiful go of lumbago[6] today, & am trotting about like Rip Van Winkle. Still we must "keep smiling" "merry & bright" "on we go again" "looking forward" etc.[7] All Love Dearest little wife

Thine now & always

Charles

x x x x x x x x x x x x x all for you & Paula

1 Paper wasn't as cheap and freely available as it is now (particularly when on active service) so he is making use of the foolscap Royal-crest-embossed paper he can get from work.

2 It does not sound like he believes it is true but the entry in the 8th Royal Berkshires war diary for 19th August 1915 says: *"One German sniper who had been sniping D Company trenches during the night was shot & killed by Major Brakspear at 4.15 AM on this day as he was crawling back to his trenches with grass & branches tied round him"*.

3 'Poor old Ted' was Charles's eldest brother **Edward Noel Napier Bartlett** (pictured *above* as a 2nd Lieutenant in the Royal Bucks (King's Own) Militia in 1893). He had died aged 44 on 17th April after 4 years suffering from 'general paralysis of the insane', a form of dementia associated with syphilis. His widow was not listed among the mourners at his funeral. It sounds as if he would have been unaware of his son Geoffrey's death in the war. → 390

4 **Hilda Bartlett**, 33, was brother Alfred's wife. Her father had taken over as managing director of the family's clothing manufacturing firm whilst his father was sitting as an MP for Leeds, but had died when she was only 4.

5 **Elizabeth Berlein**, 54, *(right)*, was an Irish farmer's daughter who had been amongst the first women to graduate from Queen's College, Belfast, reading French, English and History. She adored Leslie and it's no wonder she would have been concerned about him as his eldest brother Charlie had been killed near Ypres just 2 months before.

6 Lumbago = lower back pain. He was over six feet tall and a martyr to his long back.

7 He would have seen these phrases over and again when censoring the men's letters.

Saturday

Dearest Darling

Have not much news today I dined with A Coy last night & we had an excellent dinner. Ronald Dug & Hannah came in afterwards and we were quite late not going to bed until 11 pm.

I dont think we shall be left here more than a day or two as there seems to be some move on. The Colonel has to go up to the trenches on Monday, so it appears as if the Brigade will be sent up to a new section. Yesterday was the first time I could really test my new boots & they leaked abominably. It is a d-d shame. Ronald bought his direct from Cordings & they are much better boots & 15/- cheaper.

A real hot fine day today after the rain, and I am just off with the C.O. to see the work being done.

All Love Dearest to you & Paula & a bit for Renee

yours always

Charles

DAY
28
SAT

4 SEP 1915

Item 30
Letter to Margaret

Envelope
161 Haverstock Hill
London

FIELD POST OFFICE
4 SP
15

Sept 4th 1915

4 pm

Dearest Darling

I have just rec[d] two letters one dated Aug 30th & the other Sept 2nd. The one you wrote Sept 1st I rec[d] yesterday. What part are you going to play in Peter Pan. I dont want my wife parading as a Red Indian but if Wendy or Mrs Darling, and the salary is good I should take it.

Yes I saw about Kenneth Douglas.[1]

I dont think Birch is enjoying himself so much as he was.

I am sure Hilda's economy must be rather trying. I shall write her a line, and ask her to send me some grouse.

Poor old John he seems to be having a rotten time looking for rooms.

Yes we are at the place you think, but it is only a village 14 miles from our last spot.

The little D[r] arrived back safely last night, meanwhile the daily sick had increased

Item 31
Letter to Margaret

Envelope
161 Haverstock Hill
London

FIELD POST OFFICE
4 SP
15

to 40 per day, which will have to be cut down.

Poor old Pat you seem to have had a cheerful time rescuing him.

I dont know what regiment Lennox Napier is in but I saw one of that name had been wounded. Paula has not written me a letter for quite a long time. Well Dearest I have answered all your questions and many thanks for your letters.

> All All All Love Darling
>
> Thine for ever
>
> Charles
>
> x x x x x x x x x x x x for you
>
> x x x x x x x x x x x for Paula

1 **Kenneth Douglas**, 39, *(right)*, was a well-known actor who had been on the West End stage for over 20 years. In 1914 the lure of Broadway saw him cross the Atlantic and he also had a taste of Hollywood with a part in a Mary Pickford film. Originally booked to return home on the *Lusitania*, he'd been warned off by friends and so wasn't aboard when she was sunk on 7th May 1915 with the loss of 1198 lives. However a later trip to New York saw him on the *SS Arabic* when, at 8.32 a.m. on 19th August, a torpedo struck without warning. She sank in 10 minutes but thanks to the captain's planning and quick thinking, all but 44 were saved. Kenneth got onto the last boat but one, wearing just his pyjamas and a Burberry coat. In an interview you can hear how deeply affected he was as he describes the awful silence after the ship went down and seeing the wreckage as they rowed away. He returned to the stage but died of alcoholic poisoning in a New York sanitarium 8 years later. ➔ 394

DAY 29 SUN

5 SEP 1915

Item 32
Letter to Margaret

Envelope
161 Haverstock Hill
London

Sunday

Dearest Margaret Jane Darling

We are having quite a busy Sunday, digging trenches & practising shooting. Two companies put in church parade this morning and the other two are at it now. I had an accident last night and broke half my tooth off, it was the one who had been stopped and now I have some terrible sharp corners, which are cutting my tongue, so I am going to ride into the town where I was stopping before & see a dentist. We expect to be on the move again in about 3 days and hope to get close up to the Huns.

There was no letter from you today so I have not much to write about, if I could write all I know I am sure you would be interested but the censor might open it & I might be cashiered.[1] We had a long conference last night and although it was most important we were all so tired that we nearly went to sleep. My coffee bar is a great success and I am nearly sold out. There is a cinema performance 3½ miles off tonight but I dont think I shall go.

I have no more news, but lots of work to do. All All Love Dearest

yours now & always

Charles B

Love to Paula
Renee Billy etc   x x x x x x

1 'Cashiered' meant to be dismissed in disgrace, and it came from the time when officers had to purchase their commissions – the money was paid as a bond and if they broke the rules badly enough, they lost the chance of selling on their commissions. Even knowing this, you can see that Charles is itching to tell Margaret the details of what's going on, and though he omits some really secret stuff, there is still plenty of information in these letters for people in England to be talking about, with the chance it might reach the wrong ears.

Monday

Dearest Darling

I am still without any news. The C.O. is away, gone up to look at the trenches we are going to occupy and I am going up for the day on Wednesday or Thursday to have a look. Last night we spent framing orders for an imaginary attack, and this morning I am taking the Batt up to the trenches we have been digging where we shall practise the attack etc.

All the men are very happy today as the Field Cashier is about so they get some pay. I hope Berlein has written to his mother he promised he would. I hope to get to a dentist this evening as my tooth is rather troublesome. We are now issued with 1 respirator and 2 gas helmets each, so ought to be able to keep out any bad fumes. The big guns are making some noise today.

I hope we shall get a move on soon we are all tired of this place.

I will write later today.

All All All Love

Thine

x   X   Charles   X

DAY
30
MON
6 SEP 1915

Item 33
Letter to Margaret

Envelope
161 Haverstock Hill
London

DAY
31
TUE

7 SEP 1915

Item 34
Letter to Margaret

Envelope
*161 Haverstock Hill
London*

FIELD POST OFFICE
7 SP
15

HAMPSTEAD S.O.
8.45 PM
8 SP
15
N.W.

Tuesday
3.30 pm

My dearest Darling

    I wrote you yesterday and got a letter from you written from Winchester, also one from John. This morning I rode about 12 miles & had the remains of my tooth filed down so that I need not cut my tongue every time I eat. It was quite a nice ride & hardly touched the road all the way. There are a mass of troops up here now and wonderful improvements being made for instance there is an overhead wire running right from the back of the trenches to the front of the trenches along which hot dinners can be sent up, & wounded men sent back without anyone exposing themselves. Of course the wounded would only be sent out at night but it is a great advance on the old way of doing things.

Tomorrow I have another Court Martial to preside over, it is rather sickening out of 5 Regiments in the Brigade at present time there is only 1 other Major qualified to sit as president so I am getting my full share. Is it not about time those mattresses turned up? Not that we shall have an opportunity of using them for a week or so.

My groom Lawrence[1] has just paid 10 francs for straw for Punch to sleep on, I told him that the earth was quite good enough & I could not afford these luxuries. I have laid in a store of chocolate for our next move as we dont expect to see our transport for 3 days; however my French being so good, I have no fear of going hungry.

I have your photo in my pocket book and if I had one of Paula it would match. I have had very few letters lately, just buck a few people up to write.

    All my love is Thine & Thine only
      Now & ever
        your own
          Charles

---

1 There were at least 10 men with the surname 'Lawrence' who served as privates in the 8th Royal Berkshires and I haven't been able to further identify Charles's groom. As a Major, Charles had a groom to look after his horse and a batman as his personal servant. His batman looked after his kit and personal admin, and even sometimes cooked his food (though there was also a cook allocated to Battalion HQ), the official aim being to free up officers to do their job of leading.

Question sheets

In amongst the letters are lists of questions written by one of them with spaces to be filled in by the other. Only a few remain, but there must have been more given that some of the questions seem to be referring to news not given in Charles's letters. For

example, in Item 36 opposite, picking out **Lionel Edwards★** to enquire after his health at a time when he was unwell, but the first mention of that was in the letter that Charles sent the day after he posted off the reply to Margaret's question.

8 SEP 1915

Item 35
Letter to Margaret

Envelope
161 Haverstock Hill
London

FIELD POST OFFICE
8 SP 15

HAMPSTEAD S.O.
8.45 PM
9 SP
15
N.W.

Wednesday   Spt 8th/15

Dearest Darling

Your letter of 6th just arrived & I was glad to get it. Yes <u>Dearest</u> you go & work if you like, if you think you will be happier.

We are very busy now practising the attack under new methods,[1] and what with going up to the trenches & getting ready for a move you must not mind if you dont get a letter written tomorrow, however I will write when I get back tomorrow. Talk about a rest here, we were up at 4.30 this morning and did not get to bed last night until after 11.

I came back early 10 a.m. this morning to act as President of Court Martial, but there was only one prisoner who did not take long. I see now that all Captains with 15 yrs service have become Majors, so I shall not now be caught as often as President of Court Martials. Also all the regular Subalterns of 4 years service become Captains, and so the regulars will not be so mad with K's lot.[2] I enclose answers to your questions, and must stop now. All my love Dearest Darling. Cheer up & dont fail to write to your ever loving husband

Charles X

---

1 The new methods included the use of chlorine gas.   **2** 'K's lot' is Lord Kitchener's New Army (including the 8th Royal Berkshires) who had enlisted as temporary soldiers for the duration of the War, as opposed to the pre-war Regular Army.

Item 36
Question Sheet from Margaret & answered by Charles

How is Edwards.   Better but not well.
Do you feel better.   yes thank you
Has the lumbago gone.   Not quite.
Who is your transport Officer   Lt & Qr Mr Barrow.
Do you say a prayer for us.   yes my nypt.
Have you written to Lillian   yes but no answer. doubt if letter reached.
Have you seen Herbert or Hugh.   No.   No.
Would you like a leather waistcoat   yes in due course
(I hear they are quite the most useful things to the winter

Please answer these questions & return.

DAY
33
THU

9 SEP 1915

Item 37
Letter to Margaret

Envelope
161 Haverstock Hill
London

FIELD POST OFFICE
9 SP
15

HAMPSTEAD S.O.
8.45 PM
10 SP
15
N.W.

Sept 9th 1915

My dearest Darling

     Many thanks for two letters, one written Monday evening &
one Tuesday morning.
The grouse have arrived quite well I think, they are cooking & will be eaten cold
tonight, I think however if sent in a Game Box they would travel better.[1] I am
afraid I cannot answer your questions for if I did & the Censor opened the letter
I should get into trouble. A most terrible blow has fallen on the Regiment, and
it could not have happened at a worse time and that is the India Office have
claimed the C.O.[2] & he is ordered to leave Marseilles for Aden the day after
tomorrow. Whether his departure can be delayed for a week or so remains to be
seen, but it will temporarily give me command of the Rgt. at the most critical time
in its career.
Peter does not seem in a hurry to come out. We have not been up to the trenches
today but start at 8 am tomorrow and back tomorrow night. We are having fine
weather now but the wind has changed round which is a nuisance.
Poor old Edwardes[3] was taken off to 6th Casualty Clearing Station Hospital.[4] We
dont know what is the matter with him but fear Typhoid you might write him a
line, it can be sent over from here. The C.O. has not told Mrs. Walton about his
move yet, but she will be very pleased about it. John sent me many papers, please
thank him, I will write when I can, but if I have to take the C.O.'s place I shall
not have much time during the next week or so.

    All Love Dearest to you & Paula

          Thine

          Charles

1 Game birds could then be sent through the post unplucked with just a label round their neck (as long as they didn't leak!).

2 The C.O., **Colonel Walton★**, was a regular Indian Army officer and as such was still under the control of the India Office, though on loan to the British Army. This is what he wrote to his wife on this day: *'I received today an official from the India Office ordering me to proceed at once to Aden to take over the duties of Colonel on the Staff there, leaving Marseilles on the 11th Sept – they say that warrant & ship's ticket follow – The letter was addressed to Codford and was dated 2nd Sept & only arrived here today. I ought to have told India Office that I was leaving for France,* but forgot to do so. The ticket etc have not arrived – I took the letter up to Brigade H.Q's but the General was unfortunately out – I left it with the Bde Major who is going to show it to the General & they will fix up what I am to do. I cannot of course afford to have any trouble with the India Office – but it will be a sad blow to have to part from my Battalion just now as you will understand more fully later on. It seems decreed that I am to train battalions but not to lead them into the fight. I do not complain, but I will be sad to say farewell to them without a chance of having a go at the Bosches – & seeing how they behave. If I am to catch the boat at Marseilles I must leave here tomorrow morning – & and I dont know how I am to* get there, but shall no doubt find out in due course. Perhaps I may get a motor from here to Paris. But perhaps the General may be able to fix it up for me to stay for a fortnight more, as the Brigade Major said he was sure he would be very much upset if I had to go.'

3 Edwardes = **Lionel Edwards★**, 31. I've seen a few people with common surnames adding an extra 'e' (to make it less common?). In all official records he is 'Edwards'.

4 Charles did write the location of the hospital (Lillers) but it has been obliterated by a blob of blue pencil from a censor (and to think what else he left in). This is the only evidence of a censor I've seen in all of these letters.

DAY
35
SAT

11 SEP 1915

Item 38
Letter to Margaret

Envelope
*161 Haverstock Hill
London*

FIELD POST OFFICE
11 SP
15

Saturday

Dearest Darling

     No letter from you today this is twice this week. I got back too late to write yesterday. It was a beautiful day but very hot walking about the trenches. Fresh trenches nearer the German lines have been built since I was there last, but it was a very quiet day. One shell dropped about 15 yds from us and exactly where we had been but that was our fault as four of us had periscopes up all at once.[1] It is real good news from Russia[2] and I hope we shall soon have those fellows thinking. A shell burst on the road we were motoring up and knocked one man off his bicycle but he got up unhurt except for a few bruises. We were out practising the attack this morning and may have a dress rehearsal with empty bombs tomorrow. We got a draft of 65 N.C.O.s & men this morning but no officers. The Army Corps Commander[3] has stopped the C.O. going to Aden until he receives instructions from the War Office himself, but I am afraid there is no hope of us keeping him, for if he remained here he would be given a Brigade, however when there is a fight I expect it will be the biggest in <u>world's history</u> and he would be very depressed if he missed it. It seems a pity we cant down some of those Zepps.[4] The M.O. has just heard from his wife that one Zepp bomb dropped in the next block to her house. Is this America?[5] Well dearest Darling I must now go and inspect these new lads.

    All All All love Dearest to you & Paula

      Thine

      Charles

      X X X for you

        x x   for Paula

          x   for the rest

1 Periscopes were used to view no-man's-land and the German trenches without exposing oneself to snipers. As he points out, though, if the Germans saw a lot of periscopes going up in one place, then they could get the idea it was a gathering of senior officers and call down their artillery onto that spot.

2 The good news from Russia was that after a period of struggling against their invaders, the Russians had just taken prisoner more than 200 officers and 8,000 men.

3 Army Corps Commander = Lieut-General Sir **Henry S Rawlinson**, 51. His father had been a major-general but also the 'Father of Assyriology', finding carved inscriptions that led to the decipherment of cuneiform. Henry inherited his father's baronetcy in 1895. Without a role in August 1914, he was briefly Director of Recruiting before being given command of a division in September.

4 Zepps = Zeppelins, which had just made raids on the nights of 7th and 8th September with 44 people killed and 142 injured in Norfolk and London. The capital's few anti-aircraft guns had not come close to hitting the enemy (the airships flew way up out of range – unlike in the mock-up ***above***!). The small number of British aircraft up in the night sky did not even see the Zeppelins.

5 Mrs McGibbon was Canadian and so used to talking about cities in terms of 'blocks'. Charles obviously was not.

DAY
37
MON

13 SEP 1915

Item 39
Letter to Margaret

Envelope
161 Haverstock Hill
London

FIELD POST OFFICE
13 SP
15

CHAMPAGNE CHARLIE.

THE GREAT COMIC SONG, WRITTEN & SUNG BY
GEORGE LEYBOURNE.
MUSIC BY
ALFRED LEE.

Sept 13th 1915

My own Darling Wife

    Many thanks for both letters which arrived yesterday. You seem to be having a bad time with the Zepps, & I am glad you have got Paula away, and I shall be very pleased to hear that you have cleared out of the danger zone also, as it cannot be much fun in London. I could not write yesterday as I went into early service if you please and we then had church at 10.15, after which I inspected all Billets, stopping at C Coy's mess, who had discovered a Magnum of Roederer 1906.[1] Lunch at 12.45, and then the Colonel had all officers with our trench maps at 2 pm and he lectured & discussed the attack[2] until 5 pm when the post had gone. It is still beautiful weather and we shall remain here until it breaks. I have been thinking what with the shells out here and Zepps over London it is quite dangerous for both us, and if we took the knock who would be Paula's legal guardian. I believe the Scrub would be and then she would only learn interior economy, so I was thinking it would be a good thing if Lilian would take over the job. I will write her on the subject and you might have a talk to her. The Colonel has heard nothing further about going so we hope he will be able to stay on a bit longer.

The men are all marching 5 miles today to have a bath which I am sure they need as the only stream in this place is very muddy indeed. No sign of the beds yet. Many thanks for the fly ointment which we will try when we move up to the trenches. Ronald is up in the trenches this morning meeting a man who will operate on his left next time we go in.

Six sergeants & a Coy Sgt Major of the London Scottish have been given commissions, it makes it very hard for the regiment to carry on, they have now supplied over 400 officers out of the ranks.[3] The Germans are now painting their Aeroplanes to resemble ours, & one got over with some bombs before he was spotted. This is a true story of a German Aeroplane. "It was hit be one of our machine guns in the vicinity of - - - - - after being hit the left bottom plane slanted up towards the top & the machine listed to the right. Apparently the stay was broken. Twice it nearly turned over, & then the observer was seen to climb out into the lower plane to counteract the list. He stood up and finally lay down on the plane, & then the machine was seen to descend in a normal manner."

I think the German was a plucky devil, and I only wish he had fallen off.

Have you heard from Berlein or anyone lately?

How is Charles business doing?[4]

How do you know about Mabel Russell?[5]

Shall I write & congratulate her?

How is Paul?[6] *I have written him*

Why is the theatre off?

Have you seen Peter?

Is he not coming out?

Any news of when Bobby is coming?

Have you heard or seen Lady Crutchly?[7]

No more news Dearest All my love my Darling

Thine for ever

Charles X

1 Louis Roederer was (and still is) a champagne.

2 There is now absolutely no hiding that they are about to attack. Seeing all the men and materiel massing and with the optimism coming down from senior officers that nothing could withstand the vastness of the upcoming assault, maybe he thought that victory was inevitable whatever he wrote. He was not alone in this – Colonel Walton was similarly indiscreet when writing to his wife.

3 With the shortage of officers, men were being selected from the ranks to be given commissions. The London Scottish was a unit of the Territorial Force & would have included a lot of men of officer class who during peace-time wanted to enjoy camaraderie without having to have any responsibility & so had done their part-time soldiering in the ranks.

4 **Charles Measures**, 45, was the husband of Margaret's sister **Elizabeth** (she had turned 33 the day before). He was a jeweller, which must have been a precarious business in wartime. Both of them lived into their 90s.

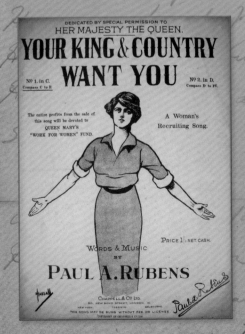

DEDICATED BY SPECIAL PERMISSION TO
HER MAJESTY THE QUEEN.
YOUR KING & COUNTRY WANT YOU
Nº 1. in C. Compass C to E   Nº 2. in D. Compass D to F♯.
The entire profits from the sale of this song will be devoted to QUEEN MARY'S "WORK FOR WOMEN" FUND.   A Woman's Recruiting Song.
PRICE 1/- NET CASH.
WORDS & MUSIC BY
PAUL A. RUBENS

5 **Mabel Russell**, *(above)*, 29, was one of the most famous actresses of her time. In a classic rags-to-riches story, she had been plucked from working in a London box office to go on the stage and had her big break when a lead actress fell ill. Huge success followed and in 1911 she married a vastly wealthy nephew of Cecil Rhodes. Only 6 months later, in trying to avoid an oncoming motorist their car rolled on a sandy verge. Her husband died from a fractured skull & she lost the sight in one eye. She overcame her injuries & returned to the stage. Maybe the gossip in this letter is about her getting together with another wealthy businessman who she would marry in 1917. After the war her husband became an MP but was thrown out of Parliament due to his agent's electoral fraud. She stood in his place, a London girl in Berwick-upon-Tweed, & was elected as only the third ever female MP.

6 **Paul Rubens**, 40, was their composer friend who had been behind many hit musicals of the Edwardian era. His recruiting song *(left)* had the refrain *'Oh! we don't want to lose you but we think you ought to go, For your King and your Country both need you so'* and raised over £500,000 for a fund to help working class women. Ironically both his parents had been born in Prussia, and only became naturalised British citizens in 1887 (though Paul was born in London in 1875).

7 **Lady Sybil Crutchley**, 49, was a grand-daughter of the 1st Earl of Leicester. A well-known amateur actress, she and Margaret had been involved in a series of charity concerts in the Northampton area in 1913.

Item 40
Letter to Margaret

Envelope
*161 Haverstock Hill
London*

Sept 13th 1915

Monday

My dearest Darling

    Many thanks for your letter written on Saturday. Paula does seem to be in demand what with Hilda wanting her also Dolly[1] & Florrie.[2] I think she might very well pay a round of visits as with luck we shall soon see which way the wind blows. I wrote you a letter this morning and ought to be on parade this afternoon but have had a phone message to wait in and see the General Commanding the 1st Division,[3] I dont know what time he is coming, but I guess it is to see if I am fit to command the Battⁿ.[4] Anyway I have just put on my cleanest tunic & breeches brushed my hair and now await his Lordship.
The Doctor was up in the North most of his leave time, and he heard you were out of town, so we must accept that as a satisfactory explanation.
Of course when letters leave here they go not direct to the field post office but to the supply columns wherever they are and from there to the field post office. Edwardes is suffering from what is called "Trench Fever" in plain English I think, and all the common sense people do also, that it is a mild form of Typhoid, but the authorities do not allow that, as it would spoil statistics for the inoculation returns for typhoid.
Well <u>Dearest</u> I have no more news. There is nothing I think I want from
    Stonecroft, unless you wish to make up the breakfast service.[5]

    Love to all & special love to you

      Thine

      Charles

1 **Dolly** = Margaret's sister Martha, 28, who had also been an actress before her 1912 wedding to William Clowes, now 39.

2 **Florrie** = Charles's sister, married to Alfie Fraser who Charles had seen in Le Havre.

3 Following General Haking's promotion to command XI Corps, the new General was **Arthur Holland**, 53, *(left)*. The son of a Major-General and the grandson of a Vice-Admiral, his original surname was Butcher. With that being a nickname for commanders who did not look after the lives of their troops, and having been Major Butcher for 12 years, he changed his name to Holland in 1910, the year he was promoted to Colonel. An artilleryman, he served with distinction in the Boer War, and as a Brigadier early in this war he had developed methods which became the standard for artillery organisation and direction. He would go on to command I Corps, be knighted in 1918, and take the seat of Northampton as an MP in 1924. Over a thousand mourners attended his funeral at which the pall-bearers were all generals or colonel commandants.

4 Colonel Walton wrote to his wife on 18th September, relaying his telephone conversation with the Brigade commander who had asked who Colonel Walton thought should succeed him as C.O.: '*I told him I recommended B* [i.e. Bartlett]. *He is a born organiser & he knows all my ideas. He is a busy man & would make a good C.O. if he would not worry them all too much by knowing too much. It is essential for a C.O. to concentrate his attention on matters of importance & not to worry with the minor details more than can be avoided. I think he realises this.*'

5 Stonecroft was the house of his half-sister **Sybilla McNair**, the eldest of his father's children. Her mother had died 2 months after giving birth to her, and she was the widow of Rev Harry McNair who had been the vicar of Aylesbury. She had died on 23rd July and with probate having been granted on 31st August, the family must have now been clearing her house. Her younger son Archibald had drowned aged 13 whilst bathing on holiday in Wales in 1910, and her elder son John was now serving as a 21-year-old regular officer in the Royal Field Artillery and had just had his wedding in June. ➔399

Sybilla

husband Harry

son Archibald

son John

DAY
38
TUE

14 SEP 1915

Item 41
Letter to Margaret

Envelope
*161 Haverstock Hill
London*

FIELD POST OFFICE
15 SP
15

Tuesday

6.45 pm

Dearest

    Have been out all day since 6.30 am so have had no time to write. I must now go down to a Supper being given by the Machine Gun Section, then feed at 7.45, & lecture on first aid at 8.45. We expect to move from here about Friday now. Edwardes is better but will not be well enough to move up with us which is a draw back. I did not have a single letter which was very disappointing. The weather here has broken at last. I am sending this off early tomorrow morning and will write again after lunch, as we shall be out from 7.30 to 12 midday practising the attack which I can almost do blindfolded. Am dining with Oldman tomorrow night as he has raised some chickens from somewhere. My handkerchiefs are now reduced to one so I hope to get some before I start for the trenches. Shall expect some nice cheery letters from you next week.

    All All All Love

    Thine

    Charles X

I wrote Paula yesterday

DAY
39
WED

15 SEP 1915

Item 42
Letter to Margaret

Envelope
161 Haverstock Hill
London

FIELD POST OFFICE
15 SP
15

Wednesday
7.30 a.m.

My Dearest Wife

I wrote you a hurried line last night & said I would write again today, but at 10 pm last night I got orders to go up to the trenches today, just to arrange a few things, so shall not be back before the post goes. It is a ripping morning and a motor ride will be very enjoyable, also I hope to be able to buy a bit of fish for dinner.

The breeches are now quite a decent fit, and so I shall cast away the old pair as they are now through in 3 places, with two leather patches sewn on them.

I have an awfully good story for you but it will have to keep for certain reasons until the end of the week. I expect I may meet some old friends today as plenty more seem to be arriving.

I have absolutely no more news. The Dr's Lecture went on until 10 pm last night, & then the C.O. talked until 10.45 so it is a strenuous life.

All love Dearest

Thine

Charles

DAY
40
THU

16 SEP 1915

Item 43
Letter to Margaret

Envelope
161 Haverstock Hill
London

Thursday

Dearest Darling

Still in the same place awaiting orders to move. We are all very fed up with the delay but it cannot be helped. Many thanks for two letters which arrived last night. I am afraid Mrs Waltons wish will not be gratified as I think the C.O. wont go for a bit yet. I am not at all certain to get command of the Regiment, when he does go, although I have been recommended for it. The idea is that Majors of the regular Batt[ns] should be brought in to command, however we can but wait and see, and I shall have no right to complain if I dont get it. We laughed at your experiences with the plumber, not that we weren't very very sorry for you, but it is so like them you ought not to have expected anything else. I do not know Schuster[1] or Gaythorne Hardy[2] the latter is since my time. Edwardes gets his letters regularly in hospital, they are sent from the supply column I believe.

I am sorry I did not make more comments on your Zep shocks but what could I say except that I think you & Renee might have gone out in the street and had a look, for if one had fallen on the house and not actually hit you you might have been buried in the debris.

I had quite an interesting day yesterday in the trenches, there was not much going on and if I told you about the days work the censor would be down my throat. I had a letter from Frank written on Saturday, but he has not much news.

Mumps has broken out in the next village, which has been put out of bounds. If we stay here much longer I shall have to have clean sheets. We had a great dinner last night with A. Coy. and I enclose the menu. We played shove halfpenny afterwards.[3]

Love to Renee & all & all Love to you

Thine

Charles X

1 **Arthur Schuster**, 64, was a physics professor who was in the papers at this time due to a libel case. Charles and Margaret's interest was because they knew Arthur Pearson, the publisher of *'Pearson's Weekly'*, the gossipy newspaper that had sullied Professor Schuster's name. In an article about women of the Anti-German Union catching spies, it had been heavily implied that because he had been found to have a wireless apparatus in his house (and was a naturalised citizen rather than a true-born Englishman), he was not be trusted. →410

2 **Geoffrey Gathorne-Hardy**, 37, had just become the first officer of the Territorial Royal Berkshires to be awarded the Military Cross, for crawling through the grass of no-man's-land to reconnoitre the German trenches in daylight. →396

3 Shove halfpenny is a game based on giving a push to coins from the edge of a board with the aim of sliding them to rest next to various scoring lines. The scoresheet is *below*, written on the back of the field postcard that was also used for the menu.

Charles Frederick Napier Bartlett

Item 44
Letter to Margaret

Envelope
*161 Haverstock Hill
London*

FIELD POST OFFICE
19 SP
15

Saturday

My dearest Darling

I missed writing altogether yesterday, I was out all day. We are not getting so much fresh meat as we should like which is not to be wondered at, half the Regiment has fresh meat one day, and half tinned, so I thought I would go & try buy some extra. I rode off in the morning and went to many places before I found a farmer with some sheep who would part with them. He had fifteen & I offered him £45 for the lot, but he would only sell at 1½ francs a kilo live weight, so I had to accept and it was arranged they should be weighed and paid for this morning.

I got back late for lunch & just as I was sitting down to write Oldman came in with a very good idea,[1] which I thought was a brainwave on his part and might save a life or two so I rode out to the range and explained it to the Colonel who there and then sent me off to the town 5 miles to buy the necessary stuff and I did not get back until 6.30 much too late to write for the post. I cannot tell you what Oldmans idea was at present as it is in connection with something we are under oath not to mention.

Well we had dinner and in bed by 9.30.

Up at 6 a.m. and drove over the farm where the sheep were all weighed with the whole family looking on much talking, and it was a most serious ceremony. After the ceremony we had to adjourn at 7.30 a.m. to the farm house and a bottle of

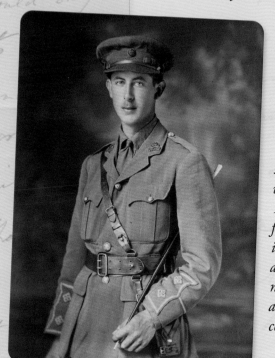

white wine & biscuits were produced. We sat round the table everyone added up the weights & made them different, the farmer & his wife had a row over it and everyone talked & eventually I paid over £44, so he would have done better to take my first offer. I then returned to billets and have since done some work and hired a yard to kill the sheep in which operation commences at 12 mid day.

This afternoon we have a Staff Ride to discuss the military situation, & tonight I am dining with a Captain Saunders, who is sending a car for me and Ronald, at a town some 12 miles off. Berlein has made an utter fool of himself by being found kicking up a row in an estaminet at 10.30 at night in company with a private soldier.[2] I have got to tell him off about it. The Colonel is disgusted and if we were not going to move soon he would have been Court Martialled. He is a fool, and it means the next time he misbehaves a Court Martial for certain. I think the boy must go off his head sometimes. Many

thanks for the handkerchiefs. Paula going to Hilda as a P.S. is the limit. The puzzle will do well in the trenches. I have not heard any more about the C.O. going yet, but of course it is only a matter of time.

If I was made Tempy Lt. Col. wouldn't Tilly be mad.[3]

  Well dearest I must stop now. All All All Love

   Thine

    Charles

1 Oldman★'s idea must be the one reported in the Battalion's war diary. The men would be wearing smoke hoods as protection against poison gas and the plan involved getting safety pins to attach them to the coat and elastic to enable them to naturally close around the throat. It just goes to show how primitive gas protection was at this stage in the War.

2 An estaminet was a French bar, and it was a strict rule that officers were not allowed to socialise with the men. **Leslie Berlein★, (opposite)**, wasn't one for rules or avoiding fun, though, and nor was he hidebound by ideas of class. **Above** is his silver cigarette lighter, engraved *'Leslie January 30 1914'* for his 21st birthday. I can just imagine him using it in the bar that night.

3 If he was to command the battalion, he'd be promoted to Temporary Lieutenant Colonel. All those who were commissioned for the duration of the War (as opposed to being regular officers) were granted 'temporary' ranks. His pathway to higher rank was rather different to those who'd stayed in the Army whilst he'd left for civvy street, and maybe Tilly's husband was a regular.

    Sunday

      3.30 p.m.

Dearest Darling

  Just got your letter written on Thursday. We have had no letters since Friday morning. I wrote you a long letter yesterday, & have no news or time to write it if I had.

I only wrote to Bathurst about a guardian for Paula, as that has to be attached to my will. I heard from Gracie today, go & see her at 22 Redcliffe Sq., also from Florrie. I think they are going to bring in a Colonel from a Hampshire Rgt. to command us, but nothing is settled. I have not dressed Berlein down yet as he went up to the trenches yesterday & is not back yet. I will give handkerchief to Paramore & will write again tomorrow.

   All Love

    In haste

    Thine

X   *Charles*

DAY
43
SUN

19 SEP 1915

Item 45
Letter to Margaret

Envelope
*161 Haverstock Hill
London*

HAMPSTEAD S.O.
8.45 PM
21 SP
15
N.W.

FIELD POST OFFICE
20 SP
15

DAY
44
MON

20 SEP 1915

Item 46
Letter to Margaret

Envelope
161 Haverstock Hill
London

8th Royal Berkshire Rgt.

7.30 A.M.   Sept 20th 1915

Dearest Darling

You are rather scored off for a letter as late last night I was ordered to go off at 8 am this morning so shall have no time to write and this is all I can do. The Regiment leaves here tomorrow and we shall not be sorry to go. I now must eat a meal as I shall not get one for sometime today and suppose I am for the trenches but shall not know until I reach Brigade HQ^{rs}.

All Love

your own

Charles

P.S. just got your Friday letter many thanks

FIELD POST OFFICE
20 SP
15

TRENCH MAP.
SHEET 36c N.W. 3 AND PART OF 1.

DAY
45
TUE

21 SEP 1915

Item 47
Letter to Margaret

Envelope
161 Haverstock Hill
London

Tuesday

Dearest

Am quite well on the move at last. Will be d-d cold sleeping in the open. I will write whenever I can. Many thanks for letters & photos rec^d last night.

All Love

Thine

Charles

FIELD POST OFFICE
23 SP
15

The Battalion marched to Bois Marquet (near Allouagne) and bivouacked there. That evening the Commanding Officer read to all officers the Battalion Operation Orders for the attack.

Item 48
Letter to Margaret

Envelope
161 Haverstock Hill
London

FIELD POST OFFICE
23 SP
15

Wednesday

Dearest Darling

We are well on the move trekked early yesterday morning and slept in a wood last night moved on early this morning and are hidden in another wood which we leave tonight and go up into back line of trenches. From there we move up in due course and I am just as sick and fed up as muck as I am being left behind with 6 other officers with the transport, the idea being that officers are valuable and all are not to be under fire at once.

As I am writing this Generals French, Douglas Haig & Rawlinson are standing within 100 yards of me.

I dont believe those people who say they like sleeping in the open, give me a bed and a roof & none of this imitation thunder & I am quite happy. It really is a most wonderful sight this soldiering and I would not have missed it for worlds.

I did not get a letter from you yesterday or today but dont expect them at present as I dont think the field post offices are open.

I will stop now it has taken me over 1½ hours to write this, the interruptions have been so frequent.

The C.O. is at a conference & everyone is nervy it just takes me all my time to keep cool answer questions and keep my temper.

All my love Dearest

Thine

Charles X

General Sir John French, 62, was in command of the whole British Expeditionary Force on the Western Front (and at odds with one of his sisters who was an ardent pacifist, suffragist & Sinn Féin activist).

General Sir Douglas Haig, 54, commanded First Army (in 1899 he had saved John French from bankruptcy & the ruin of his army career by loaning him £2,500).

Lt-Gen Sir Henry Rawlinson, 51, commanded IV Corps (including the 8th Royal Berkshires). He would go on to lead Fourth Army at the Battle of the Somme.

WILLS'S CIGARETTES.
FIELD-MARSHAL LORD FRENCH.

WILLS'S CIGARETTES.
LD-MARSHAL SIR D. HAIG.

WILLS'S CIGARETTES.
EN. SIR H. S. RAWLINSON.

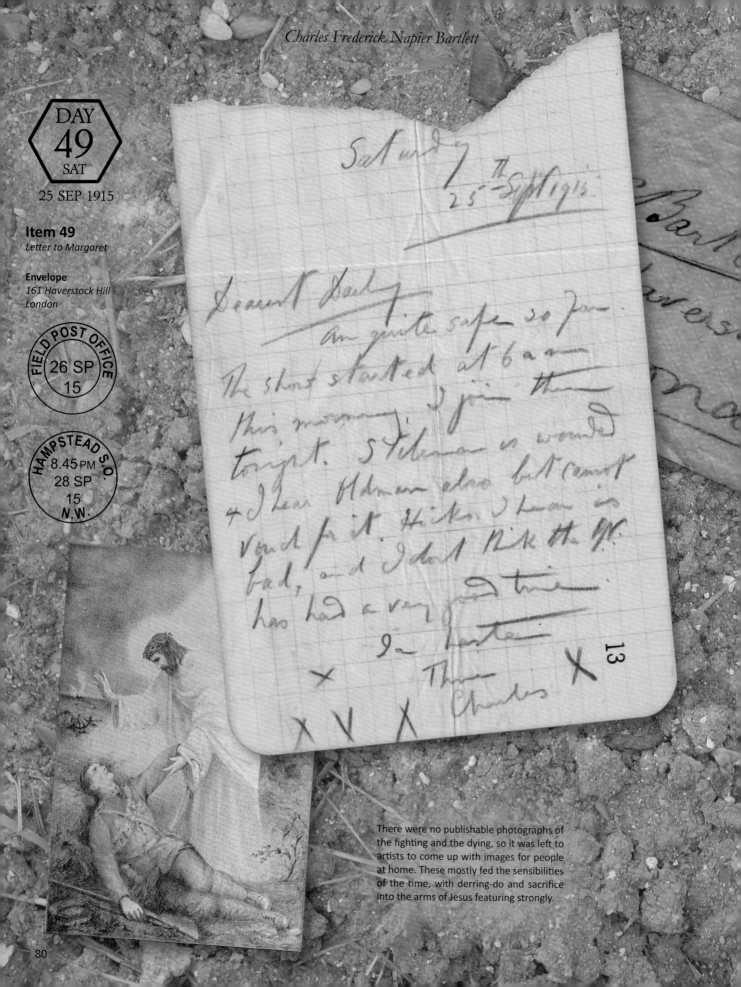

DAY
49
SAT

25 SEP 1915

Item 49
Letter to Margaret

Envelope
161 Haverstock Hill
London

FIELD POST OFFICE
26 SP
15

HAMPSTEAD S.O.
8.45 PM
28 SP
15
N.W.

Saturday
25th Sept 1915

Dearest Darling
An quite safe so far.
The stunt started at 6 a.m.
this morning, I join them
tonight. Stikeman is wounded
& I hear Oldman also but cannot
vouch for it. Hickson knee is
bad, and I don't like the Wr.
has had a very good time.
In haste
Three X
Charles

13

There were no publishable photographs of
the fighting and the dying, so it was left to
artists to come up with images for people
at home. These mostly fed the sensibilities
of the time, with derring-do and sacrifice
into the arms of Jesus featuring strongly.

GERMAN.

Guard- Pioneer. Infantry Guard Field General. Hussar. Mounted Foot Lancer. Cuirassier. Dragoon.
Rifles. Officer. Artillery Rifles. Artillery.
Officer.

20

Infantry. Train. Guard, Machine Medical Or
Gun Battery.

21

The booklet, *(left)*, was issued as a guide to the armies of the main combatants in the war. Due to their underground existence many of the British soldiers of the new armies would not have yet seen a German soldier – and in fact, as they advanced with fixed bayonets through the fog of no-man's-land, many died without ever having seen their enemy.

The map shows the front line, with the hatched area being the ground gained during the Battle of Loos. The 8th Royal Berkshires attacked left to right on an axis between Vermelles and Hulluch.

THE FACE OF THE WAR.
British Advance in the Hulluch district.

DAY
51
MON

27 SEP 1915

Item 50
Letter to Margaret

Envelope
161 Haverstock Hill
London

FIELD POST OFFICE
29 SP
15

The Trenches
Monday   27th Sept. 1915

Dearest Darling

  Just a line to tell you I am still sound in wind & limb. The Regiment has had a hell of a time but has made a fine reputation. As I daresay you guessed from previous letters we led the assault on our part of the line and out of 20 officers and 900 men, only 2 officers & 184 men finished up, but we made our objective and took four German line trenches, and if others had done as well we should have gone further on. As I told you I was kept out of the Assault with Edwardes, Coote, Spartali, Robinson Cloake & we joined up that night, ever since which we have been under heavy fire which has not done any more damage. Our officers fared as follows

  Brakspear wounded in knee
  Oldman wounded
  Hanna missing believed dead reported seriously wounded
  Tosetti wounded, not seriously
  Paramore missing no hope
  Cassells dead
  Berlein dead
  Peacock dead
  Glen missing

53

Rouse wounded

Marsh wounded

Hicks dead

Hobbs missing believed dead

Haynes missing

Allen wounded believed dead

Keable missing believed dead

Stileman wounded

Gentry Birch missing but today found alive with 20 men of his company attached to another Regiment.

It has been a ghastly business too awful to describe.

We know of no particulars as to how people met their end as the advance was made under a cloud of smoke & gas. The Camerons Gordons & Black Watch have been fighting with us & they are fine men especially with a bayonet. We have neither washed slept & been practically without water for two days. It is now starting to rain.

Leslie was the first to be killed getting out of the trenches & I dont think lived long after he was hit.

I cant write more now as of course I have a lot to do compiling lists etc, besides I am dead beat.

We hope to move out of the trenches tonight to reorganise what is left of us.

All All Love

Thine

X X   Charles X X

Tuesday

Had a bad 2 hours last night being shelled like hell very lucky just missed each time.

No relief last night & it was freezing hard, we have no coats or blankets. I really thought I was going to knock under, the most awful attack of lumbago. The Colonel leaves today so no chance of a rest. Shall be d-d glad when this phase of this great battle is over. God what a sight it has been.

Too cold to write

All Love

Charles

The Colonel & Lawrence were the only two officers to survive both did wonders.

Tosetti also spoken well of until he was hit tell Bogie Smith this phone him.

Ronald Brakspear★

MAJOR

Brewery Director

39

WOUNDED

Wilfred Oldman★

CAPTAIN

*Rancher
in South Africa*

36

DEAD

Douglas Hanna★

CAPTAIN

*Tea Broker
in Ceylon*

42

DEAD

Douglas Tosetti★

CAPTAIN

*Champagne
Merchant*

38

WOUNDED

Gordon Paramore★

CAPTAIN

Artist

30

DEAD

Hugh Cassels★

CAPTAIN

*Engineering
Graduate*

21

DEAD

Leslie Berlein★

LIEUTENANT

Law Graduate

22

DEAD

Gordon Peacock★

LIEUTENANT

*Trainee
Accountant*

21

DEAD

David Glen★

LIEUTENANT

*Engineering
Graduate*

21

DEAD

Aubyn Rouse★

2nd LIEUTENANT

*Lloyd's Insurance
Underwriter*

33

WOUNDED

Gordon Marsh★
2nd LIEUTENANT
?
22
WOUNDED

Basil Hicks★
LIEUTENANT
*French & German
Graduate*
22
DEAD

Tod Hobbs★
LIEUTENANT
Solicitor
23
DEAD

Billy Haynes
LIEUTENANT
*Ironmonger's
Assistant*
24
DEAD

Tom Allen★
2nd LIEUTENANT
Civil Servant
23
WOUNDED

Harold Keable★
2nd LIEUTENANT
*Agriculturalist
in Egypt*
26
DEAD

Donald Stileman★
LIEUTENANT
*History
Student*
21
WOUNDED

Cyril Gentry-Birch
LIEUTENANT
Town Hall Clerk
22
INTACT

William Walton★
COLONEL
Regular Soldier
50
SLIGHTLY
GASSED

Thomas Lawrence★
2nd LIEUTENANT
Mining Student
20
INTACT

The Battle of Loos saw the British Army lose the most men killed in one day in its history up to then. 8,571 died in the main attack and 1,616 in a diversionary attack at Ypres. This has only ever been surpassed by the first day of the Somme.

The photograph at the **bottom of the next page** shows the battlefield: a flat landscape with only the horizontal lines of white from the chalk of the trench parapets indicating that these fields contain thousands of men underground. Look below the white clouds of gas & shellbursts and you can just about see the little dark dots that are men attacking in the open.

Some details of the action come out later in the letters, but a lot was hidden from Charles being as he was in the rear during the assault. The great chums **Leslie Berlein★** and **Gordon Paramore★** were the first to be killed, Leslie when a shell burst upon him and his men in front of the German trenches, and Gordon being shot through the head when they had gone about 300 yards and reached the other side of the German wire entanglements. **Tod Hobbs★** and his sergeant were shot as soon as they got up to cut the wire that barred the way for their team of bomb throwers. **Basil Hicks★** was shot through the head right on the German parapet, his last words being *'Good lads, come on – straight ahead'*. **Harold Keable★**'s body was found in the third line of German trenches and the local newspaper reported that *'Major Bartlett wrote stating that he could not say how the gallant officer died as of those who were near, no-one was alive.'*

It may seem odd that he mentions only the officers and not any of the men by name, but he was a product of his time and his upbringing and this would change over the coming weeks and months of shared hardship in the trenches and with him taking over from Colonel Walton.

The only officer who died who was not in the Group Photograph was **Billy Haynes**. Charles sent the news of his death to his parents:

"His death was a great blow to us all. Not only have we lost a charming companion, but a real good officer. He was a natural leader of men, and the men of his platoon were devoted to him. When he came to us from the 4th Battalion, he came with a reputation which he certainly increased each day he was with us."

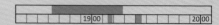

He is pictured with his father, William, 52:

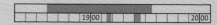

& mother, Annie, 55:

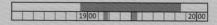

& his sister Agneta, 22, who is the only one with her eyes on the camera. She lived for another 70 years after Billy's death. During the war, she served as a nurse in a war hospital, & at her marriage in 1917 wounded soldiers made an archway of crutches and then cheered and threw confetti. Her husband was a decorated Kiwi Lieutenant Colonel who had survived Gallipoli and the Western Front, only to succumb to meningitis in May 1918 aged just 35. In her grief she went to visit his family in New Zealand, and unexpectedly fell in love and married his brother, with whom she had 3 children. She is buried with her two husbands in Reading and the grave includes the inscription *'Also in loving memory of my dear brother'*.

DAY 55 FRI

1 OCT 1915

Item 51
Letter to Margaret

Envelope
*The Old House,
Aylesbury*

Oct 1st 1915

Dearest Darling

     We are now away back out of the fire zone & d-d glad to be too. I am so busy reorganising I have not had a moment. I have written to Mrs Berlein this morning & four other parents, which was not a nice job. I rec^d two letters from you written from Windsor one of which complaining about not hearing from me. Dearest I was too busy in a trench without any head cover trying to dodge shells etc to write. The morning before yesterday a large German high explosive shell landed on the edge of my trench, and I thought "Good night all" but it did not explode which was a bit of luck.

The General has sent in my name to command this batt^n, and so I may be a Tempy Lieut Colonel soon. I have no notion how long we shall be here, I hear another Division in our Corps was badly cut about yesterday and the whole Corps may be sent back to reorganize, on the other hand we are at one hours notice to move up again if required.

The men are coming back and I now have 417, the majority of those who have returned were slightly gassed and will soon be ready for another go.

I lost my overcoat during the scrap & have not one at all and it is d-d cold. Will you go to Stovell & choose me one. He generally has the latest I want a very warm but light one.

I enclose you my cheque towards your fur coat.

     All All All Love

       In great haste

         Thine

         Charles

Item 52
Letter to Margaret

Envelope
*161 Haverstock Hill
London*

Sunday
Oct 3rd 1915

FIELD POST OFFICE
3 OC
15

Dearest Darling

      Still up to my eyes in work and no time for letter writing. Please ring up Frank & tell him so, also ask Paul when he is sending that music along. I rec[d] *3 letters from you this morning dated 28*[th] *29*[th] *& 30*[th] *for which many thanks. Apparently you have not yet had mine accounting the disasters which you ought to have had, as it was posted on the 27*[th] *instant. What on earth is the matter with last years fur coat, surely in these times that would have done. I am afraid by this time you will have had a bad time with Mrs. Berlein, Hicks etc. I was dead beat last night and slept for 11 hours without waking. I dont know where any of our wounded are. Douglas Tosetti, Stileman*[1] *and Rouse*[2] *are in hospitals near the base. I am sorry to say I now have to report Hanna as killed, I had hoped he had got off, but the Chaplain who buried him has been in so there is no doubt. We are under half an hours notice to move, but then we may not move for 2 or 3 days, anyway the rest we heard rumours of is OFF. I see the papers we got today talk a lot about Hulloch,*[3] *I never wish to see the place again, and our lot were the first there.*

More men keep arriving in driblets and I now number 470, so if I get a decent sized draft before any more of us are done in, I ought to have a fair sized Batt[n]*, as Batt*[ns] *go nowadays. This last week has been a tremendous strain on everyone and if we had not worked to death we might have moped so it is just as well.*

I hope you rang up Bogie[4] *& told him how well Douglas*[5] *has done. I would like to write him but have not a moment, I now know Douglas's name has been sent in for an award, but of course one cant tell if he will get anything or not, anyway it was a d-d fine action carrying on all day with a hole in ones leg. (you might phone him this). Give my very best love to Paula and tell her we killed some nasty Germans.*

Love to Renee Billy & everyone & with best love to yourself.

      Thine

      Charles

P.S. I enclose a letter I had from the Colonel which please keep.

1 **Donald Stileman**★ had been wounded with shell fragments in his back and foot even before the attack started. He would recover and rejoin the Battalion in early 1916.

2 **Aubyn Rouse**★, 33, had had his right arm broken by a bullet and this was the last he saw of the trenches during the war.

3 Hulloch = **Hulluch**, the village behind the German lines at their point of attack (as on the map, with the German trenches in red).

4 Bogie = **Bogie Smith**, who is mentioned regularly in the letters but who I have not been able to identify.

5 Douglas = **Douglas Tosetti**★, whose wound didn't keep him out of action for long.

Item 53
*Enclosed letter from
Colonel Walton*
(pictured **below**)

Envelope
(missing)

29*th* Sept 1915

My dear Bartlett

    I know long letters are a nuisance on service when you have so many important things to think of, but I must just write a few lines to say how full my heart is of you all in general & of you in particular. I am sure no C.O. ever had a better 2*nd* than I have had during the past year. I feel sure that you will be as good as a C.O. as you were 2*nd* & have the greatest confidence in your ability to carry out the difficult task you have in front of you. My feelings were too strong to permit me to say much when I said goodbye but I must thank you for all the help you have given me in my attempt to produce the best battalion in the New Army. If we have not succeeded at least I know we need not much fear comparison with the best. Many Battalions through whom I passed at various times during the course of the battle were grousing. I never heard a single grouse from one of our men – I felt that it would have been an honour even to be permitted to lay down one's life with our boys. No words of mine can express my admiration for & gratitude to the men the N.C.O.s & the Officers of the 8*th* R. Berks Regt. for their behaviour on the 25*th* and the following days. The conduct of the Scotties and the conduct of our men will leave a lasting impression on me and I feel I want to take off my hat to every Scotchman & to every Berkshire man. Tell them this from me will you? Please send me a line to tell me about our casualties when they are fully disclosed. I am extremely anxious to hear which officers were killed and wh. wounded – everything was so vague when I left. I felt anxious about you too as you were looking very tucked up. I hope you will soon be better. Do let me hear – Please send me a bill for anything I owe & include what I owe to King for services as groom. I suppose the Q*r* Master has got the kits & effects of the wounded & dead officers together & sent them off. The sooner he does this the easier it will be to get them away & clear the wagons. I have not heard definitely about Hicks & Paramore, Keable & Rouse whether they are wounded or killed. I think the Pioneer Sergeant should go round & mark the graves with a wooden cross with names in all known cases of officers and men. I heard that Peacock had been found & buried with the Office staff signallers etc all round. He must have been quite near to me & so must Hicks have been for they all came out of the trenches with me – only a little way behind.

General Reddie wrote me a note thanking me for the services of the Regiment and I would be glad if you would tell him how grateful I am for what he said. We were lucky to get such a Brigadier. Anyone would be glad to work for him

– and I am proud to have served under him – as I am to have commanded you & the 8th R.B.R. I see from the papers that good progress has been made at Hill 70 and that Fosse 8 has fallen to us. I wish we had been able to go through Hulluch, but I am confident that under the circs. we could not, and that if we had attempted to get in we could never have got out but would have lost our point d'appuie[1] which was so useful for the rest of the line to form on to. I am gradually getting a clearer idea of the battle into my head and I still do not think we could rightly have gone on.

Needless to say my thoughts are constantly with you, and please tell all that I have you all constantly in my thoughts & in my prayers. Let me know if I can do anything for you. In mentioning names of those who have done well I should recommend Lawrence,[2] Musto[3] and the little red headed m.g. man[4] whose name I do not know. They did fine work with the machine gun & Musto especially was cool and gave a fine example. I will never forget his honest dirty face. There was also a signaller with us whose name Musto will know who did good work. Where all did so well it is difficult to select any special names, especially as the chief part of our work was done in a thick fog. Perhaps Birch might be mentioned but I only judge from what he told me perhaps you could get more details about him from the 6th Gordons. I am afraid some of our boys who were wounded with him must still be lying out in the open if they have not been picked up by the Germans.

I am afraid you had a dreadful wet time when you came back from the front trenches, but today is fine again & I hope all got their greatcoats. I should get those buttons sewn on as soon as possible so that they may wear them in their next attack. I am certain they could attack in them & would be the better for them.

My boat goes out at 4.30 pm today (30th). Last night & this morning it did not run. Now I must go and try to get this censored and post it, in hopes you may get it some day.

May you have good fortune & success I pray most fervently, and I trust that we shall be through these cursed Germans in a day or two. I cannot thank you enough for all you have been to me during the past year but I hope you know how much I have appreciated what you have done.

Yours very sincerely

Wm C Walton

1 Point d'appui = an advantageous defensive position, used as a rallying point.

2 2Lt **Thomas Lawrence**★, 20, had taken over command of the Battalion during the first evening, despite being the youngest of the officers who had gone into action. With the C.O. suffering from gas inhalation and being ordered to the rear by the Medical Officer, he was the only fit officer left.

3 Serjeant **Henry Musto**, 38, was in the first ever photograph of the 8th Royal Berkshires, standing directly behind Charles Bartlett, *(right)*. He was tattooed with an H on his left forearm and a horse's head on his right, and had first joined the army aged 18 in 1895, serving in Nova Scotia, the West Indies, Gibraltar, and South Africa. Still a private when he left the army in 1907, he started in civilian life as a builder's labourer. He would be wounded on the Somme and become a foreman at an Army Ordnance Depôt after the war. →**401**

→**401**

| | | 19|00 | | | 20|00 |

4 The little red headed machine-gun man was Corporal **Charles Hayward**, 23, *(below)*. A cowman before the war, he was one of 4 brothers who joined up, with one being killed on the third day of the Battle of the Somme with 5th Royal Berkshires. Charles himself would be wounded on the Somme but survive the war to return to his cows. He'd married in early 1915 but his wife and 5 children wouldn't have him for long – he died aged 47 of blood-poisoning from a bone infection in his ribs and a carbuncle.

| | | 19|00 | | | 20|00 |

Item 54
Enclosed newspaper cutting

WHAT THE 8TH BERKS DID.

In our issue of to-day we are able to publish an account of the part, and a glorious part, let it be said, which the 8th Battalion of the Royal Berks Regiment took in the great advance last week-end, by which the Allies were able to make such capital progress. Although this battalion of the county regiment has only been at the front a few weeks, they have quickly been in the thick of the fray and have participated in the most successful attack for which we have been responsible during the war; and those who saw the men during their training at Reading, the excellent manner in which they carried out their drills, and their smartness generally, are not by any means surprised that they should render such a capital account of themselves. From particulars gleaned by our representative from members of the battalion who have returned to this country suffering from wounds, two platoons each of A, C, and D Companies were in the first line of their division when the charge was made. "We had orders to go over the parapet at about 6.30 a.m. on Saturday last," said a corporal. "This every man mounted and went forward. The enemy did not open fire until we got to their firing line. Then they opened a terrific fire with machine-guns and rifles. For a short period the fighting was of a severe character, but our superiority was so pronounced that the Germans discovered that further resistance was useless, and they either tried to make good their escape or surrendered. A large number were taken prisoners. At this juncture I was wounded. The enemy appeared to be completely taken by surprise. About an hour prior to the attack our artillery had opened a terrific bombardment." The story was taken up by another member of the battalion, who stated that immediately the first line of the enemy was taken the Berks and other regiments supporting them made a charge on the second line. "As soon as we got over their parapets they commenced retiring through their communication trenches as fast as they could. This line was captured without experiencing much difficulty, but on reaching the third line the Germans put up a stubborn resistance. They replied with a heavy fire, and the fighting was very severe, but by the aid of our reinforcements we were able to become masters of the situation. By this time their casualties had been very heavy. There is no doubt that the 8th Berks made a very fine charge, and we have earned encomiums of many who were in a position to judge on our excellent work." Tributes were paid to a number of officers of the battalion. One member said: "Colonel Walton is one of the best commanding officers at the front. He is beloved by us all, and an officer we admire for his fearlessness and courage. Captain Toseith is another officer who enjoys great popularity. His coolness was remarkable." Capt. Hanna, another officer, was also mentioned.

For their actions in holding a captured German trench under heavy fire at the Battle of Loos, Henry Musto and Charles Hayward were both awarded the Distinguished Conduct Medal (second only to the Victoria Cross for ranks other than officers).

Item 55
*Letter to
Colonel Walton
(kept amongst
his memorabilia
by his family)*

Envelope
(missing)

8th RBR
Oct 2nd 1915

Dear Colonel

Many thanks for your letter, like you I could not say much when you left but I never want to work with a better man than you and I hope we shall both live to talk over all this.

Am up to my eyes in work reorganizing, as we expect to move up tomorrow night (Sunday of course) or Monday morning. We went back the night you left to our original line where we were shelled for 24 hours. I was having an officers pow wow when a high explosive came plumb in the trench 4½ yds off but did not go off or there would not be a single officer left, the next night moved 3 miles back getting in wet through again at 3 am, moved on at 11.30 am 3 miles back where we are now. Total Strength 455 (for rations) Trench Rifles 317. I have 3 scouts out of 21. Bombers 53 out of 120. Signallers 18 out of 32. Machine Gunners 28, one machine gun has been returned.

Our casualties are very bad and I give you list Capts Oldman, Paramore, Cassells, Lieut Hobbs, Hicks, Peacock, Haynes, Keable, Berlein all killed Hanna missing probably killed. Rouse & Marsh[1] wounded, Allen still missing but known wounded.[2] Generals Reddie & Holland have both been round and made the most complimentary remarks about the Batt[n]. Am terribly short of N.C.O.'s, and am being harassed all round for returns. Poor Peacock[3] took all parade states & returns into the trenches and they have not been recovered, so I had nothing to work on. Gen Reddie is a ripper. Col Prichard[4] was sent home & Major Sutherland[5] commands 10th Glosters. <u>All</u> the officers pockets were rifled before they were collected & buried, a cross on each as you mention. Their kits went off directly we got here yesterday. The <u>Division</u> d-n them groused because we had eaten our iron rations & wanted an explanation in writing it was as follows "Because we were without food for 36 hours and were hungry." Oh for some officers & N.C.O.'s. Thank God I have the Sgt Major[6] & Barrow is keeping his head. Cloake[7] is a topper and Edwardes is getting his lot together, but the others are too slow for words, & cannot yet know what they want to complete, so I am having a Batt[n] inspection in fighting order this afternoon. I am just getting along but could do with a rest & wish we were going to have time

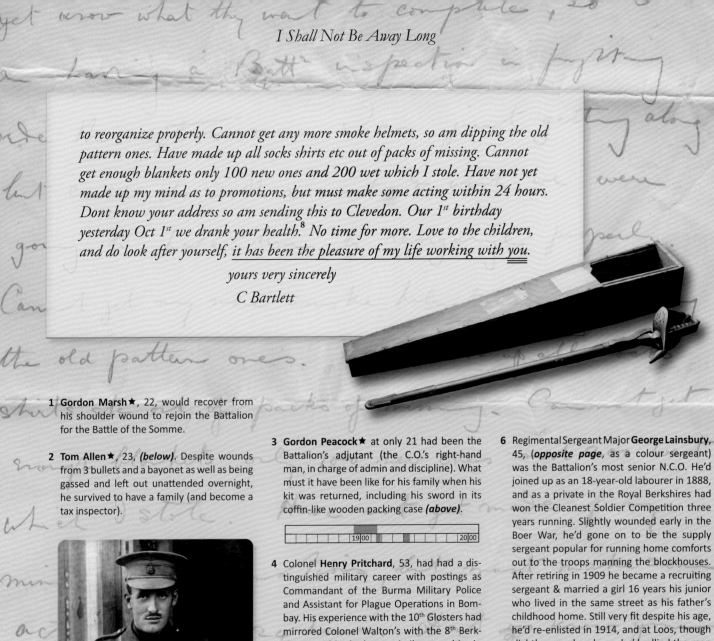

to reorganize properly. *Cannot get any more smoke helmets, so am dipping the old pattern ones. Have made up all socks shirts etc out of packs of missing. Cannot get enough blankets only 100 new ones and 200 wet which I stole. Have not yet made up my mind as to promotions, but must make some acting within 24 hours. Dont know your address so am sending this to Clevedon. Our 1ˢᵗ birthday yesterday Oct 1ˢᵗ we drank your health.*[8] *No time for more. Love to the children, and do look after yourself, it has been the pleasure of my life working with you.*

yours very sincerely

C Bartlett

1 **Gordon Marsh ★**, 22, would recover from his shoulder wound to rejoin the Battalion for the Battle of the Somme.

2 **Tom Allen ★**, 23, *(below)*. Despite wounds from 3 bullets and a bayonet as well as being gassed and left out unattended overnight, he survived to have a family (and become a tax inspector).

3 **Gordon Peacock ★** at only 21 had been the Battalion's adjutant (the C.O.'s right-hand man, in charge of admin and discipline). What must it have been like for his family when his kit was returned, including his sword in its coffin-like wooden packing case *(above)*.

4 Colonel **Henry Pritchard**, 53, had had a distinguished military career with postings as Commandant of the Burma Military Police and Assistant for Plague Operations in Bombay. His experience with the 10ᵗʰ Glosters had mirrored Colonel Walton's with the 8ᵗʰ Berkshires, and he had seen similar casualties in his battalion on that 1ˢᵗ day of the Battle of Loos, finally collapsing with the strain. Active with the British Legion after the war, he was also noted for his landscape painting.

5 Major **Henry Sutherland**, 43, originally of the Black Watch, had seen action in NW India in the 1890s. Wounded & awarded DSO earlier in 1915, he was C.O. of 10ᵗʰ Glosters on the Somme. Retired as a Colonel and became a General Commissioner of Income Tax & also a successor to Sir Douglas Haig as Captain of the Royal & Ancient Golf Club at St Andrews.

6 Regimental Sergeant Major **George Lainsbury**, 45, *(opposite page*, as a colour sergeant) was the Battalion's most senior N.C.O. He'd joined up as an 18-year-old labourer in 1888, and as a private in the Royal Berkshires had won the Cleanest Soldier Competition three years running. Slightly wounded early in the Boer War, he'd gone on to be the supply sergeant popular for running home comforts out to the troops manning the blockhouses. After retiring in 1909 he became a recruiting sergeant & married a girl 16 years his junior who lived in the same street as his father's childhood home. Still very fit despite his age, he'd re-enlisted in 1914, and at Loos, though slightly gassed early on, he'd rallied the men and organised the re-supply of ammunition, even going out in the open himself under heavy fire to collect it from the dead and wounded. Awarded the DCM, he would be hospitalised with kidney disease in February 1916 but survive until 1935. His house in Reading is now a Coral betting shop.

7 **Cecil Cloake ★**, 21, was a medical student and would prove to be a very able successor to Gordon Peacock as adjutant.

8 The Battalion was first formed on 1ˢᵗ October 1914. This reminds me of the last line of John Harris' novel *'Covenant with Death'*, though for the 8ᵗʰ Royal Berkshires it was *'One year in the making. One morning in the destroying.'*

Item 56
Letter to Margaret

Envelope
*161 Haverstock Hill
London*

FIELD POST OFFICE
5 OC
15

Oct 4th 1915

My dearest Darling

    As there is no mail today there are no letters so I cannot answer any of yours. I have no news one moment we hear we are going back into the fight and the next that we are going back further from the firing line. Anyway I wish we could move from here as we are crowded out thousands of us and the French, and not a spare inch of room anywhere. I got my first draft of one officer and 52 men today which will bring us up to over 500.

I expect you have had a rotten time with Mrs Hicks Mrs Berlein etc. The Hyde you heard of was the little chap we used to call the white rabbit.[1]

Your letter has just arrived and you are having a bad time, but I have not heard from you since you saw the Colonel.

Another awful shock has just come in. Poor old Ronald has died in No 20 General Hospital at Camiers, date of death the 2nd, and it was only the day before yesterday I wrote his mother & congratulated her on getting him home with only a hole in his leg. It is too ghastly for words & has given me the proper knock.[2]

Please phone Bogey (& Mrs Walton) and let him know and he will tell the others as I have heard from them asking for news as early as possible.

We have indeed paid a price for the small advance we have made.

    I cant write more. All Love

Thine

Charles

P.S. If you can find the Colonel ask him to drop a line to Mrs George Brakspear Ronalds mother c/o the Brewery, Henley. I think the news will kill her.

1 **Lawrence Hyde**, 21, *(right)*, is in the back row of an 8th Royal Berkshires group photograph taken in March. By May he had left, but, far from disappearing down a rabbit hole, he had joined the Royal Flying Corps and was in the air over Loos as his old battalion went into action on the first day, collecting a gunshot wound in one of his buttocks as well as a mention in General French's dispatch for gallant and distinguished service. He would be wounded again during Bloody April (another period of German air superiority in 1917), this time in the right foot, but was still flying at the war's end.

He then went from studying anthropology at Oxford, via translating Czech literature (including the literary giant Karel Čapek's dystopian novel 'Krakatit' that in 1924 was talking about atomic bombs) to his real life's work of writing and speaking on the human condition. His main theme was the failure of scientific methods, traditional religion and secular democracy to provide a true path for humanity and the need to experiment with intuition & spiritual mysticism to find a new way of life: *'Out of all this distress, uncertainty and suffering there must surely emerge a new Faith, an experience of the Mystery which is appropriate to and consistent with the demands of our twentieth-century consciousness'.*

2 **Ronald Brakspear**★ had his leg shattered by a shell but even as he was being carried off on a stretcher he was still exhorting his men to kill more Germans. His brother wrote to Charles with more details of his death (Item 63).

Tuesday
Oct 5th 1915

Dearest Darling

No time for a letter we are off again up to the trenches but I dont think we shall have such a warm time. Troubles never come singly & I have now an outbreak of itch in the Batt[n] and 50 men have just gone to hospital. It is a weary world. Am expecting Tosetti back today & jolly glad I shall be to see him. I have no other news we are all packed up ready to move & it is a nice steady rain.

All All All Love

Thine

Charles B

DAY

59

TUE

5 OCT 1915

Item 57
Letter to Margaret

Envelope
161 Haverstock Hill
London

Wednesday Oct 6th 1915

Dearest Darling

I wrote you a hurried line yesterday & Foot[1] & Co arrived with your letter just before we moved, so I brought them along with me. We made a lucky relief without any casualties, it was pitch dark & a thick fog. We started at 5.30 pm and came straight overland to the trenches themselves getting in at 11.15. We are in the reserve trenches to the London Scottish & have been badly shelled all day, one Gunner officer being badly hit and several engineers hurt a bit. Four of my lads have got hit but not dangerous. The blighters have the range to a nicety & put one on the trench just outside my dug out as Gerard[2] was bringing in breakfast. He was smothered in mud and worse still he dropped the breakfast. He thought he was a "gonner" & was quite deaf for a bit. My dug out is quite splinter proof, & it would take a big shell to get at me. There are a few 20 or 30 ft underground, but so dark & damp it is not worth it. I have a table one arm chair 2 others and a bed which is dug into the earth. It all is about 8 foot long and 4½ ft wide. The chairs make a bed for Cloak who is invaluable and a born adjutant. No pheasant or cakes have arrived yet.

DAY

60

WED

6 OCT 1915

Item 58
Letter to Margaret

Envelope
161 Haverstock Hill
London

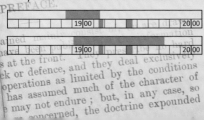

I cannot give you any further details of the dead or wounded except Dug is back with us. He is a plucky chap, & could have had a months leave easily, and why he didn't take it I cant think, as I never wish to go through another fortnight like this. It is awfully sad about Guy[3] and everyone but still we have to go through it. I had a wire from Mrs Berlein & Mrs Hicks sent on the 4th they only reached me today and they must have had my letters by now. The reason so many are reported wounded & missing in the first place is that unless death is proved by <u>an officer</u> you cannot make a "killed report" on a mans word.

You have indeed had a bad time with the parents, but still you must do your best. I would give a great deal to be home with you, as I dont think this is fighting sitting in a drain.

What a pity I did not know the Scrub was in Bethune I have been near there all the time.

I do not know if your letter was found on Leslie or not as when I had news of him his pockets had all been rifled.

I am sending back tonight for mails & hope to hear from you.

There are several rats & mice sharing my dug out with me, you see it is in one of the German trenches we captured.

There are a lot of German snipers about here all dressed in khaki which they have taken from our dead. At 3 am a French soldier was brought in as he was thought to be a German spy, but we let him go this morning.

I have no more news, and now am not sure if I shall keep command of the Rgt the responsibility is too much, and I cant see my way to pulling the Regt together unless we get away back. It is not fair on either myself or the Rgt, what can I do tonight with 326 men, 50 of which have 14 weeks service. I dont often grouse at a critical time, but this I think is the d-d limit.

Please thank Lilian for her letter, I will write her when these brutes give me a chance.

Best love to Paula & all. Thine own husband

Charles

---

1 **Eric Foot ★**, 18, *(above)*, had arrived the day before with 3 other officers and Charles has picked him out probably because he knew him from before the war (Eric's parents were at Charles's brother Alfred's wedding in 1909).

2 **Cecil Gerrard** was Charles's batman & all that remains from his records is that he survived to be sent his medals after the war.

3 Several officers named Guy were killed at Loos, but one who stands out is Captain **Guy Napier**, 31. Firstly, his surname was Charles's mother's maiden name (& Charles's middle name), & secondly he was a noted cricketer who had taken 365 wickets in 81 first class matches. Serving with the 47th Sikhs, his wounds in the left arm and shoulder at first didn't seem too bad. He kept on apologizing

for troubling the doctor, & managed to walk part of the way back but then died the same day. His wife of 2 months, Sissie, found herself a widow at 24. She never re-married & lived till 4 years after the death of Jimi Hendrix.

DAY 61 THU

7 OCT 1915

Item 59
Letter to Margaret

Envelope
161 Haverstock Hill
London

FIELD POST OFFICE 9 OC 15

Thursday   Oct 7th 1915

Dearest Darling

　No mail in again last night and no pheasant. I guess he will be a bit high when he arrives. Not much peace last night as we had digging parties out until 3.30 & 4.15 am. I sent Foot out to collect the rations & he was due back at 9.30 pm and did not get in until 11.45 pm which worried me considerably. Both sides are still shelling hard and I think I prefer the old days when the guns were limited to so much ammunition per diem. I had to go up to our front line which used to be the old German Reserve line last night to confer with the Colonel of the London Scottish.[1] I have never seen such a huge dug out before there was a huge bunk to hold two, a double iron bedstead, window door armchairs etc. The Bosches do themselves very well.[2]

I expect my lot will be taking over that bit of the line, so by the time you get this I shall be occupying that dwelling. I have not had my clothes or boots off for the last 48 hours, but managed a shave & a wash in ¾ pint of water this morning. The work last night was a rare mess up (not on our part) and no fault of our Brigade staff, but it does make one sick.

I have no more news I can write you. Please tell Lilian I have no time to write more than one letter per day during these strenuous days, as it takes me all my time going round to keep the men cheerful, which is a farce as I dont feel a bit so having got a permanent headache from this noise.

All Love to Paula & everyone

　　　Thine always
　　　　Charles

1 Lt Col **Bernard Green**, 49, the son of an earthenware manufacturer, had headed off to the Boer War with the City of London Imperial Volunteers in 1900, and again was a volunteer in this war, being hit by shrapnel in the left shoulder in November 1914. He commanded the London Scottish from February 1915 until he was replaced in August 1916 (& was again C.O. post-war). He married for the first time in 1922, his bride wearing *'a gown of cinnamon crepe romaine, draped and embroidered with old gold beads'* and *'a hat of brown velvet trimmed with heron'*. It was only just over 2 years later that he died in France, not in the trenches, but on a visit to the Atlantic coast near Spain.

2 'Bosches' was the French nickname for the Germans. Dictionaries today say it is from 'caboche' meaning 'blockhead' but a letter to *The Spectator* in September 1915 gives a more erudite if nastier explanation *(right)*.

THE MEANING OF "BOSCHE."

[To THE EDITOR OF THE "SPECTATOR."]

SIR,—The Allies—Italy and Great Britain, France and Russia—have for months been exercising their wits as to the derivation of the word "Bosche." There was not any doubt that its source, or origin, was odious, and that it was a loathing and an opprobrious term. A young Alsatian was tried by the Germans at the Court of Dessau for writing the word "Bosche," in derision of the Kaiser. The lineal descendants of the Huns could not, or did not, publish the definition, though they punished the youth. M. Théodore Joran, Professor of History, states in the *Revue des Deux Mondes* that in Littré the meaning of "Bosche" is given as ulcer: a pestilential tumour; in old Picard *boche*; in Norman *bosche*; in Bas Breton *bos, bosen*. The word is evidently derived from the Low Latin *boscia, boscium*. It is attached, according to the Professor, to the Latin, *bucca, bouche*.—I am, Sir, &c.,

THOMAS OGILVY.

Dundee.

DAY
62
FRI

8 OCT 1915

Item 60
Letter to Margaret

Envelope
*161 Haverstock Hill
London*

11.50 pm

Friday 8th

(Trenches)

My Dearest Darling

An orderly has just brought up your letters of the 5th and 6th also parcel & bandages for which many thanks. We are quite close up to the Huns in one place only a few sandbags separating being in the same trench. We have been shelled the last 24 hours without ceasing. It is a d-d awful game as one is like a rat in a drain. I am sorry about the muddle of Leslies death. As I told you, I could only make out my report on an officer's word, & of course did not see or hear from the Colonel or anyone for certain until the 27th, when I at once sent in official report copy of which I enclose.[1] I had a very nice letter from C.A.P.,[2] will you please ring him up & thank him for it. I think we are in for another push, anyway it looks like it, & we shall be used again, although not in the assault. I have not had my clothes off since we moved up from below, and am just about tired and fed up with it all.

Have just got four officers sent me from the 3rd Dorsets, all 2nd Lieutenants.[3] Why would they not send those I have trained or helped to.

All Love Dearest to you & Paula

Thine

Charles x

P.S. The Pheasant was ripping. Let us have another. Ate him early this morning.

No Cake yet or potted meat.

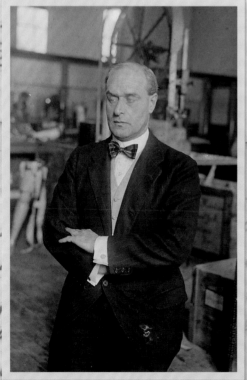

1 A telegram was sent to **Leslie Berlein**★'s parents on 3rd October saying that he was missing & *'This does not necessarily mean he is wounded or killed'*. This sparked a false hope even though they had already had reports of his death from Charles & Rev Arthur Longden. You can see the date on Charles's casualty return (***opposite***, copied using the carbon paper in his field notebook) but with so many casualties, it's no wonder mistakes were made.

2 C.A.P. = **Arthur Pearson**, 49, ***(left)*** (he did not use his first name 'Cyril'). The son of a country rector, he became one of the biggest press magnates of the Edwardian

era, founding the Daily Express & owning the London Evening Standard. He had to sell his newspaper interests after totally losing his sight not long before the war, but he was not one to give up & dedicated the rest of his life to the cause of the blind. He was made president of the National Institution for the Blind (with Charles Bartlett becoming his secretary), and founded St Dunstan's to help soldiers blinded in the war to overcome their disability.

3 It was quite common for battalions to be reinforced with officers and men from completely different regiments, particularly during the middle of a battle.

128

8ᵗʰ Royal Berkshire Rgt.

Approximate Return of Casualties
—

Officers same as last return
except Lieut BERLEIN "dead," instead
of "missing believed dead,"
Other Ranks. no alteration

C Bartlett. Myor
8ᵗʰ Royal Berkshire W. 10·20 a.m.
27·9·15.

Mater give my love to Dick
& Emili + don't worry
love to you & Dad,
Leslie.

Item 61A

Letter to Elizabeth Berlein (copied in the hand of her husband Julius. I have found copies of other letters that in this pre-photocopier era he had had to laboriously copy out by hand to send to War Office officials as he sought to find out the truth of what had happened to his son. This copy is kept amongst the family's memorabilia as well as the next letter from Margaret).

8th Royal Berkshire Regt

8th Royal Berkshire Regt
Oct 1st 1915

Dear Mrs Berlein

I am writing not only to express my own sympathy, but that of all the remaining officers over the terrible loss you have sustained by the death of poor Leslie. I know nothing I can say can make much difference to you, but I am sure you will be able to bear your loss knowing that everyone of us feel for you more than I can say. Poor Leslie was the exact type of Officer the Regiment and the Country require, he was popular with all ranks and he fell surrounded by men of his own platoon, and I feel sure that he met his end like the true soldier and sportsman he was.

The Regiment has suffered terribly out of 20 officers taking part in the assault 10 being killed and seven wounded, and out of 240 men in Leslie's Company only 101 remain.

Leslie's death took place at the commencement of the assault which his Company was leading, and the poor fellow was the first out of the trenches to go forward. His death was instantaneous so he did not suffer which is something to be thankful for. He was buried by some officers of the Scots Guards but I am unable to give you their names and there were no personal belongings on him when he was found. His other belongings I have dispatched to you this day through Cox's Shipping Agency. Once more saying how deeply I sympathise with you and asking you to remember that we are all sharing your grief.

Believe me, Yours sincerely

C. Bartlett

Obviously in writing to Leslie's mother Charles does not mention the incidents that had previously exasperated him about Leslie. Even so the news led to the collapse of Elizabeth Berlein's health, and her husband Julius, as well as dealing with his own loss, had to work out exactly what details were safe to pass on to her.

All of Leslie's belongings as well as those of his brother Charles were gathered together to be passed down through the generations of the family. Amongst them are the pictures of Leslie here and on the previous page, along with the picture of Leslie's original grave where he was buried on the battlefield. Julius Berlein visited the graves of his sons in September 1919. Leslie's body had just been exhumed and re-buried in Dud Corner Cemetery along with many others who had originally been buried all over the battlefield. Julius found the sight of all the identical rough wooden crosses most depressing and expressed the hope that the headstones that followed should not be of a uniform pattern, that each grave should be kept distinct, with parents having some say in the design. In the end, that was just not practical (and there were worries about the inequality of what families could afford) so the individuality is now down to the variety of flowers that are grown by each grave by the gardeners of the War Graves Commission.

161, HAVERSTOCK HILL,
N.W.

Oct, 1st

Item 61B
Letter from Margaret to Elizabeth Berlein

**161, HAVERSTOCK HILL,
N.W.**

Oct 1st

Dear Mrs Berlein

    I saw the Colonel today, who could tell me nothing more than we know, except that he knows that Leslie & Peacock (the adjutant) were buried. Would you like me to come down tomorrow just for the day, & I could tell you about how the advance was made, & how well everyone did. If so, just send a message & I will come down in the morning.

        Yours very sincerely

        Margaret J Bartlett

Sunday Oct 10th/15

Dearest Darling

    Many thanks for letters rec^d at 1 am this morning. Fancy you & old Bogey having lunch together, the big & the little of it. Well the Colonel would be having his wish if he was here for we are once more outside his pet village,[1] & by the time you get this we shall either be in it or not as the case may be. Anyway the little Batt^n has its usual place in the front line, much to my surprise, and I can only hope we shall not suffer as much as last time. Will you please read the enclosed & write to Ronalds mother for me and I would very much like you to go & see her, & if I come through this next scrap I will write & tell her all I can. I think they dropped him near the first German line of trenches on the Hulloch Road, which was a point he was making for. I must stop now.

    All All All Love Dearest

        Thine

        Charles

DAY 64 SUN

10 OCT 1915

Item 62
Letter to Margaret

Envelope
*161 Haverstock Hill
London*

---

1 They were opposite Hulluch again, back where they had ended up after their first attack.

Item 63
*Letter from
Ronald Brakspear★'s
brother George*

Envelope
(missing)

Oct 5th '15

My dear Bartlett

Royal Hotel
Henley on Thames

    After reading your note to my mother & your letter to Ronald you will I know be more than shocked to hear of his death. He died on Saturday the 2nd about 3 o'clock & I am glad to say that I was able to be there with my mother just half an hour before he died and he was just able to understand that we were with him. Evidently his wound got dirty as the nurses say he was in an awful state when he arrived but he was so brave about it all & on Friday they had to amputate the leg, & presumably the shock killed him. Poor old chap, it was awful to see him, but he has died a noble death. Can you give me any details or possibly say where he fell – judging from his map, it was near Hulloch. He was buried on Sunday in a little cemetery at Étaples & the last post was sounded over his grave. The box you speak of probably is one I had sent from Harrods & I'm glad to know that his greatest friend shared it. My Mother has borne it wonderfully well – she sends her love & says that if your wife & child would like to go and stay with her at Eastbourne, she would be glad to have them. Tell Ronald's men that he thought & spoke of them on his bed. Good luck & I hope you'll come back safe to your wife.

    Yours ever

    F. George Brakspear

George, *centre*, & *far right* enjoying a drink with Ronald. He would take over Ronald's role at the family brewery. *Below*, mother Florence with her donkey Nann (used for pulling a cart or lawn rollers), and Ronald's grave when visited by the family after the war.

Ronald William Brakspear ★

Brother George

Mother Florence

Oct 11th 1915

Dearest Darling

Here we are once more merry and bright. We are in what you call battle positions but dont expect to make a move until your lucky day.[1] I have a nice dug out, & have a party of pioneers[2] coming down tonight to deepen and improve it, as I have to remain in it during the assault, & conduct that part by phone from here.

Dearest I had no letter from you in yesterday's mail, surely I told you the poor old man Oldman was killed. He was wounded, & was shot while he was waiting to be dressed.

Had 4 subalterns arrive last night from the West Dorsets. They thought they had bought the Earth, & asked for food at my head quarters as if I had enough to go round.

Just after I had sent them to their companies the cake arrived 11 pm, also the other things, so I sent along for Douglas, & he & I and little Cloake ate half of it. I like these fire trenches near the Huns, as they dont shell them so much as the reserve trenches. Only 4 killed yesterday so we had a lucky day. How is Paula she has not written me for a long time but I suppose she is very busy. She would like living in these holes in the ground, but "I was never one for picnics". It is just a week since we moved, I have had two shaves & two washes each time one small cup of water doing for everything. I have not yet had my boots off or my clothes. What a life to land oneself into, but still someone has to be here. These blasted Huns are busy putting over shrapnel now. I enclose you some wires you might send on with the explanation as the families will think me rude. I have had more letters about poor old Ronny than anyone else. All love to you & Paula

Thine

Charles

P.S. Cannot find the wires they were to Mrs Berlein & Mrs Hicks & were not passed by the censor.

I enclose you one from the Colonel and one from Oldmans people. Did he make a will in your favour.[3]

DAY
65
MON
11 OCT 1915

Item 64
Letter to Margaret

Envelope
161 Haverstock Hill
London

FIELD POST OFFICE
12 OC
15

1 Her 'lucky day' would be the 13th.

2 Pioneers were troops who constructed entrenchments and fortifications.

3 This is a throwaway comment made wryly in jest (given their own financial worries) rather than any sincere belief that Oldman would have left her anything. As you will see in the enclosed letter from Oldman's brother-in-law, he left a serious amount of money that would have definitely made life more comfortable for them.

Item 65
*Enclosed
letter
from
Brig-Gen
Walton*

Envelope
(missing)

SKETCH MAP OF
ADEN, 1914–18

5, SOUTH STREET,
THURLOE SQUARE, S.W.

6th October 1915

My dear Bartlett

Many thanks for your letters. Yes. I think you have made your Sergeants' appointments wisely, & I should have done the same. The losses of officers are terrible either 12 or 13 killed so far as I can make out, & those the very pick of my brave boys. I mourn them all, & especially Brakspear. He was such a man, & such a dear fellow. And I know what a great blow the news of his death will be to you. Hanna too, alas, we can ill spare such splendid men; they were as giants amongst the many half baked youngsters who one sees in officers' uniforms. But though we mourn them as lost to us, they are not lost to the country – from the graves of her heroes this dear country of ours will be regenerated. It is in the fiery furnace of such adversities that the dross of degeneration which had set in will be melted out of the nation. We should thank God that we have such men, and preserve a firm determination to see this business through. Two things I think, all our men should be taught bombing – and all should be taught to stalk snipers in long grass. This seems absolutely necessary when they get in behind the parapet.

I am off again, to Aden, tomorrow. Not a very promising job. The mobile column went out against the Turks and indulged, apparently, in a sauve qui peut,[1] a very disgraceful affair. They are stationed at Sheikh Othman 7 miles inland, in the Hinterland. I am to try & put a little ginger into them if possible & expect some uphill work, but heaven has been so kind to me in having always given me such good fellows to help me that I can but trust that we shall get things going properly. The Sultan of LAHEJ who is under our protection has been wounded by the Turks & is now in Aden.[2] There is not much fear for Aden, but our prestige in Arabia has suffered much, & the situation is uncomfortable. Now I must end as I have much to do. My thoughts are with you all. I hope you may have a chance of doing in some of the Germans soon & getting some of our own back.

Kind remembrances to all.

Yours ever

Wm C Walton

Your wife has lunched with us twice & keeps us up in the news. It was very nice seeing her. She is going to Reading with Emmie on Monday.

1 'Sauve qui peut' = every man for himself.

2 Aden was a British Protectorate and a key staging post for ships on the way to India. The situation was even worse than he thought. The mobile column had included 400 Welsh Territorials, 300 of whom had fallen out with heat exhaustion. A relief column was sent out and when their ally the Sultan of Lahej rode out to greet their arrival, he was mistaken for a Turk & shot dead. At one point, a desperate cable was sent to London *'The Turks are on the golf course'*, but the guns of the Royal Navy ships offshore ensured that Aden didn't fall into Turkish hands, & Brig-Gen Walton ended up having a much quieter time than if he had stayed on the Western Front.

Basil Tobin Ready

his wife Hilda

their children

Fort Scoveston
Neyland
Pembrokeshire

5/10/15

Dear Major Bartlett,

Your letter does indeed bring sad news. I suppose one ought to have expected it – but never dreamt of such casualties. It is a ghastly victory when so few survive. Still we are all proud to think Wilfred Oldman did well & died as a soldier should die, & your letter will always be treasured by his family.[1] I don't know what happens about his estate, but I am executor to his late brother's estate – Russel Oldman[2] - & under the will of the latter, Wilfred was due to get some £2000[3] nearly – chiefly invested in Indian Coal. I am winding up that estate & so have money – or shall have shortly – to hand over to his (Wilfred's) executors – who are both in South Africa.[4] So if there are any debts or accounts to be gone into they might be sent to me and I could pass them on or get a power of attorney to pay for the executors if necessary.

Again our best thanks for your letter.

Yours sincerely,

B.T. Ready[5]

(Major

the Welch Rgt)

I have a great interest in the R. Berks – as my father commanded the 66th and my brother is in them now.[6]

1 I have met several descendants of Wilfred's siblings and found no trace of the letter, nor even much about Wilfred. Time and the busyness of daily life has a way of obliterating history and good intentions.

2 Russel was a plantation manager in India & disappeared from the P&O liner *SS Salsette* in the middle of the Arabian Sea on the way to Bombay on 14th January 1914, aged 36.

3 £2000 was nearly seven times Charles's annual salary in the Army, and Wilfred had been due to inherit a quarter of it.

4 Wilfred left £500 to his youngest brother and the rest was to go to his first cousin Helen Mills. His estate must have been complex because though an initial submission was made to the Probate Registry in London in 1917, it was only finally wound up in 1940, by which time both of his executors (one of whom was Helen Mills' husband) were dead and the total gross value of the estate was only £26 more than the £500 he had left to his brother, all of which cannot have been the outcome Wilfred intended when he was writing his will on the eve of going to war.

5 **Basil Ready**, 44, was the husband of Wilfred's sister Hilda. He was awarded OBE in 1918 for running an officer training battalion for the whole war. Only one of his 6 children died of old age, the others dying: in infancy in 1906; in a Lancaster bomber shot down over Berlin in 1943 aged 32; of TB in 1948 aged 30; in a car accident in 1951 aged 29; & from head injuries (after being beaten by robbers on his farm in Kenya) in 1985 aged 69, having been born the day before this letter was written.

6 The old 66th Regiment of Foot had been renamed the 2nd Battalion, Royal Berkshire Regiment in 1881, but long-held traditions die hard. His father John had survived the massacre at Maiwand in the 2nd Afghan War in 1880 (when the 66th lost 286 dead), and his brother ended his army career as General Sir Felix Ready, GBE, KCB, DSO, with 11 mentions in dispatches in three wars.

Not mentioned is that Basil was also the first cousin of Viscount Milner, an ardent imperialist & English nationalist (despite having a German grandmother) who had done much to foment the Boer War and was soon to be at the heart of government in this war.

DAY
66
TUE
12 OCT 1915

Item 67
Letter to Margaret

Envelope
*161 Haverstock Hill
London*

Oct 12th 1915

Dearest Darling

Am quite well, no news. Many thanks for two letters rec^d last night.

1. Please thank John for his letter

2. Please thank Bogey for sparklets[1] & tell him Dug is out of the next attack.

I have to send 4 officers back to first line & Dug is one. Robinson Williamson & Watson the others.[2] Dug is furious but I cant help it. Am glad you are dining with Guvnor & Bogey & hope you will enjoy yourselves. We had a hottish day yesterday & lost a few. I dont want 11 more officers at present, but I expect they will go to other Regiments. It is the Doc's wedding day. I told him he could have breakfast in bed for a treat.   All Love In haste

Thine

Charles xx

For Paula xx

FIELD POST OFFICE
13 OC
15

HAMPSTEAD S.O.
8.45 PM
14 OC
15
N.W.

On   His

1 Sparklets were little bulbs of compressed air that fitted inside a Soda Syphon to put fizz into water – perfect to go with Charles's whisky. Invented in the 1890s, they ceased production in 1981.

2 **Gerald Robinson★**, 31, had been left out of the first attack as well. A silk merchant used to trading on the Continent, he was fluent in French and German so maybe was thought too useful to risk. **Cyril Williamson★**, 27, had arrived in the week before's group, but a foot injury picked up in Canada before the war may have rendered him unfit and **Charlie Watson★**, 21, was just back from hospital with his own foot problems which would soon lead to him being invalided out and returning to Canada.

Cyril Spartali★, 27
In Commerce in India
DEAD

Clifford Salman★, 22
Trainee Priest
DEAD

Frederick Steele, 26
Motor Engineer in Beirut
DEAD

Richard Coote, 23
Barrister
DEAD

REGRET TO INFORM YOU THAT

Trenches
2 am
Oct 14th 1915

Dearest Darling

Just a line to say so far I am safe. We have had another awful dusting and done no good. Started at 2 pm yesterday afternoon and my lads went the best. I only had 360 and now can only find 112. I dont know our casualties for certain but Spartali, Salmon, Steel, & I believe Coote killed. Lawrence and Park wounded. Foot wounded & missing. Woodford, Woodthore, Holland all missing and I have not much hope for them. Self Cloak & Birch again the only ones with whole skins. It makes a total of 11 of 14 officers taken into action. Pretty sickening & depressing. We are now back in the same position as we were this morning or rather yesterday. I expect to get my lads out of the firing line at about 4 am, & hope to get back out of it tomorrow night. We were just mown down and it was beastly. I hear there are some letters for me with the first line so hope to hear from you tomorrow. Phone Mrs Birch & Mrs McGibbon their husbands are well.

All love to you & Paula

Thine in haste

Please Mrs Cloake   Charles x
     ROCHESTER
     saying her son quite safe.

DAY 68 THU

14 OCT 1915

Item 68
Letter to Margaret

Envelope
*161 Haverstock Hill
London*

FIELD POST OFFICE
16 OC
15

Eric Foot★, 18
Schoolboy
MISSING

Harold Woodford★, 22
Rubber Planter in Malaya
MISSING

William Woodthorpe, 33
Accountant
MISSING

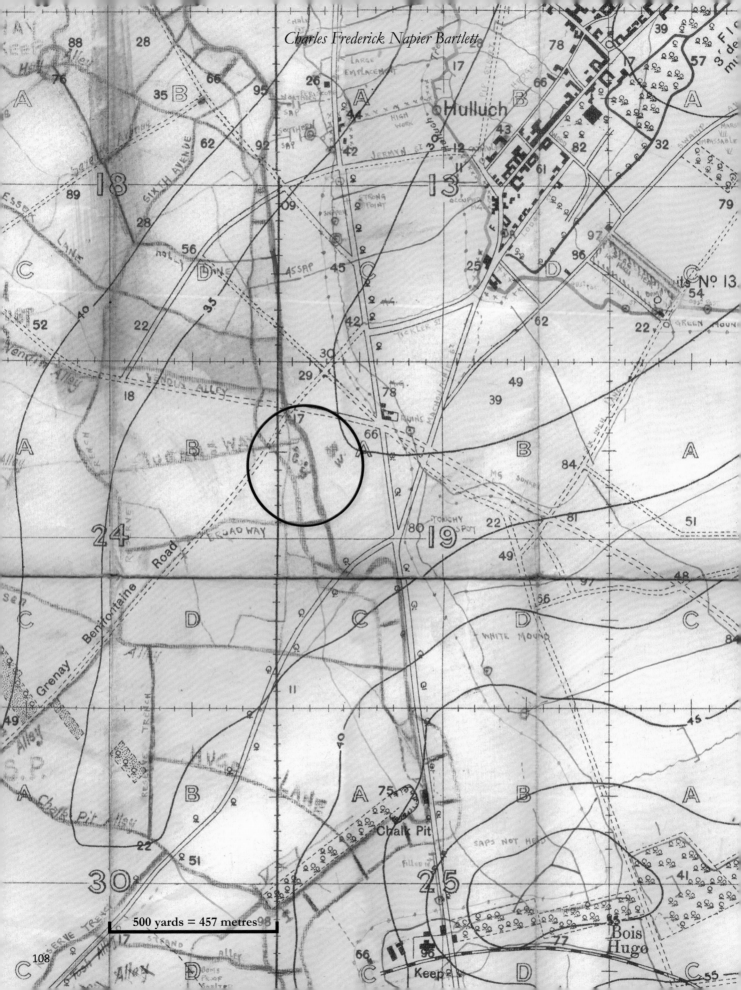

Charles Frederick Napier Bartlett

108

The black circle on the map shows where they went into action. The thick blue line is the British front line and they attempted to attack towards to the red lines of the German trenches on the right.

Of the officer casualties named by Charles, Coote and Spartali★ had sat out the first attack on the 25th and the other seven had arrived in France only days before. Of the missing, Woodthorpe & Foot★ would never be seen again, Woodford★'s body was discovered in no-man's-land ten weeks later, and Holland was found wounded with a rifle bullet through his right thigh (and would live for another 53 years).

In the *black circle* are the letters C, S & W which show where Coote, Salman★, and Woodford★ were buried (can you imagine burying a 10-week-old corpse in no-man's-land at night having emptied his pockets to send his belongings to his parents?). The British and German lines in this sector would not change significantly during the remaining three years of the war, and by the time the battlefield was being cleared of bodies, no identifiable remains could be found for any of the 7 officers killed in this attack. They are all named on the Loos Memorial to the Missing.

Richard Coote was an elder brother of George Coote★ from the Group Photograph. He had qualified as a barrister in June 1914, and was an active worker for the Radley Mission helping the disadvantaged in the London Docks. His Officer Training Corps experience meant he was a Captain and Company Commander aged only 23.

Frederick Steele, 26, was originally from Carlisle but after training as a teacher he worked at Shepton Mallet Grammar School as well as playing rugby for Somerset. A complete career change had seen him take up an apprenticeship with a rail and dock crane manufacturer back up in Carlisle and then go out to Beirut as a motor transport engineer. He was one of the 2nd Lieutenants from the 3rd Dorsets who had arrived just five days before the attack. After his death, his affairs would be sorted out by his brother because his parents were *'too old and too distraught with grief to carry on any correspondence'*. ➜411

Thomas Lawrence★ had been only slightly wounded and would be back with the Battalion that same night.

Leslie Park, 21, was another of the officers from the 3rd Dorsets, though his home was in Wigan. His father, at the time of his death in 1912, had been the Chairman of a large wholesale grocers that shared its roots with Lever Brothers. Leslie walked his mother down the aisle for her second marriage just a few months before he joined up for the war. He'd been wounded in the head in this attack but though the flesh would outwardly heal before too long, the shell shock persisted. After two years he was passed fit to join the Indian Army. In August 1918 a medical board at a hill station in India reported that he'd never been well since his arrival, with frequent headaches, occasional attacks of diarrhoea, weakness, bad sleep, nervousness, poor memory, & depression, and that a return to the English climate was essential for his recovery. After leaving the Army & finishing his training to be a solicitor, in an apt match of names Leslie Park married Gladys Field. He lived to be 80, but 2 of his 3 sons died before him, one aged 7 of appendicitis and the other as a 20-year-old Trooper in 6th Armoured Division in 1941, due to a road crash with another motorcyclist before he'd even gone overseas.

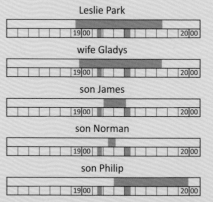

Leslie Park

wife Gladys

son James

son Norman

son Philip

Oct 15th 1915

Dearest Darling

Am quite well and left the trenches yesterday evening, after some march we got in a train & landed here at 2 am well away back from shot & shell. Will write later. If Lilian spelt her name a bit differently you would know where I was.[1]

All Love   Charles B

1 They were in Lillers.

DAY
69
FRI

15 OCT 1915

Item 69
Letter to Margaret

Envelope
(same as Item 68)

Charles Frederick Napier Bartlett *Saturday*

DAY
70
SAT

16 OCT 1915

Item 70
Letter to Margaret

Envelope
161 Haverstock Hill
London

FIELD POST OFFICE
17 OC
15

Saturday

Dearest Darling

  I wrote you a line & that was all yesterday. We are now back trying to get some rest, but of course having once more been cut to pieces I have to reorganize the Batt[n] to the best of my ability. I have the 6 officers you saw off the other day. Dug Robinson Cloake Birch Williamson & Lawrence and 464 men. It is a depressing job. I have no other news of our casualties & I fear all are dead except Edwardes & Park.
I only had 236 men with rifles & 40 machine gun men in the last show. I lost 142 of the men & 7 of the machine gunners and that with 11 officers out of 14 is pretty bad. The assault was a hopeless failure although yesterdays Daily Mail said we advanced a 1000 yds. We tried to capture one line of trenches & that was our task, by our task I mean the Brigade. The whole Brigade took part this time in the assault, each Regiment having so much front to go for according to their strength. The Brigade was not supported, & each Regiment in the Brigade lost quite half its men. We were just mown down by machine guns. We were using gas & smoke bombs to advance under, & the gas did not seem to effect the Hun I think the blighter had time to get back to his trench anyway they had some machine guns on our right flank which our gunners could not locate and they played hell with us.[1]
We were all dead beat when we got back here the night before last, nine blessed days in those trenches without taking ones clothes off & for the last 4 sleep was out of the question except when one fell asleep for an hour or so from sheer exhaustion. By your letters you seem to have been having a very busy time trotting about. I cant imagine the wifes of Taski or Clarke I suppose both had glasses and mackintoshes.[2] Poor Edwardes was hit and if you ask him where, he will probably say "somewhere in France" so if you see him be tactful & dont offer him a hard chair to sit on.[3] I dont know where he is but his home address is FAXTON, CHALGROVE ROAD, SUTTON, SURREY, so you might find out from there. Will you please write John tell him I am well also Lilian, but I have such an awful lot of work to do it is quite impossible to write. I rec[d] papers from John. Thank Gracie for her letter & will write when I can also Dolly. General Holland is coming to see me any moment so I must now stop.

  All my Love Dearest to you Paula & all

  Thine

  Charles

1 This was the sort of attack that would give British higher command a bad name, throwing in ill-prepared troops without full appreciation of the enemy defences or the advantage of surprise, seemingly with the belief that superior willpower would win through.

2 **Louis Klemantaski★**, 24, and **Wilfrid Clarke★**, 29, were in the group of officers that had just arrived and both had had their weddings on 7th October just before their embarkation for France. Klemantaski was a music critic, poet & librarian, & Clarke an assistant school master, and it looks like Charles's assumption was that their wives would therefore be dowdy intellectuals (which as you can see was not the case). Phyllis Klemantaski, 32, *(far right)*, was an artist who had been six years old when her single mother married her step-father (the identity of her real father is not known by the family). Ivy Clarke, 22, *(near right)*, was the daughter of a retail tobacconist & had been a clerk in a chemist's. She would enjoy the higher status that came with becoming an officer's wife.

3 **Lionel Edwards★** had not been in Charles's first list of casualties which is odd given that they seemed to be friends and he was one of Charles's four company commanders at the time of this attack. A rifle bullet had entered the left of his groin and exited from his left buttock, hence Charles's comment about not offering him a hard chair. The wound would become infected and need a severe

operation with a 3-month stay in hospital and regular massage and electrical treatment. He never fully recovered his health. He had two brothers. Adrian died of a brain tumour aged 9 in 1895 and Roy went missing in 1917 at the Battle of Cambrai never to return.

Lionel Edwards

Adrian Edwards

Roy Edwards

Oct 17th 1915

Dearest Darling

Many thanks for yours of 15th just received. I hope Tubby is not lost. I have no news today except Holland[1] who was missing is found wounded. I got another draft of 67 today which brings me up to 558, but what a stamp of men. I think Gracie must be crazy. She ought to work, it is not fair to herself to stop she will only mope, she ought to earn money she can do so much good with it, and she ought not to deprive the public of her work.[2] I saw you had written to poor little

DAY 71 SUN

17 OCT 1915

Item 71
Letter to Margaret

Envelope
*161 Haverstock Hill
London*

Foot. I dont know what instructions he left for his letters, so I did not touch it. I am awfully busy writing to parents, it is a rotten job but has to be done. It is quite nice not to hear shells & guns going all day and night, and when you think from Sept 22ⁿᵈ to Oct 14ᵗʰ we were under fire except for two days it was a fair strain. The Zepps seem to have had rather a good time, it seems a pity we cant counter them somehow. I liked the menu card & only wish I had had the dinner. The second pheasant has not arrived yet, but I bought two live geese yesterday.

All All All Love Dearest to you & Paula

Thine

Charles

1 **Victor Holland**, 23, was another of the officers of the 3ʳᵈ Dorsets, again without a direct connection to the county – he'd been brought up in Norfolk, his father being the Band Master of the Scots Guards who had conducted at the future King George V's wedding in 1893. Victor's wound had not involved any bone or nerve damage and he would be fit again by January and be awarded the Military Cross in October 1916 for *'fine work with his machine guns'* and going forward to take command and repulse the enemy when other officers were wounded. Twisting his knee playing football in December 1916 led to him being unable to take part in any more fighting. Following his demobilisation in Germany in 1919, he would go on to become a bank manager.

2 Gracie = **Gracie Leigh**, 40, who had appeared with Margaret in *'Miss Hook of Holland'* & *'Dear Little Denmark'* (**left**, as Ophelia). Born Lilith Grace Ellis, her father was the then well-known (but tempestuous) marine landscape painter Edwin Ellis, who died a divorced alcoholic just as she was starting to make her way on the stage. Her first big success was in 1898 in *'Little Miss Nobody'* which also featured her husband Lionel Mackinder (**opposite page**, including on the left of a cast photo in 1904). They had toured the provinces together, marrying in Manchester in 1896, and their dancing and singing of comic songs, both together and apart, had won the hearts of audiences ever since.

At the outbreak of war, Lionel was determined to join up even though at 45 he was over the age for enlistment. He bought a new toupée to make himself look younger and used his stage name rather than his birth name of Edward Stephen Harris thus making it harder to check his age. Despite having gone to public school, he refused a commission and went to France as a private at the end of November 1914. On the evening of 9ᵗʰ January, his platoon of the 1ˢᵗ Royal Berkshires was moving back into reserve when it was spotted that he was missing. A search found him with a wound in his throat from a sniper's bullet, and when lifted up and asked if he was much hurt, he simply answered *'I don't know'*, then rolled over and died.

Gracie, who was only just out of danger after a serious bout of pneumonia, was devastated, and though she would return to the stage in mid-1917, her appearances became less frequent and by the time of a 1934 magazine article it was noted that *'she lives in a country cottage and is seldom seen. The stage misses her. There is nobody today quite like her.'*

Oct 19th 1915

My dearest Darling

I did not write yesterday, I was too fed up and am still. Without any warning and without giving any reasons a regular or ex regular officer is being brought in to command. The General himself told me on the 30th that I was to keep command, and now as we have since that been cut up again they say there is too much work for me to do without any senior officers that regular officers must be brought in, & I must give way. It is damnable. I have written to CAP & told him to try & get me a job as I dont want to stay here any longer. Probably someone who was junior to me before will be brought in. All the officers are very sick about it, and the Brigade Staff say they are trying to stop it, but as I have lost all my friends except one, & there are very few of the old Regiment left I feel as if I should like to quit. I am tired out & dont mind if someone else has a turn as long as I am not asked to play second fiddle.

There is little leave going on and Birch is going the day after tomorrow, but I dont look like getting any. The General is on leave in England, & I have written to him for some, but fear it is hopeless.

I have no news, we had a dinner party last night with the Brigade Major, Staff Captain, Major Sutherland (commanding 10th Glosters) & another & had a cheery evening but I was not in form.

Tonight I am dining with the Glosters and tomorrow night with the Brigade Staff. Well well it is a rotten world at present.

All All Love to you & Paula

Thine

Charles

DAY 73 TUE

19 OCT 1915

Item 72
Letter to Margaret

Envelope
161 Haverstock Hill
London

FIELD POST OFFICE
20 OC 15

HAMPSTEAD S.O.
8.45 PM
21 OC
15
N.W.

LIONEL MACKINDER. GERTIE MILLAR. EDMUND PAYNE. ETHEL SYDNEY. GEORGE GROSSMITH Jr.
AS DR RONALD FAUSSET. AS LADY VIOLET ANSTRUTHER. AS MEAKIN. AS JOSEPHINE ZACCARY. AS THE HON GUY SCRYMGEOUR.

Item 73
Letter to Margaret

Envelope
161 Haverstock Hill
London

FIELD POST OFFICE
20 OC
15

Oct. 20th 1915

Dearest Darling

Just a line to say that Birch has departed on leave and that Douglas Tosetti & Lawrence have both been awarded the Military Cross,[1] and the Batt. Sgt. Major Lainsbury the D.C.M., so we have got our share. Phone Bogey & tell him to wire the Guvnor, Dug is rather annoyed about it, & says he does not deserve it, but I assure you his was a wonderful plucky effort going on with a hole in his leg all the afternoon and the G.O.C.[2] thinks a lot of it. I dont know if the Colonel has got anything, but I am sure he was recommended and deserved a C B if anyone ever did.[3] I dined with the Glosters last night but was not in great form being tired out, and a beastly cold, so I left them at 10 pm and returned to bed where I remained until midday today. I have heard from Edwardes he is in hospital No 1 Red Cross Hospital, Casino de la Foret, Le Touquet, Paris Plage, and does not expect to leave there for two or three weeks. Holland I have also heard of in hospital but no news of the others. Well Dearest I have no other news, I expect some more men shortly, & when I have done all the donkey work once more I suppose I shall have to hand them over.

All Love Dearest to you & Paula

Thine

Charles

Have you found Tubby & what does Paula think about it?[4]

Did you see the letter I wrote Malcolm? I told him he ought to join & I would give him a shop[5] with us.

1 The Military Cross was only awarded to warrant officers and officers up to the rank of Major. This one, *(far left)*, was awarded to Thomas Lawrence★ (his grandson has had it re-ribboned and polished since the time I first saw it). 40,260 were awarded in the First World War. They were not engraved with the name of the recipient and so when sold singly are not generally as valued by collectors as engraved medals where a definite story can be attached to them.

2 G.O.C. = General Officer Commanding (though I'm not sure if he means Reddie or Holland or Rawlinson).

3 CB = Companion of the Order of the Bath. Colonel Walton★'s CB miniature (as worn with evening dress) is *near left*. My family no longer owns the original. A medal collector once contacted me to say that he had my great-grandfather's medals. They had appeared at auction, though not with his CB or CMG. As those are not engraved with recipients' names they are often sold separately from the other medals in a group. No-one has admitted to selling them (!).

4 Tubby may be Paula's bear (see p.2).

5 A shop = a job/appointment.

Item 74
Letter to Margaret

Envelope
*161 Haverstock Hill
London*

Oct 20th 1915

Wednesday

Dearest Darling

Many thanks for your letters of the 18th & 17th recd today. Lawrence was wounded & stunned and got back to work the same night. Foot I have heard nothing of except from his father saying he is wounded & not missing, I answered it & said I was very glad, but in his case if he is alive it will be a miracle.[1] I should tell Paula about Ronald & Leslie I dont think she will realise a bit what it means. I have written to no parents yet on the 13th fight except those I <u>know</u> killed, as I can get no information at all yet back here.

Yes you did guess the right place.

That I think answers your letters which I always look forward for, & like to get. Will continue tomorrow.

Thursday

8.30 am

I have to take my lads for a route march today, & shall not be back before the post goes. We had quite a nice dinner last night at the Brigade, it really was wonderful. Oysters Soup Fried Soles Veal Cutlets Roast Chicken Charlotte Russe & Caviar on Toast with champagne and Port, also the Black Watch Band played during dinner and their pipers played after dinner. There were all the commanding officers there, & 4 others including Warlock. After dinner the Mess Sgt gave an exhibition of conjuring.[2] It was a cheery evening, & did not break up until after midnight.

That Dearest is all my news.

All All Love

Thine

Charles B

1 Eric Foot★'s father **Ernest**, 56, *(right)*, was a doctor with a practice in Pulborough. In his work he must have had to deal with sudden death but even so he could not accept that the lively boy he had seen off only a couple of weeks before was gone and that nobody knew for certain what had happened to him. There was a gulf in understanding between the people at home and the scale and conditions of what was going on in France – and just how easy it was for men to just disappear without trace & without anyone knowing the truth of their fate.

2 It seems extraordinary that anyone could enjoy such a dinner so soon after seeing their men slaughtered in front of them, but then moping would not bring their men back and in the Army, tradition takes over. They seem to be invoking the saying *'Eat, drink and be merry, for tomorrow we die!'*. Even with the stiff upper lips of the time, were they really so unaffected? I can't help wondering what they were really thinking as they watched the conjuror doing his tricks.

DAY 76 FRI
22 OCT 1915

Item 75
Letter to Margaret

Envelope
161 Haverstock Hill
London

Forwarded to: Mrs Orr,
The Cottage, Dodington,
Wellingborough

Oct 22ⁿᵈ 1915

Dearest Darling

    Am feeling years younger have just had a note from the Brigade saying I can have a weeks leave (inclusive of day I leave here & return) for the 25ᵗʰ, so expect me sometime on the 26ᵗʰ. I only hope I shall feel better than I am now. The strain & reaction is telling & I cannot eat or sleep.

    All All Love

        yrs in haste

           Charles

FIELD POST OFFICE / 22 OC 15

HAMPSTEAD S.O. / 8.45 PM / 23 OC 15 / N.W.

Item 76
Letter to
William Woodthorpe's
father, John
(from William's
army service record)

Envelope
(missing)

8ᵗʰ Royal Berkshire Rgt.
Oct 22ⁿᵈ, 1915

Dear Sir

    Your three telegrams addressed to Lieut.s Park, Holland & Steele have just been forwarded to me. I would have written you before but your son left no "next of kin" address, so I did not know where to write. I regret to say that I still have no information of your son, but it was only the day before yesterday that I heard Lieut. Holland, who was also reported missing, is in hospital, but where I am not sure. I only wish I could give you more information. He advanced with B. Coy. under cover of gas and smoke, and I believe got near the German trenches, but beyond that I cannot tell you anything more. He was with us such a short time, during the whole period of which we were in the trenches that I never got to know him, but his Company officer, who is badly wounded, spoke very highly indeed of him, and if he is lost, which I sincerely hope is not the case, not only you but the army will have suffered a severe loss.
I expect to be in London on the 26ᵗʰ instant, and if I can give you any further news will do so. My address will be 161, Haverstock Hill. Telephone 3776 Hampstead.

    Yours sincerely,

        C. Bartlett, Major

           Commanding 8th Bn. Royal Berkshire Regiment

P.S. I regret to say that the Censor will not pass any private wires reporting Casualties.

Lieut. Parke is in Base Hospital at Etaples. I regret to say Lieut. Steele is killed.

2Lt **William Woodthorpe**, 33, was the fourth of the officers from the 3rd Dorsets who had all suffered so much during the 13th October attack. He was a partner in the firm of accountants that had been founded by his father **John**, 62, *(right)*, with offices in London and Vancouver. His father set about trying to find out what had happened to him, including sending the telegrams which Charles is responding to in this letter. At the end of December he would at last get some news in the form of a report passed on by the British Red Cross Society, with the witness being named as L/Cpl Siel of the 8th Royal Berkshires:

'On Oct. 13th at 2.16 p.m. at Hulloch Lieut Woodthorpe was caught by machine gun. No-one of the Battalion got beyond Hulloch Road within 12 yards of German trenches. As the men went across I saw Mr Woodthorpe hit. He dropped at once and made one or two convulsive movements then never moved again. I was at the time in the trenches looking through my periscope and I saw the above happen.'

By this time, John Woodthorpe was in touch with his son's company commander, Lionel Edwards★ (even sending him a book to pass the time in hospital). He however said that he'd never heard of a L/Cpl Siel and with William newly arrived (and so not known to most of the Battalion) and with the smoke having made it hard to see, he didn't *'feel inclined to believe the story at all'*. One of William's brothers then visited the Lance Corporal in hospital and found that his surname was spelt 'Seal'. On hearing this, Lionel Edwards★ wrote, *'I know Seal very well, and he is a man whose word I should not doubt'* (he'd not been helped in recognising the name by the fact that the last he'd known, Seal was just a Private). It would still be another year before William Woodthorpe's death was accepted, and even in 1923 his eldest brother was writing to the War Office asking if there was any further news, but to no avail. All of William's 5 siblings survived the war, including a half-brother from his father's third marriage who was only 5 when William went missing.

Saturday

Dearest Darling

I expect to arrive London about 9 – 11 am on Tuesday morning. Will you please send my long boots & spurs to the club also any letters. Also tell Stovell to send my uniform there. I expect an appointment at War Office at 11.30 am.

All All Love

Thine

Charles

P.S. I will phone you directly I arrive but as we come by special train & boat of which I am in charge one never knows exact time or place of arrival.

DAY 77 SAT

23 OCT 1915

Item 77
Letter to Margaret

Envelope
161 Haverstock Hill
London

FIELD POST OFFICE
23 OC 15

 # ON LEAVE IN ENGLAND

Item 78

As well as spending time with his wife and daughter at home in London, Charles and his wife travelled to Reading for the Memorial Service for the Battalion. This must have been a highly charged and desperately sad occasion, and with Charles not writing about it, it comes down to reports from two local newspapers. I have decided to include them both because though both are long and report the same event, there is little that is repeated and they give different insights into the service and the times in which it took place – and show how different sets of eyes and ears at the same event can come away with different memories. The timing could have not been more poignant, the night of 31st October, though there is only mention of the following All Saints' Day rather than Halloween.

THE READING OBSERVER
Saturday 6th November 1915

The 8th BERKS.

————

MEMORIAL SERVICE
AT ST GILES.

————

When we say that a regiment has suffered heavy losses, do we remember what that means to the people at home? Every man lost to an army is also a loss to someone at home. An army can generally fill up the gaps, but who can replace the loss to the widows, maidens, mothers, and children? We have heard that the 8th Battalion Royal Berks have suffered, and the long casualty lists bear witness to the loss, but many a family in Reading has received the stereotyped notice "The War Office regrets," etc., that has meant so many heart breaks, achings, and tears.

There was a memorial service on Sunday evening for those of the 8th Berks who have fallen, and many and many that evening left a warm fireside from which a loved one was missing, braved the drenching rain and the dreary streets to find quiet and comfort in that service. It seems singularly appropriate that the festival of All Saints' Day should have been combined with the service. All Saints is to commemorate the heroes and great ones of the Church, and this year we also remember our nation's heroes who have given up their lives for freedom.

The church was filled with a congregation more than usually solemn and subdued, for there was hardly one present who had not one near and dear who was putting his life in jeopardy for his country. Many there were, too, who were mothers, widows, children, sisters or friends of those who had fallen, or who are lying wounded. There was khaki present also, for those of the Berkshire officers who were in the town attended to honour their departed comrades, and even from beneath the priestly robes of the Vicar there came a gleam of khaki.

Solemnly the service for the evening commenced; sweetly were sung the hymns applicable alike to Saints and fallen heroes, "The Saints of God, their conflict past," "How bright those Glorious Spirits shine"; sincerely a prayer for the King's recovery from his accident was raised.[1]

THE NAMES OF THE DEAD.

Then with lowered lights and over bowed heads the list of the dead was read. A long list, long enough to wring any heart not made of stone, and yet not so long to try the patience of those who listened. If any there were who might have felt impatient at the strain, there was sufficient rebuke in the words of the mother of one of the fallen officers which the Vicar read.

"Too long! we sigh. It seems scarce necessary to read in measured terms aloud their names before God's altar. Surely He will keep the loss in mind, and needs not we shall tell them name by name. And yet was it not written "He calls each one by name? . . . A year long have we watched for you, my friends, can you not watch for us one little hour."

So the list was read, officers, non-commissioned officers and men, who have won a glorious death, and as name followed name it seemed as if that mass of men who had marched over to glory were answering their names beyond.

Prayers for the wounded, sick, and missing. Another long heartrending list. Prayers for the many facing the foe. Prayers for those who have given their lives to save others, foremost of them, Miss Cavell.[2] Prayers for those bereaved, and many more who are in sore need of help and guidance at this time. Dimmed eyes and trembling lips were revealed by the raised lights as the congregation at last rose from their knees, but the hymn "There is a blessed home" was sung with a clearness that told of a great peace within.

ENCOURAGEMENT AND WARNING.

The Vicar's message in his sermon was one of cheer, telling of hope and glory for the departed. He spoke from Hebrews 12, 1, "So great a cloud of witnesses." Having recalled the vision of the saints to which these words refer, he said:

To-night we come to keep one of the most touching and beautiful of the festivals of the Christian Church, that of All Saints' Day. During the past year we have been thinking of all the evidence connected with the incarnation of the soul, its thinking of what God in His love and mercy has done for each one of us, when He came down to earth taking our nature upon Him, and living and dying for our salvation. To-night we begin to think of some return which earth makes to heaven, true, at the best a poor return to God for all His goodness and mercy to us. All Saints' Day comes at the time of the year when everything around seems to speak of decay, everything seems depressing and hurtful, like the weather today. Yet when we came in the Church, everything seemed lighted up, there was a white front on the altar, and when they sang those hymns that are so dear to us we are encouraged and take heart again, because All Saints' Day I think tells us of two things. It

speaks to us first of all great encouragement, when we are depressed and thinking how hard it is to try to be good and faithful to our baptismal covenant. When we say, "Well, it is no use trying," then comes the thought of All Saints, men and women just like ourselves, with just the same difficulties, just the same struggle, just the same failures, always the rousing to serve God better, the same coming back to God, the same devotion. Men and women like ourselves becoming in their turn the saints of God. It is a real help and encouragement to think men and women like ourselves have indeed become saints of God. So let this festival be first of all a great encouragement, cheering and heartening. Don't be pessimistic; don't let the dismal month of November depress you. Think of those who in spite of trouble, trial and temptation served God true and faithfully.

The second thought is this. Though All Saints' Day is a great encouragement, it is also a great warning. You may say to yourselves: It is no use trying, I have failed. It is a great warning that whatever other men and women have done we can do equally as well, if other men and women have suffered, so can we suffer. God knows our lot is a hard one. We have our difficulties and our own special temptations, but we must not give up, we must keep on trying, we must just have the same faith and the same loyalty as the saints on earth had.

THE MEN WHO HAD GONE.

We must also remember those of our brethren who for so many weeks worshipped in this Church of St. Giles, and who, like ourselves, grew to love the Church and its services.[3] I dare say there are a great many here to-night who can tell me many a touching last sentence in a letter or entry in a diary of those who now lie across the water. I like to think that many of those men I ministered to last winter had something to think of though they did not write it. One of our old choir boys wrote in his diary "By God's help I will pull through." And he did pull through, not in the sense he wrote it, but in a greater and truer sense, for he is now in God's Paradise. I like to think that those Testaments given out on the last occasion those men were in this church were carried, a great many of them, into action, and show signs of having been used. I myself saw those signs on many Testaments of those fallen that have come back to us in Reading. It is a great encouragement to us to think that men of the 8th Battalion worshipped in this church, because, like all men of the Berkshire Regiment, they pride themselves on serving to the honour and valour of the regiment. I am sure that when the time came for the great charge, not a single man was left in the trench. Some might have feigned sickness or made some other such excuse to remain behind, but not one held back. There was no grumbling, no grousing, even when under difficulties and in times of great privation. Surely it is a rebuke to those of us who are in our homes trying to make other people more pessimistic than ourselves by our grumblings. The words that came across the water from America are a great tribute in the characteristic slang. "The men of the 8th Battalion of the Royal Berkshire Regiment were indeed 'some' men."

Well, they have died for us and left their bodies in a foreign field that we might be in safety tonight. They are not dead except in the sense we mean it, because they live in Christ. The Church is always acting on the belief that the communion of saints, and we week by week for many months have been praying for those of our friends in the 8th Berks fighting for us. Should we stop praying when we hear that they have died of wounds or fallen in the fight, when for all we can tell our prayers have helped to make a good and noble death? We have been commending them to God's care and love, and we still have hopes of their spiritual welfare, are we not to tell them to God? Some people may have read in one of the Sunday papers the words of the Rev. R. J. Campbell:[4] "Nothing has been injured save the outer shell. No bestial hands have ever been laid upon the soul. Death destroys nothing that belongs to us, it only withdraws them from our side for a time."

Thank God, we all in this Church of St. Giles are of the Catholic faith, and because we hold this service, an intercession by prayer for the fallen, is a real and urgent thing for us to do. We are proud of those who have died for us; there can be no more noble death than theirs has been, and the only real comfort for those who mourn is that Catholic faith concerning the departed. Some of us have lost the noblest of our manhood; they have been taken from us, but they have their work to do, not here, but in Paradise. Death was glorious enough, but to-night they were living a more glorious life. They will help us here in this parish and in our homes, and they were helping us as on earth they helped England and the great Motherland. I am certain they are thinking of us and we have their love, and they wish us to live the life of sacrifice as they died the death of sacrifice. Here in this church I am certain they will be remembered and prayed for for all time.

The Vicar concluded his address with some verses written by the mother of one of the fallen officers of the 8th Berks, which began

"Lord, in this time of dark distress,
Come to our hearts and heal and bless
The war we wage that wars may cease,
And earth a temple of Thy peace,
Calm, Saviour, calm our anguished fears
And sorrow, dry the mourners' tears.
Earth's peace shall pass, Heaven's joy shall be
That men were found to die for Thee."[5]

Slowly and solemnly the banners depicting the saints were borne in procession round the church while the congregation sang "For all the Saints who from their labours rest." Then the Benediction, and, last of all, the tones of the organ reverberated through the church to the dirge that touched the hearts of all who stood there listening. It was the Dead March from Saul, telling, first of all, of the sorrow, anguish and tribulation that comes to mankind in death, then rising to a new note of gladness and triumph that superseded these things as it told of the realisation that there is something greater than death, that back of all is love, which is God Himself and all that is good and best and beautiful.

THE READING MERCURY
Friday 5th November 1915

The 8th BERKS.

MEMORIAL SERVICE AT READING.

"NOT A MAN WAS LEFT BEHIND."

Evensong at St Giles', Reading, on Sunday, will long be remembered by the devout congregation – numbering quite 1,000 – who filled the church on the occasion of an impressive memorial service for the fallen in the war, especially of those who belonged to the 8th Battalion Royal Berkshire Regiment, heroes who were also remembered in prayer on All Souls' Day. The lessons on Sunday evening were taken from Wisdom, iii; and Rev. xxi, 1-5. Psalm xc was chanted; and the hymns sung were 428, 438, 230, 437, and (as a processional) 619, A. and

M. The vicar (the Rev. Fitzwilliam J. C. Gillmor[6]) read from the pulpit the long list of names of the killed, the wounded, and the missing, connected with the parish. The collections, which amounted to over £7, were taken for the Royal Berkshire Hospital, which provides 100 beds for the sick and wounded among our soldiers. The congregation included Colonel Chase,[7] second in command of the (3rd) 4th Berkshires (representing the depôt), Mrs Walton, wife of Colonel Walton, who till recently commanded the 8th Berks, Major Bartlett (who has returned for a few days' leave from the front) and Mrs Bartlett, and the following relatives of deceased officers: The Rev. C. H. Keable and Mrs. Keable, Mr Ellice-Clark, Mrs Ellice-Clark (mother of Second Lieutenant C. Spartali), Mrs. Brakspear, etc. The Mayor and Town Clerk of Reading were prevented at the last moment from attending the service.

The vicar preached a powerful sermon from a part of the first verse of Heb. xii – "So great a cloud of witnesses." Having eloquently spoken of the "witnesses" referred to in the text, pointing out that they trusted in the same God, and used the same means of grace as ourselves, and were so commemorated in the most touching and beautiful festival of the Christian Church – that of All Saints' – the vicar proceeded: "Tonight, we think of the saints of God, we are also trying to remember before God those of our brethren who for so many weeks in the winter last past worshipped in this church, and who grew to love the church and its services. I dare say a great many here to-night could tell me of many a touching last sentence in a letter or a diary of one whose body lies across the water; but I like to think that those hundreds of men to whom it was my great privilege to minister here through last winter were of the same spirit as one of our own church boys whose last sentence found in his diary was 'By God's help I have pulled through.' He had pulled through, not in the sense, perhaps, that he meant, but in a greater and truer sense, because now he is in God's Paradise. I like to think that of the Testaments that were given out in this church on the last Sunday but one when the men were in this church, a great many were in the field of action, and showed signs of having been used – for I myself have seen Testaments of fallen men come back to their homes in Reading. It was a great privilege for us as a congregation to have had the 8th Battalion of the Royal Berkshire Regiment worshipping in this church, because – like all men who belong to the Royal Berkshire Regiment – they proved themselves worthy of the honour and the reputation and the fame of the county regiment. I may add that when the order came for the advance to be made in that terrible action there was not a single man left behind in the trenches. Some might have feigned sickness or illness; but all were only too ready to do their 'little bit' for their King and country. We are told that there was no grumbling – to use the soldiers' phrase, no 'grousing' – when the roll was called, under much privation. Surely it is a reproach to some of us who, in the shelter of our homes, are ready to make other people, if possible, more pessimistic than we are ourselves, that there were no complaints and no grumblings on that day. They were indeed – to use a common enough expression in these days which, I believe, emanated from the United States of America, but which in that sense means a great deal – the men of the 8th Battalion Royal Berkshire Regiment were indeed 'some' men! They have died for us, they have left their bodies on the foreign field, that you and I may be in peace and safety to-night. But they are not killed in the sense that they have ceased to exist. They are alive still – for all live for Christ. And the Church too, always acting upon that belief in the communion of the saints and the memberhood of the faithful departed, and we who, week by week, have for many months been praying for those, our comrades of the 8th Battalion who were fighting for us – are we to stop praying when we hear that they have died of wounds or fallen in the fight, where perhaps – who can tell? – our prayers enabled them to make that good and noble end! We have been constantly commending them to God's care and love. Have they any more need of the love of God now? Have we not to turn to God in our sorrow, and pour out our griefs and our longings for the salvation of our loved ones?" Having read some words by Mr. R. J. Campbell in a Sunday paper of that day, the preacher went on: "Let us in this church, who hold the Catholic faith, thank God because we hold this service of intercession and prayer for the fallen which is a real and a right thing for us to do. There can be no more noble death than that of our brethren has been; but the only real comfort of those who mourn the dead lies in the Catholic faith concerning the departed. You and I mourn the loss of some of the noblest sons of God and of the Empire that have been taken from us; but, believe me, they have still other work to do – not here, but in the Paradise of God. The life they were living when death came was glorious enough; but to-night they are living a still more glorious life; and they can and they will help us here in this parish and in our homes, and not only us, and will still help, as they helped, when they were on earth, England, the great Motherland. As we think of them to-night we are certain they are thinking of us, and would bid us all to live the life of sacrifice. They died the death of sacrifice. Here, in this church, on All Souls' Day, we make intercession for the departed. For all time they will be remembered and prayed for, that they may have rest and peace in the Paradise of God, a joyful resurrection, and merciful judgement at the Last Day. It has been well said that what gives to death its great solemnity is not that it changes us much but that it changes us so little. The mere fact of our passing from one stage of existence to another does not suddenly change our characters or make us fit to see God or to enter into His eternal glory. No. The faithful departed are waiting in the Paradise of God for the revelation with a yearning to know in full what here they only knew in part, being 'perfected unto the day of Jesus Christ,' and attaining unto the community of saints. In the hand of God they are with Christ. The Lord grant for them that they may find mercy in that day, and rest eternal, and that life perpetual may shine upon them."

1 King George V had been inspecting troops in France when their cheering spooked his horse. She reared twice and then fell, rolling onto the King's leg. He suffered severe bruising and possibly other damage for it is said that it affected his health for the rest of his life. Whilst returning home on an ambulance train, he insisted on performing the investiture of a Victoria Cross from his bed *(as pictured above)*.

2 Nurse **Edith Cavell**, 49, had been shot on 12th October by the Germans for aiding British & French soldiers to escape from German-occupied Belgium. Whatever the legal case for her execution (and after the war a British Committee of Enquiry did find it to be legally correct), making her a martyr was a disaster for the international image of Germany and served to reinforce their reputation for barbarism.

| | | | | | | | | | 19|00 | | | | | | | | | 20|00 |

3 The Battalion had been to regular church parades at St Giles during their training.

4 Rev **R J Campbell**, 48, *(right)*, was a radical preacher who drew crowds of thousands. A recent tour of the trenches had led to a deep personal crisis, prompting a turn from Non-Conformist Protestantism to Church of England Catholicism as well as a withdrawal from the limelight. He died in relative obscurity as a Canon & Chancellor of Chichester Cathedral having married his adopted daughter as his second wife.

| | | | | | | | | 19|00 | | | | | | | | 20|00 |

5 Leslie Berlein's mother Elizabeth was a poet but this verse seems to be more trite and clichéd than her poetry, and certainly does not have the sense of heart-rending loss and wrestling for the truth that is the hallmark of her collection '*Remembering*' published in 1921 under the pen name Katherine Moher. ➔391

6 Rev **Fitzwilliam J C Gillmor**, 47, had been the vicar of St Giles since 1911. Born in Newfoundland, the son of a Lt Colonel, he became a Territorial Chaplain to the Forces in 1908. His military links as well as the Anglo-Catholic tradition of St Giles' Church inform his sermon. He would go on to be Deputy Provincial Grand Master for the Masons in Berkshire as well as President of Reading Football Club.

| | | | | | | | | 19|00 | | | | | | | | 20|00 |

7 Lt Col **Ramsay Chase**, 53, was in the 1903 group photograph with Charles (see p.18). He'd retired as a major in 1905 & then married the 20-year-old granddaughter of the founder of Kleinwort's bank. She had grown up in the thriving German colony in Denmark Hill with her father being a manager at the bank. The start of the war had nearly seen Kleinwort's ruin due to their exposure in Germany – at the end of July 1914, £350m of bills were circulating in London, of which £120m were German/Austrian/Russian in origin, and Kleinwort's faced having to pay back impossible sums to other banks. They and the global banking system were saved by Bank of England bail-outs like those later made in 2008. The bank continues today as Kleinwort Hambros, though nearly all traces of the German community in South London have gone. Lt Col Chase did not serve overseas during the war.

| | | | | | | | | 19|00 | | | | | | | | 20|00 |

**GRAND HOTEL DU LOUVRE
ET TERMINUS**

BOULOGNE-SUR-MER

E. DELIGNY, PROP.

TÉLÉPHONE 1-43

I Shall Not Be Away Long

GRAND HOTEL DU LOUVRE[1]

ET TERMINUS

BOULOGNE-SUR-MER

Tuesday

My dearest Darling

Here we slept last night, and did not go on as no trains were running. I was lucky as when I got on board the boat I asked the purser for my cabin (not having booked one) & he said there was not one. I said this is the second time this has happened & was annoyed about it. Result Capt Lucena[2] & I had about the best cabin on board. Slept all the way over. On arrival here as no trains were running everyone ran off to this pub, who of course had not nearly room for us all. When I arrived there were about 100 officers formed up in a queue outside the Reception Office, so I wandered round got in the office by a private entrance and got quite a good room with two beds. Had some supper & to bed at 1 am.
It is raining hard here this morning and we do not move up till tonight, so dont know what to do. I wish the Guvnors friends had been about.
What a lunch we had. A good job John was not at the start.
I managed to get through a good deal in 6 days, but wish it had been longer. I am writing this with a vile pen on a copy of the Daily Mail on my knee, so that explains the scrawl.

Did I say good bye to you?

All my love Darling
Thine
Charles

Item 79
Letter to Margaret

Envelope
*161 Haverstock Hill
London*

ARMY P.O. 3
B
2 NOV 15

B. M., édit. - 603. - BOULOGNE-sur-MER
Hôtel du Louvre - Place de la République

1 The **Grand Hotel du Louvre** *(right)* was next to the train station by the docks in Boulogne. It no longer exists because the area was totally destroyed during the Second World War, with the most damage being done by an air raid on 15th June 1944 made by 297 bombers of the RAF (including 22 Lancasters of 617 Squadron 'The Dambusters' using 5.4 tonne Tallboy earthquake bombs). This stopped the docks in Boulogne being used as a base for E-boats harassing the Normandy invasion. The area was rebuilt in a brutalist style in the 1950s and '60s.

2 The only Captain **Lucena** in the Army at this time was **James**, 38, an artillery officer who had been born and married in New Zealand.

In 1912 he had become the 348th person to be awarded an Aviator's Certificate by the Royal Aero Club, with the 1st having been issued in 1910. Given the risk of flying at that time (at least 56 of the 347 people given certificates before him died in flying accidents or in the war), it's amazing that he should end up living long enough to see the first Moon landings. He died in a nursing home in Beaconsfield in 1971 aged 91.

	1900		2000

Item 80
Letter to Margaret

Envelope
*161 Haverstock Hill
London*

FIELD POST OFFICE
4 NO
15

8th RBR
Nov 4th 1915

My Dearest Darling

I had not a minute to write yesterday. We are back again where we were when I started my leave and look like being here for some time. We were kept 24 hours at Boulogne which was sickening as we might just as well have spent the time at home. Well we started at 7.15 pm and at 11.45 we were turned out at a little station about 4 miles from here, and had to wait 3 hours on the platform without any shelter. We could not walk here as we were not certain if the Brigade was here or not. Eventually I got to my quarters at 5 am. I found 5 new Subalterns which brings us now up to 30 full strength. Cloake & Robinson are on leave and Dug starts via Havre tonight so I expect you will see him. We had a nice drop of port last night, and I shall miss Dug very much when he goes. There is a great deal of work for me to do, as Klemantaski is all I have for an adjutant. We have Sgt Major Lainsbury Sgt Pickett[1] Sgt Musto & Cpl ? (the stretcher bearer) all on leave and two more going today so we are very lucky.

I must stop now & try & get upsides with my work. All my love Dearest & I wish I was still at home.

My best love to Paula & all
Thine
Charles

1 **Frederick Pickett**, 48, had got his name in the Reading papers for a string of petty offences as a boy: throwing stones, wilful damage to a tree, stealing apples, trying to steal 8 shillings from a pub till, stealing 17 live fowls from a hen roost, and burglary of pipes & tobacco from a tobacconist's (for which he got 6 months' hard labour). He joined the 2nd Royal Berkshires, and this hand-coloured photograph, *(left)*, shows him as a lance corporal in 1886. He hadn't fully mended his ways though and in 1887 ended up in Cork County Prison for 28 days for theft. He had left the Army by the time of his marriage in 1894 (when he was a railway porter in Deptford) and was a school attendance officer when war broke out. He must have joined up right away as this appears to be him in the first picture of the 8th Royal Berkshires, *(far left)* – and given his age (and bulk) my guess is that he had an admin job connected with Battalion HQ. He would survive the war to return home to his job. After he died in 1945, his children discovered that their mother was still alive in a mental hospital having been told that she had died in 1917 (the date of her admission).

8th RBR
Friday

Dearest Darling

I left on Monday & you said you would write Tuesday but so far I have not had a letter from you. This is very uphill work at present as one is expected to do in a month what we took a year to do. Nearly all my officers are "Triers" but <u>for some older ones</u>!! Dug went off last night at 11 pm & I started at 8 am this morning by going to supervise some shooting, it was a terrible show, one new officer, & not a decent Sgt left in the company.

We dont expect to move up before the 15th, and I expect you have seen the Kaiser has taken command over this side.[1] It does not look like being very peaceful, as I expect "The Huns" will try & push a bit to prevent us sending any more troops south. Tonight we have a concert & Joseph is the star turn, some concert.[2]

Klemantaski is my acting adjutant & at the present moment is having a riding lesson.[3] Tomorrow night I am being "dined" by the new officers, I shall have to behave myself.

Well dearest that is all my news

All my love my Darling

Thine & Paula's
Charles
X

Item 81
Letter to Margaret

Envelope
161 Haverstock Hill
London

ARMY POST OFFICE
5 NO
15

1 What he doesn't mean is what it looks like in this picture taken in 1913 where **Kaiser Wilhelm II** of Germany, 56, is wearing the uniform of a British Field Marshal alongside his cousin **King George V**, 50. They were both grandsons of Queen Victoria and shared a love of wearing military uniforms with their cousin Tsar Nicholas II, 47, and each of them held honorary ranks in each others' armies. The Kaiser was Colonel-in-Chief of the British 1st Royal Dragoons (now part of the Blues and Royals) and in turn King George V was a Prussian Field Marshal, Colonel-in-Chief of the 1st Guard Dragoon Regiment *(as pictured here)* and Colonel-in-Chief of the Kürassier Regiment Graf Getzler (Rhine) No. 8.

2 William Joseph ★, 32, was from a musical family and had also had some of his poems published. His surviving letters give the idea that he thought a lot of himself, but Charles obviously did not share that opinion!

3 Louis Klemantaski ★ had grown up in Hampstead, and, being able to get around by tube, tram, train and cab, he had not learnt how to ride before the war (like many of the junior officers in the 8th Royal Berkshires).

DAY
92
SUN

7 NOV 1915

Item 82
Letter to Margaret

Envelope
161 Haverstock Hill
London

Sunday

Dearest Darling

I had no time to write you a letter yesterday. I was out with the Batt[n] until 1 pm, and just as I was sitting down to write the General came along & by the time he went the post had gone.

Many thanks for three letters in all received, two yesterday, & one the day before. I am so sorry the play does not read like a success, but I should think the Evening Standard merchant was prejudiced, however notices dont count for everything. I enclose you some heather from Mrs Peacock I think she must be off her head with grief as she wrote me 5 pages of unintelligible stuff.[1] Poor old D Coy is in an awful mess, as I find now poor old Coote took all the company documents into action with him. However I spent some hours doing Birchs work in connection with this, have broken in Coy Qr Mr Sergt Read,[2] and reorganised the Coy entirely, so hope for the best. It is a glorious day here today, & if I had anyone to go for a ride with I should go for one.

Lawrence returned from leave yesterday & now all leave is via Havre an awful journey as follows

Leave Lillers 11.30 pm	Dept Waterloo 4 pm
Arr Havre 7 pm (next day)	Dept Southampton 7 pm
Arr Southampton 4 am	Dept Havre 4.19 am
Arr Waterloo 6 am	Arr. Lillers 9.48 pm

I dont know why this is unless a lot of mines have broken loose.[3]

There is a rumour that we are going to a more northerly part of the line, and I wish it was true as the trenches are very much better and it is a more peaceful existence.

The last week of training here is being devoted to practising attacks on trenches etc, as my lot average about 5 months service and dont know yet how to handle a rifle or bomb properly it is rather a farce, and I dont mind telling you I am in a bit of a funk as to what kind of a show we shall put up if we were attacked, as nothing on this earth will stop a panic.

I got a Sgt back yesterday who was slightly wounded on the 13th & from what he tells me (although officially I cannot take his word) I dont think there is any hope of Woodthorpe as he says he saw the Germans killing our wounded although he did not actually see Woodthorpe killed.

I see the Daily Express is full of the war going to end in 4 months. I wish it was true, but if they are right, I am d-d sorry for our prisoners.

We are all wondering about Kitchener, and the general idea is that he has gone East.[4]

Will you please send me my razor strop also the other two razors I have packed away somewhere, as mine are somewhat tired. Also please send novels, as it will be dark in the trenches about 16 hours out of the 24.

I had a fire in my bedroom this morning & a real good bath in front of it.

I dined with my new officers last night, & they are certainly much better soldiers than the last 8 we had from the 8th.

I have no more news, enquiries are being made about Hobbs' locket which was sent off.[5] Am glad Paula likes her doll.

> *Love to All & best love to you & Paula*
>
> *Thine*
>
> *Charles*

1 It's not surprising that **Maude Peacock**, 44, *(right)*, was off her head with grief. She had doted on her first-born son **Gordon**★ and dressed him in the most elaborate costumes as a little boy, including the one on the *far right* (along with the long hair that some boys kept at the time until they were out of infancy). She had also heard that his body had been found holding her card in his hand, so he must have been thinking of her as he lay dying on the battlefield.

2 **Stanley Read**, 22, *(below)*, a gardener, had quickly become a corporal. He came out of both attacks at Loos without a scratch ('*I have captured my longed-for trophy - a German helmet - it is a beauty*') and was now already a Company Quarter Master Sergeant. Wounded in the back & lung in March 1916, he would be unfit to serve abroad again but became an officer in 1918 & through postings in the Army Service Corps & RAF seems to have acquired the skills to become a motor engineer. He tried to join up again in 1940 but was deemed too old. He lived to be 89.

3 Sea mines floated at a level where they could be struck by ships and were tethered in place so that the people laying the mines could map where the mine-free routes were for their own ships to pass through. Mines that had broken loose were a risk to everyone, whether friend or foe.

4 **Lord Kitchener**, 65, the Secretary of State for War, was being reported in the papers as absent from London. In fact he was on his way to Gallipoli to see the situation for himself. The whole area held by the Allies on the peninsula was less than 30 square miles and all in range of Turkish artillery, so it was at great personal risk that he went, hence the secrecy. Within weeks he ordered the evacuation of the peninsula.

5 The father of **Tod Hobbs**★ had written to the War Office trying to recover his son's belongings. He'd received his valise with the kit that he'd left behind before going into action, but despite an assurance that the Germans could not have reached where he lay, all of his valuables were missing from his body except for a small heart and chain which now was lost in the post.

DAY
93
MON

8 NOV 1915

Item 83
Letter to Margaret

Envelope
161 Haverstock Hill
London

ARMY POST OFFICE
9 NO
15

8th *R.B.R.*
Monday

Dearest Darling

I wrote you a long letter yesterday, but have no more news. We are holding sports now on Wednesday instead of Thursday as we may move up on Friday, but dont expect any trouble. A staff officer told me that the latest rumour is that Kitchener had gone to Spain to arrange terms for peace. The General commanding the division sent over yesterday for a copy of "Standing Orders" for the trenches.[1] Well we have never had any so I spent half the night composing some, which you might like to read & pass on to Dug if you see him. I had no letter from you yesterday. Tonight I am dining with Warlock.

Now I must close as I am just surrounded with returns etc.

All Love Dearest
Thine
Charles

1 'Standing orders' contain general rules and instructions, in this case for whenever the Battalion was in a trenches situation. When going into the trenches in a specific location, further orders would then be issued that might supersede or add to the standing orders.

8th Royal Berks Rgt.
Nov 9th 1915

DAY
94
TUE

9 NOV 1915

Item 84
Letter to Margaret

Envelope
(same as Item 83)

Dearest Darling

Many thanks for letters rec^d yesterday. I am sorry poor little John cannot drink without after effects. I have no news. Last night I dined with Warlock or rather he dined with me at the Café de Commerce.[1] He is quite a nice man, & you ought to meet him, he is going on leave the day after tomorrow & you ought to get Goodrich to ask him to meet you. He is quite broke I think as he has nothing besides his pay. His address will be The Green Room Club,[2] so you might ask him to lunch with you at Princes one day & I will send you my next cheque from Pearson to pay for it. He is tall dark & would I suppose be wearing the London Scottish uniform. He is most amusing & some "swallower", but dont let him pay. I dont think we shall move up until Friday or Saturday now, the weather looks like breaking, & not very promising for our sports tomorrow. I was out from 8.30 to 1 pm this morning, am now (2 pm) just off to see our new Maxim gun merchants do a bit of shooting.[3] I miss Dug terribly & am also longing for Cloake to return & do my work. It is a nuisance now the post going before the mail comes in.

All All All my love Dearest to you & Paula

Thine

Charles

Post just arrived, no letter, the second you have missed this week. Please explain.

1 **The Hôtel du Commerce**, *(on right of postcard)*, was in the square near the train station in Lillers.

2 **The Green Room Club** was set up for actors in 1877. At the time of this letter it was housed in Leicester Square & stayed there until the building was hit in the Blitz in October 1940. It no longer has a permanent home and meets on an ad-hoc basis.

3 The original **Maxim gun** was a machine gun invented by Hiram Maxim in 1884. Even though the Maxim company had been bought by Vickers in 1896, and the new & improved Vickers machine gun had been adopted by the British Army in 1912, they still had Maxims when they left for France in 1914, & there was a big haroosh about Vickers charging too much and being accused of war profiteering (they cut the prices form £175 per gun to £80). I don't know whether Charles is using old lingo for the new Vickers guns or the Battalion was equipped with Maxims.

Lillers — Place de la Gare

129

DAY
95
WED

10 NOV 1915

Item 85
Letter to Margaret

Envelope
161 Haverstock Hill
London

FIELD POST OFFICE
11 NO
15

8th R. Berks. Rgt.
Wed 10 $\frac{11}{15}$

Dearest Darling

A line to catch the post. Just as I was off to bed last night orders came through that Gen Rawlinson commanding the Army Corps would inspect The Brigade at 10.30 am. I had officers up, reveille at 6 & spent 6.30 – 8.30 putting spit and polish on, and away I took my little lot. Well we stood without overcoats for 1½ hours in a nice cold rain & I still have my wet clothes on. He, the General, made a speech and praised the 8th Berks beyond everything. I will send you his report in a day or two.[1] It is too wet for Regimental sports today so we are all trying to get dry (Tommy has no change out here[2]). The mail is not in yet so I cannot answer any questions. I think I shall move up about Saturday.

Last night I appeared in Brigade orders as promoted to Temporary Lieutenant Colonel, so whether they are going to leave me in command or not I cant tell you, anyway for the present time your husband has to wear badges of rank as such, & is addressed as such.[3] Doesn't that make you laugh? It does me after all the messing about that has been going on.

All Love Dearest to you & Paula

Thine

Charles   <u>LIEUT. Col.</u>

1 General Rawlinson's address to the 1st Brigade included the following words:

   'I have been over the ground since, and standing the other day on the old first line of German trenches and taking into consideration the nature of the ground and the strongly fortified condition of the trenches, I must say it seemed to me a marvel how you managed to take the position. I can assure you no more brilliant feat of arms has ever been performed by any body of men during the present war and I am proud to have such regiments under my command.'

He may just have been using rhetoric to boost their pride but it does sound like either he had sent them into action whilst not entirely believing they would succeed, or he had not had a full appreciation of what he was asking them to do.

2 Over a year into the war, and still the supply of uniforms had not caught up with the massive expansion of the Army, and British soldiers or 'Tommies' still only had one uniform suit each.

3 His new rank badges *(left)* were a crown & star.

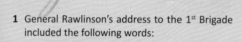

Nov. 11th 1915

Dearest Darling

Many thanks for two letters & one from Paula received yesterday. I think the post both ways is a bit irregular, as I have written each day except one. I have not gone up to the trenches today as the expedition is put off until tomorrow. We had a great concert last night. Kennerly Romford[1] sang 10 songs, & it was not over until 11 pm, and there were drinks, so it was quite a record not being in bed before midnight. You will be sorry to hear Fifi has been ill ever since my return, I dont know what is the matter with her, as I have not been able to speak enough French to find out. I should certainly go to Florrie for Xmas if I was you. I hope we shall be in the trenches at that time, for it is certain to be a peaceful period. We have another concert tonight, & tomorrow I am giving a little dinner to celebrate my new rank, after which we shall retire to the trenches to economise.

'Taski' has written to Mr. Hobbs about the locket which was sent off on Oct. 4th.

That is all my news Dearest

All love to you & Paula

Thine

Charles
x x x
x x
x x x x x x

I dont mind if you go motoring with David he is a nice chap & a gentleman.

DAY 96 THU

11 NOV 1915

Item 86
Letter to Margaret

Envelope
161 Haverstock Hill
London

FIELD POST OFFICE
12 NO
15

1 **Kennerley Rumford**, 45, *(right)*, was a baritone singer who'd studied in Frankfurt and Paris. Though he had made a name in his own right, including performances for Queen Victoria and King Edward VII, it is his wife who is more remembered by history. He had married the world famous contralto Clara Butt in 1900. She had been the first ever performer of *'Land of Hope and Glory'* in 1902 and they toured the English-speaking world with a more popular repertoire than had been his norm until then.

During the war, whilst his wife organised and sang in many charity concerts, he was running the Advanced Stores of the British Red Cross Society in St Omer. He donated his time and service, overseeing the distribution of stores to medical units as well as organising concerts in his spare time for patients and troops. He was mentioned in dispatches twice. He knew heartbreak, with his elder son dying of meningitis in 1923, his younger son committing suicide in 1934, and his wife, Dame Clara, dying before her time after a long struggle with spinal cancer in 1936. When his own time came at the age of 85, he was remembered with full and genuine affection, as an English gentleman of great charm and a lover of cricket (for many years he had been a leading light of I Zingari, an idiosyncratic amateur club that continues to this day).

19|00   20|00

DAY 97 FRI

12 NOV 1915

Item 87
Letter to Margaret

Envelope
(same as Item 86)

8th *Royal Berkshire Rgt.*

Nov 12th 1915

Dearest Darling

I had no time to write yesterday as I started by motor bus to go to the trenches at 7.30 am & got back at 7.30 pm to find your letter grousing at my short note. I am sorry but I am so short handed that I have little time some days, & today is one as we are busy putting on final touches. I have several men who are trying to get out of going into the trenches with various excuses, & I dont like it as it does not show the right spirit. Personally I hate going but then I dont say & pretend I like it.

*Well the trenches are too damnable for words, in fact the line we are going to hold is feet deep in water in most places, and the trench itself is falling in, and in this weather very little work can be done on it. We shall be within about 60 yds of the Bosch in one place.*¹ *However I dont think they can attack us as they would be drowned coming over. By the time you get this letter we shall have finished with the front line, & be back in the reserve trenches, which yesterday were stinking rather of dead Germans. However the whole show is only 5 days this time & we must hope for better weather by the next time we go in. Any amount of men now in the trenches are suffering from bad feet. I have a long pair of indiarubber boots that reach to my thighs, so hope to keep on the dry side.*

I have heard no more rumours of peace and cant see much hope of not spending Xmas in the trenches. Did I tell you according to programme we shall be spending it there, & I rather like the idea, as it is sure to be a peaceful time.

*A staff officer from the MEERUT division*² *has been in & wanted me to give up our billets, which I firmly refused. I had to report the matter to the Brigade, & the Brigade Majors reply may amuse you.*³

He is such a good chap.

Well Dearest we have one more night in bed & then five out. I will do my best to write each day.

All love Dearest to you & Paula

Thine

Charles

---

1 The map shows the area where they were going, between Loos and Hulluch. All pencil lines (blue and red) to the left are British, and their sector was from the Chalk Pit (just north of the German 'Keep' at Hill 70) to the crossroads at the top where they were closest to the Germans.

2 The Meerut Division was an infantry division of the Indian Army. In the year since arriving, they had not only taken heavy casualties but also struggled with the cold winters. They were now leaving the Western Front and were on their way to the warmer climate of Mesopotamia.

3 The Brigade Major was the Brigade's most senior staff officer, responsible for planning the Brigade's operations and administration. The initials on the bottom of the following note, 'VMF', belonged to Major **Victor Morven Fortune**, 32. At the beginning of the war he was a Lieutenant with 11 years' experience in the Black Watch. Now Brigade Major of 1st Brigade, he became a great friend to the 8th Royal Berkshires and here is suggesting that Charles tell the billeting officer of the Meerut Division to go to hell.

"A" Form.   Army Form C. 2121.

MESSAGES AND SIGNALS.

No. of Message _____

Prefix _____ Code _____ m.	Words	Charge	This message is on a/c of:	Recd. at _____ m.
Office of Origin and Service Instructions.				Date _____
	Sent		_____ Service.	From _____
At _____ m.				
To _____			(Signature of "Franking Officer.")	By _____
By _____				

TO { 1st Brigade.

Sender's Number	Day of Month	In reply to Number	AAA
* R B E 3	13th		

Billetting	officer	from —	MERRUT	division been
states	that	he	has	his
allotted	RUE St	VENANT	as	to
area	and	wishes	me	
turn	out	by	midday.	
Am	trying	to	arrange	matters
between	ourselves	if	unable	to
do	so	please	instruct	me

*Tell him to go h—
elsewhere i.e. h—
if not satisfied
send him here
M*

From	Oc. 8th Beks			
Place				
Time				

The above may be forwarded as now corrected.   (Z)

_____ Signature of Addressor or person authorised to telegraph in his name.

* This line should be erased if not required.

92146—W. & S. Ltd., London.—W 14142/641—90,000—4/15. Forms C 2121/10.

DAY 99 SUN

14 NOV 1915

Item 89
Letter to Margaret

Envelope
161 Haverstock Hill
London

8th R.B.R.
Sunday

12.30 midday

Dearest Darling

Half our journey is now completed and we are just waiting for dark before we move up into the trenches. We had an early start. Breakfast 4.45. The train journey which was timed to take ¾ hour took exactly 1¾ hours & we then marched 2 miles, & since have been waiting about in the streets for a Regiment to move out & give us their billets to rest in.

It is fine today for a change & looks as if we might get up to the trenches dry, but if the moon is as bright tonight as it was last night then we shall have to go up all the way in the trenches instead of on top, which will be wet work & take double the time.

The mail seems a bit erratic just now, and I regret to say the partridges have not yet arrived. I dont think I have any more news today. I will send you on a cheque for the wool, how much do you want? I hope this time we are up to be able to get proper crosses put on the graves of the officers who were killed on the 25th.

Well Dearest all my love to you & Paula

x x x x x Thine always x x x x
xx x x x x x   Charles x x x x x
x x x x
x   x x x x x x x x x x

Trenches
Monday

DAY 100 MON

15 NOV 1915

Item 90
Letter to Margaret

Envelope
161 Haverstock Hill
London

Dearest Darling

Here we are, we had a quiet time getting in last night and no casualties. In some places we are up to our knees in water but on the whole it is not too bad. Only one casualty so far today & that was the mans own fault, as we would climb out of the trench to do something.

The Staff has been about all day, and when the General visited A Coy he found all the officers in one Dug Out, & a man without his bayonet fixed. He immediately came to my dug out, had me out & gave me hell, which I dont mind telling you I am passing on. It froze last night which helped dry the place up a bit. We have been well shelled most of the day but no damage done.

I am looking forward to getting rations up tonight as I hope there will be a letter from you. Also maybe a partridge.

Well Dearest I have no other news. I dont like the cold, never did and never shall.

All All All Love Dearest to you & Paula

Thine

ˣ ˣ ˣ   *Charles*   x x x

x x xxx x

xxx

P.S. My groom is going on leave & wants some money, I have none up here & thought I had my cheque book, but have not, so if he turns up please give him £2– (Two pounds)

All Love once more   *Thine*

Tuesday

Nov 16ᵗʰ 1915

Dearest Darling

Many thanks for your letter. Yes at the present moment I am wearing Ronny's coat, & when we get back out of discomfort I will write to Mrs. Brakspear. You will be amused to hear our new C.O. walked in last night his name is Major Dalby of the KRR's & is quite a nice fellow.[1] I am very sorry to have to give up command but am very glad to have an officer of experience with me. I now revert to major again which is rather a scream.

I cannot write any more tonight as the Staff has just come in & if I dont send this off now it will have to wait until tomorrow.

All Love my Darling

Thine

Charles

Love to my little Paula

What a scream Lilian taking her to Northampton.

DAY
101
TUE

16 NOV 1915

Item 91
Letter to Margaret

Envelope
161 Haverstock Hill
London

LONDON N.W.
12.15 PM
NOV 20 15

135

Charles Frederick Napier Bartlett

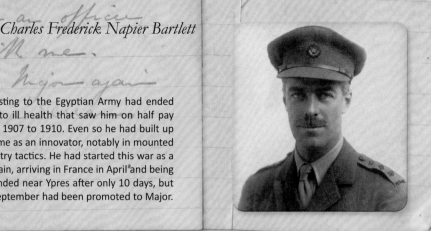

1 KRR's = King's Royal Rifle Corps, which had originally been raised as the Royal American Regiment in New York in 1755. Major **Gerald Dalby**, 35, *(right)*, was an Etonian who had entered Sandhurst in 1898, four years after his elder brother was drowned there in a boating accident. During the Boer War he was badly wounded in the left wrist, and a posting to the Egyptian Army had ended due to ill health that saw him on half pay from 1907 to 1910. Even so he had built up a name as an innovator, notably in mounted infantry tactics. He had started this war as a Captain, arriving in France in April and being wounded near Ypres after only 10 days, but by September had been promoted to Major.

DAY 102 WED
17 NOV 1915

Item 92
Letter to Margaret

Envelope
161 Haverstock Hill
London

8th *R.B.R.*
Wed Sept 17th 1915[1]

Dearest Darling

I have not much news for you, living the life of a rat in a drain does not lend itself to much. Last night I was down in our front line and it was quite an amusing sight. We had a party putting out wire[2] in front of our lines, & the Germans had the same, neither fired a shot, in fact the Germans shouted "if you dont fire we wont". It is an awful farce but what can we do except obey orders. Our new C.O. is quite a nice man not old, & I should think quite clever. I am very sorry not to have got command but am very glad to have got an officer with experience even if he is senior to me.

The Berkshire Women Volunteers under Mrs Henderson are going to look after the interests of the 8th Battn, but I expect she will have told you this, but it must not stop you getting on with the work. The Government are now issuing leather waistcoats, so you need not worry about them so much. With this weather we shall never have too many socks, & Balaclava caps mittens and gloves seem to be more in demand than anything at present. This morning we have been shelling the enemy's lines hard with the result that they have been hurling back at us a lot of heavy stuff, which although it cannot penetrate my present dug out jut shakes the ground & is most unpleasant. We are being relieved tonight and it is raining and hailing like fun it will not be a very pleasant job, but anyway we shall get a bit further back. I hope by this time you will have lunched with Warlock, & that you will have enjoyed yourself.

Dearest I dont think I have any more news, except the partridges turned up yesterday in the middle of dinner, so we ate the lot, and they were much appreciated.

All my Love Dearest to you & Paula

Thine

xxxx xxx x x x Charles x xx xxxx

1 Fuddled by the cold, he's put September but with the reference to the new C.O. it must be November.

2 i.e. Barbed wire for the defensive entanglement.

Nov 18th 1915

Dearest Darling

     I simply cannot understand you not hearing from me as I have written every day except one, when Taski wrote. The posts are irregular at present. I got three from you at 3 am this morning. By now you must have received my letters. Thank goodness we get out of the trenches tomorrow night for six days and then in for another 12, but in a much cleaner & "healthier" part of the line.

You have not heard that I was made a Tempy Lt. Col & now am the simple Major again.

I hope luck will come my way and I shall get a job in the dry somewhere as this wet weather & damp dug outs gives my old back absolute hell.

It was freezing hard this morning & tonight is raining hard, and I have to go out in it. The last 5 days I have lived in waders up to my thighs.

Dearest I have no more news. I shall bath & wash about midnight tomorrow.

    All my Love Dearest

    Thine now & always

    Charles

    x x x x x x x x x x x

x x x x x x x x
x   x
x *For Paula* x
x x x x x x x

DAY 103 THU

18 NOV 1915

Item 93
Letter to Margaret

Envelope
161 Haverstock Hill
London

FIELD POST OFFICE
19 NO 15

8th Royal Berks Rgt
Nov 20th 1915

My dearest Darling

    Many thanks for your letter recd this morning enclosing one from Dugs Father[1] and Booseys wire, also another just arrived enclosing Mrs Waltons Johns Tillys. This Colonel job is a nuisance as I have had letters from heaps of people in and out of the Regiment.

I am told by the Brigade it is a mistake on the part of G.H.Q.[2] and if I made a

DAY 105 SAT

20 NOV 1915

Item 94
Letter to Margaret

Envelope
161 Haverstock Hill
London

fuss I should probably keep command, but I am so thankful to have a man of experience that I really dont mind, except for the false impression it may give other people. We had a comfortable relief last night & no casualties, getting back here about 10 pm when we had a jolly good dinner, and this morning a fine hot bath and clean clothes.

If I write any more I shall miss the post. As you can imagine we are up to our eyes refitting.

     All All All my Love to you and Paula

       Thine

       Charles

       xxx for Paula

       xxx for you

FIELD POST OFFICE 20 NO 15

1 Dug's father, **Max Tosetti**, 71, *(left)*, despite the Italian name, had been born a Prussian in Saarbrücken in 1844, the son of a district court clerk. Emigrating to England at the age of 23, he started out as a shipping agent. His business grew to control the import of most of the Grand Marque Champagnes into London, enabling the purchase of a large hall set in a well-wooded park in Cambridgeshire.

2 G.H.Q. = General Head Quarters, i.e. the staff commanding the British Expeditionary Force.

DAY 106 SUN

21 NOV 1915

Item 95
Letter to Margaret

Envelope
161 Haverstock Hill
London

FIELD POST OFFICE 21 NO 15

       Sunday

My Dearest Darling

     Many thanks for letter just rec*d*. I write every day but when in the trenches it is not easy to catch a regular post. I cannot write much today as the horses are waiting, and I have to go 4 miles to arrange to wash the men.
Re my promotion, a protest has been sent in, and we must await results.
Maj Dalby is an awfully nice man, and has himself written saying I have been badly treated. I will write daily but dont expect much as we are only out for 6 days and there is an awful lot to be done. I have not seen Warlock yet but hope to soon. His Regiment is 2 miles away. All All Love Dearest to you & Paula

       Thine for ever

       Charles B

     xxxx For you

     xxxx For Paula

8th *Royal Berkshire Rgt*
Nov 22nd 1915

My dearest Darling

      Many thanks for the partridges, which arrived this morning on the person of one Warlock. I had not much time to talk to him as the General was about but he seems to have enjoyed his lunch. I have no news, I can get no satisfaction as to why Dalby has been brought in, & although I have put in a protest the General refuses to send it on. I have written C.A.P. on the subject and asked him if he can find me a job through Sir Reginald Brade,[1] so if you pass St Dunstans[2] you might go and see if you cannot put some pressure on, as this infernal cold is most unpleasant. We go in on Thursday for 12 days and you can imagine what my poor old back will be like at the end of the time I dare not think. Dug's company is so far off I see little of him now, & although Dalby is a very nice man it is not the same thing. He naturally is introducing the system and customs he has been used to, and altogether it is "pas le même chose".[3]

As John wishes to be the forwarding agents for all wooleys etc. I should just let him be so. I hope letters are arriving more regularly now. You have no idea how many letters I have congratulating me on getting the command, & still they keep coming in. I hope we shall find some nice tame Bosches[4] against us when we go in the trenches on Thursday night, & I hope you will work a nice soft billet for me. Could you not ask Sir R Brades secretary to find out why I was given the command of the Rgt, and another man brought in at once.

    All my love Dearest to you & Paula

    Thine

    xxxxxx Charles xxxxxx

Item 96
Letter to Margaret

Envelope
*161 Haverstock Hill
London*

FIELD POST OFFICE
23 NO
15

---

1 **Sir Reginald Brade**, 51, *(right)*, had been a civil servant since 1884 and was knighted in January 1914 a few days before being appointed as Secretary of the War Office. Since the outbreak of the war he had had to deal with a huge expansion of his role and of his staff. Having had a bed made up in the corner of his office, he made himself available at all hours to cheerfully give of his knowledge & vast experience to every enquirer. With the strain of his job & with nearly no holiday taken during the whole war, his health broke down in early 1919 & he was forced to resign, but remained Secretary & Registrar of the Distinguished Service Order until his death. ➜391

2 **St Dunstan's** was in Regent's Park, in a house lent by the German-born American financier Otto Kahn. It had been set up by Arthur Pearson to give support to blinded soldiers and teach them new skills to make the most of their lives. It continues today as Blind Veterans UK.

3 pas le même chose = not the same thing.

4 Different German regiments came with different reputations, ranging from the *'fierce & gigantic'* Prussian Guards, to the Saxons who were described by a Royal Berkshires' private as being *'fairly quiet and a bit playful'*.

DAY 108 TUE

23 NOV 1915

Item 97
Letter to Margaret

Envelope
161 Haverstock Hill London

FIELD POST OFFICE
23 NO 15

8ᵗʰ Royal Berks Rgt
Tuesday Nov 23ʳᵈ 1915

Dearest Darling

 I have no further news for you. It is simply d-d cold & miserable out here. I wonder if you could get hold of Sir R Brades secretary who told you that you could communicate with me through him, & ask him to find out why I was gazetted[1] to the command of the battalion on Nov 16ᵗʰ, being antedated to Sept 29ᵗʰ & then on Nov 15ᵗʰ a new man is brought in, when there has not been a single word said to me about it, or any reasons given. This action on the part of G.H.Q. simply makes me look a fool especially as I keep on appearing in the local papers as having been given command.

Do you think General Sir Charles Crutchly[2] could do anything for me. I am tied down out here, and the general does not want to forward my protest much as he would like to. In fact there is some d-d dirty work somewhere, and if you could manage to get someone to take up the case I think I should very probably be reinstated, but officially I can do no more, so it is up to you to worry the nice secretary boy you spoke of, General Sir Charles, & C.A.P. and all going well something ought to turn up, but you must work hard and see what you can do. I am glad you are going down to see Dorothy give her my best love. What has happened to Vi Gold ? Let us know how Tony is![3]

 All love to you and Paula

  Thine

  Charles

1 Army appointments & promotions were announced in the London Gazette, so they were referred to as being 'gazetted'. In this case, 24ᵗʰ November would see the cancellation of the notice he describes, then on 9ᵗʰ December it would say that he had been a temporary Lt Col from 30ᵗʰ October to 14ᵗʰ November. The bottom line was that he was back to Major.

2 Maj-Gen **Sir Charles Crutchley**, 58, *(left)*, was the husband of Lady Sybil who had become friendly with Margaret through the theatre. After joining the Army in 1874, he had been on campaigns in Egypt and the Sudan, where he was severely wounded. From 1887 to 1909 he was on the Recruiting Staff at the War Office, finally as Director of Recruiting. He was now Lieutenant-Governor and Secretary of the Royal Hospital at Chelsea, the home of army pensioners. His only child, Gerald, a godson of Queen Mary, had been wounded and taken prisoner in January whilst with the Scots Guards.

3 Dorothy was brother Edward's widow, **Rose Annie Dorothy Bartlett**, 42, and **Vi Gold** was her twin sister. I wonder if Tony is a familiar nickname for their brother Capt **Vivian Rose**, 46, who had only just been found as a prisoner of war in a hospital in Belgium, having been missing since the Battle of Loos. The two world wars would have a devastating effect on the Rose family. ➔ **406 Rose**

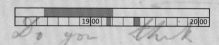

Item 98
Letter to Margaret

Envelope
161 Haverstock Hill
London

8th Royal Berkshire Rgt.
Wednesday
Nov 24th 1915

Dearest Darling

No great news, we have postponed going into the trenches for 24 hours as General French is going to inspect the Brigade this afternoon. Next tour of trenches we are lucky as we start with 3 days in the front line, 3 days in the support line, 3 more days in front line & the last period of 3 days in the reserve line where we shall have houses or at least cellars to live in, & then a further period of 6 days rest.[1] Dalby and I dined with C Coy last night, who gave us an excellent dinner with champagne and port, and we were all in bed by 10 pm. The weather is fine, but it is no longer freezing with the result that the mud is too awful. Tomorrow we go up to the trenches to see the line we take over, & the next night we move the Battn up. The papers do not seem to have any good news. The Doctor goes on leave tomorrow, so you may see him. I must say he has worked splendidly & we have had less sick men than any other Battn in the Brigade. Next time we come out for our 6 days rest we shall be back further than we are now in a dull village with very bad accommodation. The pheasants were excellent. A Dundee Buzzard cake[2] would do us a nice bit of good, & of course any more birds there are about would be much appreciated. Wouldn't Louie like to make a large jar of home made potted meat? Now I must go & get ready for Gen Sir John French.

All All Love Dearest to you & Paula
Thine

XXX   Charles   XXX

---

1 This gives a good idea of the structure and routine of the infantry in the trenches. It wasn't just the one line, there was defence in depth. Different units were in each of the front line, the support line and then the reserve line, with communication trenches linking to the exit from the system, out of sight of the enemy. Each line came with a different set of jobs and a different level of required alertness towards the enemy.

2 So many people misspelled the name of '**W & G Buszard**' that they had an entry for 'Buzzard' in the London directory to point people to their shop on Oxford Street. Famous worldwide for their wedding cakes, they also did a good business in fruit cakes to the front. One was described in *The Bystander* as a *'rich nourishing pabulum of the colour of old mahogany, surmounted by a weighty crown of sugared icing and pretty conceits, which at first sight would appear to deny penetration to anything but a direct hit from a 12-inch shell'.* →393

DAY
111
FRI

26 NOV 1915

Item 99
Letter to Margaret

Envelope
161 Haverstock Hill
London

Nov 26th 1915

Dearest Darling

No letter from you yesterday. I could not write yesterday as I was up in the trenches all day, and did not get back until 6 pm.
I have a very comfortable dug out this time in fact the best I have ever had.
You will be glad to hear that the General commanding the Division has at last taken up my protest & has forwarded same suggesting I should be reinstated.
I have no other news & have to go round & smell all billets to see that they are left clean.
I will write you a long letter tomorrow, but as I shall be in the trenches you will not get it the day after you get this.
This time we are fairly close to the Bosche, Dug's company being within 30 yds of them in places, my own headquarters being 1000 yds back & very deep.

All All All Love Dearest

Thine

Charles

X X X X X X X Paula

X X X X X X X you

DAY
112
SAT

27 NOV 1915

Item 100
Letter to Margaret

Envelope
161 Haverstock Hill
London

8th R.B.R.

Sat.   27.11.15

6.30 pm

Dearest Darling

I promised to write you a long letter today, but my hands are too cold & I have not had a moment. We had a rotten relief last night, we only had 4½ miles to go & get in position. We started at 3 pm & finished at 10.30. It snowed, it rained, it froze & did everything beastly and was pitch dark so bad that the guides who were sent out to meet us lost their way. I have been twice round our front line today (a 3 hour job each time) & shall go round again tonight.
It is freezing hard & the trenches are full of water with a nice thin coating of ice which one treads through every time. We have had a lucky day today only one man

with a bad scalp wound, and the last regiment who held this bit of line averaged 8 killed & several wounded per day. Our casualty was the mans own fault, & ought to have kept his head down.

I hope you are urging on "my protest" as officially I can do no more than send in my formal protest, but if anyone takes it up I am bound to be given the command again, or another new regiment at home. We dont look like getting any dinner tonight, these Tommies are fools, I dont know what food is sent up to the trenches, it is not my business, & as long as we are all well fed I dont complain. Last night we had fish & sticks, for breakfast we had kidneys & eggs & bacon, and for lunch fish chops & sardines on toast, and now we are told there is no dinner until rations arrive, which many be any time, not even a drop of water to make soup with. All we have is some Tinned tongue, Tinned asparagus, and Paté de Fois Gras, why simply because Dug who is within 30 yds of the Germans & I know is eating pheasants tonight should we rough it. Your letters 24th & 25th just arrived. Dearest I am sorry about the lugs but cheer up.[1] If you let the house at a profit all well & good.[2] I am glad you are going out. It is just rotten about my promotion, I only hope either you, CAP or the General will raise a protest and I shall not appear so incapable as the Gazette makes out. I have no time for more.

> All my love Dearest to you & Paula
>
> Thine for ever
>
> x x x x x x x Charles x x x x x x
>
> P.S. will answer Paula's letter tomorrow.

1 Use of the word 'lugs' for 'ears' doesn't imply the deepest sympathy for the health problem she must have told him about.

2 It seems extraordinary given his current circumstances and accommodation that he was having to think about sub-letting his house to help make ends meet, especially as it meant his wife effectively becoming homeless and dependent on the good will of family and friends.

DAY
113
SUN

28 NOV 1915

Item 101
Letter to Margaret

Envelope
161 Haverstock Hill
London

FIELD POST OFFICE
29 NO
15

Sunday

5 pm

Dearest Darling

A dreadful calamity, our censor stamp has been accidentally destroyed, at least so I hear, but being in the trenches I cannot vouch for it. However last night I sent my letter to the Brigade to be stamped & I am told if I put our number on it will reach you so let me know. We have had a very quiet day today & so far no damage has been done. I was round at 5.45 this morning, & my word it was cold, but all the officers were well and cheery.

This afternoon I have been looking at the trenches we go to tomorrow, & as soon as I have finished this & had a cup of tea I am off on my rounds once more. It takes me about 2½ hours to get round, so I shall get back about 8 pm dinner, early bed as I shall be out again at 6 am. I shall not get the post until my return, so cannot answer your letters which arrive today. I have written Paula but have no more news. I hope you are jogging up CAP & co.

All my Love Dearest

Thine

Charles

x x x x x x x x x

x x x x x x x x x x

x

Sunday

My darling Paula

Many thanks for your letter which I thought was very nicely written & showed much improvement.

It is very cold here and we have now been in the trenches two nights and again tonight. These three nights the men have to be out all the time night and day without any cover whether it is raining or as it is now freezing. Then tomorrow we go out to another lot of trenches where the men live in holes in the ground where they sleep all day & work all night, after that three days we go up again to the trench where the men have to be out all the time for another three days, then we all go back to a village where we live in cellars for 3 days by day & work all night. After that we go back to a village for a weeks rest when we shall be able to shave and wash, which by that time we shall not have done for 12 days. How would you like not to have your clothes off or not to be washed for 12 days?

We have been very lucky so far this time only one man being wounded. I am afraid I shall not be home for another two months but the time will soon pass away. I hope your new Dolly is quite well, give her my love.

There is such a lot of ice now on the puddles in the trenches, & it is not quite thick enough, so breaks when you walk upon it & the water is so cold & often up to our knees.

Give my best love to Mummy & I hope Nanny Louis & Ethel are all quite well.

Your loving

x x x x x   Daddy x x x x x

145

DAY
115
TUE

30 NOV 1915

Item 103
Letter to Margaret

Envelope
*161 Haverstock Hill
London*

Nov 30th 1915

Dearest Darling

Many thanks for your letter received at 1 am this morning saying you will do all you can & stir up General Crutchly etc.

I am sorry you did not like my joke about the eight guineas.[1] I did not mean John to supply all the money for wooleys & will send a cheque as soon as Barrow who is on leave returns.[2] As for sending 10/-[3] to Pat Walton, the Colonel was very kind to me & if I do a little for his family occasionally I shall do so if I want to. I give you every penny of my private income & as good a time as I possibly can, & when I am living up to my knees in water I do not appreciate your lecture. If you spend money occasionally on others I dont lecture you & I will be allowed to spend 10/- or £5 of my money if I like without any jawing. We had a terrible relief last night pouring with rain & trenches up to our knees in water and although it started at 5 pm it was not complete until after midnight, & we returned to rest rather miserable.

It is a beautiful day today but the water and mud is too dreadful for words. The mice and rats run about our dug out like good 'uns.

I have heard no more about my promotion yet & am afraid it will have to come from your side.

I should like some more socks if you have any, as my trench boots just wear them out, & I use about 4 pairs per diem.

That is all my news
All Love to you & Paula
Thine
x x x x x Charles x x x x x

1 The joke about the 8 guineas is missing. A guinea (named after the area in Africa where the gold for the original coins came from) was one pound & a shilling, or 21 shillings.

2 The Quartermaster James Barrow★ was in charge of the Battalion's pay and accounts.

3 10/- was 10 shillings (i.e half a pound or nearly 9 days' pay for a private). Notes of this low denomination had only existed in England since the start of the war (replacing coins made from gold that was needed for the war effort). They were issued by the Treasury. The Bank of England only took over the issue of all notes in England in 1921.

Dec 1st 1915

Dearest Darling

Many thanks for yours of Nov 27th recd late last night. I am sorry you cannot afford to send a cake so dont worry. I wont suggest anything else & shall not expect anything more, so you can make your mind quite easy. If what money you get is not sufficient I am sorry. I have no more, & you get a very much higher percentage of all the money I get than most wives do, so I dont think there is any necessity for you to sit & grumble in front of fire when I am in an infernally damp dug out with shells dropping all around. It was beastly wet last night again, but I did not go out. Dalby went out until 1 am & I did the early morning work. Johny Pawson turned up here this morning being attached to the Brigade for instruction & Arthur Llewellyn I hear is also here, so expect I shall see him either today or tomorrow. I have just had a shave and washed my face & feel much cleaner. We are beginning to get a better system of getting letters and papers in the trenches and actually got yesterdays London papers at 11 am this morning. The Bosche is still quiet.

You remember the horse poor Peacock used to ride.[1] Well he was bringing up water last night & was shot, so we only got ½ rations. Well Dearest that is all. Please dont grouse any more, there is enough discomfort here without getting any from home.

All Love

Thine

x x x x x x Charles x x x x x

DAY
116
WED

1 DEC 1915

Item 104
Letter to Margaret

Envelope
161 Haverstock Hill
London

FIELD POST OFFICE
2 DE
15

1 I have 3 pictures of Gordon Peacock ★ on his horse. I don't know the horse's name but in this picture he looks like he is smiling for the camera. During the war, Britain lost over 484,000 horses due to war wounds, disease & exhaustion.

Item 105
Enclosed question sheet returned to Margaret

Nov. 26th.

Are you meaning the tummy bands not yet as my drawers are
" " " " Bandage. not yet. lined.
Will the gloves do.
What do you mean about cheque & motor! my joke.
What do the men want for Xmas. Socks & wooleys.
CB.

Item 106
Undated letter to Margaret referred to in Item 105

Dearest

Mail just come in. Here is the cheque
to pay for lunch & also the rent phone
motor car etc. Have written once if I add
any more you will be another day
without money.

Yrs
Charles

X Puss

Dec 1st 1915

7.25 pm

Dearest Darling

I wrote you this morning but have a chance to get a line out tonight. We have had a lively day & been shelled hard, but no casualties at present, although I hear the transport has been damaged a bit again.

There is no news really, it is very cold & thank goodness looks like drying up a bit. I dont know how long it will be before you hear after this, as we move up to the front line again tomorrow night, so there may be a bit of a delay. Anyway all my love Dearest to you and Paula.

Thine, in haste,
Charles

Item 107
Letter to Margaret

Envelope
*161 Haverstock Hill
London*

FIELD POST OFFICE
2 DE
15

Dec 3rd 1915

Dearest Darling

Many thanks for your letter and enclosures which will be rather amusing if GHQ say that is the fault of the War Office. I am sorry I dont answer your letters more fully. I mean to, but it is not because I do not read them as I read them all twice & always look forward to getting them more than anything else during the day. Re your Pyrhea of Gums[1] please go & see Harold before you let anyone start playing with your mouth, once they start heaven knows when they will finish & I know two men out here now who are infinitely worse since they were treated.

Last night we came up to the front line again & it was the worst night we have had yet, I was round until 1 am & came in with mud & water up to my waist even my tunic under my mackintosh was caked with thick mud & I simply had to have it scraped off.

The men poor devils stuck it magnificently and I met some carrying rations & water in mud up to their knees, who were absolutely dead beat 1000 yds from their destination. One boy was absolutely crying with exhaustion, and I had to talk to him for 10 minutes when he smiled & said "I'll stick it the 8th Berks

DAY
118
FRI
3 DEC 1915

Item 108
Letter to Margaret

Envelope
*161 Haverstock Hill
London*

FIELD POST OFFICE
3 DE
15

are never beat". They are a fine crowd. Arthur Llewellyn is out here stopping at Brigade HQ but I have not been able to get up as far as this.

The Buzzard cake was excellent & we much enjoyed it. Thank God we have only two more nights of this, & if we get out with less loss by sickness than 50 we ought to be thankful. It really is terrible, Rain, Rain, Rain. One thing the d-d Germans must be worse off as their trenches are lower than ours. I am glad your inside is not bad, but I fail to see how you can say it is my fault about no war babies.

Dearest I have no more news please go & see Harold before you start letting that firm pull your mouth about. All Love Dearest

Thine

xxxxxx Charles xxxxxx

P.S. If anyone complains about not having heard from me, I have been too "fed-up" to write, as until I hear from the General I have no explanation as to my promotion being cancelled.

1 Pyorrhea is an old name for gum disease caused by bacteria.

Item 109

Article in the Reading newspapers quoting a letter written on 3rd December 1915 to the Mayor of Reading, **Leonard Sutton**

The following is an extract from the letter sent by Major Bartlett to the Mayor:—

'We are at present doing 12 days in the trenches, when we go back to rest billets for a week to clean up and rest. The weather is awful. One is up to one's knees in water in the communication trenches and where there is no water the trenches are deep in mud. The colonel in command of the battalion says he has never seen such a fine lot of men; as he says 'You never hear a murmur,' and when the last drafts have had more training and experience there will not be a finer body of men in the line. It really is wonderful to see these lads, keen as mustard: it does not matter to them whether they are in the firing line, or trying to clean up filthy trenches, or cooking their food in pouring rain, they never grumble. At one o'clock this morning I met a ration party coming down a trench knee deep in water and mud. One man was carrying two water cans, and a sack of coke, besides his rifle, full equipment, and extra coat. He was resting, and I asked him if he was 'done.' He replied 'Nearly done in, sir.' I said 'Stick it,' and he replied 'Stick it; Sir, of course we shall stick it; the 8th Berks are never beat.' That shows you the spirit of our lads, and while there is that spirit we shall never be beaten. I think I have talked enough of ourselves now. Christmas Day this year in the trenches will be a very different one to last year, when the town entertained us all so splendidly, but, never mind, we hope Christmas, 1916, will see the majority of us back. Personally, I hope to get a little leave this Christmas time, as my last leave was nearly all spent 'on duty.' The Germans are putting some heavy stuff over us to-day, and already have put my candles out twice with concussion, which is a bit of a cheek on their part, and these shells are too near to be healthy.'

Leonard Sutton, 52, (*above*, in bowler hat), was not only the Mayor of Reading but also a partner of the family firm, Sutton's Seeds. He'd started out as a keen student of agriculture and to expand his knowledge he spent two years in Germany studying methods of seed production and visited California & South Africa. By 1914 Sutton's Seeds were one of the biggest seed merchants in the world, with premises covering six acres right in the centre of Reading.

Leonard bore unimaginable loss in his lifetime. His wife died aged 31 not long after the birth of their sole daughter in 1900, & during the war four of his five sons were killed within 18 months, aged 21, 20, 19 and 21. Eric was shot by a sniper near Loos in April 1916. Victor was killed when rounding up prisoners after a charge in Palestine in November 1917. Alexander had only been a month overseas when he was killed near Passchendaele in January 1918. Eustace was serving with one of the three Field Companies of Royal Engineers that had been raised by his father in 1914 when he was killed organising HQ soldiers into a counter-attack during the German Spring Offensive in March 1918. Even the survivor, Noël, his eldest son, would have to go through the sinking of the ship transporting him and his men across the Mediterranean in May 1918.

Elected Mayor three times and involved in every aspect of civic life, Leonard explained that he found hard work & time to be the principal healers for grief and loss. A modest man, he refused high honours, getting just a CBE in 1920. His daughter May would be the one to continue the family tree. ➔412

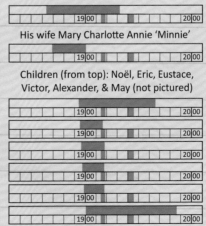

Leonard Goodhart Sutton

His wife Mary Charlotte Annie 'Minnie'

Children (from top): Noël, Eric, Eustace, Victor, Alexander, & May (not pictured)

DAY 119 SAT

4 DEC 1915

Item 110
Letter to Margaret

Envelope
161 Haverstock Hill
London

Saturday. Dec 4th 1915

Dearest Darling

We got no letters at all yesterday. And tonight if there is a mail it will be too late to answer any questions. The weather is still awful and if it goes on there wont be any trenches left. Even our deep dug out is leaking hard & although I try & sleep under the table with a mackintosh sheet over the table it gets on to me somehow. I was up in our front line until 10.30 last night & started off again at 6.30 this morning, & shall go up again this evening, but it is just one long wade. I have had to cut off my mackintosh so that it reaches just above my knees, as it got so heavy that it was impossible to walk. Last night one man's boots came off in the mud & we simply could not find them, so he had to be sent out of the trenches. The General was round this morning & said it was worse than last winter. In our front line it is not quite so bad, of course one stands in water but there are one or two ledges & places where one can sit down in comparative dryness, but the Batt^n on our left I believe they have to sit in it & a lot of their trenches fell in this morning uncovering a lot of dead Germans, who smelt awful. Tonight we are amusing ourselves by sending the Germans messages written in German to say that if any of them surrender (i) they will not be shot coming over if they dont come more than 3 at a time (ii) they will be well treated (iii) they will be well fed (iv) if they dont come they will either be killed or cripples for life. These messages are being thrown over in old bottles cigarette tins etc and it will be quite interesting to see if any come along. A good many are coming in every day. I am sending you copies of General French's & General Rawlinson's speeches[1] which when you have read will you send on to Mrs. Walton to forward to the Colonel who I am sure will like to read them. They will appear in the Reading papers so you need not bother to copy them if you want to keep them. All our officers are keeping wonderfully well also the men, how they do it without a dry rag I cant think. My shirt has not been dry for 3 days as my mackintosh is just a sponge now & the rain is soaked into my tunic, so I sit, when I am in, in a British warm[2] & dry my tunic, but have no change.

The light railway that our rations are pushed up on has been washed away, so what time, if any, we shall get our food tonight remains to be seen. The Dumping ground where are rations are brought for us to fetch is roughly about a mile from the front line, & the last night or two it has taken the ration party 6½ hours to go & fetch them, & then some of the party get so exhausted that they are liable to drop them & then the "poor dog gets none". We go into reserve billets tomorrow night, if we can swim to them. We have had so far a lucky day only two wounded & those not badly. A heavy bombardment all day on our part & the Bosche has retaliated a bit, but not much on our sector of trenches. Well dearest I have no more news. Let me know which day you are going to NORTHAMPTON to Xmas.

All my love Dearest to you & Paula

Thine

x x x x x Charles x x x x x

1 In General French's speech he talked of *'the splendid battle'* and the 1st Division's history in the war so far: *'The terrible losses which you have suffered has caused the Division to change its individuality several times over.'* *'I can only tell you that if the results of the Battle of Loos are not appreciated now, they will be in the future. It was one of the biggest battles that the British Army has ever won.*

To see what a difficult ground it was and how strongly fortified were the trenches it was all the more praiseworthy to take them as you did. I can only regret the losses that you suffered. I am quite sure that you had honour by that which you have won, in future generations it will not be forgotten that you worked hard for your country.' He wasn't to know how forgotten the Battle of Loos would

become. Four days after this mention in Charles's letter, he was forced to resign.

2 The British warm is a heavy woollen overcoat *(opposite)* that first appeared in 1914. If you had the money it was possible to have it made of camel vicuna wool (like llama) with a fur lining made from wallaby or muskrat, the top of the range costing 15 guineas.

8th R.B.R.

Dec 5th 1915

Dearest Darling

Just a line to say so far all is well. We are just waiting for the Black Watch to relieve us & then off we go & sleep in a house tonight. The worst of it is no one has arrived to remove our blankets cooking pots etc, so we dont look like having a very pleasant evening. We had one lad shot this morning through the back of the head, he is just alive and that is all, and I fear will not get over it, he was such a nice boy, and one of Dug's best.

We have had a fine day today, but last night was as bad as usual, and the water is still pouring into our Dug-out, so nice for the people who have to sleep here tonight.

We have had no letters or papers for days, this will be the 4th day unless we get some when we get back tonight.

One man shot himself through the foot last night, I think he was just "Fed up" and did it on purpose, anyway he will have to be tried for it by court martial.

I have absolutely no news.

All my love Dearest to you & Paula

Thine

x x x x x Charles x x x x x

DAY
120
SUN

5 DEC 1915

Item 111
Letter to Margaret

Envelope
161 Haverstock Hill
London

FIELD POST OFFICE
6 DE
15

DAY
121
MON

6 DEC 1915

Item 112
Letter to Margaret

Envelope
161 Haverstock Hill
London

FIELD POST OFFICE
7 DE
15

Dec 6th 1915

Dearest Darling

I rec^d two letters from you last night for which many thanks. We were relieved the night before last, the rain was awful, & although we only had two miles to go the last company did not get in until 12.30 am, having taken 6 hours to fight their way through the mud. The home made potted meat has arrived. Tell Louie it is excellent & thank her. Douglas and Dalby are just living on it. We have it for breakfast lunch and dinner, so it will die an early death. We have quite good billets here & wish we were remaining, but have got to back a bit further tomorrow where officers & men will not be nearly so comfortable & under the same amount of shell fire. Many thanks also for the handkerchiefs which are most useful. My application for retention of the rank of Lieut Colonel has been turned down by the 4th Corps Commander.[1] I have not time today to deal with it but when we get back I shall put in again asking reasons for it. We had splendid arrangements for the men the other night when they came in. They were all dead beat, and as each lot came in they were led straight to their billets where there was a fire in each billet. Two dry blankets on some straw, a packet of cigarettes on the top of the blankets, & each man got 1½ pints of hot soup, & they were as happy as bugs on a rug. Last night we had to find large fatigue parties[2] and some of them did not get back until 6 am. It is very hard work, and the men are marvels the way they stick it. There are some new regulations out about leave. I have not studied them thoroughly yet, but by a casual glance I see a loop hole by which I may not have to wait 3 months. However more of that anon.

All my love Dearest to you & Paula

Thine

x x x x x x Charles x x x x x x

(yours)   (Paulas)

1 The 4th Corps Commander was still General **Sir Henry Rawlinson**, *(left)*. The motivation for Charles still pursuing his promotion seems to be more that his loss of rank looked bad than actually wanting the extra responsibility. The extra pay that went with the rank might also have been welcome.

2 Fatigue parties did all the jobs that kept the Army functioning, such as carrying up equipment and supplies, usually in the middle of the night when they couldn't be observed by the enemy.

Item 113
Letter to Margaret

Envelope
*161 Haverstock Hill
London*

8^(th) Royal Berks Rgt.
Dec 9^(th) 1915

Dearest Darling

      I missed writing yesterday, as we were moving back, and the posts did not start. I have just rec^d a long letter from you, which I will read again & answer tomorrow, also one from Paula which please thank her for. We are back in the worst billets we have had since we have been in France,[1] and I would rather be in the trenches. Last night just as we were going to bed the dirty Bosche started shelling us with some nasty heavy shells. One came, & made a hole in the house next to ours, & another fell about 25 yards from my bedroom in the garden. In fact it was quite a nasty business. However we are all alive this morning. I dont mind these shells in the trenches as one expects them, but when one is "at rest" in billets & have to go to sleep with the d-d things whistling over the house it is a bit thick. I have not been able to find out much about leave yet, but hope to get home early in the new year. I dont think much hope for Xmas as we shall be in the trenches at that time, but you might let me know if you are going to Northampton, if you are shutting up the house or not, as I might arrive and want some clothes. When in the trenches one never gets notified if one has leave or not until it is time to wade out & either just catch or just miss the train 10 miles off. I have no other news, I have seen nothing re Curzon[2] in the papers.

      All my love Dearest to you & Paula

      Thine

    x x x x x x   Charles   x x x x x x
    x x x x x x x x x x x x xx

1 They were in the town of Mazingarbe, some 3 miles behind the nearest part of the front line.

2 **Frank Curzon**, 47, *(right)*, was an actor-turned-theatre-manager who at this time was being sued in a court case concerning the rent for the Prince of Wales's Theatre, one of several West End theatres in his stable. He had a flair for picking successful plays (one of which was *'Miss Hook of Holland'* that had featured Charles's wife) and news was just coming out that he was soon to produce *'Please Help Emily'* starring two of the biggest names of the day,

Charles Hawtrey and Gladys Cooper. Having been divorced by his first wife in 1909 (for adultery, though he had first tried to divorce her by falsely alleging a long-standing infidelity), he married the star of *'Miss Hook of Holland'*, Isabel Jay. He had also started owning and breeding racehorses and would finally have a great success with 'Call Boy' winning the Derby in 1927. It was a last hurrah in a bad year. His wife had died suddenly in Monte Carlo in February and he himself was so ill that he cut a frail figure when personally congratulated by the King at Epsom and only lived for another month.

4248 A ROTARY PHOTO. E.C.   MR. FRANK CURZON.   FOULSHAM & BANFIELD.

DAY 125 FRI

10 DEC 1915

Item 114
Letter to Margaret

Envelope
161 Haverstock Hill London

FIELD POST OFFICE
10 DE 15

8th *Royal Berks Rgt.*
Dec 10th 1915

Dearest Darling

There was no letter from you yesterday, in fact all I had was a bill for cigarettes. Last night was quite peaceful, in fact I dont think the Huns sent over any shells at all. This morning I have been sitting on a General Court Martial the accused being an officer, who was being tried for being drunk in the trenches.[1]

I have not been able to find out any more about leave, but it does not sound too promising, as there are only 3 majors including myself, for duty in the Brigade. However I must hope for the best.

It is still raining and water is all over the roads.

I hope to get out for a ride this afternoon, I badly want some exercise, & my feet are not in great trim for walking, having lived for so long in waders.

There is absolutely no news to give you.

I have heard nothing about Clarke.[2] I wrote his wife and she answered saying she had heard nothing also. We dont know if he has crossed to England or where he is.

Well Dearest, now a little lunch.

All the men are washing & having their hair cut with horse clippers so we have no parades today.

All love Darling to you & Paula

Thine

x x x x x x Charles x x x x x x

1 The officer was 2Lt **Stephen Lucena**, 28, and his life was a saga of bad luck and tragedy. He was 13 when his gentleman farmer father suddenly died aged 34, and 21 when his grandmother died having been shot by the estranged ex-husband of his aunt. In the meantime, Stephen had finished his schooling (including a year in Germany), and first joined the Army in 1906. He resigned as a Lieutenant in the Army Service Corps in 1910 to go into business, but things can't have gone well because in January 1914 he rejoined the Army as a private in the Royal Sussex. He'd made it up to Corporal when he arrived in France on 12th August 1914 and was a 2nd Lieutenant when on 25th January 1915 a mortar shell exploded near him, with the concussion causing temporary blindness, nerve shock & insomnia. By August he was said to have recovered and returned to the trenches. On 19th October he was found to be drunk in a town behind the lines, & his first court martial was on 11th November (9 days after his first cousin Capt James Lucena shared a cabin with Charles on the ship back to France). →399

2 **Wilfrid Clarke★**, (*left*, joking about in Sandhill Camp), had been made Brigade Trench Mortar Battery commander on 25th November. Three days later whilst preparing a fire mission, he was caught in heavy shelling and buried unconscious. A passing ration party found him and dug him out, and he woke up in hospital in Le Touquet 5½ days later, suffering from shellshock & concussion. He would be deemed fit enough to return to the Battalion the following May.

8ᵗʰ R.B.R.
Dec 11ᵗʰ 1915

Dearest Darling

Many thanks for two letters recᵈ this morning written 6ᵗʰ & 7ᵗʰ. It indeed must have been a funny concert, and as long as your sense of humour lasts I am sure you will enjoy those shows.

Well we had quite a peaceful day yesterday, & there was no shelling near us. The Bosche put a few into the next village. Klemantaski[1] has gone to hospital, but only because there is no accommodation for officers here, and I found him sleeping in an empty hut on the floor with a bad go of dysentery. Really some of these young officers want nurses, they have no idea of personal comfort or feeding themselves properly, with the result that their health naturally gives way. It is very dull here, all the men are taken for fatigue, & it is hopeless to try & get any training done. Yesterday afternoon I went for a ride with Dug, who has received his parcel, and Punch nearly had me off about 6 times. He shied at everything & nearly refused to pass some motor lorries, which he usually passes without a murmur. We dont expect to go actually into the trenches until 17ᵗʰ or 18ᵗʰ, but shall move up a bit closer on the 15ᵗʰ, where we shall be much more comfortable than here.

Thank heavens it is fine today & I hope to get off for a walk this afternoon.

Well Dearest I have no more news, except to pass the evenings we have to play Bridge.

All love to you & Paula

Thine

x x x x x Charles x x x x x

DAY
126
SAT

11 DEC 1915

Item 115
Letter to Margaret

Envelope
161 Haverstock Hill
London

FIELD POST OFFICE
12 DE
15

1 **Louis Klemantaski★**, (*right*, holding a score by his favourite composer Meyerbeer) was a sensitive poet and far from a natural soldier. How many of his comrades would have written like this?:

> Ah, I remember, now, one summer night,
> When all the street was wrapped in silence deep,
> You, late-returning, in the candle-light,
> Framed in the window, stood – a lure to keep
> My eyes from delving in my books uncouth.....
> Your clothes had fallen down: I marked the grace
> Of every muscle in your body smooth:
> The straight, fair back: the shoulders broad: the face
> Mobile & chaste: the supple hips: the thighs,
> Pallid & slim: the breasts, so small & white:
> The arms, distangled, wavering to the skies
> In a long aura, as swallows winged to flight.
> Then, as day quickly sinks beneath night's pall,
> So quickly fell your night robe over all!

157

DAY 128 MON

13 DEC 1915

Item 116
Letter to Margaret

Envelope
161 Haverstock Hill
London

FIELD POST OFFICE
13 DE 15

Monday Dec 13th 1915

Dearest Darling

     Just got your letter of the 11th. I hope you are not ill, let me know at once. It is a pity you did not go down to Dorothy you might have had a rest. I have been with the General for ages so have only 5 minutes for post. We go up to the trenches tomorrow but it looks like a quiet time. I dont know about leave, & all letters due in London on or before the 25th have to posted on the 17th, so I shall not be able to let you know. Anyway you will send all my uniform British warm, Boots etc. to the club,[1] as there is just a chance I might get away on the 23rd, but it is rather remote & depends how much I can "weedle" the Divisional Staff.
It wont make any difference to your plans & you are not to mention it to Paula or the Fraser family[2] at any price, as if I do get away they will have the surprise of their lives. Let me know which day you go please.

All All All <u>Love Dearest</u>

Thine in haste

Charles

x x x x x x x x x x x x

Paula & you

---

1 The club = The Badminton Club.   **2** The Frasers were his sister Florrie and her daughters aged 13, 10 & 8.

DAY 129 TUE

14 DEC 1915

Item 117
Letter to Margaret

Envelope
161 Haverstock Hill
London

8th R.B.R.
Dec 14th 1915

Dearest Darling

    Had a busy morning handing over these billets & now a bit of lunch & then back to the Trenches and very glad we shall be to get there, & finish another spell.
I have absolutely no news, except when I was wandering about last night with Dug we found some DM '06 in a shop & promptly bought two bottles, but being in a sober frame of mind, we only drank one last night.
There was a chance of going on leave on the 18th but I did not take it, as I did not feel like starting back on Xmas or Boxing Day, & when the next chance will occur I know not. I do hope you are feeling better & will let me know what is the

matter with you. I have only seen Warlock once since he returned & then I met him in the street. When not in the trenches they have always been billeted in a different village to us.

Dug is trying to pull your leg, & I dont know what regiment Hay is commanding now, but he was for "Home Service" only.

All love Dearest to you & Paula

Thine

Charles

x x x x x x x x x x x

FIELD POST OFFICE
14 DE
15

Thursday Dec 9th

For how long are you out of the trenches: *no longer.*

When do you go in them again: *now.*

How are the gloves: *very well thank you.*

Was Clarke wounded: *yes, no one knows how.*

When do you expect leave: *G.O.K.*[1]

Have you got the socks & toothbrush: *yes thanks.*

Have you seen Worlock lately: *nothing to speak of.*[2]

How is A Llewellyn: *only spoke to him on phone, sounded fatter than ever.*

Does Dug appreciate Renée sending things: Nothing to do with you (with

apologies) ask little Carrie, Douglas[3]

How is Cloake: *In the pink, as it leaves me at present.*[4]

Does he get any potted meat: *when it reaches him.*

How is your back: *Does not feel like increasing the population.*

Was Capt Hay in the Seaforths: *Not in his youth.*

Item 118
Question Sheet
from Margaret
& answered
by Charles
(& Dug)

Mr. WORLOCK.

1 G.O.K. = God only knows.

2 **Frederick Worlock**, (**left**, playing Benvolio in *'Romeo & Juliet'* in 1911), had just been promoted to Captain in the London Scottish. He would get through the Somme with only a minor wound and the award of the MC, but on the evening 28th March 1917 when leading his company in the dark up to do a night's work in the trenches, a heavy shell fell amongst them, killing 10 outright and wounding 39, five of them fatally. Frederick was hit by a piece of shell in the right arm and even after two operations he was left with a lot of pain and very little use of his fingers and thumb. Being only fit for desk work, he was sent at first to the Meteorological Office. In early 1918 he wrote to the War Office to ask for a better post as he was finding it hard to support his household of wife, child and mother. He also said that if he could return to acting, he would be able to earn enough to pay his debts and support his dependants. What he didn't mention was that he was also in the process of being divorced by his wife, having deserted her and later she had evidence of his adultery at the Waldorf Hotel. In the end, the Army let him go in May 1918 and he returned to the stage. He moved to the U.S. in the early '20s, becoming the third of the four husbands of the notoriously difficult actress Elsie Ferguson and appearing on Broadway and in Hollywood films playing an array of lords, landowners, judges, inspectors, governors, and senior officers, as well as a Roman senator in *'Spartacus'*. One of his last films was the 1961 Disney cartoon *'101 Dalmatians'* in which he voiced a henchman of Cruella de Vil as well as a police inspector.

3 This answer was written in Douglas Tosetti's hand and it looks like some match-making was going on to get him together with Renée (and he was having none of it).

4 *'In the pink, as it leaves me at present'* was another cliché that Charles would have seen from censoring the men's letters – it meant being in excellent health or high spirits.

DAY 130 WED

15 DEC 1915

Item 119
Letter to Margaret

Envelope
161 Haverstock Hill
London

FIELD POST OFFICE
? DE 15

8th R.B.R.
Dec 15th 1915

Dearest Darling

We had quite a nice "relief" last night although it was rather late. In fact it started at 4.15 & did not finish before midnight.
I have not been through the trenches today my inside being all wrong, & I am at present full of calamil[1] waiting to get rid of it.
The Transport Officer has just come in to say one of his horses has been shot so cannot wait for letters.

In haste
all love to you & Paula
Thine
Charles

1 Calomel was a mineral that was then commonly taken as a laxative (that was before they realised how toxic it was – it's a chloride of mercury!).

16th Dec

Dearest Darling

No time for a letter, as am just waiting for a car. Have got a chill & am run down so was cleared out of the trenches last night, & am being sent on today to a Clearing Hospital, I dont know where, probably where Edwardes was. I will let you know as soon as I do, anyway I shall get letters pretty quickly, but it will probably knock my leave on the head.

All love Dearest

Thine

xxxxxx Charles xxxxxx

Paula   you

DAY 131 THU

16 DEC 1915

Item 120
Letter to Margaret

Envelope
161 Haverstock Hill
London

FIELD POST OFFICE
17 DE 15

Friday

Dearest Darling

Just a line to let you know I am in a Field Hospital having my inside cleared out, very comfortable & looked after by proper nurses, none of your fancy bits.

We are in a double lined tent with plenty of blankets. If we had been in Billets & not in the trenches, I should not have retired "sick", but being in the trenches there was nowhere else for me to go.

I will write more tomorrow, but today it is rather difficult.

All All Love to you & Paula

Thine

xxxxxx   Charles
Paula
xxxxxx

DAY 132 FRI

17 DEC 1915

Item 121
Letter to Margaret

Envelope
161 Haverstock Hill
London

ARMY POST OFFICE
18 DE 15

Item 122
Letter to Margaret

Envelope
*161 Haverstock Hill
London*

No 12 Casualty Clearing Hospital[1]
Saturday

My dearest Darling

Just got your letter of the 14th & Renee's of the 13th for which please thank her.

I am very glad the operation has gone off alright you were an old duffer not to tell me, but buck up & get well for Xmas or Paula will be so disappointed. I am getting on famously & am out of bed today, but it is not very exciting here as there are only tents, no sitting accommodation or fires. I expect to get back to the Rgt on Monday night, so shall not know anything about my leave until then, when I dont suppose any letter will reach you until after Xmas.

Lawrence rode the horse over, & brought your letters, and as the poor sisters have only had fresh fish twice in 6 months or something terrible like that I sent him on to where he could get some. There is only one other officer here, and they are not taking in any more as the tents are going to be repitched on dryer ground.

The food here is quite good but the cook does not touch our Regimental cook.

They buried a man who was run over by a motor lorrie just outside here. He was wearing a Lancashire Rgt's uniform & there was nothing to identify him except a Roman Catholic Cross, so the Regiment was asked for the name of missing men, & he could in no way be identified, until they dug him up again & then discovered he was a German spy, the dirty dog.

Well Dearest keep quiet & look after yourself. I dont know when I shall see you but I expect between Xmas & the new year.

All All All Love to you & Paula

Thine

x x x x x x Charles x x x x x x

Paula   you

1 Nº 12 Casualty Clearing Station was then in Hazebrouck, 21 miles from the Battalion's position in the Loos sector. A CCS was a brief stop in the medical chain – they either got someone fit enough to return to their unit or stabilised them for evacuation to a hospital. In Charles's case it must have been decided that he would benefit from a rest at home and he was soon on his way on leave.

 ON LEAVE IN ENGLAND

1916

DAY
148
SUN

2 JAN 1916

Item 123
Letter to Margaret

Envelope
161 Haverstock Hill
London

?
B
3 JAN 16

HÔTEL MEURICE[1]
35, RUE VICTOR HUGO
BOULOGNE-SUR-MER

2.2.16[2]

8 pm

Dearest Darling

So far alls well, but what an awful crossing. I never knew what it was to be really sea sick before. I just perspired through all my clothes, & reached for all I was worth bring up about a quart of flem & that was all. I think we must have eaten some bad food last night as I nearly fainted on the train. As usual we are hung up here until 1 midday tomorrow when we go on. However I have a good room & dont mind as I am not yet feeling my best, and can do with a good nights rest.

10 am Monday[3]

Am taking it easy. I had no dinner last night, but was bad all night. However feel a little better, & shall get on this afternoon.

Have just ordered some chicken, & must now get up & dress.

All my love Dearest, I will write tomorrow, there is no news here.

Thine
Charles

1 **Hôtel Meurice** *(left)* appears to have been another victim of Second World War bombing.

2 In his run-down state, he's got the month wrong (if it had been February, the day after the 2nd would have been a Thursday, not a Monday as here).

3 Did he borrow a pen from the hotel staff to begin the letter? The next day, it looks like he's used the blue pencil he had for censoring the men's letters.

4.1.15[1]

Dearest Darling

Just a line, I arrived last night & slept with the Transport. I
reported at the Brigade office, & when the General saw me, he made me go & see
the London Scottish D[r], as ours was in the trenches. My temperature being on 95
I am being sent back for a weeks rest again. Certainly I feel rotten & cannot eat,
but hope to be back for the move. As we are all the time in the reserve trenches
it does not matter & Dalby has gone on leave & the General says Dug is quite
capable of carrying on this present tour. I will let you know where I land to.

All All Love

Thine

Charles

1 A typical New Year mistake – it was 1916.

DAY
150
TUE

4 JAN 1916

Item 124
Letter to Margaret

Envelope
161 Haverstock Hill
London

FIELD POST OFFICE
JA 5
16

Thursday[1]

Dearest Darling

I am back in an officers rest home for a few days.
My temperature has gone to normal & I hope to be out before the Rgt moves back
to rest, in other words training.
I have quite a large room in this Chateau with dressing room attached, &
Lawrence brings my letters over each day as it is only about 10 miles off.
He was over this morning but brought no line from you.
In peace time the grounds of this place must have been just wonderful, as there is
a large lake, & a moat running round the place.[2]
I think we must have all eaten something wrong, as Jim was bad & you looked
far from well.
I am quite anxious to hear how Paula liked "Alice & Wonderland," so write me
full account.
Everything seems very quiet in this part of the world, and I hear the trenches are
in a fairly good state. Dalby got away on leave alright. I hear that we shall go
back in some village near the town we were before, so we shall not be able to drop

DAY
151
WED

5 JAN 1916

Item 125
Letter to Margaret

Envelope
161 Haverstock Hill
London

FIELD POST OFFICE
JA 6
16

in & see Fifi & Germaine "of an evening like". *Dearest I will try & think of some news & write tomorrow. If I dont stop now I shall fall asleep & miss the post.*

All Love Dearest Thine

Charles

xxxxxx
xxxxxx } *for you*   xxxxxx
xxxxxx } *For Paula*

Environs d'HOUDAIN.— Château d'Olhain.

Collection Cayet-Delautre.

1 See the next letter for why I've made this Wednesday not Thursday.

2 The Battalion were in the old German front line where they had gone into action on 25ᵗʰ September. Take a line 10 miles from there & you find the magnificent **Château d'Olhain**, *(left)*, exactly as described by Charles. You pass through a large courtyard and then cross a drawbridge over the moat to reach the castle proper. Dating from the 15ᵗʰ century, it has seen many wars: besieged by the French in 1641, partly demolished by the Spanish in 1651, taken by the Dutch in 1710, and requisitioned by the Allied Armies in both World Wars.

DAY
152
THU

6 JAN 1916

Item 126
Letter to Margaret

Envelope
161 Haverstock Hill
London

Thursday Oct 6ᵗʰ 1915[1]

Dearest Darling

     Lawrence has just ridden over with your letter of the 3ʳᵈ, which I was glad to get. I am sorry you & Jim had such a rotten time & felt so bad, but I am sure I felt worse. I am still in this rest camp and have been out morning & afternoon. Tomorrow I shall try a really decent walk, & if well after that shall make for the trenches on Saturday or Sunday.

There are one or two nice fellows arrived, & last night we has some real good Bridge.

It is truly sad about Pat Walton,[2] *but you must just take her out in the Easter Holidays as you suggest.*

The breeches are to just go & be cleaned. The cleaning will be sure to shrink them, and then they will be just right. I have not felt like writing yet, and so have not written anyone but you, but hope to make a start tomorrow. The papers are too dull for words, and there does not seem to be anything going on here. Did I tell you that Moss got hit by a shell in three places, but not serious, at least not dangerous.[3] *He* is somewhere in hospital, & if he is sent to England you must go & see him, but I will let you know. I am very anxious to hear about Paula & Alice in Wonderland. I am glad you are going to Florrie you ought to get a real good rest there, and I should not hurry back if I was you. To get a bath here, you have to go into a stable where there is a boiler, & some long baths, apart from the discomfort of getting there & back there is not much the matter with them. We are called here at 8. Breakfast 9. Lunch 1. Tea 4.15. Dinner 7.15. Drinks only allowed at lunch & at & after dinner up to 10 oclock, & at 10.30 we are sent to bed, & I have read all the magazines here. I see in the Daily Mail today "Tommys Author is Nat Gould",[4] so you had better send all my books to Mrs Hendersons hospital.[5]

All All All Love Dearest to you & Paula

> Thine for ever
>
> Charles

1 The date he's written is a sign that his illness is making him all over the place mentally. The postmark along with the talk of 'Alice in Wonderland' ties it to the first week in January 1916 and that Thursday was the 6th. Both this and the previous letter were marked Thursday but with the mentions of Lawrence coming over in both letters and the round-trip ride being 20 miles, I think they must have been different days and I've put them in the order of their postmarks.

2 By the time I read this letter, my Gran, Pat Walton, had died so I never got the chance to ask her about this (and so much else). So many of the young men she'd spent time with in her summer holidays had been killed and I would not be surprised if she had had a breakdown.

3 Private **John William Moss**, N° 13357, was reported wounded in the papers a couple of weeks after this date. For Charles to be picking out a private who was known to Margaret, it seems likely that he was some kind of personal servant to Charles. He was discharged from the Army on 30th July 1917 and there is no sure sign of him after that.

4 **Nat Gould**, 58, *(right)*, had sold millions and millions of his *'clean, manly & sincere'* horse racing tales with titles such as *'The King's Favourite'* and *'The Wizard of the Turf'*. His second son Herbert was a Captain in the

RAF who shot down 6 German planes before going missing in August 1918.

5 **Phyllis Henderson** (*above*, in the front row 5th from left), the wife of the Chief Constable, had just taken over as the commandant of a new soldiers' convalescent home in Reading, despite having responsibility for a 9-year-old stepson and three of her own children aged 5 & under. Her brother Alan would be killed in German East Africa in June 1916. She would also lose her youngest child Alister in the next war when during a night take-off in pilot-training his plane hit some trees.

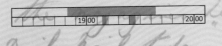

DAY 153 FRI

7 JAN 1916

Item 127
Letter to Margaret

Envelope
161 Haverstock Hill
London

FIELD POST OFFICE
JA 8 16

Friday 7th /15

Dearest Darling

Many thanks for your letter of the 4th just arrived.
I am glad Paula enjoyed the Theatre, & should have liked to have heard some of her remarks. Yes Mrs Guy I believe has money, anyway I hope so for her sake.[1] I am sorry you are not up to the mark but I hope by the time you get this you will be alright. I felt quite frightened when I saw Renee's hand writing & thought you were ill again. I am feeling much better & have gone into strict training & mean to have a busy month's training when we get back to rest.
There is absolutely nothing to do here except play bridge.
I went for a 5 mile walk this morning, & have to work out some plans for training, so shall not be too dull, I have sent for the horses tomorrow, & hope to get into Bethune & get my hair cut tomorrow.
Post just going.

All all love to you & Paula

Thine

x x x x x x Charles x x x x x x

1 Mrs Guy is likely to be **Constance**, the wife of Guy Napier (as back on p.96). Her husband's estate was £786 14s 3d. In terms of her own family, her father had cut his throat whilst a patient at Bethlem mental hospital in 1898 leaving £3241 9s 7d. Her mother (who was from the Coolidge family of Boston, USA) died in 1906 leaving £8731 11s 2d. All three of her sisters died young (aged 3, 18 & 5) leaving only Constance and her brother Neville to inherit. Constance died in a nursing home in Eastbourne in 1975, leaving £20,731.

DAY 154 SAT

8 JAN 1916

Item 128
Letter to Margaret

Envelope
161 Haverstock Hill
London

Saturday

Dearest Darling

There has been no mail in today. I am getting on fine and am feeling fitter than I have been for months. I shall be ready to go back on Monday & shall be another man. I had the horses over this morning & went for a ride for an hour. It was very cold, but did my liver a lot of good. You will be glad to hear I have written the Colonel a regular budget of news all about the Regiment that ought to interest him quite enough.
When are you going to take Paula to "Where The Rainbow Ends"?[1] There are some fairies there, or have I forgotten all about it.
A Captain Waters of the Stock Exchange has arrived here, he is quite a nice person, & we seem to be the only two who have baths in the morning certainly

one or two have them in the evening, but the remainder oh my Lord. Well Dearest I have absolutely nothing to write about. We talk shop all day, and just grouse. I was not even allowed to ride into the town to get my hair cut today so shall have to wait until we get away back to rest.

All All All my love Dearest to you & Paula

Thine

x x x x x x Charles x x x x x x

1 *'Where The Rainbow Ends'* was a children's play that was a staple of the Christmas season from 1911 into the late 1950s. The story is of the journey of four children in search of their parents. They travel on a magic carpet and are joined by St George of England in shining armour to help overcome all the fantastical difficulties on their way, not least the dragon. This production at the Garrick Theatre had made a change from the original, where a character who becomes an ally was no longer a German, but a Frenchman who received the loudest cheer of the performance when he defended the honour of the Union flag.

Sunday 9.1.16

Dearest Darling

Many thanks for your note of the 6th. I am sorry you are back in bed, but you dont give yourself a chance. Why not make up your mind to have a complete rest, and cut gadding about for a bit. From Northampton you might go on to Dorothy for a bit, however I know it is no use lecturing you, so I wont, but I dont want you to overtax your strength & be a chronic invalid for the rest of your life.

I am much better & really move up to meet the wily Bosche tomorrow night. So far we have been lucky this tour, as I heard from Dug today that we have had only 1 killed & 4 wounded, and as we have been doing all the working parties, it is very good.

I have absolutely no news, I won 10 francs at Bridge last night, & shall probably lose it tonight. Thanks for enclosing Paula's postcard, I think she must have been writing against time.

Well Dearest I will try & get a line off on my way up tomorrow.

Give my love to Florence & the family.

All All All Love to you & Paula

Thine

Charles

x x x x x x x x x x x x

DAY
155
SUN

9 JAN 1916

Item 129
Letter to Margaret

Envelope
c/o Mrs A J Fraser
Woodside
Hardingstone
Northampton
(Margaret was staying
with Charles's sister
Florrie Fraser)

DAY
157
TUE

11 JAN 1916

Item 130
Letter to Margaret

Envelope
c/o Mrs A J Fraser
Woodside
Hardingstone
Northampton

FIELD POST OFFICE
JA 12
16

Jan 11ᵗʰ 1916

My Dearest Darling

　　Once more I find myself in the trenches having entered under
cover of darkness last night, and I find the Battⁿ has dug a new reserve trench
since they have been up, & the Corps Commander[1] complimented them on the
splendid work they had put into it.
I went for a tour round before breakfast this morning, all the N.C.O.'s & men
seemed quite pleased to see me back & there were many "Good Mornion's Sir Glad
to see yer back", which if not very military was quite pleasant. I dont think I can
have been severe enough, & shall have to look to it in the future. We move back
the day after tomorrow. The trenches we now occupy are much improved since we
were last here, & I have quite a comfortable bedstead, and a very good stove, also
the walls have been covered with tapestry (in other words sandbags) which if not
ornamental keep the rats from climbing over ones face. So far today the Bosche
has left our lines alone, so I went & called on The Camerons this morning and
The Black Watch this afternoon. We are not going back to our old Rest Billets, but
to a village 3 miles away, so shall be not able to drop in & see Fifi & Germaine.
Dalby, Taski & Joseph are all on leave, & two more go when they come back, so
I hope we shall work everyone off while we are at rest, so that I shall not have to
wait, when it comes to my turn. I hope by this time you are feeling better. Bobby
must have had something quaint to do with all this secrecy about it.
The trenches are in very good order, & as dry as a bone, but it looks rather like
rain tonight, however I hope it will blow over.
Barrow is sick, also the Sergt Major. The last official reports for sickness & "Trench
　　Feet" have just been issued & through the whole Division we are less
　　by more than half of any other Battⁿ.[2]
Well Dearest I have no more news.
Love to Flo & the kids & with best love to you & Paula

　　　　　　Thine

x x x x x x　　Charles x x x x x x

1 The Corps Commander was now Lt-Gen
Henry Wilson, 51, *(left)*. Known as *'the
ugliest man in the British Army'* due to
an old facial wound, his pre-war planning
(including many visits to scout the ground
of what became the Western Front) was
key to the deployment of the BEF in 1914.
Politically active, he would become Chief
of the Imperial General Staff in 1918 and
was assassinated by the IRA after unveiling
a war memorial in London in 1922. He is
buried in the crypt of St Paul's Cathedral.

2 Due to all the water in the trenches, the
cold, & poor hygiene, men would develop
'trench foot' (where their skin would start
rotting) unless there was strict discipline
with regular foot inspections, and drying &
airing of the feet. The Battalion's average
daily figures were just under a man a day.

1900　　　　2000

Jan 12th 1916

Dearest Darling

  Just a line to hope you are feeling better, & to tell you I am very nearly at the top of my form. I am much better, & my nerve is as steady as a rock and I dont bob a bit. The Bosche has put over some heavy stuff today, but I dont think has done much harm, at least not as far as this Brigade is concerned. We have had another beautiful day, & if it only holds up for the relief tomorrow night, we shall do very well.

We have had another draft and are now nearly a 1000 strong again. The other Battⁿˢ in the brigade are also being made up to strength, so it looks as if this Division will be having a hand in the next push.

Your two letters of Saturday & Sunday have just arrived for which many thanks. I am sorry you are not much better.

Give my love to Scrub if you see him. He is a lucky dog to get out of the scrapping, but now I am fit I dont suppose I should be happy if I was away from my little lambs.

Well I have no more news I will send Taylor & Lowne[1] a cheque when I have earned it. Your letters were brought up by the acting QM[2] who I have a lot of orders to give to, & who takes this back with him.

  All All Love to you & Paula

  Thine

  x x x x x x Charles x x x x x x

---

1 Taylor & Lown was a livery stable on the Finchley Road in London. As well as looking after people's horses, since 1910 they had offered motor vehicle sales and maintenance.

2 QM = Quarter Master. With James Barrow ★ sick, someone-else was acting for him.

DAY
158
WED

12 JAN 1916

Item 131
Letter to Margaret

Envelope
c/o Mrs A J Fraser
Woodside
Hardingstone
Northampton

FIELD POST OFFICE
JA 15
16

Octʳ 14th 1916

Dearest Darling

  I recᵈ a line from you on my arrival last night at Noeux Les Mines, where we stopped one night & came on here (Allougane) where we rest for one month.[2] Have had a long day and shall be very busy tomorrow & Sunday so dont expect much in the way of news.

I am sending this by an officer who is going on leave, as there is no mail out today. We had a good relief last night, no casualties, & got back to Noeux by 9 pm, the men getting in by 10 pm so it was good quick work. Billets here are good,

DAY
160
FRI

14 JAN 1916

Item 132
Letter to Margaret

Envelope
c/o Mrs A J Fraser
Hardingstone
Northampton

I have quite a decent room with clean sheets & electric light, & the mess for Head Quarters is clean if nothing else. Tomorrow we hope to hire some furniture & be more or less comfortable for the time we are here. Dalby returned last night & had a crossing of 7½ hours. We are all a bit done tonight, and as usual had to fight for billets. I had 3 disputes over 3 places. I only wanted 2 of them, but fought for 3, won the two I wanted, & gave way over the other one.

All Love Dearest to you & Paula

Yours ever

Charles B

---

1 Again he's put October instead of January.

2 1st Division had been relieved in the forward zone by 47th Division, and the 8th Royal Berkshires first went back to Nouex-les-Mines, one of the larger towns in the area, 5 miles behind the front line, and then to Allouagne, a smaller village some 8 miles further back.

DAY
163
MON

17 JAN 1916

Item 133
Letter to Margaret

Envelope
*161 Haverstock Hill
London*

Jan 17th 1916

Dearest Darling

I am afraid I have not written for two days but what with settling down, & so many alterations in the companies & the various establishments I have not had time to get a line off to anyone.

Now about your letter of the 13th & "Gadding About". I dont call going down to the country gadding about as you rest there, but when in town you do too much, every day you are at something or the other, & you ought to make up your mind to rest so much each week.

I am dropping Bathurst a line about my American securities, but as he holds a power of attorney I expect he has done all the necessary work.

Duglas will not be starting home for at least a week, as Coy Officers have to go one at a time, & Captain Lawrence is at present on leave. Please thank Paula for her letter. I will write her tomorrow.

We are moving our Head Qr Mess as we were living in the Mayors house, & whilst I was having a bath this morning the Lady Mayoress dashed into my room wringing her hands, & gnashing her teeth & wailing "Le Marie is dead", so we have had to clear out, while all the relations are coming for the funeral, and like the Irish they hold a kind of wake.[1] However we return there on Friday. I am

WILLS'S CIGARETTES.

MARSHAL JOFFRE.

sending this over by Cloak who is going on leave, but we have not been able to get him more than 7 days.

Joffre the French C in C[2] is coming round on Thursday, & so I suppose we shall all have to line the streets, & look pleasant, which is waste of a day. I hear that we are not for the next push, but that this division is going to be kept for the time the line is broken, & then we shall go through and chase the Hun back into his own country. It may be safer, but will be very uncomfortable. Have you seen or heard anything of the Doc's wife? We are all rather fed up here, & think we have had enough war to last us for some time. We cannot get hold of any papers with the honours list in, so if you have a copy would you send it along. I have absolutely no news.

All All All Love Dearest to you & Paula

Thine

xxxxx Charles xxxxx

---

1 **The Mairie in Allouagne**, *(below right)*, has since moved to a more modern building. The Mayor (the French should be 'Maire') was **François Bailly**, 59, a farmer (and son of a farmer) who had been in office since May 1912. I have not found a picture of him but as a 20-year-old at the start of his five years of full-time military service, he was described as being 164 cm (5' 4½") tall with blue eyes and light brown hair, an oval face with rounded chin and forehead, a medium mouth and a big nose. Having reached the rank of corporal in the cavalry he left the Army in 1882, and the following year married Augustine Philomène Bouxin, with their twins, Léon & Elise, being born the year after. It looks like Charles has mis-identified the woman who interrupted his bath because Augustine Bailly had died in 1913 and François Bailly's death registration describes him as her widower (i.e. he had no 2nd wife). With Charles only having arrived two days before, he may not have been totally familiar with who everyone was, and perhaps the early morning bearer of bad news was the Mayor's housekeeper. →389

(Pierre) François Bailly

| | | | 19 | 00 | | | | | | | 20 | 00 |

Augustine Philomène Bailly née Bouxin

| | | | 19 | 00 | | | | | | | 20 | 00 |

2 The French Commander-in-Chief, Général **Joseph Joffre**, 64, *(above)*, was the son of a barrel-maker from the Pyrenees. As an 18-year-old he had seen action against the Germans during the Siege of Paris (1870-71) and then went via French Indochina, Formosa (nowadays Taiwan), Timbuktu, and Madagascar to become Chief of the General Staff in France in 1914. He was known as 'Papa' by his troops but, though he was a step-father, the only child he claimed as his own was born to his second wife whilst she was married to her first husband. His offensive tactics at the start of the war nearly led to total disaster, with 22nd August 1914 alone seeing 27,000 French soldiers killed in the Army's worst day of the whole war. He did not like to visit battlefields or hospitals or to have his routine of eating and sleeping be disturbed when at his HQ.

ALLOUAGNE - Mairie

Jan 19th 1916 [1]

Dearest Darling

No news but just a line to say all is well. I forgot to tell you about our new Subaltern who came out with a tin helmet & a steel waistcoat to protect himself from the bullets & before he had been out a week he got one in the seat, rather funny I think. He was not in this Battⁿ but the 5th I think.

I have spent nearly the whole morning chasing out men who thought they were sick this morning, really some of these shirkers are the limit.

I had a great night last night with my coffee bar and sold "hot chips" until we could not cook them quick enough.

Tonight we have a lecture on the duties of NCO's, which I suppose I must take an interest in & try and be present at.

We are busy putting spit & polish on for old Joffre and have to march 3 miles & line the streets for him.

Cloake went off in high glee last night and I am only sorry they would only give him 7 days. It is a drizzly rain today, & altogether things are very dull.

Cant think of anything more to say

All All All Love

Thine

xxxxxx Charles xxxxxx

1 It must be the 18th from the postmark on the envelope.

DAY 164
TUE

18 JAN 1916

Item 134
Letter to Margaret

Envelope
161 Haverstock Hill
London

FIELD POST OFFICE
JA 18
16

DAY 165
WED

19 JAN 1916

Item 135
Letter to Margaret

Envelope
161 Haverstock Hill
London

Wednesday
Jan 19th 1916

My dearest Darling

A beautiful day, and I went for a long ride with Dalby round our training area and feel better. Your letter of 16th just arrived saying that you have had no letters for a day or two but when we make a big move like the last the posts are apt to be delayed as moving forty thousand men is no small job.

Monsieur Le Marie is still dead & the funeral has been put off until Friday, which is really rather awful, as he is beginning to turn some, & we dare not leave the house for fear of offending the people. He is in a room just under mine and all day & all night the villagers come in & sprinkle him with holy water.

Tomorrow we are parading for Joffre, & by our orders we shall be standing about for at least two hours. I have absolutely no news, except I forgot to complain I had no letters yesterday.

All All All Love Dearest to you & Paula

Thine

x x x x x x Charles x x x x x

FIELD POST OFFICE
JA 19
16

Friday

Dearest Darling

    Some rush on today. We had an awful day yesterday, bitterly cold raining & no overcoats. We had to stand for 2¼ hours waiting for Joffre, who came slowly by in a closed car, and the windows were so smothered in mud that he could neither see us or us see him.[1] It was a terrible farce. This morning I have to leave at 9.30 as I am president of a Court Martial about 4 miles off, & from what I hear it looks like Death for one or two poor devils. The General is coming round any moment on a surprise inspection. However I got wind of it & all is well. I have 2 companies on roast meat & two vegetables for every man so my part is all in order. Churchill[2] goes on leave tomorrow, so I will send letter by him. Herewith GOC so no more.

Thine

Charles

DAY
167
FRI

21 JAN 1916

Item 136
Letter to Margaret

Envelope
*161 Haverstock Hill
London*

FIELD POST OFFICE
JA 21
16

1 **Joffre** getting into his Renault car, *(right),* in less muddy times. His driver in 1914 had been a two-time winner of the French Grand Prix whose breakneck chauffeuring had been the talk of the French press but Joffre had since lost him to the Air Force.

2 **Harold Churchill**, 21, had been a dental student and was a bit of a rarity amongst the officers of the 8th Royal Berkshires in that he was actually from Berkshire. Born and raised in Reading, his father was a private secretary at Sutton's Seeds.

DAY
168
SAT

22 JAN 1916

Item 137
Letter to Margaret

Envelope
161 Haverstock Hill
London

FIELD POST OFFICE
JA 22
16

Saturday

Dearest Darling

There was no letter from you yesterday and that is the second miss this week. I had quite an easy Court Martial yesterday the accused would give evidence he was not asleep, & so nearly messed up his case altogether. However I hope he will live to fight another day as he was such a nice looking young fellow, & this was his first mistake.[1]

The other prisoners I had to postpone as there was not sufficient evidence.

The General was quite pleased on the whole, but complained that the men sleeping on floors had straw to sleep on, and the regulations only allow straw for those sleeping on bricks or stone floors, but why the poor devils should not be as comfortable as possible I cant make out.

May I please have my washing, as one of my shirts has gone on leave to England by mistake with another officer. I only want a thick shirt. I shall be very glad when Cloake comes back, the boy acting for him is too uppish for words.

The Funeral went off very well and they tell me was a huge success, people came for miles, & all had a good hearty meal. We are having a dinner party tonight. The Brigade Major, Col Sutherland, & Col Hamilton.[2] We have sent the Mess Corpl 10 miles in one direction to buy fish. The little Doc 9 miles to get some DM, and the acting adjutant 3 miles to buy some asparagus, also some mushrooms & truffles, the menu is as follows:

Tortere Claire[3] (the real stuff brought back by Dalby)

Soles Frit

Poulet en Casserole avec champignons

Asparagus

Meringues with hot chocolate

Scotch woodcock

I am tired of this place, it is too dull, & the town is just too far to go to. However we go out for a trek for 4 or 5 days soon and practice open warfare, but as the ground is nearly all under water & what isn't is under cultivation, I dont know how it will work out.

I have absolutely no more news other than this.

All my love Dearest to you & Paula

Thine

x x x x x x Charles x x x x x x

Jollows.

*Tortue (Clare   (the real stuff brought
Soles Frit.   back by Dally)*

Scotch Woodcock

1 The court martial that took place in Allouagne on 21st January was of Private **William Neil** of the 1st Black Watch. He was accused of 'Sleeping on Post', found guilty and sentenced to be shot. However, in the Remarks column in the register is the note 'not confirmed', i.e. the sentence was not carried out. The only Private William Neil I could find in 1st Black Watch had N° 2106, arrived in France on 1st December 1914, was wounded in May 1915 & discharged to the Reserve on 31st January 1919.

2 Lt Col **John Hamilton**, 46, had just returned as C.O. of 1st Black Watch having been replaced after the Battle of Loos. He was a 1st cousin of General Sir Ian Hamilton, who had led the invasion of Gallipoli.

3 A tourtière is a meat pie traditional for the festive season in French Canada, made using cloves, mace & nutmeg and shortcrust pastry.

Item 138

Letter from the Bartletts' solicitor Algernon Bathurst (included because it's not the sort of thing you think of First World War soldiers having to think about while on active service)

TELEPHONE
"HOLBORN 347."
TELEGRAMS–SPARELY, HOLB, LONDON.

HORES, PATTISSON & BATHURST.

H.A. HORE.
ALGERNON BATHURST.
W.E. LUARD PATTISSON.
EDMOND L. PATTISSON.

Enc:

48, Lincoln's Inn Fields.

London 21st January 19 16.

Dear Mrs. Bartlett,

  The Trustees have decided that it would be well to sell all the American securities belonging to the Trust and to reinvest the proceeds in the British Government 5% Exchequer Bonds.

  This is considered to be a very wise move at the present time as American securities stand at a high price, and the effect of the reinvestment will be to give a larger income. I therefore enclose a Form of Request which perhaps you will kindly sign and return to me if you approve, and we can sign it as Attorneys for your Husband.

    Believe me,

    Yours sincerely,

    Algernon Bathurst

Mrs. Charles Bartlett,

  161, Haverstock Hill,

    N.W.

DAY
170
MON

24 JAN 1916

Item 139
Letter to Margaret

Envelope
161 Haverstock Hill
London

FIELD POST OFFICE
JA 24
16

Monday

24th Jan/16

Dearest Darling

Many thanks for your letter of 21st just recd. I did not write yesterday as there was no post out, and this morning I have been rushed off my legs. Someone seems to have made a mess of running the Brigade Recreation Room, so the General has ordered me to take it on, & I have had a morning at it. As I wanted to make some alterations such as a hole in a wall, to save about a quarter of a mile, I had to see no less than three French officials.

I am so sorry you are not fit, and I hope you will soon be your old self again. I am not quite satisfied with myself, as I cannot get my inside to work with the regularity it ought. We had a great dinner on Saturday night, and yesterday I lunched with Dug at Germaine's Café which was rather a large order one bottle leading to another, but we were on our best behaviour. When we got back about 5 pm I found a command for one to dine with the General, so I had to iron my trousers and once more put on my best behaviour.

Yes the potted meat arrived while I was sick, so it was all gone when I got back. The Pork Pie met the same fate.

I will write a longer letter tomorrow, at present the office is too full of work.

All All All Love Dearest to you & Paula

Thine

xxxxxx Charles xxxxxx

DAY
172
WED

26 JAN 1916

Item 140
Letter to Margaret

Envelope
161 Haverstock Hill
London

Jan 26th 1916

Dearest Darling

I did not get a letter off yesterday, as I was out all the morning, having to try by court martial a man who was asleep on his post. However as there was a legal flaw in the evidence he left a free man, which was lucky for him.[1] William is the Christian name of William's cousin. Dug goes on leave tonight, that is to say if his leave comes back from the Division in time. He has had to start off in a hurry owing to the trek the Brigade has to take part in which starts on the 5th. The General has asked himself to dinner tonight, but owing to short notice I dont think he will be so well done and I should like him to be. Yesterday at lunch time the General sent for me and asked me to go straightaway to a town & arrange the Brigade Boxing competition, which was the real reason I did not get a letter off in time. This afternoon I am giving my "Farewell Performance" on the football ground. We cant raise 11 officers without me so play I must.

Cloak comes back tonight also Lawrence. It is very sad about poor old Bogey, but I suppose the port & brandy must have an outlet somewhere and at some time.

We had a Colonel from General Head Quarters of the forces in France to lecture us the other night, and he did not seem very optimistic as to the state of things over here, and informed us there would be some hard fighting to be done in the spring. However another Staff officer was much more cheerful, and thinks another 6 months ought to see the beginning of peace.

We drank damnation to the German Emperor last night on the occasion of his birthday.

When we go back to the line, we go into quite a different sector, where I hear the trenches are in very good order, and which I believe is quite a comfortable spot, so I expect we shall soon be going up to have a look. However we shall have to take over from a London Territorial Division, and they never put much work into the trenches.

I am quite sick of this place and after all arranging Recreation Rooms, & Boxing Tournaments is not what I came out here to do.

Well Dearest I have no more news, all my love to you & Paula

Thine

xxxxxx *Charles* xxxxxx

1 This must be Private William Neil again (from p.177).

FIELD POST OFFICE
JA 26
16

Jan 27th 1916

Dearest Darling

No letter from you today. Well I played my Farewell Game of football yesterday and I really think it is my last. I lasted well until half time, after which I retired to goal. However we beat the Sergeants by 2 – 1, and they were betting 2 to 1 on themselves. I was very done after the game, developed a frightful headache & retired to bed, and did not wait up for the generals dinner. However alls well that ends well and this morning I am alright again.

DAY
173
THU
27 JAN 1916

Item 141
Letter to Margaret

Envelope
*161 Haverstock Hill
London*

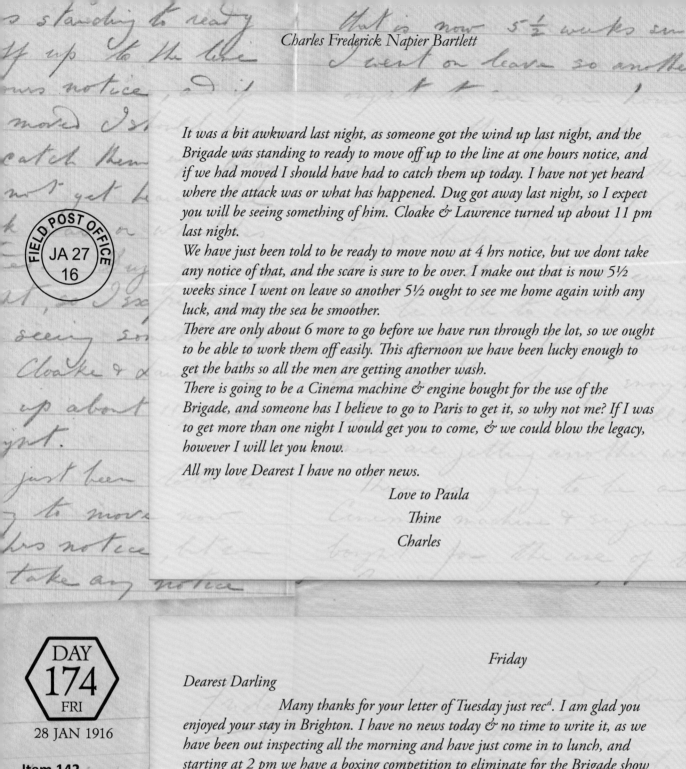

It was a bit awkward last night, as someone got the wind up last night, and the Brigade was standing to ready to move off up to the line at one hours notice, and if we had moved I should have had to catch them up today. I have not yet heard where the attack was or what has happened. Dug got away last night, so I expect you will be seeing something of him. Cloake & Lawrence turned up about 11 pm last night.

We have just been told to be ready to move now at 4 hrs notice, but we dont take any notice of that, and the scare is sure to be over. I make out that is now 5½ weeks since I went on leave so another 5½ ought to see me home again with any luck, and may the sea be smoother.

There are only about 6 more to go before we have run through the lot, so we ought to be able to work them off easily. This afternoon we have been lucky enough to get the baths so all the men are getting another wash.

There is going to be a Cinema machine & engine bought for the use of the Brigade, and someone has I believe to go to Paris to get it, so why not me? If I was to get more than one night I would get you to come, & we could blow the legacy, however I will let you know.

All my love Dearest I have no other news.

Love to Paula

Thine

Charles

FIELD POST OFFICE JA 27 16

DAY 174 FRI

28 JAN 1916

Item 142
Letter to Margaret

Envelope
161 Haverstock Hill
London

FIELD POST OFFICE JA 28 16

Friday

Dearest Darling

Many thanks for your letter of Tuesday just rec^d. I am glad you enjoyed your stay in Brighton. I have no news today & no time to write it, as we have been out inspecting all the morning and have just come in to lunch, and starting at 2 pm we have a boxing competition to eliminate for the Brigade show which takes place on Sunday. Tonight we are going into the town to hear Kennerly Rumford & his party.

Tomorrow we are playing a football match, but I shall not take part.

All All All love Dearest to you & Paula

Thine for ever

x x x x x x Charles x x x x x x

Sunday

Dearest Darling

      We are all in a fluster today. We are at an hours notice, with a lot of motor busses waiting to take us away in case we are wanted. However I have not yet started fussing about my own personal comfort and until I do there is no need for you to worry. However I am very busy seeing that everyone else is ready. Also I am personally standing by to proceed to ?? name of place not stated and what I am being sent off for I know not, however it is all in the days work, and will be a nice safe jaunt. The Brigade Boxing competition takes place this afternoon which is rather amusing, and I hope will not be interfered with. I have just written rather a clever letter to the Mayor of Reading, asking for some wheeled stretchers, which I hope we shall get.[1]
I have no more news.

      All All All Love to you & Paula

      Thine

      xxxxxx Charles xxxxxx

      No mail in today

DAY
176
SUN

30 JAN 1916

Item 143
Letter to Margaret

Envelope
*161 Haverstock Hill
London*

FIELD POST OFFICE
JA 30
16

1 His appeal to Leonard Sutton was successful, with the Mayor organising fund-raising including a concert by the band of the Grenadier Guards. The wheeled stretchers, known as Furber hand ambulances (**below**, named after their inventor Capt Harold Furber of the Welsh Regt) cost £19 each and by 1st April the Mayor's Fund had raised £65, including £5 from the Mayor himself and a guinea from Mrs Walton. A sergeant writing home said he could now transport 40 wounded men in the time it would have taken to carry 20 on traditional stretchers.

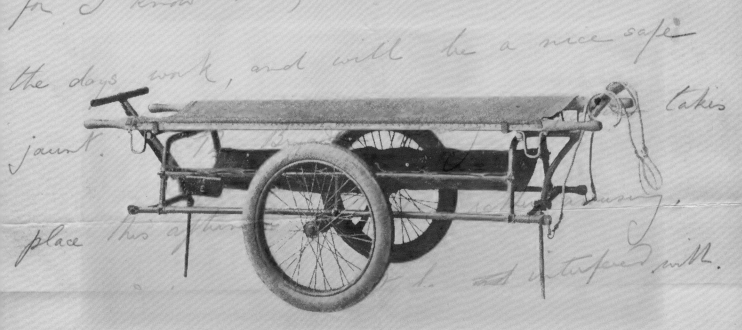

DAY
179
WED

2 FEB 1916

Item 144
Letter to Margaret

Envelope
161 Haverstock Hill
London

ADRESSE TÉLÉGRAPHIQUE
RITZOTEL·PARIS

PARIS · 81
2-2
16
R.DESCAPUCINES

Hôtel Ritz
Place Vendôme
Paris[1]

Feb 2ⁿᵈ 1916

Dearest Darling

    I have not been able to write for two days as I have seem to have been all over France the last two days. We arrived here last night & leave again at midday today. I must have been somewhere near the Scrub, but had no time to look for him. We have 4 hours train journey from here & then, if we are lucky, 50 miles back to our Regiments in a car, but we may have to stop the night with another division. Beyond carrying letters to various chiefs we dont know what our exact mission has been. Capt Rycroft of the Black Watch is with me, such a nice chap,[2] & if the weather had not been so cold, all would have been well.
I am afraid our trip here now will be cancelled as I have to order the cinema this morning. Things here are fairly exciting, what with being at one hours notice to move, & Zepps being busy here, also the Germans very lively all the way along the line, it looks as if we shall be busy.

    All Love Dearest to you & Paula

      Thine

    xxxxx Charles xxxxx

1 Paris is 115 miles from Allouagne. **The Ritz Hotel,** *(left)*, first opened there in 1898. It was bought by Mohamed Al-Fayed in 1979 and was the last place Princess Diana dined before her death in 1997. Rooms are now from £880 per night.

2 **Julian Rycroft**, 23, had been in the newspapers nationwide in 1913 when, after being pulled over on his motorbike and failing to produce his licence, he explained to the magistrates that his dog had eaten it. Being an officer and a gentleman, his word was believed and the case was dismissed. During the war, he would rise to command a battalion at the age of 26, with awards of DSO, MC and Belgian Croix de Guerre. He was also badly wounded and that brought about his early retirement from the Army and a move to take up farming in South Africa. It wasn't enough to recover his health though and he died in 1928 aged 35. His wife (who had lost her only brother in 1921 also from war wounds) died of TB only four years later, aged 36, leaving two orphaned daughters aged 10 and 7 (both going on to have long lives with 7 children and 13 grandchildren between them).

HEADQUARTERS
32ND DIVISION[1]

January[2] 3rd 1916

Dearest Darling

Just a line to tell you I am on my way back to the Regiment, where I hope to arrive tonight. Last night we got to Amiens having travelled 4½ hours from Paris, without dinner & when we arrived at 11 pm we went to three hotels, & could get nothing to eat or drink, & eventually went to bed having drunk plain water from the tap, & trusted to providence there were no typhoid germs in it. It was quite a nice motor run out here this morning, & this part is much nicer country than where we are, many more trees and not such a flat country. It has been quite an interesting expedition, but at the present moment with two Division Generals[3] & 4 Staff Colonels in the room I am not feeling my best. I will write again tomorrow, this is just to let you know I am well, and feel all the better for my tour.

All Love Dearest

Thine

In haste

Charles B

xxxxxxxxxxxx

DAY
180
THU

3 FEB 1916

Item 145
Letter to Margaret

Envelope
*161 Haverstock Hill
London*

FIELD POST OFFICE
4 FE
16

---

1 32nd Division's HQ was in Senlis le Sec, 3 miles from Albert down in the area of the Somme, 80 miles from Paris, with 35 miles more to get back to Allouagne.

2 Should be February.

3 The commander of 32nd Division was Major-General **William Rycroft**, 54, *(near right)*, who was the father of Charles's travelling companion. Visiting on this day was Major-General **Edward Perceval**, 54, *(far right)*, commander of 49th Division, who were due to take over part of the line in this sector. Rycroft would stay with 32nd Division through the Battle of the Somme before being posted to Salonika in November. His final job was as Governor of British North Borneo. He died two years before his son. Perceval would also stay with his division through the Battle of the Somme but was forced to give up his command through ill health in 1917. He commanded a battalion of the Home Guard in the Second World War when aged 80.

DAY 181 FRI

4 FEB 1916

Item 146

Letter to Margaret

Envelope
161 Haverstock Hill
London

Feb 4th 1916

Dearest Darling

I got back last night after an adventurous drive, having 1 burst tyre & 3 punctures, on the way home & did not get in until 10.30 pm when I found 4 letters from you, which I will read again & answer in detail, but this morning I have been so rushed, & have such a lot to do getting ready for the trek. It was a most interesting tour, & very nice to see another part of the line. I have never seen so many soldiers since I came out and feel rather glad I am not in that part of the line. I have not rec^d my washing or my pants, so I suppose they have gone to glory. Dalby is out this afternoon, so I have to do office work, so no more now.

All All All Love

Thine

Charles

DAY 183 SUN

6 FEB 1916

Item 147

Letter to Margaret

Envelope
161 Haverstock Hill
London

Sunday

Dearest Darling

I have never been so busy, & of course owing to the move the post has been altered without any notice, so I shall have to write again after lunch. We are really off tomorrow on the trek, but I am under orders to be President of a Court Martial on Tuesday so may come back & sleep here tomorrow night.
Please thank Paula for her letter.
Owing to new rules I have had to make all the various Regimental accounts into one, & I have been going through figures until my head is fuddled. However Barrow says they are alright, & he ought to know.
Dug seems to have enjoyed himself, & you seem to have seen a good deal of him. How does Renee like him? He has not mentioned her to me hardly, so I dont understand the game.
I am now put in charge of the Brigade "Recreation", as the two Padres who run the show cant get on, so I have to keep the peace. I will write more fully later & answer your letters.

All Love Dearest

Thine in haste

xxxxxx Charles xxxxxx

x one extra as it is Sunday

DAY
186
WED

9 FEB 1916

Item 148
Letter to Margaret

Envelope
161 Haverstock Hill
London

FIELD POST OFFICE
FE 9
16

8th R.B.R.
Feb 9th 1916

Dearest Darling

At last I have a chance to sit down & write you a letter. Yesterday I had to go about 8 miles & was president of a Court Martial, tried 8 men & did not get back until 6.30 when I had to go & see the General, as we are having a horse show here next Sunday afternoon. I have to be president of Court Martial every Tuesday & Friday until the end of this month at this place, which is a hospital which is kept for men who have "self-inflicted wounds". At present there are 92 of them there, it sounds a lot but really does not average half a man per regiment, & I dont suppose more than 25 per cent are wilful, but still they all have to be tried.[1]

I am now answering your letter of the 29th. I once more repeat I have not got my washing. Your question about a man Court martialled & sentenced to death is a bit of a conundrum, but I think the real answer is that he is just reported Dead in the usual way, as if had been killed in action.

I quite like the Ford story in your letter of the 30th.

You never told me much of your conversation with Paul, & when are they going to be married. Maurice Brett was asking me the other day when I was in Paris. He is APM there, & I had to go to him for a permit to get the Cinema out of Paris. He was very sick about it all & says Paul is treating Phyllis disgracefully, & it is very awkward for them all, I quite agreed with him, but I had to as he was the only person I could get a permit from, & he was not supposed to give me one.[2]

You seem to have had a royal time with Dug who seems to have spent most of his time with you & Renee.

Next time I come home we will go away for a few days, as from past experience one gets no rest in London none here, & one begins to get a bit tired. I think I shall try & borrow Philip's house, it is so nice. You were wrong in your letter of the 1st I certainly did go to Bronay but did not stop there. We visited the Head Quarters of the French 10th Army, and they do do themselves very well. I am glad "Pink Petty"[3] went so well with the Flying Corps. I am afraid Paula will not appreciate the board for her back for many days, & it will soon cease to be a joke. I think I have now answered everything except about Foot. We have only one Woodhouse[4] in the Rgt. He is Coy Sgt Major of A Coy. I believe Miss Foot met a man in hospital, & the man told her Coy Sgt Major Woodhouse might know something about Foot, so Miss Foot wrote to Woodhouse, who was in the trenches, & sent the letter back to Coy Qr Mr Sgt Brand,[5] who sent it to Barrow & he wrote to Mrs Foot saying that although Foot was reported "missing" there was, not in his opinion, much hope. Mrs Foot has also been writing to Lieut Lawrence, & he has given her all the information he can.

I have spent 2 hours this morning cross examining anybody who could know anything & have found out absolutely nothing, & we never shall until the war is over. When we go up to the trenches on Monday we shall go into a new part of the line, on the right of where we were before, & I believe it is fairly healthy there, but we shall follow the Londoners, & they always leave the trenches in bad condition. I have written Paula a letter & I think have answered all your questions. I really am sorry for Mrs Foot, but we have all done all we can, & we are hoping she will soon get some news from someone else.[6]

All All All Love Dearest

Thine

xxxxxx Charles xxxxxx

1 Again, there is not much detail left about self-inflicted wounds and the subsequent courts martial, as sections reporting about them in Divisional orders have been redacted. Men who were fed up with life in the trenches could contrive to get sent home by shooting themselves in the hand or foot. Accidental discharges during the handling of firearms were not unknown so it was possible they might get off with just the wound, but the military authorities were not very forgiving. On the dates that Charles gives, he must have been in Aire-sur-la-Lys where there was a Casualty Clearing Station with barges on the canal kitted out with beds in 'wards'. Perhaps some of these barges were quarantined to stop these men of 'lower moral fibre' from 'infecting' the rest. Nearly all the men tried there on these dates were found guilty and sentenced to between 14 & 84 days of Field Punishment N° 1 (as described on p.60).

2 **Paul Rubens**, 40, *(above)*, was in a relationship with a big star of the Edwardian stage, **Phyllis Dare**, 25 (*far right*, in her younger days with another star, her sister **Zena**, now 29). Phyllis had been cast in Paul's show *'The Sunshine Girl'* in 1912 and he then wrote a number of songs just for her. In January 1915, at Charles's invitation, Paul had performed with Phyllis during a recruiting concert in Reading, where she put on a recruiting sergeant's cap and led men off to join the Army (➔**407 Rubens, Paul**). The reason behind Paul's on-off behaviour towards Phyllis would become apparent later on. Major **Maurice Brett**, 33,

was an Assistant Provost Marshal (in charge of military police) in Paris but he was linked to Charles by being married to Phyllis' sister Zena (hence the family gossip). It is unlikely that Charles was aware of the professional & personal secrets that were hidden beneath the surface of Maurice Brett. ➔**392 Brett**

3 *'A Pink Petty from Peter'* is the song on p.22 from Paul Rubens' *'Miss Hook of Holland'*.

4 **William E B Woodhouse**, 35, a church sexton, had enlisted at once in August 1914. His wife lived a long life of great misfortune. ➔**414**

5 **Herbert Brand**, 29, was a master tailor which was a useful skill to have for the Battalion. He came through Loos unscathed, but would be wounded on the Somme in November 1916, requiring 18 weeks in hospital. Commissioned in the 6th North Staffordshires in January 1918, he was badly gassed 6 weeks from the end of the war but survived to return to his wife and children and to civilian tailoring.

6 **The Foot family** would never find out for sure what happened to Eric. ➔**394**

MISSES ZENA AND PHYLLIS DARE.

1. **Has Mrs McGibbon come back here!**
   No
2. **Did you notice my remark re a present for the spring in 2 or 3 letters ago!**
   Yes
3. **Have you found out any more about your washing!**
   No
4. **Why doesn't Dug write to Renée!**
   For the same reason you have not written to me.
5. **Is he been on Gemain again!**
   Not 'arf.
6. **Do you know if Dug suffers from varicose veins!**
   Yes, downstairs. Refer to the Vet R.C.
7. **Does he suffer from ingrowing toenails!**
   A sure thing
8. **Has he moss on his teeth!**
   Yes, except when opening & shutting his mouth.
9. **Has he moss in his ears!**
   A rolling stone gathers no moss (they come out at night)
10. **Does he stuff his navel with cotton wool to keep out the cold!**
    It is not really a navel but a Berkshire Button[1]
11. **Ought Renée to get in supply of pickaxes to remove same!**
    Why not try a Mills Bomb[2]
12. **Do his feet smell!**
    Renée ought to know (when toes turned down)
13. **Does he still use Bromo or Daily Mirror!**
    Theatre Programmes
14. **Does his hair harbour vermine!**
    What hair are you referring to?
15. **If so – what sort!**
    HEN BIRDS.
16. **Is he fond of white mice!**
    For scouting purposes.
17. **How often is he manicured!**
    Depends on the surroundings.
18. **Has he hair on his chest!**
    Why ask, seeing is believing.
19. **If so – nothing doing!**
    Hasn't this been done?
20. **I know for a fact Renée is not going in for Baloons, but for what!!!**
    Try Babies
21. **Please number & answer questions on this sheet**

Item 149
*Question Sheet
from Margaret
& answered
by Charles
(mostly on the back)*

*(undated but probably
from around this time
given the references to
his lost washing and
Dug & Renée)*

**1 Royal Berkshire
Regiment button**

**2 The Mills Bomb was
a type of grenade
introduced in 1915**

DAY
188
FRI

11 FEB 1916

Item 150
Letter to Margaret

Envelope
161 Haverstock Hill
London

Feb 11th 1916

7 AM

Dearest Darling

    Many thanks for letter. How dare you miss writing for two days? Luckily for you we missed a mail for one day, so I only missed one day, but dont do it again. The letters are the only break in the day. It is snowing if you please this morning, & I have a long ride to do, which will be most unpleasant. I dont expect to finish the Court Martials until 7 pm, when I shall ride back to town, dine there & come back here after dinner, when I shall hope to find a letter from you. I have no more news.

    All All All Love to you & Paula.

    Thine

    x *Charles* x

DAY
189
SAT

12 FEB 1916

Item 151
Letter to Margaret

Envelope
161 Haverstock Hill
London

Saturday

12.2.16

Dearest Darling

    Many thanks for letter just rec^d. I am glad Paula loves her skipping. I quite expected Mrs Walton would have told you that the C.O. had heard from me, as I am sure it is time I had an answer.

There is no news here. We do not move up to the trenches until Wednesday & then the Brigade is in reserve the first week, so we shall not really be within 30 yards of the Bosche until the 20th, & then the bit of line we have been given is quite the best in the neighbourhood.

On Monday there is a big Field Day, so I shall not get a line off that day. Tomorrow the Divisional General is lunching with us, which means no ordinary cooking & then the Horse Show, after which the match between Punch & some unknown horse in the Black Watch.

The men are having their last wash today, at least Bath.

    All All Love Dearest to you & Paula

    Thine

    Charles

    xxxxxxxxxxxx

Monday
7 AM

Dearest Darling

We have a big parade today, & shall not be back before the post goes, so just a line before we start.

We had a very disappointing day yesterday. The Race did not come off as the officer in the Black Watch scratched at the last minute. We took only one 1st two 2^{nds} & one 3rd prize in the Horse Show, which was sickening as we deserved much more. So many marks were given in each competition for the length of time horses & men had been in this country, so we were handicapped out of everything, as I am sure we have a far better lot of horses than any other Regt.

Two more nights here & then up again, but I dont think there will be much doing in our part for some time. Well I must get up now.

All Love Dearest to you & Paula

Thine

xxxxxx Charles xxxxxx

DAY
191
MON

14 FEB 1916

Item 152
Letter to Margaret

Envelope
161 Haverstock Hill
London

Given Charles's lovey-dovey nature, it might seem strange that he makes no mention that it's St Valentine's Day, but if you look at the newspapers of the time you can see that it just wasn't the thing that it is now.

8th R. Berks. Rgt.
Feb 17th 1916

Dearest Darling

Here we are up again in the line, but not actually in the trenches.[1] We have quite good billets, and are just 3 miles from the Germans, who since our arrival have not taken any notice of us, but if they do we have a "Funk Hole" or dug out to run into until they cease shelling. It was no ordinary move yesterday, I rode the whole way and it never ceased raining & was blowing a gale that you could hardly ride against. Tiles from the houses were being blown off, & I saw two carts turned over, in fact I have never seen such a gale. There are still several natives left here, & one or two shops even. It is the same village as we stopped in on the night of the 29th Sept when we left the trenches on our way back for the 4 days rest we got then. I have quite a nice billet, the old lady who lives next door lent me some beautiful sheets, and I had quite a nice bed. Of course the electric light has been shot to pieces, & there is only one pane of glass left in the

DAY
194
THU

17 FEB 1916

Item 153
Letter to Margaret

Envelope
161 Haverstock Hill
London

windows, but with a nice fire I was quite comfortable. Gerrard has a mattress he found somewhere & sleeps outside the door.

We are going up into the line tomorrow to see what the trenches are like, & then we move up on Sunday. It is most extraordinary but every time this Regt moves it is nearly always on a Sunday. We are then 3 days in the front line 3 days back here, 3 days in the front line and 3 days in some old cellars between here & the front line. Then 6 days somewhere back, either here, or where we used to go before.

As far as I can make out Batt^n H^d Q^{rs} are never in the trenches in this sector but always in the cellar of some old house or other, so we ought to be fairly comfortable. Well dearest this is all my news. All All All Love Darling to you & Paula.

Thine

xxxxxx Charles xxxxxx

1 They were in Les Brebis, one of number of dormitory villages that had been built in the area of Bully-Grenay just before the war. The *corons* (miners' cottages) were laid out on a rectangular grid of avenues with young trees and central amenities, and would be almost completely destroyed by the war's end.

DAY 195 FRI

18 FEB 1916

Item 154
Letter to Margaret

Envelope
*161 Haverstock Hill
London*

Friday

Dearest Darling

No time for a letter today. I am just off to the trenches to look out a road for bringing up rations etc.

I had no letter from you yesterday, in fact there was no mail at all.

The d-d Bosche shelled this place yesterday, & knocked down the house next to mine, & killed two horses in a stable where I nearly put Punch.

It is very wet & the trenches are over knee deep in water, so once more we have to take our waders.

I will write again tomorrow.

All All All Love

Thine in haste

xxxxxx Charles B xxxxxx

Feb 19th 1916

Dearest Darling

I rec'd three letters from you yesterday dated 14th 15th & 16th, also some Bystanders,[1] which made us laugh until we cried. The Pictures of this war by Bairnsfather[2] are too funny for words. I see they are published in an album, & I wish you would buy us one & send it out, after having a good laugh yourself. They are all so true especially the one "If you know a better hole go to it". I am sorry you are grousing about the short letters, but I have been kept on the run so much lately. Of course I think Malcolm a mug & have no patience with him, not being able to join the army because so many people at Allens were dependent on him & then he leaves them for a most risky speculation. I am very glad the concert was such a success. I should have ridden Punch myself if I had been obliged to, that is if my opponent would only race owners up[3] I was going to but not otherwise.

I rode the old horse one or two fast gallops, & although I am riding practically every day I was quite stiff after them. I went all round our line of trenches yesterday with Cloake, and although they are in a very bad state the lot we go into first are the safest we have yet been in. In several places one cannot even see the Bosche trench. While we were out yesterday the D-d Bosche put some shells over, & got 3 of our men, but none fatal, but I am afraid one will have to have his leg off. They were all together sitting on the latrine. Then in the afternoon our best pair of heavy draught horses, which we brought out from England got frightened & ran away, one of them colliding with some iron railings & killing himself. Then I lost 5 francs at Bridge, & just as I was going to bed I had to fetch the Dr to a man who was in the next billet to me & he had got appendicitis & had to be sent to hospital, so altogether it was not a red letter day for us.

I had a long letter from Phyllis Dare yesterday who says you leave her & Paul severely alone, so you must go & see them.

1. Have you seen anything of little Moss in Endil Street[4]? If not would you pop in & see how he is?

2. Has Louis forgotten how to make Potted Meat?

3. Is Buzzards closed?

4. Did not you say something about Dried Fish?

5. I am not drinking whisky now there is none to be bought within miles (at least 20). It is very sad. Tell John.

Our Padre is getting a bit of a nuisance, and will not look after his own business, but will try & run the Battalion.

DAY
196
SAT

19 FEB 1916

Item 155
Letter to Margaret

Envelope
161 Haverstock Hill
London

FIELD POST OFFICE
19 FE
16

They have cut down the postal arrangements here for outgoing letters, so you will understand if this takes an extra day or so to travel.

Our Head Qrs in the trenches this time are in a house & so we shall get some fresh air, but we sleep in the cellars. I have no more news.

All All All Love to you & Paula

Thine

xxxxxx Charles xxxxxx

1 *The Bystander* was a weekly magazine featuring reviews, cartoons and short stories, published from 1903 to 1940.

2 Capt **Bruce Bairnsfather**, 28, *(above)*, had been in Belgium with 1st Royal Warwicks when he sent in a drawing to *The Bystander*. It was published in January 1915 but by the time his fame really started to take off he was in hospital with shellshock after a near miss during the 2nd Battle of Ypres in April. His recovery was helped by concentrating on producing more drawings. He was delighted that *The Bystander* had taken him on at £4 a week but in the end that didn't work out well for him because though they increased his weekly rate, they held the copyright for his work and it wouldn't be him who made a fortune when they'd sold over 2 million of the *'Fragments from France'* books of his drawings by the end of 1917. It opened doors to an interesting life in the worlds of books, lecture tours, theatre and films (he directed a silent movie called *'Carry On Sergeant'* in 1928) and he was employed as official cartoonist to the American forces in Europe during the Second World War, but his life ended in reduced circumstances and relative obscurity.

3 If horse owners could just pick their best jockey and not ride themselves, Charles obviously didn't fancy his chances.

4 **Endell Street Military Hospital** had been set up in what had been a workhouse in Covent Garden and was entirely staffed by women suffragists. In fact one of the head doctors had served time in 1912 for throwing a brick through a window in protest at a cabinet minister's anti-suffrage stance. Being the daughter of Elizabeth Garrett Anderson & the niece of Millicent Fawcett, Dr Louisa Garrett Anderson had obviously been brought up to believe she could make a difference, and she and Dr Flora Murray would oversee the treatment of over 24,000 soldiers and upwards of 7,000 operations in the four and a half years the hospital was open.

The Bystander, September 15, 1915.—No. 615. Vol. XLVII

The BYSTANDER

THE ETERNAL QUESTION

"WHEN THE 'ELL IS IT GOING TO BE STRAWBERRY?"

(Plum and apple is the only jam known throughout the Expeditionary Force)

BY CAPT. BRUCE BAIRNSFATHER

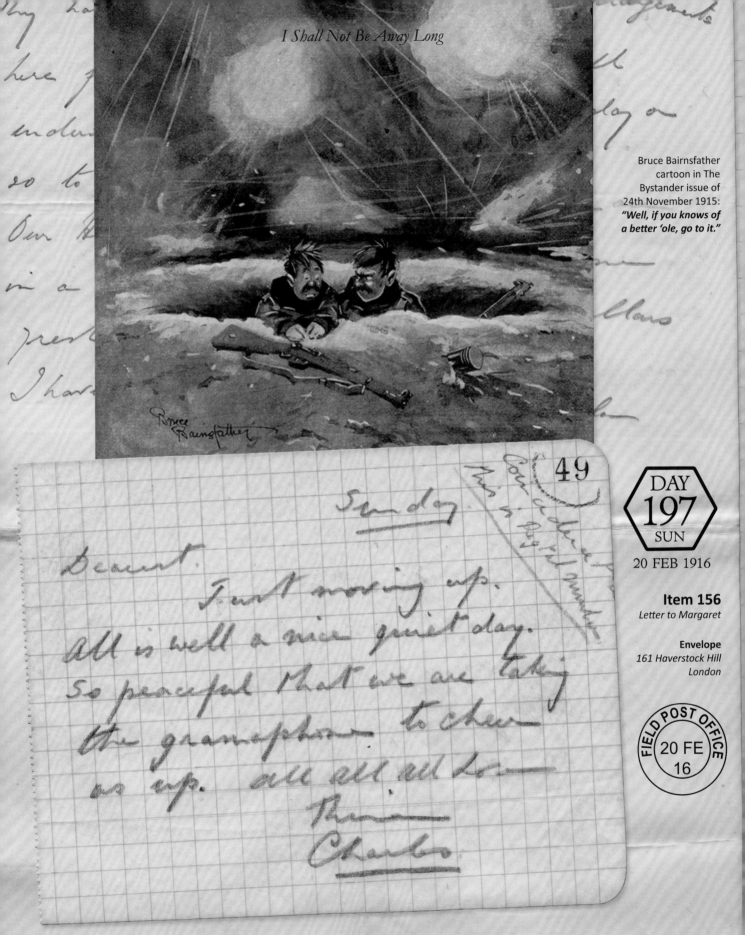

I Shall Not Be Away Long

DAY
197
SUN

20 FEB 1916

Item 156
Letter to Margaret

Envelope
*161 Haverstock Hill
London*

FIELD POST OFFICE
20 FE
16

The Royal Berkshire Regiment were previously known as the 49th Regiment of Foot, hence the note of the coincidence with the number of the page from his field notebook.

DAY
200
WED

23 FEB 1916

Item 157
Letter to Margaret

Envelope
*161 Haverstock Hill
London*

*Forwarded to:
Theydon Lodge
Theydon Bois
Essex*

FIELD POST OFFICE
24 FE
16

HAMPSTEAD S.O.
10.15 PM
26 FE
16
N.W.

Feb 23rd 1916

Dearest Darling

 I did not write yesterday, as all I received from you was a terse note saying you were not going to write as you had only rec^d one letter from me in four days. That was a nice letter to get having sat through as heavy a day's shelling as we have ever had with the exception of the battles. However luck was with us, & we only lost 3 men. I was out round the line from 5.30 to 10 am, & all day there was the most fearful excitement everyone on the alert, & the Huns attacked but not very near us. The battery behind our Head Q^{rs} had over a thousand shells put into them, & houses all round us were being knocked about. In the evening it quieted down & I went round half our line, Dalby doing the other half from 9 – 11.30 pm after which we came back, & as I was not for "early rounds" this morning I returned to my cellar & slept until 9.30 am being woken up by the guns again, & another Artillery Duel is going on.[1] *It is snowing hard, & it will make it very difficult to get about, as the trenches are far from good.*

I heard from Scrub yesterday, & he hopes to get home about the middle of March, so I hope I shall be over with him. I had a long letter from Walton which I will send home in due course. Stileman turned up again yesterday afternoon, both his toes are stiff, & I doubt if he could do much marching, but what does that matter for this hole in the corner warfare.[2] *Tomorrow night we go back into Rest Billets for three nights after which I hope things will be more peaceful in this line, as it is really quite a nice bit to hold.*

It is now snowing so hard all is peaceful as no one can possibly see where the shells are falling. I shall have a nice time getting about tonight, & once more shall have to put on my waders.

 I have no more news.

 All Love

 Thine

 xxxxxx Charles xxxxxx

1 Artillery in the First World War is often associated with its effect on infantry, but a big part of their role was in finding and destroying the enemy's artillery to prevent it firing on their own infantry. Flash-spotting and observation from aircraft, balloons and in the forward trenches or other vantage points as well as sound-ranging were used to locate enemy guns and direct fire onto them, sometimes leading to artillery duels where the infantry were just onlookers, as here. Being an artilleryman was not a soft option, as shown by the fact that over 53,900 British artillerymen died in the war.

2 As well as the damage to his foot sustained at the Battle of Loos, **Donald Stileman★**, *(left)*, had bits of shrapnel in his back that his grandchildren would be able to feel through his skin when he was in his nineties.

Feb 25th 1916

Dearest Darling

   I have not written for a day or two as after being 3 days without a letter I was rather "fed up". I have told you before now that when the Division moves the post is apt not to be regular, so as you knew the Division was moving your letter was most uncalled for. We have had two nights out of the trenches & go back tomorrow, all is fairly quiet here, but all leave has been stopped, I suppose because the French seem to be having a nice time down South.[1]

I am sure I wrote & told you that Moss was in Endell Street Hospital, because you wrote & told me you were going to see him one day, but owing to rain or something you did not.

I am afraid the days of Fresh Fish are over here in fact supplies are very hard to get. Whether it is because there are so many more troops in the county, or lack of labour I dont know. As you say we have tried smelling the whisky cork, but with 4 inches of snow on the ground & none procurable for a radius of 20 miles it does not give much satisfaction. However I suppose we shall survive, & I daresay someone else will cheer us up.

I dined with the General last night but did not get any news of interest, except we are in the trenches for at least 3 months this time.

I have no more news.

I am sorry if I worry you asking for things & I must apologise for not having a larger income.

  All Love

  Yours

  Charles

DAY 202 FRI

25 FEB 1916

Item 158
Letter to Margaret

Envelope
161 Haverstock Hill
London

FIELD POST OFFICE
25 FE 16

1 The Germans had attacked the French on 21st February, the first of the 303 days of the longest battle of the war, the **Battle of Verdun**. Taking place 150 miles south-east of Charles's current location, it was centred on a network of forts which the Germans knew the French would defend at all costs. The Germans' declared aim was to bleed the French white but the staunch French resistance ensured the soil would be stained almost equally with the blood of both sides.

As an indication of the place of the battle in the popular consciousness of the time, during the next 3 years over 3,000 British babies (both male & female) would be given the forename 'Verdun', including nearly 900 who had it as their first name (and one called Loos Verdun Leather went on to a long career in the Navy, though unsurprisingly he was known as 'Ted').

Item 159
Letter to Margaret

Envelope
*161 Haverstock Hill
London*

FIELD POST OFFICE
26 FE
16

Feb 26th 1916

Dearest Darling

     I did not write you a very nice letter yesterday, as I did not think yours was very nice, but I have a better one from you today.
I cannot think who would have taken you to see the Fights. Who did? & why did you go? I am sure those things are not in your line.
I hope the kippers, for which many thanks, will arrive today, as we are without rations tomorrow, none being issued to any one, as we are all supposed to eat up our iron rations. Of course the village has found out, & to buy enough rump steak for 6 of us for two meals I had to pay 19 francs.
We had some show here last night, & blew up 3 mines[1] under the dirty Bosche & did them a bit of no good. Two of them got chucked about 30 yds, & landed on our barbed wire, which could not have been very pleasant for them. Tonight we go up into the front line again, & shall have to keep our eyes open, as they will be wanting to get a bit of their own back.
A heavy thaw set in this morning, although the snow is thick on the ground there is any amount of mud & slush about, & the trenches will be damnable.
I had a line from Mable sending me some priceless stories, a copy of which I enclose.

    All Love Dearest to you & Paula
    Thine
    xxxxxx Charles xxxxxx

1 We now think of military mines as being small devices that explode when stood on or driven over, but the origin of the name comes from shafts being dug like coal mines under the enemy and packed with explosive for a much bigger blast.

Item 160
Letter to Margaret

Envelope
*161 Haverstock Hill
London*

Feb 26th 1916

Dearest

    As this is the last chance of getting a letter off to you before the 28th I am writing to say that all is well.
The kippers have arrived, & we may have one or two for the sake of old times, when we come in from our rounds about 2 AM. On the other hand we may have them for breakfast. As if the thaw is not bad enough it has started to rain, so we

are in for a ripping time. I have got a beautiful new pair of field boots, water tight & lace up to my knees, & I have neither to pay or owe for them. I think they were put on our supply wagon by mistake. I got a pair for Dug also. The D^r bought a similar pair & had to pay £4-10-0 for them so he is rather sick about it. There has been no mention of leave again, but I hope it will soon be open again, as I may get blocked & have to wait.

All All All Love

Thine

Charles

FIELD POST OFFICE
27 FE
16

32

Feb 27th 1916

Dearest Darling

    I have absolutely no news. We moved up to front line last night, and although it was thawing and raining while the relief was being carried out, it was freezing hard again by midnight. I went out at 5 AM and it was so slippery getting about was very difficult. Breakfast at 9 with some excellent kippers, for which many thanks, & also some Devonshire Cream, which F A Simonds sent me from Sidmouth. Apparently he has been ill and has been there to recoup. The Artillery have moved a gun up near our headquarters, & at the present moment the Hun is trying to locate it with shells, so we have retired to the cellars.

We can get no news here as to what is happening Verdun way, all we get is from the Local Papers. Our first Batt^n has come into the line somewhere on our right, so I may see some of them.

I have just sent a message by carrier pigeon asking the Brigade Major to come & eat a kipper for breakfast tomorrow.

All All All Love

Thine

xxxxxx Charles xxxxxx

DAY
204
SUN
27 FEB 1916

Item 161
Letter to Margaret

Envelope
161 Haverstock Hill
London

FIELD POST OFFICE
28 FE
16

DAY
205
MON

28 FEB 1916

Item 162
Letter to Margaret

Envelope
161 Haverstock Hill
London

FIELD POST OFFICE
29 FE
16

Feb 28th 1916

Dearest Darling

Many thanks for your letter received this afternoon. I have no news. One funny little incident – the Brigade on our left took a prisoner and two Tommies, one a Lancashire lad & the other a Welshman both claimed to have taken him, and were fighting as to who should lead him back. Eventually the Lancashire lad won & was followed down the road by the Welshman using awful language. Suddenly comes running down the road an excited Black Watch man saying have you seen a prisoner, & when he found the Lancashire lad with him he exclaimed What the b—y hell are you doing with that wee Laddie? sure he's a German, and why the hell did God give you a bayonet if was not to stick into him?

The mails are all "anyhow" & I daresay a few never reach. I did not hear from you yesterday at all.

Yes do send the book along or the bit you want me to read.

You say the kippers went off gaily yesterday morning, they were gaily finished this morning. I shall not be able to write tomorrow, as I leave the trenches early to go & see some new toy away back which throws liquid fire at the Bosche.[1] We blew up another mine an hour ago, but I have heard no results. We hear the French have done a wonderful counter attack Verdun way.[2]

All All All Love
Thine
xxxxxx Charles xxxxxx

Love to Paula. When will she write?

1 The new toy that threw liquid fire was not like a modern flamethrower with one man carrying a tank on his back and squirting streams of burning fuel at close range. What Charles was going to see was known as a **Livens Large Gallery Flame Projector, (left)**. Being 17 metres long & 2.5 tonnes in weight, it was the opposite of portable, requiring 300 men to transport it to the front line and assemble it in a shallow tunnel dug up near to the enemy's trenches. It consisted of fuel tanks and a 36 cm diameter pipe with a nozzle which came out onto the surface from the tunnel. Being vulnerable to shellfire, with a maximum range of 90 metres and only being capable of firing a total of three 10-second bursts, it was found to be impractical on the few occasions it was deployed and use of it was abandoned.

2 The rumour mill had inflated tales of a French counterattack – an attempt to re-capture Fort Douaumont on 26th February had failed and the situation was still desperate.

Feb 29th 1916.

70

Dearest Darling,

What on earth do you want to go & stay with The Tweens for. What can they think of you? & what on earth is the attraction.

I went many miles this morning to see this new invention & then it was not working so had our journey for nothing. However it was a fine day & so we had a nice bus ride, & some fresh air, & it was quite a change from the trenches.

We had quite a nice little bombardment of the Boche last night, having 6 machine guns, & 6 field guns playing on a party for a minute. The field guns fired about 60 shells & the others got off about 3500 rounds, so they had a warm time.

71

As you know we have always to carry an emergency ration, & the other day orders were given we were to eat this ration in lieu of the ordinary ration. One Tommy I heard say to another "Bill you know why we aint got no rations today" Bill said "No". Tommy said "because some fool officer forgot there were 29 days in Feb this year & forgot to order extra ones".

Many thanks for pictures which arrived last night, & we had a hearty laugh.

I had a letter from Bizzy tonight who seems better. The Relief has just started, no more news. all all all dove

Thine

Charles.

DAY
206
TUE
29 FEB 1916

Item 163
Letter to Margaret

Envelope
*161 Haverstock Hill
London*

FIELD POST OFFICE
1 MR
16

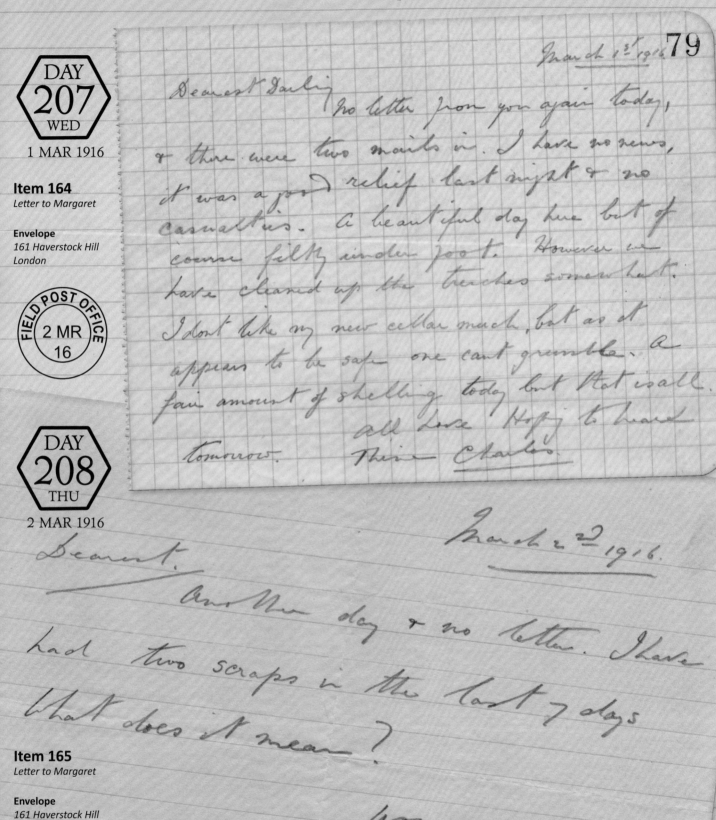

March 1st 1916

Dearest Darling

No letter from you again today, & there were two mails in. I have no news, it was a good relief last night & no casualties. A beautiful day here but of course filthy under foot. However we have cleaned up the trenches somewhat. I don't like my new cellar much, but as it appears to be safe one can't grumble. A fair amount of shelling today but that is all.

All love. Hoping to hear tomorrow. Thine Charles.

DAY 207 WED

1 MAR 1916

Item 164
Letter to Margaret

Envelope
161 Haverstock Hill London

FIELD POST OFFICE 2 MR 16

DAY 208 THU

2 MAR 1916

March 2nd 1916.

Dearest.

Another day & no letter. I have had two scraps in the last 7 days what does it mean?

Yours
Charles.

Item 165
Letter to Margaret

Envelope
161 Haverstock Hill London

FIELD POST OFFICE 3 MR 16

I Shall Not Be Away Long

P.S. I am sorry there are no shops here that I can buy you a birthday present, so I enclose a French Note, which is only worth 5<u>d</u>., & which is only changeable in one town. However it may do for someone's stamp collection.

DAY
209
FRI
3 MAR 1916

Item 166
*Letter to Pat Walton
(found amongst her
memorabilia in
my parents' loft)*

Envelope
*c/o Miss Wiltshire
The Lawn
Clevedon
Nr Bristol*

FIELD POST OFFICE
3 MR
16

BÉTHUNE
CHAMBRE DE COMMERCE
0.50 CINQUANTE CENTIMES 0.50
SÉRIE 127

The PS is all that remains of this letter to my grandmother,
above centre in a dark skirt amongst girls from her small
boarding school 'The Lawn'. School Principal, Winifred Wiltshier, 39,
must have had her hands full being surrogate mother to so many whose
fathers were away in the war. She stayed Principal until 1931 & never married.

Winifred Wiltshier   19|00   20|00

Patricia Walton   19|00   20|00

Charles Frederick Napier Bartlett

DAY 210 SAT

4 MAR 1916

Item 167
Letter to Margaret

Envelope
161 Haverstock Hill
London

FIELD POST OFFICE
4 MR 16

Saturday

Dearest Darling

    I could not write yesterday. I got 3 letters given to me in a snow storm from you, so I apologise for not writing. We had a bad relief yesterday, rain & snow all the time, I was wet through from 2.30 pm until I got to bed at midnight. I was reading your letters riding along in a snowstorm, & I have them to read again, all except the paper of questions, which I dropped, & I could not get off to get it, so you must write them out again. There was some heavy fighting close to us last night, but I dont know what has happened. We are inches deep in snow again & it is still snowing. I had a letter from Mrs Tate who seemed very pleased at hearing from me, & she sent me two dirty stories both of which were chestnuts. I will write more fully tomorrow, I must now go to "orders", after which I retire to make up a bit of sleep. Last night there was too much noise, & when I tell you that we are back in Brigade Reserve you can imagine there was some. Thank Paula for her very well written letter. All All All Love

Thine
xxxxxx Charles xxxxxx

DAY 212 MON

6 MAR 1916

Item 168
Letter to Margaret

Envelope
161 Haverstock Hill
London

Monday

Dearest Darling

    I had no letter from you yesterday, and I was unable to catch the post, as I was out all the morning. We are still having a lot of snow & what the trenches will be like I dread to think.

I may, but am not at all certain, be leaving the Regiment for two months, and going to the Base as an Instructor. The General has not made up his mind, the trouble being I am too senior, however I would not mind a change at all, as I dont think our lads will be wanted for any real fighting at present. The C.O. has recommended me, and if I dont go, I dont know who else there is in the Brigade, who has been out as long as I have, & has the necessary qualifications. Last night Dug & I went to the Gunners Mess[1] & played Bridge.

Tonight we are having some of the subalterns to dinner. We have had several promotions. T.B. Lawrence & Robinson to be Captains. Footman, Phillips,

Churchill, Cox, Beale & Baker all to be first Lieutenants.[2] I am sorry poor old Klemantaski did not get his second star, but all those other lads had just as much service, & are after all more capable.

I have a charming landlady in my present billet, who comes in every morning & lights a fire for me to get up by. This place has been quite peaceful & no shells have been near us since we arrived.

Sgt Evans, the man who used to box for us, has been awarded the DCM. The other day we exploded a mine, & buried two of our people & Evans went out under fire, dug out one man & brought him back, & then went out and dug out the other & fetched him in.[3]

The Cake arrived from Buzzards last night & will be much appreciated, I must write to Lilian & thank her. Have you heard about the woman bus conductor, who was expostulating with a man for smoking inside the bus & said "Do you want to get me into trouble?" The man replied "I dont mind if I do, which is your day off?"

> Well Alll Alll Allll Love
>
> Thine
>
> xxxxxx Charles xxxxxx

FIELD POST OFFICE 6 MR 16

1 Gunners Mess = the mess for the Artillery officers.

2 I'll introduce these officers in more detail later.

3 **Elias Evans**, 27, *(right)*, was from Briton Ferry on the River Neath between Swansea and Port Talbot. He was a well-known boxer in the area and when younger had made his living in a boxing booth (i.e. a tent that travelled with fairs, where the house boxers would take on challengers from the audience or fight exhibition bouts). By the time of the war, though, he was back in Briton Ferry and working in the Steel Works as a smelter. Being used to the hot and heavy work at the furnaces stood him in good stead when he joined the Army.

The citation for his DCM says that it was an enemy mine that had exploded (though there is no mention of this in the Brigade war diary and the British did explode a mine on 28th February). A newspaper reported he had dug nine men out, working for hours without his shirt on under heavy fire from the Germans. Whatever the truth of the details, there is no doubt that it was a heroic effort justly rewarded.

As well as the DCM, he was presented with a gold watch when he went back home on leave. Soon after this action he transferred to 173 Tunnelling Company, Royal Engineers, where his strength and ability were applied until the end of the war. He would return to the Steel Works for the rest of his working life and live to be 86. On the gravestone he shares with his wife and parents-in-law, the letters 'D.C.M.' are proudly inscribed after his name.

DAY
213
TUE

7 MAR 1916

Item 169
Letter to Margaret

Envelope
*161 Haverstock Hill
London*

FIELD POST OFFICE
7 MR
16

March 7th 1916

Dearest Darling

No letter from you today. It is still snowing and the weather is too vile for words. I have been out all the morning watching our machine guns practising and our bombers bombing and have just finished lunch, topping up with a slice of Buzzard cake & a glass of port, and now I have to go & see the General, who is about 3 miles away. As the going is bad I am walking, what energy. However I expect I shall find out if I have got the job at the base or not, but rumour was not very encouraging on the subject last night.

Tonight Dug is giving a dinner party, I have offered to lend him some knives & forks, but he does not want them, so how he is going to feed us all I do not know. Tomorrow we shall go up & have a look at the line we shall have to occupy the night after. Anyway we do our 9 days in the front lines this time straight off, so we shall get a consecutive 9 days in the Rest Billets next time, but I am afraid they will not be here.

I have no more news.

All Love Dearest to you & Paula

Thine

xxxxxx Charles xxxxxx

DAY
214
WED

8 MAR 1916

Item 170
Letter to Margaret

Envelope
*161 Haverstock Hill
London*

FIELD POST OFFICE
? MR
16

8.3.16

7.30 AM

Dearest Darling

Just a line to say alls well. We are just off to look at our new line of trenches we take over tomorrow night.

I am afraid I have not got the job as instructor, as it has to be a Captain. However I have been offered another job which I have not considered sufficiently to discuss. It is a quite new billet & would want a lot of organising, and from what I can make out it would be more safe than interesting. However I will be able to tell you more tomorrow.

All Love

In haste

Thine

x Charles x

March 10th 1916

Dearest Darling

I could not get a letter off yesterday as I had to leave Rest Billets at 9 am, & was President of a Court Martial & had 7 cases to try.[1] After that I had to go to Brigade HQ, leaving there about 7 pm for the trenches. We rode up nearly all the way at times being quite close to the Bosche. We have a complicated bit of line.[2] I started out at 10 pm last night & got back at 4 am leaving again at 9 am & am just back, 12.30 midday.

It is a lively spot but not much danger with a little care. I had to sit in a dug out for ¾ hour this morning as they were peppering a trench I wanted to go down. Dug has rather a lively bit of line to look after. I will write more fully but must stop now if this is to catch todays post.

All All Love

Thine

xxxxxx Charles xxxxxx

DAY 216 FRI

10 MAR 1916

Item 171
Letter to Margaret

Envelope
161 Haverstock Hill
London

FIELD POST OFFICE
11 MR 16

---

[1] Of the seven cases he tried in Les Brebis, six were for soldiers of the 10th Glosters (4 for absence and breaking out of barracks, and 2 for self-inflicted wounds – and all were found guilty). The other case was for Sergeant **Henry Turner**, 31, of the 8th Royal Berkshires.

Henry had originally tried to join the Army as a boy but had been turned down for not meeting the minimum chest measurement. He managed to get into an Artillery unit in the Militia aged 18½, but left after 49 days to join the Royal Marines. He was based in England from 1903 to 1910, when he was invalided out, still a private but noted for very good conduct and ability. He then returned home to Limehouse near the docks in London.

At the beginning of the war, his previous military experience meant that he was soon promoted to Sergeant after enlisting with the 8th Royal Berkshires, and he was an acting Company Sergeant Major by the time the Battle of Loos was over. Being described as a *'very gallant fellow'* who *'always volunteered for dangerous work'*, it must have been a very serious incident that saw him being court-martialled here for drunkenness. With Charles's shortage of good NCOs, it would have pained him greatly to have to sentence Turner to be reduced to the ranks, though this was later remitted to demotion to Corporal.

Cpl Henry Turner would be killed on 3rd May by a shell falling at his feet. Notification that he had been awarded the Military Medal for his work at Loos arrived on 7th June.

[2] Their new sector was to the south of Loos in the centre of the map *below*.

DAY
217
SAT

11 MAR 1916

Item 172
Letter to Margaret

Envelope
161 Haverstock Hill
London

FIELD POST OFFICE
11 MR
16

March 11th 1916

Dearest Darling

Many thanks for two letters received last night. The most important thing at the moment is will you please send me out two sets of underclothing & a shirt or two. By the time they will arrive the warm weather will be here. It was truly a terrible accident that befell me this morning. I was in a sap

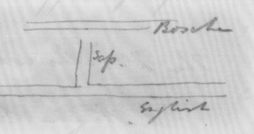

at 5.30 am this morning (for sap see illustration) when I was taken violently short, and could not get back to a latrine with the result there was an appalling accident in my breeches, so when I did get

back to the trench I had to cut off my pants & throw them away. All I had to wash in was snow, but now I have got back to Batt^n HQ, & had a good wash with hot water & a complete change I feel better, but I had to cut off the tail of my shirt. With regard your letter of the 8th, I think you & Renée must have been drinking very heavily, because I still cannot make out why a Rhinoceros is like a centipede. However it may be that the letters got very wet in transit, & the writing was very hard to read. Poor Col Graehame[1] commanding the Camerons was killed yesterday by a big shell which just happened to land plumb in the trench, as he was walking back from our HQ^{rs} to his. The D^r who was with him was blown some distance along the trench, but otherwise than being much shaken was untouched. The kippers have arrived & were excellent eating, for which many many thanks.

All All All Love

Thine

xxxxxx Charles xxxxxx

I am writing to Paula

Possibly the most extraordinary and surreal of all these letters. The crux of the main incident is that when he was so suddenly caught short, he was in a sap. As his drawing shows, a sap was a trench dug out into No-Man's-Land, the idea being to be able to observe and listen to the enemy more closely. Through all this, Charles had to keep deadly quiet or risk having German fire directed onto him.

1   Lt Col **Lawrence Graeme** CMG, 43, *(left)*, was a male line descendant of the second son of the 1st Earl of Montrose, who fell at the Battle of Flodden in 1513. He'd served throughout the Boer War, and became C.O. of the 1st Camerons in May 1915, taking them through the Battle of Loos. His father, also a Lt Col, who had fought through the Indian Mutiny, never got over his loss and died in 1917.

Item 173
Letter to Margaret

Envelope
*161 Haverstock Hill
London*

March 11th 1916
3.50 pm

Dearest Darling

  I have written you one letter today, & have just received another from you written on the 9th. Pte Gerrard, c/o Major Bartlett, 8th R Berks Rgt is quite sufficient address & will get him a day quicker than otherwise, as the men only get their letters in the trenches if all is quiet, and we have a mounted groom waiting at the Field Post Office 7 miles back. Directly the mail arrives the Hd Qrs letters are given him. He rides full tilt to Brigade Reserve 3 miles, where a cycle orderly waits for him & he bicycles 2 miles to the mouth of the trench & a runner is waiting there who runs down 1¾ miles to our Head Qrs, & that is the way we manage to get our letters, when they do arrive at the Div. Post Office. Perhaps rather luxurious but horses bicycles & men all have to be exercised. It is 9 days in front & support line, but here the support line is so close it does not matter, & now the Reserve billets have been done away with as being too far away, so the whole 12 days we are up close. Also the Brigade Reserve billets have been moved up, so when we are back for 6 days we shall still have these d-d shells whistling over our heads. Well I have no more news. All All Love

     Thine
     Charles

FIELD POST OFFICE
12 MR
16

March 12th 1916

Dearest Darling

  Just a line to say all's well. We had a quiet night last night, but had no luck this morning two men getting badly hit, one killed & I fear the other wont last long.[1] I hear I may be given command of the Divisional Company, about 400 NCO's & men, I dont know what the work is exactly but I dont think I shall have much to do with the trenches, if I get the job, but then again I may be too senior. Anyway another Major has turned up for the 10th Glosters so there is some chance. It is a beautiful day today, but as we are underground & have no intention

DAY
218
SUN

12 MAR 1916

Item 174
Letter to Margaret

Envelope
*161 Haverstock Hill
London*

FIELD POST OFFICE
13 MR
16

of putting our noses out, it does not make much difference, & the worst of it is that we have run out of oil, so are all in a bad temper trying to work with one candle. I hope Paula will give you some nasty conundrums after my letter about the stork. What about your Family Tree, have you discovered you belong to the Stuarts or to the Bosche. Personally my family were woolpackers & money lenders I think.[2]

All All All Love

Thine

xxxxxx Charles xxxxxx

1 A sign of how accepted this sort of incident had become is that it does not merit an entry in the Battalion's war diary. Unless an officer or lots of casualties were involved, most of these incidents just ended up in the numbers of dead and wounded totalled at the end of each month. To be able to identify the men in this incident requires a look in the records of the Commonwealth War Graves Commission (CWGC). I haven't been able to identify the man who was wounded (a few men of the 8th Royal Berkshires died in this period, and this one may have survived), but the man who died was Pte **G Crawford**, Nº 18813.

The CWGC have no further details about him – not a first name, not an age, not an address or next of kin. I found that this applies to thousands of British dead even though they had been formally identified. The reason for this is that the policy was not to include these details unless they had been verified by their families, which was sensible given that lots of men had signed up under false names and ages which the Army had not checked on enlistment. The Army had provided the details they had on each man, but with so many men to bury and register (a process that was still continuing into the 1930s) by the time a lot of families were being written to, they were no longer at the known contact address – and with no verification, the details could not be included in the register. Index cards did exist for each man with the details given by the Army, but a paper shortage in 1942 led to the decision to pulp them all. The sole piece of paper that led to George Crawford's full identification was amongst over 6 million pension index cards that were nearly destroyed by the MOD but saved by the Western Front Association in 2012 and only put online after the War's Centenary.

George Crawford was actually Joseph Crockford, born in south London, the son of a labourer. Two of his elder brothers were regular soldiers killed in 1914 at Mons and in East Africa, and Joseph must have joined up with an alias to beat the rule that said he was too young to serve overseas. He was still just 19 when he was killed. By coincidence, the day I started researching him was 12th March 2018, 102 years to the day that he died.

2 Discussion of Charles and Margaret's family trees follows in a few letters' time.

DAY
219
MON

13 MAR 1916

Item 175
Letter to Margaret

Envelope
*161 Haverstock Hill
London*

March 13th 1916

Dearest Darling

Many thanks for your letter of 10th I recd last night, but I have not had one from you today. Last night we had a good relief, & got back to the support line by 10.15 pm, but owing to rations losing their way did not get any dinner until 11.15. Bed at 12.15 in a dug out about 30 ft below the ground. It is an old German one & very comfortable with two bunks in it. This morning it was like a hot summers day, and we went out to find 3 of our companies, who while in support, are under the orders of another Battn. Well we wandered *for hours in trenches sometimes up to our knees in water, & eventually found D Coy, & then started back to find Dug & Robinson's, but it was no good. In this sector none of the trenches are marked, they are knocked in daily, & are all among the Ruins. I dont suppose there is one whole house standing in the place, & certainly not a pain of glass. At last we climbed into the open, & ran to the church, or what is left of it, which is 4 walls about 40 ft high,[1] & from that point we got into another trench, & wandered home. Owing to the clear day there was so much shelling going on it is far from pleasant. We were all wet through with perspiration, & I have got no change, so am sitting in a dug out on the trench level with my overcoat on & a rug round my legs to keep me warm trying to get dry. It is a rotten existence. The ground just shakes every time a shell drops anywhere near, & I shall be very glad when one side or the other gets a move on. The worst part is we are all getting "lively".[2] I think these old German dug outs have many too many inhabitants, which are not on the regimental strength. I had a letter from James Hay who is out here somewhere but I cannot gather from his letter where; he has had to revert to Captain on coming abroad, but has some staff appointment.*

> *All All All Love*
>
> *Thine*
>
> *xxxxxx Charles xxxxxx*

1 The church in Loos-en-Gohelle, as shown in these postcards, was completely destroyed in the war. Its former site is now a car park next to the Town Hall.

2 By 'lively' he means 'lice infested'.

La Guerre 1914-15-16
Visé Paris

LOOS (P.-de-C.) - Les ruines de l'Église de Loos.

Edition Deschamps - Béthune

6 — Loos-en-Gohelle (P.-de-C.)
L'Eglise

F. Alemon, Béthune — Cliché G. L.

Item 176

Enclosed question sheet from Margaret answered by Charles

> **What about the gramophone** – *not heard a word*
>
> **What is Gerrard's Christian name** – *Cecil*
>
> **What is Gerrards number[1] - ?**
>
> **Did you get the 2 Bystanders** – *yes, thank you*
>
> **Did Dug get my letter** – *Have not seen him for days except in trenches & too busy to talk about home*
>
> **I have just sent off 2 more Bystanders. Have you got them** – *No*
>
> **Is it cold out there** – *D-ly[2]*
>
> **Do you want any socks** – *No thank you*
>
> **" " " " Handkerchieves** – *Yes please*
>
> **" " " " gloves** – *No thank you*
>
> **Have you heard from Scrub again** – *yes, he still hopes for leave*
>
> **Have you sent me the C.O.'s letter** – *Not yet.*

1 At this time, each Regiment assigned each man an ID number (Gerrard's was 14284). This meant that if they changed Regiment they had to have a new number. In 1920, it changed so that each man was centrally assigned an Army number which they kept for their entire service.

2 D-ly = Damnably.

DAY
220
TUE
14 MAR 1916

Item 177

Letter to Margaret

Envelope
*161 Haverstock Hill
London*

FIELD POST OFFICE
14 MR
16

March 14th 1916

Dearest Darling

Just a line to tell you the Bystanders arrived last night, for which many thanks but no letter. I have no news. I have not got the job I was after, a personal friend of the Division has got it, at least so I have been told, so I suppose I shall just have to go on being a "walking understudy" until the end of the war. It is another hot day today, and I dread to think what the smells will be like in the summer. The rats here are in thousands, & any time I expect to see my bed being walked away with. I did a tour this morning, & managed to find Dug's company, he said that he had had a postcard from you & that was all. I will write later in the day, when the post comes in, & I have heard from you.

All All Love to you & Paula

Thine

xxxxxx Charles xxxxxx

DAY
221
WED

15 MAR 1916

Item 178
Letter to Margaret

Envelope
*161 Haverstock Hill
London*

Dearest Darling   *March 15th 1916*

Many thanks for yours of the 11th, which came in yesterday afternoon. I am glad you went & saw Dug's sister, as Dug much appreciates you doing so. You will be sorry to hear that Robinson & Gardenner have both been hit this morning. Robinson several times in the face, and Gardenner in the thigh and a broken wrist. The Dr has just gone off to patch them up, so I can give you no further details this post.

Lucky Scrub to get home, I wish to heavens I was with him. We move up to front line tonight for 3 days, & I shall see more of Dug, as his company is in reserve and in cellars quite close to our H.Q. The Bosche is very lively today, & has got 6 of the Glosters already, d-n him.

If leave had not been all stopped up here I should have been home now.

Cpl Fullbrook got the "Croix de Guerre", a French military cross for bravery. There was one given to the Brigade, and as our Stretcher Bearers did so well on the 13th, & the Cpl was in charge of them, when it was given to us I recommended him. The Dr has got no honour yet, although he deserves one, & when the honours list comes out I hope he will get something.[1] Cpl Fullbrook has misbehaved himself since & is now a full duty Cpl.[2] I am afraid I shall not get much news today, if I have to rely on what you get from the Linders.

All All All Love Dearest to you & Paula

Thine

Charles

x

1 It seems strange that this is the first mention Charles makes of **Dr Peter McGibbon**'s actions at Loos. He had led stretcher bearers between the lines at great personal risk and succeeded in rescuing many wounded men, even being wounded himself on both 25th September and 13th October. He would be awarded the Military Cross in the King's Birthday Honours on 5th June.

2 **Albert Fullbrook**, 26, *(right)*, had joined the Royal Navy aged 18 and left as an Officers' Cook 2nd Class after 5 years' service (17 months of which was on the battleship HMS Prince of Wales as part of the Atlantic Fleet). At Loos, he had been with Peter McGibbon in no-man's-land tending to the wounded (who included Frenchmen from the flank of their attack, hence their award of the Croix de Guerre, *far right*). Despite having to go back to full duty (i.e. front line infantry rather than stretcher bearing), he would make it through the war to become a carpenter like his father. His only daughter was born a month before he went into action at Loos and he got to see her have 4 children of her own.

Item 179
Letter to Margaret

Envelope
*161 Haverstock Hill
London*

FIELD POST OFFICE
16 MR
16

Peter McGibbon

| | | | | | 19|00 | | | | | | | | 20|00 | |

Mabel McGibbon

| | | | | | 19|00 | | | | | | | | 20|00 | |

March 15th 1916

Dearest Darling

There was no mail at all yesterday, not even a paper. You will be glad to hear Robinson & Gardenner are not badly hit. Robinson will be back in a week or so,[1] and Gardenner has a nice wound, which may give him a stiff wrist for the rest of his life, but will give him a whole skin for the next three or four months at least. I think everyone wanted to change places with him as he got in the ambulance last night, at least some said so (self included) and the others would have if they dared.[2]

A worse blow has fallen & that is the little D[r] has been sent to the Base for employment in a hospital there, where he will have some operating work to do. The order came suddenly yesterday afternoon & he went last night. It was bound to come as he has done very well here, and our sick is always less than any other Rgt thanks to his careful handling, so he deserves a good job, and I expect his wife will be very pleased that he is out of range. We shall miss him from a medical point of view very much, and at heart he was a good little soul.[3]

We had quite a good relief last night, and did it in record time. It was a very light night, but as there was only the HQ & one company to go over the open it did not matter. We moved down with a Company of Black Watch that was going down to the front line on our left, and a man near me got a nice couchez[4] bullet in the left arm, just my luck or I might have started for home.
We finished the relief by 8.40 pm and at 9.45 Dalby & I went round the trenches and pottered about until 1 am. It was a glorious mine. We have a sap 65 yds long, which is a tunnel under ground running out from our front line under the Boche. I went up to the end as I was told one could hear them working, but I could hear nothing. I have just spent an hour making out all the meals for the next 6 days, it is so hard to get a change, & our Mess Cpl is a fool. My dug out or cellar here is very damp, so I am having the earth taken away this morning, & the pioneers are coming up to lay a floor tonight. I have found a lovely looking glass[5] 4ft x 3ft in one of the shattered houses, which is a great addition. All All All Love

Thine
Charles xxxxxxxxxxxx

1 **Gerald Robinson★** did return quickly.

2 His assessment for **Eric Gardenner★** was less accurate. If he could have seen the future of Eric's wound going septic, years of misery from the epilepsy it induced and an early death aged 44, he wouldn't have been so ready to swap places with him.

3 **Peter McGibbon,** *(opposite page)*, was affable but no-nonsense which may explain Charles's assessment. He would not stay at the base hospital for long, resigning his commission in June, and after a year at a hospital in London, he returned to Canada. In the general election of late 1917 he was elected as a Unionist MP and was noted for his efforts on the behalf of ex-servicemen. He & Mabel endured further heartbreak in 1919 when their second child also died as an infant, the day after she was born. They both devoted themselves to the people of Muskoka District in Ontario. As well as Peter's busy medical practice (which often involved doing operations on people's kitchen tables in outlying areas), both put huge energy into the church and local schools and societies. Though defeated in the 1921 election, Peter returned as a Conservative MP in 1925, 1926 & 1930, finally losing his seat in 1935 in the Liberal landslide during the depths of the Depression. Both their funerals were attended by hundreds of mourners and a stained glass window, *(right)*, was dedicated to their memory with the words *'He laid his hand on them and he healed many'*.

4 It looks like he's spelt 'cushy' as 'couchez'. That French word may be to do with lying down and taking it easy, but actually 'cushy' comes from the Army's time in India and the Urdu & Persian word 'kusi' for 'pleasure/convenience'.

5 Saying 'looking glass' for 'mirror' seems as quaintly outdated as 'wireless' for 'radio'.

March 16th 1916

My darling Paula

    Mummy tells me that you can now add up, I can hardly believe it, so I am sending you some sums to add up for me. You will be sorry to hear we have lost our cat, I do hope a nasty German has not caught her. Yesterday 2 of our officers were wounded, but not badly, and one of them will be able to come home to England for quite a long time. We are having beautiful weather now. Poor Punch was nearly hit by a shell the day before yesterday, the shell falling about 20 yds from his stable; I have not seen the horse for 7 days as when we are in the trenches I have not time to go back as he is now nearly 3 miles away. How is your big Dolly! & has she had a cold while all the snow was on the ground.

        Now I must go out
           Best love
              Paula Darling
          from
             your loving
              Daddy

DAY 222 THU

16 MAR 1916

Item 180
Letter to his daughter Paula

Envelope
Same as for Item 179

Item 181
Letter to Margaret

Envelope
*161 Haverstock Hill
London*

Dearest Darling   *March 16th 1916*

     I wrote you a line this morning, but have had 3 from you just arrived, the 12th 13th & 14th letters. I am sorry you are disgusted with me, but I am not going to climb out of trenches with missiles flying about even at the expense of my underclothes. I can get new underclothes but not a new skin. Your remarks about magnums of champagne I do not appreciate as I have not seen one since we came up a fortnight month nearly ago.

I am glad the Scrub has got his leave, mine I am afraid is hopeless. We have so far had a quiet day & no casualties, but the lot on our left have been dropping in for it a bit.

I went down to the support line with the General this morning but have not yet been up in front, but shall spend a few hours up there tonight. I had a line from Alec Bosman,[1] & they are moving to a house on Camden Hill, but I suppose that means the one near Kensington.[2] I have had no other letters. I dont understand Readie's husband getting leave, any way it sounds hopeful, & when it does open there are only two in front of me, & probably only one.

All All All Love

Thine

Charles

1 **Alec Bosman**, 37, the son of a Dutchman who had made his fortune in Hong Kong, was the managing director of The Morgan Crucible Company, a maker of graphite crucibles (for the high temperature heating of metals) and carbon brushes (a key component in electric motors), items which were vital for new technologies being used in the war effort. The current incarnation of the company has 85 sites across 30 countries.

2 He means Campden Hill which is an affluent area just west of Kensington Palace.

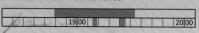

Item 182
Letter to Margaret

Envelope
*161 Haverstock Hill
London*

DAY
223
FRI
17 MAR 1916

        1 pm.   *March 17th 1916*

Dearest Darling

     Post just going & have had the Brigade Major here all the morning & no chance to write. We had a nice walk last night looking for trenches which only exist on paper.

We had another officer, Davenport, such a nice boy, hit this morning, and so we are getting more than our share. However I hope he will be alright, but I am afraid his skull may be slightly cracked.[1]

We shall be 8 tonight to dinner in this cellar, as the Brigade Major & another staff officer have asked themselves and we are going to explore after dinner. Best love will write later.

> Thine in haste
>
> Charles

FIELD POST OFFICE
17 MR 16

---

1 2Lt **Sydney Davenport**, 23, was an analytical chemist from Windsor whose family was ripped apart by the war. Though this wound was not too severe (he'd be back by June), his younger brother Lance had been killed in a charge on Hill 70 in Gallipoli in August 1915, & his elder brother Robert would be blown up by a shell on the Somme in August 1916, the shellshock seemingly breaking his health & leading to his early death in 1923 from a burst ulcer. Sydney himself would be badly gassed in September, the effects of which permanently weakened his heart. He ended the war fit only for sedentary work in the Anti-Gas Department of the Ministry of Munitions. He did get married in 1918 but his daughter was only 14 when he died at the age of 42.

Both his sisters had long lives. Cecilia, the oldest of the 5 siblings, was a nurse who married an American oilman and emigrated for a time to Mexico. Younger sister Lilian never married and lived to be 99.

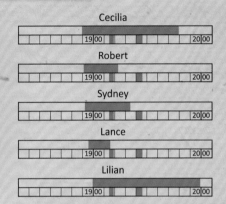

Item 183
Letter to Margaret

Envelope
161 Haverstock Hill
London

FIELD POST OFFICE
18 MR 16

March 17ᵗʰ 1916

7 pm

Dearest Darling

Have just got your letter having been out ever since I wrote you this morning. You are a silly old thing about your family tree. I was only joking and what I said about my family is quite true. If you go & look at the tombstones at Buckingham, you will find all my ancestors described as woolpackers, & what is a private bank but a money lender. I really would like to know your tree, so dont be silly but send it along.[1] Am sorry about the Motor Bill. I dare say by this time Bathurst will have paid it.

I hear leave will open again shortly, rather a nuisance as I shall have to take mine during rest period.

> Must stop now.
>
> All All Love
>
> In haste
>
> Thine
>
> Charles x

---

1 Following on from this and the mention in Item 174, the story of Charles & Margaret's family trees is on p.419.

Item 184
Letter to Margaret

Envelope
*161 Haverstock Hill
London*

FIELD POST OFFICE
18 MR
16

March 18th 1916

Dearest Darling

Hooray. Get my clothes out. Civilian ones for choice. Leave is coming again on the 20th. There are two officers before me. I hope to arrive at the end of next week. I hope to hit Scrub off & have written Lilian to send me a wire if I shall miss him, in which case I will put in a special application. We had a nice walk last night, & went within 30 yds of the Bosche trench in the open. It was so misty one could not be seen. However we had miles of tape we laid out to mark where new trenches should be dug & did some good work. We got back at 1.30 just in time to meet a funeral party of one of our men, so I had to attend that, which was an extraordinary experience, as he was buried quite close up, not being time to take him back, as thank God we vacate this bit of line tonight, & shall not be here again for a month.[1] I have written Bathurst & told him I am taking you & Paula to the sea for a day or two, & to make necessary arrangements. We will also take Lilian. All All All Love

Thine

Charles x

1 The burial took place at what is now St Patrick's Cemetery in Loos (patch of green at ***centre left of map***). You can see that the area was risky in daylight because there are blue lines of British trenches throughout the town. The red of the German front line is about 1500 metres to the west, and because Loos was in a bulge in the line so the red lines curve left down below the town off the bottom of this map, the closest part of the German line was actually only 1000 metres to the south of the cemetery.

The funeral was for Private **Walter Heaver**, 26, who had been a cart driver on a farm near Newbury before the war. He was the eighth of 10 children, and ended up having at least 34 nieces and nephews. Two of his nephews, born in 1917 and 1919, were named Walter. One of those died of malaria in 1944 aged 24, his battalion having been with the Chindits in Burma & India, and the other lived to be 94.

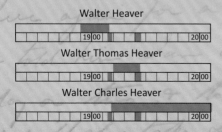

Walter Heaver

Walter Thomas Heaver

Walter Charles Heaver

Scale 1:10,000

March 19th 1916

Dearest Darling

Many thanks for underclothes, which arrived last night. I had two basins of hot water this morning & some strong carbolic soap, stood out in the open & had a clean wash. However the first thing when I get home will be a Turkish Bath, so please have all clothes ready to meet me there. Our new cellars are not good, and we cannot move about by day at all. There was a scrap on last night on our left & I believe the Bosche got back some trenches, but if they have been retaken I dont know, but am anxious to as I know our 5th Batt^n was one of the Regiments doing the counter attack.[1] We had a very bad relief last night, it was very light, & the Bosche put a lot of stuff over. One company lost 2 killed & 6 wounded before they could get into the trenches again, & we had a Transport Driver badly hit. The result was a very late night, & 2.30 am before we could turn in. I found a man swinging a huge hammer this morning & looked as if he was just hitting a lump of wood, but when I got up I found he had his vest on the wood, & was slaying lice. Not a nice story.

All All All Love to you & Paula

Thine

Charles x

---

1 Having been on alert all night, at 3.30 p.m the 5th Royal Berkshires had moved forward to relieve another unit in the front line trenches, losing 6 men wounded in the process.

March 20th 1916

Dearest Darling

Just a line this morning. Rec^d two letters from you & will write you about the extract from the book later.
One more night up here, & then back for 6 days, during which I shall start on leave. We had another rotten night last night the Bosche wounding several, & amongst them two very good NCO's. I am fed up with this sector.

No time for more now.

All All All Love

Thine

Charles x

DAY
225
SUN

19 MAR 1916

Item 185
Letter to Margaret

Envelope
161 Haverstock Hill
London

DAY
226
MON

20 MAR 1916

Item 186
Letter to Margaret

Envelope
161 Haverstock Hill
London

 # ON LEAVE IN ENGLAND

Phyllis Dare in a promotional picture from around this time. She was appearing in the title role of Paul Rubens' musical *'Tina'*, and I can imagine that Charles might have chosen it as a welcome distraction.

4/5/16[1]

Item 187
Letter to Margaret

Envelope
*161 Haverstock Hill
London
(hand-delivered)*

My dearest Darling

As I wrote you I had to stay 24 hrs in Boulogne, and when
I left I found I could have caught a boat 24 hours later & caught the same boat.
Well everything went well on the journey, absolute comfort, & I arrived at 7 pm
at the Station & rode 8 miles to Brigade HQ where I found that Dalby could not
get away until tonight so I slept with the "first line" in comfort, & came up this
morning. We are in a new subsector[2] and I have been all round this afternoon
& returned very very hot, as it is a beautiful summers day. We have had 2 killed
& 5 wounded today, which is a bit of bad luck. I have 2 more nights here, 3
in support, & then we go back for 6 days rest (so called), so now you know my
movements. By this time you will have seen Dug the lucky dog, as he gets this week
and it does not count as leave,[3] and I expect he will be over again a month from
now. We have the most filthy cellar here, all six eating in it, & 4 of us sleeping in
it. Dalby is taking this letter with him which will save a day, & you may get it
tomorrow night.

I am going round tonight, & again at 5 am
tomorrow as I find that is the quietest time.
The Bosche has just been trench mortaring us
badly again, but I dont think done any damage
& we have put some real heavy stuff into his
trench. Well Dearest All All All Love

Thine

Charles

Love to Paula xxxxxx
xxxxxx

1 He's fuddled from the travel again. It should be 3/4/16.

2 They were now in Maroc, another of the dormitory
   towns for miners in the area of Bully-Grenay.

3 **Douglas Tosetti★**, *(right)*, was on his way to
   Buckingham Palace to be presented with the Military
   Cross by the King (an event commemorated by this
   photograph). This trip back to London was in addition
   to his normal leave entitlement.

DAY
241
TUE

4 APR 1916

Item 188
Letter to Margaret

Envelope
161 Haverstock Hill
London
(posted in England)

?
8 PM
5 APR 16

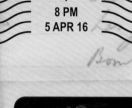

April 4th 1916

Dearest Darling   *4.30 pm*

    I missed the post this morning, as I had to go round the line with the General, and we started at 7.20 am, and got back at 2.30 pm. I think we looked into every nook & corner of the front, support & reserve lines, and I am dead beat, as I was out late last night & at 5 this morning. However TB Lawrence is off tonight to see the King, so I am sending this by him.[1] I spent 2 hours on the double Crassier this morning, and it really is not a nice place.[2] Dug's subaltern Footman seems to have done very well up there as the Acting Brigadier told me he had dubbed him "King of the Crassier". Now a message has just come in to say Kenneth Gunn the Brigade Bombing Officer has just been sniped there and died at once, "Taski" was I believe talking to him at the time. He was such a nice lad, had been out since the commencement & had been home twice wounded. It is rotten luck. His brother is home now getting his Military Cross.[3] I had a very nice letter from the little Doc, who wished to be remembered to you, and he is now at Bouglogne, & although I was there 24 hrs I did not know it. I shall go round again tonight, & not in the morning, as I think I have seen quite enough in the short time I have been up. Today we have had no casualties so far, & although D Coy had a good bit of stuff thrown at them nothing was done.

    I have no more news.

        All All All Love

        Thine

        xxxxxx Charles xxxxxx

1 **Thomas Lawrence ★** was off for the investiture of his Military Cross at Buckingham Palace.

2 **The Double Crassier**, *(below)*, consisted of two slag heaps from the coal mine workings. In 1916 they were 22 metres high and even then were a major feature of the flat landscape of the Loos Battlefield. By the time coal production ceased in 1986 they would be nearly seven times taller, becoming the highest slag heaps in Europe. Today they dominate the landscape and are the centrepiece of the UNESCO World Heritage Site that preserves the history of the generations of miners who created them.

3 **Kenneth Gunn**, 30, (*left, top,* an engineer) and brother **Marcus**, 25, (*left, bottom,* an insurance broker for Lloyd's) had signed up as privates in the London Scottish the day after the declaration of war, and both had been wounded at Messines on 1st November 1914. On their recovery, both were commissioned in the Black Watch. At Loos Kenneth got bomb wounds in the left arm & neck whilst Marcus had earned his MC for supporting attacks with machine gun fire and rescuing many wounded men. Marcus would not survive his brother by long, his company being nearly wiped out by a British trench mortar barrage on the Somme on 3rd September 1916.

DAY 242
WED

5 APR 1916

Item 189
Letter to Margaret

Envelope
161 Haverstock Hill
London

FIELD POST OFFICE
5 AP
16

5ᵗʰ March[1] 1916

Dearest Darling

I have not yet recᵈ a letter from you, but have had only one from the Mayor of Reading dated 31ˢᵗ. A quiet night last night and so far nothing doing today. I did not go round last night as owing to 3 men of a party, who were lent to us last night to do some work, being killed[2] I was very late, as I had to turn out some of our men to bring them in, & waited myself until I had seen it done. This morning I have been round making up my great mind as to what work we shall do the three days in reserve. I have absolutely no news & as lunch is being brought in (only bully beef today) I will stop.

With All All All Love

Thine

Charles

xxxxxx

xxxxxx

1 From the postmark, it's definitely April.   2 There was nothing in the Battalion's war diary about this incident.

DAY 243
THU

6 APR 1916

Item 190
Letter to Margaret

Envelope
161 Haverstock Hill
London

FIELD POST OFFICE
6 AP
16

April 6ᵗʰ 1916

Dearest Darling

I was surprised to get no letter from you yesterday but hope for better luck today. We finished up very quietly last night in the front line & completed the relief without any further casualties. This morning I have been a tour, & supervising the work. Last night a "special order" came out from the Division saying that the GOC Division congratulates the 1ˢᵗ Brigade on the remarkable improvement of the trenches since they have been in occupation. The Bosche has been fairly busy this morning and although I thought I had now got my nerves fairly under control, he fairly made my heart jump into my mouth, as I was returning home. The brute got 4 shells in just close to Baker & I, and we hopped out of the trench, & ran like stags through the village to a cellar we knew of where we waited until he had finished. Well that is all my news.

All All All Love Dearest.   Thine always

Charles B

Love to Paula xxxxxx

xxxxxx

Item 191
Letter to Margaret

Envelope
161 Haverstock Hill
London

FIELD POST OFFICE
7 AP
16

April 7ᵗʰ 1916

Dearest Darling

  Many thanks for your letter enclosing tie, which arrived last night. Also for writing Mrs Hicks etc from whom I hope you will get suitable replies. Last night we had a very wet night which interfered very much with our work, however it is fine today and I hope to complete before we go out tomorrow. Only one casualty yesterday & that was a cook back with the first line, who got rather a nasty bit of shell in the leg. I went round early this morning and it was quite nice walking, and am now waiting for the C.O. of the Rgt that is going to relieve us tomorrow night. It looks to me as if the authorities at last have found some way to cope with the Zepps getting at London.[1] *Little Cloake*[2]*'s servant brought a lamp into our cellar at 4.30 this morning, when we thought we would have another half hours sleep, but when we got up we found the lamp smoking hard and that we were smothered with a layer of soot. Thank goodness I had all clothes which I had not got on in bed with me. Tonight I am dining with Rycroft whose cellar is only about 100 yds from us. It is quaint there are 3 Battⁿ H Qʳˢ within 400 yds, but one cannot get about much in the daylight. Please thank Paula for her letter, which I will answer soon. Hope you have had a good time with Dug.*

    All All Love

    Thine

    xxxxxx Charles xxxxxx

1 The dark early hours of 1ˢᵗ April had seen the first time that a Zeppelin had been brought down over England. One of ten raiders that night, it had been punctured by anti-aircraft shells before having a tussle with an aircraft carrying a new weapon. Ranken darts were high explosive dart-tailed missiles weighing a pound each which needed to be dropped from above the Zeppelin so they could fly down onto it. There are confused reports as to how effective they were in this case, but whether it was the shells or the darts, the Zeppelin's structure was weakened and it fell into the sea near Margate. One of the crew drowned and the other 18 were surprised not to be shot when rescued from the sea just before the Zeppelin sank.

2 'Little **Cloake**★' was 5' 6½" (169 cm) tall and when he joined up in September 1914 had weighed only 8 st 12 lb (56 kg), so he was considerably smaller than Charles. (I haven't found a record of Charles's height but in photographs he is taller than most – definitely over 6' (183 cm) – and he regularly makes a point of referring to smaller people as 'little').

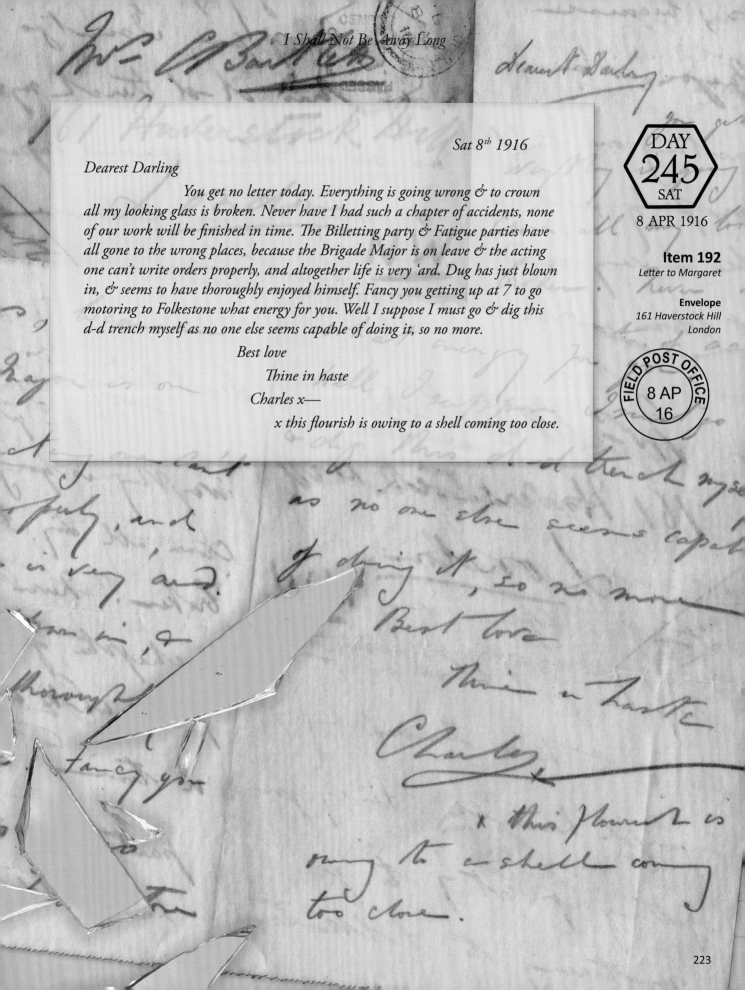

Sat 8th 1916

Dearest Darling

You get no letter today. Everything is going wrong & to crown all my looking glass is broken. Never have I had such a chapter of accidents, none of our work will be finished in time. The Billetting party & Fatigue parties have all gone to the wrong places, because the Brigade Major is on leave & the acting one can't write orders properly, and altogether life is very 'ard. Dug has just blown in, & seems to have thoroughly enjoyed himself. Fancy you getting up at 7 to go motoring to Folkestone what energy for you. Well I suppose I must go & dig this d-d trench myself as no one else seems capable of doing it, so no more.

Best love

Thine in haste

Charles x—

x this flourish is owing to a shell coming too close.

DAY
245
SAT

8 APR 1916

Item 192
Letter to Margaret

Envelope
161 Haverstock Hill
London

FIELD POST OFFICE
8 AP
16

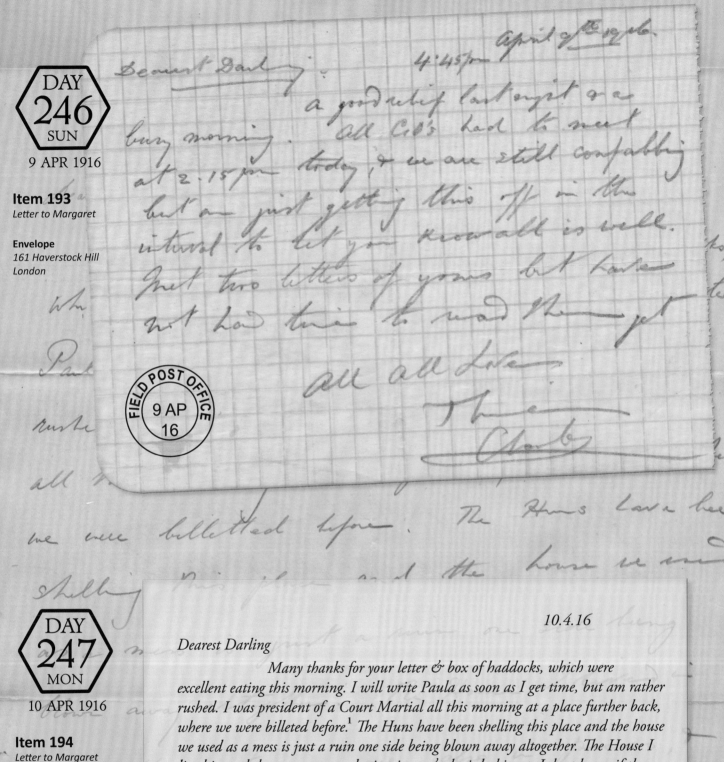

DAY
246
SUN

9 APR 1916

Item 193
Letter to Margaret

Envelope
161 Haverstock Hill
London

FIELD POST OFFICE
9 AP
16

Dearest Darling —   4:45pm   April 9th 1916.

a good rest if last night & a busy morning. All C.O.'s had to meet at 2.15pm today & we are still confabbing but are just getting this off in the interval to let you know all is well. Just two letters of yours but have not had time to read them yet.

all all love
Thine
Charles

DAY
247
MON

10 APR 1916

Item 194
Letter to Margaret

Envelope
161 Haverstock Hill
London

                                        10.4.16

Dearest Darling

Many thanks for your letter & box of haddocks, which were excellent eating this morning. I will write Paula as soon as I get time, but am rather rushed. I was president of a Court Martial all this morning at a place further back, where we were billeted before.[1] The Huns have been shelling this place and the house we used as a mess is just a ruin one side being blown away altogether. The House I lived in and the next one are also in pieces, & the inhabitants I dont know if they are alive or not, it is a d-d shame, they were such nice people. It is a beautiful day, & I think we have rec[d] our daily shelling which was not at my end of the village.

Thanks for reminding me about my birthday,[2] I am going to have a party consisting of Dug, Cloake, Col Lewin cmdg the Gunners,[3] Col Sutherland, Maj Clowes,[4] Major Arbuthnot[5] & Phillips. We ought to have a jolly evening. Our mess room is not big enough, so Dug is hunting the village to find one. I have got to go out this afternoon to look at a new bit of line, in fact have about 3 days work to do to scout the whole front. Well Dearest once more many thanks.

All All Love

Thine

xxxxxx Charles xxxxxx

FIELD POST OFFICE
10 AP 16

1 The accused at the court martial in Les Brebis was 2Lt **Hubert Corke**, 22, of the 10th Glosters. He was the son of a country vicar and had left his third year of training as an electrical engineer to join up in Sept 1914, arriving in France just after the Battle of Loos. Court martialled for *'Neglecting to obey a battalion order'*, he escaped with a severe reprimand. 9 days after this letter he was at the entrance to a dug-out when he was hit in the back by a shell splinter that entered his lung and killed him.

2 On 12th April Charles would become 38.

3 Lt Col **Henry Lewin**, 43, *(right, top)*, had spent a large part of his career employed by the Egyptian Army (including some time as military secretary to the governor-general of the Sudan) and was a Major at the start of the war. He was now in command of 25th Brigade, Royal Field Artillery. His wife of three years was the daughter of Field Marshal Earl Roberts, the Army's Commander-in-Chief during the Boer War, and his 1-year-old son was named Frederick Roberts Alexander Lewin after both the Earl and the Earl's son Freddy who had been killed in the Boer War and awarded the Victoria Cross. Through his father-in-law, Henry became a good friend of Rudyard Kipling and their correspondence on matters military and literary still survives. He would retire in 1929 as a Brigadier General, CB, CMG and Knight of the Légion d'Honneur. From 1940 to 1942 he led a battalion of the Wiltshire Home Guard. His wife succeeded as Countess Roberts in 1944 but the title became extinct on her death as their only child Freddy had been killed in action as a Lieutenant with the Irish Guards in Norway in 1940.

4 **George Clowes**, 33, would become a great pal of Charles's & together they were called *'The Twa Bings'*, the same nickname as given to the Double Crassier by the Jocks. He was a cousin of Margaret's brother-in-law William Clowes, both being great-grandsons of William Clowes, the 'Prince of Printers' who went from printing the casualty lists of the Peninsular War to setting up the world's largest printing works in London. George was up at Oxford when an uncle died and it was decided he should enter the family firm. So at the age of 19 he started out as a reader's boy getting to know every part of the business, eventually ending up as chairman and managing director, a man who cared for his staff and was esteemed by them in turn. Meanwhile he had a parallel career as a part-time soldier. In 1900 he had joined the London Scottish as a private and in September 1914 went to France as a Captain in command of a company. He was now on the staff of 1st Brigade & would finish his Army career as C.O. of the London Scottish with the DSO & OBE.

5 **George Arbuthnot**, 51 *(left, bottom)* had been in the 1st Royal Berkshires with Charles (see the 1903 photograph on p.18). His father was an Artillery Major General who as a junior officer had commanded two artillery pieces at the Battle of Inkerman in the Crimean War. Father and son made a tour of the Crimea battlefields in 1910 (the Regimental Museum has an album of his photographs of Berkshires' monuments and graves, all of which have since been obliterated due to the Nazi invasion in 1941 in which one gun fired 7-tonne shells). He helped form the 5th Royal Berkshires at the start of the war and, though wounded in October 1915, he would survive to the age of 87.

DAY
248
TUE

11 APR 1916

Item 195
Letter to Margaret

Envelope
*161 Haverstock Hill
London*

April 11th 1916

My dearest Darling

Behold me in one of my very worst tempers, and am just fed up to the teeth with soldiers.

I have got to turn the Battⁿ out & do a nights digging again. The Brigadier has protested about it, but no good. The Division say it has to be done so there is an end of it. What it means is that out of six days rest, three nights are spent digging trenches, and the men go back to the trenches more tired than when they came out. Last evening we exploded a practice mine that is we made a crater exactly like we do when blowing up Bosche, and it was most interesting the earth just went up like a huge water spout about 150 ft in the air fell all round leaving a crater about 30 yds wide. It was a grand sight, & although I was 100 yds away I thought at one time I should be smothered in earth. When we go up to the trenches again we do not go to the sector we were in last time, but to the line we were in the time before, and not only that we have got the quiet bit of it to look after, at least I hope it is still quiet.

Dug is in great form, and we had a great game of Bridge last night with Robinson, & a doctor man. Today we were going up to look at some new country, but as it is pelting with rain we shall not go unless it clears up. Our officers Riding class is a quaint sight to see, but we are getting on nicely thanks to many falls, & making them ride without saddles.

I have no more news.

All All All Love

Thine

Charles xxxxxx

April 13th 1916

Dearest Darling

Many thanks for letters of 8th 9th & 10th recd yesterday none today. Talk about Rest! Oh Lord. Yesterday I was hard at work all day until 7 pm & then we had the birthday dinner, present Self, Dug, Cloake, The Padre, The Doc, Phillipps, Maj Arbuthnot, who used to be in 2nd Battn & now Town Major here, Col Sutherland & Col Lewin, son of the man where I first went to school.[1] A quiet evening & we broke up about 11.30. Called at 6.30 this morning, & spent the morning in the trenches where we go tomorrow night. This afternoon I was supposed to go & look at a new line, but cannot get away, as I have all relief orders to work out, & tomorrow I am again president of a court martial with 8 men to try, & start the day at 6.30 am by riding round the reserve line of another sector, court martial from 10 to about 5, then do Dalby's work, & push off to the trenches about 8 pm, dine in the trenches then go round the line and by about 3 am hope to have finished. All leave is again stopped, but the reason does not effect us in any way, & I hope to have some peace in the next few days, even if it is in a cellar. I did not write yesterday but I was so rushed all day. Please thank Paula for her letter & present, and thank you for the cake. All All All Love

In frantic haste

Thine

Charles

DAY 250 THU

13 APR 1916

Item 196
Letter to Margaret

Envelope
*161 Haverstock Hill
London*

*Forwarded to:
Grosvenor Hotel
Swanage
Dorset*

FIELD POST OFFICE
13 AP 16

HAMPSTEAD
8 PM
15 APR 16

1 **Col Lewin's father William** had been a retired Commander in the Royal Navy and headmaster of Hazelhurst, a prep school for 24 boys in Frant, near Tunbridge Wells.

15.4.16

Dearest Darling

I simply had not a moment to get a line off last night or during the day as I was courtmartialling hard all the time. We had a very good relief last night, and a very quick one one man was hit rather badly but that was all. We have a very long line this time and I started round with Cloak at 10.30 pm, & did a very thorough tour of inspection with the result we did not get back here until 3 am. Before I left the front line I phoned back to our HQ with the result Gerrard had a beautiful breakfast waiting for us consisting of liver & fried eggs & bacon with some hot tea. Yesterday we had hail, and it was a very cold day. Today

DAY 252 SAT

15 APR 1916

Item 197
Letter to Margaret

Envelope
*161 Haverstock Hill
London*

is light but very cold. Dug is very well and as usual is holding the sticky part of the line. The Huns blew up a mine last night in the sector we were in last time, but I have not heard what happened. I have not heard from CAP yet & perhaps he is waiting to hear before writing me. I have had no time to write to Miss Coultate or anyone, but after we have settled down here hope to have more.

There is no more news.

All All All Love to you & Paula

Thine xxxxxx xxxxxx

Charles

Item 198
Letter to Margaret

Envelope
161 Haverstock Hill
London

April 16th 1916

Dearest Darling

Rec[d] two letters from you today dated the 13th & 14th the latter from Swanage. I am glad Gen Montgomery[1] spoke so well about us, & it seems so funny after all the praise we have rec[d] there have been so few awards. Since writing yesterday I have had a busy time and shall be glad to get to the reserve line for 3 days tomorrow night. Last night I went my rounds & thought I was going to get a few hours sleep but on arrival back here I found our chief mining officer and he told me he was going to explode a mine close to us at 5.20 am this morning, so all arrangements had to be made for that, then at 3 am the Brigade rang up & I had to get every watch in the Batt[n] set to the exact second, at 5 we were waiting for the mine, & at 7 I had to get up & go & play round the line with the General until midday, when I got back, receiving visitors about the relief tomorrow until 1 pm when I retired to sleep, & did not wake up until your letters were brought in at 3.30, since when a wash shave & tea & now feel better. The mine went up alright but I dont know the extent of the damage, but several arms legs etc were sworn to as having been seen in the air. I am rather afraid there is a German one running under our bit of line, & am having a mining expert down tonight, & for the present have contented myself by withdrawing the men from the neighbourhood of it.

I have not seen so much heavy shelling since Sept as has been going on today, at least from the Bosche & the other big tower[2] has been knocked down, which is a nuisance as it was such a good land mark at night. I dont think much damage has been done as far as life is concerned, we had 6 hit yesterday & 3 so far today, but I have a little scheme on at day-break tomorrow which I hope will cost the Bosche a few lives. Well Dearest I have no more news.

> All All All Love to you & Paula
>
> Thine always   xxxxxx   xxxxxx
>
> Charles

1 There were a few Generals called Montgomery in the Army in 1916 (and Monty of El Alamein fame was at this time only a Brigade Major).

2 The tower was a part of the mining infrastructure that dominated the town of Loos-en-Gohelle, *(right)*, and was known as 'Tower Bridge' by the Tommies.

> April 18th 1916

Dearest Darling

Many thanks for letter rec^d yesterday. I missed writing yesterday. We were having rather an exciting time & did not know how or what was going to happen any minute. However we were relieved at 11.30 pm without anything happening at all, & besides a small mine going up at 3 am nothing happened to the people who relieved us & they had no casualties. Terrible weather again. I have been round the reserve line this morning but the weather is too bad to do much work, & this afternoon I hope to sleep. I have not seen Readie's husband, one seldom sees anyone outside ones brigade, as we all have our areas, & seldom have time to leave them. Another box of haddocks arrived last night, so I suppose you have taken the hint, but please vary them with kippers, anyway very many thanks, I had a beautiful poached egg on the top of one of them this morning. Well Dearest if I write more I shall miss the post. All All All Love

> xxxxxx
>
> Thine
>
> Charles
>
> Love to Paula
> xxxxxx

DAY 255 TUE

18 APR 1916

Item 199
Letter to Margaret

Envelope
161 Haverstock Hill
London

FIELD POST OFFICE
18 AP 16

DAY
256
WED

19 APR 1916

Item 200
Letter to Margaret

Envelope
161 Haverstock Hill
London

19ᵗʰ April

Dearest Darling

Very busy handing over to Dalby & no time for a letter. I hear
I have been recommended to go as Brigade Major to the Munition Workers at
home, & that is a very good job. Will you see your friend at the War Office & see
if he knows anything about it, as I know absolutely nothing more at present.

Yours for ever
in frantic haste
Charles

Forwarded to:
The Hydro Hotel
Eastbourne, *(right),*
(it's still there but
with less lawn and
more conservatory)

DAY
257
THU

20 APR 1916

Item 201
Letter to Margaret

Envelope
The Hydro Hotel
Eastbourne

20.4.16

My dearest Darling

Many thanks for yours of 16ᵗʰ recᵈ last night. I had rather a
busy day as Cloak was seedy & retired early.[1] As I hurriedly wrote you yesterday I
know nothing more of the job as Brigade Major of Munitions except that it is a
home job and I believe well paid, but I can only expect to be amongst the "also ran"
as there are sure to be a lot of people with lots more influence than I have after it.
Are you at the Hydro as a guest? & where is Paula?
We go up into the front line tonight for 3 nights, & hope for a quieter time this
time. The Rgt who is in now has had bad luck losing a good many wounded & two
officers killed. The weather here is vile, & I have just been into a cellar, & found 2
subalterns who were on duty last night wearing kilts made of sandbags and trying
to dry their soaked clothes. It is also bitterly cold and altogether rather depressing.

All All Love
Thine
Charles xxxxxx

1 'Seedy' was then used to mean 'unwell'.

quite the dirty Bosche was when he suddenly put
15 shells at us in less than ½ minutes.

April 21st 1916

Item 202
Letter to Margaret

Envelope
*The Hydro Hotel
Eastbourne*

FIELD POST OFFICE
21 AP
16

Dearest Darling

A line to let you know so far all is well and we have completed one night out of 3 in the front line. It was no ordinary relief last night. I was walking down the Road with the C.O. & saying how quiet the dirty Bosche was when he suddenly put 15 shells at us in less than ½ minute. I ran to the nearest hole, & was glad when I heard Cloake shouting "Here's a trench" & we nipped in pretty quick. The blighters had got us nicely but beyond Dalby getting his cheek grazed none of us were touched. We have an officer & 5 men of the Fleet[1] attached to us for two days. I took the officer round last night, and it was an eye opener for him. He did not believe or said he would not have believed it if he had not seen it, & said he would much rather be on his ship than in a trench. I cant find out anything more about Munition Work, and am afraid there is not much hope. It is a pity but cannot be helped.

Dug is in great form, and has got the easy time these three days.

Kingerlee has just this moment been hit but dont say anything about it until you hear more from me, as I know no details. A sniper got him, & the bullet went in through the cheek and out at the neck, so I am afraid it sounds bad.[2] I hear leave opens again on the 25th and that the date the whole of our division leave the line is the 15th, so if that is so we shall have only one more tour of 12 days to do when we have finished this, & shall be the Reserve Brigade for the last 6 days, which is rather nice, as it gives one time to clean up before going right back, & I also hear we shall go back to our nice village. Well Dearest this is all my news, I am just off to have a look at the wounded lad, but the post will have gone before I am back.

All All All Love

Thine

xxx Charles xxx

1 **The Royal Naval Division** had been raised in August 1914, mostly from the thousands of men of the Naval Reserve for whom there had not been berths on ships. They saw action at the Siege of Antwerp in 1914 as well as Gallipoli in 1915 and had just arrived on the Western Front. After many casualties, few of the men now had seagoing experience, but although they would fight as infantry for the rest of the war, they maintained naval traditions, with naval badges of rank and sailors allowed to wear beards (whereas soldiers were not).

2 Lt **Cyril Kingerlee**, 20, *(right)*, had had a difficult start in life with his mother dying when he was 3. The war started a month after his 19th birthday and he joined up at once, though he did not arrive out with the Battalion until October 1915. The bullet had entered just below his nose on the left side, gone through his jaw bone and tongue and come out below his right ear. He would be back with the Battalion in February 1917. More terrible experiences awaited him but he would become the living embodiment of why you should never give up. →**398**

Item 203
Letter to Margaret

Envelope
*161 Haverstock Hill
London*

*Forwarded to:
The Hydro Hotel
Eastbourne*

April 22nd 1916

Dearest Darling

(i) I have not the Breeckes[1] }

(ii) " "   "Tunic }

(iii) The scheme has not gone,[2] too busy with mines.

(iv) I have written Lilian

(v) The weather is damnable

(vi) I have not had my clothes off for a week to see how my eczema is.

(vii) What baby.

Now having answered your questions I can tell you we got Kingerlee off last night by motor ambulance and with luck he will recover. The bullet went through his cheek & neck and missed by a hairs breadth two places which could have proved fatal, and unless any unforeseen complications set in, he ought to be right again in 4 or 5 months. With regard to your lodgers it is hard to advise as it is not only what they pay you, but what they bring in at odd times. However you have your books and you could make out a statement as to how much it cost to live when they came to you & how much it costs now. How is the garden wall getting on? Yesterday we had to blow up a gallery[3] as the Huns gallery was getting too near us, but beyond burying a few live Bosche & raising the ground a bit nothing happened, although we were very busy and ready in case anything occurred.

We have heard no more about leave and as Asquith has again postponed his decision, he may think it wise not to let the military over until the question has been settled,[4] as I hear that was one of the reasons that leave was stopped.

I am writing to Kingerlee's father, so you need not worry.

The Trenches are awful again flooded out & in some places they have collapsed until one is on the ground level.

I have no more news, I cannot understand CAP not answering my letter.

All All All Love

Thine

xxx Charles xxx

1 'Breeckes' is Charles combining the spelling of 'breeks' and 'breeches', i.e. trousers.

2 The scheme is as mentioned in Item 198. He never does explain what it was.

3 'Gallery' = an underground shaft in a mine.

4 **H. H. Asquith**, 63, *(left)*, Prime Minister since April 1908, had been putting off a decision about whether to extend conscription to include all men of military age (it had applied to single men since March). With concerns about whether the Army was going to continue to have enough men, the Cabinet (a coalition since May 1915) was hugely divided between those for an immediate fixed decision in law and those wanting a more flexible approach that only brought it in when there was no other choice. The impasse threatened to bring down the Government. In the end, full conscription would come in in May, but Asquith only lasted out as Prime Minister until December. His eldest son Raymond, an early volunteer, would die from a shot to the chest in September.

Easter Sunday/16

Dearest

All well, leave front line tonight. C.O. & Cloak both out & am having a busy morning & post is just going.

All Love
Thine
Charles

DAY 260 SUN

23 APR 1916

Item 204
Letter to Margaret

Envelope
161 Haverstock Hill
London

Forwarded to:
The Hydro Hotel
Eastbourne

April 24th 1916

Dearest Darling

I did not get a letter off yesterday. We had a quiet relief last night but a very late one, which was only to be expected considering the state of the trenches. However I managed to breakfast at 9 this morning after getting to bed at 3, & since have been watching our lads making wire entanglements, which we are going to cart up & place 30 yds in front of our front line tonight. I had some shirts & socks from Lilian yesterday for which I must write & thank her. The Bosche is putting a lot of stuff over this morning, & a lot is going into Rest Billets, which cannot be very pleasing for those there.

Yesterday afternoon they hit our house, & removed what was left of the roof. We were all in the cellar & it was not a very comfortable ten minutes.

I heard from C.A.P. who says the man who he spoke to about special leave has not been very favourable, so I suppose I shall have to work it from this end.

DAY 261 MON

24 APR 1916

Item 205
Letter to Margaret

Envelope
161 Haverstock Hill
London

Forwarded to:
The Hydro Hotel
Eastbourne

I have no more news, it is a beautiful day, & the Bosche has a perfect ring of observation Balloons all round us.[1]

> *All All Love*
>
> *Thine*
>
> *xxx Charles xxx*

1 Observation balloons were used by both sides to spot for their artillery and spy on the enemy. Sited a few miles behind the lines so as to be out of range of direct fire, they were surrounded by anti-aircraft guns to dissuade attackers. Sitting in a basket under a hydrogen balloon at a height of up to 1,500 metres tethered to the ground by a 15 mm diameter steel cable was not for the faint-hearted. The observers had wired telephones to relay information or strongly suggest they be speedily winched back down to the ground if they saw enemy aircraft.

Item 206

Enclosed note from Margaret, writing out a passage from 'Gordon's Letter' (My guess is that Gordon worked in the War Office)

I expect I could find out if your husband was going to get his Mun. job if I knew more precisely what it was. Do you know who has applied for him. I presume it is the Ministry of Munitions but I should like to know for certain before I bother them.

234

April 26th 1916

Dearest Darling

  No letter from you today. I have no news. We are spending an afternoon basking in the sun, reclining on our long basket chairs, which we have had brought up from the first line. It is a curious world. This place was a kind of model village each house holding two families.[1] *Of course there are no civilians here now every house is empty & not a door or pane of glass in the place. Where there were no cellars they have dug them out, & we all live in them. One or two houses are luckier than others & the best one has three whole rooms, which we use as our mess. The houses are all about 25 to 30 yds apart. The house next to us caught it a bit this morning and there were a few wounded who did not get in in time when the Bosche started shelling. All around us are our Batteries, & they are at the present moment firing direct over us & are about 250 yds from us. The air is full of aeroplanes and the Bosche is occasionally having shots at them, with the result fragments of shell occasionally are heard dropping on the roofs. On these very bright days the Bosche shoots in the morning & we shoot in the afternoon, as the sun is right for them to observe in the morning & not for us, but it is vice versa in the afternoon. However by way of a change he has just put 4 large crumps*

DAY
263
WED

26 APR 1916

Item 207
Letter to Margaret

Envelope
161 Haverstock Hill
London

Forwarded to:
The Hydro Hotel
Eastbourne

FIELD POST OFFICE
27 AP
16

235

in a mine about 600 yds away. Another quaint sight all round is the observation Balloons. We can see 6 Bosche & 3 of our own. The sun is ripping. The C.O. is asleep also Cloak, & Dug is writing to his sister but looks like dropping off any minute. My chair is right next to a hole which leads into a deep cellar in to which yours truly pops directly any trouble commences. It is a curious existence and I dont know if you will understand it from this description. We dont sit out like this when the Battⁿ holds the front line, but only on peaceful days when in support. Tonight we are relieved by another Brigade & go back for 6 days rest (so called). Then we have another go of 12 days, & I am afraid we have not got the nice quiet bit of the line, but go back to the spot where we were when I returned from leave. We are going to do 6 consecutive days in the front line & then 6 in support. However with mines being let off nearly every day it is difficult to know from one week to another what the line will be like. (I thought so, Dug is asleep). Well Dearest I have no more news. This sleep is infectious. Lilian I believe is at Stableford Bridgnorth Salop, if you think this letter would interest her send it on. I must write & thank her for shirts socks & a letter, but at the present moment sleep is imperative. I was up in the trenches until 3 am this morning trying to take an interest in a new trench being dug, but really all the time shivering with fright.

> All All All Love
>
> Thine
>
> Charles

This is one of my favourite letters. He truly conjures up what it was like to be there on that day, sitting in the sun with the big guns firing overhead. Not only is there the strangeness of his situation but the complete honesty of his reaction to it all, his love for his friends, and his fear.

1 They are back in Les Brebis. You can get an idea of its original orderliness from the pre-war map, *(left)*. When the families first moved in to their new homes, they can never have imagined that they would turn into the desolate picture of destruction on the *previous page*.

DAY 264 THU
27 APR 1916

Item 208
Letter to Margaret

Envelope
161 Haverstock Hill
London

27/4/16

Dearest Darling   3.15 pm

  I wrote you a long letter yesterday telling of a quiet time. As the old saying "What a difference in the morning". We were relieved last night at 9.45 & returned back to rest billets where we had supper & bed at 2 am. At 4.30 am the d-d Bosche were shelling like the devil, the houses each side of us were hit. We retired downstairs, & got everything ready for a counter attack. I was in pyjamas & sent Gerrard upstairs to get my clothes, when I dressed. Then a round

Forwarded to:
The Hydro Hotel
Eastbourne

around billets & the shelling stopped, so I was brave enough to go up & have a bath. After that all kinds of rumours & no one allowed to leave billets. Shelling going on, & one of our very best NCO's killed.[1] However now we hear the "Other Lads"[2] who are Malcolms friends, have <u>re</u>captured the trenches & we are once more at the situation called "normal". We are at one hours notice & the C.O. and I are getting on our horses & going for a good gallop after a rather strenuous few hours.

All All Love

Thine

xxx Charles xxx

PS Just got 2 letters from you & one from Paula

The lad who has been through 16 engagements is a worse liar than Asquith.

FIELD POST OFFICE
27 AP
16

HAMPSTEAD
1.15 PM
29 APR 16

1 L/Cpl **John Henry Caladine**, 21, *(right)*, the son of a bricklayer, and the eldest and only brother of 3 girls from Abingdon, was a greengrocer's errand boy in 1911, fighting for his life and being wounded at the Battle of Loos in 1915, and then killed by a shell in a ruined miners' village in 1916. His youngest sister Dorothy had a son she named John.

2 Above *'Other Lads'* Charles has faintly written *'Irish'* – I think he may be conveying his English prejudice.

Edith May Elizabeth Caladine

| | 19|00 | | | 20|00 |

Emily Rose Caladine

| | 19|00 | | | 20|00 |

Dorothy Helen Caladine

| | 19|00 | | 20|00 |

| | 19|00 | | 20|00 |

April 29th 1916

Dearest Darling

       I did not get a letter from you yesterday, so I did not write. This is a rotten rest & we caught it again yesterday, and at 4 am this morning the dirty Bosche started attacking again. We sleep out in the garden as our rooms upstairs are in a direct line of where the shells come from. The afternoon the day before yesterday I rode out as I told you & we were having a nice fast gallop when Punch put his foot in a shell hole & nearly came down, he kicked my right ankle recovering himself, so I had to sit all yesterday with my ankle in cold water. It was a beautiful hot day & if it had not been for shells it would have been very

DAY
266
SAT
29 APR 1916

Item 209
Letter to Margaret

Envelope
161 Haverstock Hill
London

pleasant. Last evening I dined with the General, there was quite a party of us, 12 in all. There was an attack going on at the time, but we sat out, & listened to the band which had frequently to stop as the guns were making such a noise. It was rather quaint as the fight was going on only 3 miles off & shells dropping around at irregular intervals. I enclose you a menu. We shall not be sorry to get back in the trenches as there one can get out of the way in a dug out but here it is not a pleasant feeling never knowing which house is going to catch it next.

Well Dearest I shall hope to hear from you today.

All All Love

Thine

xxx Charles xxx

1st Infantry Brigade

MENU - 28/4/1916.

Ox Tail Soup

Fish (sole).

Spinich - with eggs & toast.

Joint - Mutton
Vegetables.
Peas, Cauliflower & Potatoes.

Asparagus with butter.

SWEETS.
Caramel Pudding.
Macedona Fruit Jelly.

SAVOURY.
Anchovies with eggs.

Coffee.

Desert.

****

DAY
267
SUN

30 APR 1916

Item 210
Letter to Margaret

Envelope
161 Haverstock Hill
London

FIELD POST OFFICE
30 AP
16

April 30th 1916

Sunday   7.30 am

Dearest Darling

Not much news this morning. We had a peaceful day here on the whole yesterday. The dirty Bosche had the impudence to attack & he used gas, but the wind changed around & he got it blown back on his own dirty self. They must have used a lot as we smelt it back here which is 3 miles from the place where they attacked. They never got into our lines at all yesterday & I believe a great many were killed. We hear from reports by the Flying Corps that they are massing a lot of troops in front of us, but I dont think they will attack near here, or they would never have used gas yesterday. We had few shells over yesterday; one was rather close to us & a bit got Dug who was walking with me on the head, but it glanced off his cap, & beyond a bruise that is all. I am writing this letter laying in bed. It is a beautiful morning & so far very peaceful; we have had 8 shells over us about an hour ago, but no damage done, & as we sleep in the garden with a large house behind us it would be rotten luck to get one at all. Dug & I are going for a ride today. We think we will go & see Eugénie about 11.30. Lunch at Bethune & have a sleep there in the afternoon then go & have dinner with Fifi & Germaine returning here in the cool of the evening. I cant ride Punch as he has not yet recovered.

I wish they would send back the first Brigade to put down the riots in Dublin. Really the Irish are dirty dogs and rotten fighters.[1] Has Malcolm been called up yet? How has he avoided it?

Two more nights here & then back again. Cant help thinking it is very nearly time I had some more leave, but have not yet thought out an idea to obtain it.

All All All Love

Thine

xxxxxx Charles xxxxxx
Paula   you

1 The *'riots in Dublin'* were **the Easter Rising**, the biggest revolt against British rule in Ireland for over a century. Beginning on 24th April, six days of fighting saw the deaths of 66 rebels, 143 British soldiers and police, and 260 civilians, as well as a total of over 2,600 wounded. Many of the civilian casualties were caused by the British Army using artillery and heavy machine guns in built-up areas, and an inability to distinguish friend from foe in the chaos.

DAY
268
MON

1 MAY 1916

Item 211
Letter to Margaret

Envelope
*161 Haverstock Hill
London*

FIELD POST OFFICE
2 MY
16

Dearest Darling   *May 1ˢᵗ 1916*

    I have written you one letter which I thought you could send on to Gordon. I sincerely hope I shall get something soon as I am thoroughly tired of hanging about with the dirty Bosche throwing lead at one. We had a fine ride yesterday & did not get back until 1 am. We dined away back & left there at 10.15, & came slowly home through the woods where the nightingales were singing too wonderfully for words. It seems a bit hard if I am going to be sent to command another Battⁿ after having trained this one from the beginning. Personally I dont think I am any more efficient now to command a Battⁿ than I was when Dalby came in November, in fact I think less as I am sure I am more frightened than I was.   *Well Dearest All All Love*

                Thine

    *xxxxxx Charles xxxxxx
    Paula*

DAY
270
WED

3 MAY 1916

Item 212
Letter to Margaret

Envelope
*161 Haverstock Hill
London*

                May 3ʳᵈ 1916

Dearest Darling

    All quite well. We returned to trenches last night, & are busy today, as the Rgt is having a show tonight, which might be rather fun. I leave the trenches tomorrow & am going to Brigade HQ for 10 days to do Major Clowes work while he is on leave.

There is no other news. I will write direct to Durham tomorrow, & make some arrangements for you.

           All All Love

            In Haste

            Thine

    xxxxxx Charles xxxxx

FIELD POST OFFICE
3 MY
16

DAY
271
THU

4 MAY 1916

Item 213
Letter to Margaret

Envelope
(missing)

May 4th 1916

Dearest Darling

    Many thanks for two letters received this morning. I am sorry you have had a row with your lodgers for I hate rows. I have told you I have rec^d both breeches & tunic for which many thanks also for the Bystanders & Tatler[1] just rec^d. We had quite a nice little show last night. I have never seen such a flame of fire as went up when the mine was exploded. We killed several Bosche & nearly got one home alive, but the party could not get him over so had to strip him. He was an enormous fellow.[2] Young Footman who took out the raiding party did extremely well & is sure to get an immediate award.[3] We lost one man officially reported as "missing believed killed",[4] but must have accounted for 20 or 30 Bosche easily. It was hard to tell, as they bombed 3 dug outs, & although they heard much squealing there was no way of telling how many were inside.[5] Well that show was over at midnight, after which I came down here to B^de H.Q. where I expect to stay for about 12 days until Clowes comes back. It was a pity I could not get down here a day or two ago to get the hang of the work as I had only an hour with him before he departed, & am at present a bit in the dark. Well Dearest I will write more tomorrow. At present moment I am a little fussed as the General & Brigade Major are both out, & several curious conundrums have to be answered.

All All All Love

Thine

xxxxxx Charles xxxxx

1 *Tatler* was described as *'an illustrated journal of society & the drama'*. It later merged with *The Bystander* & was described by one editor as *'an upper class comic'*. The current editor is a great-grandson of Field Marshal Haig.

2 Two British mines in the Double Crassier were found to be close to German mines so it was decided to explode them and use that as cover for a raid to get prisoners for identification. At 8.30 p.m. the mines went up and surrounded by an enormous barrage of shells and bombs, one officer and 15 men entered the German trenches. As well as bombing 6 dug-outs, they seized a very big man they had wounded, and whilst a delaying party of 4 men threw bombs to cover their retreat, an attempt was made to drag him back. He was lifted up a ladder but then they got tangled in the wire and found it impossible to get him through, so stripped him of his coat and equipment and left him.

3 Lt **David Footman**, 20, *(right)*, would indeed be awarded the Military Cross for this raid, just one event in his very colourful life. ➔**394**

4 One of the delaying party was known to be badly wounded or killed but because he had three German bodies lying on top of him, he had to be left behind. His body was never found and the name of Private Ernest Moore is on the Arras Memorial to the Missing. His real name, though, was **Edgar Martin**. ➔**400**

5 I was shocked when I first read this description of the *'squealing'*. It sounds as if he saw them more as animals to the slaughter than human beings.

DAY
272
FRI

5 MAY 1916

Item 214
Letter to Margaret

Envelope
161 Haverstock Hill
London

FIELD POST OFFICE
6 MY
16

Friday May 5th 1916

Dearest Darling

Many thanks for yours of the 3rd just come in. I am having a nice time, as Clowes who has gone on leave has let his clerk go also, so I am rather like a fish out of water. However so far I have only made one error. Touching wood we have had comparative quietness here & very few shells anywhere near us. We (the Berks) are doing another raid tonight & hope to catch a live Bosche or two. I heard from Paula this morning & she seems to be thoroughly enjoying herself. Dug will be getting his leave in about a week to ten days time so I expect you will be seeing something of him. I have heard nothing more of Munitions & am afraid that that is all off. I hear we move a bit down the line next time we go in which is rotten luck, as it means after the months rest we shall come back to our present sector which is not nearly so healthy as the other. I have absolutely no other news, except Germaine Fifi & Co do not look their best in the hot weather.

All All Love

Thine

xxxxxx Charles xxxxxx

DAY
273
SAT

6 MAY 1916

Item 215
Letter to Margaret

Envelope
(Same as for Item 214)

May 6th 1916

Dearest Darling

Tis our wedding day. I am wondering if I shall get a letter from you about it. Being at Bde H.Q. I managed by sending a motor cyclist to the 1st Army H.Q. to get a wire off which I hope will reach you in due course. The General & Brigade Major are both out & I am in charge today, so am very busy & d-d important. There is no news we are putting up another mine this afternoon. The Bosche must be getting d-d sick of being buried. Not nice weather it is blowing a gale. Last night I went up to the trenches to examine Bomb stores etc, so even here one is never out of them for long. We are all expecting a move on account of what is going on around us, but it looks as if it will be a move back, as the Division is not being filled up by any means. Well Dearest many happy returns of the day. I will write if I can later.

All All All Love

Thine

xxxxxx Charles xxxxxx

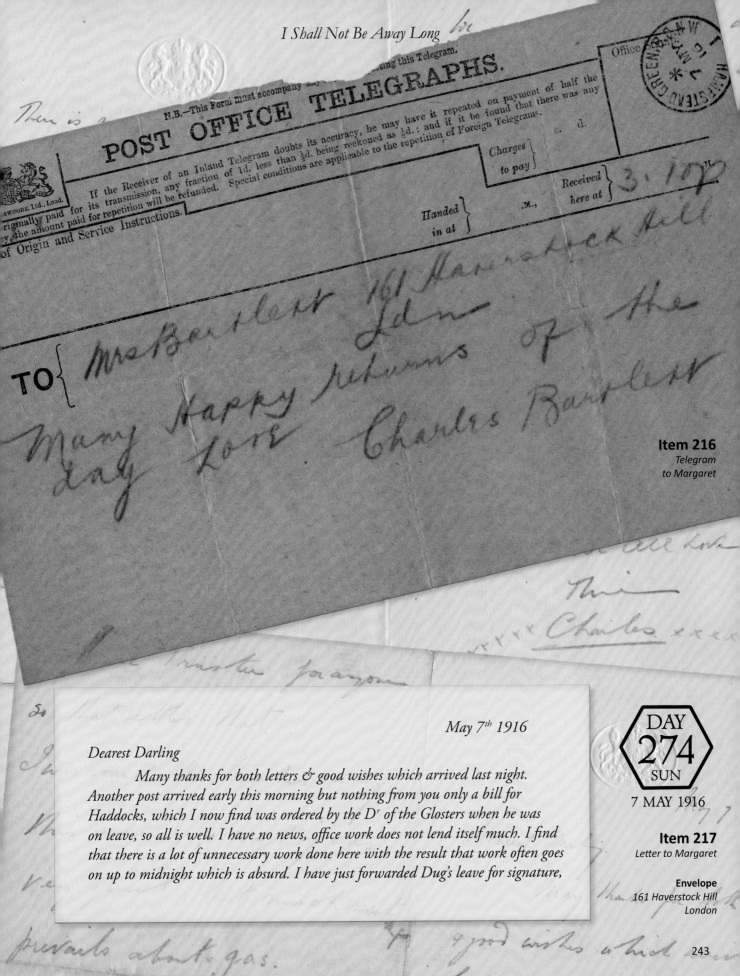

POST OFFICE TELEGRAPHS.

N.B.—This Form must accompany any enquiry respecting this Telegram.

If the Receiver of an Inland Telegram doubts its accuracy, he may have it repeated on payment of half the amount originally paid for its transmission, any fraction of 1d. less than ½d. being reckoned as ½d.; and if it be found that there was any inaccuracy, the amount paid for repetition will be refunded. Special conditions are applicable to the repetition of Foreign Telegrams.

TO *Mrs Bartlett 161 Haverstock Hill Ldn*

Many Happy returns of the day Love Charles Bartlett

Item 216
Telegram to Margaret

with all love
Tui
xxxx Charles xxxx

May 7ᵗʰ 1916

Dearest Darling

Many thanks for both letters & good wishes which arrived last night. Another post arrived early this morning but nothing from you only a bill for Haddocks, which I now find was ordered by the Dʳ of the Glosters when he was on leave, so all is well. I have no news, office work does not lend itself much. I find that there is a lot of unnecessary work done here with the result that work often goes on up to midnight which is absurd. I have just forwarded Dug's leave for signature,

DAY 274 SUN

7 MAY 1916

Item 217
Letter to Margaret

Envelope
161 Haverstock Hill London

so with luck he ought to get off on Tuesday night, & be in London on Wednesday night the Lucky Dog. I saw one of the chief officers of the Division who could tell me no more about that job of Brigade Major to Munitions than anyone else, all he could tell me was my name was forwarded. Where are your P.S.'s going ? I am not going to hand my affairs over to the public trustee for anyone so that settles that.[1] I was round the trenches early this morning, & everything was very quiet, but much excitement prevails about gas.

All All All Love To You

Thine

xxxxxx Charles xxxxxx

[1] The public trustee was a trustee appointed by a court to administer the affairs of a trust if there are no-one willing or appointed to do the job (e.g. for an existing trust in life or someone's estate after death). It further points to Margaret having concerns about their financial situation.

Item 218
Letter to Margaret

Envelope
(Same as for Item 217)

FIELD POST OFFICE 8 MY 16

DAY 275 MON 8 MAY 1916

Date 8.5.16

FATIGUE and CARRYING PARTIES.

No.	Strength	Report to	At	Time	Found by	Remarks.

Dearest.

All quite well no time for letter

Thine

Charles xxx

244

May 9th 1916

Dearest Darling

No letter from you again today. I nearly missed the post altogether last evening as I had rather a busy day. I had to go up to the trenches and got delayed. The GOC Division rang up & asked me if I would take command of a regiment of Suffolk Terriers.[1] I dont know if I shall get it, but I had to say "yes", as if one does not take what is offered one may be passed over for some time to come. I dont know where this Rgt is ? or anything about it, & the choice is between myself & one other, but as I have no connection in any way with the Suffolks my chance is very small. Dug leaves today, & I am sending this by him. I did hope to dine with Dug in Bethune tonight, but am afraid Fortune will be out, so shall have to stay here. It would be rotten luck to go & command a Batt[n] down YPRES[2] way at present, & I would rather have one of the Berkshires, but it cant be helped. Anyway it shows they now mean to give me one, although I would sooner have a more peaceful job. We have not been shelled here for the last 2 or 3 days, & I am beginning to feel quite brave again. We are looking forward to the Rest, although mine looks a bit "off" at present.

All All Love

Thine

xxxxxx Charles xxxxxx

---

1 Suffolk Terriers may sound like a breed of dog, but he means a Territorial (i.e. pre-war part-time volunteer) battalion of the Suffolk Regiment.

2 He had never been to Ypres but it was legendary as the definition of miserable hell, with the British Army defending a bulge in the line and the Germans able to spot for their artillery from the surrounding higher ground, and a low water table meant that the mud was all-consuming.

10.5.16

Dearest Darling

I have had no letter for 3 days now, so dont know what is going on. I got very wet last night up in the trenches, but today is a beautiful day. I have heard nothing further about a new Rgt but dont expect to for a few days. By the time you get this you will have seen Dug & got all the news. It is just hopeless to try & write a letter in this office. It is one continual stream of people coming in & telephones ringing. I hope when Clowes comes back I shall remain on here

FIELD POST OFFICE
10 MY 16

until I get something definite. I have been exactly 3 hours writing this letter now. Robinson is hoping to go on leave on Sunday next, but with 2 other Captains away I have not yet been able to persuade the General to sign it. Well Dearest there are only 8 men in the office now.

All All Love

Thine

xxxxxx Charles xxxxx

Paula

DAY
278
THU

11 MAY 1916

Item 221
Letter to Margaret

Envelope
(missing)

May 11th 1916

Dearest Darling

Many thanks for two letters rec[d] this morning. Of course I am very fond of you even after 8 yrs of married life. I have not heard anything more yet about a new job, except the Chief of Staff was saying last night I should not remain in this Division much longer. There are rumours going about that leave stops on the 28th and after that date no more letters will be sent home only post cards,[1] so if there is anything in these rumours our months rest looks a bit off. Dug has got his 10 days. If you see him tell him the General commanding the Corps has just sent for his "raiding party" to congratulate them, & I had to tell him they were all on leave,[2] so he is going to see them another time. I am alone this morning and so rather busy. I think I should prefer this job to commanding a Batt[n] but no such luck. If only someone would send for me over the munitions job quickly I should be delighted. I am sorry to say I am FED UP with this bloody war.

All All All Love

Thine

xxxxxx Charles xxxxx

The map on the left shows the small area where Charles had spent most of his time during the past several months (it's from the centre left of the map on the right, behind his message).

1 In an attempt to increase security, field postcards only had multiple choice answers to be ticked off with basic information to allay the fears of those at home without giving away the sort of information written in letters.

2 It wasn't just medals that were given for good deeds. The GOC of 1st Division had given all the men in the raiding party 'green tickets' (i.e. combined leave and railway tickets which were green in colour).

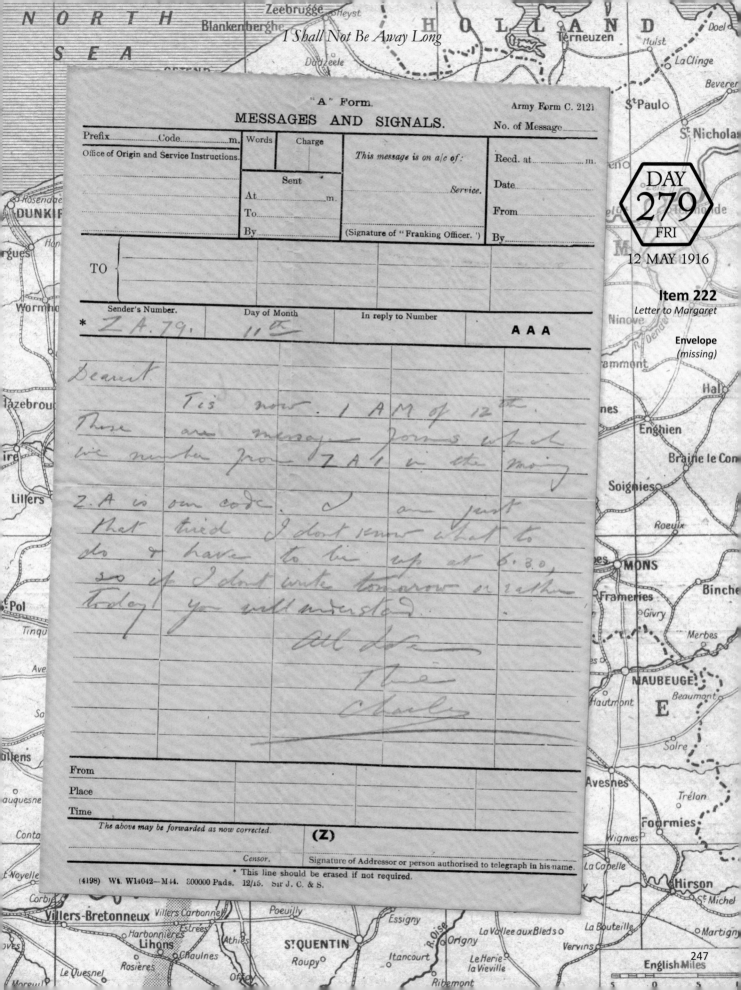

"A" Form.

Army Form C. 2121

MESSAGES AND SIGNALS.

No. of Message

Prefix	Code	m.	Words	Charge	This message is on a/c of:		Recd. at	m.
Office of Origin and Service Instructions.							Date	
			Sent			Service.	From	
			At	m.				
			To				By	
			By		(Signature of "Franking Officer.")			

TO

Sender's Number.	Day of Month	In reply to Number	
* Z A. 79.	11ᵗʰ		A A A

Dearest

Tis now. 1 A M of 12ᵗʰ.
These are message forms which
we number from Z A 1 in the morning

Z.A is our code. I am just
that tired I dont know what to
do & have to be up at 6.30,
so if I dont write tomorrow or rather
today, you will understand.

All Love
Thine
Charles

From			
Place			
Time			

The above may be forwarded as now corrected. **(Z)**

Censor. | Signature of Addressor or person authorised to telegraph in his name.

* This line should be erased if not required.

(4198) Wt. W14042—M44. 200000 Pads. 12/15. Sir J. C. & S.

DAY
279
FRI
12 MAY 1916

Item 222
Letter to Margaret

Envelope
(missing)

DAY 279 FRI

12 MAY 1916

Item 223
Letter to Margaret

Envelope
(missing)

12.5.16

Dearest Darling

*Tis midnight. I did not get a letter off today. What with a relief tomorrow night & going to take over a new part of the line life is rather strenuous. We now are not going to get our months rest, so all arrangements have been cancelled, but by tomorrow everything may be altered again. I personally cannot think that we shall take part in any push of any sort until the men have had a rest, I am sure they are not fit for it, that is speaking of the Division as a whole. This afternoon I went & had a look at our new bit of line,[1] it is a quaint place, you are within 300 yds of the Bosche & can walk about the ruins in comparative safety, as no bullets can hit one owing to the ground, but of course shells there are a bit of a nuisance. Our front line is quite close to Bosche, but what I refer to is the Batt*n* HQ. I read your letter about Frank.[2] He is rather the limit. I am afraid I have not time to go Bankrupt at present & after all said & done he invested (or agreed to the investments) the money in the things that dont pay, he sits at home in absolute comfort, he has no lives dependent on him, even his son has d-d bad manners, & not all his money will educate him any better than Paula, so he had better shut up, & come out here, & after a month or two he would go home, & say nothing was too good for him. We had a nice bit of shelling here yesterday. In fact it kept me at B*de* HQ all the afternoon, when I ought to have been elsewhere. My landlord spent the entire afternoon in the cellar. However all quiet again today. I heard from the Div, in fact I saw them tonight that nothing more had been heard about the Suffolks, but I could not possibly hear for another 24 hours. Well Dearest & now to Bed.*

All All All Love

Thine

xxxxxx Charles xxxxxx

Paula's

---

1 They were moving into the trenches at Cité Calonne, another of the dormitory towns of miners' cottages near Bully-Grenay.

2 I was thinking this might be Frank Curzon, who Charles could have had business dealings with in relation to their theatre connections, but Frank Curzon does not appear to have had a son (as pointed to in this letter) from either of his marriages, so I think this must be another Frank (as mentioned in other previous letters).

Item 224
Letter to Margaret

Envelope
(missing)

Sunday March[1] 14th 1916

Dearest Darling

      4 pm & have sat the entire day in this office. Many thanks for your letter, but you seem to be having a bit of worry with servants & P.S.'s. There is just no news, we dont even know now if we are going to get our rest or not. I have heard nothing further and although I am not keen on getting a Terrier Batt[n] I know nothing of I am rather tired of being continually recommended & getting nothing. I shall of course do nothing about going Bankrupt, until I came home, & dont think there will be any trouble about. Re Dolly coming to live with you, would it not be better to go & stay with her for the summer months. I should have thought William would have got exemption.[2]

Well Dearest the General has just shouted for me to go out so I must stop.

All All All Love

Thine in haste

xxxxxxx Charles xxxxxxx

1 Should be May (14th March was not a Sunday).

2 Conscription had come into force on 2nd March. The original Act applied to single men or childless widowers aged 18 to 41. Margaret's brother-in-law William Clowes, being married, was safe for now, but the rules were about to change. From 25th May, married men would be eligible too, so it sounds as if Margaret & Dolly were making plans to stay together for moral support should they both be left on their own.

Item 225
Letter to Margaret

Envelope
(missing)

Monday 15th 1916

Dearest Darling

      I have had no letters today neither has anyone else, so we are all alike. I am afraid we are all done out of our rest anyway for the time being, and I am very busy taking over the new bit of the line. We are going to have a beer bar and sell beer lime juice etc within 300 yds of the Bosch, which I think will be rather fun.

Last night the General & Major Fortune were both dining out when the alarm went, which very nearly upset me, however I finished my whisky & soda, then proceeded to make all the Brigade "stand to" in their billets. However after half an hour the scare went off and we "stood down" again.

I think the Bosche did try to get into our line but failed hopelessly.

I was going for a motor drive tonight to get some fresh air but now cannot get away. I will write Paula in a day or two, at present I am not writing to anyone & shall not until we get settled down in the line.

All All Love

yours

xxxxxx Charles xxxxxx

Paula's

DAY
283
TUE

16 MAY 1916

Item 226
Letter to Margaret

Envelope
(missing)

May 16th 1916

Dearest Darling

No mail in today, but tis a beautiful day. We are moving down to our new bit of line on the 18th, & apparently remain there for 18 days. All idea of rest remains in the air still & no one seems to have any ideas as to what is going to happen. I am dining with the Black Watch tonight, & last night we had a dinner party here which was interrupted by 3 Camerons dragging in what they thought was a German spy but turned out to be an officer of another Brigade in a very intoxicated condition. I have received the papers for which many thanks & they are most acceptable, as one gets less here than with the Regiment. Having only been out of the line 5 days this time everything has been an awful rush and none of the 6 days arrangements fit in. I am at present trying to get 250 men washed in 5 baths in 5 minutes or some equally hard conundrum.

Well Dearest I have no other news. I hear that the scare about "Postcards only" is off.

All All All Love

Thine

xxxxxx Charles xxxxxx

Paula's

18th

Dearest Darling

  Many thanks for letter. I am so sorry you have been worried with these bills but never mind. I cant think who can have spent the money. I have had an awful 2 days, moving a Brigade for the first time is no joke. However we are all ready to move at last & at 5 pm we push off. With luck we shall have a more peaceful time. Anyway we are in for 16 days, and for the present I am remaining with the Brigade Staff, & hope to move on to something else. The heat here is intense and I am glad to say our HQ at the new place is a large Chateau with a beautiful shady garden. Clowes came back this morning & seems to have had a very good time. I am so sorry for Dug, it is bad luck to arrive home, & find so much sickness. I have no other news.

    All All Love Dearest

    Thine for ever

    xxxxxx Charles xxxxxx
    Paula's

DAY
285
THU

18 MAY 1916

Item 227
Letter to Margaret

Envelope
161 Haverstock Hill
London

FIELD POST OFFICE
19 MY 16

May 19th 1916

Dearest Darling

  Many thanks for your letter of the 17th recd this morning, which was very quick. Well we moved into our new quarters[1] last night, & had a very good relief, but two officers of the Black Watch got hit one rather badly in the knee,[2] the other was a new youth, who only arrived yesterday & was going into the trenches for the first time.[3] It is a beautiful house this, but has been rather knocked about, & there are very few panes of glass left, but as long as the weather lasts like this there is nothing to complain about. I have a man hard at work putting in glass, & we have put up a summer house in the garden, & I am having a second

DAY
286
FRI

19 MAY 1916

Item 228
Letter to Margaret

Envelope
(same as for Item 227)

of the kindest hearted men going. The only thing he knows about is horses but will do anything to try & help on...

one put up to sleep in. As you say it is a wonder where all the troops are and why we are not sent out for a rest. I will send you the 15/- and something for Paula's holiday if you will let me know when & where Her Ladyship is going. Marcus Gunn returned from leave the night before last & brought a beautiful salmon with him which was a nice change. I am going round the line this evening just to have a look. There are only about two bad places in it, & neither of them are in our piece of line, but in the other Battalions. We are a cheery party here as Fortune is one of the nicest men you ever met, Clowes is a very nice man, when you know him, but he takes a lot of knowing, and Marcus Gunn is Brigade Machine Gun Officer & the only other is Paddy O'Dowd an Irishman, who is most amusing and one of the kindest hearted men going.[4] The only thing he knows about is horses but will do anything to try & help one. I had a letter from CAP asking me to get a months leave to come back & help him as he heard our Division was going out to rest, but as we dont seem as if we are it is not much good. Of course I made him write it, but I may be able to use it later. Well Dearest that is all my news.

All All All Love

Thine

xxxxxx Charles xxxxxx

Paula's

1 Brigade HQ was located opposite the church in Bully-Grenay and later he describes being billeted in a chateau nearby.

2 It was Capt **Philip Hugh Lumsden Campbell Colquhoun**, 23, *(left, bottom)*, who had been wounded in the knee (and also in the neck). He would be back in France in January 1917. After the award of an MC and a spell as an instructor, and only 8 weeks from the end of the war, he was killed by a sniper while pointing out the objectives for the day's attack to his platoon commanders. Before the war he'd been a tea planter in Assam and had been recommended for the Indian Army when he was killed. His elder brother Ernest had returned from Bulawayo to join up and was killed in 1917 leaving a 2-year-old son.

3 2Lt **William Bucknall**, 22, *(left, top)*, indeed had only arrived the day before. He would recover to join the Royal Flying Corps, be injured in an air accident in August 1917 and wounded in December 1917. Returning

to the Black Watch in 1919, he was a Lt Col when wounded in the Middle East in 1940 before leading the 1st Worcesters in action in Eritrea during 1941. Awarded OBE in 1948, he was twice married and lived to be 87. His younger brother Richard survived the First World War only to be killed in Singapore just before the surrender in 1942.

4 Capt **Richard 'Paddy' O'Dowd**, 40, was born in Dublin but grew up in England and settled in Bath. Two of his three sisters died in their thirties before the war. In March 1918 he would leave the 10th Glosters to work with horses supplying ammunition to the artillery, and then after the war he returned to his job at Lloyds Bank. When he died in a nursing home in 1942, he was serving as a private in the Home Guard and his home was named 'The Battlefields' (it was on the site of the Civil War Battle of Lansdowne, and contained ample stabling for his beloved horses).

20.5.16

Dearest Darling

Many thanks for yours of 18ᵗʰ recᵈ this morning. You seem to be seeing a good deal of Dug and I hope the old man is enjoying himself. I had a line from John & shall answer him in a day or two. I dont think the work at Lilian's club will suit you very well but we shall see how you get on! The Dirty Bosche raided the Brigade next to us last night & walked off with an officer 1 man & a machine gun. They had a good many killed but caught our men in the middle of a relief.¹ As you say I did have a strenuous time for a bit, but now the others are back things are very much easier, which tells you I am still at Brigade HQ, although how long I remain I do not know. I went up the line yesterday afternoon & found them all very comfortable, men in the front line coming back 100 yds having a cold bath & then returning.

I am sorry you dont like the envelopes, & I am even out of those now, so shall have to use message envelopes until a new supply arrives.² I am really beginning to think about leave.

All All All Love

Thine

xxxxxx Charles xxxxxx

Paula

DAY
287
SAT

20 MAY 1916

Item 229
Letter to Margaret

Envelope
(missing)

---

1 The officer captured was Lt **Charles Davidson**, 26, son of the hallkeeper of the Royal College of Surgeons in London. He was in temporary command of a company of the 1ˢᵗ South Wales Borderers as they went in to take over the front line at 9 p.m. He'd put down his pack in a dug-out and was just heading out to check all the sentries had been posted, when the Germans started an intense barrage. As the barrage raised onto the support line, he shouted at his men to line the parapet, but already German soldiers were upon them. As he went to attack one, he was hit on the head from behind and blacked out. He came to to find 6 Germans standing over him holding clubs and shovels. They had dragged him into a sap and from there took him further back until he eventually found himself in a prisoner-of-war camp.

In April 1918, he would be transferred to neutral Holland but only made it home in January 1919. He described himself as an actor and was on a ship to America in 1923, but at the time of his marriage to a dancer in 1930 he was the proprietor of a café in Hollywood. It seems they gave up on their dreams in 1932 and returned to England. In 1939 he was working as a travelling salesman of disinfectants.

2 A lot of the envelopes from around this time are missing so it's difficult to know which ones Margaret found so offensive. Here are a couple of examples, *(right)*, including one of the message envelopes.

253

DAY
289
MON

22 MAY 1916

Item 230
Letter to Margaret

Envelope
(missing)

May 22nd 1916

Dearest Darling

I did not write yesterday for the very simple reason that I could not get back in time to catch the post. I had gone down the lines with Fortune, and while down there the D-d Bosche made an attack on our left (not on our Brigade) and put an awful bombardment of shells all over our new lines and on all the support lines & communicating trenches leading up to them. We were dodging about for 4 hours before we got back & then got home weeping copious tears as the dirty dogs were chucking gas shells. The gunning went on all night and is still going on. We did not take much clothing off and did not get much rest. They are pitching some real heavy stuff about 100 yds from our house, where they think there is a gun, but there isn't.

Clowes & I have just been out to look at the holes, but before we got to them we heard another one coming and did the white rabbit act back to our hutch. The Bosche took some trenches yesterday and I hear we counter attack this afternoon so I expect there will be some more gunning. As you say we seem to be followed by Bosche, whenever we get into a quiet bit of the line, the Bosche choose that time to annoy us. The last Brigade that was here for 21 days had hardly a shell over them and our casualties are not good reading.

The weather is much too fine for fighting and one ought to be sitting out in the garden, but with these things dropping 100 yds away the pieces of brick etc make it impossible.

A man has just blown in and asked if he can put up an anti aircraft gun in our garden. I had to say "yes" but I am sure it means trouble. I hope you will have had a pleasant lunch with Bathurst, and not be too much worried. I knew you would regret that last set of sables[1] you bought and those 3 last dinner gowns you got from Paquin[2] were quite unnecessary. I dont think I have any more news, Clowes & I are holding each others hands and pretending we like it, but we are both trying to think of some method of getting a job at home without pretending we want one. You might give me more news of Malcolm. He must surely go before a proper medical board, & I do hope he gets caught. Edwardes does not sound very cheerful,[3] and altogether the outlook is not very hopeful.

All All All Love

Thine

xxxxxx Charles xxxxxx
Paula

254

ups an anti air craft guns in our garden. I had to say "yes" but I am sure it means trouble. I hope you will have had a pleasant lunch with Bathurst, and

1 Sables are a type of marten hunted in Russia for their dark fur which was much valued in the fashions of the time.

2 **Paquin** was one of _the_ leading Paris fashion houses with a branch in London & a clientele of famous actresses and courtesans.

3 **Lionel Edwards★** was out from hospital but still recovering slowly from being wounded in October.

regret that last set of sables you bought and those

23.5.1916

Dearest Darling

    I am feeling a little better thank you at the moment. I think "some war" is going on for we have had some real proper shelling for the last 48 hours. I have not been out of the office today, as I was trying men by Court Martial all the morning.[1] At 4 am the Dirty Bosch started this morning & I got out of my bed, which was in the garden pretty quick, & just after I got out a great bit of shell came & has made an awful mess of my mackintosh sheet & a hole through my bed. I guess I scored off the dirty Lop Ear[2] pretty well. Anyway this battle ought soon to be over, but we have had very little sleep the last two nights so shall not be sorry. No letter from you today. There are a lot of our big guns round our HQ which make an awful noise and those are what the Bosche are trying to get at so we are well in it, but my luck is still with me.

I only wish Malcolm had been here. I dont think somehow I shall sleep out tonight, not that a roof or a wall or two is much protection, as the shell that annoyed my mackintosh made a hole in the ground about 4 ft deep & 7 ft broad & that in real hard ground. Well such is life. If it continues much longer we shall move further back.   *All All All Love*

        Thine

    xxxxxx Charles xxxxxx
    Paula

DAY
290
TUE
23 MAY 1916

Item 231
Letter to Margaret

Envelope
*161 Haverstock Hill
London*

FIELD POST OFFICE
23 MY
16

Black Watch
cap badge

---

1 The courts martial were all for drunkenness and included Sgt **Robert Bain**, 30, of 1st Black Watch, who was reduced to the ranks as a result. He'd been born illegitimate in Fife, with his mother being a pithead worker who soon after married a coal miner who then gave Robert his surname. At 17, he joined the Black Watch and was still a private 9 years later when he returned home to coal mining & to get married. Called up from the Reserve the day after war was declared, he was wounded in the right foot on 20th September 1914, and then had his shoulder broken at Loos in 1915. Three months after his demotion for drunkenness he would be promoted back up to Sergeant and awarded the Military Medal for his bravery on the Somme. As soon as the war ended, he was released to return to coal mining and what sounds like a tempestuous relationship with his wife. By 1928, both were alcoholics. One day, having given his wife his disability pension, he came home to find her so drunk he had to carry her to bed. The next day he gave her his week's wages and on his return was so incensed to find her drinking again that he picked up the 4-pound axe that was near at hand & hit her twice on the head. She recovered but he was sentenced to 18 month's hard labour. It is possible that he is the Robert Bain who died in the poorhouse in Kirkcaldy in 1942.

2 Lop Ear = traditional lucky rabbit?

Item 232
Letter to Margaret

Envelope
*161 Haverstock Hill
London*

FIELD POST OFFICE
25 MY
16

May 25ᵗʰ 1916

Dearest Darling

    I did not write yesterday as there was absolutely nothing to write about. I recᵈ your letter of the 22ⁿᵈ. Dug was with me when your letter arrived and we had a hearty laugh at your idea of having a room at our chateau, as a few minutes before your letter arrived a d-d great shell had landed in the garden & knocked over about 6 trees. There is not a pane of glass left & yesterday what was left was dropping about, so now we are going to see what we can do with some talk. I am sorry Paula is seedy & I hope she will be better. I have written her & sent her £3-0-0 and will send her some more at the beginning of next month. Last night we were all rather depressed, so the General said he would have a dinner party, & a Cinema show, so in the midst of shells dropping you could have seen us eating & drinking champagne with a cinema show going on at the end of the room. It was quite a nice distraction, but at midnight we had to get busy with the mining officers, & I hope that this morning a good few Bosche have found themselves buried.
It is very quaint Claud Hamilton turning up again. Dug seems to have enjoyed himself very much, & I am so glad that his Father is so much better, and it seems as if the operation on his sister may do her all the good in the world. Scrub is lucky to get home again so soon, and I think he is a mug to give up his job. Poor old Punch has got highly nervous with all this shelling, & I am seriously thinking of sending him further back.

    I have no more news.
      All All All Love
      Thine
      Charles

Item 233
*Enclosed Question
Sheet from Margaret
answered by Charles*

May. 22. 4a.

Did you get my letter about C. Hamilton ! yes
" " " " the red lamps ! yes, we have one to march Bde H.Q
" " " the papers . yes. Thank you.
" " " Simonds' parcel ! yes it was broken
Are you staying with the Brigade for good ! I have not a notion
Did you get Paula's letter . yes & answered today

May 26th 1916

Dearest Darling

A more peaceful day today. Just got your letter of 23rd with enclosure from Bobby, which makes me smile. About Malcolm I dont think I shall ever be able to be friends with him again, & I only hope he has to go up in front of a proper Medical Board.

While up the line yesterday afternoon the Bosche put a shell into a shop just at our gates, & the shop is no more, the old woman who runs it was outside at the time, & got off with half a hand blown off & nothing more. It is Dug's Father's birthday, so we have sent him a wire, which may or may not arrive. I am afraid our quiet spot is rather the opposite at present, but no matter as it shows that we must be doing a lot of damage to make the Bosche retaliate so much. No more news. Just off up the line for a walk, as we think it is the safest place to take exercise at the present time.

All All All Love to you & Paula.

Thine for ever

xxxxxx Charles xxxxxx

910 . La Grande Guerre 1914-16. — Bully-Grenay
près Béthune. Le bombardement.
Visé Paris 910.
"Phot. Express."

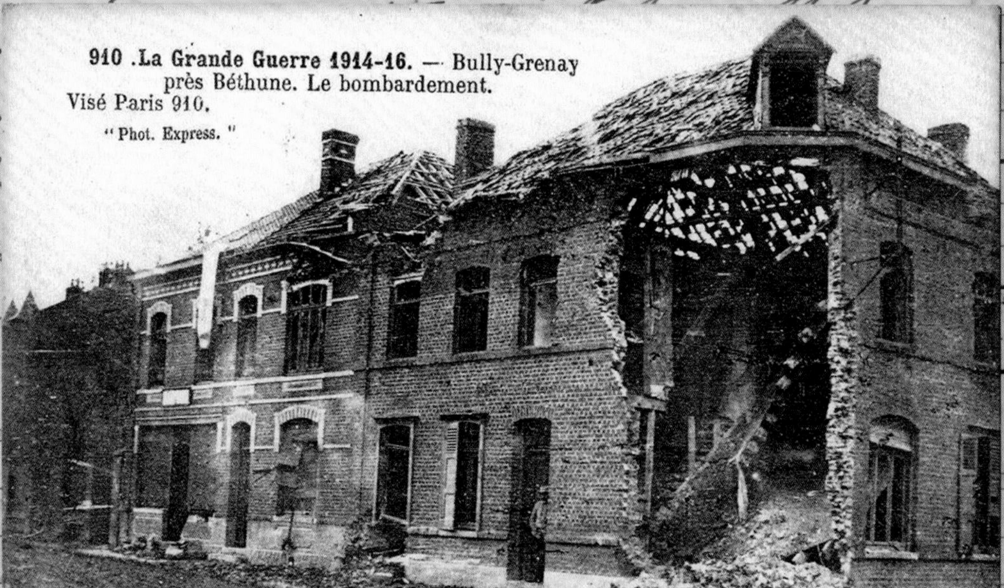

DAY
294
SAT
27 MAY 1916

Item 235
Letter to Margaret

Envelope
161 Haverstock Hill
London

FIELD POST OFFICE
27 MY
16

May 27th 1916

Dearest Darling

I received your letter of 24th this morning. I think it is a good thing you have let the house, and at 3½ gns[1] per week, it ought to pay. I suppose you will have an inventory taken and do it in a business manner, or is it all a friendly proceeding, either one thing or the other, I dont mind which, but dont have any half & half measures. I note your plans but dont expect me home between the 20th & 30th, for this reason, that if the Division goes out at the end of the month, Dalby will go on leave then, and I shall go back and command, and if the Division does not come out I dont expect I shall be able to get away. However everything is so "in the air" at present it is no use your trying to make any but plans for yourself and I will fit mine in accordingly.

A deserter came over and gave himself up to Dug's Coy at 2 am this morning, but we were not allowed to cross question him. I had a busy morning Court Martialling this morning, and since then have been up the line, and this afternoon have a good deal of office work to do as Clowes is out.

The Bosche has been quieter as far as we are concerned at HQ the last day or two, but, we are going to give them perfect hell this afternoon, & expect we shall get a bit back. Well Dearest I think a little writing paper & envelopes would be useful, as I simply cannot remember to send for any.

All All All Love

Thine

xxxxxx Charles xxxxxx

PS I will write you about Bathurst tomorrow.

1 gns = guineas

258

Sunday 28ᵗʰ 1916

Dearest Darling

    Am very tired today. We were up last night very late as the dirty Bosche attacked, and whats more took on the 8ᵗʰ Berks. Poor old Klemantaski was killed and 12 men & 16 wounded, but they put up a fine fight and not a Bosche got into our line. Everyone from the Corps General downwards is very pleased with the Battⁿ, and it was a great show. We killed a nice lot of Bosche, & I will send you on a full account. We were shelled again here for 4 hrs early this morning, and altogether had a lively time, but as the Bosche had a nasty jab in the eye we may now get a little peace. We were up against the Prussian Guard, so I think the lads deserve every credit.[1]

I dont quite understand your letter. Do you mean now that you want to let the house permanently to the Vaughans[2]?

Well I must stop now, I am getting all the clothing & equipment etc from the dead Bosche to send down to the Division.

All All All Love

In haste

Thine

xxxxxxxx Charles xxxxxx

Paula   yours

DAY 295 SUN

28 MAY 1916

Item 236
Letter to Margaret

Envelope
161 Haverstock Hill
London

FIELD POST OFFICE
? MY 16

1 At 9.45 p.m. **Louis Klemantaski** ★, *(right)*, had taken 15 men out to repair the barbed wire just in front of their trenches at Cité Calonne (in the area marked K on the map and aerial photo **below**, just south of the railway line). Heavy trench mortar fire suddenly opened up at 10.30 p.m. and a raid by over 30 Germans tried to enter the British line. Some of the wiring party were able to jump back into the trenches but Louis was amongst those killed out in the open. The Adjutant, Cecil Cloake ★, wrote, '*To me he was an oasis from whom I always drew refreshing thoughts & soothing words. His cheery nature and wonderful kindness, which was ever the same to all, won him the affection of both officers & men*'.

2 **The Vaughans** were Tommy, 46, & Lillian, 32, & their 1-year-old son. Tommy was theatrical manager to Frank Curzon. ➔**413**

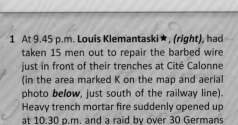

DAY
296
MON

29 MAY 1916

Item 237
Letter to Margaret

Envelope
*161 Haverstock Hill
London*

FIELD POST OFFICE
29 MY
16

May 29th 1916

Dearest Darling

    Many thanks for letter of 27th rec'd today. I wrote Paula days ago, so she ought to be satisfied by now. It is beautiful weather but the wind is blowing towards the Bosche, so all is well.

I have not been able to get hold of an official copy of the attack but will send one when I do.

There is no news except we are not going to get out of the trenches at the end of 18 days & dont know when we shall get out. Footman who did so well on the raid has been awarded the Military Cross, Cpl Smith the DCM[1] & two privates the Military Medal,[2&3] so we did very well.

    No other news.

        All All All Love Dearest

           Thine
      Paula's
      xxxxxx Charles xxxxx

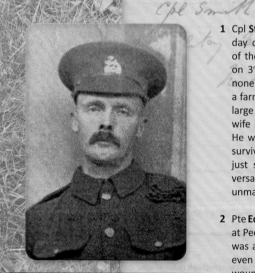

1 Cpl **Stephen Smith**, *(left)*, turned 40 on the day of this letter. He had been in charge of the delaying party during the night raid on 3rd May, throwing bombs until he had none left to throw. Before the war, he was a farm labourer and then a cart driver for a large water mill in Newbury, and he and his wife had lost their only child as an infant. He would be wounded on the Somme but survive to become a gardener. His wife died just short of their golden wedding anniversary and they are buried together in an unmarked grave in Newbury.

2 Pte **Edward Edwards**, 22, was a biscuit maker at Peek Freans' factory in Bermondsey (so it was apt that he'd joined 'The Biscuit Boys' even though he wasn't from Berkshire). The wound he'd received during the 3rd May raid wasn't his first of the war and it wouldn't be his last. →394

3 Pte **Cyril Ruff**, 20, was the fifth of the ten children of a firewood dealer called King George Ruff (who had been so christened by his father, a labourer called King Ruff). At the age of 15 he was the operator of a steam-driven stamp that cut out metal parts to make carriages. Three of his brothers also joined up, with 1917 being a bad year for them: in January the eldest was invalided out with the heart disease that would kill him in 1921, in September the youngest was killed near Ypres, and in December the other left the Army with dysentery from service in Gallipoli and Egypt. Cyril himself would be gassed and wounded in the left arm on the Somme in September 1916, by which time he was a L/Cpl and applying for a commission. He was invalided out but recovered to resume work as a coach builder and get married to the nurse who had tended him during his recovery. →408

Letter missing from
Margaret's numbered sequence

May 30th 1916

Dearest Darling

    I have absolutely nothing to write about. I went to poor old Taski's funeral this morning, which could not be held before, as it was only last night I was able to find the Rabbi. We have had a quiet morning this morning so am feeling braver than usual. This afternoon I am going up the line to put up notice boards etc, or rather see they get to the right place. I hear that I am likely to remain at Brigade HQ's at present anyway, but hope something definite will come along soon. No letter from you today. However I dont think anyone has had any today, although the papers have come in. I am writing Bathurst that I will not settle anything until I get leave or am having a more peaceful time. I simply have not the time to worry about private affairs at present & as far as I can see there is nothing urgent.

       All All All Love

       Thine

    xxxxxx Charles xxxxxx

DAY
297
TUE

30 MAY 1916

Item 238
Letter to Margaret

Envelope
161 Haverstock Hill
London

FIELD POST OFFICE
30 MY 16

Before the beginning of years
There came to the making of man,
Time with a gift of tears,
Grief with a glass that can,
Pleasure with pain for haven,
Summer with flowers that fell,
Remembrance fallen from heaven,
And madness risen from hell.
Strength without hands to smite
Love that endures for a breath
Light the shadow of night
And life the shadow of death.

And the high gods took in hand
Fire and the falling of tears
And a measure of sliding sand
From under the feet of the years
And the froth and drift of the sea
And the dust of the labouring earth
And bodies of things to be
In the houses of death and of birth

And wrought with weeping & laughter
and fashioned with loathing & love
With life before and after
And death beneath and above
For a day and a night & a morrow
That his life might endure for a span
With travail and heavy sorrow
The winds of the north and south.
They gathered us unto strife
They breathed upon his mouth
They filled his body with life
Eyesight & speech they wrought
For the veils of the soul therein
A time for labour and thought
A time to serve and to sin
They gave him light in his days
and love and a space for delight
And   and length of days
And night and a sleep in the night
His speech is a burning fire
With his lips he travailleth

The last unfinished poem from Louis Klemantaski's poetry notebook

DAY
298
WED

31 MAY 1916

Item 239
Letter to Margaret

Envelope
161 Haverstock Hill
London

May 31st 1916

Dearest Darling

Just rec[d] your letter of the 25th. Peace reigns more or less again and we hope to get out of the line on the 2nd for eight days rest. Dont get in a fuss, if there is an attack I have to remain at the Brigade HQ behind & drive back all stragglers or shoot them,[1] so at present I am quite safe. To prove to you how quiet we are, we are having a dinner party tonight with the Band playing, & I only hope the dirty Bosche hears them. A man called A J Fraser[2] who was in the 1st Batt[n] called on me yesterday and I missed him, however I hope to be able to ride over & see him this afternoon or one day next week. Could you please send me out the thin pair of khaki breeches there is about somewhere. I am very short & do not want to order any more. No official report is being made about the raid. I saw it was referred to in yesterday's Morning Post. All All All Love to you & Paula.

Thine

x Charles x

1 He may just be being flippant but this does look like an acknowledgement that it was an accepted practice in extreme circumstances for British officers to summarily shoot British soldiers if they were found to be running away in the midst of a battle. The only written evidence I've seen about this is in Brigadier-General Frank Crozier's book '*The Men I Killed*', in which he admitted shooting men out of hand and was quite blunt about its necessity: '*Men will not, as a rule, risk their lives unnecessarily unless they know that they will be shot down by their own officers if they fail to do or if they waver.*' (In a peculiar twist to an extraordinary life, Frank Crozier became an ardent pacifist in the 1930s.)

2 **Alexander James Fraser**, 35, *(right)*, knew Charles from his pre-war service (and was not to be confused with another A J Fraser, Alfred James, husband of Charles's sister Florrie). Born in India, he served in the Boer War with 1st Brabant's Horse. Arriving in France in November 1914 as a Captain with the 2nd Royal Berkshires. he was wounded at Neuve Chapelle in March 1915, but rejoined in June and would survive the war, retiring as a Major with the Military Cross. Notable for his monocle along with his fastidious appearance, he was the last survivor of the 1903 group photograph on p.18. His Colt .476 calibre Model 1878 Double Action revolver (*left*, at 2/3 scale) is in the Regimental Museum.

June 1*st* 1916

Dearest Darling

We are not writing much today. We are too frightened. Do you know Bairnsfather's picture of "a Farm House Somewhere in France" our Chateau is beginning to resemble that.[1] The dirty Bosche put one in our office this morning, but I was out of the room. Poor old Major Skinner[2] got badly hit, otherwise we are all "nicely thanks". In the midst of shells we joke so dont worry. Every time a gun goes off more plaster & muck falls down, so we are filthy dirty.

Well dearest I am now going out for a ride to avoid trouble for a bit.

All All All Love

Thine

Charles

DAY
299
THU

1 JUN 1916

Item 240
Letter to Margaret

Envelope
161 Haverstock Hill
London

FIELD POST OFFICE
1 JU
16

Bystander copyright.

" Dear ———. At present we are staying at a farm. . . ."

1 I think he means the picture above: *'Dear —, At present we are staying at a farm...'*

2 Major **Alexander Skinner**, 36, *(right)*, was the second-in-command of 10th Glosters and had only arrived the day before at Brigade HQ on temporary attachment. Really, though, he was Indian Army, born in Bengal, the son of a Colonel. His parent regiment was the Indian 5th Cavalry, but he spent a lot of the war with the Glosters, recovering from his wounds to become C.O. of 1st/5th Glosters for the first half of 1917 before being reclaimed by the Indian Army. Awarded the DSO in 1918 he finished up as C.O. of the Indian 3rd Cavalry, retiring in 1931 to live in Cheltenham. During the Second World War, he was a Group Commandant for the Royal Observer Corps, organising volunteers to monitor aircraft flying over Western England.

Item 241
Letter to Margaret

Envelope
*161 Haverstock Hill
London*

Forwarded to:
*Hill Close
Studland Bay
Swanage*

FIELD POST OFFICE
2 JU
16

Friday

Dearest Darling

> *Just a line to say all is well with our little H^d Q^{rs}. We had a pretty bad time yesterday, and the Regiment had awful bad luck last night. Poor old Barrow was killed,[1] the Transport Sergt[2] & 6 men, 6 other men wounded, 8 horses killed & 4 wounded, which wasn't a bad effort on the part of one shell. It all happened as rations were being taken up. I may go to Paris on Sunday for a night. I said in the midst of shelling yesterday that I was fed up & thought 2 days in Paris would do me good. I meant it as a joke but the General said you can go if you like, and if there is an officer going from the Division I may go with him. Anyway it would be out of shell fire for a few hours, as I have had enough to last me some time. We move back from here this afternoon to our old H Q^{rs} & although that was not very good it was peace perfect peace compared with this.*

> *All All All Love*

> *Thine*

> *xxxxxx Charles xxxxxx*

1 **James Barrow ★** left a wife and 5 children, *as pictured*. Next to James is his elder son, George, still looking very young. He was called up in late 1917 & was among many 18-year-olds who were rushed over to France in the desperate times of the German Spring Offensive in April 1918. Captured only days after his arrival, he was put to work just behind the German front line. He lived to be awarded an MBE as a civil servant in charge of medical supplies for the Army in the next war.

2 Sgt **Arthur Brown**, 29, born in Yorkshire, was an iron worker. Married in 1907 in Wolverhampton, he left a son aged 4 & a daughter aged 2. His wife Daisy, 29, never re-married and lived to be 73.

James Barrow ★

His wife Alice

Their children

Arthur Brown

His wife Daisy

Their children

June 3rd 1916

Dearest Darling

   Just a line to say I am off with a Capt Arnold[1] 1st Division Staff to Paris for one day. I am jolly glad to be out of the way of shells for a bit. It is a beautiful day and we ought to have a nice motor drive. I shall go & visit the Blind Institute in Paris,[2] & have baths every 4 hours, and a jolly good dinner. Things are very quiet this morning & you would not know there is a war on. I must try & send Paula a Doll but the shops may not be open when we arrive tonight & tomorrow is Sunday.

All All All Love

Thine

xxxxxx Charles xxxxxx

Paula

DAY
301
SAT

3 JUN 1916

Item 242
Letter to Margaret

Envelope
161 Haverstock Hill
London

Forwarded to:
Hill Close
Studland Bay
Swanage

1 **Allan Chomondeley Arnold**, 23, had joined the Army in 1912 and would serve in France, North Russia, Waziristan, Scotland, Turkey (as Military Attaché throughout WW2), & India, retiring as a Major General, CIE, CBE, MC. He has a brief Wikipedia page in Slovenian but not in English.

2 **The Institut National des Jeunes Aveugles** (National Institute of Blind Youth) was founded in 1784 and was the first special school for blind students in the world. Louis Braille studied and taught there in the early 19th Century. For a time it was housed in the National Opthalmology Hospital mentioned in the next letter.

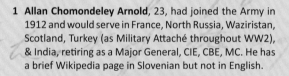

FIELD POST OFFICE
3 JU 16

June 6th 1916

My dearest Darling

   Here I am back again & much refreshed after 48 hours absence some good baths & two excellent dinners. We had perfect weather and motored about 50 miles to AMIENS on Saturday morning getting there at 1.30. Had lunch there caught the 3.20 train arriving in Paris at 6 pm. We stopped at The Continental[1] and after a nice bath we dined at The Ambassadors[2] & saw the Revue that was not up to much. On Sunday morning I went to see Maurice Brett & got some introductions to the Chief Blind people, and as Arnold was busy in the afternoon I slept, & went for a walk. That night we dined at The Ambassadors, & we retired to bed by 10.30. Monday I spent from 9 – 12 at the Blind Hospital[3] which is more or less on St Dunstans lines but very much more

DAY
304
TUE

6 JUN 1916

Item 243
Letter to Margaret

Envelope
Hill Close
Studland
Dorset

FIELD POST OFFICE
6 JU
16

economically run and then caught the 1.15 train back to AMIENS. That was a slow train and did not get in until 6 pm when we were met by a Major Carey who motored us back to the 1st Corps HQ where we dined, & eventually fetched up here at 10.30 pm. This place has quite quietened down, and I dont believe the Bosche ever meant to make a big attack here, & that all the shelling was just a "Blind" to distract attention from elsewhere. I will be quite polite to Mr Heale if he turns up. As far as leave is concerned, at present only junior officers are allowed no C.O.'s 2nd in Command or Adjutants being allowed to apply, so until that is altered I can make no plans, however after a blow like I have had I can last a few more weeks without grumbling. What looked like a naval defeat appears to be a naval victory now, so things are brighter all round.[4] I will write to Tommy Vaughan in a day or two, but now I must write a long letter to CAP about blind French soldiers.

I am sure a few weeks at Studland[5] will do you a lot of good, and I hope to get down there for a few days when I do get away. All All All Love Dearest to you & Paula & love to Eileen.

Thine

xxxxxx Charles xxxxxx

1 **The Hôtel Continental** looked out onto the Tuileries Garden. It is now known as 'The Westin Paris - Vendôme' and a night in one of its 440 rooms costs from £380.

2 **Les Ambassadeurs**, a restaurant/nightclub in the Hôtel de Crillon at the end of the Champs-Élysées was a centre of entertainment for the aristocracy, as depicted by Henri de Toulouse-Lautrec and Edgar Degas in the late 19th Century. It closed in 2013.

3 The 'Blind Hospital' near the Place de la Bastille is now known as the **Quinze-Vingts National Ophthalmology Hospital**. Founded in 1260 by King Louis IX, it took in blind poor people, housing them with their families and giving them help and training. The ever-increasing number of blinded French soldiers meant that another hospital had to be opened in the east of Paris in mid-1916.

4 The British and German Navies had met in the North Sea on 31st May. In the 36 hours of the **Battle of Jutland**, the British lost 14 ships and over 6,000 sailors killed whilst the Germans lost 11 ships and over 2,500 killed. On the face of it, that seems to be in favour of the Germans, but the damage inflicted had a bigger impact on the smaller German Navy and it would not venture out again to challenge the Allied trade blockade during the rest of the war, and for that reason the Battle of Jutland can be counted as an Allied victory despite the huge losses incurred.

5 Studland Bay in Dorset is famed for its sandy beaches. The house where Margaret was staying, **Hill Close**, *(left)*, is on a slight ridge about half a mile from the sea. Built in 1896, inside it has an Art Nouveau feel given a bit of a rustic twist by low doors in a farmhouse style. It is currently valued at £3 million.

HOVSE · AT · SWANAGE · FOR · A · SVTRO · ESQRE.

June 7th 1916

Dearest Darling

     Am rather rushed today. Fortune & Clowes are both out, and I am now also doing "Town Major" while that worthy is on leave. Do you see that C Gentry Birch has got the military Cross?[1] I am sorry you are depressed but cheer up, things are quite bright here now and everyone has their tail up. It is bad news about Kitchener but cannot be helped.[2] The GOC has just been round presenting medal ribbons to officers, & I had to call out their name. I have never heard such drivel as he talked.[3]

Footman is again on leave to get his military cross, & has only been back in the country 3 days, the lucky dog. Well Dearest I will write more tomorrow.

     All All All Love

     Thine

     xxxxxx Charles xxxxxx

DAY 305 WED

7 JUN 1916

Item 244
Letter to Margaret

Envelope
Hill Close
Studland
Dorset

FIELD POST OFFICE
7 JU 16

1 **Cyril Gentry-Birch**'s Military Cross was for his actions at Loos over 8 months before. **→396**

2 Field Marshal **Earl Kitchener**, 65, *(near right)*, had disappeared in the sinking of the cruiser HMS Hampshire, just one mile off the coast of the Orkneys. He'd been on a secret mission to reassure the Russians and the whole affair would lead to as many conspiracy theories as the killing of JFK. The prosaic truth is that a German mine likely caused the sinking. There would be legal wrangles over his estate which included his collection of fine porcelain.

3 The GOC was Major-General **Peter Strickland**, CMG, DSO, 46, *(far right)*. In September 1914 he took over as C.O. of the 1st Manchesters when they stopped in Cairo on their way from India. Wounded in November 1914, ten days after arriving at the front, he was not out of action for long, soon being given command of a brigade, & then being gassed in September 1915. He had just taken over 1st Division at the time of this letter, & would lead them through the rest of the war. Known as 'Old Hungry Face' by his soldiers, he had a fearsome temper, huge energy and a great will to succeed. Knighted in 1919, he was the last British soldier to uphold martial law inside the UK when for 3 years he commanded 6th Division in Ireland, ordering the executions of several IRA members & once closely escaping death in a targeted ambush. He ended his career as a Lt-Gen, in command of British forces in Egypt, where he had served for much of his early career. **→412**

WILLS'S CIGARETTES.

LATE F.-M. EARL KITCHENER.

DAY 306 THU

8 JUN 1916

Item 245
Letter to Margaret

Envelope
Hill Close
Studland
Dorset

FIELD POST OFFICE
8 JU 16

June 8th 1916

Dearest Darling

Just rec[d] your letter of June 5th. I am sorry you have not fixed up a house yet. I am very glad Scrub has got a Batt[n][1] & he ought to do well with one and I dont think Hilda has anything to worry about as C.O.'s jobs are looked upon as quite the best, & even in action one has a nice dug-out.

I think this job of Town Major is money for nothing, so far I have been at it 24 hours & have had absolutely nothing to do except write one letter. It suits me down to the ground as I now have two offices, & can spend my time walking between them. The only thing is the General knows a Town Major's job is nothing, so I have my usual other work to do as well. You will have not found as many letters from me as you expected as I did not write from Paris as the letters from there would not have arrived before those I wrote when I got back. All leave has now been cut down to 7 days for everyone. I have not yet thought out a plan to overcome this order but hope to, by the time I can put in for leave. Everything is very quiet here. Tonight I am going over to dine with Dug, I have not seen him for nearly a month except just to pass him in the trenches. We are having a new Brigade attached to us for instruction, so in the course of a few months we may get out to rest. "Touching wood" we have not had a shell in this place today, and I think the Bosche must be rather worried about the Russians.[2] Dreadful news about K and who will take his place.[3] With any luck after another push or two we ought to be beginning to see the commencement of the end. Well old Lady we are still very cheerful.

All All All Love

Thine

Paula

xxxxxx Charles xxxxx

Paula has not answered my letter

---

1 Brother Alfred had just taken command of 1st/4th Oxfordshire & Buckinghamshire Light Infantry, who were in training with attacking manoeuvres in the area of Agenvillers, a small village near Abbeville, 13 miles from where the River Somme enters the sea (and only 5 miles from the battlefield of Crécy where in 1346 the English Army and their longbows had inflicted a heavy defeat on the French).

2 On 4th June, the Russians had launched the **Brusilov Offensive**, one of the biggest battles in history, named after its architect General Aleksei Brusilov, 62. His new tactics included the use of several points of attack on a broad front with short bombardments co-ordinated with storm troops and with reserves held close up for immediate follow-up of success. Attacking in western Ukraine centred on Lviv, the first 72 hours saw an advance of 50 miles and the capture of 200,000 prisoners and 700 heavy guns. Similar tactics used at the same time elsewhere might have seen the collapse of the Austrian-German forces. The Germans managed to recover with disastrous casualties for both sides, more than during the Somme or Verdun, and it was the Germans who would learn and apply the tactical lessons long before the British or the French.

3 K = **Kitchener** - his place as Secretary of State for War was taken by David Lloyd George, but 'K' was a totemic figure for the British Army, and it could be argued that no-one else did come close replacing him in the eyes of the public during the rest of the war.

June 9th 1916

Dearest Darling

All is still quite peaceful and quiet. I had a nice little dinner with Dug last night. The C.O. was there, Marcus Gunn & 7 others. It was a quiet evening and we were back in the office by 10.45 pm, & did not drink Champagne. Tomorrow the Brigade goes into the line again and we remain here. There was just a remote chance that I started home on leave today, as a wire came in this morning to say one C.O. & one 2nd in Command could go at a time, so being thoughtful I tried to push off so as not to keep anyone else waiting, but alas someone remembered I was doing "Town Major" so my style was decidedly cramped & I dont look like being the first, second, or third. However I would rather come home in July as I dont want to spend all the time in town. I wrote to my niece yesterday. I went up in the trenches this morning, not because I liked it but because I was told to. However as I never heard a shell I came back with my tail still up. I have no more news.   All All All Love

Thine

xxxxxx Charles xxxxxx
Paula's

DAY
307
FRI

9 JUN 1916

Item 246
Letter to Margaret

Envelope
Hill Close
Studland
Dorset

FIELD POST OFFICE
9 JU
16

June 10th 1916

Dearest Darling

No time for a letter today. A 1000 "Pigmies" in other words a Batt[n] of Welch Bantams have arrived for instruction, & already half of them have lost their way.[1] We had a thunderstorm this morning & as if we have not enough missiles in the way of shells & bullets flying about, a thunderbolt arrived in the village. I am having a lot of fun today with officers wet through arriving & coming to see me in my capacity as Town Major to find them billets. Of course there is not half the necessary accommodation, & they would all like to be rude to

DAY
308
SAT

10 JUN 1916

Item 247
Letter to Margaret

Envelope
Hill Close
Studland
Dorset

me but dare not. Poor old Barrow's accounts are in a muddle, I am sure if he was alive they would be alright, but at present I am responsible.

All All Love

In haste

Thine

Charles

X

1 The battalion that had arrived for instruction were the **15th Welsh** and he refers to them as pygmies because they were all under 5' 3" (160 cm) tall. That had been the minimum height for soldiers at the start of the war but with the shortage of manpower, smaller men were allowed to form Bantam battalions (named for the small but aggressive chicken). Many of the 15th Welsh were miners and very strong, but one problem was seeing out of the trenches. If they built up the fire steps then taller soldiers coming in after them would find themselves exposed, so they were ordered to stand on two sandbags instead.

**DAY
309
SUN**

11 JUN 1916

Item 248
Letter to Margaret

Envelope
Hill Close
Studland
Dorset

Sunday June 11th

Dearest Darling

What weather again, it is raining in torrents & the trenches must be awful. I hope to get away at the end of ~~next~~ this week & if so I will come straight to Studland as a few days peace & quietness would do me good. Things are still very quiet here which is a good thing as with all the "Pigmies" attached to us the trenches are pretty full. I went up the line last night after the Brigade had gone in, and except for the rain had quite a pleasant walk getting home at 1 am, & I then slept from 2 – 9 which was not a bad effort. I received the breeches yesterday for which many thanks. Is the house shut up if so you might send a key to The Badminton Club so that I can get some clothes. It is impossible for me to say which day I shall get away but hope to leave about Friday, but I _shall_ leave the first available opportunity.

I have no more news. All All All Love

Thine

xxxxxx Charles xxxxxx

DAY
310
MON

12 JUN 1916

Item 249
Letter to Margaret

Envelope
*Hill Close
Studland Bay
Swanage*

FIELD POST OFFICE
12 JU
16

June 12th 1916

Dearest Darling

I have no news today. I dont believe I ever told you that I bought you a hat in Paris. I was so sick of seeing people in black I thought a dash of colour might cheer us up a bit. Yesterday I spent the day in the office & was besieged with officers wanting billets & there were none for them. In the evening I rode over to the Division[1] to try & find out when there was a chance of getting away on leave, and found out nothing, and after dinner I went up the line & saw Dalby & arranged with him to go as soon as I could get permission from the Division, so that is how I stand. Then when I come back I go & command the Rgt while Dalby is on leave after which I come back here & do Clowes work, while he does Fortunes & by that time it will be Clowes turn to go on leave & so I hope to avoid trenches for some time to come. Many thanks for Picture which made me laugh a good bit. You know in letters we are not allowed to say where we are, in fact I am trying a man by Court Martial tomorrow for writing home.[2] I have not written to General Walton. Just got your letter blaming me for not writing from Paris. I told you the reason so see no cause for complaint. I am sorry if I did not thank you for the writing pad, but you will see that the paper is out of proportion for the envelopes. I did not buy Paula a Doll, I could not find one, & only had a few minutes to spare when the shops were open on Monday morning.

    Well Dearest no more news.

    All All All Love

    Thine

    xxxxxx Charles xxxxxx

    Paula's

1 1st Division HQ was in Noeux-les-Mines about 4 miles away.

2 It's likely that the court martial didn't happen the next day because the registers list none that took place in Bully-Grenay on that date, and possibly that was because, as you will see, he managed to get the leave he was hoping for.

Five days leave !

Taxi !

 # ON LEAVE IN ENGLAND

STUDLAND BAY. NEAR SWANAGE

L. D., B., 838. - BOULOGNE-sur-MER. - Perspective du Quai Gambetta

HOTEL FOLKESTONE

I Shall Not Be Away Long
BOULOGNE-SUR-MER

(BRANCH HOUSE : IMPÉRIAL-HOTEL)

TELEP. 226
TEL. AD. FOLKESTONE-HOTEL

DAY 321 FRI

23 JUN 1916

Item 250
Letter to Margaret

Envelope
c/o Mrs Spottiswoode
28 Tite Street
Chelsea
London

ARMY P.O. 3
B
23 JUN 16

HOTEL FOLKESTONE[1]

BOULOGNE-SUR-MER

23.6.1916

Dearest Darling

We crossed yesterday, & I met a lot of men I knew. We were not permitted to have a drink although the boat did not go until 4 pm. I am staying here with Harry Lindermere[2] who is in the ASC & a member of the Badminton. It is quite a nice pub overlooking the harbour. We were escorted over yesterday and passed two hospital ships for England, and by the way the men were cheering I do not think they could have been very bad. There was a draft of 50 Berkshires going out to the 5ᵗʰ Battⁿ on my boat but no Berkshire officer with them. You will be glad to hear that "Imperial Continental Gas Coy"[3] stock has gone up considerably & it might start paying again next year and as we get the best part of 150 or more out of it, the sooner the better says I. Well at beginning of war our unearned income was roughly £820 per year which is the average the income tax is worked on. Deduct income tax and it leaves roughly 640, deduct 140 for Imperial Continental 500. House rent 80, making 420, and 12 times 35 makes 420, so you see how we stand. The American shares were sold at a good time and we get a slightly higher income from the 5% Government Bonds, so that means a few pounds, so it is a tight fit. However I will send you a fiver to complete Paula's holiday and you are to have the benefit of the "Letting" so I hope you will get along. These French pens are too awful for words so excuse scrawl.

Love to my niece, and All All All Love to you & Paula

Thine
Charles

Having let out their home, Margaret is now staying with the mother of her friend and fellow performer **Betty Spottiswoode**, 21, *(right)*. Betty's father Hugh was director of a renowned printers & publishers, chairman of *'Tatler'* & *'The Sphere'* and of various charities, director of the Royal Academy of Music & of Broadwood pianos, and had died suddenly the previous August aged 51.

1 **The Hotel de Folkestone,** *(opposite, bottom)*, was another dockside Boulogne hotel which would not survive the Second World War.

2 Lt **Harry Lindemere**, 40, was the son of Louis Lindheimer, a German immigrant. ➔399

3 The **Imperial Continental Gas Association** was a London company with expertise in manufacturing gas from coal for use in heating and lighting (this was before the general availability of natural gas). Before the war they had gas works in Antwerp, Brussels, Berlin and Vienna, all of which were now behind enemy lines. Two months after this letter, the German government nationalised all of the company's assets in Germany (their biggest market), which can't have been good for Charles's income. The company received compensation after the war and continued until 1987 when it split into two companies, one of which was Calor.

DAY 322 SAT

24 JUN 1916

Item 251
Letter to Margaret

Envelope
28 Tite Street
Chelsea
London

FIELD POST OFFICE
24 JU 16

24.6.1916

Dearest Darling

No letter from you yet, but I found 4 written before you knew I was coming home. I arrived back last night, and we are all very busy. I am going up the line tonight to see Col Dalby, but cannot hope to carry out our plan just at present as I dont think it would be a suitable opportunity, but I might just as well start the ball rolling. Dug has got his majority[1] will you let Bogey & The Guvnor know. All All All Love *Thine in haste*

xxxxxx Charles xxxxx
Paula

1   i.e. Douglas Tosetti had just been promoted to Major.

DAY 323 SUN

25 JUN 1916

Item 252
Letter to Margaret

Envelope
28 Tite Street
Chelsea
London

June 25th 1916

Dearest Darling

Many thanks for two letters recd today. I am sorry but I can do nothing towards getting anyone a commission nowadays. I could have some time ago but at present it is contrary to orders, the idea being that those men who are suitable will be recommended by their own C.O.'s and the authorities do not want to be worried by applications from men who have waited to be fetched.[1] We are rather busy here at present, but only on paper. I am sorry Hilda is fussed, but she will get over it and after all a C.O. of a Battn is the best job out here. I have sent in my application and will let you know how it progresses. It was really rather funny this morning. The Bosche was putting over one or two shells and as they seemed to be getting nearer I got out of bed & had a look out of the window to see where they were going and the first person I saw was George Clowes craning out of his window. However beyond putting one into our servants billet (& they were out) nothing happened and we both retired to our little beds.
This daylight bill[2] is a nuisance as it puts us back with our work, and we have so many hours work to do when it is dark that we are having breakfast now between 9 am & 10 am.

Today I had a lot of men to try by Court Martial, and managed to do 5 in 1½ hours which wasn't bad. Give my love to my niece.

All All All Love to you & Paula

Thine

xxxxx Charles xxxxx

Paula

1 Volunteering to enlist obviously indicated the keenness looked for in an officer, while waiting to be conscripted did not.

2 The Daylight Saving Bill had received Royal Assent on 17th May, and the clocks had been put forward an hour for British Summer Time for the first time ever on 21st May 1916.

27.6.16

Dearest Darling

Just rec^d your letter of 23rd & am glad the children are stopping on for a fortnight, it will save my fiver???? I will address after tomorrow to Hill Close. My application for the 9th Batt^n has been strongly recommended & forwarded so I have hopes. It has got as far as the 1st Corps it then goes to the Army, & then to GHQ & perhaps home then & again perhaps not, but we must wait & see. I have not written to Harvey as I can do no good now, & really after all the life is not so bad, & why should these lads have commissions before the men who have had 2 yrs of fighting. I expect you will see more of what is going on in the papers than we shall know out here, as we only get the wildest rumours. I have had a filthy cold, but with a strong dose last night & a great deal of port & whisky I think I have drowned it. I went up the line this morning but not far, & am ashamed to say I have not yet been round our front line.

I must write Paula a letter. We are fairly busy thank you, & have not been shelled at all the last 48 hours. I found Gerrard asleep on my bed last night, & caught him 3 beauties with my cane. Love to my niece & All All All Love to you

Thine

Charles

DAY 325 TUE

27 JUN 1916

Item 253
Letter to Margaret

Envelope
28 Tite Street
Chelsea
London

275

DAY 327 THU

29 JUN 1916

Item 254
Letter to Margaret

Envelope
28 Tite Street
Chelsea
London

FIELD POST OFFICE
29 JU
16

29.6.16

Dearest Darling

    Some more writing paper something like this please, it costs 1/- & has a picture of a Battleship on the cover.[1] Well many thanks for three letters, two rec[d] yesterday & one today. You seem to be having a good time dancing & I am glad you are saving up for my next leave. Paul married what a "catastroff".[2] I did not write yesterday, as I had to get a Batt[n] of Pigmies out of the trenches, & another Batt[n] in, so was out the whole day. They are jolly little beggars, and ought to put up a good fight. I dont think letters will be stopped at all anyway I hope not. You need not fuss about the 8th we dont expect to do any real pushing until we have had a months rest, & according to latest ideas that looks like being in August. How is my niece I love her very much. I got a wonderful medical certificate from the Assistant Director of Medical Services[3] recommending me for duty with the Home Establishments, so I have increased hopes. I shall be interested to hear what Razzle is like.[4] I have lost my torch which is a nuisance as I fall over carts & horses on my way to bed. I am afraid we have heard nothing about Lille out here, and although the Bosche are certainly having a rotten time I fear it is not true.[5]

Well Dearest I must now do a job of work.   All All All Love

        Thine

        Charles B

        x x x x x x

1 A pad of Dreadnought writing paper can be seen on p.6.

2 **Paul Rubens** & **Phyllis Dare** had decided to get married at the end of the run of her current show *'Tina'*, with Phyllis planning to then retire from the stage.

3 The **ADMS (Assistant Director of Medical Services)** was a Division's head doctor. In the case of 1st Division this was Col **Stuart Macdonald**, 55, a Scot who had served in Malta, the Punjab Frontier, and during the Boer War. He would end the war as a Major-General, CB, CMG, Croix de Guerre and become Honorary Physician to King George V. He never married. His medals sold at auction in 2003 for £1750 and were then sold by a dealer in Canada for $6,400 in 2015.

4 **'Razzle-Dazzle'** was a revue that had just opened at the Theatre Royal, Drury Lane (it would later transfer to the Empire Theatre, Leicester Square, **as pictured**). It celebrated the glitz of the stage (one of the performers appeared in a diamond dress), but *'going on the razzle-dazzle'* also pointed to a wild night out (it would be the next year before 'dazzle' was used to describe the outlandish geometric patterns that were painted on ships as camouflage).

5 **Lille**, the city known as 'the Manchester of France' for its industry, was 6 miles behind the German front line. Newspapers reported broadcasts from a wireless station that said it was in London and told of the Allied capture of Lille. This was soon shown to be a German ruse, though the Germans were forcing Lille's civilians to evacuate the city at this time.

DAY
328
FRI
30 JUN 1916

Item 255
Letter to Margaret

Envelope
Hill Close
Studland
Dorset

June 30th 1916

Dearest Darling

  Many thanks for yours of 27th just recd. We have not yet heard anything about letters being stopped & I dont see why they should be. Paul's marriage tickles me very much and I am still betting even money.[1] It is wonderful how some people get passed unfit for active service, personally I dont think I was ever examined or I might have escaped, however I am glad I did not. Halton Camp Tring[2] is quite close to Aylesbury so we might have gone over to see him, but I dont understand how he is a Major & Adjutant. I had a letter from Cox today saying I was overdrawn so I suppose some cheques from France have arrived. Anyway I told Cox not to worry & to take my pay from July in settlement. Razzle Dazzle does not sound very exciting. We got a rather good gramophone record from the "Bing Boys" called "Just one more little drink" which we played & acted to at 2 am this morning with the result that we sat up an extra half hour longer than necessary.[3]

My recollections of Bognor do not lead me to think that you will go there. I used to go over & play cricket there when I was at Storrington and did not think much of the place.

Clowes and self are pretending to be brave and are going up the line this afternoon, not that we like it, but to pretend we take an intelligent interest in our work. Is Phyl Bedells married? If not when is she going to be?[4]

We are all rather "Fed Up" today, we have no news and the weather is beastly, and I think we should even welcome a Bosche shell to wake us up. I have never known the dirty Bosche so quiet, although they gave the next village to us a bit of a doing last night. After being here now 4½ months we have now dug ourselves a nice "Funk Hole" outside Brigade HQ & the more they knock the house about the safer the Funk Hole will be, as the bricks can only fall on top of the Dug Out. Well Dearest I have no more news. All All All Love

    Thine

    Charles

1 **Paul Rubens** and **Phyllis Dare** had a famously on-off relationship.

2 **Halton Camp** was on land owned by Alfred de Rothschild. The Royal Flying Corps landed there on an exercise in 1913 and since 1914 it had been an Army camp. It went on to become one of the biggest RAF stations in the UK. Its closure was announced in 2016.

3 The hit revue **'The Bing Boys Are Here'** had opened in April & featured the song *'Another little drink wouldn't do us any harm'*.

4 **Phyllis Bedells**, 22, *(right)*, a prima ballerina who would be a founder member of the Royal Academy of Dance, was appearing in *'Razzle-Dazzle'*. Her marriage would be blighted by a hidden aspect of the First World War. →**390**

Item 256
Letter to Margaret

Envelope
Hill Close
Studland
Dorset

1.6.16[1]

Dearest Darling

Not time for letter writing today. Have just been President of a Court Martial, & now have to write orders to move a Batt^n of Pigmies out of the trenches & get another one in. I never could write orders, & the result will probably be that both Batt^{ns} will be lost.

We have had excellent news.[2] Everything is very quiet up here & everyone seems very cheerful.

Must stop now.

yours in haste with all love
Charles X

FIELD POST OFFICE
1 JY
16

---

1 Actually 1st July 1916.

2 The excellent news is the opening of the Battle of the Somme, some 30 miles to the south of his current location.

Item 257
Letter to Margaret

Envelope
Hill Close
Studland
Dorset

FIELD POST OFFICE
2 JY
16

2.7.16

Dearest Darling

Not much time to write, as we are getting ready to move back for a period of rest which we are looking forward to. However I expect the post will be a bit erratic for a day or two, but by the time you get this we shall be away back reclining in basket chairs and generally having an easy time. The Brigade Major came to my room this morning to find me but I was out, however he said here had he been for 5 months in a tiny room & finds me in a huge room with beautiful large windows and a beautiful garden. Everything is very quiet still here. The Bosche did put a shell in our garden of our Mess this morning, but besides breaking the windows no damage was done. Well Dearest I have no more news.

All All All Love

Thine

Charles x

3.7.16

Dearest Darling

   A hurried line. I have been over away back making arrangements for our move tomorrow,[1] so dont expect a letter for a day or two after you get this. It is a nice village where we are going. You still seem very unsettled as to where you are going to live. I heard from Edwardes today & they are very short of officers,[2] so I might be sent there anyway, but should hate to go as a Coy Commander, which would be out of the frying pan into the fire, however one must "wait & see".

   Post just going.

   All All Love

   Thine

   Charles

DAY
331
MON

3 JUL 1916

Item 258
Letter to Margaret

Envelope
Hill Close
Studland
Dorset

Forwarded to:
28 Tite Street
Chelsea
London

1 They were going to Barlin, with billets in Cité de Fosse 7, another village of miners' houses. **2 Lionel Edwards**★ had just joined the 9th Royal Berkshires, a training battalion, at Bovington Camp in Dorset.

5.7.16

Dearest Darling

   Many thanks for this paper & two letters rec[d] last night. We moved back here yesterday & it was "some move". I was soaked to the skin and we had a long day. I dont think we shall be here more than a day or two & will then move a bit further back. Yes the news is good. What I meant about "not fit for active service" is that it seems that anyone who does not want to come out can get a medical certificate, & that was all. I am very well, but no Medical Officer up in the front can recommend any officer to go home on account of ill health, so I got our old ADMS to say "I have this day examined Major C.F.N.B. & recommend that he should be transferred to the it would be for the benefit of the service that he should be transferred to the Home Defences & take over the appointment for which he has been recommended." Rather a nice way of putting it. It would be very amusing to see Paula with Lilian, I think Lilian would get a bit tired towards the end of the day. I am now going out for a ride partly business partly pleasure. There is no news we only hear a rumble in the far distance.

   All All Love

   Thine

   xxxxxx Charles xxxxxx

DAY
333
WED

5 JUL 1916

Item 259
Letter to Margaret

Envelope
c/o Mistress
Betty Spottiswoode
28 Tite St
Chelsea
London

All's well but much too busy to write as the whole division is on the move. I did from 6 am to the following day at the station loading ⅓ of the Div and left there at 10 pm getting to bed this morning at 6 am up at 9.30 & we expect to move again this afternoon & the country beautiful & quiet. The news seems very good

H.Q as

two lett

DAY
336
SAT

8 JUL 1916

Item 260
Letter to Margaret

Envelope
28 Tite St
Chelsea
London

FIELD POST OFFICE
9 JY
16

8.7.16.

Dearest Darling

     All's well but much too busy to write as the whole division is on the move.[1] I did from 6 am to 10 pm the following day at the station loading ⅓ of the Div and left there at 10 pm getting to bed this morning at 6 am up at 9.30 & we expect to move again this afternoon. The weather is fine & the country beautiful & quiet. The news seems very good and everyone seems very pleased.[2]

Love to my niece & Best Love to you & Paula

        Thine always
        xxx Charles xxx

1 Their move had been: march 11 km to Fouquereuil, train 50 km to Doullens, march 17 km to Naours, then this day march 12 km to Molliens-au-Bois.

2 Did he really believe they were suddenly being rushed down to the battle area to follow up on success?

DAY
337
SUN

9 JUL 1916

Item 261
Letter to Margaret

Envelope
28 Tite St
Chelsea
London

FIELD POST OFFICE
9 JY
16

            Sunday
12 mid day   *9.7.16*

Dearest Darling

     Just up after a long lay in bed. We are in the best chateau we have been in since I have been in France, but am afraid we shall be turned out & the place used for a Divisional HQ as it is too large really for us.[1] I got two letters from you yesterday, & you seem very unsettled still in your plans, but I suppose you will find some place eventually. News seems to keep good still. I wonder if the Scrub has been in the push,[2] it is so difficult to find out where any unit is, but our casualties do not seem to be very heavy.[3] Anyway I think we have the Bosche stone cold, or he will be soon. He is certainly finished as far as air fighting is concerned.[4] There is very little news. Our new band is beginning to play quite nicely. Marsh has arrived, I dont know if I told you.[5]

Well Dearest that is about all for the day. Your own husband sends his love to his loving wife.

        Thine
        xxxxxx Charles xxxxxx

1 The **Chateau des Marronniers** *(right)* in Baizieux is now a hotel used as a base for visiting the Somme battlefields.

2 Brother Alfred's battalion were indeed down on the Somme, but a scheduled attack for 3rd July had been cancelled and they had since been holding front line trenches that were full of water from the pouring rain.

3 The Army rumour mill was obviously not working. It is over a week into the

battle and he doesn't seem to have heard of the disaster of the first day, with the British Army losing 57,740 men, killed, wounded or missing.

4 The Allies certainly had air supremacy at this point, but again he was under-estimating the Germans, who would re-organise their air force and regain the upper hand in 1917.

5 **Gordon Marsh** ★ had recovered from his wounds received at Loos.

DAY
339
TUE

11 JUL 1916

Item 262
Letter to Margaret

Envelope
28 Tite St
Chelsea
London

Forwarded to:
Ashley Cottage
Ashley Road
Thames Ditton

FIELD POST OFFICE
12 JY
16

July 11th 1916

CHELSEA.S.W.
11.15 AM
15 JUL 16

Dearest Darling

This battle seems to be upsetting the post a bit as I have only had one letter the last three days. Well we seem to have settled down here for a few days and I sincerely hope we shall not have another move for a bit. Considering the men had been in the trenches their marching has been wonderful, and in my Batt[n], we only had one man fall out.

I had a nice sleep this afternoon, having nothing else to do. I met a great friend of Pat Gold's the other day, a man named Gilbey, who knew all the Golds Roses etc.[1] Paula has had quite a good bit of sea side this year. Did I ever tell you I saw Connie at Cox's on my way through, she looked very well.[2] I am getting a bit fussed about this leave business being stopped as it looks as if I shall be more than my three months this time unless it opens soon. There is no news here and even the papers are not regular, but I should think something will have to give somewhere soon, as masses of troops are supposed to be coming out. I will write Paula soon but at the present moment I have a lazy letter writing fit on.

All All All Love

Thine

xxxxxx Charles xxxxxx

1 **Patrick Gold**, 27, *(right)*, was first cousin of the husband of Vi Gold (who was born a member of the Rose Family) & his father was named Alfred Gilbey 'Argo' Gold, hence there was likely a family link to this Gilbey that Charles had just met. Patrick had taken a shrapnel bullet in his right arm at Loos on 13th October and was not fit for further active duty. His

brother Alec, adjutant of 5th Royal Berkshires, had just been killed on 3rd July. Patrick would return to surveying and marry twice.

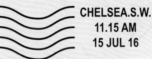

2 **Connie Bennett**, 23, was the youngest of Margaret's sisters, and had married in 1912.

Charles Frederick Napier Bartlett

DAY
341
THU

13 JUL 1916

Item 263
Letter to Margaret

Envelope
28 Tite St
Chelsea
London

Forwarded to:
Ashley Cottage
Ashley Road
Thames Ditton

13.7.16

Dearest Darling

Once more on the move, so dont expect a letter for a day or two as our Divisional post office is closed. Dalby is sick so I am once more commanding the Batt[n]. Hence I am very busy as we have no officers with previous experience of moving troops. Dug I have made 2nd in Command, so we are having some time in our spare moments. I have heard nothing from you but owing to the push we are told not to expect anything. Dug sends his love. I am hoping to see the sea in a day or two.   *All All All Love*   *Thine*
          P.T.O   *Charles*

On the back is this note from **Douglas Tosetti** ★, not seeming to have a problem with referring to 'the Bosche' despite his Prussian ancestry.

'ullo, ow are you — Sorry for the Batten when it has to fall back on me as 2nd in command but I think we shall be able to look after the Bosche, and ourselves afterwards, first off to bed — I don't think. All the best to you a little Curri' when you see her

DAY
343
SAT

15 JUL 1916

Item 264
Letter to Margaret

Envelope
*28 Tite St
Chelsea
London*

March[1] 15th 1916

Dearest Darling

 Thank goodness we are now <u>really</u> back at rest. All this time we have been on the move and had a turn in the biggest battle of the war. We were suddenly taken out of the trenches at our old place and moved every day for 4 days until we arrived at a place which John knows of and since then have had a real hard time.[2] Dalby was hit the first day,[3] so I had to leave the Brigade & take command, and we were the last three days in the front line of the advance. Two officers killed, & 5 wounded or shell shocked[4] and about 150 killed & wounded with a very small proportion of killed. It was a ghastly show, the smell was too awful, & the battle of Loos was a mere nothing in comparison. However we got back at 4 am this morning, & I slept until 12.30 midday, & have since had a bath & clean underclothing so feel very much better. We were holding a piece of line while the troops on our right moved round so had a comparatively easy time. The village we took was levelled to the ground, & all the time we were in possession of the village Bosche kept on crawling out of cellars which we did not know of, but they had no fight left in them, & were glad to be captured. We took two Bosche Doctors & there were about 100 wounded Bosche. The Bosche D[r] told me the first night "Tonight I am your prisoner tomorrow you may be mine this is the third time I have been taken". It was quite true the village had been taken & re-taken twice. However it is now safely in our possession & the Bosche D[rs] & the wounded we sent back to one of the prison camps. It is a wonderful sight this huge battlefield, and the noise is too deafening for words. I have just seen poor old Ronald's brother, he is in the Motor Transport.[5] Our new tin helmets have saved any amount of lives, and it seems a pity we did not have them before.[6] The whole Batt[n] did extraordinarily well, and thoroughly deserve a rest for they were a very weary lot coming out,[7] and the dirty Bosche put a new kind of gas shell over us as we were coming out, which was most unpleasant.

Well Dearest I have a lot to do.

All All All Love

Thine

xxxxxx Charles xxxxxx

FIELD POST OFFICE
15 JY
16

---

1 From the postmark, it is July.

2 They had been in action at Contalmaison.

3 i.e. **Gerald Dalby** was not sick as he'd told her in the previous letter.

4 He names the casualties in a later letter.

5 **George Brakspear** had originally joined the Navy in May 1915 but after Ronald's death had taken a commission in the Army Service Corps, arriving in France in March 1916.

6 Often forgotten is that for the first 22 months of the war, the only head protection most British soldiers had was cloth caps. Helmets started arriving in late 1915, but because production of munitions was the first priority of industry, it was only just before the Battle of the Somme that there were enough helmets for each man to be issued one individually.

7 They were now back in Albert, about 2 miles behind the start line for the 1st July attack.

Item 265
Letter to Margaret

Envelope
28 Tite Street
Chelsea
London

FIELD POST OFFICE
16 JY
16

July 16ᵗʰ 1916

Dearest Darling

Recᵈ two letters today, & the one in which you said you had not heard, & that you supposed I was having too good a time to write made me smile a good deal. I am now very busy reorganising and getting kit etc made up again but we dont expect to be called on to have another go for some time, & then it will be our turn to be in reserve so you have nothing to worry about. Poor old Punch was hit the other day, & has two pieces of shell sticking in him, which has made him rather nervous, & not easy to ride, but he will settle down in a day or two. We seem to be pushing on very well and heaps of Bosche prisoners come through daily.

I have to give a lecture tonight on the recent fighting & discuss it all with my officers, so no more for today.   *All All All Love*

Thine

Charles

Letter missing from
Margaret's numbered sequence

FIELD CENSOR
165

Item 266
Letter to Margaret

Envelope
28 Tite St
Chelsea
London

July 18th 1916.

Dearest Darling,

Just a line to say "all's well". We are sitting in a very wet wood, but don't expect to be doing any fighting for the present. The news seems exceptionally good this morning, and I do hope the end will soon be in sight. I wrote to Paula. There is no news I can give you so with all all all love

Thine

Charles x x x x x x

x x x x x x

FIELD POST OFFICE
19 JY
16

They were now in Bécourt Wood, two miles from Contalmaison, off the bottom left of this map (which was marked up by Cecil Cloake ★).

The good news was that the day before, the British had captured Ovillers and Bazentin Wood (but at a cost in casualties of 5,121 & 9,914 respectively).

18. 6. 17

Item 267
Letter to Margaret

Envelope
28 Tite Street
Chelsea
London

FIELD POST OFFICE
19 JY
16

18.6.17[1]

Dearest Darling

I wrote you this morning & have no more news, but just send this line to thank you for this writing paper, which if we dont move too quickly will be useful. I forgot to tell you our new QM has arrived and seems to be quite a success.[2] *I have not seen anything of Tweens Rgt but as there are troops in every conceivable hole & corner for miles & miles it is not to be surprised at. Now the weather has cleared this wood is not such a bad spot. I have just had a letter from Bogey saying he hopes we are enjoying our rest. ??? Well well c'est la guerre. Yes, that is the same Houldsworth. I heard he had had both legs broken but was expected to live. I am very sorry about it.*[3]

All All Love

In haste

Thine

Charles

1 From the postmark, it's 18.7.16.

2 The new Quartermaster, Lt **Cecil Moon**, 34, the son of a cloth seller, had served as a private in the Boer War, surviving capture at the Battle of Diamond Hill in 1900. He signed up again with the Army Ordnance Corps in 1903 (with a tattoo of a vampire on his left arm) but left after the birth of his son in 1906. By 1912 he was a music hall manager in Bolton with two convictions for neglect of his wife (including a sentence of one month's hard labour) and one for riding a bicycle without a light. He went to France in July 1915 as an Artillery Battery Quarter Master Sergeant & was commissioned for this new job with the 8th Royal Berkshires a month and two days before this letter. →**401**

3 Lt Col **Arthur Holdsworth**, 40, *(left)*, had stood next to Charles in the 1903 1st Royal Berkshire's group photograph on p.18, and ***below left*** you can see them sitting together in Gibraltar in 1901. Both were in the Battalion polo team that won a cup and played at Madrid on the occasion of King Alfonso's coronation in 1902. In 1914 he was captain & adjutant of 3rd Royal Berkshires in Reading. Appointed Lt Col & C.O. of 2nd Royal Berkshires in December 1915, he led them into action on the first day of the Somme. Can you imagine what his parents thought when they received these words from the Medical Officer about their eldest son?:

'Your son was wounded early by a shell. The whole of his heel was blown away, but he kept on for six hours walking on his toes, when he was hit by a bullet just above the knee, the bullet smashing his thigh bone . . . I think his courage and endurance in carrying on for six hours after his left foot was shattered were marvellous. 1 wish we could have saved his life, but I fear there was not much hope.'

His mother was able to arrive at his bedside before he died on 7th July. He was buried 40 yards from Ronald Brakspear ★ at Étaples.

Charles.

July 20th 1916

Dearest Darling

Could not get a line off yesterday. Cloake was sick & has had to go back for 2 or 3 days rest. Scrub has just been in to lunch & we have had a nice old talk. He has been lucky so far & not suffered much. Our Brigade is going to have another go tomorrow, but we are in reserve, & dont contemplate any trouble. I have had a letter from Paula, who seems to be enjoying herself, also from Lilian, who seems delighted to have her. If you dont get a letter for a day or two dont fuss because if I was damaged you would be notified before any letter from here could possibly reach you. All All Love

Thine

Charles

? 5 PM 24 JUL 16

DAY 348 THU

20 JUL 1916

Item 268
Letter to Margaret

Envelope
28 Tite Street
Chelsea
London

Forwarded to:
Imperial Hotel
Hythe
Kent

FIELD POST OFFICE
21 JY 16

July 21st 1916

Dearest Darling

Just a line to say alls well, & we are not fighting but in reserve. Scrub moved up also last night but was in reserve too – a fact which we congratulated ourselves on. The whole Division expects to be relieved before you get this, & the only reason we may not be is that our casualties are so light we might be kept in the line a bit longer. I got a draft of 164 Derby[1] recruits yesterday, & a poor looking lot they are, & I believe absolutely without discipline, but I gave them all a nice lecture, & now hope for the best. Lilian seems to love having Paula. I have never seen so many guns in my life they are nearly touching one another & average a gun to every 30 yds, so poor old Bosche is having a rough time. Well Dearest no more news.

All All All Love

Thine

Charles

CHELSEA.S.W. 11.15 AM 26 JUL 16

DAY 349 FRI

21 JUL 1916

Item 269
Letter to Margaret

Envelope
28 Tite Street
Chelsea
London

Forwarded to:
Imperial Hotel
Hythe
Kent

FIELD POST OFFICE
22 JY 16

---

1 **The Derby Scheme** was an attempt to see if Britain's manpower requirements could be met by volunteers or whether conscription was needed. Named after the 17th Earl of Derby (the Director General of Recruiting), the survey in November and December 1915 involved men attesting as to whether they would enlist if required. 38% of single men and 54% of married men said No, so conscription was introduced. Meanwhile those who had said Yes were now arriving at the Front after their few months of training.

July 22ⁿᵈ 1916.

July 22ⁿᵈ 1916

Dearest Darling

      A beautiful day for a battle. Last night we moved up into an old Bosche dug out which is built in the side of a hill and goes back in the ground about 30 yds, so feel nice & safe. The dirty dogs gave us a dose of gas last night & we had to wear helmets for about an hour, otherwise we are being left severely alone. I think another night or two will see the Division back at rest. The noise & smell is I think beginning to tell a bit on everyones nerves. The guns never seem to cease firing and dont even trouble to dig themselves in but just sit out in the open & fire day & night. I think we have a lot of new troops against us now, & fresh ones, as they seem to be fighting jolly well now although it is not nice to have to admit it. I am afraid from what I hears Scrubs crowd got a rather unpleasant time, but as his Battⁿ was in reserve I dont expect they suffered much.[1]

    All All Love

      Thine always

        Charles

CHELSEA.S.W.
8 PM
26 JUL 16

1 Brother Alfred's Battalion had tried an attack at 1.30 a.m. on 19th July but lost direction in the dark and, finding themselves under fire in only a shallow trench at daylight, the attack was abandoned with a loss of 12 killed and 88 wounded.

July 22ⁿᵈ 1916

Dearest Darling

      Just recᵈ two letters from you written on the 18ᵗʰ. I thought you would be happier thinking I was resting & could do no good knowing we were pushing. Now you understand our little joke about the sea & the Bosche.[1] Also why I sent my spare kit home, so that settles that.
Dalby was slightly wounded, but am afraid will lose one or two fingers. Snell[2] & Maggs[3] were the lads killed. Morris,[4] Churchill,[5] Lunn[6] were wounded. Joseph[7] collapsed, and Cox[8] was taken for the flying corps, so our numbers are diminished. I think the Bosche have a lot more guns now, and anyway are giving us a bit of a doing this afternoon, however sitting right inside the inside of a hill is very safe.[9]

    All All All Love

      Thine

       Charles

CHELSEA.S.W.
8 PM
26 JUL 16

1 He's referring to his letter of 13th July.

2 2Lt **Francis Saxon Snell**, 29, *(above)*, was a Cambridge analytical chemistry graduate, killed by a burst of shrapnel when reconnoitring the enemy position. →411

3 2Lt **George Maggs**, 27, *(below)*, was a clerk in the Reading Biscuit Factory and a prize-winning athlete. He had just written home saying, *'The countryside is beautiful and marching is made pleasant by the continual change of scenery.'* His part in the action is told later in a press report but this is what Donald Stileman★ wrote to his parents:

 'He was sitting in a trench with several members of his platoon when a 5.9" shell came in the middle of them and your poor son had both legs broken and a wound in his side. We gave him some morphia and before he was taken off by the stretcher bearers he knew he was dying and asked me to write to you. He was unconscious most of the time and died quite peacefully, trusting in his Saviour.'

4 2Lt **Cyril Morris**, 23, a schoolmaster, was knocked over when the nose cap of a shell struck him on the chest, but got away with severe bruising & would be back in February 1917. One of the few to escape the German Spring Offensive unhurt, he briefly took over command of the remains of the Battalion. During the advance of August 1918, a bullet caused a through & through flesh wound in his right calf, but he survived to become a chartered accountant. His only brother was killed near Arras in July 1917.

5 Lt **Harold Churchill**, 22, had been hit on the head which led to shell shock with severe headaches, giddiness and nausea. He would recover to rejoin the Battalion in January 1917 and survive both the German Spring Offensive and the 'Spanish' flu in 1918 to become a dentist and have a family.

6 2Lt **Cyril Lunn**, 20, *(above)*, knocked out cold by a shell fragment in the back, was left with shellshock. Even after arriving in Salonika in 1917 he was still having bouts of unwellness and was invalided home in 1918. By 1927 he was a chemistry researcher at King's College, Cambridge, but died in a motorbike accident in Wiltshire. There were skid marks for 117 feet & 2 pins were found to be missing from the front forks. His pillion rider Vera, though badly hurt, survived him by 55 years.

7 2Lt **William Joseph★**, *(above)*, had walked into Battalion HQ weeping and in a state of complete nervous collapse. After being given a strong drink he was sent on to the Casualty Clearing Station. He would recover only to be killed in May 1918.

8 Lt **George Cox**, 23, *(below)*, who'd joined up from a plantation in Borneo, would become an air ace, downing 5 enemy planes whilst flying a Sopwith Camel, and strafing ground troops forming up for attacks (awarded the MC in 1918). He stayed in the RAF (including flying as an instructor), was awarded the Air Force Cross in 1940, retired as a Wing Commander, and became Assistant Manager of Prestwick Airport (MBE in 1958).

9 They were in the support line in Shelter Wood a mile south-west of Contalmaison.

Item 272
*Letter to CAP,
i.e. Sir Arthur Pearson,
who forwarded it
to the parents
of Gordon Marsh★
(whose son
showed it to me)*

Envelope
(missing)

22.7.16

My dear Chief[1]

    *I am afraid I have been very remiss about writing but we have been on the move & too busy for words. We heard one day that the whole division was coming out of the trenches & thought that after being in for 5 months we were going to have a rest, but we were pushed into trains, & then marched & marched until we landed in the big push, & have now been in it for 11 days. The first day the C.O. was wounded so I had to leave my staff job, & come back & command. So far we have been very lucky, only 2 officers killed & 5 wounded and about 140 other ranks, and as we were in the village that was taken & retaken 3 times we were lucky. I found over 100 wounded Bosche in the village & a Bosche D*ʳ *& two students looking after them. The Bosche D*ʳ *was quite a nice chap, & told me "Tonight I am your prisoner but probably tomorrow you will be mine" however we still hold the village & I suppose he is on his way to Donnington Hall.*[2]
The Battle of Loos was nothing to this and you cannot imagine the noise stink or number of dead about. It is awful, & rather gets on ones nerves. However we have another go tonight, & I hope after that the Division will have a rest for a bit, for the men are done. You will be glad to hear Gordon Marsh has done extremely well, & I have just sent in his name for an "immediate award" of a Military Cross. I sent him out with a small party to capture a wood which he did & consolidated the position & held on to it for 48 hours under intense shell fire until he was relieved. It was a plucky bit of work. The Bosche have got some fresh troops here & a very different lot to those we were up against 10 days ago. These blighters do know the way to fight & whats more are putting up a jolly fine fight, but from what we gather from prisoners they think they will be beaten now, & never realized how many guns & men we had. I got my first batch of Derby Recruits yesterday, & am not favourably impressed with them, but shall know more about them by this time tomorrow. Please give my love to Chips.[3]

        Kind regards to Mrs Pearson

            Believe me

              *Y*ʳˢ *ever*

            Charles Bartlett

and you cannot imagine the noise
stink or number of dead about. It is

1 **Sir Arthur Pearson**, *(opposite, top)*, as well as being Charles's chief at the National Institution for the Blind was **Gordon Marsh★**'s uncle by marriage. **Lady Ethel Pearson**, 45, *(opposite, bottom*, in her younger days) was the sister of Gordon's mother, and indeed it is likely that this connection with the Pearsons through to Charles Bartlett had led to Gordon being commissioned into the 8th Royal Berkshires, hence the report on him in this letter. Gordon Marsh★ would receive his MC in the 1917 New Year's Honours, Sir Arthur having been made a Baronet in the Birthday Honours in June, and Lady Ethel would become a Dame in the 1920 Birthday Honours for her work with St Dunstan's. Sir Arthur Pearson died in 1921 after slipping in his bath before breakfast and hitting his head on the taps.

2 **Donington Hall** near Derby was being used to house POWs. It is now the HQ of Norton Motorcycles, right next to the Donington Park motor racing circuit.

3 **'Chips'** was the nickname of Sir Arthur Pearson's personal assistant, **Gladys Mace**, 26. She would soon be delivering an invitation to join St Dunstan's to a young officer blinded by a bullet the day after this letter, a young officer who she would go on to marry and who at the age of 24 would take over as Chairman of St Dunstan's after Sir Arthur's death. She and Ian Fraser (later Baron Fraser of Lonsdale) would share the helm of St Dunstan's for 52 years.

| | | | | | | | | | 19|00| | | | | | | 20|00| |

DAY
351
SUN

23 JUL 1916

Item 273
Letter to Margaret

Envelope
28 Tite Street
Chelsea
London

Forwarded to:
Hotel Imperial
Hythe
Kent

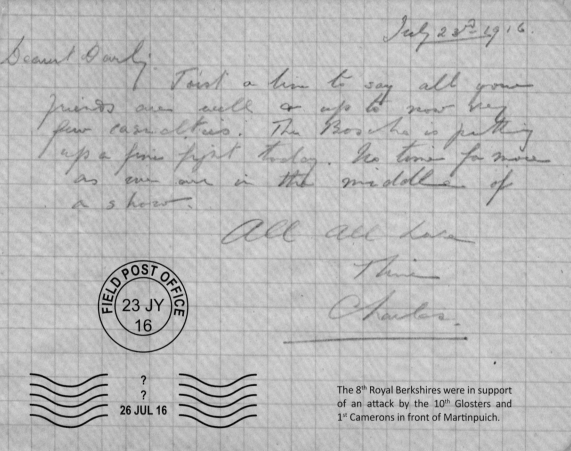

July 23rd 1916.

Dearest Darby

Just a line to say all your friends are well & up to now very few casualties. The Bosche is putting up a fine fight today. No time for more as ever are in the middle of a show.

All all love

Thine

Charles.

FIELD POST OFFICE
23 JY 16

? ?
26 JUL 16

The 8th Royal Berkshires were in support of an attack by the 10th Glosters and 1st Camerons in front of Martinpuich.

tomorrow. Please give my love to Chips
Kind regards to Mr Pearson
Believe me
yrs ever
Charles Bartlett

DAY
352
MON

24 JUL 1916

Item 274
Letter to Margaret

Envelope
28 Tite Street
Chelsea
London

Forwarded to:
Hotel Imperial
Hythe
Kent

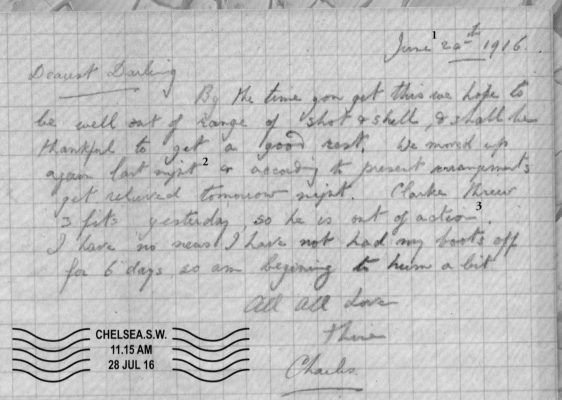

June 20th 1916. [1]

Dearest Darling

By the time you get this we hope to be well out of range of shot & shell, & shall be thankful to get a good rest. We moved up again last night [2] & according to present arrangements get relieved tomorrow night. Clarke threw 3 fits yesterday, so he is out of action. [3] I have no news. I have not had my boots off for 6 days, so am beginning to hum a bit.

All all love

thine

Charles

CHELSEA.S.W.
11.15 AM
28 JUL 16

1 From the postmark, it's July.

2 They were back in the front line at Contalmaison.

3 **Wilfrid Clarke ★**, *(left)*, was back from being wounded in November, but the damage to his neck must have caused more damage than was realised, & the rigours of active service had jiggered things up and caused him to fit. He would not serve in the trenches again, becoming an instructor in a Physical Training & Bayonet Fighting School *(as above)* – no doubt a relief to his wife who was now 5 months pregnant.

1900   2000

Letter missing from
Margaret's numbered sequence

DAY
356
FRI

28 JUL 1916

Item 275
Letter to Margaret

Envelope
28 Tite Street
Chelsea
London

FIELD POST OFFICE
28 JY
16

July 28th 1916

Dearest Darling

   Many thanks for your letter rec[d] this morning saying you had got as far as Hythe.[1] I seem to be busier than ever now we are all out at rest. We can just hear the booming of the guns & that is all. Yesterday we had an afternoon in AMIENS. The General, and 3 C.O.'s and old Clowes. Clowes & I lost the General soon after we got there & had a most amusing time & many champagne cocktails before dinner, & then we all dined together & came home. It was some dinner but there was no DM. The General was in great form. Today Dug Cloake Lawrence, Phillips, Robinson & 4 others have gone in to have a good dinner. We were all just like school boys yesterday & thoroughly enjoyed ourselves.

Outside my tent I have a little pen with 4 chickens inside. I got 2 dead ones yesterday & 4 alive so hope to get 2 meals without meat. I hear that the push is going on until the end of Sept, which is not very pleasant. Also I now have the strongest Batt[n] in the Bde, which is rather a nuisance as it means first go. I had a draft of 50 men yesterday all of whom were slightly wounded on July 1st, so they have not had a very long holiday. If you can find Footman[2] or Beale,[3] go & see them, they are such nice lads & have done so well. I miss them very much as they were d-d good officers. Well Dearest

I have no other news.

   All All Love

   Thine

   xxx Charles xxx

1 As written on the previous letter's envelope, Margaret had been staying at the Hotel Imperial in **Hythe** (on the Kent coast). There she would have often been reminded of the war, as the town was home to the School of Musketry (so named until 1919 even though the Army had swapped muskets for rifles over 50 years before). The School moved to Warminster in 1969 but the Army still uses the firing ranges and even now you can often hear the pop pop of shooting when on the seafront.

2 **David Footman** had bits of high explosive shell in his right forearm and hand, with some pieces still needing removing even in December.

3 Capt **Cyril Beale**, 27, *(right)*, from Bournemouth, was from the family that owned Beales, said to be the first department store in the country to have its own Santa. The tradition had started in 1885, and Cyril became the first Father Christmas to arrive anywhere by plane *(above)* after he took over Advertising and Events in 1912. Joining the Battalion as a 2Lt in October 1915, he was soon a company commander. On 26th July a shrapnel splinter had cut into his upper left arm and chest, and nerve damage would leave him with numb fingers & thumb. Over the next 3 years he would be assessed by medical boards in London, Bournemouth, Aldershot, two camps in Wiltshire, & Norwich, before at last being released as unfit by the Army in 1919. He had married in 1917, and returned to the family business, had 3 children and became President of both Bournemouth's Chamber of Trade and its Rotary Club. Beales department store still had 22 branches in 2020 before Covid-19 accelerated their closure.

Item 276
Letter to Margaret

Envelope
28 Tite Street
Chelsea
London

Forwarded to:
Calvados
Hythe
Kent

July 29th 1916

Dearest Darling

> *Many thanks for two letters rec^d today, and glad you are having some summer weather. Here the weather is just beautiful, & if it wasn't for the fact that sooner or later we have to go back into the "inferno" life could hardly be more pleasant. I have lost touch with the Scrub which is a pity. I really could not put up with being his junior so have become a Lieut Colonel again, which I am sure will amuse you. Dug is now 2nd in Command, so it is a nice little syndicate. I have no other news & am supposed to be patronising some sports, so better toddle off there.*

All All All Love

> *Thine*
>
> *Charles*

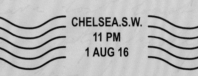

FIELD POST OFFICE
29 JY 16

CHELSEA.S.W.
11 PM
1 AUG 16

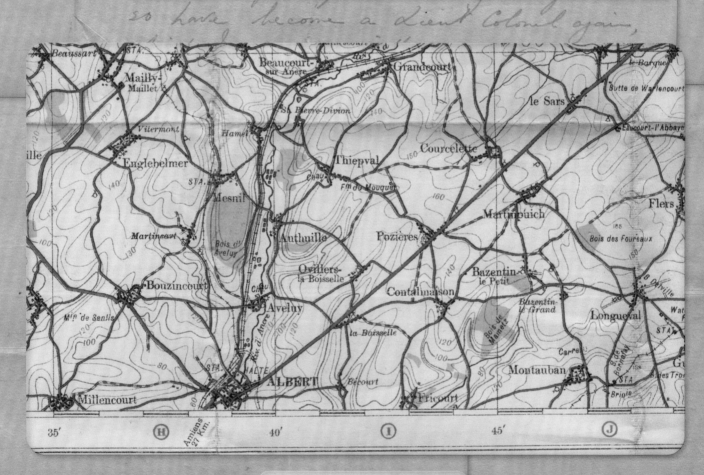

Item 277
Letter to Margaret

Envelope
*28 Tite Street
Chelsea
London*

*Forwarded to:
Calvados
Hythe
Kent*

Aug 1ˢᵗ[1] 1916

Dearest Darling

Many thanks for your letter, but so far no photo has arrived. The weather here is simply gorgeous, & today being Sunday we are doing very little work. We had a little dinner party last night. Clowes, Col Sutherland & Hatfield[2] the vet coming to dinner, & the menu consisted of Lentil Soup, Fried fillets of Sole & Shrimp Sauce, Devilled Chicken & fresh Peas, Duck Paté & salade, Stewed Currants & Cream and Caviar on Toast. Tenants Lager Beer & Port. We had the band to play which consists of about 5 fifes & 3 drums, but is rapidly growing again. The whole show was quite a success. On the 4ᵗʰ there is a divisional horse show. I shall show Punch & poor old Ronnies horse,[3] but dont expect Punch will do anything as he is badly marked at present. If there is a jumping competition I ought to nearly win it on Ronnies old horse.
The Brigade sports went off very well, but my lot did not do very well, only getting one first prize two 2ⁿᵈ & three 3ʳᵈ.
There is no news, I have been wracking my brains for the last 10 minutes, so with all all all Love, I remain

Thine

Charles

CHELSEA.S.W.
8 PM
2 AUG 16

FIELD POST OFFICE
30 JY
16

1 From the postmark it is 30ᵗʰ July, which fits with his mention of it being Sunday.

2 Capt **Robert Hadfield**, 45, of the Army Veterinary Corps, had been out since June 1915 and at this time was serving with 1ˢᵗ Division. An unsung but vital part of the Army, the vets must have been stretched to breaking point, with their unit war diaries showing a continual catalogue of large numbers of sick and wounded horses. Robert Hadfield was out in France to the very end of the war, and then returned to his wife and daughter and took up a veterinary practice in the Lake District. His First World War campaign medals came up at auction in 1997 but did not sell.

Nine days before this letter Robert's brother Charles had been killed after falling under the wheels of a motor-lorry in Manchester despite its speed being no more than 4 miles an hour (this being not long after the loss of Charles's son James who fell ill while serving in Salonika & died of appendicitis in Alexandria in March, aged 19).

3 Ronald Brakspear★'s horse, *(above)*, went by the name of Topsy.

DAY 360 TUE

1 AUG 1916

Item 278
Letter to Margaret

Envelope
28 Tite Street
Chelsea
London

Forwarded to:
Calvados
Hythe
Kent

FIELD POST OFFICE
1 AU 16

Aug 1st 1916

Dearest Darling

I am that busy I simply have no time for letter writing. What with Inspections and Training one is busier than when fighting Bosche. Yesterday we had Divisional Commander & today the Corps Commander.[1] Started this morning at 6.30. We may be going to AMIENS[2] for dinner tonight, that is if we can get a car. Your photo has just arrived for which very many thanks and it is I think very good. I will take it with me wherever I go. The Follies[3] came & gave a show last night from 6 – 8 pm after which the Brigade had a dinner party of 18 which was quite amusing. No more officers have arrived yet which seems a pity as I am badly in need of them.

I am still addressing to Tite Street, so let me know when to alter.

All All All Love

Thine

With many thanks

Charles

CHELSEA.S.W.
2.15 PM
4 AUG 16

1 The Commander of III Corps was Lt-Gen **Sir William Pulteney**, 55, *(below)*. A highly respected officer who had been C.O. of 1st Scots Guards during the Boer War, he led III Corps from August 1914 until February 1918 when the strain started to tell on him. He would marry for the first time in 1917 aged 56 and serve as Black Rod, responsible for the buildings & services of the Houses of Parliament, from 1920 to 1941. Tributes to 'Putty' after his death recalled his sense of duty but also the joy he brought with his infectious laughter.

2 Amiens was 17 miles from their location in Albert.

3 The Follies, *(above)*, was the theatre troupe of 47th Division who started giving concert parties in February 1916. The leading 'lady' was Corporal Leslie Ward, 23, who would lose his left hand in the German Spring Offensive in 1918.

Aug 2nd 1916

Dearest Darling

　　　　This "rest cure" is getting rather strenuous. I was out with the Coys until midnight last night, & this morning we were out from 7.30 – 12 midday, C.O.'s conference from 2.15 – 3.30, and now we have to go & practice the attack from 5.30 to 9.30 pm, after which we do it again in the dark from 1.30 am to 4.30 am, & tomorrow afternoon another Divisional scheme from 1.30 pm to 8 pm, so we are busy some. I got a short note from you this morning but cannot read your address so please write it more plainly.

The weather is still beautiful, and a little less work, & a motor to get about in life would be delightful. Dug is in tremendous form just now. I had a nice parcel from Cuckoo[1] this morning, if you are writing please thank him, I shall not have a moment today or tomorrow.

　　　　All All Love

　　　　Thine

　　　　Charles

CHELSEA.S.W.
9.15 AM
7 AUG 16

---

1 Charles's nephew's widow thought that Charles was known as **Cuckoo** but this shows it can't have been him, and, if it was the nickname of one of the brothers, by a process of elimination it must be John.

Aug 3rd 1916

Dearest Darling

　　　　Many thanks for your letter. You are wrong, we are still at rest & hope to be for another 7 or 8 days. You see we had a very long spell in before. Got home this morning at 5 am after doing a good nights work. We are out again now 1.15 pm to 8.30 pm & are going to have a dinner party tonight when we get in. No time for more.

　　　　All Love

　　　　Thine

　　　　Charles

CHELSEA.S.W.
11.30 AM
7 AUG 16

DAY
361
WED

2 AUG 1916

Item 279
Letter to Margaret

Envelope
28 Tite Street
Chelsea
London

Forwarded to:
Calvados
Hythe
Kent

FIELD POST OFFICE
3 AU
16

DAY
362
THU

3 AUG 1916

Item 280
Letter to Margaret

Envelope
28 Tite Street
Chelsea
London

Forwarded to:
Calvados
Hythe
Kent

Item 281
Letter to Margaret

Envelope
*28 Tite Street
Chelsea
London*

*Forwarded to:
Calvados
Hythe
Kent*

Aug 4th 1916

Dearest Darling

    This is the last sheet of writing paper I have, so please let me have another bobs[1] worth, as none is procurable here. I rec[d] two letters this morning, & am much amused at you & Betty being run in & you will be lucky if you get off under a couple of quid.[2] I was talking to the Corps General yesterday afternoon & dont expect to go into the line for another 8 or 9 days, & then for 3 weeks, which means 2 weeks up, & 1 in Div reserve, & of the 2 weeks 1 week will be in the front line & the other in support, so it wont be too bad. However I expect we shall want reorganising a bit at the end of it. I have quite lost the Scrub, & all I know is that he is away back resting. This afternoon there is a divisional Horse show, & I am jumping poor old Ronnies horse in the jumping, & if it was not for a wall there is to be negotiated I think I might stand a chance.

Dug & I both ate something that has upset our tummies, & we were awake most of the night sympathising with one another. There is no other news. I am glad Paula has taken to bathing & enjoying it. Tell Betty I am not surprised she has to get a registration card to go to Dover,[3] the only remarkable thing is that she does not have to have one to go anywhere.

    All All Love

    Thine

    xxxxxx Charles xxxxxx

1 'Bob' is slang for a shilling.   **2** Had Margaret & Betty committed a motoring offence, to be run in by the police?   **3** The security for Dover was higher given its importance as a military gateway to France.

Item 282
Letter to Margaret

Sunday
6/8/16

Dearest Darling

    Many thanks for yours of 3rd & also one from Paula. I still dare not write to Hythe as I dont think Calvados is sufficient address. I did not write yesterday as my tummy was out of order & spent a day in bed, but am at the top of my form today. Have just eaten an enormous lunch & am preparing for sleep. Dug & Cloake have gone to "town", but I could not get a way, as there is a C.O.'s conference at 6 pm, & the bus would not get back in time. It is beautifully hot again today. Someone has started a rumour that the whole Division is going to India, but I am afraid it is too good to be true. It would just be ripping to go there for a winter nice warm climate & no shells.

However we can look forward to nothing more than 21 days in the trenches again. The news today is exceptionally good, & the Australians are doing wonderful work.[1] Thank Paula for her letter & I will write her soon.

All All All Love

Thine

Charles

CHELSEA.S.W.
5.45 PM
9 AUG 16

Envelope
28 Tite Street
Chelsea
London

Forwarded to:
Calvados
Hythe
Kent

FIELD POST OFFICE
6 AU 16

1 The Australian 2nd Division had just taken a network of German trenches east of Pozières. Even with careful preparation involving the digging of assembly trenches for an attack at dusk, the Division had had 6,848 casualties in 12 days.

July[1] 7th 1916

Dearest Darling

No letters at all today and we hear there are none for two days which is rather a blow. More good news last night namely we dont go up again until the 15th by which time I shall have a good deal more confidence in the men. Last night I dined with one of my old Colonels who is commanding a division and we had a rare old talk over old times.[2] I had not seen him since Khartoum days. We are out tonight again doing night work, and tomorrow night we hope (by we I mean the 4 Colonels Tut Tut) all to dine together in town. I am having the men inoculated again by degrees, but so far have not been done myself yet, & dont think I want to feel seedy for 2 or 3 days, & as I drink so little water, it really does not matter much.[3] We are at last getting some more tents, so if the weather does break up it wont matter. I must say we have been very lucky. I was afraid at one time I was going to lose Cloake, as he is quite up to taking a staff job, but now I hear no officers are to leave their Regiments until after the push. Well Dearest that is all.

All All All Love to you & Paula

Thine

Charles

CHELSEA.S.W.
11.15 PM
10 AUG 16

DAY 366 MON
7 AUG 1916

Item 283
Letter to Margaret

Envelope
28 Tite Street
Chelsea
London

Forwarded to:
Calvados
Hythe
Kent

FIELD POST OFFICE
7 AU 16

Charles Frederick Napier Bartlett

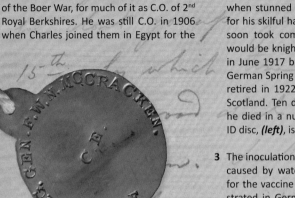

1 Actually it was 7th August (the anniversary of his original embarkation for France).

2 Maj-Gen **Frederick McCracken**, CB, DSO, 56, *(left)*, had fought in Egypt and the Sudan in the 1880s and then from beginning to end of the Boer War, for much of it as C.O. of 2nd Royal Berkshires. He was still C.O. in 1906 when Charles joined them in Egypt for the last posting of his Army career. In February 1914 his 16-year-old son fell ill and died during a visit to Switzerland. Six months later while in command of 7th Infantry Brigade at the Battle of Le Cateau he became probably the first General Officer casualty of the war when stunned by a shell but won plaudits for his skilful handling of the rearguard and soon took command of 15th Division. He would be knighted and take over XIII Corps in June 1917 but was sacked following the German Spring Offensive in 1918. He finally retired in 1922 after a period as C-in-C in Scotland. Ten days before his 90th birthday he died in a nursing home in Croydon. His ID disc, *(left)*, is in the Regimental Museum.

3 The inoculations were against typhoid fever, caused by water-borne bacteria. The idea for the vaccine had originally been demonstrated in Germany in 1896, with the first typhoid vaccinations being made in 1909, by the US Army.

Item 284
Letter to Margaret

Envelope
28 Tite Street
Chelsea
London

Forwarded to:
Calvados
Hythe
Kent

Aug 8th 1916

Dearest Darling

Just recᵈ yours of the 4th & had quite a budget of letters today Lil Flo Cuckoo Bogey Dalby all writing at once. We had a long night show last night, & this afternoon we are off to Town. The Brigade Major invited Dug too so we shall have a merry afternoon & evening. Tomorrow night we are out again all night, & it is really getting to be all night work, so we are guessing what we may expect when we get back. However sufficient unto the day etc, & we are all looking forward to a top-hole dinner. Prices here are awful, 12 francs for a tiny chicken now & eggs over 2d a time. I suppose I shall get your address some time. I dont approve of Betty toying with Canadian officers, she is too young. There is a lot of gunning going on in the distance, & the amount of ammunition being used must be enormous. Weather still beautiful. I have no more news.

All All All Love

Thine

xxxxxx Charles xxxxxx
Paula's

CHELSEA.S.W.
11.30 AM
11 AUG 16

DAY
369
THU

10 AUG 1916

Item 285
Letter to Margaret

Envelope
28 Tite Street
Chelsea
London

Forwarded to:
Calvados
Hythe
Kent

Aug 10th 1916

Dearest Darling

   Many thanks for yours of the 7th. The post is very curious as I have had your letters, & no one else, except those who hear from Folkestone, have had any, so there is some good reason for you to stay there. The weather has broken at last but the rain is rather welcome, as the dust was getting too awful for words. We are still very busy either doing attacks by day or by night, and when not practising one is out looking at the ground, so one has not a minute. Dug was out with me this afternoon, & we were riding back to camp, when as Dug puts it he meant to go one way & his horse another, and the horse won, so Dug I found in a hedge. However no bones broken. Have just heard of Bertie Hendersons death, he married Dorothy's sister, it really is awful.[1] *This way the Bosche has been quieter the last 36 hours, but seems to be massing a lot of men in front of us. The Brigadier's horse came down with him, & he is laid up with a strained ankle. I heard from Pat Walton the other day the first time in ages.*[2] *We are just off to practise another form of attack, & are using trench mortars, rifle grenades bombs etc & if someone does not get damaged I shall be much surprised.*[3]

  All All All Love

  Thine in haste

 xxxxxx Charles xxxxxx
   Paula's

CHELSEA.S.W.
11.30 AM
14 AUG 16

FIELD POST OFFICE
10 AU
16

1 **Albert Henderson**, 46, *(right)*, appears with Charles's brother Edward in the Bucks Militia photo that is on p.406 along with details of the Rose family. His wife Mary was the sister of brother Edward's widow Dorothy. He had been in France with the 10th Royal Warwicks since July 1915, was awarded the MC in June 1916, and took command when his C.O. was wounded during their first attack on the Somme on 3rd July. They were under heavy shellfire on 23rd July when at 9.45 a.m. he was killed. His wife was working in a YMCA near Le Havre at the time. She was initially awarded a pension of £140 a year & a gratuity of £300 but after some wrangling about what rank he actually held, this was changed to the rate for a Lt Col, £180 a year plus £450 (though he's on the Thiepval Memorial as a Major). He had not been invested with his MC and in line with the King's recent decision that in such cases the next-of-kin should receive the insignia, his wife was offered the option of a parade with a General but instead chose to have his MC sent to her in the post.

2 This is the last mention of my Gran, Patricia Walton. I don't know if they ever met again.

3 Hand thrown grenades had the disadvantages of a short range and great risk to the throwers. Weapons had therefore been developed that infantry could use to provide their own local fire support without having to communicate with the far distant artillery. A trench mortar was a tube on a base-plate aimed upwards with a bipod & could fire up to 25 5-kg bombs a minute a distance of up to 700 metres. A rifle grenade included a rod that fitted down the barrel of a rifle and could be fired up to 200 metres. I have seen men listed as casualties during training, and with the imperfections of the kit and a lack of the modern concern for health & safety, men must have been getting damaged when practising all the time.

Aug 11th 1916

Dearest Darling

Many thanks for two letters written on the 8th & 9th. I like the way you say use my brain. How was I to know that CALVADOS was such a well known house in HYTHE that the name of the road was not required. However I suppose since you & Betty have been there it has attained some reputation.

This is a strenuous rest but the men are getting very fit and I feel confident we shall put up a good show, which is more than I thought a fortnight ago. Tonight we are having another camp concert, & tomorrow Regimental sports, which I think will about complete our training. The Italians seem to be doing well.[1] I quite remember your birthday is the 23rd, & will try & find you a blouse or something if I get into AMIENS again. We are having another practice with Trench Mortars again this afternoon, it was quite good fun yesterday & no one was damaged exactly why I cannot tell you, as lumps fell all over the place. Let me know if you hear any more of the Scrub. I am hoping leave will open up again in about a months time in which case Cloake & Dug have to go & then I shall consider it my turn.

All All All Love

Thine

xxxxxx Charles xxxxxx
Paula

[1] On 6th August the Italians had launched an offensive in what became known as the Sixth Battle of Isonzo. It would be counted a victory as they captured the town of Gorizia (near today's border with Slovenia), but with 21,000 dead versus 8,000 Austrians killed, it came at a cost.

Saturday

Dearest Darling

No letter from you this morning. Am still very busy & may have to go up to the line tomorrow to have a look round to see where we go when we move up on Monday night. I hope not as I was looking forward to having a last dinner in the town. We had a most successful concert last night, & are having sports this afternoon, and all the men are having final baths & clean clothes tomorrow, which will be the last they will get for three weeks. The heat gets more every day & I expect the smell will be fairly strong.

I found we've a very good comic singer last night, one of the new draft, so good is he that I am leaving him out of the trenches. Well Dearest I have no more news.

All All All Love

Thine

Charles

FIELD POST OFFICE
12 AU 16

14.9.16.[1]

Dearest Darling

     Many thanks for writing paper. Yesterday after church parade Dug Self Cloake the D^r & Phillips[2] all went into Town & had lunch, which was quite nice.

Have just had a storm, the first we have had since we came out of the line, it was rather welcome as it will lay the dust for the march up this evening. We are in reserve the first few days, & after all we may not be in the line for as long as we thought we should have to be.

I am awfully sorry about Renée's brother,[3] & will write to her when I get up.

Also poor Louie will be very upset. However, on the whole things look brighter, & the Bosche cant stand the strain much longer, the great thing being to dodge them until they do give up. Well Dearest I have no more news.

All All All Love

Thine

xxxxxx Charles xxxxxx

DAY **373** MON
14 AUG 1916

Item 288
Letter to Margaret

Envelope
Calvados
Hythe
Kent

FIELD POST OFFICE
14 AU 16

1 Actually 14th August (he mentions having church parade the day before, i.e. on a Sunday, so this is a Monday, and 14th September 1916 was a Thursday).

2 Lt **Frederick Phillips**, 39, *(right)*, had been born in Dublin to a Scottish father & a Welsh mother. He'd served through the Boer War as a private in the Imperial Yeomanry and then stayed on in South Africa, finishing as a Lt in the Transvaal Mounted Rifles, having fought in the Zululand Rebellion of 1906. In 1914 he was a metallurgist working with cyanide to extract gold, and arrived back in England to join up in October. He went to France in January 1915 as a private in the 6th Inniskilling Dragoons and was commissioned into the 8th Royal Berkshires in October whilst in hospital with lumbago. He took over the Battalion Transport after Loos & also trained the pipers and drummers of the Battalion band. →**401**

3 With thousands of casualties occurring at this time, this mention of Renée's brother does not give much of a further clue about Renée's identity.

Charles Frederick Napier Bartlett

DAY
375
WED
16 AUG 1916

Item 289
Letter to Margaret

Envelope
Calvados
Hythe
Kent

FIELD POST OFFICE
16 AU
16

16.9.16[1]

Dearest Darling

Had no letter from you for two days. We arrived up here in reserve last night. It is not a nice spot, as outside it is decidedly unhealthy on account of shells, & inside there is a plague of flies, and it is also infernally damp; however we must expect these things in the big push?

We got in yesterday without any casualties but soaked to the skin. This morning I have been round our front line, it is a curious position in one place we are in the same trench as the Bosche he holding one bit, & us the other, and I guess he will have to go. There is a rumour that we are only in for 10 days, but even if were true, it might be an unmixed blessing, as there are worse places. However I am an optimist at present, & think that anything might happen any time as Austria cannot stand the strain much longer, & if she gives in the end must be in sight. The C.O. I relieved yesterday was a pal of Scrubs[2] but I have lost sight of the latter, but I expect by this time he is having another go somewhere. At the present moment the D^r & the Adjutant are slapping flies by thousands which are falling & sticking in my hair.

Love to Betty & All All Love to you & Paula

Thine

Charles

1 From the postmark it's actually 16.8.16.

2 Scrub's pal was Lt Col **Charles Collison**, DSO, 45, (**left**, in 1915), the C.O. of 11th Royal Warwicks. An ex-regular who had retired as a Captain in 1911, he is notable for being the first battalion C.O. to publish his memoirs after the war (with a mention of *'Lt Col Bartlett'* for this handover). After over 3 months on the Somme, he would be invalided out on 25th September, with his medical officer saying he needed a complete change and a rest. When he died in 1935 (of a heart attack on his local golf course), his obituary was written by the man who had taken over as his Signalling Officer just five days before this letter of Charles's. This was a certain **A A Milne** (right, then aged 34, and already an established writer), & I can imagine that Charles must have met him, albeit briefly, during the handover of the Battalion HQs. It would be 3 months later that Milne himself would be invalided home with trench fever, and 10 years before the first appearance of *Winnie the Pooh* in print. Milne's obituary of Collison showed a great love for his old colonel and his eccentricities, including his fastidiousness and *'humorous detached irony'*. This is no better illustrated than by Collison's description of the latest fashion in officers' caps (as worn by Milne, **below**) as being *'a cross between that usually to be seen on the heads of Breton onion-sellers and a mufti cap after being worried by a bull-pup and then thrown in a pond.'* ➔ 393 Collison

17th Aug. 1916

Dearest Darling

So far all's well. We are not very comfortable but still cheerful. I wont write more as I doubt if the orderly will be able to get through with this, & there is no news.   All All Love

Thine

Charles

x x x Paulas   x x x yours

No letter from you, but none for anyone these days.

DAY 376 THU

17 AUG 1916

Item 290
Letter to Margaret

Envelope
*Calvados
Hythe
Kent*

19th August 1916

Dearest Darling

Rec[d] your letter of the 14th in the middle of a push yesterday.[1] We were in a bad way being sent forward before we were ready & lost a good many. Bissley,[2] Conyers[3] & Harrison[4] were killed, Stileman,[5] Prout,[6] Harvey,[7] Goodship,[8] Pitt[9] & Sumpster[10] wounded & we lost 150 other ranks killed & wounded, so I am now once more reduced to 7 officers for actual work with their companies, but hope to get some back from courses in a day or two. I am sorry you did not appreciate my joke about your birthday present, & think I am mean. However we never shall agree on that point.

Col Longridge[11] the Chief Staff Officer of the Division was killed yesterday, & each Batt[n] in our Brigade has suffered pretty badly.

We are all pretty tired, but hope to be relieved tomorrow. I have no more news. I will write and wish you many happy returns tomorrow.

All All All Love

Thine

xxxxxx Charles xxxxxx

DAY 378 SAT

19 AUG 1916

Item 291
Letter to Margaret

Envelope
*Calvados
Hythe
Kent*

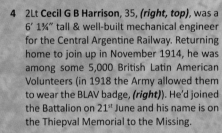

1   They had attacked just north of Bazentin-le-Petit. Details are in the report that follows.

2   2Lt **William Bissley★**, 28, *(left, top)*, was a school teacher from Maidenhead. His wallet was removed from his body and returned to his wife, but his remains were never recovered and his name is on the Thiepval Memorial to the Missing.

3   2Lt **Walter Neville Conyers**, 26, *(left, below)*, was born into a family that had lived in Bermuda for some 300 years. After finishing his schooling in Canada he stayed to start work in banking & insurance before returning to Bermuda in 1913 and enlisting from there in 1915. After joining the Battalion on 25th June, he'd been knocked out for 3 hours when a bullet hit his steel helmet in July, and then was killed in August. His name is on the Thiepval Memorial to the Missing. His nephew was named Walter Neville Conyers in his memory and kept this photograph of his soldier uncle on his desk. Also kept was his uncle's swagger stick (as held in the photograph) which lived atop the fridge and was brought out when his children misbehaved, leading to chases around the kitchen as they tried to avoid its lashes. ➜394

4   2Lt **Cecil G B Harrison**, 35, *(right, top)*, was a 6' 1¾" tall & well-built mechanical engineer for the Central Argentine Railway. Returning home to join up in November 1914, he was among some 5,000 British Latin American Volunteers (in 1918 the Army allowed them to wear the BLAV badge, *(right)*). He'd joined the Battalion on 21st June and his name is on the Thiepval Memorial to the Missing.

5   Lt **Donald Stileman★** was wounded the day before his 22nd birthday. He is pictured *(right, bottom)* with his intrepid father, a bishop & missionary. A bullet in the right arm left him with a *'dud hand'* but he would go on to be an inspiration to his family and to me.

6   2Lt **Douglas Prout**, 25, was grandson of an internationally-known pioneer of scientific farming methods such as the cultivation of heavy clay soils using chemical fertilisers. After school Douglas started out in banking, but was soon touring the country as an actor in repertory theatre, appearing in Belfast, Burnley, Leeds, Liverpool, Middlesbrough & at the theatre on the West Pier in Brighton (later a set for *'Oh! What a Lovely War'*). He'd joined the Battalion on 2nd April and his wound on 18th August must have been minor because he was soon back in action.

7 2Lt **Stanley Harvey**, 22, the only child of a London schoolmaster, had arrived in France in May, not long after the death of his mother. A bullet had entered the inner side of his left arm and exited at the back just above the elbow, amazingly without hitting any bone. The inflammation and nerve damage would take time to heal, so it wasn't until late 1917 that he returned to the Battalion. During the German Spring Offensive in 1918, he led a charge along a trench against an enemy bombing party & was shot dead at the same instant as he fired point blank at a German.

8 2Lt **Gilbert Goodship**, 27, *(left, top)*, had been hit by a bullet in the chest which missed his lung but then cut into his right arm. He'd be back in France in April 1917. ➔ **396**

9 2Lt **Douglas Pitt**, 24, *(left, bottom)*, a bank clerk, had first gone to France in October 1915 as a private in the Honourable Artillery Company, with some time spent providing the guard for General Sir Douglas Haig's HQ. After seven weeks at Cadet School, his commission in the 8th Royal Berkshires was gazetted on 2nd August. He arrived with the Battalion on 4th August, was wounded while on fatigue on 17th August and died in hospital on 24th August. His last letter home includes this ***drawing*** of his right collar badge (he was still revelling in its newness) & he asks if his father wants a fountain pen for his birthday on the 17th. Instead his father would receive Douglas's effects, including his dentures.

10 2Lt **Frank Sumpster**★, 28, *(right, top)*, had a gunshot wound to the shoulder. He would return in October 1917, but was killed on the first day of the German Spring Offensive in 1918, leaving a month-old daughter.

11 Lt Col **James Longridge**, CMG, 41, *(right, centre)*, was the grandson of the inventor of a barrel design used in all guns above 3-inch calibre in the Royal Navy. He'd left a desk job at the India Office to go on active service in France & had been Chief of Staff of 1st Division since July 1915. His body was brought back and buried in Albert & his ***gravestone*** bears the badge of his Indian Army regiment, the 43rd Erinpura. His family dedicated a shrine to him in St Paul's Church, Exeter, in 1917. That church was pulled down in 1936 and its site is now under a vast shopping centre. His brother Archibald, an army chaplain, died in October 1918 of pneumonia following gas poisoning and influenza.

Item 292
*Report by Charles
(from the
Battalion's
War Diary)*

<u>*APPENDIX NO. 3.*</u>

*ACCOUNT OF THE OPERATIONS BY THE
8th (SER) BATT. ROYAL BERKSIRE REGIMENT
ON THE AFTERNOON OF THE 18th AUGUST 1916.*

1. *During the relief our Artillery bombarded our front line so as to make intercommunication between the Companies impossible. LANCS TRENCH from S.2.c.9.2. to S.2.c.8.3. was badly knocked in and this prevented our platoon which was to attack from 70TH AVENUE from getting into position and also prevented us from occupying LANCS SAP. An attempt was made to get some men across this portion of trench by crawling but was unsuccessful owing to the activity of enemy snipers. The trench at S.2.d.3. was also flattened, burying most of one platoon and a machine gin section and making communication between the two companies impossible. The third Company on the right of the road at S.2.d.6.2. got into position without casualties.*

2. *At 2-45 p.m. the three Companies did a frontal attack on the enemy's Intermediate Line. The report of the Officer Commanding the left Company who returned wounded was to the effect that the smoke sent out by the 15th Division blew across our front so that they could not tell in which direction they were going. The remains of the Company afterwards joined up with those that were left of the other two Companies who had reached a shallow trench about 100 yards in front of out front line and had started to consolidate, it being impossible for them to progress further owing to machine gun fire. Captain BIRCH was the only Officer with this party and he tried to hold on to the trench with the men he had but was very heavily shelled and forced to retire to our own line again.*

The failure to reach the objective seems to have been due to

(1) Lack of time for sufficient organization and for all ranks to get some knowledge of the ground.

(2) The intensity of the enemy's machine gun fire which caused many casualties especially in the right company.

(3) The loss of so many Officers.

C Bartlett, Lieut Colonel
Commanding 8th Royal Berkshire Regt.

On the ***map opposite*** you can see Lancs Trench (where they were shelled by their own artillery), Lancs Sap and the Intermediate Line marked up (the first two being in grid square S.2.c, with the Intermediate Line crossing right over into grid square S.2.d).

DAY
380
MON

21 AUG 1916

Item 293
Letter to Margaret

Envelope
Calvados
Hythe
Kent

FIELD POST OFFICE
21 AU
16

21/7/16[1]

Dearest Darling

    This is to wish you very many happy returns of the day, & to hope we shall spend the next one together. Last night we got out of the front line, & are now back in reserve, & I doubt very much if we go up again until we are made up again. We lost Bissley, Harrison & Conyers & Joy[2] killed; Stileman, Pitt, Harvey, Prout, Goodship, Sumpster, & a Cadet officer (who had just arrived & dont know his name[3]) wounded. So I now have 7 company officers left instead of 24, 7 Sergeants instead of 32, and 13 corporals instead of 32 and altogether 350 instead of a 1000, so the outlook is not very promising as God only knows where the officers & NCOs are coming from. However I suppose with a little sleep we shall cheer up. The last place was quite the hottest corner we have yet struck. There was no outstanding feature on anyone's part. I am very sorry for Mrs Bissley, as I think he had only been home once since he was married, & was well overdue for leave.[4] I hope you will have rec^d the birthday present alright. Gerrard has lost my washing things, but have got another supply & I am now going to shave & wash the first time I have touched water for 5 days. I have also sent for my bath which I propose to put in a shell hole, & have a good wash but that wont be up until tomorrow. Many thanks for Paula's photo I will write to her soon. It is a great pity one has not a camera here as the sights have to be seen.[5] I hope Johns tea party was a success. We ate two tinned ducks & a tinned chicken when we got out last night, which he had sent us, & they were mighty good. You & Betty seem to be having a good time, for which I am very thankful, & only hope I shall be home before you break up the party. There seems to be some fuss going on over the Chelsea Pensioners, does it affect the General in any way.[6]

The authorities have now ruled that Dalby has substantive rank, so if he comes back I shall once more find myself a Major, but I think it is extremely doubtful.[7] However it is a bit of a strain during this heavy fighting and might be much safer if he did. Well Dearest I have no more news.

      All All All Love

      Thine

      Charles

1 From the postmark & content it's 21/8/16.

2 2Lt **Edward S Joy**, 25, *(left)*, was the son of the Yorkshire Post's commercial manager in London. He ended his school days in a Jesuit college in Bruges before joining the colonial department of an employers' liability insurers.

Having gone out to reconnoitre on the 20th he was shot in the head. He managed to continue only to be shot again. One of his men tried to bring him back in and two others volunteered to go out and help but it was too risky to let them do so once they heard for sure he was dead. His youngest brother George had been badly wounded on 1st July, but would live until 1974. ➔ 397

3 The cadet officer is not in the war diary.

4 **William Bissley★**'s wedding had been in December & his only leave after his honeymoon was a few days in April. What Charles would not have known was that, as he wrote this letter, William's wife Muriel was in labour, and Will & Mu's only child Betty, *(right)*, would be born the following day. Charles's letter to William Bissley's family was quoted in the local paper: *'By his death the Regiment has lost a plucky and very popular officer and his work during the fighting is deserving of high praise. We all feel we have lost a brave and true friend.'* His wife never re-married and lived to see 4 grandchildren and 8 great-grand-children (and they have since been followed by 14 great-great-grandchildren).

5 It was against orders for British soldiers to have cameras on active service. Even those who broke the rules tended to take pictures that shielded those at home from the reality of what was going on. The truest representation that I have seen of the horrors of the war is in the often shocking stereoscopic photographs in the Museum at Sanctuary Wood near Ypres.

6 The current fuss was about servicemen's pensions in general, not just the Chelsea Pensioners for whom General Crutchley was responsible. Parliament was debating who should pay for topping up the standard pension in cases where wounds had led to a need for greater aid, whether this should fall to the State or to private charities. In the face of strong opposition the government conceded to its duty.

7 Dalby having 'substantive rank' meant that he was a permanent Lt Col. Each Battalion had a fixed establishment of the different ranks it was allowed (which included only one Lt Col), so with Dalby still on the books of the Battalion despite being wounded, it meant that Charles was currently only a temporary Lt Col.

Item 294
Letter to Margaret

Envelope
Calvados
Hythe
Kent
(no date or postmark but must have been enclosed with another letter around this time as her 28th birthday was on 23rd August)

Charles Frederick Napier Bartlett

DAY 382 WED

23 AUG 1916

Item 295
Letter to Margaret

Envelope
Calvados
Hythe
Kent

FIELD POST OFFICE
24 AU 16

23.8.16.

Dearest Darling

Rec^d your letter of the 18th yesterday, but could not get any letters away, so did not write, at least to you as I have had so many letters to write to parents etc, and am very busy making up stories or rather putting stories into military language to obtain some immediate awards for the men who have done well. The three men who got the Distinguished Conduct Medal in the first fight all got hit last time, also the two who had earned it before, which was bad luck.[1] I think we shall be going up to hold the line again for 4 or 5 days after which the whole Brigade will go back into reserve for 4 or 5 days, and then the whole Division will come out of the fighting, and reorganize in peace & quietness. I am glad Doll met Florrie, but am sorry if Paula is going to be like Helen as I was hoping for better things.[2] I have not written Renee yet, & I think will leave it for a bit under the circumstances.

Today is your birthday, & I am thinking of you, & wishing you many happy returns. Bless you. I suppose you will be able to beat me at golf when we get back. I had a bath this morning in the open outside my dug out, ready to run in at the first shell arriving, but none came. All All All Love

Thine

xxxxxx Charles xxxxxx

---

1 The DCM men from the first fight were Lainsbury, Musto & Hayward. Those who had earned it before that must have been serving with other units (& maybe even in the Boer War) before joining the 8th Royal Berkshires.

2 It sounds as if Margaret's sister Dolly had met Charles's sister Florrie for the first time. Florrie's eldest daughter **Helen**, 14, would go on to found a company of Girl Guides and marry an officer who'd been wounded in the

war and who would retire as a Lt Col after the Second World War to become secretary of Northants County Cricket Club.

B.E.F.[1]

25./8./16[2]

Dearest Darling

I received yours of the 21st this morning and as you say you dont seem to have much news. About letting the house for the winter will the Vaughans take it on or to whom will you let it? as I should think it would be difficult. What has happened to William Clowes, is he going to be called up?[3] and surely by this time Malcolm ought to have had another examination. The weather here is beautiful & now we have cleaned the place up a bit, if it was not for the noise life would not be so bad. A heavy bombardment has just started & the Bosche is sure to retaliate in a few minutes, so I will get the orderly off with this while I can & then retire to my cave.

All All All Love

Thine

xxxxxx Charles xxxxxx

DAY 383 THU

24 AUG 1916

Item 296
Letter to Margaret

Envelope
Calvados
Hythe
Kent

FIELD POST OFFICE
24 AU 16

---

1 B.E.F. = British Expeditionary Force, i.e. the British Army on the Western Front.

2 Probably the 24th, from the postmark.

3 The rules had changed to include conscription of married men up to the age of 41. Margaret's brother-in-law William Clowes was 3 weeks short of his 41st birthday. I have not found any sign of him doing any military service. He

was a banker which should not have been an occupation to give him protected status and an exemption. Processing all the applicants for exemptions was a massive undertaking. There were 2,086 Military Service Tribunals formed around the country and by the end of June 1916, 748,587 had applied to them, only just less than the roughly 770,000 who joined the Army during the same period. Proceedings of the tribunals were reported in

the local papers so the public could see who had been exempted and either understand why those men were not in uniform or give them a hard time if they did not approve of the reason for their exemption, which could be due to the national importance of their work, or business or domestic hardship, or medical unfitness, with only about 2% of those applying for exemption doing so on the grounds of conscientious objection.

Item 297
Letter to Margaret

Envelope
Calvados
Hythe
Kent

FIELD POST OFFICE
26 AU
16

26/8/16

Dearest Darling

Have no news which is good news. We have not had a mail for two days, except one line from you which I was glad to get, but your letters are too short nowadays, are you too busy or what? There is a mail in today, but if I wait to get back to HQ for it I shall miss the post. Dug & I were discussing the question of grouse. Have you or Jim eaten any yet? Cooked I believe they travel quite well. Well we have got to get through a few more days which ought to be fairly easy & then I hope for a little peace & quietness. We had a nasty night last night & the night before, but no harm done although we had to finish our dinner underground, & instead of port we had to put on our gas helmets.[1] All in a days work.

All All All Love

Thine

Charles

P.S. I think Paula owes me a letter.

1 The **gas helmets** would have been as ***below***, just a gas-permeable hood chemically treated to filter out the nasties, with an exhaust valve fed from a mouth-held metal tube. You may have seen this very famous image before, but do you know the story of the man who took the picture? **→392 John Warwick Brooke**

DAY
386
SUN

27 AUG 1916

Item 298
Letter to Margaret

Envelope
Calvados
Hythe
Kent

FIELD POST OFFICE
28 AU
16

27/8/16

Dearest Darling

Just got a letter from you written on the 23rd but apparently you had not recd mine of the 19th or my birthday present. I am not sure about letting the house altogether, we have to live somewhere, & under the present circumstances our Landlords might take a lower rent. I asked Bathurst to find out about this, & I dont want to go back to a flat especially after having lived in the open for practically two years. Also there would be the expense of refurnishing. How much a month are you drawing from Bathurst now? as with the house let there might be a little accumulating.

Captain Fenner was hit this morning, he was in charge of all our Lewis Guns, & an invaluable officer.[1] Curse the Bosche. I have had no reinforcements & now the Brigade is again in the front line it is very hard for those that are left however it is only for a few days. The flies are d-d awful & as it has been raining they all seem to have taken cover in our dug out. You might send me a few cigarettes we can get none here except De Reszke[2] & I am getting sick of them.

All All All Love

Thine

Charles

PS Have not the Vaughans got the house until the end of Oct?

1 Capt **Harold Fenner**, 27, *(right)*, was born in Fiji, went to school near Sydney and followed his father into working for the Colonial Sugar Refining Company in Fiji. With the Battalion since October, he had now been wounded in the right knee and right buttock. He would return in June 1917 only to be shot in the head during the German Spring Offensive in 1918 whilst sniping at trench mortar men preparing to fire on his company's position. He woke up to find himself being treated by German stretcher bearers, & was a prisoner in Germany until late 1918. Having resumed his work in Fiji, he was on a visit to Sydney in the 1920s when he realised he couldn't bear to return home without the woman who would become his wife. Even such an obviously brave man hesitated to pop the question until told he would be a fool not to by a family friend. They were married in 1926 but his health started failing in the early '30s and after an operation to remove his gall bladder he died when his son was aged 7.

"De Reszke"
The Aristocrat of cigarettes

2 **De Reszke cigarettes**, available since at least 1904, were manufactured by a Russian in Piccadilly and named after the Polish star tenor Jean de Reszke who despite worrying for his voice liked a smoke and endorsed their *'delightful and harmless qualities'*. The brand would be sold in 1927 to Godfrey Phillips, the tobacco company that coincidentally was founded by Louis Klemantaski's grandfather.

Captain H. R. Fenner
Royal Berkshire
1915.

DAY 387 MON

28 AUG 1916

Item 299
Letter to Margaret

Envelope
Calvados
Hythe
Kent

FIELD POST OFFICE
28 AU 16

28/8/16

Dearest Darling

    All's well so far. Am very busy making final plans for what will be I hope our "Farewell Performance" in this line for a bit. I had hoped we should not be required but it seems they cannot do without us. The weather has broken and the going is very heavy. Have you visited any of my wounded lads yet? I believe Beale Footman & Weedon[1] are all in one hospital at Fenner[2] I expect will go straight home so you might try & find out.

We shall all be glad to get away back out of hearing of the guns, as we have now had this incessant din since July 12th although when we were out before the noise did not effect us much. Dont ask Fenner where he was hit if you see him.

The Reading Mercury of Aug 19th has a wonderful true account of our doings, & where they got it from I can't think.

        All All Love

          Thine

          Charles

1   2Lt **Frank Weedon**, 38, had started his adult life as an architect but when his father died in 1904, he had taken over the family coal merchant's business in Wallingford. Out in France since December 1915, he was now in hospital because the 4th & 5th toes of his left foot had been badly cut by glass whilst bathing in a river on 19th July. They would be healed by September but he then needed an operation to sort out his piles in October, these small bits of bad luck combining to be long term good luck because he missed most of the carnage of the Somme and only returned to the Battalion in January 1917. Then before Passchendaele he was posted to the Inland Water Transport, where his civilian expertise was put to use in the important job of transporting supplies on the canals. So he survived the war to return to his business and wife and two young daughters.

2   The hospital name has been left blank.

This report includes some repetition from before but I've included it because it gives an idea of the public face of Charles Bartlett in contrast to the writings in his letters.

Local newspapers had much greater importance at the time than they do now, as shown by the fact that Charles was seeing this report when over in the trenches in France (can you imagine any present day soldier getting his local paper when abroad?). They carried national stories and might be some people's only source of news.

Particular emphasis in the Reading papers was given to stories of the soldiers of the Royal Berkshire Regiment, this despite the fact that even just the 8th Battalion had men recruited from London, the West Midlands, & South Wales, with officers from all around the world.

Item 300
*Charles's report in
The Reading Mercury*

Reading Mercury

Saturday 19th August 1916

The ROYAL BERKS.

EXPERIENCES IN THE "GREAT PUSH."

Descriptions have been published in this paper of the doings of several of the Berkshire battalions in the "great push." The following story, which we have gleaned, deals with another of the units of the Royal Berkshire Regiment:–

After having been continuously in the trenches since February, and during which period they had had a most gruelling time in some of the hottest parts of the line, the battalion were relieved, as most thought, to go back for the long-promised and long-looked-for rest. They went out with their reputation as a fighting unit greatly increased, as the number of awards show, viz., 1 Military Cross, 3 D.C.M.'s and 4 Military Medals, besides several cards and mentions – all for good work in the trenches, such as making raids, resisting raids, and other little "stunts" to "put the wind up" the Boche and to generally demoralise him. At one point the battalion completely stopped an enemy raid in force, and received congratulations. It is said that this is the only time an enemy raid has not succeeded in getting at least one in the trenches. At another place a very successful raid was made by the battalion, and so well did it succeed that the German official communiqué announced that "the English attempted an advance at ____" while the "English" consisted of Second Lieutenant D. J. Footman and eight men. For this great and daring work this gallant officer received the Military Cross, while one of the party received the D.C.M. and two others the Military Medal.

Great was the joy of the men when the relief was completed and the trenches were gradually fading away into nothingness, and the dozen or so miles back to "rest," and no "Stand to's" and "Sandbag filling," was done in record time, with whistling and singing all the way. However, the next morning saw all hopes of a rest dashed to the ground and the battalion preparing for more strenuous work and a five days' trek and bivouac southwards. It was apparent to all what was meant, and they were to "do their little bit" in the "great push." The five days' trek was accomplished in great style, and on a certain night the battalion proudly and cheerily left in battle array for the village of ____, still held by the Germans. They halted that night in the old German line, and were able to see and form an idea of the nature of the fighting and also of the power of our artillery, for the German trenches were nothing but a series of craters, while German dead, equipment and rifles and all sorts of debris, not forgetting the dozens of helmets to be found everywhere, taught them of the fierceness of our attacking forces. The village of ____ had been taken a few hours previously, and the battalion, with their comrades, were to be sent to hold it at all costs and consolidate it, as it had already been taken and retaken three times. In reconnoitring the position before going in, they had the great misfortune to lose a very brave and promising officer in Second Lieutenant F. Saxon Snell, who was killed instantaneously by shrapnel.

At nightfall the battalion moved up into the village, and the sight that met their eyes was one which the men say they will never forget. The Germans were shelling the village with all sorts of shells of all sizes, and changing the monotony of the burst of "Crumps," "Pip Squeaks" and shrapnel with gas and tear shells. Of the village itself, not one house was left standing, but three or four cellars, which had been reinforced by the Germans when in possession, were still intact. These the Germans were now doing their utmost to destroy, and the air was full of brick dust, and bricks were everywhere vying with the shrapnel and bullets to find their "billets." The dead and dying of both sides were everywhere lying amongst the other debris, while the smell was anything but inviting. One Tommy, when asked his opinion of the place, said that it reminded him of a huge slaughterhouse and rag and bone shop rolled into one.

During one of the enemy's "strafes," the C.O. was badly wounded in the hand, having a most miraculous escape from being killed. One cellar was used as a dressing station, and the M.O., in taking over, found to his surprise the place already occupied by a German doctor and about 20 of the enemy's wounded, who had been there with hardly any food for ten days, during which time the ownership of the village had been in doubt. This German M.O., we are informed, was a most worthy member of this worthy profession, and helped in attending to the wants of our wounded. After well regaling them with bully beef and biscuits, jam and tea, these wounded, together with the German doctor, were taken to the rear of our lines and sent away under escort. One or two other officers had something in the nature of a scare in going down cellars and finding little groups of demoralised Germans. These were also sent away under escort. Little groups of Germans were turning up in all sorts of places, some showing fight, but the majority willingly surrendered.

The battalion soon set to work in digging themselves in and generally preparing for the anticipated counter-attack. It was ascertained that the enemy were holding a trench only 50 yards away, and in their hurry to get out of this "midnight scrap" when the Berks attacked, the Germans left behind them a couple of machine-guns and several thousands of rounds of ammunition. Another company, while on its prowls, captured a field gun. Meanwhile, the rest of the battalion had reinforced the other companies, and by daylight had pushed on another 200 yards, the enemy showing but little fight, and several coming in and surrendering. The next morning the enemy attempted a counter-attack, but it was repulsed with heavy loss, so terrific was the fire from machine-gun and rifle. One batch

of prisoners who were captured said that so terrible was our artillery fire that they had been cut off four days, and were without officers, food, and stretcher-bearers.

In resisting this attack, Second Lieutenant G. Maggs and 14 men had some hand-to-hand fighting with a party of between 20 and 30 of the enemy, his men using the bayonet with great effect, while the gallant young officer used his revolver to great advantage. Not one of the enemy party escaped, and it was a great loss to the battalion when Second Lieutenant Maggs was mortally wounded by a shell, after resting in the trench from his very strenuous and exciting time. He was a most fearless officer, loved by officers and men alike, and one the battalion could ill spare.

Not content with holding the village, the motto was to push on, so that afternoon saw Second Lieutenant Goodship and Second Lieutenant Marsh, each with a small party, move off to take two small woods, which they accomplished with very little loss. Second Lieutenant Lunn (of Caversham) was wounded in an attempt to take some trenches. The next day was spent in making the new position more secure and dealing with small attacks on the positions, none of which were successful, however, for nothing could shake the doughty Berkshires from their newly won ground. During all this time the enemy were shelling the positions unceasingly, and every one agreed that it was the most hellish bombardment they had ever experienced. This was responsible for most of the casualties, only a small percentage suffering gunshot wounds, and those were in most cases slight wounds. No doubt the steel helmets were responsible for the saving of lots of lives.

Thus, in four days, the battalion had not only made the village secure, but had advanced for a distance of 400 yards. On being relieved, they went back for a four days' bivouac in a wood just behind the village, and still within shell fire, while every night they were treated to a bombardment of gas shells, none of which, however, had any other effect than causing a few tears and causing every one to perspire in their gas helmets.

After the four days' respite, which consisted of fatigues of carrying wire and ammunition, etc., up to the front line, the battalion moved up and joined up with the Australians at ____. It is remarkable that the Anzacs had a battalion of Berkshires on their right and another on their left. The artillery had bombarded the positions at intervals for days before, but at 6 p.m. on July 24th a furious bombardment set in, which lasted without a second's cessation till just before 12.30 a.m. All previous bombardments were child's play to this, for the very earth shook, while the German position looked to be one long mass of flame. Every one crouched in his little funk hole which he had hastily dug for himself with entrenching tools, and waited impatiently for the barrage to lift and get out. The bombardment increased in intensity just before the half-hour till it seemed that the very earth was being moved by some giant hand, while it appeared that the very sky was wreaking vengeance on the Hun and was raining shells. It seemed impossible that even a worm could exist after such a bombardment. At last the minute had arrived for the first line to go forward. The enemy artillery were pouring out all their vengeance and making "No Man's Land" a perfect inferno. The Germans in the trenches were very quiet till the wire was reached, when dozens of machine-guns seemed to rise from the ground and poured out such a hail of bullets as to cause a temporary stoppage. However, this was only very temporary, and with a few words of encouragement from the officers, the whole line

swept down on the enemy. The fighting was terrific, and the enemy were there in hundreds and were using bombs and other devilish devices with impunity. In places they were driven out, but came back again and again, using hundreds of bombs. By this time our bombers had got to work, and slowly but surely the enemy were driven back. Just before dawn the last of the enemy were driven out or killed, and the work of digging in and generally making the place more secure against a counter-attack was proceeded with. The fight had been long and fierce, but once again the Berkshires had shown the Germans that they are more than a match for them when it comes to close quarters. The next day was spent in watching and waiting for the German counter-attack, but other than a very violent bombardment nothing happened, owing, no doubt, to a barrage which was continually kept up by our artillery. In fact, for every shell the enemy sent over, our artillery repaid fourfold. After another day of watching, the battalion was relieved, no doubt to again put its spoke in the wheel of this great offensive when called upon.

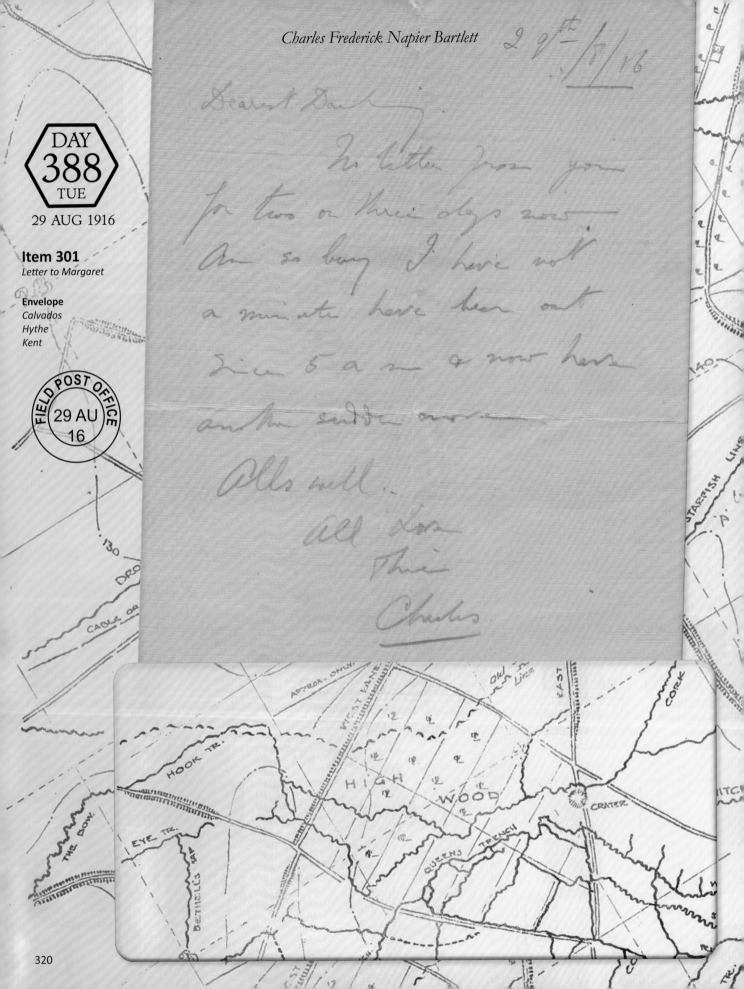

Charles Frederick Napier Bartlett

29ᵗʰ /8/16

Dearest Darling,

No letter from you
for two or three days now —
Am so busy I have not
a minute have been out
since 5 a m & now have
another saddle over —

Alls well —

All Love
thine
Charles

DAY
388
TUE

29 AUG 1916

Item 301
Letter to Margaret

Envelope
Calvados
Hythe
Kent

FIELD POST OFFICE
29 AU
16

DAY

392

SAT

2 SEP 1916

Item 302
Letter to Margaret

Envelope
c/o Mrs A Fraser
Hardingstone
Northampton

FIELD POST OFFICE
2 SP
16

Sept 2nd 1916

Dearest Darling

> *Many thanks for your letters which I found on my arrival back the night before last or rather at 4 am yesterday. We have had a hard time & have to go up again for 48 hours this afternoon.[1] The Bosche has been very active with shells & gas & nearly did me in the other night but with encouragement from old Dug we crawled out of it. However the Bosche gave us another dose last night & we are all just tired of it. We gave the Bosche hell when he tried to come into our lines the day before yesterday & killed them good & plenty. I had three men killed last night & two of them were Sergeants which is just my cursed luck.[2] This blasted gas has made all our food taste bad, & altogether we are not very pleased with life. We are all crawling with lice & vermin of all kinds, & if you could see us catching them in our spare moments, & rubbing powder into our clothes you would be sorry for us. When we move up tonight we go into a new place half of the Batt[n] is attacking tomorrow & we all hope to leave the line the day after. I have sent up an officer & some pioneers to dig me a nice hole in the ground. I think I know a nice bank behind which I ought to be comparatively safe. The last place I was in was very deep & the only dug out that held out, I have never seen such shelling. I built up there a nice latrine with two thicknesses of iron roofing covered with sandbags, & the dirty Bosche blew the whole thing to atoms. I have no more news, my writing is worse than usual as I have to wear a smoke helmet.*

> *All Love to Florrie & the kids*
> *& All All All Love to you & Paula*

> *Thine*

> *xxxxxx Charles xxxxxx*

Margaret is with his sister Florrie.

1 They had been in the front line in High Wood from 29th to 30th but owing to the continuous rain and very muddy conditions, the proposed attack was postponed and they returned to Mametz Wood. ***On the inset map on the facing page***, at bottom left you can see 'Bethell Sap' which was approved as a trench name by 1st Divison HQ on 1st September. It led to me wondering if it was a tribute to his wife's stage name, but he doesn't mention that he's named a trench after her.

2 The men who'd been killed were:

Sgt Walter Folley, 21, single, a plumber's mate from Maidenhead.

| | | | | 19|00 | | | | | | 20|00 |

Sgt George Swinden, 23, single, a machine tool maker from Smethwick, near Birmingham.

| | | | | 19|00 | | | | | | 20|00 |

Cpl Thomas Wort, 24, married, a gas fitter from Birmingham.

| | | | | 19|00 | | | | | | 20|00 |

DAY
393
SUN

3 SEP 1916

Item 303
Letter to Margaret

Envelope
c/o Mrs A Fraser
Woodside
Hardingstone
Northampton

FIELD POST OFFICE
4 SP
16

2.30 pm

3/9/16

Dearest Darling

There is a chance to get a line out so this is to say Dug & I are quite well. We are in the middle of a fight. One of my companies went over at 12, & I am afraid is cup up.[1] Capt Lawrance[2] wounded & I believe Lieut Edens[3] killed, but dont say so yet. Baker[4] is wounded. However we seem to be doing very well, but I dont look like having much left to command.

All Love

In haste

Thine

Charles

Some fight its going on for miles.

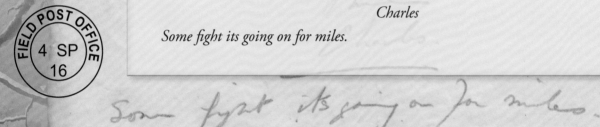

1 As in turning over a cup when finished?

2 Capt **John Lawrance**, 42, (differently spelled and no relation of Capt Thomas Lawrence ★), was a mining engineer who had served in the Railway Pioneer Regiment during the Boer War. He'd recover from his shoulder wound, be awarded the MC and rejoin the Battalion in March 1917. In December 1917 he was invalided out with gastritis, soon after leading D Company into action at the Battle of Passchendaele. He returned to South Africa and died in Port Elizabeth in 1962.

3 2Lt **Lionel Edens**, 19, *(left)*, was from Oxford and as a boy had been a chorister at St John's College. Charles Bartlett wrote to his parents, *'Only two nights before his death*

he had done very valuable patrol work and all his work, whether in the line or out of it was extremely good. By his death we have all lost a good friend and it is no exaggeration to say that he was one of the bravest officers it has been my luck to meet. His disregard of personal danger and his determination had already begun to make their mark and his men would have followed him anywhere. His death was instantaneous and he fell cheering his men on.' His father wrote to try to recover his belongings, including *'a parcel containing pyjamas and socks posted to him on Aug. 31 which must have arrived after his death.'*

4 Lt **Geoffrey Baker**, 26, was a bank clerk. The shell fragments he'd taken in his upper right arm would see the beginning of a long & bitter relationship with the Ministry of Pensions, with his file running to 450 pages. ➔389

Sept 4ᵗʰ 1916

Dearest Darling

Just a line to tell you that we are still going strong although this is the 24ᵗʰ day of this shelling. Yesterday we had a bad time in casualties losing Edens & Chambers[1] killed. Baker Lawrence Prout[2] wounded and Marsh[3] and Davenport[4] gassed, so I now have 4 company officers left. We also lost 130 men out of the remaining 280 so my command is dwindling some. However I hear a draft of over 250 arrived yesterday, so we shall be able to keep going.[5] We were to have been relieved tonight but are not now until tomorrow, & I have to hold onto the front line tonight with what is left of my crowd, & what is left of the Camerons who are much in the same state. Poor old Dugs company has been cut to pieces and only about 12 or 15 men remain. You might let the Guvnor know he is very well. Please thank Bogey for the Tomatoes, which were much appreciated. I had a line from Scrub asking me to meet him in PARIS yesterday.

All All All Love

Thine in haste

Charles

DAY 394 MON

4 SEP 1916

Item 304
Letter to Margaret

Envelope
c/o Mrs A Fraser
Hardingstone
Northampton

FIELD POST OFFICE
4 SP 16

1 2Lt **Cleveland Chambers**, 22, *(right)*, joined the Battalion on 4ᵗʰ August with Douglas Pitt who he had served with in the Honourable Artillery Company (HAC). Charles says in this letter that he had been killed, but again there were no officer witnesses so he was posted *'missing believed dead'*. One private interviewed in hospital said that he had been in a shell hole with Mr Chambers who had been slightly wounded in the head and then saw him killed instantly as he got up to go to the dressing station. Charles responded saying, *'I can only add that the ground where 2Lt Chambers was believed to be killed was carefully searched for his body, on or about Sept 20ᵗʰ 1916, by an officer, but no trace could be found. I consider that Nº 21528 Pte F Smith's report is probably correct.'* On this basis, his death would be officially accepted in December. Imagine the shock when his family were told 18 years later that his body had been found. He was identified by an ID disc found in a purse with his old HAC Nº and part of his name still readable, confirmed by his dental records. His headstone was put in place in 1937, nearly as many years after his death as he had lived on Earth. His aunt placed an 'In Memoriam' notice to him in

The Times every year from 1917 until her own death in 1944. His name is still on the Thiepval Memorial to the Missing.

2 **Douglas Prout** had returned after his wound on 18ᵗʰ August, but this time he was posted *'wounded & missing'*. His death would be confirmed on 10ᵗʰ October, and his name is on the Thiepval Memorial to the Missing.

3 **Gordon Marsh** ★ would always be troubled by the effects of the war. In an effort to find a better climate for his damaged lungs, he went to India and then to Kenya, where he lived for the rest of his life.

4 For **Sydney Davenport**, see Item 182.

5 He may have had the numbers, and all would have been trained men, but still it seems to be asking a lot to keep going when success in the attack comes from teamwork and trust in one's commanders built from concentrated practice together.

Item 305
Letter to Margaret

Envelope
c/o Mrs A Fraser
Hardingstone
Northampton

B.E.F.

Sept 7th 1916

Dearest Darling

We got out of the line the night before last all that was left of us ie. Self Dug Robinson Lawrence Birch Sarchet[1] & Oliver[2] and 130 N.C.O.s & men, and very glad we were to get away. Our losses were thus Edens killed, Chambers believed killed, Capt Lawrance wounded, Baker wounded, Marsh & Davenport gassed, so we are now practically the same as after Oct 14th last year. The Division comes out for rest on the 11th, so we may have to go up in support for one or two nights. The new N.C.O.'s & men are toppers, and make me feel very confident. I could not write yesterday as I was very busy in the morning and then was on a court of enquiry all the afternoon finding out why one of our guns killed some of our own men.[3] You seem rather peevish because I asked you about the house money. Really I dont grudge you a penny & you know it but I only thought if you had saved a bit you might have been able to manage a trip to Paris while we are out that is if leave does not reopen. However I wont say any more. I think you might go & see my wounded officers, it would be a nice little bit of attention, & it does not matter if you know them or not, and you could tell them the news. It was a pretty long spell up 24 days in front of the guns and I think we all feel a bit shaken. I fear we shall go no further back than before which is a bore. Will you let me know exactly which Batt^n the Scrub belongs to as he must be somewhere near & I cant find him under a month unless I get his regiment. I think he is 1/4 OXFORDS but am not certain.[4] I will write again tomorrow. There is an enormous gun which keeps popping off & makes me jump every time. I am indeed "jumpy" & am longing for the 11th.

All All All Love

Thine

Charles

xxxxxxxxxxxx

---

1 Lt **Hugh Sarchet**, 21, was a trainee accountant and the son of an Army chaplain. → **409**

2 2Lt **Arthur Oliver**, 28, joined up in September 1914 despite having a wife and 16-month-old son. Illness would lead to a period of home service from late 1916 till May 1918, and then on 8th August 1918, the first day of the final British Offensive of the war, a piece of a high explosive shell entered the outside of his right heel & exited through the sole of his foot. Though his heel bone had been pulverized, they tried to save his foot but after 16 months of treatment, with 7 operations to remove bits of bone & daily dressing with hydrogen peroxide, his right leg was amputated above the knee. He eventually escaped the Army in April 1920 to become a bank clerk again.

3 No records of courts of enquiry seem to remain. Their aim was to learn from mistakes and this one must have been for the attack on 18th August (see Item 292).

4 Scrub's Battalion was 1st/4th Oxfordshire and Buckinghamshire Light Infantry. Charles was back out of the line in Bécourt Wood and Alfred was 6 miles to the north in the front line east of Auchonvillers.

Sept 9th 1916[1]

Dearest Darling

There is a d-d gun firing so close that it is quite impossible to write & I have got a splitting head from the noise. Thank goodness there is only another 48 hrs & then away back. I got another draft of 220 today but have not seen them yet. I think now we are so strong we shall have another push before settling down for the winter.

I have no other news. A brand new Batt[n] is just going by, looking so pleased with themselves, they are right up to strength, & "where ignorance is bliss tis folly etc". Poor devils.

All All All Love

Thine

xxxxxx Charles xxxxxx

DAY
398
FRI

8 SEP 1916

Item 306
Letter to Margaret

Envelope
Woodside
Hardingstone
Northampton

FIELD POST OFFICE
8 SP
16

---

1 From the postmark, it must be 8th September.

Sept 10th 1916[1]

Dearest Darling

Just rec[d] one letter from you, which you didn't date but you evidently wrote the day after you had seen the Zepp. The weather is beautiful, & if it was not for the noise all would be well. The dirty Bosche had the impudence to put some shells in our wood last night but did no damage. Tomorrow we move back & under new arrangements we go further back the next day which is quite good news, as we are going to a village on a river where we shall be able to get clean once more. I cant get any more news of my wounded & missing officers and am beginning to give up hopes.

One Batt[n] of the Brigade had to go up this morning to do some dirty work, but I am thankful to say it was not my turn. The flies here are beastly & am sure spread illness. A lot of Bosche prisoners have come by today and they looked a poor looking lot. If old Alfie is not going to get leave until after the Push I should think he will have to wait some time. In our Army leave has not started again & I fear

DAY
399
SAT

9 SEP 1916

Item 307
Letter to Margaret

Envelope
Woodside
Hardingstone
Northampton

it wont while we are out this time. Our first seaside party went off this morning, & I hope to be able to send some more at a later date.

I think I get more fed up daily with this war & badly want a change. My latest draft of 220 were nearly all 1/5 Cheshire Terriers & many of them have 2 yrs service so they will be useful. I had all their Cheshire badges off & have labelled them BERKS. Thank goodness none of them have been in the line before and I shall be greatly surprised if after a month with all this fresh blood we shall not be able to give a pretty good account of ourselves. Officers is now my cry and although I have tried every proper channel & every other way to get some, none come. Love to all at Woodside & with best love to you & Paula.

> yrs ever
>
> xxxxxx Charles xxxxxx

Enclosed is a Bosche field post-card for someones stamp album.[2]

1 From the postmark, it must be 9th September.   **2** The German field postcard is no longer enclosed with this letter.

Item 308
Letter to Margaret

Envelope
Woodside
Hardingstone
Northampton

Sept 10th 1916

Dearest Darling

> Just a line to say we are out thank the Lord,[1] & I have just had a bath & found the most wonderful collection of animals, so am writing Lilian Vaughan to send me some of the shirts I sent home.[2] Tonight I sleep in a house for the first time in 10 weeks. You might enquire if you can afford to come to Paris & if you can then enquire if it is possible to get there. Now to get some food.
> We push off at 7 tomorrow, & go into Army Reserve which is good.

> All All All Love
>
> Thine
>
> xxxxxx Charles xxxxxx

1 They were back in Bécourt Wood.   **2** I wonder if Lilian Vaughan knew when she let the Bartletts' house that she would have to attend to the administration of Charles's wardrobe.

Sept 13th 1916

Dearest Darling

I missed writing yesterday as I was joy riding. Colonel Rose had asked Col Hamilton & Col Sutherland to dine with him in the town and they suggested I should go too, so he called for me & away we went, & had a jolly good dinner. The prices here are getting worse. 13 francs for a chicken, & they were asking 12 francs for a medium sized lobster. It is raining & the majority of billets wont keep out the rain so we are in for a bad time. I have never seen so many troops about and something will have to give but I sincerely hope we shall not be dragged into it. I dont see what Florrie has to worry about not hearing from Alfie. I write because I think you like to know that I have successfully dodged the shells each 24 hours but as he does not have to do that I dont suppose he has much to write about. We have bought ourselves all new knives forks spoons etc, two table cloths tumblers & china tea cups & are pretending we are at home, but the imagination has to stretch a bit, as our table is made out of biscuit boxes, & the manure heap outside the window attracts the flies a good deal. The men are being paid today the first time for a month, so I expect the canteen will do well. Well I have no more news.

Love to all & best love to you & Paula.

Thine

xxxxxx Charles xxxxxx

DAY
403
WED

13 SEP 1916

Item 309
Letter to Margaret

Envelope
Woodside
Hardingstone
Northampton

Forwarded to:
Nithsdale
Burgess Hill
Sussex

FIELD POST OFFICE
13 SP
16

HARDINGSTONE
17 SP
16

6t0. Albert (Somme) — La Rue de Nemours - Nemours Street

R Lelong, 21, Rue St-Martin, Amiens

They had marched some 5 miles back to billets in the village of Millencourt. On the way they went through Albert, *(left)*, to which it looks like Charles then returned for his dinner. With the town having been shelled for 2 years it's extraordinary that any restaurant managed to continue in business and it's no wonder the prices were so high.

Item 310
*Letter to one of
William Bissley's brothers
(from William Bissley's
army service record)*

*With all the paperwork
necessary for so many
dead and wounded
I can't help wondering
how Charles had the time
to do his actual job
of commanding
the Battalion.*

Sept 13th 1916

Dear Mr Bissley

    I recd your note & enclosed form, which I am obliged to return unsigned. Although I knew your brother very well and would do anything in my power to help his wife, I have never had the pleasure of meeting her, so I cannot sign a certificate that I have known her for some years. If the words "and the widow" are taken out it would make all the difference.
I am glad to say we are back at rest now but cannot expect a very long period.

            yrs sincerely
            C Bartlett comdg.
        8th Royal Berkshire Rgt.

DAY 405 FRI

15 SEP 1916

Item 311
Letter to Margaret

Envelope
Nithsdale
Burgess Hill
Sussex

FIELD POST OFFICE
15 SP
16

Sept 15th 1916

Dearest Darling

    I got three letters from you last night written on the 7th 10th & 11th. I did not write yesterday as I had such a tremendous lot to do. I dont like the look of your Asiatic Body Cord[1] & think I should prefer the lice, but after having all my clothes boiled & my "flea bag"[2] disinfected I am now clean once more. Bogey sent me some patent stuff, & as I woke up last night scratching I applied some with vigour with the result I have jolly well blistered myself and suffered agony. Poor old Ronny's brother lunched with me yesterday, and did I tell you I met Owen Backler[3] the other day, he is a great pall of T.B.V.s. All leave to Paris has been stopped, so that's that for the present. I think the old Bosche is getting the surprise of his life today[4] but so far we have had no news. Some of my new officers will be alright I think, but one or two seem a bit casual. Yesterday the Divisional Commander came round without notice and I met him as I was riding onto the ground. One of the new lads was leaning on his stick in a casual manner, so the G.O.C. jumped down my throat & said "When I come on parade I dont want to see officers leaning on their sticks" & I quickly replied "Neither do I sir", which rather defeated him. Well I have no more news. Train Train morning noon & night.

    Love to Doll
    All All All Love to you & Paula
    Thine
    xxxxxx Charles xxxxxx

1 The Asiatic Body Cord was developed by a chemist's in Edinburgh to get rid of lice. Based on an Indian folk-medicine device it was a cord of plaited wool impregnated with a mixture of one part yellow beeswax and two parts mercury ointment. Worn around the waist it was said to be *'like a gas attack on the vermin'*.

2 His 'flea bag' was likely a sleeping bag made from canvas, wool and camel hair, affordable only to officers, and heavy to carry (but he had a servant to do that).

3 Captain **Owen Backler**, 35, had a life full of difficult hurdles to overcome. ➔388

4 The surprise for the Germans was the new British secret weapon: tanks, used for the first time on this day. Interesting that he should know about them & the timing of the attack, but it must have been difficult to hide these noisy lumbering monsters and he was a senior officer with contacts to find out what was going on. They were a significant development in the effort to break the deadlock of trench warfare but were very slow (only 1 mile per hour over broken ground) and prone to breaking down (only 9 of the 32 tanks in this attack made it across No-Man's-Land). The war would end before they had a chance to develop into a fully effective weapon.

DAY
407
SUN
17 SEP 1916

Item 312
Letter to Margaret

Envelope
Nithsdale
Burgess Hill
Sussex

FIELD POST OFFICE
19 SP
16

Sept 17ᵗʰ 1916

Dearest Darling

Just recᵈ yours of the 13ᵗʰ. I am sorry Florrie is so "fratchy".[1] I am afraid she takes after the poor old Mater.[2] We are still here & very nice it is today. I spent the entire morning writing to parents & wives of the men who have been awarded D.C.M.'s & Military Medals, & not lived long enough to hear of it.[3] I see the English papers have notices of the new Caterpillars or armoured cars, they are great & can climb over any trench & will even get over a wall, and once inside only a direct hit by a big shell has any effect. I heard from Dalby, & he does not expect to be back for some time, & may now have to have two fingers off. Col Hamilton has been given a brigade,[4] & Victor Fortune has gone to command the Black Watch.[5] I went to church parade this morning. Poor old Dug had a parcel this morning from the office & said to me, now we can have a nice smokestick, but when he opened it, it was soap for lice. I have no other news. Paula owes me a letter.

All All All Love

Thine

Charles

1 Fratchy = quarrelsome, irritable.

2 His mother, **Sarah Emily née Napier**, (*left*, in earlier life) had been born in Bahia in Brazil, the daughter of a merchant. She was a widow for 25 years before her death in 1913.

3 This seems to be an exaggeration. 3 DCMs and 13 MMs had been awarded to men of the 8ᵗʰ Royal Berkshires in September, and though a number of those had been wounded, I've only found one who had been killed. That was Cpl **Thomas Wort**, as already named on 2ⁿᵈ September. His wife told the local paper that she had received a letter, stating,

'Your husband was awarded the Military Medal for coolness and gallantry during a German raid on our trenches at ____ on May 27ᵗʰ. He and his gun team were largely instrumental in beating off the raiding party. His officer also told me that when he was killed he lost a very gallant and promising young non-commissioned officer, whose place he would find it hard to fill.' →**415 Wort**

4 Brig-Gen **John Hamilton**, DSO, would command brigades in the 51ˢᵗ (Highland) Division before retiring to his family's estate near Aberdeen in 1921 & dedicating himself to public works. A very well-loved figure, he was deeply hurt by the loss of his only son Alistair who was killed on Crete in 1941 whilst serving as a company commander with the Black Watch.

5 Lt Col **Victor Fortune**, DSO, commanded 1ˢᵗ Black Watch until January 1918 and would end the war as a Brigadier-General. He is most famous for being the Major-General in command of 51ˢᵗ (Highland) Division during the fall of France in 1940. Cut off and unable to be evacuated he surrendered with over 10,000 of his men and stayed a prisoner for the rest of the war. He turned down three offers to be repatriated. Even after having a stroke in 1944, he would not leave his men & was knighted in 1945 for his dedication to them, though his health was broken. →**395**

Sept 15th 1916.

Sept 18th 1916

Dearest Darling

      Just a hurried line to tell you we are on the move again, & have to go back to the line. We move up tonight & take over tomorrow night. It is pouring with rain & I am not very much looking forward to it. However it is something to have had 6 days out, so we must not grumble, but be proud of the fact that we belong to a Division that has the reputation of always obtaining its objective, even if on that account we do get more than our share. I hope my new lads go alright. I should have liked to have had them to train a bit longer but no matter we must chance it.

                      All All Love
                      Thine in haste
                      Charles

DAY
408
MON

18 SEP 1916

Item 313
Letter to Margaret

Envelope
c/o W. Garfitt Clowes
Nithsdale
Burgess Hill
Sussex

even if on that account we do get more

6

19/9/16

Dearest Darling.

      Just a line to say so far, so good. We had a very wet march up, it poured the entire time & all the night, & the men had very little shelter. We had an old barn, & half of it was dry, & by keeping a fire going all night, we were pretty dry & warm. We move up to the front line at 4 pm but the Batt⁰ is in support the first day or two. The trenches must be full of water, & it is still pouring with rain. Writing pads have run out again so please let us have another shillings worth. The new Brigade Major[1] is a great pall of Scrubs, which is a coincidence.
         All all all love
           Thine in haste
             xxxxx Charles xxxxx

DAY
409
TUE

19 SEP 1916

Item 314
Letter to Margaret

Envelope
c/o W. Garfitt Clowes
Nithsdale
Burgess Hill
Sussex

1 The new Brigade Major was Captain **Robert J B Yates**, 33, of 22nd Cavalry, Indian Army.

20/9/16.

Dearest Darling,

Writing in a hole in the ground. All's well. Weather awful, could not complete relief last night so spent night by the side of a road. May go up tonight, but 16 men this morning & 1 officer wounded. What a life. Heard from Bethel; don't know yet what I can do for him. All love

Thine
Charles.

DAY 410 WED
20 SEP 1916

Item 315
Letter to Margaret

Envelope
Nithsdale
Burgess Hill
Sussex

FIELD POST OFFICE
21 SP 16

21/9/16

12

Dearest Darling,

Just a line to say "all's well." Found a nice dry dugout last night, but expect to get moved on today. Please thank Lilian Vaughan for shirts, & John for socks. The mud here is awful, & it takes 6 horses to do 2 horses work, & rations are a great difficulty. However we must not grumble. Boy is well but I fear I had a few men gassed last night. All all all love

Thine
Charles. xxxxxx

DAY 411 THU
21 SEP 1916

Item 316
Letter to Margaret

Envelope
c/o W. Garfitt Clowes
Nithsdale
Burgess Hill
Sussex

FIELD POST OFFICE
21 SP 16

Sept 23rd 1916

Dearest Darling

I did not write yesterday, I had nothing to say and was feeling "Fed Up". We had a bitter blow yesterday our D[r], Captain Peto, one of the nicest men I have ever met, & as brave as a lion had his leg blown off yesterday & died during the afternoon.[1] It is awfully bad luck. For 4 hours yesterday we could get neither in or out of Brigade Head Quarters the shelling was so heavy. I have had 2 companies up & 2 back this time self being back of course, so far have been lucky & only lost 40 and so far no officers. Tonight my two front companies are relieved, & the whole Batt[n] is in support, but much too close up to be pleasant. I had a letter from Bethel[2] asking me to apply for him as an officer, because he then says he will get a commission, but at present am not able to say that I can, as Dalby is really still boss, & feeling runs rather high on the subject, but I will do what I can. His division[3] is the one we relieved & a nice mix up they were in, and never cleaned up their wounded which was about as disgraceful a thing as I have seen out here. God knows how long we are in for, we have obtained both our objectives already, so I suppose we shall get some fresh ones. Anyway it does not sound much like Paris. I was over the ground this morning we were fighting over last time, & the Bosche must have lost heavily according to the amount of dead still laying about. Cloake has got the Military Cross.[4] Dug is very fed up today, and quite annoyed because we ran into some tear shells this morning which made him weep, also because I would not visit the front line, so he has gone off by himself; he is really a difficult person to keep alive, & will walk into trouble as sure as fate one of these days. I am rather disappointed with my new men, & if I had only had them a month to train and then let them in gently I am sure they would have done well, but to have to chuck the mob into this real hot fighting, it is a bit of a strain on them. However so far they have not had to go over, but carrying heavy loads in pitch darkness under heavy shelling when one has had no experience must be a bit trying, & I am sure I should chuck my load down & run to the nearest shell hole if I had to do it. I heard from Bogey yesterday, & he sent off some grouse on the 16th which have not yet arrived, which is most distressing. I dont seem to have had a letter from Paula for a long time. If William has got exemption until Jan he will just be in time for the end of this push in Feb, as I believe we are pushing all the winter. It is a beautiful day & I am sitting writing in the sun, but not far from my funk hole, as the Bosche are putting some of their heaviest about, & have splashed us twice already. My friends just left me, & I was

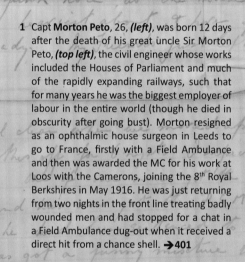

beginning to feel clean when we moved up, but as I have not had my clothes off for 6 nights I expect to begin scratching again soon. One of our men got the Military Medal the other day and has now got the D.C.M. and is also wounded, also he had been sentenced to 2 yrs imprisonment, so he has got a funny mixture to go on with.[5]

I have no other news so as Tommy says "Will now close, hoping this will find you in the pink as it leaves me at present".

All All All Love

Thine

Charles

PS Love to Doll & William

PPS Is Doll any fatter[6]

1 Capt **Morton Peto**, 26, *(left)*, was born 12 days after the death of his great uncle Sir Morton Peto, *(top left)*, the civil engineer whose works included the Houses of Parliament and much of the rapidly expanding railways, such that for many years he was the biggest employer of labour in the entire world (though he died in obscurity after going bust). Morton resigned as an ophthalmic house surgeon in Leeds to go to France, firstly with a Field Ambulance and then was awarded the MC for his work at Loos with the Camerons, joining the 8th Royal Berkshires in May 1916. He was just returning from two nights in the front line treating badly wounded men and had stopped for a chat in a Field Ambulance dug-out when it received a direct hit from a chance shell. ➜**401**

2 **Bethell Robinson** was Margaret's only brother, aged 30. Married in 1912, when he described himself as a secretary, he had joined up as a private in the Civil Service Rifles (a Territorial unit of the London Regiment). Nicknamed 'All Bloody Gentlemen' because of the class of their recruits, a lot of them might have been looking for commissions. Bethell never would become an officer and was an Acting Corporal when he died of pneumonia in an Egyptian hospital in October 1917.

3 1st Division (inc. 8th Royal Berkshires), had just taken over the front line to the north-east of High Wood from 47th Division, whose infantry battalions were all from the London Regiment (inc. 1st/15th Civil Service Rifles).

4 Charles's recommendation for **Cecil Cloake**★'s Military Cross read as follows:

'On the afternoon of the 18th August, when the Battalion had suffered severe loss, Captain & Adjutant C. S. CLOAKE went forward under heavy shell and rifle fire; reorganised two Companies which had lost all their officers, selecting good positions for them to hold. His quick appreciation of the situation, combined with his cool courage was a fine example and restored a much needed confidence to the men at a most critical time. His constant devotion to duty has never been more marked.'

Cecil Cloake never attended an investiture for his MC, it eventually being posted to him in 1921, but he wore the ribbon on his tunic and then stuck it onto a page of his war memoirs:

5 This is only a glimpse of the unusual life of Pte **Walter Yates**, DCM, MM, aged 26. ➜**415**

6 This points to Margaret's sister **Dolly** being pregnant. She & **William** already had a 3-year-old daughter, but if this was a pregnancy it can't have gone to full term as the next of her 3 children wasn't born until September 1918.

Martha 'Dolly' Clowes née Robinson

(Herbert) William Garfit Clowes

24/9/16

Dearest Darling

　　　Just rec^d your letter of the 20th. As I wrote you yesterday I heard from Bethel but cannot do anything until we get out from this d-d hole, which I hope will be at the end of the month. I should have thought by the 20th you would have heard that we were at it again. However no great damage yet, I have so few officers that the Bosche have not found one yet, and only 60 other ranks done in. Dug had a letter from Renée saying she was marrying John the 21st of this month. Is this so??
We had grouse from Bogey yesterday, & partridges from the Guvnor, so are doing pretty well. Leave is opening for worn out officers at the rate of about 1 per Regiment per 10 days, but I shall not be able to get away until we have finished this tour & reorganised, which will be towards the middle or end of October. In haste.

All All All Love
Thine
Charles

DAY
414
SUN

24 SEP 1916

Item 318
Letter to Margaret

Envelope
*c/o W. Garfitt Clowes
Nithsdale
Burgess Hill
Sussex*

FIELD POST OFFICE
26 SP
16

A.D.M.S.　　　　　　　　　　24.9.16
Dear Colonel,

　　　On behalf of myself and all the officers of the Rgt, I am writing to say how sorry we are for you and your corps over the loss of Captain Peto. His loss has been a bitter blow to us for every officer, N.C.O. and man loved and respected him. No words of Colonel Dalby's or mine could express how much we appreciated his work while he was with us, and we feel certain, knowing his good and gallant work that you have lost one of your most valuable officers.

yrs sincerely
C Bartlett comdg.
8th Royal Berkshire Rgt.

Item 319
*Letter to
Col. Stuart Macdonald,
Assistant Director of
Medical Services,
1st Division*

*(Kept amongst
Morton Peto's
memorabilia
by his family)*

Not only was Charles writing to relatives. Here he is writing to Morton Peto's immediate boss in the Division, part of his military family.

Item 320
Letter to the father of Morton Peto

(Kept amongst Morton Peto's memorabilia by his family)

> B.E.F.
> 24.9.16.
>
> Dear Mr. Peto,
>
> On behalf of myself and the officers of the Rgt, I am writing to offer you our deepest sympathies over the loss of your son, who was our Medical Officer. Your son was loved and respected by every officer, N.C.O. and man of the Battalion, and his death has been a severe blow to us. No words of mine can express our admiration for the work he did while with us, and his gallantry under fire was proverbial. Always quiet nothing was too much trouble for him, and we have lost not only a gallant officer but a great friend. Once more let me say how sorry we all are for you and believe me.
>
> yrs sincerely
> C Bartlett, Lt. Colonel,
> Comdg. 8th Royal Berkshire Rgt.

Morton Peto can't have updated his next-of-kin details because his father had died the previous November. His mother had also died in 1915 so it would have been one of Morton's 6 elder siblings who opened this letter.

DAY
416
TUE

26 SEP 1916

Item 321
Letter to Margaret

Envelope
c/o W. Garfitt Clowes
Nithsdale
Burgess Hill
Sussex

Forwarded to:
The Goring Hotel
Grosvenor Gardens
London

> Sept 26th 1916
>
> Dearest Darling
>
> Some battle going on just at present, but my lot are in support & I hope we shall not be wanted. Yesterday we celebrated the anniversary of Loos by giving the Bosche absolute hell, so he is trying to get a bit back on his own. No news of when we come out, but we hear that when we do come out, it will not be for long, & that we are going no further back than before, so it is rather depressing. I got no letter from you yesterday & did not write one myself as I was not feeling like it. There is no news I can think of. I am anxiously waiting to hear about Renée. I threw out a feeler to the General about Bethel yesterday but it did not go very well. His cousin is in the same boat & he wont apply for him, so I must try another way.   All All All Love to you & Paula
>
> Thine
> Charles

FIELD POST OFFICE
27 SP 16

DAY
418
THU

28 SEP 1916

Item 322
Letter to Margaret

Envelope
c/o W. Garfitt Clowes
Nithsdale
Burgess Hill
Sussex

Sept 28th 1916

Dearest Darling

      I had two letters in which you seem rather terse at not having heard from me, but I expect you will have got a lot altogether. The sudden move up the line rather upset things, & yesterday we had another sudden move and got moved back for which we were truly thankful.[1] We dont know what is going to happen to us, but are sincerely hoping for a rest but there are rumours we are going to another part of the line. The vital question of leave is still under consideration but when it does open two other C.O.'s have to go before me. You might let me know your plans how long you will be at Burgess Hill, as I think a day or two in the country would do me good. I must stop now, we did not get in until 10.30 pm last night & then were drenched, & now I have to interview more new officers.   *All All All Love*

                   Thine

                   Charles

1 The Battalion had moved back into billets at Bresle, 4 miles west of Albert, well out of the firing line.

DAY
419
FRI

29 SEP 1916

Item 323
Letter to Margaret

Envelope
Nithsdale
Burgess Hill
Sussex

Sept 29th 1916

Dearest Darling

      I recd yours of the 25th today. I expect the postal delay is owing to the battle which is growing larger every day, & the fields are a wonderful sight. The ground we were first fighting over is now a large camp, & a railway has been laid right up to it. We move from here in two days, but dont know where to, except that it is further back. Cloake goes on leave tomorrow, but we can get no information as to whether there will be a second edition or not. We went into town last night & had a good dinner by We I mean Dug, Col Sutherland, Phillips & two Black Watch officers, but unless someone lends us a car we are too far to ride. The Follies are giving a show tonight, which ought to be amusing.

I am thinking of going to Scotland if I get leave as I get an extra day by so doing, but dont know who I want to see there. The weather here is awful again, & if it continues will put a stopper on the fighting, as supplies will not be able to get up. Well I have no more news.

All All All Love

Thine

xxxxxx Charles xxxxxx

Paula's

FIELD POST OFFICE
29 SP
16

DAY
420
SAT

30 SEP 1916

Item 324
Letter to Margaret

Envelope
Nithsdale
Burgess Hill
Sussex

FIELD POST OFFICE
1 OC
16

Sept 30th 1916

My Darling Wife

Many thanks for letter & pad received today. You will be glad to hear we are moving back on the 3rd to a town near the sea about 40 miles back, & we have been promised three weeks rest, which if it comes off will be wonderful. I have had another dose of writing to parents which is a nasty job. The weather has cleared up, and if it keeps fine we ought to have a good time. Cloake got away on leave, & I hope to now when the other C.O.'s come back, but there are no definite orders on the subject at present, & compared to other people I have had leave quite recently. The Follies gave a very good show last night, & are giving another one tonight. Our new Brigade Major is dining with us tonight, & we are having a grouse pie. I have no other news.

All All All Love

Thine

xxxxxx Charles xxxxxx

Item 325
Letter to Margaret

Envelope
Nithsdale
Burgess Hill
Sussex

FIELD POST OFFICE
5 OC
16

Oct 4th 1916

Dearest Darling

     I dont think I have missed writing for 3 days before, but as there was no mail going out, it was not much use. We had an 8 hours motor bus ride and it rained some. However I am now living in a large chateau[1] with a huge double room & dining room all to myself. The owner is an old solicitor & seems quite a nice old thing. We have the use of the dining room for a mess, & altogether are very comfortable. I have applied for Dug to go on leave tomorrow in which case I should be starting in about 12 days time, as he only gets 7 days & I should have to await his return. If he does not go, I go when the others come back, & as they have been granted an extension I dont know when they do return, so we are not really much forrader. The General has also an extension & when he comes back he will be acting Divisional General while the other man is on leave. The Scrub was round this way the other day, & I think has gone up to the line again. Yates met a French lady, a mutual acquaintance of theirs, who said the Darling Boy had been to see her. N.B. The Lady is over 60.[2]

I am up to my eyes in work today so excuse scrawl.   All All All Love

        Thine

        Charles

1 They were in **Franleu**, near to Abbeville and the mouth of the River Somme. The chateau, *(right)*, was overlooked by the church tower from which the 7th Argylls would observe the advancing Germans before their last stand in June 1940.

2 Charles seems to be hinting at some impropriety with this mutual acquaintance of brother Alfred & the Brigade Major, **Robert Yates**, though both of them were married and both had exemplary careers. In fact, Robert Yates is the only officer for whom I've ever found a full career's confidential reports, and all are in the form of: *'An excellent officer. Keen & energetic. A hard worker'* with only one exception in 1914 being *'inclined to let his duties slide for his own pleasures'*. That, though, I think reflects his interest in riding and sport. Wounded in 1917, he ended the war as a major, DSO. His last post was as C.O. of 1st/6th Gurkhas, and in 1931 he retired to Aberdeenshire.

FRANLEU — Le Château

DAY
425
THU

5 OCT 1916

Item 326
Letter to Margaret

Envelope
Nithsdale
Burgess Hill
Sussex

FIELD POST OFFICE
6 OC
16

Oct 5th 1916

Dearest Darling

Rec[d] two letters from you today dated Sept 29th & 30th. You seem to like the Goring Hotel.[1] The mail is most erratic nowadays. I am frightfully busy training once more and it really is uphill work. I was at it from 6.45am to 9.30 last night and started again at 6.45 this morning. I do not understand Scrub's promotion. I thought he was a "substantive Major" & if so would only be a Tempy Lieut Col, but if he is only a substantive Capt he becomes a Tempy Major with permission to wear the badges of rank of Lieut Col, while commanding a Batt[n]. Personally I am a substantive Major with temporary rank of Lieut Colonel but if Dalby comes back I revert once more. My promotion this time is different to last when I was made substantive. It is all very difficult but what it really means is that when doing higher command work you get temporary rank of one step up.[2] You have not told me what you are going to do this winter, & I am most interested to know, so buck up & let me know. It looks to me now that I shall not get away until Dug comes back, & as he has 10 days I shall not be able to start before the 16th or 17th. I wish rather I had gone myself as he had had the chance before & did not take it, and I should not be surprised if we were run up the line again before I finish my leave even if I start it.

I have just had two more officers arrive, one has been a policeman at Windsor & Plymouth for 6 years, & been out 1½ year.[3] The other was "home service"?? I should think on the "Combing out" principle Master Malcolm would be caught out, anyway I hope so. My acting Adjutant has been away all day today, so I am now going to turn in & do his work.

Love to Doll & all there & best love to you & Paula

Thine

Charles

PS Let me know how long you are at NITHSDALE for, & where you go to from there.

1 **The Goring Hotel**, *(above)*, had opened in 1910, being said to be the first hotel in the world with all rooms en suite and with central heating. It would become the US Army HQ in London in 1917. It's not far from Buckingham Palace and Kate Middleton stayed there the night before her wedding. With only 69 suites and rooms, it is the height of luxury, with a night's stay now starting at £380.

2 The aim of the Army's system of promotion seems to have been to avoid paying out too much money to people, with only substantive (i.e. permanent) ranks getting full benefits in terms of pay, pensions and gratuities paid on death or injury. With so many casualties, survivors could be promoted more quickly than the system was set up for, hence the confusion Charles describes.

3 The 2 new officers are not listed in the war diary, but the ex-policeman was 2Lt **George Easton**, 25. He had been a Lance Corporal in the Military Foot Police, arriving in France in May 1915. He would survive to marry a war widow and become a traffic examiner and fuel inspector for the Ministry of Transport.

19|00 20|00

Sunday Oct 8th 1916

Dearest Darling

Just rec^d three letters from you written on Sunday Monday & Tuesday from the Goring Hotel, where you seem to be doing yourself pretty well. We are hard at work training, and as there is nothing else to do & nowhere to go it is just as well. Each Batt^n is in a different village so one does not see much of anybody. I am dining with the Brigade tonight, & am hoping that the Brigadier comes back tomorrow, and then we shall get something definite about leave, but I hope to be able to start about the 16th. What are you going to do about Paula, is she going to winter at Burgess Hill or what. The Zepps do seem a bit busy, but I hope they will leave London alone now they have had a few smashes.[1] Poor old cuckoo, I think he had better try St Dunstans for a job. Fancy Paul being really ill, where is Phyllis.[2]

Sorry cannot write any more have been called out & post will have gone before I get back.   *All All All Love*

Thine

xxxxxx Charles xxxxx

DAY
428
SUN
8 OCT 1916

Item 327
Letter to Margaret

Envelope
Nithsdale
Burgess Hill
Sussex

FIELD POST OFFICE
8 OC
16

1 Since the start of September, four Zeppelins had been brought down (as *below*, near Potter's Bar). Though fighter aircraft still found it difficult to make contact in the dark night air, the thing that was making the difference was the introduction of explosive and incendiary bullets. Normal machine-gun bullets just made holes in the individual gas cells of the airship, but these new bullets set fire to the hydrogen resulting in a much more devastating effect. It was the beginning of the end of the Zeppelin raids.

2 **Paul Rubens** gave the idea that his weak physique was due to the erratic habits of a musician (he said one of his recreations was *'getting up late'* and his telegraphic address was *'sleepy'*) but in fact he was suffering from TB. It was this that had been behind the on-off nature of his relationship with Phyllis Dare. He had been confined to bed since being seized by a serious attack when they were out house-hunting a month before. Following the advice of doctors, their engagement would be called off in early November.

 # ON LEAVE IN ENGLAND

DAY
442
SUN

22 OCT 1916

Item 328
Letter to Margaret

Envelope
*Ladies United
Services Club,
Curzon Street
London*

Sunday

Dearest Darling

There has not been a post in or out since I arrived back, &
there is none today, but I am dining with the Divisional General tonight so
am hoping to get this off from there. Well we arrived back to the same place at
3.30 am the following day after a nasty crossing which nearly proved fatal to me
however I held on and we dined in Boulogne & caught the 9.30 pm train on.
Since I got back I have not had a moment to call my own. I am on parade from
9 to 1 and 2 – 4 and it is some job now. Generals are all over the place and even
this morning we had an inspection, which went very well until he inspected the
transport, and then he really did have cause to complain, so I have literally spent
the afternoon looking at the men cleaning harness etc. I have stopped all their
leave and feel so depressed about the whole show I dont know what to do. It is
simply because Phillips the transport officer is on leave & the men were too d-d
lazy. Rumour has it that we remain here for another week or so, & then return
to where we came from, but that may be all altered. I have no more officers and
it will be uphill work if some more dont arrive. The Padre is on leave so the Mess
has gone to pieces,[1] in fact I think that self Dug & Cloake being away at the same
time has just about put the Batt^n back a month, and I am very unhappy about it.
Well the car has just come to fetch me.

All All All Love

Thine
Charles xxxxx

Margaret is staying at the **Ladies' United Services
Club** in Mayfair. There were plenty of clubs for
military men at this time, but not for their ladies,
and, with many military wives being engaged in
charitable activities, the need arose for a place
to provide them with the facilities they needed
when they were in London. The Club opened in
November 1915 having occupied the Washington
Hotel, a completely new building that had only
opened in 1913. Ladies qualified for membership
by being *'nearly related to officers of both Services
who hold or have held commissions'* and, as an
added incentive, officers on leave were allowed
to stay as guests of their wives. It would close
amongst scandal in March 1919 after the owner
of the building issued a writ for substantial costs

for rent against the club, despite the fact that
she was also the governing director of the club.
Over 2000 paid-up members lost out, and she
ended up re-opening the hotel having doubled
the price for rooms to take advantage of the post-
war scarcity of hotel rooms. The hotel continues
today as The Washington Mayfair.

1 In addition to his duties as Padre, **Rev Arthur
Longden**, *(right)*, was Mess President for the
Battalion. As such he was in charge of running
the Officers' Mess. In normal times he must
have done a good enough job as eleven days
after this letter Charles would sign the form for
the renewal of Arthur's contract as an *'Acting
Chaplain engaged for duty abroad'*. ➔399

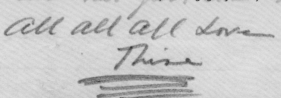

DAY
444
TUE

24 OCT 1916

Item 329
Letter to Margaret

Envelope
*Ladies United
Services Club,
Curzon Street
London*

Oct 24th 1916

Dearest Darling

    Never have I had such a time since I returned. What with inspections and training I have not had a minute to call my own, and have to return to office after dinner. I now have 3 platoons of my best company isolated with German Measles,[1] & one case of diphtheria, so I have sanitary officers bobbing round all day, after that Dug is laid up with a bad knee, and on the top of everything we have orders to move on again, and I believe we are going back to where we were. Reports are being called for all day long on various points connected with the move, and I have both the Q[r] M[r] & transport officer away, so Cloake and I are doing the whole thing practically. My best company commander is also in bed, so we are a real happy family. And it is just pouring with rain and we are paddling about in gum boots. I have no woolly waistcoats of any sort will you please post me out one, also my leather one would be most useful. I sent off a letter yesterday by the Court Martial Army expert who was over trying our deserter,[2] who got off with 5 yrs penal servitude, so this makes the third, & I have not had one from you! No more news that I can tell you.

    All All All Love

    Thine

    Charles xxxxx

1 **German Measles** got its name from being identified by German doctors in the 1700s, rather than being anything derogatory about the Germans. It was not a serious illness but was highly infectious and cases needed to be quarantined to avoid it spreading and affecting the Army's ability to fight.

2 The deserter was Pte **John Butler**, 23, who'd been a driller for a motor manufacturer in Coventry before the war. He must have been considered an efficient soldier to be with the Battalion when it first embarked for France in August 1915, and he was wounded at the time of the Battle of Loos. His sentence is marked in the Court Martial register with an S, which points to a suspended sentence (otherwise men might favour prison to staying in the frontline). He would be killed in June 1917 and his name is amongst the four Royal Berkshires listed on the Memorial to the Missing In Nieuport, *(below)*, at the northernmost end of the Western Front.

DAY 446 THU

26 OCT 1916

Item 330
Letter to Margaret

Envelope
(missing)

Oct 26th 1916

Dearest Darling

No letter from you today. I am up to my eyes in work. More than half the Battⁿ has now got German Measles, including the Doctor, and I spend my time isolating people and answering the sanitary officer's 1000 & one questions. I am very worried at not hearing from you.
Please write.   All All All Love

Thine

Charles

DAY 448 SAT

28 OCT 1916

Item 331
Letter to Margaret

Envelope
*Nithsdale
Burgess Hill
Sussex*

*Forwarded to:
Ladies United
Services Club,
Curzon Street
London*

28.10.16

Dearest Margaret

I am not pleased at not hearing from you. I have plenty of worries here without you adding to them. The Division goes into the line on the 30th, but my Battⁿ is being left behind for 10 days owing to German Measles. I enclose the cheque in re-payment for what you lent me. I will write again when I hear from you.   All All Love

Thine

Charles

FIELD POST OFFICE 28 OC 16

BURGESS·HILL – S·O·SUSSEX 11.30 AM 31 OC 16

345

Item 332

Letter from
Margaret to Charles
(looks like her copy
kept after sending,
labelled 'My answer')

(no envelope)

Nov 2nd

Dear C

Many thanks for cheque which arrived today – & so you are not pleased with me, & have enough worries without me adding to them – Well - that is one of the reasons I haven't written, because I thought you would worry less if I didn't worry you with letters – another reason is – that I have been expecting an explanation of your behaviour – ever since you went back as you have had ample time to think it over.

I want you to be sensible; & for the last time – I want you to give me a full detailed account of all that has happened, & tell me the truth – however unpleasant it may be. I think after everything – this much is due to me. Perhaps then we can see our way to clear things up & start afresh. I want to know for how long it has been going on – who she is & where you stayed – etc. Of course if you – after thinking it over seriously – find you cannot give it up then we had better separate. It certainly seems rather foolish to think that because you won't speak up everything must be upset – but I will leave it to you to decide & shall hope to hear from you soon. I am sorry you are not pleased with me, but it is hardly my fault.

M

Item 333

Letter to Margaret

Envelope
Nithsdale
Burgess Hill
Sussex

Nov 9th 1916

My dear Margaret

I rec^d your letter of the 2nd yesterday, and really you might think I have been ~~having~~ living with another woman for ages.

Your questions. How long has it been going on.

Answer one night.

Where did I stay. Well you saw it yourself. Who was she?

No one you know and it would not be fair to say who it was and you cant expect me to. All I can say is that I have only heard once from her since the episode, & when I was over this time I did not even see her. I believe you thought it was Miss Mace, but I assure you we are not friends in that way at all. You must know I am much too fond of you to run a second establishment, even if I could afford to. I have apologised to you once, & do so now again, & after all I do do all I can for you, but if you cannot forgive me, I quite understand it is all my fault.

I went to Paris with Dug on Sat. to see Lewthwaite, and had a decent dinner, but did not go to a show or anything, and as we got there late on Sat & had to leave early Monday did not have much time.

I have had to move the Field Ambulance Hospital over here, which has been a lot of extra work, and meant all rebilleting.

On Monday night our train coming back was bombed for about ½ hour, and some real big ones were thrown, but none touched us. However it was not a pleasant experience. Cloak is away, also Sarchet, so as there is no other Adjutant with experience I am doing it myself which entails more work.

I had a nice long letter from Paula.

Our Padré is leaving us & as he runs the Mess & the Canteen it is a nuisance, but he will return when we get back to the line, which I hope will not be long now. I hate it when I am there, but dont like being left out of it when the others have to go.

Well that is all my news. I hope to get a letter to say I am forgiven, & then we can start afresh.

> All Love
> Still Thine
> Charles

Forwarded to:
Moray House
Adelaide Rd
Surbiton

With all the *'Thine'* and *'All Love'* and Xs at the end of his letters, it comes as a bit of a shock that he should even be thinking about a liaison with another woman, especially when on leave and reunited with his wife. He makes it clear that it was not with Miss Mace (i.e. Sir Arthur Pearson's personal assistant known as 'Chips', as in Item 272) but history does not record who it was instead.

There is of course no excuse for his behaviour, but as you have seen from the many divorces among Charles's peers, a lot of marriages broke down during the war, and it's got to be said that all-male public schools have a lot to answer for in terms of attitudes to women and sex, even through to the present day. David Footman gives an idea of public school male thinking of the time in his memoir of his early life:

'...I thought a lot, fervently, about girls and so I imagine did most of us. We were completely lacking in experience. All we had to go on were hearsay, novels and dirty stories and our ideas were consequently muddled.' ... 'Love, for us, was one thing and the excitements of copulation quite another. There were not only ladies in the world. There were others – shop girls, tarts, Frenchwomen. One should make hay while the sun shone.'

'When I was in the Army I was to find that permissiveness (for males only, of course) was the general rule. Exhortations to chastity were to most of us an empty sound. Fulminations regarding venereal disease were a matter not of morals but of common sense; a few elementary precautions and there was little danger of a dose of the clap. Married men were supposed to be loyal to their wives and they usually were. Otherwise it was a free for all. Should amateurs be unavailable or unappetising there was a wide choice of tarts. It was accepted that everyone should have his greens. I once shared a billet with a middle-aged subaltern of impeccable respectability – he was cashier in an insurance office – who told me he always had a woman every three weeks: he found it good for his lumbago.'

I doubt whether Charles using that excuse would have gone down too well with Margaret.

Meanwhile, the Battalion was still isolated in Franleu, but it seems that the German measles outbreak was all but over as they were spending their time in training with special emphasis being put on 'The Battalion in the attack'.

THE LADIES' UNITED SERVICES CLUB,
CURZON STREET,
MAYFAIR, W

Nov 24th

Dear Charles

I received your letter of the 9th, & I haven't answered it earlier as it required a lot of thought.

I accept your apology & I would like to be able to forgive you as you ask but it isn't an easy thing to do. My feelings are more or less numb just now but in time, & with your help, I hope to be able to feel differently about it all. For the present we had better leave things as they are, but when you are next home it is essential that we should talk things out & decide once & for all how things are to be in the future between us. I am sure you have not forgotten the promise we made to each other that there shall be no fusses. Let us just talk quietly about it & try to come to a definite understanding. I feel that this is my due, & I'm sure you will understand, & agree to that too.

M

I am seeing Alfie on Monday, & then going back to Burgess Hill.

Dec 8th 1916

My dear Margaret

A line to thank you for your letter, which I am afraid I have not by me now, as after we finished a very trying tour in the trenches I succumbed to an infernal chill & am now in hospital. I dont know what more there is to discuss but you shall have it your own way. However I dont expect to be home until the end of Jan. We had a good few casualties while we were up the line. Cloake was hit, & several men near us killed, I think it was the nearest shave I have had yet.[1] The weather is awful. I am sending you a cheque when I can get out for Paula's Xmas present.

yours ever
Charles

After their quarantine, the Battalion had taken the train from Gamaches to Albert and arrived back on the Somme battlefield near Bazentin-le-Grand on 28th November. After a few days working on fatigues they went into the front line near the Butte de Warlencourt on 1st December. With so much rain having formed such terrible mud that communication trenches were impassable, the occupation of the frontline had to be carried out by crossing most of the way in the open. When relieved on 5th December they returned to huts in Bazentin-le-Petit.

1 This incident is not in the Battalion war diary, which is rather strange as **Cecil Cloake ★**, *(right)*, was the one writing the entries. In his own memoirs he only mentions being wounded once, on 18th August. A shell splinter sliced open the scalp on the back of his head. It was dressed there and then and he needed no further treatment, but in old age the scar would occasionally break open and discharge, making him think that a small piece of shell was still lodged in the bone.

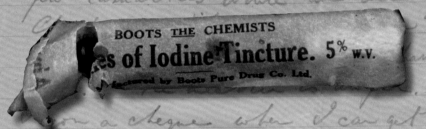

BOOTS THE CHEMISTS
of Iodine Tincture. 5% w.v.
factured by Boots Pure Drug Co. Ltd.

Dec 11th 1916

Rest Camp

My dear Margaret

Many thanks for your letter of the 6th just rec.d. I have no cheque book with me in this place, but expect Pearson's cheque any day which I will send you. I dont know about leave. I am anxious to get back to the Batt.n, & make some alterations & improvements which are most necessary from the experience of our last tour, or I should have been home now instead of this place, as I was offered leave. However I hear the Division will be coming out at the end of the month for a rest, & I expect all C.O.'s will be sent off first. I am trying to get Cloake away for Xmas, as he badly wants a rest, & being hit the other day did not improve matters for him. The weather is too awful for words & the only thing to be said for it is that it has stopped my Batt.n doing an attack, which I was not looking forward to, but we may have to do it yet. You might send Gerrard something for Xmas, he does not deserve it, having lost a pair of boots of mine but no matter he wept about it. Please thank Paula for her letter, & hoping you will all have a merry Xmas.

yrs ever

Charles

DAY
492
MON

11 DEC 1916

Item 336
Letter to Margaret

Envelope
161 Haverstock Hill
London

FIELD POST OFFICE
12 DE
16

DAY 501 WED

20 DEC 1916

Item 337
Letter to Margaret

Envelope
161 Haverstock Hill
London

(blank cheque still enclosed unused)

FIELD POST OFFICE 21 DE 16

20.12.16

Dearest Darling

A line to wish you all a merry Xmas. I am still in this infernal hospital & unless I can get better in a day or two am afraid I shall be sent further down. My tummy will have nothing to do with me, & although I am on a strict diet cannot digest anything. CAP's cheque has not come to hand. So try & cash the enclosed. I have not cashed a cheque since I went to Paris, & so I hope it is good.

Once more all good wishes

yrs ever

Charles

PS I have no cheque form of any sort so you must take this to Mr Stewart. I have written him.

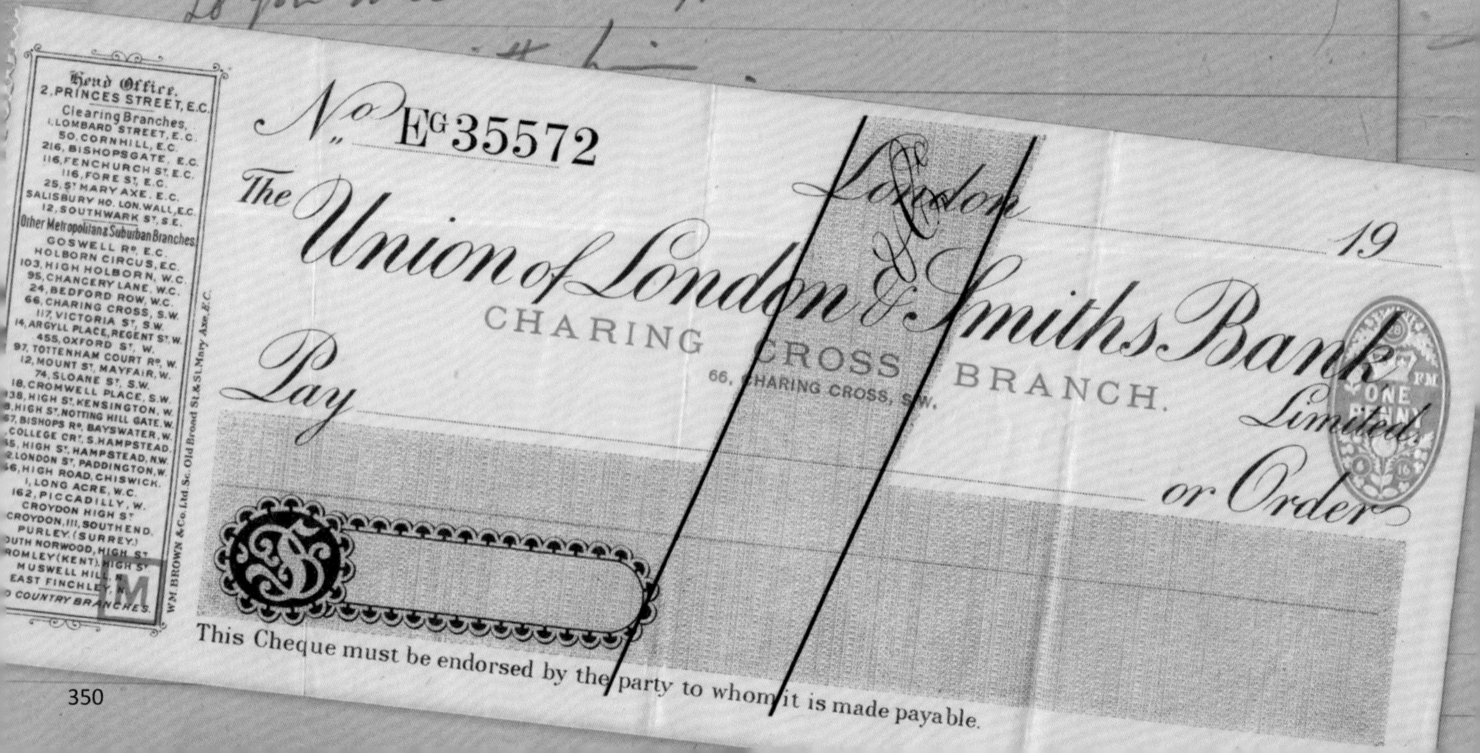

Head Office, 2, PRINCES STREET, E.C.
No EG 35572
London 19
The Union of London & Smiths Bank Limited
CHARING CROSS BRANCH.
66, CHARING CROSS, S.W.
Pay
or Order
ONE PENNY
This Cheque must be endorsed by the party to whom it is made payable.

DAY
507
TUE

26 DEC 1916

Item 338
Letter to Margaret

Envelope
161 Haverstock Hill
London

26.12.16

Dearest Margaret

> *A line to say I leave hospital today, & very glad to get away. I go up to front line until the 30ᵗʰ, when the Division comes out. Not much of a Xmas, one letter from Lilian, & nothing else. I hope Paula got her watch in time. Gerrard I find has not unpacked a single garment since I have been here, so when I wanted some trench clothes this morning I found everything <u>mouldy</u> & <u>damp</u>, & impossible to put on, so I have sent him back to his company.[1] Cloake is at duty now, & was not badly hit, I was next to him at the time. It still rains, & I hear my men are getting trench feet as hard as they can.[2]*

> *All Love*

> *Thine*

> *Charles*

> *Love to Paula xxxxxx*

1 As Charles's servant, Gerrard would have spent his time in Battalion HQ, so being sent back to his company to do the job of a standard infantryman would not have been a welcome change.

2 At the end of their time at rest in Franleu, every man had been given instruction in how to prevent chilled feet and frostbite, and the Medical Officer gave a demonstration in the use of whale oil (when rubbed into the feet, it provided a barrier to the water). Trench foot could lead to such damage (as pictured, **right**) that a man would have to be invalided out of the Army. Being caught with trench feet having not taken appropriate precautions was therefore viewed by the Army in a similar way to self-inflicted wounds.

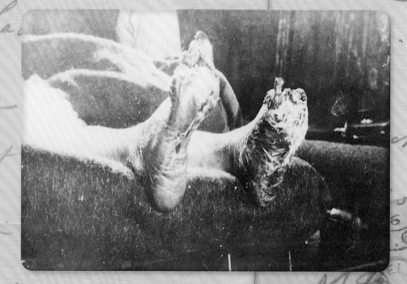

351

Item 339
Letter to Margaret

Envelope
*161 Haverstock Hill
London*

FIELD POST OFFICE
28 DE
16

Dec 27th 1916

My dearest Margaret

Many thanks for yours & Paula's letter. I hope the cheque did arrive in time, anyway it will have arrived by now. I have not yet been up to the Batt^n, & am living at Brigade H^d Q^{rs}.[1] The General commanding the Division told me today that I was to go on leave as soon as his application for me to proceed returned from G.H.Q., so I may start any time unless he changes his mind, which he is not given to. He asked me the reasons why I did not want to go, & exactly what was the matter with the Batt^n, & I told him that they were suffering from inexperience etc. However he had it out, & all the company officers have had their leave stopped until matters straighten out, & the Brigadier is investigating one tomorrow. It is all very worrying, but they only have themselves to blame. I suppose a change will do me good, but to be sent off without having a chance to see them is not very pleasant. However I suppose everything will turn out alright in the end but I would have liked to see this trouble through myself.
I heard from Bathurst the other day, who seems to want to find you something to do. I will try & let you know if I do start soon, but as I said before this is special leave for C.O.'s, & is sent direct from G.H.Q.[2]

All Love to you & Paula
Thine
Charles

1 Brigade HQ was in huts at Bazentin-le-Petit. These would have been **Nissen huts** (as in the picture, *left*). Their design was the brainchild of Major Peter Nissen, 45, a Canadian born in the USA, the son of a Norwegian emigrant. Using curved corrugated steel sheets, a hut could be packed in a standard Army Wagon and erected by 6 men in 4 hours. They had first gone into production in August 1916, and over 100,000 were made during the First World War.

2 Charles was soon on his way home on leave.

 ON LEAVE IN ENGLAND

1917

Whilst on leave, Charles's name appeared in the London Gazette amongst those who had been awarded a Mention in Despatches by Field Marshal Sir Douglas Haig. His name was listed with 28 other officers and men of the Royal Berkshire Regiment, including his late friend from his pre-war service, Arthur Holdsworth.

DAY 527 MON

15 JAN 1917

Item 340
Letter to Margaret

Envelope
161 Haverstock Hill
London

Jan 15th 1916

Dearest Darling

    Arrived here safely after an awful journey at 5 pm yesterday and was too late for the post. I have had a raging tooth ache ever since I started with the result I feel like nothing on earth. I was violently ill on the way over & retired to bed at Calais the moment I got there, after which I was only first up in time to catch the train. I will write more fully later today but the post is just off.

I did not enjoy my leave much, did you?

        yrs

        Charles

xxxxxx Paula

DAY 529 WED

17 JAN 1917

Item 341
Letter to Margaret

Envelope
161 Haverstock Hill
London

17.1.16

Dearest Darling

Am on the move at a moments notice. We are off to a quiet spot will try & get a line off tonight to explain.

all Love

Thine

Charles.

Sunday 21st 1917

Dearest Darling

Having travelled hard for three days we got back here yesterday. I went to Paris the first night, but we got there very late & had to leave the next day, and then went to see men etc at the Base.[1] I saw Mr Lewthwaite, and as we were getting in the taxi to go to the base, who should drive up but C.A.P., but beyond shaking hands had no time for any more. I got 3 officers at the base but no men, and on the return we had to come via Paris or a longer route, so we took the longer to avoid changing stations in Paris and were due in at 9.50 pm, but the train was late, & we eventually got put out 2½ miles from our town at 2.40 am with a 20 mile drive and a snowstorm. Such is travelling in this country. However we found a pub at 4 am & waited for a car which came at 10.30, & got back here yesterday at 1. I had a lot to do, as we move back the day after tomorrow, and this morning I was out at 7 am. What with Dug Cloake Sarchet away I have taken on about as much as I can manage, & being sent down to the base did not improve matters, as it was one continual travel. I have no senior officers but hope to get back Robinson & Lawrence. When we get back I hope to get time to write a few letters, but have laid out my day now commencing at 6.30, & finishing at 7.30 pm & bed directly after dinner.

Best love to Paula & yourself

Yours ever

Charles

DAY 533 SUN

21 JAN 1917

Item 342
Letter to Margaret

Envelope
161 Haverstock Hill
London

FIELD POST OFFICE
22 JA 17

Again, he's suffering from beginning-of-year-itis and put 1916 on the dates of the previous 2 letters, and for this letter has not included the month (but 21st January 1917 was a Sunday) and the trip he describes is from this time according to the Battalion's war diary.

Since the beginning of January, the Battalion had been billeted in Albert and employed in improving the roads outside the town.

1 Charles visited Nº 46 Infantry Base Depot in Rouen in order to make personal contact with the commander there so as to explain in detail what the Battalion's needs were in terms of men and equipment. Rouen is on the train line that roughly follows the River Seine from Paris out to Le Havre on the coast. On the way Charles would have passed Giverny, the village on the Seine where through the years of the war Claude Monet had been painting his water lilies, *(right)*.

DAY
537
THU

25 JAN 1917

Item 343
Letter to Margaret

Envelope
*161 Haverstock Hill
London*

25.1.17

Dearest Darling

    Many thanks for your letter. You tell me to write you a nice letter and I would if I could, but the cold is so intense I can hardly hold a pencil, and to complete my trouble both my big toes are slightly frost bitten. We had a good march here the day before yesterday, & were well shelled just before we left but had no casualties, and the only shell that would have finished off some of us did not go off. We are here until the 4th[1] & then move up into a new area, but do not actually take over the front line until about the 12th. We have to do 5 hours training per day, and of course I am so cold by the time I have been out an hour that by the end of the day I am just a frozen bit of flesh. However Dug Cloake & Sarchet being away I have not a minute to myself, & I think should find some excuse for a holiday. My teeth are beginning to go back again, as I simply have not the energy to use the sprayer. My bad tooth is getting better & only aches on occasions. There are no windows & in fact I have never felt the cold so much in my life before. I can say no more, but will try & find time for a more cheerful letter tomorrow.

    All All All Love to you & Paula

        Thine

          Charles

1 They were in Warloy, 5 miles west of Albert.

DAY
542
TUE

30 JAN 1917

Item 344
Letter to Margaret

Envelope
*161 Haverstock Hill
London*

30.1.17

Dearest Darling

    Many thanks for yours rec[d] last night. My word the cold is too awful and standing about for 5 hours daily will be the end of me. I have lost now my transport officer who is down with pneumonia, so there is not a single one of the headquarter staff here except myself hence no letters being written, but I am very fond of you all the same.

    All All All Love

      Thine

       Charles

31.1.17

Dearest Darling

I know you will think I have been slack in writing but what with this intense cold and so much to do it is impossible. I am sending this by our Doctor who I have told to ring you up & give you all news. You might ask him to lunch at the Pic he is such a nice fellow, & I enclose one pound to pay for lunch. My troubles are not over. Phillips has gone down with pneumonia and he is a great loss. This is our list of Headquarters, so you will see what a lot of help I have now.

C.O.	Self	
Major Tosetti		*on leave*
Capt Cloake	*adjutant*	*on sick leave*
Lieut Sarchey[1]	*assistant adjutant*	*at a school*[2]
Lieut Phillips	*Transport officer*	*sick*
Lieut Byrne[3]	*Medical officer*	*on leave*
Lieut Moon	*Quartermaster*	*on leave*
Rev Longden	*Mess President*	*on leave*

I am dining with the General tonight and the Black Watch tomorrow, and to go out on these cold nights is most unpleasant. If you see Lilian or John or anyone I ought to write to will you tell them I will do so as soon as I can. We move up on the 4th but not into the line until about the 9th. My tooth is still a bit of a worry & I have to go to the dentist again on Friday. All the canals are frozen, hence a shortage of coal. Well I have nothing to say but thank goodness I am luckier than some C.O.'s, who are sleeping in tents.

All All All Love to you & Paula

Thine

Charles

DAY 543 WED

31 JAN 1917

Item 345
Letter to Margaret

Envelope
161 Haverstock Hill London

(Posted in England)

? S.W.
5.15 PM
2 FEB 17

1 He has spelt 'Sarchet' phonetically (the name comes from the Channel Islands).

2 There were schools of instruction to teach the skills necessary to use items of equipment and undertake different roles within the Army. Possibly Hugh Sarchet was learning the job of Adjutant (he would take over from Cecil Cloake★ in early 1918).

3 Lt **Charles Byrne**, 23, had served as a 'dresser' on a hospital ship before becoming a medical officer in the RAMC. He would be captured in the German Spring Offensive in 1918 and be noted for his excellent work for his fellow POWs. Rejoining the Army in 1939, he was awarded the OBE for his work during the fall of France including volunteering for the rescue party after the sinking of the Lancastria.

DAY
546
SAT

3 FEB 1917

Item 346
Letter to Margaret

Envelope
161 Haverstock Hill
London

3.2.17

Dearest Darling

Many thanks for yours rec^d yesterday. We are still shivering & my poor old feet are more sore than ever. Tomorrow we move 12 miles, which will be no easy march with the roads in such a bad state. I am trying to make up my mind to have a bath tonight, but am rather funking it. We have a big brigade field day today which will be a cold job.

Am too cold to think of anything more at present.

All All All Love to you & Paula

Thine

Charles

DAY
548
MON

5 FEB 1917

Item 347
Letter to Margaret

Envelope
161 Haverstock Hill
London

5.2.17.

Dearest Darling

Arrived yesterday here, and push on the day after tomorrow. Am pursuing the Scrub all the way up the line, he left a note for me, & I have sent my orderly to try & bring him back to dinner, but personally I would not move out in this cold if I could avoid it. Many thanks for waistcoat. Toes are d-nable, & am wearing boots sized 10 instead of 8. Shall not want shirt at present. Am sending Bogey Harrods bill to deal with. I should think Paula might have some stockings with that sovereign. Have not used the sprayer, the spray would freeze between the time it left the nozzle & reached my teeth. Lilian's socks not yet arrived. Writing Mrs Hicks when we get to the end of our journey. Gerrard has a nasty cold, but refuses to leave me. The last two marches only one man fell out each time & then he fainted before doing so. Not a bad record. A draft of 103 arrived today but dont come under my command until the 8th.

All All Love

In great haste

Thine

Charles

Love to Paula, I hope she will get a prize. Is the 1st class the top or bottom one, & how many are there?

8.2.17

10 p.m.

Dearest Darling

Am trying to write in semi-darkness. Dug has just arrived & seems well. We have been marching hard for two days. Lunched with Scrub yesterday, & caught up my Battⁿ afterwards.[1] He moves up the line today & takes over the right sector of his Division, I go up in 6 days & take over left sector of my division, so we shall be next to one another. Will write more tomorrow. D-n the cold. Feet better but no voice left.

All All Love

Thine

Charles

DAY 551 THU

8 FEB 1917

Item 348
Letter to Margaret

Envelope
161 Haverstock Hill London

1 The Battalion had marched south of the River Somme to take over a new area from the French 24th Division. Stopping first in Cerissy, they were now in the huts at Camp Olympe not far from Chuignes. On the way they had been led by their band who at one point stopped to play them past as they gave the salute to the French General who was in the company of the commanders of III Corps, 1st Division & 1st Brigade. The war diary notes that this period's weather was the coldest they had experienced so far in the whole of the war.

10.2.17

Dearest Darling

Working like the devil to keep warm, & get ready for the trenches. Yesterday with the exception of ½ hour for lunch I was out from 9 am to 5.30 pm. I went up towards the front line yesterday afternoon, & my word there has been some fighting in this district, one sugar factory was battered to pieces. I believe the communicating trench leading up to the front line is over 2 miles long. However I expect to take the officers up tomorrow to have a look round. Cloake returned yesterday, but is being taken at once for staff work, however I get Sarchet back today, so hope to ease off a little myself. I dont think I have had such a hard fortnight for a long time, and with 3 moves thrown in it has been no joke. Poor old Paul I hear he has gone,[1] but have not seen it in the paper, in fact have not seen a paper for ages.

DAY 553 SAT

10 FEB 1917

Item 349
Letter to Margaret

Envelope
161 Haverstock Hill London

FIELD POST OFFICE
11 FE 17

Little Byrne is back & said he rang you up, but could not catch you, & was so rushed that he was sorry not to meet you. As we are settling down in the trenches you might send me a writing block. As you can imagine having gone into a new district there are at present no canteens or conveniences of any sort. Well Dearest I must now be off.

All All All Love
Thine
Charles

Song
THE SLEEPY CANAL.
PAUL A. RUBENS.
"MISS HOOK OF HOLLAND."

By the side of the sleep-y ca-nal. You and I. 'Neath the sky:

1 With the decline in his health, **Paul Rubens** had withdrawn down to Cornwall and died there on 5th February. It would not be until 1919 that **Phyllis Dare** would fully resume her stage career. Her last show would be with Ivor Novello and she retired after he died in 1951. She never married.

| Paul: | 1900 | 2000 |
| Phyllis: | 1900 | 2000 |

DAY
554
SUN

11 FEB 1917

Item 350
Letter to Margaret

Envelope
161 Haverstock Hill
London

Forwarded to:
c/o Lady Crutchley
Royal Hospital
Chelsea
London

Sunday.
11.2.17.

Dearest Darling

    Just rec[d] your letter written on Monday saying poor old Paul has gone. Thank goodness he did not have to suffer like poor old Syb.[1] We are on the move again tomorrow but when we settle down in the line I will write to Mrs Rubens.[2] At the present moment I am just too busy for words, as of course the majority of officers & men are new to this kind of warfare we are going back to. Both the Major General & the Brigadier are very pleased with the way the Batt[n] has trained on during the past month, & both have told me so which is something. I wish you would send me any cuttings out of the papers, you have about poor old Paul, as I have not seen a notice at all. I was counting up the officers I have had under me since we came out and although we always seem to be short, it comes up to the awful total of 92. Tomorrow we have our final bath for 3 weeks, and what the trenches will be like when the thaw comes I dread to think. I have only two bad toes now but have lost my voice not through cold but shouting. Would you like to send out a parcel of those little sausages, they would travel nicely in this weather & go well in a dug out.

No more news

All All All Love to you & Paula

Thine

Charles

1 Syb = his elder half-sister **Sybilla** who had died in 1915.

2 **Jenny Rubens**, 64, lived in Kensington with her husband Victor, 79. She had two sons serving in the Army & yet it was the one who hadn't joined up who died during the war. Paul's brother Walter, who was also

a composer, had gone to Gallipoli in 1915 as a Lieutenant in the Essex Regiment, but though he survived the war, his health was broken. He died on the French Riviera in 1920, possibly also of TB, and TB had led to their other brother Herbert being invalided out from the Army in 1918, though he would live until 1963. ➜**407 Rubens Family**

14.2.17.

Dearest Darling

Moving up into the front line this afternoon. I have not actually been round it but am going up early with Cloake in a closed motor to do so. Yesterday we went to Batt^n HQ and learnt all we could about it. It appears to be quite a quiet spot although the Bosch greeted us by putting one shell through the mess & one in the kitchen. Letters seem to take a long time yours about 6 days. I started this letter at 9 am & it is now 12 midday, & so many people here I must give up.

All Love

Thine

Charles

DAY
557
WED

14 FEB 1917

Item 351
Letter to Margaret

Envelope
*161 Haverstock Hill
London*

They were in now in Chuignes.

Item 352
Letter to Margaret

Envelope
(Same as for Item 351)

15.2.17
2 pm

Dearest Darling

Arrived here yesterday afternoon and it has been peace perfect peace.
The Engineers rebuilt our HQ last night and I slept in my corner and never heard
a sound. All this morning I spent in the line, which is alright now, but I dread
to think what it will be like when it thaws. However it is nice to be able to walk
about without having to dodge shells all the time. I will try & write you a long
letter tomorrow, but now I must get some sleep, as I shall be out again tonight.
The men have started quite well, & as long as we start with strict discipline it will
be much easier afterwards.
You are quite right about Connie.[1]

In great haste
All All All Love
Thine
Charles

1 Margaret's sister **Connie** had married a bank clerk who in December 1915 had attested that he was willing to join up under the Derby Scheme. It is likely he had recently received his call-up papers as he would be mobilised 3 weeks after this letter. He survived the war but Connie fell for a decorated Australian infantry captain who became the co-respondent in the filing of her divorce in 1919 and whom she would marry in Sydney in 1926.

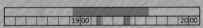

Item 353
Letter to Margaret

Envelope
161 Haverstock Hill
London

Army Form C. 2121.

GNALS.   No. of Message

17/2/17

Recd. at............m.
Date..............
From..............

Dearest Darling

I wrote Paula a line yesterday & meant to write you on my
return, but it took me over 6 hours to get round yesterday as there was what you
read in the papers considerable artillery activity on both sides. The thaw has I fear
started, and I only hope it will be gradual. I have had no time to write letters, as
I have had such a lot of work to do, and these French trenches are so complicated,
it is worse than the maze at Hampton Court to find ones way about. Also I am
carefully studying the Bosche line with a view to annoying him the next time
we come in the line. We go back into reserve tomorrow for 4 days. Did I tell you
Williamson came out again, but has gone home sick; this is his third attempt, &

A A A

he has now lived on the army 2½ years, & not been in a trench.[1] I wrote Bathurst yesterday as the Blind people sent me their cheque in error, so I sent it on to him. We have not had an English post for days, & know very little of what is going on. Now I must about my business.

All All All Love to you & Paula

Thine

Charles

1 2Lt **Cyril Williamson** ★ , *(right)*, would soon be transferred to the 9th Worcesters in England, and arrived again out in France in 1918, but 4 days after the Armistice. Demobilized in 1919, he would be back in uniform during the Second World War.

19.2.17

Dearest Darling

I did not write yesterday as I only got up at 5 am in the morning and got to bed at 1 am. We are out for 4 days rest, which looks like being 4 of the hardest days work we have had for a long time. We are still in cellars but not so comfortable as when up in the line. I am just a little bit fed up, there seems to be no rest, & one has to keep up to a high pitch to keep the others up at all. Dug is sitting writing with a cat asleep on his shoulders, & as the cat is "expecting" I dont think it is very nice. I simply have not had a minute to write to other people, but hope to when we get back in the line again. Please thank John for some socks & Turtle soup which have just arrived, also I hear a parcel from Lilian is in the stores. The slush & dirt is awful, & we all have terrible "Trench coughs". Dinner menu for tonight as we have guests consisting of gunners who are shooting over our heads next week & must be propitiated consists of Turtle Soup

Salmon Cutlets

Roast leg of Mutton

Scrambled eggs & Anchovies

with Vermouth Whisky & Port

All All All Love

Thine in haste

Charles

DAY
562
MON

19 FEB 1917

Item 354
Letter to Margaret

Envelope
*161 Haverstock Hill
London*

Feb 2²ᵈ 1917

DAY 565 THU
22 FEB 1917

Item 355
Letter to Margaret

Envelope
*161 Haverstock Hill
London*

FIELD POST OFFICE
22 FE 17

Feb 22ⁿᵈ 1917

Dearest Darling

No time for letter writing. We have had no mail for two or three days. Thank goodness we go back in the trenches tomorrow as this 4 days rest is a farce. I may go to a C.O.'s conference next week which may mean a journey to Havre but it is not yet settled. Two more officers[1] today so I am getting on, but there is a lot of sickness about. I am still voiceless & a running cold. Will you please send me two boxes of "Pinelyptus Pastilles". Proctors sort is the kind to ask for, "At all stores & chemists", "No others any use".[2] Will write tomorrow.

All All All Love to you & Paula

Thine

Charles

MADE IN GREAT BRITAIN
**PROCTOR'S
PINELYPTUS PASTILLES**
(BRONCHO-LARYNGEAL)

FOR
**ASTHMA
CATARRH
COUGH**
DIRECTIONS:— TAKE ONE
FREQUENTLY DAY OR NIGHT

FOR
**CHEST
THROAT
VOICE**
REGISTERED
AT HOME AND ABROAD.

RECOMMENDED BY
Mᵐᵉˢ SARAH BERNHARDT, MISS ELLEN TERRY, SIR HENRY IRVING, ETC.

PROCTOR'S PINELYPTUS DEPÔT, NEWCASTLE ON TYNE, Eng.

1 The two officers were 2Lt **Cyril Morris**, back from being wounded in July, and 2Lt **Eric Johnson**, 21, who had been studying engineering at Cambridge in 1914. Initially rejected by the Army on medical grounds, Eric at first served at the Royal Aircraft Factory in Farnborough as a research assistant on the strength and weatherproofing of wing fabrics. At last commissioned in December 1916, he would be taken prisoner during the German Spring Offensive in 1918, but survive to become a chartered civil and mechanical engineer, get married and have a daughter he named Lesbia.

2 **Proctor's Pinelyptus Pastilles** were made by a chemist in Newcastle for *'clearing the throat and giving tone and strength to the voice'*. First advertised in 1898, with endorsements from the like of Sarah Bernhardt & Sir Henry Irving, they are still available today, with the slogan: *'As used by Lords, Ladies, Principal Public Speakers, Singers and Members of Parliament for over a hundred years'*.

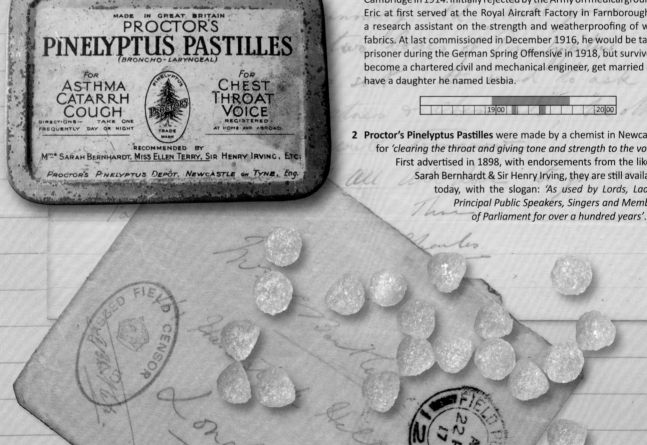

Item 356
Letter to Margaret

Envelope
*161 Haverstock Hill
London*

*Forwarded to:
Nithsdale
Burgess Hill
Sussex*

24.2.16.[1]

Dearest Darling

> We have had no letters for days, and as I leave tomorrow for the Army School where I shall be until the 4th unless I hear from you today I shall not until my return. The old Bosche got very windy yesterday and put over a lot of shells without doing any damage except spoiling our savory as the kitchen got knocked in just as we were finishing dinner. The trenches are in an awful state. I got stuck in one yesterday & had to be lifted out, and the men seem to spend their entire time digging each other out. Dug had a narrow shave yesterday from shells dropping within 10 yds of him and to avoid them he had to lie flat in the bottom of a trench which was half full of water. You never saw anyone in such a mess as he was when he got back.
>
> Three Bosches came in the day before yesterday two were very poor specimens and seemed to know nothing, and as Dug put it "If they couldn't give better information why not shoot them". Well I have a lot of news but owing to the Censor shall keep it to myself.

> *All All All Love to you & Paula*
>
> *Thine*
>
> *Charles*

HAMPSTEAD S.O.
9.30 AM
28 FE
17
N.W.

1 Should be 1917.

26.2.17.

Dearest Darling

> Received 5 letters from you & 1 from Paula last night. Am sorry I have not given you much news lately but when one is living in mud up to ones knees & doing only what one is forbidden to write about, it is rather difficult to say much. I am on my way now to the Army School where I shall be until the 4th, & dont think I shall get any letters until I return. I will write Paula again tomorrow. All All All Love

> *Thine*
>
> *Charles*

I hope Paula is better

FIELD POST OFFICE
26 FE
17

Item 357
Letter to Margaret

Envelope
*161 Haverstock Hill
London*

4th Infantry School of Instruction[1]
B.E.F.
28.2.17.

Dearest Darling

My word this is the place for me and I would not mind being here for the duration of the war. There are 24 of us and it is quite nice to associate with soldiers again. I have a good billet with sheets which I have not seen since I got back. Have met several old friends and the work is most interesting. Thank goodness it goes on until the 7th, so you can write up to then judging by how long this takes to reach you. I have still no voice and if I am not better at the end of this course I shall have to lie up for a bit. I hope Paula is better and is getting on well at her school. Today we are going to do a tactical scheme which I am feeling rather nervous about. We are carted about all over the country in motor buses & I believe finish up this afternoon in the town where we may get a bon dinner. The Messing is the only bad part of this show, but that may improve and anyway there is none of the d-d noise of shells dropping all around one. Well Dearest I have no more news.

All All All Love to you & Paula

Thine

Charles

FLIXECOURT (Somme – Le Château

1 **The Fourth Army School of Instruction** was in a chateau, **(right)**, at Flixecourt, a little town halfway between Amiens and Abbeville. It had opened in February 1916 with the idea of standardising methods across different units. The C.O.s' courses enabled the sharing of frontline experiences as well as giving the chance for a rest.

Army School

1.3.17.

Dearest Darling

Just rec^d yours of 23rd. I am afraid no kippers or sausages will be coming on here. My voice is worse, in fact is a mere whisper, & although I feel fairly fit unless it improves I shall have to go for a rest cure. Yesterday afternoon we all went for a long bus ride & saw some French works, which were just marvellous, then had a good dinner & got back here 11 pm. Left here at

---

DAY 571 WED

28 FEB 1917

Item 358

Letter to Margaret

Envelope
161 Haverstock Hill London

ARMY POST OFFICE
MR 1 17

DAY 572 THU

1 MAR 1917

Item 359

Letter to Margaret

Envelope
161 Haverstock Hill London

9 am in motor buses & inspected a Musketry School, attended a lecture from 2.30 – 4.30, just had tea & now another lecture from 5.30, so we are kept pretty busy. For pity's sake hurry up the cough lozenges, as they are my only supplement for cigarettes. I hear 3 bales of socks have turned up from Mrs Hicks, but have not seen them or heard officially, really she is a marvel.[1] I am glad Paula is better. I sent Bathurst a further cheque so your spring requirements look in the distance, but I will do my best. Where do you think I ought to reach you on your birthday?[2] I dont know & cant gather from you how long letters are taking.

All All All Love to you & Paula

Thine

Charles

---

1 **Ellen Hicks**, 57, was the mother of Lt Basil Hicks★ who was killed at Loos. 17 months after his death and she hadn't given up, and was doing what she could to support the men of her son's Battalion. Her other son was a Navy pilot and would survive the war, but she would never have grandchildren and only outlived the end of the war by two years.

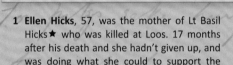

2 Margaret's birthday was 23rd August so it appears that he is confused, but we'll see later that it is his attempt at a ruse.

4th Army School
March 7th 1917

Dearest Darling

We have had no opportunity for writing the last few days, as we have been touring about all over the country looking at Camps etc. Two nights we stopped at LE TOUQUET, and really had not only an interesting but most instructive time, and we got back here last night. There is an address by the Army Commander this morning, & then we may all push off to PARIS to visit the French Sandhurst,[1] but the C.I.C.[2]'s permission has not yet arrived. This conference has been a real joy, & we all have enjoyed ourselves immensely. It is such a change to get into a Mess of 24 where there are no Temporary Gentlemen,[3] although it may be a bit snobbish to say so. I wrote to you about Connie, I dont mind her staying for a bit while near town, but do not want her with you always. No letters have been forwarded from the Batt[n] for a week, so I cannot answer any questions there may be. Col Gordon who is commanding the

DAY 578 WED

7 MAR 1917

Item 360
Letter to Margaret

Envelope
c/o Lady Crutchley
Royal Hospital
Chelsea
London

Welsh Guards is taking this letter over. He is such a nice fellow.[4] *Well Dearest I have no more news. I have still no voice.*

All All All Love to you & Paula

Thine

Charles

xxxxxx

1 Sandhurst's Royal Military College provided training for officers of the British Army. The French equivalent was **Saint-Cyr**, founded in 1802 under Napoleon, & located at this time just to the west of Paris near Versailles. It is now 200 miles away in Brittany.

2 C.I.C. = Commander-in-Chief, Field Marshal Sir Douglas Haig.

3 There were a lot of officers with temporary war-time commissions who before the war would not have been considered to be of officer class (i.e. they probably worked for a living as opposed to gentlemen who lived on their invested wealth), so they were jokingly referred to as *'Temporary Gentlemen'*.

4 Lt Col **Douglas Gordon**, 33, after serving in the Boer War was Superintendent of Gymnasia in London from 1908- 1912. In 1914 he had been a Captain in the Scots Guards and was now two months into being C.O. of 1st Welsh Guards (DSO in 1918). He would become Equerry to the Duke of Connaught in 1921.

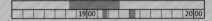

DAY
581
SAT

10 MAR 1917

Item 361
Letter to Margaret

Envelope
161 Haverstock Hill
London

Hotel Ritz

Place Vendôme

Paris

10.3.17

Hotel Ritz
Place Vendôme
Paris

10.3.17

Dearest Darling

I have heard nothing of you for a week but hope to when I get back tonight. I sent you off a small hat yesterday which I hope you will like. All yesterday I spent in bed, & am still feeling rotten, but have to get back somehow today. I am still voiceless, & my throat is beginning to trouble me a good deal, so I dont quite know what to do. Will you send the Caledonian Club[1] *£1-1-0. All the Black Watch belong to it, & insisted I should join, and as it is only one guinea I thought I would.*

All All All Love

Thine

Charles

1 **The Caledonian Club**, then in St James's Square in London, was struggling due to the deaths of so many members in the war. It would also soon be having a crisis meeting following the death of its proprietor, but great efforts by its membership gave it a new lease of life and it continues today for those having a *'close association'* with Scotland. Though Charles's father's first wife had been Scottish, his main qualification for joining seems to have been the friendship of a lot of officers of the Black Watch.

DAY
583
MON

12 MAR 1917

Item 362
Letter to Margaret

Envelope
161 Haverstock Hill
London

FIELD POST OFFICE
13 MR
17

March 12ᵗʰ 1917

Dearest Darling

     You will be surprised to hear that I am now on my back in No 2 FA[1] with a temperature of 101, & no voice. I have tried to get the best of it & not leave my work, and that was one of the reasons I went to PARIS to consult a specialist, but it is no good & I have to retire from the contest for a time. The A.D.M.S. is trying to arrange for me to go to Lady Michelham's hospital at MENTONE[2] so that I shall still be on the strength. If I do wives are allowed out there but not to sleep in hospital, & all patients have to. However it is not definitely settled, but think it over & see Bathurst. I should very much like you to come out there, I dont know if Bathurst has any money, but sure to, & I believe there is or was some to come from poor old Paul.[3] I am pretty certain to move from here to somewhere tomorrow either a Casualty Clearing Station or the Base. It is most disappointing as everyone is so pleased with the Rgt at present, it is a nuisance to leave it.

     All All All Love to you & Paula

Thine

Charles

P.S. Not a good position to write in.

---

1 Nº 2 FA = Nº 2 Field Ambulance, which was then in the huts of Camp Marly near Chuignes.

2 **Lady Michelham**, 34, had been born Aimée Geraldine Bradshaw, the daughter of a wealthy grandee in Devon who later owned Powderham Castle near Exeter. Aged 17 she had married the even more wealthy Herbert Stern, a 48-year-old financier who had inherited £2 million from his father in 1887. He was a racehorse owner & art collector, but also a shrewd investor who had increased his inheritance many fold despite giving away huge sums to charities & in 1905 had been created Baron Michelham. In 1915, he promised £1000 to any airman who shot down a Zeppelin, & he financed two convalescent homes for officers at the Grand Hotel, Cimiez, & Cap Martin Hotel near Mentone on the French Riviera, as well as taking over the Hotel Astoria in Paris as a British hospital. It was Lady Michelham herself who was doing a lot of the hands-on work, including running an ambulance train from the front to their facilities. In this picture, *(right)*, she is wearing the Order of the League of Mercy, the Médaille d'honneur du travail (in Gold), & the Légion d'honneur, alongside some of her 19 yards of pearls. She would be mentioned in dispatches twice & awarded the 1914 Star (the lack of a higher honour has the whiff of a snub by the British Establishment). ➜400

3 **Paul Rubens** made no mention of Charles or Margaret in his will.

DAY 584 TUE

13 MAR 1917

Item 363
Letter to Margaret

Envelope
(same as for Item 362)

13.3.17.

Dearest Darling 2 pm

Just rec*d* letters dated March 1, 2, 5 & 7. I wont go into them now, as I only have a minute to post & hope to get this off by the Div. mail. I was told this morning that I should proceed to South of France as soon as they heard there was a vacancy, so if you would care to come, chance the channel, & get rid of your exzema so much the better. I will let you know when I start. Yes dearest I am much happier.

All Love
Thine
Charles

DAY 585 WED

14 MAR 1917

Item 364
Letter to Margaret

Envelope
161 Haverstock Hill
London

ARMY POST OFFICE
15 MR 17

No 2 F.A.
14.3.17

Dearest Darling

Now to answer some of your letters. March 1*st*. The Conference was to interchange ideas, & meet different Corps & Army Commanders. The sausages & kippers arrived in due course, the sausages would have lasted another 2 days & the kippers another 3, of course I was not in at the death but they were much appreciated, & for which many thanks. Now for March 2 letter which deals with spots. I am very sorry for you & can only suggest a change to the Riviera. Now for March 5*th*. What I meant you to write & say was my birthday is in Aug but Paula's is on the ? day of March, but you did not rise.
Of course I am much happier, & am hoping to see you at MENTONE before long. It is settled I go as soon as there is a vacancy & my temperature has been normal for 48 hours so I hope to start the day after tomorrow. Could you not get Jim Lady Sybil or even Lilian to come out. It is an awful journey of course, as it now takes 8 hours from Calais to Paris, where you would stop one night, & then 22 hours on. Well put your thinking cap on and I will let you know when I start. If you were to come alone Zena Brett[1] would look after you in PARIS. His office is in PLACE

de ST HONORE near the Ritz, and if you arrive in Paris station get hold of one of the Military Police, tell them you are a C.O.'s wife, & make them look after you. Provide yourself with food, there are no dining cars, & you can only take as much luggage as will go on the rack & fill the corridor. I am very sorry for poor old Dug as the Major General has sent another C.O. to command during my absence.[2] I have protested but am afraid it is no use. It is an awful bit of bad luck, as he did so well last time, & I consider most unfair. My address will be "Officers Convalescent Home" Cap Martin Hotel, MENTONE so you can write & let me know your ideas on the subject. If you come please bring me 2 pairs white flannels & shoes, if not please post them on receipt of this, no other civilian clothes allowed. Give my best love to Paula, after lunch (Bengers food[3]) & a sleep I propose to write to Her Ladyship.

yrs with all my love

Charles

1 **Zena Dare** had retired from the stage after her marriage to Maurice Brett in 1911. She was currently with him in Paris & in fact spent 3 years nursing French wounded in the American hospital there, only taking time out to have her third & last child in March 1916. She returned to the stage in 1926 & appeared in many long-running productions, ending in her longest run of all as Mrs Higgins in the original West End production of *'My Fair Lady'* for 2,281 performances from 1958 to 1963. After all that she professed to being a nervous person who had never enjoyed acting but liked the life it gave, loving the people she met and the money she earned. She was on Desert Island Discs in 1957 (with her chosen luxury being a mink coat), and Eamonn Andrews surprised her at a curtain call in 1963 for *'This Is Your Life'*.

2 Lt Col **Cornelius Asgill Shaw Carleton**, DSO, 33, *(above right)*, had the look of the rugby forward he had been for Gloucester. In 1914 he was a Lt in 2nd Welsh, having served in Nigeria and Egypt. After a series of daring recces he was wounded on 25th September 1914 and awarded the DSO. Back as a Captain in 1st/6th Welsh in November, he took over command when his C.O. was killed at Loos in October 1915. He did not seem committed to this transfer to the 8th Royal Berkshires & would go back to 1st/6th Welsh in July. In April 1918 he became C.O. of 2nd Welsh, being wounded after one week, & 6 weeks after his return to them in August he was wounded again, but would survive to the age of 81.

3 **Benger's Food**, *(right)*, was a hot milk preparation that included enzymes to ease digestion. One slogan was *'It is retained after every other food has been rejected'* & it was a *'boon to Invalids and the Aged'*. First advertised in 1883, it was made in Strangeways in Manchester into the 1960s.

DAY
586
THU

15 MAR 1917

Item 365
Letter to
Margaret

Envelope
(same as for
Item 364)

No 2 FA
March 15th 1917

Dearest Darling

    No luck Lady Michelham's home at Cap St Martin is full at present. However a wire has been sent asking when there will be a vacancy and we expect to hear tomorrow when I will let you know. If I get there <u>I do hope you will be able to come</u>. I have had no news of you for 3 days of you. My temperature is down to normal at last but I cannot sleep and dont feel merry or bright.
4.30 pm Just rec^d your letter of the 9th, the posts are getting too awful for words. Fancy poor you getting up with the lark, & then not having any potatoes. I am sending Bathurst another cheque but I am afraid it wont arrive by the same post as I am pushing this line off now in the Div. H.Q. bag.

      All All All Love to you & Paula

        Thine

        Charles

DAY
588
SAT

17 MAR 1917

Item 366
Letter to
Margaret

Envelope
161
Haverstock Hill
London

March 17th 1917

Dearest Darling

    No news about a vacancy at MENTONE, and as you can imagine there is some excitement going on here what with the Bosch retiring[1] & the Russian Revolution.[2] I am a bit better & my temperature is down but I am still very weak, & can only speak in a whisper. I had no letter again from you today, but one from John, who does not seem very well. This is a deadly dull place & I shall be glad to get away from it. One only has mud to look upon, & the unceasing guns to listen to. I do hope to get some news tomorrow.

      All All All Love to you & Paula

        Thine

        Charles

FIELD POST OFFICE
18 MR
17

1 Realising that their resources were stretched, in October the Germans had started to build a new defensive position (the dotted line on the map, **right**). This would shorten their line by 18% and, along with a more efficient and robust design, enable them to free up over 10 infantry divisions and 50 artillery batteries for redeployment. British aerial reconnaissance had spotted the new defences in January 1917, but although they had published a full set of maps of what they dubbed *'The Hindenburg Line'* by 13th March, it was still quite a surprise when the Germans started a pre-planned withdrawal the day before this letter. In their wake they left a trail of devastation so that although the Allies took the shaded area on the map, all buildings and bridges were rubble, there was poison in the wells and booby-traps had been laid.

2 Everyone talks about the October Revolution, but it was eight months before that that the protests and strikes and riots had started, with the Tsar abdicating two days before this letter. Shock waves went through the British Royal Family and no doubt contributed to their decision to at last renounce all their German titles in July (nearly three years after the war began) and change their name from Saxe-Coburg-Gotha to Windsor. Further revolt in October would see Lenin setting Russia on the road to Communism.

Item 367
Letter to Margaret

Envelope
(same as for Item 366)

March 17th 1917

7 pm

Dearest Darling.

Just rec'd orders to move at once to MENTONE, come & join me if you can.

All Love

Thine

Charles.

Item 368
Letter to Margaret

Envelope
161 Haverstock Hill
London

And so we come to the last letter that Charles Bartlett sent his wife from France. He's in Nº 5 Casualty Clearing Station at Bray-sur-Somme and was soon on his way 485 miles to the Côte d'Azur, right down in the south-east corner of France.

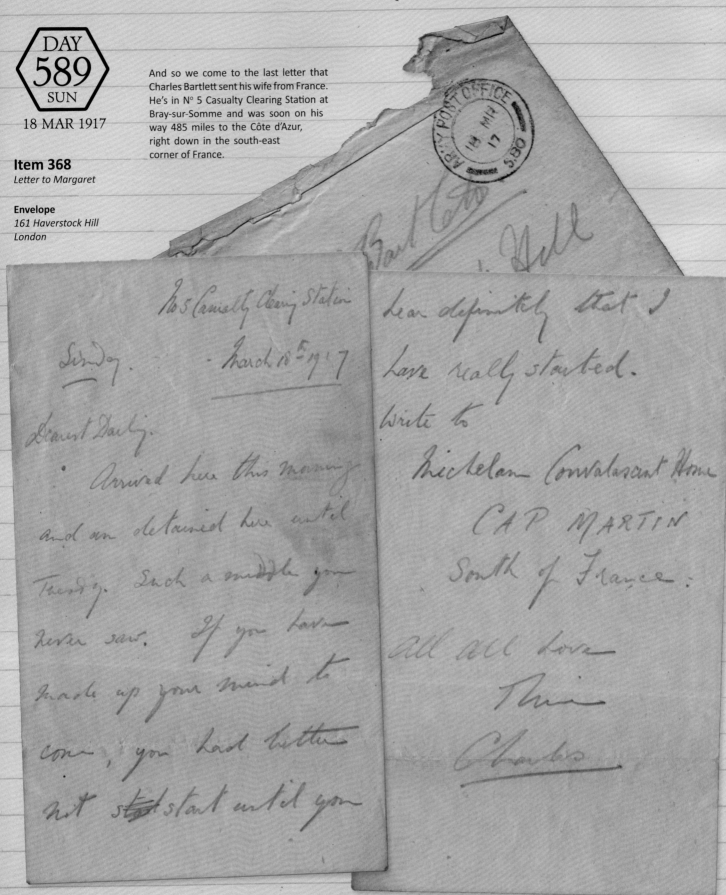

No 5 Casualty Clearing Station
— March 18ᵗʰ 1917

Sunday.

Dearest Darling.

Arrived here this morning and an detained here until Tuesday. Such a muddle you never saw. If you have made up your mind to come, you had better not start start until you

hear definitely that I have really started.

Write to

Michelam Convalescent Home
CAP MARTIN
South of France.

All all love

Thine

Charles

Life after the Letters

Having had such detail of Charles's life and thoughts over the previous year and a half, it comes as something of a shock that the letters end and there are but a few crumbs of information about the rest of his life. For reasons you shall see, not much is known about him by his family. What there is has been put together from Army Lists, the London Gazette, local papers, and civic records along with items kept in his adjutant Cecil Cloake's notebook of memoirs and a small number of glancing personal recollections from people who knew of him.

Charles's destination for his convalescence was the Grand Hôtel du Cap Martin, *(right)*. It was on the tip of the headland halfway between Menton(e) and Monaco on the French Riviera (near the Italian border, hence Nice is 'Nizza' on the map, **below**). It had been built in the 1890s by an English company funded by the founder of Black & White Whisky and during La Belle Époque saw many distinguished visitors, including Emperor Franz Joseph I of Austria & his wife Sissi, and King Edward VII and his family when he was Prince of Wales.

Lord and Lady Michelham paid all expenses for the British officers staying at Cap Martin Hotel for up to three weeks, with as many as 200 being resident at any one time. It was run just like the first rate hotel it was, with civilian waiters, an orchestra playing at tea and dinner, and fine wines being served at the sumptuous meals.

924. ~ MENTON. ~ Grand Hôtel du Cap Martin

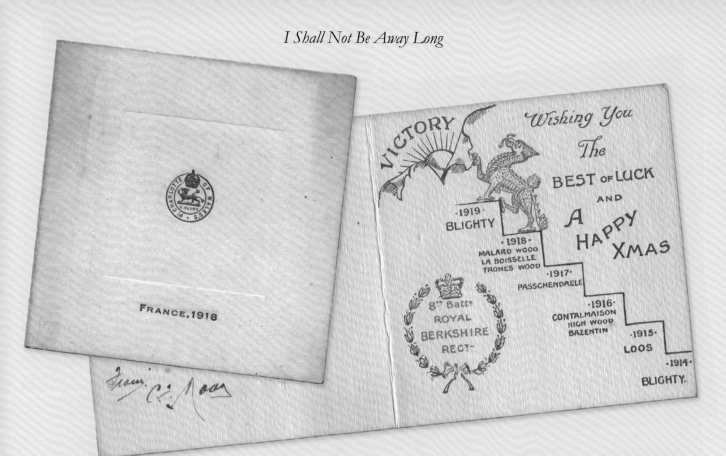

Margaret travelled to join Charles during his convalescence. As you can see in the photos, **opposite**, she is the centre of attention as they pose with other recuperating officers on the Promenade des Anglais during a visit to Nice. I wonder if they were as relaxed as they look.

No doubt the time went by in a flash and Charles and Margaret must have returned to real life in London some time in April 1917. It appears to have been decided that Charles needed a rest from the front line because in May he found himself back to the rank of Major with a Home Service battalion of the Green Howards (officially 17th Alexandra, Princess of Wales's (Yorkshire) Regiment) based in Chelmsford. That unit was disbanded later in the year but even so, he managed to avoid any more shells and ended the war in the employment of the Ministry for National Service. He'd got the safe job that he wanted but I wonder how he felt as his old Battalion suffered through the battles of Passchendaele and the German Spring Offensive. The group photograph, **(below)**, shows the Battalion's officers in August 1918. Not a single one of them was in the Group Photograph taken in May 1915 – and the suffering was not over: in the last 100 days of the war, they lost 12 more officers killed and 23 wounded. The 8th Royal Berkshires had not entirely forgotten him, though, and after the end of the war he received a Christmas card, **above**, from his old Quarter Master, Cecil Moon (sitting 3rd from left, **below**).

Charles eventually left the Army for good on 23rd December 1921. After all the wrangling about his rank when on active service, it must have been gratifying to be told that he had been granted the rank of Lieutenant Colonel in retirement (though no doubt that was tempered by the fact that for most of the previous five years he had been badged and paid as a Major!).

Back in civvy street, all was not well with Charles's home life. The picture on the **right** tells a story. Paula is wearing a special hat for a christening whilst in the background her parents appear disengaged (and that is emphasised by the way that the photograph has selectively faded to cast a miasma over Charles and Margaret). Margaret's professional stage career had ended with the war (though she would continue as an amateur through the rest of her life) and Charles looks diminished and lacking his pre-war vigour – and of course his cheating had cast a pall over their marriage. The year after he left the Army, he left Margaret. She wrote to him at the Badminton Club:

24th November 1922

Dear Charles,

I am making this last appeal to you to reconsider your decision, which I hope and pray may not be final. Is it not possible for us to make a fresh start. Even if you retain no affection for me I beg you to think of Paula's future and her love for you.

I implore you to come back and make a home for us and I promise to do everything in my power to make you happy, and forget the past.

Yours,

Margaret

His reply was brief:

December 7th 1922

My dear Margaret

I am sorry for the delay in answering your letter but have been giving the same due consideration.

I regret to say that I find it quite impossible to return to live with you again.

Yours,

Charles Bartlett

And so Margaret went to court, at first to petition him to come back, and then, in April, to commence divorce proceedings, this time accusing him of adultery. She didn't know the other woman but said that the liaisons had occurred on the 4th, 5th, 14th and 15th April. The divorce became final on

26th May 1924, though things rumbled on about the final settlement into 1926.

Meanwhile Charles was working as an organiser for the National Institution for the Blind and later the Greater London Fund for the Blind that was founded by Sir Arthur Pearson in 1921 – and other than the fact that Charles would visit Paula to take her out from her boarding school in Sussex, the rest of the 1920s are a blank.

In 1930 he is in the Electoral Roll at 23, Ruvigny Gardens, a small terraced house in Putney. Things must have been bad for him to have moved south of the river and it appears that this was a boarding house, with a landlady 10 years his senior and a high turnover of other occupants. Though registered there several times over the next decade, there are gaps and my guess is that it allowed him to have a base in London without too many ties.

In May 1932, Charles's name was in the papers connected with a fraud trial. His address was then given as a farm in North Devon but the initial hearing was in Marylebone Police Court and related to a man who had placed ads offering posts as a steward or stewardess for a high-class country club near Hastings. A number of applicants had each been told that they had got the job and had paid sums varying from £50 to £200 as *'cash security'* only to find that the job didn't exist, that their money had gone and the address given for the country club was the accused's cottage. The accused had named Charles as agreeing to be the chairman of the club. In the witness box, Charles stated that the proposition had been put to

him and he had been induced to introduce the accused into the Badminton Club but that he had not given any authority for the use of his name in any way. Typically of the local papers of the time, though it was said that the accused had pleaded guilty to all charges except one, I can find no follow up that gives what happened to him or how Charles was viewed in the whole matter.

The next view of Charles in the historical record is at Paula's wedding in November 1935. He gave her away at the Holy Trinity Church, Brompton, as she married Jack Cameron, the youngest son of the doctor of a tuberculosis sanatorium in Angus in the wilds of Scotland. Despite all that had happened, Paula labelled Charles's picture *'Daddy'*, **(opposite, top)**, though she also wrote *'Dad'* for her new father-in-law. The colour scheme for the wedding was gold, with Paula's ivory taffeta dress brocaded with gold threads, her fashionable halo headdress edged with gold and the three bridesmaids in pale gold lamé frocks. The reception for the 300 guests was held at the Ritz and luckily for Charles he didn't have to foot the bill – it was hosted by a friend, Mrs L B Smith. Labelled *'Smithie'* by Paula, maybe she is the widow of the Bogie Smith mentioned in Charles's letters, but the Smith name dreaded by family historians makes it difficult to be sure. Charles's wedding present was one of the 25 cheques given to the newly-weds.

Two years further on and the next glimpse of Charles's life is given by the letters he wrote to Cecil Cloake as shown on the following pages.

Paula   Margaret

'Daddy'

'Dad' = father-in-law Dr Hugh Cameron

'Smithie'

'Aunts Flora & Chatty'

WORTH.
HELE
BRADNINCH
DEVON.

Oct 9th/37

Dear Cloake.   GENERAL IDEA.

First Division B.E.F. DINNER
seventieth Annual Dinner
Mayfair Hotel London 7.30 for 8 pm. Nov 5th/37
Decorations will be worn.

SPECIAL IDEA.

You are to be General Dalby's guest, and he has asked me to get in touch with you and ask you and any other 8th Berks to come as his guests and wants to raise an 8th Berks Table. I hope you will be able to attend. I am trying Edwardes, Rouse and Robinson. Do you know any others?

Dalby's town address is 23 Rutland Court. S.W.7 if you want to write to him, but will you also drop me a line here as I must let George Clowes, who runs the dinner know.   Yours very sincerely,

C. Bartlett.

WORTH
HELE
BRADNINCH
DEVON.

Oct 21st /37.

Dear Cloaker.

Thanks for yours of the 16th. I have now heard from Edwardes that he is coming, also Rouse is certain and I believe Robinson will turn up.

I did not write Beale as I heard from Delly again definitely naming the five of us, so I suspect he thought 5 guests sufficient.

You will receive a Ticket in due course, and don't forget to bring it along with you.

It will be a pleasant outing for me and I look forward to seeing you all. Farm life is very interesting, but not exciting. The other morning a Cow was shouting her heart out for the Bull, and because I kept her waiting 2½ hours, when I got her there she would not look at him. Ungrateful Bitch. However Pork is up and 62 pigs went off yesterday. 200–300 Chicken every Wednesday. I tell you this is some intensive farm and I wish I had a financial interest in it instead of being a paying guest.

yrs &c.
Charles Barkley.

The first letter with its use of the phrases 'GENERAL IDEA' and 'SPECIAL IDEA' is a reference to how military plans and orders were put together at the time of the First World War.

Notably absent from the names in these letters are Charles's great pal, Dug★, and his old C.O. Brig-Gen William Walton★.

Douglas Tosetti★, *(right)*, had managed to survive everything until 21st March 1918, when, during the desperate fighting at the opening of the German Spring Offensive, he sacrificed himself in an effort to locate a German machine-gun so that his men had a chance of escape. He was shot through the head and chest and died instantly. His body was never found after the war.

Brig-Gen **William Walton★** had survived the war, finishing his Army career in India with operations against the Mahsuds and Waziris on the North West Frontier in 1919 and a spell as Inspector of Infantry in 1920. After being very active in local civic life in Weybridge, his last two years had been blighted by heart problems and he had died 6 months before the dinner.

His wife **Emmie** had become an alcoholic, but after her daughter confronted her, she gave up drinking overnight and survived her husband by 12 years.

Of the others mentioned in this last letter of Charles's, three would not survive long after this reunion with their war service contributing to their early deaths:

Aubyn Redmond Rouse ★

Lionel Huddlestone Edwards ★

Cyril Elmes Beale

The three others named would make significant contributions to the war that was just about to start:

Gerald Dalby had managed to keep his fingers on his right hand despite two of them being badly broken at Contalmaison in July 1916. His grip had been weakened as a result but still it wouldn't prevent him playing polo. He was now a Major-General, and though he'd served on the Staff in the latter part of the war and had been steadily

promoted thereafter, his most significant contribution had been as a pioneer in the reform of basic infantry tactics, training and equipment, firstly as the Chief Instructor at the Small Arms School in Hythe in the 1920s and then as a brigade commander in the 1930s. Not only did he develop *'battle practices'* with live ammunition, but he experimented with clothing and equipment to enable infantrymen to be more agile in action. He succeeded in halving the weight carried compared to the norm in the First World War and his impact can be assessed by the fact that when *The Times* only published a 6-line obituary for him, the distinguished military historian Captain Basil Liddell Hart wrote in with a more fulsome tribute that closed with the words: *'Innovators of Dalby's kind contributed far more than most of the high commanders to the better course of events in the next war'*. He had been awarded a CB in 1936 to go with his DSO from 1917 and would command a Territorial Army division briefly before retiring at the end of 1939 and becoming a Colonel for the Home Guard in London during the next war.

Gerald Robinson★ would work in inter-services intelligence, including looking for information about V1 launch sites.

Cecil Cloake★, *(left)*, had qualified as a doctor with a practice in Wimbledon and as such would be called to attend many incidents during the aerial bombing of the Second World War.

Cecil's son John, who would have been just about to turn 13 when Charles Bartlett visited his home at the time of the dinner, remembered meeting him and described him as a *'relaxed affable chap'*.

At the time of writing these last two letters in 1937, Charles was staying at Worth Farm, in the countryside just north of Exeter. Given that he says he is a paying guest and following on from his Devon farm address in 1932, it looks like he enjoyed the country life as an escape from the city. Without a tie to a permanent home, he might as well pay for lodgings in Devon as in London.

Charles would have had a lot in common with his host at Worth Farm. Bob Wellington had served as a Captain in the Royal Field Artillery, being awarded the Military Cross for his part in the Battle of Loos and then being posted for home service having been gassed on the Somme. The fact that it affected him deeply is alluded to by the story told that on one visit to a neighbour, *'He said he could do with a whisky, and then he drank the whole bottle!'*. He would not have been in alone in needing the prop of alcohol to deal with the nightmare of the war, and I can imagine him and Charles sharing a few stories and some solace over a bottle of whisky (➜**413 Wellington**).

In September 1939, just after the beginning of the Second World War, a register was conducted of the British population, and in it Charles is listed as being back at 23, Ruvigny Gardens, in Putney. He was now 61 years old and didn't give any occupation other than *'Lt Col late Royal Berkshire Rgt, Retired'*. One of the reasons for the register was to be able to co-ordinate rationing, and that started for bacon, butter and sugar in January 1940. Amazingly Charles's ration card for this time is still held by his family, **(right)**, which appears in stark contrast to the menu from the 1st Division Reunion dinner from 1937, **(above right)**. It shows that he had already moved on to a hotel in Earl's Court. It wouldn't be long though before he was forced to settle down by the illness that would lead to his end. Years of enjoying the good things in life had caught up with him. He moved in with Frances Hale, who he'd known for a long time from his work with the National Institution for the Blind where she had been a secretary. She lived on Putney Hill, half a mile from Ruvigny Gardens, and that is where both of them were living when they got married on 9th November 1940.

It seems likely that it was a very quiet wedding. The venue was Wandsworth Register Office and the witnesses were Alec and Gladys Bosman (his friends mentioned in the letter of 16th March 1916 on p.214). Frances at 44 was 18 years Charles's junior and by this time would have been more nurse than wife. Charles's arteries had furred up, and, with the poor circulation caused by that, he developed gangrene in his right leg and had to have it amputated. In fact he was not well from the time of their wedding onwards, being unconscious for the whole of Christmas 1940 and finally dying of pneumonia in Putney Hospital on 28th December with his new wife by his side. His body was cremated at Putney Vale crematorium and his ashes scattered in the grounds of his old family home at Peverel Court.

I have found no memorial to him nor have I found his will or army service record. He could have been another of those people who served their country in the First World War only to be almost completely forgotten by history. I'm sure he would have been utterly surprised to find his spontaneous jottings gathered together as they are in this book. Few of us leave such a transparent record of our complexities as human beings. His faults are laid bare and I have variously heard of him described as *'a bit of a rogue'*, *'the black sheep of the family'* and there is no doubting that he was led by his enjoyment of sensory pleasure whether that was food and drink, or singing and laughter, or the company (and more) of women. Though that could lead to others getting hurt in his wake, it is also true that he was generous and good company, with another remembrance being that he was *'a damn fine host'*. I'm sure he would be happy with that as an epitaph.

Menu.

Variétés Scandinave
Saumon Fumé d'Ecosse

Consommé Double Monte-Carlo
Brindilles au Chester
Velouté Chiffonnette

Filet de Sole Wladimir

Vol-au-Vent de Ris de Veau Royal
Pommes Nouvelles
Mousseline Favorite

Faisan d'Ecosse sur Canapé
Salade Hermine

Bombe Napolitaine
Frivolités

Café

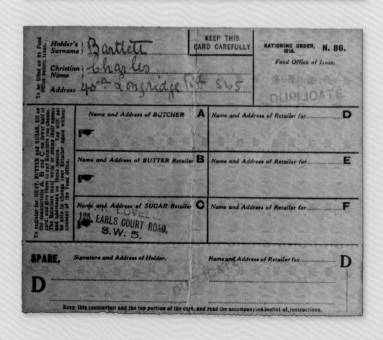

Lieutenant Colonel Charles Frederick Napier Bartlett

12th April 1878 – 28th December 1940

Army officer,

Bon viveur,

Survivor of the Battles of Loos and the Somme,

Bit of a rogue,

Champion of the blind,

Damn fine host,

Letter writer.

So, what happened to Charles's immediate family after his death? His widow Frances never re-married, and though I have the feeling that he had married her with the idea that what remained of his worldly possessions would go to her, she certainly did not inherit massive wealth. In fact in her final years, after she had retired to Bognor Regis, her niece ended up paying for her nursing. She died in 1974.

Frances Mary Bartlett née Hale

Charles's first wife Margaret also did not marry again, but despite all that had happened at the end of her marriage she kept the Bartlett name for the rest of her life. She also kept her ex-husband's letters from the war though the only copies she held on to of her own letters were the two in late 1916 from the time she had caught him cheating on her. She did not hold back in her condemnation of him with a story coming down through the family being that he had got her manicurist pregnant, and his presentation as a persona non grata means that details of his life are almost absent from the family's memories. Margaret's feelings are laid bear by the rip across his photograph on the previous page.

No doubt Charles's divorce had cost him a pretty penny and there were further dealings in court to finalise the settlement which paid for the upkeep of Margaret and Paula. He can't have seen Paula much following her marriage in 1935 because after honeymooning in Paris she went straight out to the Philippines, her husband Jack having a job as an agent for an insurance and shipping firm in Manila. There she had a son and then life got turned on its head with the Japanese invasion in December 1941. Manila was captured on 2nd January 1942 and Paula and her husband and young son were interned by the Japanese.

Margaret did not to hear any news of them for over three years. During that time she kept herself busy by working for the Red Cross at St James's Palace in London and she bought a notebook in which she wrote unposted letters to her daughter and grandson in order to keep their memory alive. Then on 6th February 1945 came a miracle – Paula was at last able to write home after liberation by the Americans. Not only had all three of them survived but they were now four, with a new son having arrived on Boxing Day (as pictured *above*). After being on starvation rations they were reduced to just skin and bones, with Paula

Margaret Jane Bartlett née Robinson

Lady Sybil Mary Crutchley née Coke

Gerald Edward Victor Crutchley

Betty Crutchley née Spottiswoode

Rosalie Sylvia Crutchley

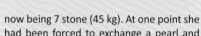

now being 7 stone (45 kg). At one point she had been forced to exchange a pearl and diamond pendant plus a platinum, diamond and pearl ring for one kilo of rice. Even so she returned to the Philippines after the war and her daughter was born there.

Of her friends mentioned in Charles's letters, Margaret was to stay in touch with the Crutchley family and Betty Spottiswoode for the rest of her life. In fact they became as one when Betty married General and Lady Crutchley's son Gerry in 1919, with their engagement being announced once he'd been moved from a prisoner-of-war camp in Germany to internment in Holland in early 1918. He became a well-known cricketer for Middlesex and also appeared with Betty and Margaret in amateur theatre productions with the Windsor Strollers, and with the Old Stagers as part of Canterbury Cricket Week. Also starting out in those productions was their daughter Rosalie Crutchley who had been a bridesmaid at Paula's wedding and went on to a prolific acting career with her last film role being as a brusquely inquisitive guest in *'Four Weddings & a Funeral'*. Her brother Edward became the executor of Margaret Bartlett's will in 1962. One bequest that was not in Margaret's will was the passing down of a flair for the stage that would see one of her grand-daughters become a dancer with the famed Radio City Rockettes precision dance company in New York.

Charles's unmarried siblings John and Lilian are more remembered for the manner of their deaths than for what they did in life.

John Bartlett went to stay at the Oxford home of his brother Alfred for Christmas 1938. He'd gone to bed after a party on Christmas Day but was found gassed in his bed the next morning. Alfred's theory was that he made a mistake when turning off the gas fire in his bedroom. As well as the tap for the fire, there was one for a gas ring and it seems that John had tried to turn off the fire with that one, and when that did not extinguish the fire, he tried the other tap. That worked but he then didn't close the gas ring tap that he had inadvertently opened. Great pains were taken to stress that it was an accident with one paper's strange headline being *'Normal Man's Letters About Future Plans'* due to Alfred giving evidence that John had seemed normal when he retired to his room after the party and had written two letters referring to upcoming arrangements before turning in.

John Francis Napier Bartlett

Lilian Bartlett was at her home in the village of Little Gaddesdon in Hertfordshire on the last night in October 1944 when the wireless set in the kitchen caught fire. She rang for the fire brigade from her bedside telephone but by the time they arrived she had collapsed and her live-in companion-housekeeper was found lying on the floor in the same room having gone to try to help her. Neither could be revived and were judged to have died from carbon monoxide poisoning.

Lilian Emily Bartlett

Both John and Lilian's names were added to family grave in Stone churchyard, and it is notable that Charles's was not, even though their deaths occurred either side of his.

Sister Florrie's husband Alfie survived the war as a Major in the Royal Army Service Corps (though he'd lost a brother killed in May 1915). From late 1917 he had served in Italy with awards of the DSO & Italian Croce di Guerra. He returned to his job as Outdoor Manager and Superintendent of Transport for a major brewery in Northampton, and ended up as their Managing Director. One of their granddaughters would become the

wife of firstly a baronet and secondly the British High Commissioner in Cyprus, and another granddaughter is now Baroness Iliffe, her husband being the owner of a 9,000-acre estate in Berkshire and a media empire that includes 38 local newspapers.

Florence Mary Fraser née Bartlett

Alfred James Fraser

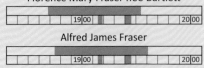

Brother Alfred also made it through the war, remaining C.O. of 1st/4th Ox & Bucks Light Infantry until August 1919, except for three 2-month absences. He took part in the 3rd Battle of Ypres after which he was awarded the DSO, and then went with his Battalion to Italy in November 1917. In June 1918 they were attacked by the Austrians during the Battle of Asiago and though their line was penetrated on both flanks and communications were breaking down in all kinds of chaos, he kept a cool head and enabled his Battalion to hold out so that eventually the Austrians were beaten off and the line fully re-established.

Alfred James Napier Bartlett

(Dorothy) Hilda Bartlett née Barran

For this he received a bar to his DSO and the Italian Croce di Guerra. Alfred was appointed Chief Constable of Cumberland and Westmorland in 1925 but by 1927 had returned to Oxford where he became secretary of the county's Territorial Army Association, being awarded the OBE on his retirement in 1946. One day in 1954 he got on the wrong side of a policeman when parking his car. He told the constable that he would only be away for five minutes while he got to a cup of tea. *'You won't get a cup of tea in Banbury in five minutes on market day'* came the reply and after he didn't return for 35 minutes, he found his case up in front of the magistrate with a £2 fine for parking in a no-waiting street being the result. Such was the nature of local newspaper gossip at the time and it must have seemed just so much fuss about nothing after all that he'd been through in the war. He survived his wife by 6 years and when he died in 1956 he was the last survivor of the seven Bartlett siblings.

His elder daughter Elizabeth became a Senior Commander in the ATS (the women's branch of the Army) in the Second World War and married a priest whose church had been destroyed in the Blitz on Coventry (and who later became Bishop of Singapore and then Bishop of Wellington in New Zealand).

His second daughter Kit was a matron at St Bartholomew's Hospital in London.

His son Dick followed him into the Ox & Bucks Light Infantry before switching to the 7th Parachute Battalion in the Second World War. At ten to one in the morning on D-Day 1944, he jumped out of a Stirling aircraft and landed in an apple orchard some miles from his drop zone and separated from most of the company he was supposed to be commanding (he only found his servant and a signal corporal to link up with). He eventually rejoined his Battalion in the area of Pegasus Bridge at ten o'clock that night. For the next two weeks he was heavily involved in the fighting before being wounded in the arm and evacuated. After the war he was in Cyprus during the emergency and finally took part in the Suez invasion in 1956 after which he decided to leave the army and head out to Rhodesia with his young family. In the end, though, he only outlived his father by two years, succumbing to cancer aged 38 in 1958.

it would be Dick's sons who I'd meet in Johannesburg and who would lead me to finding all these letters and giving the great uncle, of whom they'd never heard, a form of immortality.

Additional
Stories

BACKLER, Owen Key. Born in 1880 in Southsea, near Portsmouth, he was the grandson of a long-standing keeper of the Royal apartments on the Royal Yacht *Victoria & Albert*. His father was a money collector for a gas company who scooted off to America before Owen was 10. Owen's mother supported her 3 kids by selling fruit, but died when he was 14, leaving him effectively an orphan. In 1900, aged 19, Owen joined the Army as a private in the 10th Royal Hussars. That only lasted a year before he was discharged as medically unfit, despite having not seen any active service. Back in civilian life he went up the ladder from being a junior clerk to a career in newspaper advertising with a home in Holland Park in London.

Whatever his prior medical problems, he was said to be in very good health when he joined up in October 1914 and he arrived in France as a Captain in the Army Service Corps in July 1915, working on the delivery of supplies for 19th Division. In January 1916 he came down with pleurisy after being gassed, and his subsequent insomnia and depression led to a medical officer saying that he needed *'complete rest in a quiet country place'*. By the time he bumped into Charles in September he'd been back in France for two months but six weeks later he would again be on his way home, this time with shell shock. He'd been in charge of a train using a narrow gauge railway to take supplies into Ypres when it came under heavy shell fire. He wasn't hit by any projectile but the concussion had a serious effect and even into the 1920s he was highly emotional and nervous, with broken

sleep and lack of concentration such that he could not return to his pre-war job in the London newspaper world. Even with his commanding officer confirming the truth of his story, his efforts to get a wound pension from the War Office fell on deaf ears, not least because of the absence of a physical wound, and when he looked for the medical officer who had initially treated him, he found that he was dead.

Meanwhile his condition had not been helped by the death of his wife in February 1918. In fact his wife must have been a worry for most of their marriage, having first needed hospital treatment for mental illness aged 17, and then in 1909 (five years after their marriage), an attack of noisy violent incoherence led to her being sewn up into blankets to restrain her before she was committed to Bethlem mental hospital (as pictured **above** – the building now houses the Imperial War Museum). She was confined to a padded cell where she sang and shouted herself hoarse, but after a month's treatment with a sleep-inducing drug she returned to normal and was soon able to go home. In early 1917 she had appendicitis as well as having one ovary removed, then towards the end of the year she started to behave strangely again. By this time she was described as *'almost obese'* and whilst waiting for admission she smashed a glass photo frame and sustained cuts to her thumbs. Again she was held in a padded room and in her restless state kept stripping herself and got very little sleep. On the ninth evening after her admission, she collapsed and despite administration

of drugs to stimulate her heart, she died at 1.35 a.m., aged 43.

She was not the only one in her family to have mental difficulties. Her brother Eardley was an engineer working with new technologies, manufacturing a car in 1899 and a training apparatus for aspiring flyers in 1912, but he too spent time in Bethlem hospital, with the notes on his admission in 1913 remarking, *'He confesses to having acquired syphilis at the age of 14 from a housemaid!'* as well as describing his agitated listing of all sorts of inventions and schemes that were going to make him a fortune. At one point he tore his clothes into pieces because he said they did not fit him, and attacked the staff after accusing them of starving him. Soon after that he escaped from the strong room and ran down a gallery before being subdued. Even so, 11 days later he was released uncured and ended up in an asylum in Essex where he died in late 1915, aged 42, of General Paralysis of the Insane caused by syphilis.

My guess is that Mabel's other brother would also have been a cause of vexation to Owen. Named Noel Pemberton Billing, he had gone from stowing away aged 13 on a ship bound for Africa to starting an aircraft manufacturer before the war that made aeroplanes that looked amazing but flew terribly (after he sold the company to his works manager it turned into Supermarine, later maker of the Spitfire). He flew for a period in the war but gave it up to become an MP in 1916, on the imperialist, anti-Semitic, anti-homosexual side of right wing, & in 1918 ended up in court after accusing Margot Asquith, wife of the former Prime Minister, of being involved in a lesbian affair as part of a German conspiracy he dubbed the *'Cult of the Clitoris'*. He resigned his seat in 1921, though his continued antics would earn him a Times obituary in 1948 that ended, *'His constant & dismal appearances in the Courts had begun to pall, and the public found little to admire in a man so persistently combative.'*

Despite all that he married into, Owen clearly loved his wife and placed a notice in the Times in 1920 with the words *'In loving memory of my dear wife Mabel'*. He did eventually return to working in Advertising & Publicity on a freelance basis and finally died of a stroke aged 76. ➔329

Owen Key Backler

| | | | | | 19|00 | | | | | | 20|00 |

Mabel Barrow Backler née Billing

| | | | | | 19|00 | | | | | 20|00 |

BAILLY, (Pierre) François. Being the only French person that I could identify of the many that Charles must have met during all his time in France, I thought I'd put some effort into finding out about the Mayor of Allouagne, François Bailly. Doing family history research on the Continent is not as easy as in the UK because records tend to be held locally rather than centrally and most are not searchable online, and people also generally don't seem to be as interested in genealogy. Maybe there have been too many problems around people's ethnicities that they'd rather let it lie.

In this case, though, I was lucky to find a website containing some names and dates for François Bailly's family and to add to the luck the website owner knew his way around the records and was happy to help me as I got nowhere with enquiries to the present-day Mairie. During my visit to Allouagne I did however find the family grave, *(right)*, though as you can see it doesn't have the names and dates and photographs that are so common on French graves. Who knows the stories hidden beneath its grand exterior. →**173**

BAKER, Geoffrey. It's unusual to be able to see inside someone's body when you know their life story but you've never seen their face but that's what we have here with Geoffrey Baker's x-ray, *(right)*. The shell fragments that were left in his upper right arm are clearly visible, but it was 5 weeks before this was seen because his x-ray got mixed up with that of another man. The delay led to his wounds not healing as they might have done and he spent 5 months in hospital and was much handicapped thereafter, having sustained some nerve damage. After the war he went to work in a bank but found writing difficult even into the 1930s. His lengthy correspondence with and about the Ministry of Pensions became increasingly sneering and bitter. Even so, it is difficult not to be amused when he writes, *'I think you will agree with me that my case is one over which the Ministry of Pensions has shown absolute carelessness...'* and the recipient is a 'Miss B Careless' (Beatrice Careless started work at the Ministry in 1920, never married and died in 1967 aged 95). There is more Carry-On style naming later on when he is examined by a medical officer called Major Dick. A lot of the wrangling was about the degree of his disability with an initial assessment of 70% being downgraded to

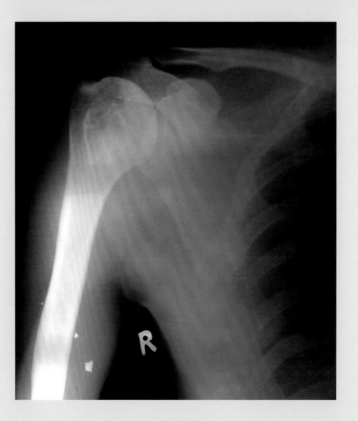

40% in 1918 with a consequent effect on the size of his pension. Finally, after much persistence, in 1933 his permanent award was set at 50% disability.

At the start of the Second World War he was running a hotel near the Somerset coast and in 1940 when he was called up from the Reserve, though a slight weakness was noted in his arm, his overall fitness was assessed as A1. That didn't last for long: in 1943 he developed fibromyalgia (a painful inflammation of the soft tissue in his back along with general weakness). He credited this to inoculations he'd been ordered to have by the Army. And so began a whole lot more wrangling. Even today the cause of fibromyalgia is unknown, but the Army said it wasn't their fault, that his teeth were in a decayed state which affected his general health whereas he said that another officer who'd had the jabs at the same time as him had also had a reaction, even if not as severe. The bottom line was that he was no longer fit to serve, and after leaving he tried to get the Army to admit responsibility for his condition and award him a further pension. The Ministry of Pensions' stance after many medical boards was that he was *'temperamentally hypochondriacal & anxious & over-concerned about himself'*. Through all of this he continued to received his First World War disability pension and that only ceased on his death in 1952, at which point a note was made in his file: *'no deductions are required to be made by this Dept.'*

Geoffrey's brother Kingsley had died of wounds while resisting the German Spring Offensive in March 1918. His nephew Peter was shot down whilst flying an unarmed artillery-spotting plane during the Battle of Anzio in Italy in February 1944 and died from his burns six weeks later. After wars the focus can often just seem to stay on the dead but remember also the many wounded survivors whose suffering both physically and mentally went on and on. For Geoffrey Baker it lasted 36 years. ➜**322**

BARTLETT, Geoffrey Edward Rose, (above, right). Charles's nephew had at first been thwarted in his dream of a career in the Royal Navy when a medical discovered that he had an intermittent heartbeat. Instead he joined the Merchant Navy and sailed twice around the world in his teens. The start of

the war saw rules being relaxed and he had been a midshipman on the battleship HMS Bulwark for 3 months when her magazines suddenly exploded whilst she was moored at Sheerness. All but 12 of her crew of 750 were killed in the accident. No trace of his body was ever found. He was 19. ➜**62**

BEDELLS, Phyllis. She made her debut on the stage aged 13 as the first oyster in *Alice in Wonderland* in 1906 and went on to become Britain's first prima ballerina. The picture **below** is a long way removed from

Ian Gordon Macbean

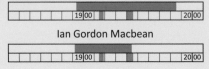

the ugliness of war that had such an effect on the husband she married in February 1918. Ian Macbean had joined the Army as a regular officer in 1910 and arrived in France with the 2nd Sherwood Foresters on 11th September 1914. Nine days later during a counterattack to regain some trenches from the Germans he was wounded. I have found no details of his wounds but when back in London he also ended up needing treatment for syphilis (which required notification to the War Office's Director of Personal Services who quaintly had the code name *Seemliness*). His young man's urge to sow his wild oats while he was still able would have grave consequences later on but in the short term meant that he was not with his Battalion when 766 of them were killed, wounded or captured during a German attack on 20th October. Returning in March 1915 he lasted 18 days before being shot through the sole of his right foot when out on patrol. Fit again in March 1916 he went on to serve on the staff in Salonika. He ended the war as a Major with the MC and in December 1918 was presented with the Order of the White Eagle 5th Class by the Crown Prince of Serbia, though the very next day saw him admitted to hospital with dysentery. Thrown into the deep end as a Brigade Major amongst the troubles in Belfast in 1920, he struggled until relieved by a more experienced officer and soon after that he was compulsorily retired as the Army down-sized to peacetime levels.

In 1928 he was working in the British Legation in Peking when he was bitten by a rabid dog. He managed to survive but his health was beginning to decline when in 1939 he tried to join up again (by which time his uniform had been *'ravaged by the moth'*). He refused to recognise anything was wrong despite weight loss from his normal 9 stone down to 8 stone as well as bouts of giddiness, a lack of inclination for work and a *'history of injudicious spending'*. Tests confirmed the cause to be the onset of General Paralysis of the Insane due to syphilis.

Cruelly the result of his youthful recklessness had come back to slowly kill him over the next five years and he would not live to see his daughter Jean follow in her mother's footsteps as a celebrated dancer and inspiring ballet teacher. ➜**277**

BERLEIN, Elizabeth, *(below).* It is hard to pick just one poem from her collection, but this one illustrates the sort of questioning that is not present in the verse read out at the memorial service in St Giles'. →**122**

1914.

I WILL not give my son for the world's sake ;
　O God, that sacrifice I cannot make,
Quicken the mighty future with Thy Breath
I will not give—even to creative death.
Can'st Thou not save the world, or must *I* give ?
Must my son perish that the unknown may live ?
Christ died, O God, a sacrifice for men,
Can *love* ask such a sacrifice again ?
Nay, God forgive, yet 'twas a *father* gave
His one, His only Son mankind to save.
It is a *mother* pleads ; yet Mary knew
And willed the sword that pierced her own heart through.
Speak Martyr-Mother weeping by the Cross
Is there a Power can turn to gain, our loss ?
Must we give—freely ?　Is the will the price
That changes suffering to sacrifice ?

*　*　*　*　*　*　*

I do not know, I only know that he,
The son who went, will not return to me.

BRADE, Sir Reginald Herbert. His grave, *(right)*, is hidden in the depths of the Surrey woods in the churchyard of St John the Baptist, Okewood. Not even close to any centre of population and with the surrounding trees providing an additional buffer to the outside world, its stillness and quiet is a far cry from Whitehall where he spent his working life. If he wanted to forget all about it (and in turn be forgotten) then this was the place to come. The grass is strimmed to shortness but the damp air is a perfect environment for the lichen that grows on his grave and someone casually glancing in the churchyard would be unlikely to notice that here was buried someone so vital to the British war effort in the dark years of 1914 to 1918. →**139**

BRETT, Maurice Vyner Balliol, (*right*, with his wife Zena Dare). Maurice had passed out top from Sandhurst and was an aide-de-camp to General Sir John French before the war. After arriving in France in 1914, he had used his office in Paris as the base for a small spy network he was secretly running to provide intelligence for his father, Lord Esher. Originally known as Regy Brett, Lord Esher, *(below)*, avoided high office in favour of being a high-powered string-puller behind the scenes. Ever since the days of Queen Victoria (whose letters he had edited for publication) he had had the ear of the monarchs and had particularly influenced European affairs in the times of Edward VII. Privately he had even more secrets with a series of infatuations with adolescent boys and young men, stretching back to his time at Eton. He couldn't forget the idyllic nature of his school days and would often visit Eton where the boys were advised against taking long walks alone with him or his friend, the promiscuous paedophile, Lord 'LouLou' Harcourt. When the mother of an Eton pupil threatened to go to the papers about advances made to her son, LouLou drank an overdose, but the resulting inquest covered up his suicide and Regy made sure to extract LouLou's child pornography collection from his library before it could come to wider notice.

Even more shocking is that the greatest infatuation of Lord Esher's life was for his son Maurice. This led to an uncomfortable third person in Maurice's wooing and then marriage of Zena. Even so Maurice took on the job of editing his late father's papers for publication, but was only part of the way through that task when he suddenly

MISS ZENA DARE AND HER FIANCE, THE HON. MAURICE BRETT.   ROTARY PHOTO, E.C

died having had a heart attack whilst out grouse shooting on his Scottish estate. He had tickets to see his wife Zena Dare on stage in Glasgow that evening but the news of his death was not broken to her until she returned to her hotel after her performance. ➔**186**

BROOKE, John Warwick, *(right)*. At the age of 15 he had signed up for 12 years with the Royal Navy but bought himself out in 1910 after 9 years in which he had served as a signalman, spending time in the cells on 6 occasions (at least one of which was for going on the run) and ending up with a tattoo of a woman on each arm. By 1914 he was a press photographer but went to France as a cavalry signals sergeant in 1915, getting the DCM in 1916 for repeatedly repairing the phone wires as all around him were becoming casualties from heavy shellfire. In July 1916 he was commissioned as one of the first two official war photographers on the Western Front (confusingly the other one was named Brooks, so they were each jokingly referred to as 'Brooks-or-Brooke'). He survived taking pictures over all the front line and returned to his press work, only to die aged only 42 of TB in 1929. His wife, who was left penniless with two children aged 13 & 4, then tried to get some support via the War Office. She said the TB must have come from his war service, but in fact when he joined up in 1914 it was noted that he had a fluid swelling of the scrotum which is associated with TB and that had got worse throughout the war.

It could have seen him stay at home but even after an operation he was anxious to return to his duty of documenting the war. In the end after considering Brooke's *'good service record and the widow's initiative in finding employment'* (she was a cashier in a restaurant), she was awarded £20 in *'small fortnightly instalments'*. Between 1916 and 1918 John Warwick Brooke had taken over 4000 photographs many of which are **the** photographs that define our view of the war and which you see over and again. Having taken the pictures under government contract, he would have received none of the presumably substantial fees that would have accrued over the 50 years they were in Crown copyright. He was however visited by the King and Queen when ill in hospital in 1917 and congratulated on his work, and no doubt he was grateful for his MBE in 1918 & OBE in 1920. ➔**314**

BUSZARD, W & G. William Buszard had actually died aged 31 in 1884, but his brother George kept his initial in the company name as well as taking in his three children (though two of them died aged 23 & 33 before the First World War). George had one son, Stanley, who maybe he thought would one day take over the family business, but his success worked against him as it meant he could afford to send Stanley to Medical School – and then the war intervened. Stanley was killed in action on 8th December 1917 in the battle to recapture Jerusalem, dying the day before the Turks withdrew. By this time, other people were running the business of W & G Buszard anyway, and it was then taken over by the Aerated Bread Company in 1918. The site of their bakery and hugely popular tearooms on Oxford Street is now the flagship store for JD Sports. ➜141

CARTER, Francis Charles, *(above)*. He is at the centre of the 1903 group photograph on p.18. Both his sons died as a result of the war. The younger, Gerald, was on board the submarine C33 which was presumed to have struck a mine and sank with all hands when attempting to ambush a German U-boat in the North Sea on 5th August 1915 (his 29th birthday). The elder son, Herbert, served throughout the war, being awarded the Military Cross and reaching the rank of Lt Col. After the Armistice, he used his fluency in Russian to help train White Russian forces and it was in Vladivostok in Siberia that he fell ill with pneumonia and died on 28th February 1919, 6 weeks before his only daughter was born. Herbert's widow, who was born a Guinness, went on to marry and have two further children with John Slessor who ended his distinguished RAF career as Chief of the Air Staff. ➜42

COLLISON, Charles Sydney. His view on the British steel helmet is also worth quoting:

'One would like to know just how many men are now walking about who would have been in their graves but for this hideous but effective head-dress. As for its designer, only the prayers of the countless thousands who owe their present happiness to this hat can save him from being haunted to his death by the spirits of all the artists and lovers of the beautiful that have ever existed.' ➜304

George Buszard

Stanley George Buszard

Herbert Francis George Carter

Gerald Ernest Berkeley Carter

CONYERS, Walter Neville. In 2016 Walter's great-great-nephew Alex was working in London and through family connections was asked to attend the commemoration of the Centenary of the first day of the Battle of Somme as a representative of the Governor of Bermuda. He is pictured, *(right)*, in front of the Thiepval Memorial to the Missing with Captain Paolo Odoli, who was aide-de-camp to the Governor and whose great-great-uncle had survived the battle. Alex's traditional Bermudan attire caught the attention of Dan Snow who interviewed him as part of BBC Television's coverage of the event. ➔**306**

DOUGLAS, Kenneth (born as Kenneth Douglas Savory). For someone so very famous in his time, little remains of him now. No copies are now known to exist of the film he made with Mary Pickford, *'A Girl of Yesterday'*. There are no pictures of him in the National Portrait Gallery, though there are 14 of his wife, the actress Grace Lane. The only recording I have managed to find of his voice is one where he is not playing a part but instead is describing that fateful day when the SS Arabic was torpedoed (you can hear it on YouTube if you search for "Sinking of SS Arabic"). His son Gerald Savory would go on to have an important part to play in the creative development of television as Head of Serials and then Head of Plays at the BBC in the 1960s and 1970s. ➔**64**

EDWARDS, Edward. Even prior to re-joining the Battalion out in France on 4th October 1915, he had suffered his first wound due to falling from a train in April (with the resulting heavy grazing to his left arm needing four days in hospital). His second wound came during the 3rd May raid, this time in the arm and neck but it must not have been too major because he was able to go on leave soon afterwards and get married. His third wound would come on the Somme in August, again in the arm but this time more seriously and he'd be 6 months in England before being posted to join the 7th Royal Berkshires in Salonika (in

Greece) in March 1917. His fourth wound was to his left thigh in May 1917, needing 2 months out, and then in November 1917 he caught malaria (as did 37% of British troops who served in Salonika). After recovery, he was in a malaria rest camp in Dublin for 6 months before going back out to France in September 1918. He managed to avoid any further damage before his demobilization in April 1919, but the combined effect of his war service can't have been good for

his health and he died from heart disease in 1929 aged 35. His widow was left with 5 children under the age of 12 (with another having died of pneumonia as an infant). She worked as a laundress to support her family and lived to be 91. ➔**260**

Edward Edwards

| | | | | | 19|00| | | | | | | | 20|00| |

Harriet Martha Edwards nee Stocker

| | | | | | 19|00| | | | | | | | 20|00| |

FOOT family. *(See panel opposite).*

FOOTMAN, David John. Not only was his life colourful but it was also full of secrets that did not make it into his obituary in *The Times*. That starts with a description of his academic life at St Antony's College, Oxford, which he entered at the age of 58 & where he became the first director of the Russian & East European Centre specialising in the study of the Soviet Union. It mentions his First World War service with his MC and wound on the Somme (missing out that he was taken prisoner during the German Spring Offensive in 1918) before going on to talk about his work for the Consular Service in Yugoslavia and Egypt for a decade after the war, his marriage to his second cousin & subsequent divorce (but not his frequent adultery that let to that divorce), his staying in the Balkans to talent spot local folk singers for HMV, and his novel writing (his 1936 comedy *'Pig and Pepper'* was said to be *'much funnier than Kingsley Amis'* when picked in a *Guardian* list of neglected treasures in 2007). The rest of his career is then rather glossed over, saying that from 1935 he was with the Foreign Office (being awarded a CMG), before joining St Antony's in 1953, and had written a number of well-regarded biographies and histories, with particular focus on Russia.

Missing from all of that is the small matter of his work in the Foreign Office being for the Secret Intelligence Service and that during the Second World War he became head of Section I in MI6, responsible for the procurement and evaluation of foreign political information. Renowned for his intellect, he is said to have had a dominating influence on the SIS for nearly 20 years. However, as his life drew to a close, it wasn't this that he chose to write about but rather his early life up until the First World War (his memoir being entitled *'Dead Yesterday'*). Near the end of what is quite a personal analysis of his bafflement with life, he does give a hint of his later career when discussing the class system: *'After World War II the Old Boy Network came under heavier fire, following the*

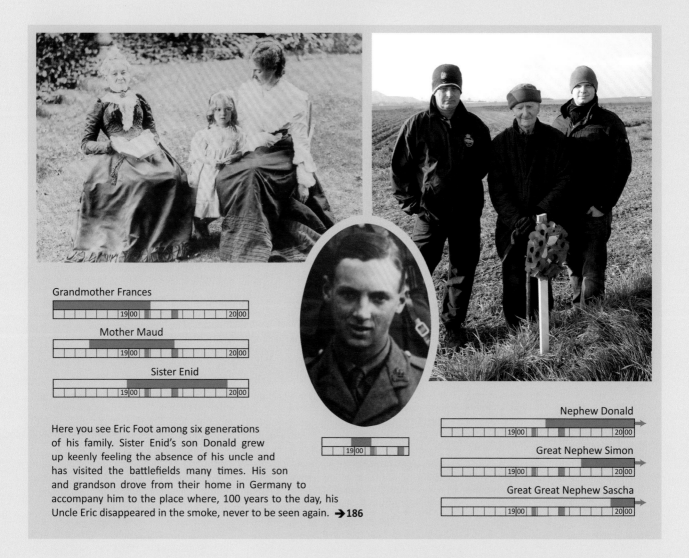

Grandmother Frances

Mother Maud

Sister Enid

Nephew Donald

Great Nephew Simon

Great Great Nephew Sascha

Here you see Eric Foot among six generations of his family. Sister Enid's son Donald grew up keenly feeling the absence of his uncle and has visited the battlefields many times. His son and grandson drove from their home in Germany to accompany him to the place where, 100 years to the day, his Uncle Eric disappeared in the smoke, never to be seen again. ➜186

Burgess and Philby affairs.' While admitting that the system was *'unfair'* and *'offered opportunities for abuse'*, he defended it for having allowed the British Empire to run mostly successfully *'with far less personnel and far less talent than would otherwise have been needed'*. He neglects to mention that it was he who had been involved in the recruitment of both Burgess and Philby and that their very public defections led to him being forced out of MI6 in 1953. Like so many intelligence workers of that time he seems to have taken his secrets to the grave. ➜241

FORTUNE, Victor Morven. He stands in the centre of this picture, *(right)*, taken at the time of his surrender to General Erwin Rommel who poses alongside him in Saint Valéry-en-Caux in June 1940. ➜330

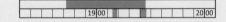

GATHORNE-HARDY, Geoffrey Malcolm, (above). The grandson of a former Home Secretary, as a boy growing up in Mayfair he'd lived next door to the Rawlinson family, though the future General Sir Henry Rawlinson was 14 years his senior. Aged 22, he set off for the Boer War as a Private in a unit of the Imperial Yeomanry known as 'the Millionaires' for the wealthy gentry it contained. Two months after their arrival in South Africa the whole unit was captured after being cut off and besieged for 4 days. Geoffrey lost a finger and went into captivity along with four lords, an MP, the son of the Archbishop of Canterbury, the nephew of the First Lord of the Admiralty & a future Prime Minister of Ireland.

After his return to England he became a barrister and in March 1914 he married Kathleen Goschen, the niece of the aforementioned First Lord of the Admiralty, whose German roots were in Leipzig from where her merchant banker grandfather had immigrated exactly 100 years before.

Geoffrey's brother Alfred would be killed at the Battle of Loos in 1915 and in September 1917 he himself was hit in the left foot by a bomb dropped by an aeroplane with the wounds being so severe that amputation was necessary the next day. On Armistice Day in 1918, his father, a former MP and Railway Commissioner, was found by his servants dead in his smoking room at the family home, Donnington Priory in Newbury. The ink was not yet dry on the diary entry he'd just completed and there was a bullet wound to his head & a revolver by his side. Having been told by a specialist that he had not long to live, he had taken his fate into his own hands.

Geoffrey did not let his disability get in his way. He was a crack shot and loved hunting and fishing in wild country. He

had a great interest in Norway having been there before the war, and as well as being fluent in Norwegian, he became an authority on its early history and during the Second World War assisted the Norwegian government in exile. A leading light at the start of the British Institute for International Affairs (now more commonly known as Chatham House), in 1934 he wrote *'A Short History of International Affairs 1920-1934'* in which he tried to extract the learning for future generations. Another world war later in 1950 he published the 4th edition of this book, extended to cover up to 1939 and concluding: *'Ideological disarmament and the rediscovery of mutual tolerance are the crying needs of the hour. Till this problem is solved, the motive behind our efforts for peace is basically nothing but fear, and a world which seeks peace with no higher motive than this is perhaps ripe for annihilation by the atomic bomb.'*

His wife lived to be 100 but with no children from him or his brother and sister, Donnington Priory left his family and is now the headquarters and showroom of a fine art and antiques auction house. ➔75

GENTRY-BIRCH, Cyril. Seeing him towering head and shoulders above his second wife, *(opposite, centre)*, it's difficult to imagine how he managed to get through active service in two world wars without being picked off, particularly when you consider that he went over the top twice at Loos, as well as at the Somme and Passchendaele, and was caught up in the maelstrom of the German Spring Offensive. It was such a maelstrom that he was officially reported as killed, and the Regimental History still has him listed amongst the dead despite his having been found in a German prisoner-of-war camp soon after. His company had managed to hold off three German assaults when he took a bullet in the lung, eventually waking up to find two German stretcher bearers attending to him. Repatriated at the end of 1918, and demobilised in late 1919, he was back in the Army in 1922, this time as a regular in the Cheshire Regiment. His inter-war service included spells in India, Malta and Palestine and then he was back in France in September 1939. More good fortune saw him missing Dunkirk as he had been posted to instruct at the Cheshires' infantry training centre and then in September 1940 he became C.O. of the 2nd Cheshires and embarked with them for the Middle East in May 1941. After voyaging around the Cape of Good Hope and a spell in Cyprus, they were deployed in the defence of Gazala in

February 1942, but again Cyril's luck held out as, just a month before the Germans attacked and decimated the 2nd Cheshires, he was posted to become Commandant of the Middle East Camouflage Training and Development Centre, and he served in training roles for the rest of the war.

His first wife having died in 1939, he re-married out in Alexandria in 1944 where his bride Linda was a sister (and later matron) in Queen Alexandra's Imperial Military Nursing Service. Cyril retired after the war as a Colonel and went on to serve as a district councillor in Henley. He and his wife remained active with charities into very old age and he was remembered as a very correct very polite upright gentleman of the old school. He'd come along way from being a council clerk in 1914. ➔267

GOODRICH, Louis. Though he'd been a professional actor for 12 years before the war, he was no head-in-the-air thespian. He'd been born at Sandhurst with his Army father on his way to being a Major-General. Despite having first embarked for France as a private in December 1914, when Louis became adjutant of an Officers' School in 1917 he had all the bearing of a professional soldier and was known as a keen disciplinarian. He would get an MBE for his service there, and afterwards when he met drama critics who had been cadets at the school, he'd beg them humorously to let bygones be bygones when writing their reviews of his shows and to forget the days when he had severely dealt with them on parade. His first wife filed for divorce in 1917 on the grounds of desertion and frequent adultery with various women. Marrying again in 1918, he went on to appear in films as well as in the theatre as both actor and playwright. With storm clouds gathering in 1938, he tried to join the Officers' Emergency Reserve but was told that at the age of 66 he was too old. ➔54

GOODSHIP, Gilbert Reginald. His father was an umbrella maker and also the verger at St Giles' Church in Reading, with Gilbert being involved in all aspects of church life, including as Captain of the Church Lads Brigade and a bell ringer, as well as working at a big ironmonger's from the age of 14. He was also a Territorial private in the Berkshire Yeomanry and had reached Sergeant when he was commissioned in May 1915.

In France for only 7 weeks before being wounded on the Somme, Gilbert ended up in hospital for 6 months and was left with muscle wastage and nerve damage. During the German Spring Offensive in 1918, his platoon was surrounded but they held out until their ammunition was all gone and only 6 of the original 21 were left alive. He survived being a prisoner in Germany for the rest of the war, returning debilitated by the poor conditions and lack of food to find that his second child had arrived in his absence. He didn't stay in Reading for long, moving to Nottingham (where his third child was born), then Harrow and Amersham (where he ran a grocer's and hardware shop with his wife) before finally settling in the village of Grundsiburgh in Suffolk in 1956. One constant throughout his long life was bell-ringing. Everywhere he lived he rang and taught and conducted ringing. It must have been a solace to him after all that he had been through in the war and his legacy continues through all that he passed on in his kind and patient way to the next generations and also in the

sixth bell to be installed at Offton Church in Suffolk for which he led the fundraising. His obituary in the bell ringers' weekly journal 'The Ringing World' noted that, not long before his death, a visiting band had found itself a ringer short and even though his health had been poor all year and he was far from well, *'he turned out and rang the treble faultlessly to a quarter peal'.* ➜307

JOY, Edward Sydney. Charles Bartlett wrote to Edward's father, & his letter was quoted in the Reading Mercury:

'It is with the deepest regret I write to tell you of the death of your son, who fell on the 18th. He was carrying out some important reconnaissance work when he was sniped, and the only slight consolation I can offer you is that death was instantaneous. Although he did not live to bring back the information, his courage and pluck enabled him to get sufficiently far forward for him to obtain same, and the scout who was with him brought back the required information, so without your son's fine example I am confident he would not have done so.

I have lost by his death a most promising young officer, whom it will be difficult to replace. On behalf of every officer I send you our sincerest sympathies, and assure you how deeply we feel for you, as not only have we lost a good officer, but a true friend.' ➜311

KEATING'S. Their insect-killing powder was formulated from the ground-up flowers of certain species of chrysanthemum & tansy. By the 1930s with the trenches filled in and household living conditions improved throughout the country, demand for their insect powder dwindled and they needed to do something else. The Second World War saw them moving into precision engineering but that too went into decline in the late 1970s. Their motto could be 'Adapt or Die' because the present day sees them as a scientific engineering firm that beat some of the biggest names in Europe to be awarded the contract to make key components for the European Space Agency's new generation of weather satellites – a long way from killing lice. ➜50

KINGERLEE, Cyril Henry. After surviving the Battalion's attack at Passchendaele in November 1917, he became an instructor at 5th Army Infantry School. Many of the men he taught were young conscripts who went on to bear the brunt of the German Spring Offensive in March 1918, and that weighed heavily on him for the rest of his life.

After the war he kept his military moustache to hide the scar from where the bullet had entered his face in April 1916. He started up one of the first cine film processing companies and married in 1925. Just three years later his wife died from poisoning of the liver (possibly as a complication of pregnancy or from a now-discredited pain relief drug). Her death combined with all he'd been through in the war led to an outpouring of grief that was almost too much to bear. In an effort to take him out of himself, his father arranged to take him to the Albion Hotel in Brighton for Christmas and that is where his luck changed when he met Elaine Nind, who was also there for Christmas with her parents and four sisters. Her initial sorriness for him turned into a deep love and they were married in the summer of 1931. His troubles were not completely over though. Their honeymoon only lasted one day as he had to return home on finding that his business partner had embezzled all his company's assets and disappeared. Despite his best efforts the business went into liquidation just before the Second World War and then he

was in uniform again, *(above, bottom left)*, serving with an anti-aircraft battery in Colchester. His big piece of luck, though, had been finding a companion who remained steadfastly with him through the rest of his life and you can see the love they shared in the picture taken on their Golden Wedding anniversary, *(above)*, and in the 2 children, 5 grandchildren and 9 great-grandchildren from their marriage, eleven of whom are amongst those shown ***below*** at his son's wife's 70th birthday party. →231

LINDEMERE, Henry. His father Louis Lindheimer was from near Frankfurt and had come to England in the 1870s, marrying an Englishwoman who'd been born in Florence and having six sons, two of whom were born in Paris. Perhaps in the face of anti-German prejudice or just from a desire to fit in, Henry, along with the rest of his family, changed his name to Lindemere before 1901. He followed his father's commercial lead and became a stockbroker, while also making a name for himself as a racehorse owner. In 1907 however he gave all that up to go to Canada. Two of his brothers ended up staying there for the rest of their lives but for whatever reason it was not for him and he returned to stockbroking in London, and got married in 1910. Less than two years later his wife died due to disease in her adrenal glands not long after the birth of their only daughter Beryl. Maybe delayed by the need to care for Beryl, he didn't join up until October 1915, and would see out the war using his equine expertise with the Horse Transport in the Army Service Corps, finishing as a Captain. He married again in 1924 to a Liverpool school master's daughter 24 years his junior. He divorced her for infidelity in 1931, and not long after that their elder daughter died aged 6 of a bowel obstruction caused by a congenital defect. Their younger daughter Anita was aged only 13 when Henry died in 1940.

Henry Lindemere né Lindheimer

In an interesting twist of fate, both of his surviving daughters ended up with very German surnames, or rather the same very German surname. At the end of the Second World War, Beryl married Martin Adolf Sobernheim. He had been born Jewish in Berlin and managed to escape the Nazis only to find himself interned by the British. The fall of France in 1940 had led to an outbreak of paranoia and in July he and some 2000 Jewish and anti-fascist German refugees along with a smaller number of Nazis and POWs were put on the *SS Dunera* to Australia. The now infamous voyage saw the internees abused, beaten and robbed by their British guards. Stories of their treatment and their pale and emaciated appearance on their arrival in Australia led to courts martial for their guards and Martin was amongst those soon on their way back to freedom in the UK. He was married to Beryl Lindemere for nearly 39 years and after her death in 1984, he married her half-sister Anita. ➔273

LONGDEN, Arthur, *(below)*. Before the war he'd been secretary for the Northern Province of the Church of England Men's Society, providing a social meeting place for men in a Christian setting. He would be awarded the MC in the 1918 Birthday honours and survive his 4 years in France to return to his wife and children. After a spell in a parish near Wigan, he took over the parish of St Breock, a tiny village in Cornwall. He was rector there for 31 years and that is where he and his wife are buried. Not much about him has come down to the family members I contacted. I gave them the three long letters of condolence I'd found that he'd written to bereaved families (one of them is in my first book). The only remnant they had of him was this rather lovely picture taken in a relaxed moment in later life. ➔343

LUCENA, Stephen Evelyn. At his first court martial he was found guilty but got away with a severe reprimand. Ten days later he was found drunk again, this time whilst on duty in the trenches at 1.30 a.m., and with that being a more serious offence, he was dismissed from the service at his next court martial, presided over by Charles Bartlett. Most people might have collapsed at that point, and he was clearly struggling, but in August 1916 he joined up again, this time as a gunner in the Royal Garrison Artillery. He was wounded in the back in June 1917 but it was not too serious and he returned to France in September. Even when the war was over, and having survived all that, he decided to stay on in the Army, eventually leaving as a Lance Sergeant in 1922.

The next year he was on a ship to Canada and the only definite remaining 'sightings' of him are in the voters' list for Toronto in 1935, and his death notice that appeared in the paper on Christmas Eve 1949. This gives his home address as a rather run-down rooming house which was only 200 metres from the location of a *'Stephan Lucene'* in the 1945 voters' list at the House of Providence, a huge hostel that sheltered 700 of Toronto's poor. His luck had obviously not improved. There is an anomaly though. In the death notice he is listed as *'Major Stephen E Lucena'*. Had he seen further military service in the Canadian Army? It's hard to know. Canadian military records of that era are only accessible to next of kin. Stephen only had one sibling, his younger sister Theodosia. In an effort to see whether she had any living descendants I discovered that in 1917 when she was 24 she had been admitted to Bethlem mental hospital. In late 1915, she was doing unpaid war work on farms when she was operated on for appendicitis and soon after that she started suffering from delusions. A change of air to the seaside had seen her improve but then one day she falsely accused her mother of killing her animals, threatened her with a stick, and cycled from Bexhill to London where she was found lost and wandering by police. Delusions continued where she thought she had had a baby but said she was a 14-year-old girl, and she was often agitated, noisy and violent. Not getting any better,, she was taken to East Sussex County Asylum in 1919, where she still was in 1939, and she died in a mental home run by nuns in Plymouth in 1976 aged 84. Her notes make mention of a great aunt, an aunt and a cousin (all on her mother's side) who also had been certified insane.

Both Stephen and his sister were dealt terrible cards on top of terrible cards. I never met them but I will not forget their stories and I will make sure to count my luck. ➔156

Stephen Evelyn Lucena

Theodosia Gladys Lucena

McNAIR, John Kirkland. Charles's nephew would survive the war and in the Second World War became a Brigadier on the Staff of the Joint Staff Mission in Washington DC (1942-44) before taking over as Director of Graves Registration and Enquiries at the War Office (1944-46). ➔73

MARTIN, Edgar. Having found that Private Ernest Moore was the only man from the 8th Royal Berkshires posted as missing in action on 3rd May 1916, I looked him up in the Register of Soldiers' Effects and my interest was piqued when below his name I saw the note *'alias Martin, Edgar'.* His total effects of 8 pounds, 9 shillings and 8 pence were paid out to his brother George Martin and two sisters under their married names, and that was enough for me to be able to find him and his family in the censuses and get his birth certificate.

Edgar Martin was one of the 9 children of a plumber and was born in East Grinstead in Sussex in 1883. His medal card as Ernest Moore said he arrived in France on 5th December 1915, at which point he would have been 32. So why was he serving under an alias? He wasn't under age, so was he on the run from something, maybe even something criminal? I then had the great good fortune that a search for Edgar Martin turned up his Army Service Record. He'd signed up under his original name in Manchester in 1909, becoming a driver in the Army Service Corps. His previous job was as a brewer's labourer and he was 5' 3" (160 cm), just under 9 stone (57 kg), with a sallow complexion, hazel eyes, light brown hair, and a scar on the bridge of his nose. The latter might have come from a brawl as his record noted that he was later arrested on two occasions, for assaulting a police constable in 1909 and for drunkenness and riotous behaviour in 1911. In August 1911 he left the Army but having stayed on the Reserve, he was mobilized at Aldershot three days after war was declared in 1914.

After arrival in France on 22nd September, he'd become a driver for the wagon train of the 2nd/8th Gurkhas but in March 1915 his haemorrhoids became so bad that he was hospitalised and shipped back to England. When recovered he joined a company of the Army Service Corps in Basingstoke, but on 20th July he was found to have been absent from the mule lines when acting as line orderly and sentenced to 5 days confined to barracks. Then, on 24th July 1915 he deserted – and it must been very soon after that he enlisted with the Royal Berkshires in Reading in order for him to be going out to France with them in December. This didn't make sense – why would a man on the run from the Army join the Army?

Further searching found that one of his brothers, Edward George Martin, had joined the Royal Sussex Regiment before the war and had been killed at the Battle of Aubers Ridge on 9th May 1915. Had

Edgar Martin alias Ernest Moore

Edward Godfrey Martin

Edgar decided he wanted revenge and so taken it into his own hands to change from a supporting role to being a fighter? Why couldn't he have just asked for a transfer? Going back to his Army Service Record, there is a further clue. On 20th May 1913 he had married Rose Maud Burton. She was originally from near Haslemere in Surrey but in 1911 was working as a housemaid in Worthing – not too far from East Grinstead but still a long way from the Register Office in Manchester where they were married. In 1930 she wrote to the War Department to ask whether her husband Edgar Martin had been killed in action. The reply went out that as far as they were concerned his whereabouts were still unknown after his desertion in 1915. Their left hand didn't know what the right was doing, because whilst his last will and testament must have led to the discovery of his alias (he wrote it as 'Ernest Moore' and only made mention of his siblings), no link was made to his earlier service under his original name nor to his wife. Who knows what his reasons were for what he did but the outcome was that Rose received no widow's pension and when she re-married to ladies' tailor Leon Godel in 1943 she was forced to say she was unmarried and use her maiden name. She lived until 1975. I wonder if she ever knew what happened to her first husband.

As a result of all the confusion he sowed, Edgar Martin appears on the Memorial to the Missing in Arras as *'Moore E.'* and on his home town memorial in East Grinstead

as *'Edgar Martin'* (as shown in the pictures ***above***). Local historians have found the details of his brother but nothing about him. No doubt they gave up when they didn't find him listed by the Commonwealth War Graves Commission and missed the very subtle clue on the memorial itself with the letter 'G's of their names linking the two brothers together in death. ➜241

Rose Maud Godel was Martin née Burton

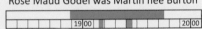

MICHELHAM, Lady. Her husband would die in 1919, leaving her £15 million. In June 1924 she went to the Rodeo Show that was part of the British Empire Exhibition at Wembley and whilst there her attention was caught by one of the performers who *'gallantly doffed his 10-gallon hat to her while bulldogging a steer'.* In February 1926 they were married, but seven months after that, she fell ill with liver disease. She lasted only four more months before dying in Paris aged 44, having just auctioned her first husband's considerable art collection (including 'Pinkie' by Sir Thomas Lawrence ***(opposite, top left)***, which realised the then record price of 74,000 guineas, about the same amount that their London mansion in St James's had just raised at auction).

Her second husband, Fred Almy, wasn't quite the rough cowboy that it might appear from the description of his *'bulldogging'* (i.e. throwing the steer to the ground by seizing its horns and twisting its neck). He

was from a long-standing and well-to-do Long Island family, but he appears to have had a wild streak running right through him. Firstly he rejected a life in the family wool business to be a stoker for locomotives on the railroad, being dubbed the *'Millionaire Fireman'*, and then he upped sticks to Arizona where he set up a successful ranch from scratch. After his marriage to Lady Michelham, his nickname became the *'Cowboy Millionaire'* (there had been a 1909 film of that name, the plot of which mirrored their trans-Atlantic and culture-clash romance) but he did not stay the millionaire for long, getting through his $50 million inheritance in 10 years (not helped by the Wall Street Crash). In the meantime his love life was no less tempestuous. A month after his wife's death, he attended a fashion show in Paris and a month after that he was on a ship back to America with one of the models as his new wife (and was caught bringing in cases of alcohol during Prohibition). His new wife divorced him in 1939 having become sick of his antics and with all the money gone. Still he managed to make it through to his death in 1965 without becoming completely destitute.

There are more complications with Lady Michelham's family than can be told here, but the current Lady Michelham lives in Switzerland & continues her predecessor's tradition of robust philanthropy. ➔369

MOON, Cecil Frederic. I thought I'd picked him out from a 1917 group photograph, *(above)*, as he is the only one in the picture wearing Boer War medal ribbons, a Lieutenant's rank badges and had the shape of a Quartermaster who didn't have to do a lot of running about. To be sure, though, I thought I should see if I could find confirmation. Ordering his service record from the MOD started me on a trail of discovery that included his using aliases to have relationships with at least six women who were not his first wife (including at least one bigamous marriage). I have so far found that he fathered nine children, all of whom he abandoned in infancy, and a lot of those children's descendants have been trying to find out the truth about him without realising that they have other close relations doing the same thing. I have confirmed that this is indeed him in the 1917 group photograph but along the way have uncovered enough extraordinary stories for another book. ➔286

						19	00									20	00	

MUSTO, Henry John. His wife Elizabeth endured much hardship and loss in her long life. Of the four children she had with her first husband, one girl died as a baby, two girls were taken in by Barnado's when her husband came down with TB and after his death in 1904 they were sent off to Canada. Only her one-year-old son stayed with her and was taken in by Henry Musto when he became her second husband in 1908. She had two further sons with Henry in 1909 and 1913 and cared for them whilst he was away in the First World War. One of those sons was then killed in 1943 when the workers' bus he was travelling in was hit by an engine shunting wagons at a level crossing in Didcot's Ordnance Depot. She outlived Henry by 13 years and finally died in 1966 aged 91. ➔91

Elizabeth Musto née Greenwood

						19	00									20	00	

PETO, Morton. I was so moved by the expressions of loss after his death that I decided to contact his family even though he wasn't in my original group photograph. I managed to find his nephew, also called Morton Peto (in memory of his uncle), and wrote to him. When we spoke on the phone, he told me that he had recently retrieved a box from the loft containing his uncle's memorabilia, including the diary he had kept during his two years in France written on scraps from his field service book. That had formed the basis of a memoir put together by his uncle's younger sister and having re-read that for the first time in many years, he'd decided to get it properly typed up. He had just put down the first draft after reading it when my letter arrived. The coincidence left him pretty shattered, but still he agreed to meet me and I was able to share what I had found and in turn he provided me with Charles Bartlett's letters of condolence, as well as the photograph of his uncle. He himself had followed in his uncle's footsteps by serving as an Army medical officer during the Second World War, including 18 months in the Western Desert. He went on to be a county GP and recalled that during house visits he saw on display a lot of the *'memorial of a brave life given for others'* scrolls from the King like the one he had for his uncle Morton. ➔334

PHILLIPS, Frederick David. He was able to avoid capture during the 1918 German Spring Offensive (and was awarded the MC) but not long after that he left the Battalion to become a mounted military policeman, ending his Army career in 1919 as the Deputy Assistant Provost Marshal of 36th Division in the rank of Captain. He married at the end of the war and in 1925 returned to the gold mines in South Africa with his wife and two young children. ➔303

RADFORD, (Maurice) Clive. There are three extraordinary stories that I found when researching Clive Radford. Firstly, he was the brother of probably the most famous music hall star at the beginning of the war. Basil Hallam Radford appeared under the stage name '**Basil Hallam**'. He'd started out in the theatre playing minor Shakespearian roles, but by 1914 he'd moved into musical comedy and it was in April that year that he personified the role that would make his name, appearing in *'The Passing Show'* with 16 dancing girls and singing,

> I'm Gilbert, the Filbert,
>   The knut with a 'k',
> The pride of Piccadilly,
>   The blasé roué;
> Oh, Hades, the ladies,
>   They'd leave their wooden huts
> For Gilbert, the Filbert,
>   The colonel of the knuts.

As PG Wodehouse explained in an article at that time, a 'knut' (pronounced 'nut') was the *'descendant of the Beau'* or Dandy, beautifully turned out, living on his father's money and cultivating *'a certain air of world-weariness'*. *'His chief forms of relaxation are dancing and bread-throwing'*. Basil as Gilbert the Filbert, **(below)**, caught this trend to a T, and he was soon all the rage, with the 15-year-old future Queen Mother writing to a friend for pictures of him and receiving letters from another friend, Lady Lavinia Spencer (great aunt of Lady Diana), signing herself *'Basilette'*. The brutal realities of the war and the heightened valuing of duty and sacrifice would see the knuts go out of fashion. Basil himself saw the result of that when still performing in 1915 and being presented with white feathers and other 'suggestions' that he should be doing his bit. Little did his accusers know that he had tried to enlist right at the start but been rejected as unfit by the Army. An injury to the arch of his foot when he was 9 meant that he needed a steel plate in his right boot and when he and his American dancing partner introduced the Foxtrot to London, he was doing it through the pain. Even so, he was still trying to join up and in September 1915 succeeded in getting a commission in the Royal Flying Corps to act as an observer in the balloons that were winched up behind the lines to spot for the artillery and note information about the enemy positions. He did this despite suffering from 'sea sickness' nearly every time his balloon was in the air. In April 1916 he was sent home with an inflammation of his bowels and at the beginning of May he had an operation to try to sort out his crippling leg problems. His bone-setter attempted to get him to take a longer rest to recover but his reply was, *'I must go back to the boys whether I am well or not'*. So it was that in August 1916 he found himself in a balloon that broke free from its moorings as it was being winched down in a high wind. It quickly gained height and started to drift towards enemy lines much to the horror of the thousands of soldiers watching on the ground. Little did they know as they saw the drama unfold that one of the men in the basket was someone they knew from the music halls and from concert parties behind the trenches. There is some debate

as to exactly what happened next, but the majority of eye-witness accounts tell of one man jumping out of the basket and landing safely by parachute but that something went wrong as the other tried to jump, possibly getting his parachute caught in the balloon's rigging, and then suddenly dropping like a stone from over 3,000 feet. He hit the ground a few yards from an officer of the Scots Guards who searched his body and on finding his cigarette case discovered he was Basil Hallam. It seems so desperately unfair that a man who had brought so much joy to so many should die in such a miserable, frightening and very public way.

Basil and Clive's parents were to go through more misery in June 1918 when, in a strange twist, Clive, *(above)*, was named as a co-respondent in a very widely reported divorce case, despite having been killed in action nearly three years earlier.

In a bid to find an explanation for the erratic behaviour of his wife, a Captain William Myers had searched his house and found, tied up with ribbons, a collection of letters from a Captain in the Gordon Highlanders, and from Clive Radford.

I think it's fair to say that William Myers' wife Agneta could be described as 'lively' (she was familiarly known as 'Jimmie' and liked to drive about in a cowboy costume). Maybe that is the very thing that attracted him to marry her in 1911 when he was 33 and she was 19. He had had problems with her erratic behaviour even before coming back on leave during Christmas 1914 and finding her not at home. When she did turn up in the New Year she brought with her two officers *'to see the horses'* and, not long after, she returned to London with them. It turned out that one of those officers

was Clive Radford and he had completely fallen for her. At the end of his leave she gave him a lift down to Folkestone, and then, at his invitation, wangled her way on board the boat with the promise that she would not set foot in France, only to do so after getting a permit from the French authorities as Clive's 'sister'. She returned on the next boat but he was soon writing to her: *'Listen, go to some really good place and have a really good miniature of yourself done and mounted in a good locket ... Your ring is a firm fixture. I can't remove it even if I wanted to. They noticed it here and wanted to know if I were married. I said, "No, but that I wished I were." And so I do if only it were to you I were married...'.* Their correspondence continued until June 1915, when Clive sent her what the judge called *'a beastly dirty postcard'*, writing, *'It might amuse you, darling'* but by that time Jimmie had moved on in her affections and he never heard from her again.

The case involving the Captain in the Gordon Highlanders included a particularly bizarre story in which Jimmie had one day rung him up pretending to be her maid, saying that she and her sister had started off for Gallipoli by aeroplane but had been shot down over Swindon and her sister had broken her neck while she had had a leg amputated. They then borrowed a stretcher, sprinkled it with bullock's blood from the butcher, and were bandaged with their faces made pale with powder in time to give the Captain one of the shocks of his life. Other evidence was insufficient for the jury to find Jimmie guilty of adultery with him but they did pronounce guilt in the case with Clive Radford and that was enough for the divorce to go through.

Jimmie married again but died in 1939 after an operation for kidney disease just three years after the birth of her third child (each child having had a different father).

The divorce case was not the last of Clive Radford in the afterlife. In November 1928, the War Office received a letter saying, *'A report has been received that Capt Radford is still alive and is in a mental home, having been taken prisoner when lying wounded.'* The letter was from the General Secretary of a society set up to help ex-servicemen with mental problems but when he was spoken to on the phone, he could add no further details – and after a check with the Imperial War Graves Commission who confirmed that Clive had been buried in Vermelles, the case was closed. Who knows where the original report came from, but

there can be little doubt that he had been killed. His death was categorically reported in the war diary of the 1st Royal Berkshires, so there must have been a reliable witness. In addition an inventory of his effects returned from the front listed only a single item: *'One Identity Disc'*. ➔45

REDDIE, Anthony Julian, *(above)*. At the beginning of the war, he was a major with the then unusual distinction of having seen no active service in his 22 years in the Army (though he'd won many polo cups and shot a lot of big game in India). That soon changed after he arrived in France on 13th August 1914 with 1st South Wales Borderers, and he had had to take over command on 1st November 1914 when his C.O. was wounded in the middle of desperate fighting during the First Battle of Ypres. After his promotion to command 1st Brigade, he would lead them for over two years. Being among the observers at the trials of the first tank back in England in February 1916, it was his favourable report that was possibly the first detailed analysis that General Sir Douglas Haig read about the new weapon. After a six month break with the reserves in Wales, in April 1918 he returned to command a Yorkshire Territorial Brigade in France for the rest of the war. In 1919, having been mentioned in dispatches seven times and awarded CMG, DSO and Légion d'honneur, but with the Army shrinking to peacetime numbers, he reverted to being C.O. of 1st South Wales Borderers and then was a Territorial Brigadier for 4 years before his retirement in 1928. During the Second World War he was an area organiser for the Home Guard in the Scottish Highlands. ➔55

ROBINSON, Bethell. Margaret's father had started playing for Preston North End (PNE) in 1880, at the beginning of their first season playing association football (previously their games had been cricket and rugby). After centuries of free-for-alls with different local rules, the Football Association had started to regularise the game. Even so, tactics took a while to develop and when Bethell was first in the team, he was one of six forwards. One 14-1 defeat led to a re-think and he moved to full back where he remained for the rest of his career.

You can see he has the look of Margaret in the 1882 team photo *(above, back row 2nd from right)*. He stands next to the bowler-hatted team manager William Sudell, a key figure in the development of the modern game in terms of tactics and organisation and in the introduction of professionalism. At that time the FA didn't allow players to be paid and clubs were trying to get round this by 'employing' players in local businesses. Bethell himself had been assistant to the Town Clerk of Preston before taking the job of Club Secretary of PNE in 1883. In that capacity he helped to bring the club into profit that season but also famously opened the letter from the FA that accused them of professionalism and led to them being banned from the FA Cup in 1884. The floodgates would not hold though, and it was only the next year that the FA passed a motion allowing players to be paid.

Meanwhile William Sudell had also been bringing in players from Scotland, such that Bethell was squeezed out and forced to look for other clubs to play for. He turned out for Preston Zingari, Blackburn Olympic, Farnworth Standard, Halliwell, Accrington, & Church before finally being picked up by Bolton Wanderers. So it was that he was in their defence on the first ever day of the Football League, 8th September 1888, when they lost 6-3 to Derby County. Strangely, given the qualification rules that had been introduced, he also played for West Bromwich Albion (WBA) in the FA Cup in 1889. That included the semi-final against his old club, PNE, who won 1-0 on their way to doing the first ever League & Cup double without losing a game (and thus cementing 'The Invincibles' name they'd earned due to their long unbeaten streaks since 1886).

Bethell became the captain of Bolton Wanderers whilst continuing to play for them over the next two seasons (and also in another FA Cup semi-final loss with WBA in 1891) but he had also followed the route of many footballers in becoming a pub landlord, taking over the Crown & Cushion in Bolton. It was there in May 1891 that the police made a raid as part of a co-ordinated operation across Bolton to crack down on illegal betting. Bethell was found guilty and fined £5 as well as having his

license endorsed. Perhaps it was this that convinced him to move his family down to Chiswick where he set himself up as a (legitimate) horse-racing betting agent.

When the First World War came, with his wife having died and his five children all grown-up and making their own ways in the world, he joined up despite being in his mid-50s. As far as I know he didn't see any action but was posted out to Burma with a battalion of the Rifle Brigade that was made up of older men. The idea was that they could best be used for garrison duties around the Empire and thus free up younger men to do the fighting. He reached the rank of Company Quartermaster Sergeant before returning home and becoming an estate agent in Hammersmith. In 1921, at the age of 60 he married a 33-year-old typist who had divorced her husband for deserting her just after the war and they moved to Southend-on-Sea. Long after his playing days were over he was talked of in hallowed terms in the papers, but after his death in 1931, the Lancashire Evening Post incorrectly remembered him as one of the Invincibles and the only allusion on his grave to his football fame is the trophy-shaped ornament that has been somewhat roughly re-fixed in place *(above)*. ➔20

ROSE FAMILY. Sir Philip Rose (1816-1883), a solicitor made a baronet in 1874, had been the first recognised agent for the Conservative Party, and a close friend and adviser of Prime Minister Benjamin Disraeli. He was also the High Sheriff of Buckinghamshire in 1878, four years before Charles Bartlett's father held that office, which gives an indication that the families moved in the same circles of society.

They were to become even more closely connected when Sir Philip's grandson Vivian & Charles's brother Edward became friends whilst serving in the Royal Bucks Militia (as pictured in the fabulous photograph of young officers in 1892, *(below)*: Vivian is at bottom left, Edward is at bottom right pointing with his thumb at the silliness going on in the centre, and Albert Henderson, who is mentioned later in the letters, is sitting in the centre holding the dog). The closeness was further sealed when Vivian's sister Dorothy married Edward Bartlett in 1894. Dorothy must have thought she was set for life having combined her family's great wealth with that of her new husband and received over 300 presents from those at the heights of society who attended her wedding, including a Maharajah. The joy would not last. In 1904 her youngest brother John died of pneumonia aged 15. In 1914, her elder son Geoff was killed in the explosion of HMS Bulwark. In 1915 her husband Edward died having gone insane as a result of catching syphilis. In 1916 her sister Mary's husband Albert Henderson was killed during the Battle of the Somme. In 1917 her brother Vivian died in a hospital in Shepherd's Bush having been wounded and taken prisoner at the Battle of Loos in 1915 (his left arm had been amputated and he never got over a splintered fracture of his right thigh despite returning to England in a prisoner exchange in late 1916). In 1934 her twin sister Violet died (11 years after her divorce from Quiller Gold, a cousin of Patrick Gold from p. 281). In 1941, Dorothy herself was killed during the worst night of the Blitz (10th-11th May 1941, the same night as the brother of Charles's solicitor). She was amongst 99 members of a Californian sect who were hit by a bomb whilst worshipping the moon beneath a glass roof in York Terrace next to Regent's Park. Perhaps she had taken to the occult to look for answers that her family's Catholic faith could not provide.

(Rose Annie) Dorothy Bartlett née Rose

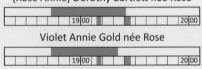

Violet Annie Gold née Rose

This was not the end of the bad luck for the Rose family. In 1943 Vivian's grandson Peter was watching cricket at Downside School when one of a pair of low-flying Hurricanes crashed into the crowd. He was among 9 boys killed alongside 15 wounded, resulting in the dying out of the male line of the Roses back to Vivian's father. → 140

RUBENS, Paul. *Above*, on the left you can see Phyllis Dare as she stands on the stage in Reading Town Hall and looks out over the audience under the flags of Britain and her allies. Whilst Paul played the piano, she sang his song *'Your King & Country Want You'*. Once the men had seen the reality of joining up they would parody the end of its refrain *'We shall cheer you, thank you, kiss you, when you come back again'* as *'Oh! We'll hate you, boo you, hiss you, if you sing it again!'*. Cecil Cloake★ got in trouble with the military authorities when a newspaper published one of his private letters in which he protested the use of sexual emotion to encourage recruitment. Many of the boys who had joined up that night were now dead on the battlefield, as he had seen with his own eyes. ➔186

RUBENS family. Paul's grave, *(right)*, is in Hanwell, West London, ringed by a hedge that is still trimmed. His brother & parents have been added below his name. ➔361

Paul Alfred Rubens

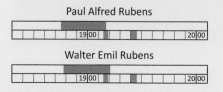

Walter Emil Rubens

(Paul) Victor Rubens

Jenny Rubens née Wallach

RUFF, Cyril. Cyril and his wife Dorothy had two sons but one died as a baby in 1928 so it is only their elder son Kenneth who appears with them in this picture of the family in uniform during the Second World War, *(below)*. Cyril was a Lieutenant in the Home Guard (note the First World War medal ribbons on his chest, including that for his Military Medal on the left, and his collar badges based on the Staffordshire knot, a local symbol going back to Anglo-Saxon times). He also took it upon himself to organise the collection of donated goods for needy causes such as the people of Coventry during the Blitz. The depot for these efforts was the ironmonger's shop, *(right)*, that his father had established in Smethwick in 1919 and which Cyril took over in the early 1930s, running it for over 25 years. He is remembered by his family as being 'old-school' and could be somewhat remote, but you can hear the voice of a real enthusiast in the 1956 newspaper interview about his hobby, when he says that he *'cannot resist old kitchen sinks - you know, the real thing, hand-fashioned well over a hundred years old and weighing anything up to five hundredweight'* and

he would *'travel miles to get a really good piece.'* Not only that, but he and his wife then filled them up with their collection of alpine plants. After I read that I looked at the background of the wartime photograph with new eyes and realised it was a fuller portrait than I first thought. Not only does it show the family but also the many hours of shared devotion involved in creating the garden in front of which they sit. ➔ 260

SARCHET, Hugh le Gallienne. He was an 18-year-old articled clerk to an accountant in London when he joined up in November 1914. Out in France since October 1915, he would be awarded the MC in January 1918 and then become Adjutant just before the opening of the German Spring Offensive. During the first attack on 21st March he stayed behind at Battalion HQ to destroy all secret papers. Whilst doing so he was attacked and had to kill several Germans with his revolver before making his escape.

In the attack of 4th April he was seriously wounded at the same time as his C.O. was killed and was never to be seen alive again.

Meanwhile his younger brother Lionel had arrived in France in November 1915. He became a trench mortar specialist, and as Chief Instructor at the III Corps Bomb & Trench Mortar School in July 1918 he was sent to teach a short course in America. By his special request he returned to the front line in September and was killed on 23rd October. Two days before the Armistice his mother Emily discovered the news of his death in a casualty list in the paper and having heard of Hugh's death from his banker also before any notification from the War Office, she wrote them a strongly worded letter saying, *'You will not be surprised that I should ask for a complete explanation for it is unforgivable that such gross incompetence should exist in any department in this the 5th year of the War, and that any parents should be treated with such scant courtesy or feeling.'*

She would have been familiar with the workings of the War Office as her husband William had been an Army Chaplain since 1896. A Wesleyan Methodist, he had served in Gibraltar, Devonport & Portsmouth, and then was in France all the way through from August 1914 to November 1918. In that whole time he had only been designated as 'Acting Chaplain' as there was no fixed establishment for Wesleyan chaplains in the Army like there was for Anglicans and Catholics. Even after his exemplary service in which he had been awarded both MC and OBE, they dodged giving him a permanent commission because at 55 he was deemed too old. This had serious implications for his pension when leaving the Army in that as only an acting Chaplain he would not be eligible for one at all. Things came to a head in 1922 when he became completely deaf. Unable to continue in his ministry and having lost money due to that year's failure of McGrigor's Bank, he was faced with an impoverished retirement and was reduced to begging in his letters to the Army, saying that he'd spent his life savings on keeping his sons at good schools in the hope that they would later provide for him *'but now all that is ended'*. Eventually after a letter of support from General Henry Horne, commander of 1st Army, he was awarded a disability pension of £126 a year and lived out his days in his birth place of Guernsey.

Rev. William Sarchet had been present at the funeral of his son Lionel in 1918. It seems amazing to me that after all he had been through in the war, his faith had stayed strong enough to chose the epitaph that he did for his son's grave, *(left)*. ➔324

William Henry Sarchet

Hugh le Gallienne Sarchet

Leslie Lionel Sarchet

SCHUSTER, (Franz) Arthur, *(above)*. This is not the place to go into the details of his achievements in physics, but a hint of his brilliance can be seen in these words from the one of the world's greatest ever physicists, James Clerk Maxwell, when offering the 24-year-old Arthur Schuster a job in 1876: *'It would do us all great good if you were to come and work in the Cavendish Laboratory the very prospect of your coming has caused all our pulses to beat about 1 per minute quicker.'* He was renowned for the variety of his interests and, among many other things, he was the first to use X-rays practically when called in to locate the bullet in a woman's head after she had been shot by her husband. He also coined the word 'antimatter', the idea of which had been first suggested by William Hicks, another alumnus of the Cavendish Laboratory under Maxwell, and coincidentally the father of Basil Hicks★ from the Group Photograph. Like William Hicks, who was a founder of what became Sheffield University, Arthur Schuster's contribution to scientific research and education in this country was immense and reaches through to today, not least through his establishment of a laboratory in Manchester which under his successor, Ernest Rutherford, became a renowned centre for physics.

When war broke out in 1914, he had been on his way out to the Crimea to observe the total solar eclipse. Turning around in Constantinople, he returned home into what became something of a personal storm. Firstly he and his family were the subject of anti-German prejudice despite the fact that they had come to England in 1870 after Prussia annexed their home city of Frankfurt and had been naturalised British citizens for 39 years (and in fact he and his two brothers all had sons serving in the British Army). Added to this was the fact that Arthur had a wireless installation in his house. Its purpose was to receive time signals from the Eiffel Tower and even though it was not sensitive enough to receive signals from Germany and was only a receiver so unable to transmit, it was packed away and eventually confiscated by the police. With public ignorance of the new wireless technology and the general paranoia of the time, this was used as a further stick to beat him with and, after reports appeared in the press, life became very difficult for him, as he describes on a visit to his club in London:

'...it was with fear and trembling that I entered the Athenaeum a few days later and selected a solitary place in the coffee-room. I was leaving again directly after luncheon, and as I was putting on my coat in the hall I suddenly felt someone stepping up behind to help me. Surprised at this politeness, which is somewhat unusual in the Club, I turned round and looked into the kindly face of Lord Roberts, with whom I had no personal acquaintance. The hall was then full of members of the Club, and it was obvious that the action was intended to be, and in fact was, a demonstration.'

Field Marshal Lord Roberts being the retired Commander-in-Chief of the British Army meant that this demonstration carried no little weight, and with the Royal Society also having passed a resolution fully backing his loyalty, it must have been deeply frustrating to have the whole business with his wireless apparatus dredged up again in July 1915 with the article in *Pearson's Weekly*. He was once again exonerated by the judge in the libel case, and, nine days before this mention of his name in Charles's letter, he had been greeted by cheers when, as the President of the British Association for the Advancement of Science, he had stood up to speak to their annual meeting. In front a banner depicting science as a female figure veiling her eyes amidst the guns he gave an address entitled *'The Common Aims of Science and Humanity'*. His words have a clear resonance with our own times:

'I must ask you to reflect whether the achievement of wealth and power, to the exclusion of higher aims, can lead to more than superficial prosperity which passes away, because it carries the virus of its own doom with it. Do we not find in the worship of material success the seed of the pernicious ambition which has maddened a nation and plunged Europe into war? Is this contempt for all idealistic purposes not responsible for the mischievous doctrine that the power to possess confers the right to possess, and that possession is desirable in itself without regard to the use which is made of it? I must, therefore, insist that if we delight in enlisting the wealth accumulated in the earth, and all the power stored in the orbs of heaven, or in the orbits of atomic structure, it should not be because we place material wealth above intellectual enjoyment, but rather because we experience a double pleasure if the efforts of the mind contribute to the welfare of the nation. The hunger for intellectual enjoyment is universal, and everybody should be given the opportunity and leisure of appeasing it. The duty to work, the right to live, and the leisure to think are the three prime necessities of our existence, and when one of them fails we only live an incomplete life.'

The very same day as this speech he received a telegram saying that his son Leonard had been wounded at Gallipoli. Luckily it was only a slight wound in the forearm and Leonard would serve through the rest of the war, become the chief of administration for BBC television right at its beginnings in Alexandra Palace before the Second World War and live to be 95. One of Arthur's sons-in-law would not be so fortunate, dying of wounds in 1917 a month after arriving at the front.

Arthur himself would continue his research but also dedicate himself to the administration and promotion of science. Having been Secretary of the Royal Society from 1912 to 1919, he was key in the foundation of the International Research Council, being Secretary from 1919 to 1928 and doing much to further his ideals of co-operation in science for the benefit of all humanity. As well as a knighthood in 1920, he was awarded several prestigious Royal Society medals and honorary doctorates.

Sadly materialist nationalism was again resurgent at the time of his death in 1934 and the Second World War would see his son's only child dying of wounds received when assaulting a German gun position in Italy in 1944. Arthur Schuster's legacy lives on, though, not least in the Schuster Building at the University of Manchester which opened in 1967 and now houses the School of Physics and Astronomy. ➔75

SNELL, Francis Saxon. He'd married just after joining up in November 1914. The book 'War Letters of Fallen Englishmen' (published in 1930) includes this to his wife:

'. . . . R. and F. are such ripping fellows, and yet they look upon the Bosch as just so much unutterable vermin; they have no sort of pity or compunction for them; the more they kill the better. Once L. came into our mess, and he said in his open boyish way, "And you know there was a rather rotten story about that raid last night (it was a raid on the German trenches). "What was that? said R. and F. "Why," said L., "they captured a German officer, and were taking him back to our lines, and he had his hands tied behind his back, and a chance bullet hit one of the men forming his escort, and so they turned on him and killed him.

"I don't see anything rotten about that," said R. (and F. backed him up). "More Bosch you kill the better."

"But," expostulated little L., "he was a prisoner; and it was only a stray bullet that hit his escort, and his hands were tied behind his back; and he could not defend himself; and they simply killed him just as he was." "And a damned good job too," says R.

It's rather awful that, you know, for it means this; — that not only hard cruel uncharitable men like some we have met — but even lots of awfully nice chaps, have simply put the Germans outside the range of all human sympathies whatever; not in the heat of anger, but deliberately, in their calm considered moments.

There is no question whatever about a man like R. being affected by, or of his catching feelings from, the crowd of other people. And there must be thousands and thousands like him. . . . '

Looking at the list of officers who were with the Battalion at the time, it looks like 'little L' must have been Cyril Lunn (5' 6" = 168 cm tall), with 'R' Gerald Robinson ★ and 'F' David Footman. Both these last two had spent time studying at schools in Germany with David Footman later writing:

'I was unmoved by anti-German propaganda, by the thesis that Germans were basically evil, of which one heard something in World War I, though without the stridency it attained in World War II. After all I had spent nearly seven months in the Kaiser's Germany and had found it a pleasant country to live in. There was a degree of paternalism; certain things were forbidden but nothing that I myself had any desire to do. For certain groups, for the officer corps for instance or the more fashionable student corporations, there were rigid codes of behaviour of which parts were admirable

and parts absurd. But for the ordinary run, German society, as I saw it, was refreshingly free from taboos.'

All of which is interesting when you consider that Francis Saxon Snell's wife Amy's maiden name was Spiegel and anti-German feeling had led to her whole family changing their name to her English mother's maiden name of Ralfs early in the war. In fact her father was Hungarian (and a missionary aiming to convert his fellow Jews to Christianity) and all his children were born in England. Amy lost her father in 1913, her husband in July 1916 and her brother in September 1916 (he died after being hit in the face by shellfire on the Somme). She never re-married. Her husband is commemorated by the beautifully carved panelling that surrounds the altar of St John the Baptist Church at Cookham Dean near Maidenhead, including the **above** design with his initials. ➔**289**

STEELE, Frederick James. He wrote his will in Rouen on 6th October 1915 on the way to the front. Leaving everything to his two brothers and his mother, he also included the instruction to 'buy Miss Gwen Whelan a piece of jewelry of value of £5' with her address in Kingston in Surrey near to another school where he had taught. I wondered if Gwen found happiness with anyone else.

The only Gwen Whelan I found in Kingston was married on 2nd November 1917, with the marriage index listing her as both 'Gwen Whelan' (how she'd signed the register) and 'Anastasia Gwendoline Maud Whelan' (her full name also given in the register). She had married Gordon Miller, a private in the Royal Canadian Dragoons. Sadly where I first saw their marriage certificate was in the records of their divorce. He had made it through the war without any disability caused by enemy action but had picked up a sexually-transmitted disease in 1919 and by the time of Gwen making her divorce application in 1925 she had evidence of his adultery with three other women.

After their divorce, things didn't go well for Gwen's ex-husband. In 1928, he was named as committing adultery with another man's wife in another divorce case, and by the time of the Second World War he was an inmate in a mental hospital. On 13th October 1955 he was living in another mental hospital when he went out for a walk and disappeared. He had recently begun to feel unwell and was about to have tests, but after his body was found (on New Year's Eve by children playing on the grounds of Wentworth golf course) the only disease that was found was gallstones. He had however taken the equivalent of 250 tablets of aspirin.

I have found no definite trace of his ex-wife Gwen after their divorce. Certainly she doesn't appear with her full first names and if she just called herself Gwen along with either the surname Whelan or Miller, then are too many in the indexes to be able to pick her out. With the cost of ordering records and no definite clues, I've decided to let her be. Wherever she ended up, I wonder if she kept the piece of jewelry that Freddy Steele left her. ➔**109**

STRICKLAND, Edward Peter. Not mentioned in his biography so far is his private life. In the summer of 1918, he married Barbara, the widow of a brother officer from his original regiment, the Norfolks (Capt Francis Cresswell, adjutant of the 1st Battalion, was named in the very first casualty list of the war, having been killed during the Retreat from Mons in September 1914). They had a daughter christened 'Lavender' (though, given how that could be abbreviated, it's no wonder she was known by her second name 'Jane'). He also took on Barbara's two daughters, one of whom would go on to be Lady Billa Harrod, the redoubtable saviour of many Norfolk churches through her campaigning and fundraising. In turn her son Dominick Harrod became BBC TV's economics correspondent in the 1970s, and coincidentally was one of the best friends of Brig-Gen William Walton★'s grandson Ned. ➔267

SUTTON, Leonard Goodhart. The grave stones, *(below)*, in the family burial plot in Reading were rather overgrown when I arrived. I was thinking that this would provide an image I could use to illustrate how nature and the passage of time are no respecters of human history, but, as luck would have it, the best photograph I took was after I'd ripped away the ivy and brambles, and that just seems to be right.

You can see the whole family named. The survivor of the boys, Noël, lived for 47 years after the war and, having no children, would be the last descendant of Leonard to serve on the board of Sutton's Seeds. There were no dates or details for the youngest of the family, May, and I felt I needed to find out what happened to her to make the story complete. She seemed to have disappeared without trace from the British civil records and I was despairing of finding anything when I came across a notice in the *Reading Observer* in November 1923 saying that she was engaged, with the marriage set to take place in Nairobi.

The name of her husband-to-be rang a bell: Major Frederick Chater-Jack, DSO, MC, and when I looked him up I realised where I'd heard of him. He was Spike Milligan's C.O. during the Second World War, as featured in *'Adolf Hitler – My Part In His Downfall'*. He was a great contrast to Spike's first C.O. (the very officious one nicknamed *'Leather Suitcase'*). Major Chater-Jack had served with great distinction in the First World War and he was an officer who Spike Milligan *'would have followed anywhere'*. He ended the Second World War as a Lt Col with a second DSO for his service in Italy. He and May have had 4 daughters, 9 grandchildren, 17 great-grandchildren, and 10 great-great-grandchildren. There may no longer be a Sutton running the company that bears his name, but, even with all the terrible things that have happened, Leonard Goodhart Sutton is remembered through the family that has grown from his love. ➔151

VAUGHAN, Tom Benjamin and Lillian. Tom Vaughan was from Lancashire and in his youth he had become firm friends with Frank Curzon when they worked together as junior clerks in Frank's father's oil company. After Frank departed for the stage and started into theatre management, he convinced Tom to join him as his manager. Tom's likeable manner and business ability saw him fulfil the same role for the stars Gladys Cooper and Gerald du Maurier as well as for the American impresario Gilbert Miller. He was the manager of the Prince of Wales's Theatre when Margaret (as Peggy Bethel) appeared in productions there before the war. 1927 would be a terrible year for him – not only did he lose his great friend Frank Curzon in July but his Irish actress wife Lillian died in October aged 43 (she had been receiving treatment at a specialist private sanatorium on the Norfolk coast where lots of fresh air was seen as an important part of the cure for TB - the widow of Julian Rycroft (see p.182) would also die there). Tom only survived his wife by 8 months and both of them are buried in the churchyard in Hampstead, marked with the cross in the centre of the photograph *below*. They left two orphaned boys aged 13 and 9. The younger of those boys would become a Navy flier in the next war and was killed with his mechanic when their plane stalled in a climbing turn and crashed near Crawley on 31st August 1940. ➜ 259

Tom Benjamin Vaughan

| | | | | | | 19|00 | | | | | | 20|00 | |

Lillian Vaughan nee Farrell

| | | | | | | 19|00 | | | | | | 20|00 | |

Thomas Francis Gerald Vaughan

| | | | | | | 19|00 | | | | | | 20|00 | |

John Gilbert Vaughan

| | | | | | | 19|00 | | | | | | 20|00 | |

WELLINGTON, Robert, *(above right)*. At the age of 16 he'd gone out to work in the office of a family business in Constantinople but it didn't suit his health and a doctor advised that he ought to lead an outdoor life. He therefore returned to England and joined Wye Agricultural College in Kent.

In 1912, at the age of only 22, he was asked to head up a new fruit experiment station at East Malling in Kent. At the start there was a 23-acre field with nothing in it except a muddy farm track, but with hopes and ideas and hard work he set about turning it into a suitable environment to

undertake *'the study of problems met with in the actual culture of fruit trees and bushes'*. An example of one of those problems was that standard apple trees were so big as to make it difficult to pick the fruit efficiently, so he collected dwarf rootstocks from home and abroad with which to experiment and develop trees that were smaller but had similar yields. The resultant Malling rootstocks & their successors are used in nearly every part of the world where apples are grown commercially, & around 90% of apple orchards in Western Europe are grafted onto the Malling-9 rootstock developed under his tenure before the First World War.

Even after he joined up for the war, he still theoretically remained director & after a dose of gas left him unfit for active service in 1916 he became head of the Fruit Section in the Ministry of Food Production despite still being only in his mid-20s, and was awarded an MBE in 1918. On leaving that position, he moved down to Worth Farm in Devon (where Charles Bartlett stayed in 1937) and, whilst raising a family, continued his pioneering work in the growing of fruit, in particular cider apples, blackcurrants and Royal Sovereign strawberries. His efforts to branch out and grow cauliflowers led to an incident that illustrates his gruff, tough character and powerful personality. He had gone to a wholesaler with his harvest of cauliflowers and was offered a pitifully low amount of money in return. Despite saying that he couldn't make any money at that rate, the wholesaler wouldn't budge, so he took all his cauliflowers to his local market place and gave them away for free. In one

| | | | | | 19|00 | | | | | | 20|00 |

fell swoop the market for cauliflowers was ruined and the wholesalers were forced to deal with him. No wonder he was known as 'the Boss' amongst his family.

He moved down to Cornwall in 1945 but still continued an active interest in the advance of horticultural science, not least in his continued association with the East Malling Research Station.

On 10th November 1965 he drowned in the sea near his home. The verdict was suicide. It sounds like it would not have been out of character to decide his own fate when he found himself no longer fit to do what he wanted. If you enjoy eating an apple today, think of this man whose work you likely hold in your hand. ➜ 383

WOODHOUSE, William Edward Basil. He has a special place in my heart because it was he who brought back the chalk Berkshire dragon that was an important feature in my first book. The dragon had been carved into the 1st Line of German trenches near Hulluch which the 8th Royal Berkshires had taken on 25th September 1915. You can see him looking as pleased as punch posing next to his trophy on a visit back home from the trenches, *(right)*.

He was the second of the eight children of a cowman from Bray, then a small rural village on the Thames near Maidenhead. It therefore seems unusual that his eldest sister Ethel married a Swiss upholsterer called Emile Hungerbuhler and kept her surname throughout her long life despite possibly attracting anti-German prejudice. Also unusual is the fact that when William's youngest sibling was aged about 3 their father took up with another woman and in 1911 was pretending to be married to her whilst living 35 miles away in a village near Witney in Oxfordshire. He had another five children with her – in fact when 33-year-old William joined up in 1914 his newest half-sister was just a few months old.

William himself had married in 1906. He only had one child, Keith, who died in 1913 of acute 'water on the brain' aged 3. William continued in his job as sexton at St Michael's, looking after the fabric of the church and maybe even digging graves. Having joined up in August 1914, he went to France in August 1915 as a Company Quarter Master Sergeant and soon after the Battle of Loos was promoted to Company Sergeant Major, the most senior NCO in a Company of over 200 officers and men. In April 1916 he would be wounded in the left hand and the wall of his abdomen, requiring a stay in hospital in England. On recovery he could have been sent to another battalion but at the special request of his officers he came back to his old Company in July 1916. He got away with being slightly wounded in November 1916 but on 24th February 1917 his luck ran out when he was hit by a shell in the trenches and killed. At his parish church the Russian Contakion (an Orthodox hymn to the departed) was sung in his memory and the bell ringers rang a muffled peal. His name was added to his son's grave in the cemetery at Bray, *(right)*, with note being made of the symmetry that his end had come near the village of Bray on the Somme. Today this memorial is missing, presumably destroyed by vandals, though the surround for his mother's grave still remains.

William was the second husband that his wife Violet had lost. Born in Reading, she was first married to Sussex sailor William Harris in 1898. When he died in 1903 he was the Captain of a boat of the Newhaven-Dieppe service and had had TB for 2 years. Returning to Berkshire, she'd married William Woodhouse and then after his death, she went back to Sussex and in 1928 married master builder and undertaker Arthur Woolger (whose father had coincidentally been the undertaker for her first husband's funeral). He died 12 days after the declaration of war in 1939 but still she survived for another 28 years. ➔186

Violet Ann Woolger was Woodhouse
was Harris née Rookley

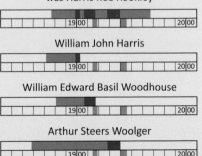

William John Harris

William Edward Basil Woodhouse

Arthur Steers Woolger

WORT, Thomas. His wife Susannah was left a widow at the age of 26, with a daughter aged 2 (having lost 2 sons as babies in 1913 and 1915). The War Gratuity she was paid for her husband's death was £10 (i.e. a few months of his wages, but still not very much for the loss of her family's bread-winner). She would have been entitled to a widow's pension but it would have been fairly meagre (indeed it took the government a while to catch up with the prob-lem, with the Ministry of Pensions only being created in December 1916). Whatever pension she was receiving would have stopped when she married again on Christ-mas Day 1917, though she would possibly have then received another one-off gratuity. With her new husband John La Touche she had six more children (including another boy who died as a baby) but died in 1930 of pneumonia and heart failure aged 39.

As an example of how attitudes to Remembrance have changed over time, consider the fate of the memorial to the staff of the City of Birmingham Gas Department where Thomas Wort was a fitter. It was erected in 1921 in the Gas Hall, *(right)*, and then, after that was turned into Birmingham Museum and Art Gallery, it was moved to a landing, then to storage, and then to the grounds of the British Gas Social Club which then became a private Sports Centre. In 1994 the sculpture of Victory on the top of the memorial was stolen by metal thieves. A refurbishment was undertaken in 1999 but by 2012 it was covered in moss and nearly hidden by grass clippings. It is now in pieces in a Museum store where no-one can read its inscription *'Let those who come after see to it that their names be not forgotten'*. ➔330

YATES, (George) Walter, alias George Yates, alias George Hawkins. Even with no name given in Charles Bartlett's letter, the com-bination of MM and DCM awarded on the Somme made it easy to pick out Pte GW Yates (Nº 18567) from the war diary (and in fact he was one of only two men in the whole war to get that combination whilst serving with the 8th Royal Berkshires). Less easy was piecing together the rest of his complicated story.

He'd arrived in France on 12th October 1915 and, unusually as a private, had got a special mention in the Battalion's war diary as a result of leading out a patrol on the night of 4th May 1916 (the day after David Footman's raid on the Double Crassier).

On discovering a German working party he returned to get a team of bombers together and after crawling back within 4 yards of the enemy, he started bombing them, and then pursued them until he ran out of bombs. It was noted that he had done persistent good work on night patrols and as a reward the GOC of 1st Division gave him a green ticket to go on leave. What was not mentioned was that Walter had been court-martialled just 11 days before for violence to a senior officer and been sentenced to two years' hard labour as well as being reduced to Private from the rank of Corporal. It says how much his work was valued that his prison sentence must have

been deferred and he was back to leading patrols so soon afterwards.

His MM was for his actions during the Battalion's first attack on the Somme in July, when he managed to carry messages across the battlefield despite heavy shell fire. He escaped untouched and tended to the wounds of his com-rades who were not so fortunate. His DCM was for later in the bat-tle when he was tasked to carry messages, rations and ammunition to an advanced strong point under intense shelling. Coming back from his second trip he was shot at by a German who hit him in the leg at the second attempt. Even so, Walter made it back to deliver his messages before going to get his wounds seen to.

In trying to find what happened to him next, a check of the medal rolls showed that he had initially forfeited all his medals having been convicted of desertion 6 days before the Armistice. Also noted was that they had been reinstated in 1936. Intrigued, I started a wider search in the old newspapers online. It was difficult because 'Walter Yates' is not exactly a rare name, but a small item in the 31st October 1928 edition of the *Nottingham Evening Post* caught my eye. Under the headline *'Derby Chief Constable & Alleged Deserter'* it said:

'"It took them a long time to find me," was the reply of Walter Yates, a caravan dweller, at Derby to-day, when asked if he had anything to say as to why he should be remanded to await an escort.

It was stated that he had been a deserter from the 2nd Berkshire Regiment since May, 1921.

Mr. A H. Domleo, one of the magistrates: I blame the system. I object to the whole proceedings.

The Chief Constable: There is more to it than meets the eye.'

And that was the whole article, leaving more questions than it answered and with no follow-up in further editions. Even a longer article in the *Derby Daily Telegraph* on the same day didn't add much more detail except to say that he had deserted from being stationed in Dublin and that the magistrate's objection was on the basis that he felt it unfair that the Army should still be allowed to have jurisdiction over this man after he had been free for so long. Walter was also said to have remarked *'I have been expecting it'* to the police officer who put him under arrest. This seemingly innocuous remark has more meaning once you get to know some of the rest of his story.

Of course it wasn't definite that this was 'the' Walter Yates I was looking for, but something that gave it a greater likelihood of being the right man was that when he appeared in a newspaper casualty list in September 1916 (with his Royal Berkshires' number of 18567) he was listed as coming from Derby. Still, it was not much to go on and everything I tried seemed to come up a blank. Thinking I might have to give up on him, I then received a tip as part of a different search at the National Archives. If a soldier left the Army after 1920 their record was kept in a different place to all those that were destroyed in 1940, and if it still existed, their name would appear in the Military Discharge database on Ancestry. I looked him up and there he was, but still I thought I was a long way away from actually seeing his record. When I first started my Group Photograph research, you needed to have the permission of the soldier's nearest next-of-kin to be able to get a transcription from the record of a soldier who served after 1920. I started to think of what I could write in a letter to the MOD to try and get them to bend the rules in this case. After all it was all a long time ago and everyone who served in the First World War is now dead. And then I discovered

that the MOD had already worked this out for themselves and changed the access rules. All that was required was proof that the soldier in question had been born over 116 years ago. Well, I didn't have that but I thought there was a good chance that they would discover this to be true when they looked in Walter Yates' records – 116 years ago was 1901 and I couldn't believe that he would have been younger than 14 when he went to France in 1915. So I sent off my cheque for £30 and waited and hoped.

On my return home after Christmas there was my best present, an envelope of photocopies from his records and with the hints they contained I was at last able to put together a fuller picture of his life.

He was born on 2nd May 1890 (though on every form I've seen he made himself out to be younger). He was named 'George Yates' by his unmarried mother Rebecca who was a potter's rinser & didn't identify his father on the birth certificate. He soon got a father though when in late 1891 his mother married Meshach Norwood Hawkins (also known as John) who had just got out from 9 months in prison for theft (and by 1911, Rebecca had given birth to 16 children, 11 of whom had died, not helped by living in slum conditions in Derby).

Walter first joined up in Derby on 18th August 1914 but was chucked out after 2 months having already absented himself for 2 weeks. His brother Harry died of wounds received during the Battle of Neuve Chapelle in March 1915 and maybe

that was the spur for Walter to have another go at joining the Army in June 1915, this time down in Reading where they wouldn't know about his previous bad behaviour.

As already noted, the bad behaviour re-surfaced in 1916, and it got worse. As well as the violence to a superior officer in April 1916 he had gone absent but avoided a trial for desertion by order of Brig-Gen Reddie. After recovering from his wounds from the Somme, he was with the 3rd Royal Berkshires in Portsmouth when he deserted in December 1916. Caught after 6 months on the run he was sentenced to 56 days in prison before transferring to the 6th Royal Berkshires in France. In November 1917 he was again caught absent without leave and sentenced to 84 days Field Punishment Nº 1 (later cut to 42 days). On the disbandment of the 6th Battalion in February 1918 he was posted to the 5th Royal Berkshires but deserted again 10 days before the start of the German Spring Offensive. Caught at the end of April, he was held awaiting trial for 6 months and then sentenced to 6 months hard labour, though this was soon commuted to 42 days Field Punishment Nº 1, and, not only that, in April 1919 his sentence of 2 years' hard labour from April 1916 was cancelled and he was discharged from the Army. Amazingly, the Army signed him up again the very next day. By this time, as well as a very bad disciplinary record, he had scars from a bullet wound on his left forearm, and from shrapnel wounds on his left cheek, around his right eye, and below

The medals of Walter Yates: DCM, MM, 1914-15 Star, British War Medal, Victory Medal

his left knee, but the DCM & MM proved he was a fighter and that must have been what counted.

Things seem to have been fine discipline-wise during a nine month tour in Mesopotamia with the 1ˢᵗ Royal Berkshires and he was even promoted to Lance Corporal soon after being transferred to the 2ⁿᵈ Battalion in Dublin but then in late 1920 he went AWOL again. As well as being busted back down to private, he did 14 days' detention in the guardroom and then, only a week after getting out, he was violent and insubordinate to a senior officer. Back in the guardroom waiting to go off to 2 years' hard labour, he managed to escape – and that was the last the Army saw of him until he was found in Derby in October 1928.

What I have not mentioned so far is that in October 1914, Walter had got married, just after being chucked out of the Army the first time. His wife Ruth also enjoyed picking fights, with convictions in 1919 (when she threatened to stab a policeman with a hat pin when resisting arrest) and in 1927 (for fighting in the street on a number of occasions, for one of which she laid the blame on her mother-in-law). These last incidents may not have been unconnected with Walter. A report appeared in the paper, naming him as *'George Yates, alias Hawkins'* (i.e. his mother's married name) and saying that he had drawn a knife on Ruth in a pub and said, *'If you don't come back to me I'll stick this through you'*, at which point he'd struck out and cut a hole

in her coat. At this time they had been living apart for over two years and Ruth was staying with another man. The magistrates bound Walter over for 12 months but within 3 weeks he was back in court, this time having been nabbed stripping lead from the roofs of some houses in Nottingham. He was sentenced to three months in prison. A year after his release was when he was captured as a deserter and handed over to the Army and to me that points to Ruth having dobbed him in to get him off her back, hence his comment at the time. Having been picked up by the Army, he spent 10 days in the guardroom at which point the GOC ordered his release without further formalities except deductions from pay and he was discharged from the Army.

I don't know what happened to Ruth but in May 1939 Walter joined the Territorial Army and was then living in Bristol with a different wife – and following her up unearthed a whole other extraordinary story. Edith was married to John Cartledge in Derby on 1ˢᵗ August 1914. Her husband joined up soon after but the Army didn't keep him for long as the epilepsy he shared with his siblings worsened to the point where he was having 2 or 3 fits a day. He and Edith went on to have 10 children and then on 12ᵗʰ June 1934, dressed in a white blouse, navy blue serge coat, black skirt, green hat with green and black rosette, light stockings and black shoes, she left her 5-year-old son playing in the front room, walked out of the house and disappeared.

Her husband professed that the reason for her disappearance was a complete mystery, but to me it seems obvious that she was at the end of her tether. Her first born son had died of gastritis and convulsions aged 7 months in 1916, and then all of her last 3 sons had also died as infants (in 1930, 1931 & 1932, of measles, premature birth and pneumonia). She fetched up in Bristol with Walter and had 4 more children with him (all being registered with both the Cartledge and Yates surnames, with one girl dying aged 3 in 1941 of meningitis). She was also convicted of helping another woman procure an abortion in 1943 and died in 1962 of cancer of the cervix with both Yates & Cartledge on her death certificate. Even just the bare bones of her story point to a life full of misery beyond my understanding.

Meanwhile Walter's return to the Army had not lasted long. In October 1940 he was declared unfit and so was discharged for the last time. His medals ended up in the Regimental Museum, but it's unclear whether he himself took them in or it was one of his family after his death in 1958. Like all medals they are but a facade on a reality that is unimaginable except to the person who wore them. The sole hint that these belonged to a rule-breaker is the silver rosette on the ribbon of the 1914-15 Star. It was only meant to be worn on the ribbon bar of men who'd served in France & Belgium between 5ᵗʰ August & 22ⁿᵈ November 1914 but I don't suppose that Walter Yates cared much about such niceties. ➔334

MARGARET JANE ROBINSON
WIFE OF BETHELL ROBINSON
DIED 26TH JANUARY 190
AGED 38 YEARS

B

AGED   YEARS

Charles and Margaret's Ancestors

Margaret's mother's grave, *(opposite)*, is broken from the vertical and lying flat in the burial ground in Chiswick in contrast to the Bartlett family tombs, *(below)*, in Buckingham old churchyard, which although they have not always been cared for, now have Grade II Listed status. You can read the names & dates of Charles's Bartlett grandparents and great-grandparents (as well as his father's first wife and other members of the wider family), but, contrary to what Charles says, none of the inscriptions say anything about their occupations (an example is on the **next page**).

The power of the Bartlett family in Buckingham dates from about the time that the last Stuart King, James II, was deposed in the late 17th Century (which makes me think of Charles's joking reference to the possibility of Margaret being descended

from Stuarts – strange that they should be grouped together with the current enemy 'the Bosche' over two centuries later but it goes to show that it's not just the Northern Irish who have long memories about this).

Tanning was where things started for the Bartletts. A messy and smelly business, it not only involved the removal of rotting flesh from the animal hides but also the use of dog urine and faeces to do the curing. It wasn't good for anyone's health, not least because the effluent from the process went straight into the River Ouse, even if that was downstream from the town centre. By the late 18th Century the Bartletts were well set not only in business but in civic affairs, with two of them being elected Bailiff (the original title for 'Mayor') in this period. By now they had diversified into woolstapling (preparing and dealing in wool), and after

the canal came to Buckingham in 1801 they also established themselves on the new wharf as coal merchants, having recognised that steam-powered engines would be important to their business.

By 1812, they had also gone into banking with Charles's great-grandfather John giving his name to the Bartlett and Nelson bank which printed its own 'Buckingham' banknotes over the next 50 years. The family was now seriously wealthy with interests in land and property. Charles's grandfather Edward was described purely as a banker rather than being involved in the grubbier businesses, and *'his penetrating mind and liberal heart were always at the service of his native place. Every project calculated to benefit the poor, assist the industrious, to aid benevolent or religious institutions, or to amuse his more opulent neighbours, was*

readily and spiritedly supported by' him. He laid the foundation stone of the church in nearby Gawcott, and it may not have been a coincidence that Gawcott was the birthplace of George Gilbert Scott who, early in his stellar architectural career, was commissioned by Edward to add the semi-circular Keeper's House to Buckingham Gaol. To the *'sorrowing gloom of all'* Edward died after a very short illness at the age of just 35, and the esteem in which he and his wife were held is shown by the stained glass windows in Buckingham church that were dedicated to their memory, *(opposite)*. They depict King Edward the Confessor and Elizabeth of Hungary, royal saints who shared the Bartletts' names and were also renowned for their Christian charity (funnily enough Edward the Confessor is also the patron saint of difficult marriages, more relevant perhaps to Charles than his grandfather).

Charles's father John Edward Bartlett was only nine when his father died, but even though he left Buckingham soon after his first marriage in 1857, he continued in the traditions of this long-standing Buckingham family.

In the face of all that I can understand how Margaret would not be leaping to show Charles her own family history. There does not appear to be anything to be ashamed of, it was just that it was not

as grand by comparison with the Bartletts. It would be interesting to know how far she was able to trace it back in those times before online genealogy databases, but the story from the beginning of the 19th Century onwards appears to be of working class families making good. I've only found one of her forebears going back to her great-grandparents who was not born in north Lancashire (and he was born only just over the border in Cumberland). In among some very English surnames (Robinson, Parker, Porter, Parrington, Wilson) only her great-grandmother Elizabeth Breckel has the hint of anything exotic like the Bosche, but she spelt it 'Brakell' at her wedding and it seems likely from other families in the area that it's just a variant spelling of the local name 'Breakhill' (others I've found in the area being Breakall, Brekel, Breckell).

There were at least two Bethell Robinsons before the one who became Margaret's father. Elizabeth Breckel had married the first of those and when he died young she supported herself by running a lodging house in Fleetwood, then a developing port on the Lancashire coast. Her son Bethell had gone from engine smith and millwright to become a furniture maker and dealer (at one time employing three others in his business), and then was employed as an insurance agent. This last change happened

after his son Bethell's footballing exploits and though there wasn't the money in football that there is now, I wonder if being part of that world had expanded his horizons of possibility (or maybe business wasn't so good and he needed whatever job was available).

Margaret's mother, born Margaret Jane Parker, had started out as a cotton weaver, the daughter of a tinplate worker. Tinplate was then used to make kitchenware and other household goods and by the end of his working life not only was her father Richard Parker self-employed but he was employing others. His first wife before her early death had been a dress maker but by the time of his second marriage it looks like his new wife didn't have to work to add to the household earnings. In turn, Richard Parker's father had progressed in his lifelong trade to become a master shoemaker employing ten men.

Measured on their own terms, Margaret's forebears seem to have been successful in their lines of work, but there is no getting away from the fact that they were still poles apart from the Bartletts, and the bottom line is that, given the social boundaries of the time, if Margaret had not made it as an actress and singer on the West End stage it's unlikely Charles would have met her let alone taken her for his wife. ➔215

Charles Frederick Napier Bartlett

STATEMENT

OF

INCOME TAX ADJUSTMENT.

A.

D PAY DEPT.

Financial Year—1st April, 191**6**...., to 31st March, 191.**7**....

Name *Major C. F. N. Bartlett*   Unit *R. Berks. Regt*

	PAY.			TAX CHARGED.			REMARKS.
	£	s.	d.	£	s.	d.	
June Qr.	72	16	–	–	–	–	
	17	10	–	–	–	–	
Sept. „	73	12	–	–	–	–	
	32	4	–				
Dec. „	73	12	–	6	5	–	
March „	103	10	–	9	11	6	
Total .... £	373	4	–	15	16	6	
Abatement allowed (see under)	120	–	–	–	–	–	........Tax refunded
Tax at 1/3 in £ the £ on	253	4	–	15	16	6	Authorised by the:—

Statutory Allowances admitted.

Abatement	.... £ 120 : – :
Children	.... £ : :
Life Assce.	.... £ : :
Small Income relief	.... £ : :

£ 120 : – : –

A.

The above relief has been allowed provisionally, subject to the receipt of instructions from the Commissioners of Income Tax, War Office, or the receipt of relief claim.

MESSRS. COX & CO., Army Agents,

(Income Tax Dept.), Charing Cross, S.W. 1.

3,000. Cbd. CX 573 5/17.

Late Additions

I had laid out most of the book when I first saw some material that I just had to include. A lot fitted into the existing structure and the rest is here as a reprise and reminder. Somehow the pictures mean more when you've read all the story of Charles's war.

Opposite: They say that the two sure things in life are death and taxes, but still it seems bizarre to me that being in a war zone under constant threat of death is treated as a job from whose earnings it is still necessary to pay tax to the government who is paying you in the first place, and that the requisite paperwork must be completed as in this tax statement for Charles that covers the period he was on the Somme.

Right: Out of lots of pictures of Paula I've picked this particularly beautiful one.

Below: Looking at how old Paula is as she sits in the goat cart, this is from about 1913. Charles is between Margaret's sisters Dolly **(right)** and, I think, Connie **(left)**. Both were married in 1912 and so the other men are quite likely to be their husbands. The post-war christening photograph on p.378 looks like it shows Dolly holding her second child (born in 1918) with Connie on the right and the doting father, William Clowes, on the left – and he looks like the man on the right of this picture so possibly Connie's then-husband George Bennett is the one looking rather detached on the left.

This page: Given the fame of Margaret's father as a footballer I was surprised at how few pictures were available of him. I eventually tracked down Bethell Robinson's appearance in the team photo on p.404 and now here are pictures of him in group photographs that are both literally and figuratively miles away from his time playing football in Preston. Here he is in his late fifties as a Company Quarter Master Sergeant in Burma in about 1916. These might even be from the period when he was in Port Blair in the Andaman Islands where his unit was guarding a convict settlement. It was a dull job in difficult conditions with many British soldiers ending up in hospital due to disease. To me, Bethell looks unbearably sad and ground down by life, but even so he must have been lifted by the seemingly irrepressible spirit of the local children, indeed one seems to be sucking on what might be Bethell's pipe, *(right)*.

Opposite: This is the 1913 Christmas card that at last gave me the key to identifying Charles's Irish friend Malcolm who so irked him by avoiding military service. His home, 55, Antrim Mansions, is just off Haverstock Hill, 500 yards from Charles and Margaret. Malcolm Wilson was the same age as Charles and grew up in Belfast. Having started his working life there with the printers David Allen & Sons, he was promoted to their London office and became well-known in the arts and theatre world for his work in the production of posters and publicity material as well as for his *'charming and fragrant personality'*. I have found no sign of him doing any military service, though two of his brothers worked with the YMCA in France as priests, one dying of a skull fracture after the car he was in lost a wheel and crashed near Le Havre in March 1918.

Left: Paul Rubens is a victim of the fickleness of fame. In the decade before the war, his music was all the rage and helped to define the era, yet now there is barely a person who knows his name. The scraps of paper on these pages give witness to the state of his place in the cultural memory, with the brutality of the war no doubt having played its part in obliterating the genteel aura that went before. Something of his story and his music can be heard in a half-hour feature about him broadcast in Australia in the 1950s. Search *YouTube* for "With A Song in My Heart Prg#23 (Paul Rubens)" – it's even got an excerpt of *'A Pink Petty from Peter'*.

Below left: Peggy in checked dress and white bonnet in Paul Rubens' show *'Dear Little Denmark'*.

Below right: Peggy on the right as Mina in *'Miss Hook of Holland'*. Music from both the shows featured here was in the repertoire of the orchestra on the Titanic in 1912.

Opposite: Peggy's score for *'A Pink Petty from Peter'*, to go with the words on p.22.

Left: Betty Crutchley (née Spottiswoode) to the left of her mother-in-law Lady Sybil Crutchley and Margaret. All were leading lights in many productions of two of the foremost and oldest amateur theatre companies in Britain, The Windsor Strollers and The Old Stagers. Margaret had left her 'Peggy Bethel' stage name behind, being listed as 'Margaret Bartlett' but known to all as 'Peggy'. She was well reviewed in the wide variety of roles she played, and even ended up in Aberdeen for a season of plays in 1942.

Below: Peggy in August 1939 in *'The Twelve Pound Look'* by J.M. Barrie. She plays the ex-wife of a self-important man who escaped her marriage by becoming a typist only to then by chance be hired to answer letters for him on the eve of his knighthood. His second wife helps him practise the dubbing with a sword but her predecessor's example soon starts to appeal.

Opposite: A scene from *'Tilly of Bloomsbury'*. In 1924 and 1925 Peggy was in productions playing the heroine, a starving poor girl who turns the head of an upper class gentleman (played by Betty Crutchley's husband Gerry). The two leads have opportunities to become quite *'expert at the osculatory art'*, here under the disapproving eye of the gentleman's snobby sister. The reaction of Peggy's ex-husband in real life is not recorded.

Following in Charles Bartlett's Footsteps

Following in Charles Bartlett's footsteps wasn't just about finding pictures and information for this book. I'm interested to see what remains of us after we leave this world and I like to see if I can get a feeling of what it might have been like to be the person who had stood in a particular place all those years before. With Charles Bartlett this was not easy. I could find the locations but sometimes it felt as if he had been erasing history as he went with whole buildings having disappeared or the environment having so radically changed as to eliminate all feeling of its past. Some of these absences or changes have been mentioned in the notes with the letters but I've picked out a few in more detail here. There were even two places where I did actually get a feeling of his presence.

The outside of Charles's birthplace, Peverel Court, may have stayed almost the same throughout its existence but inside it is no longer a family home. However comfortable it may be for its elderly and cared-for residents, it has the feel of an institution with notices on doors, rooms that are offices and wall-to-wall brown carpet with metal tread-edges on the stairs.

Charles was not baptised in the church near his home in Stone but in Aylesbury. His father had initially lived there after leaving Buckingham and appears to have remained a member of the congregation even after moving into Peverel Court. The font in St Mary's Church, *(opposite)*, is famed as one of the 'Aylesbury fonts' that date from the late 12th Century. It was found buried in three parts during the total refurbishment of the church not long before Charles's arrival in the world. Another refurbishment in 1978 saw the church being gutted, with the pews removed, and the installation of new wooden flooring and a refectory area with plastic seats. The day I visited had the bustle and singing of a children's group and the clink of crockery for morning coffee.

The Buckinghamshire Lunatic Asylum, for which Charles's father chaired a committee and which was such an important institution in their village of Stone, closed in 1991 and nearly the whole site was

demolished in 1994, leaving only the chapel, now derelict with keep-out fencing around it.

The family grave, *(left)*, stands on its own at the edge of the churchyard in Stone. It bears the names of John Edward Bartlett and his wife Sarah Emily – *'They rest from their labours, and their works do follow them'* – and their children Edith Constance – *'Blessed are the pure in heart for they shall see God'* – and John Francis Napier and Lilian Emily but not that of their son Charles Frederick Napier Bartlett. When Charles knew it before the First World War, the churchyard would no doubt have been immaculately kept by then-affordably-paid staff. Today it is down to volunteers who must be busy earning a living elsewhere and whilst it is by no means overgrown, I had to pull ivy from the grave.

Charles's two prep schools have had very different fates. Hazelhurst School is now a private home (it housed Canadian troops during the Second World War and closed not long thereafter). Lockers Park School still has its original schoolhouse and chapel but they are now but a part of a large campus of modern buildings as the school has expanded to take 170 pupils.

Charles's old house at Rugby School is still there but it is no longer known as 'Donkin' after his housemaster, and since 1992 it has been a boarding house for girls.

Inkerman Barracks in Woking (the scene of the 1903 group photograph) became the headquarters of the Royal Military Police after the Second World War but then was demolished in the 1970s and replaced by housing.

The original St Saviour's Church in Paddington where Charles & Margaret were married was demolished in 1972 and replaced with a new church.

The Royal Berkshire Regiment no longer exists, having merged with the Wiltshire Regiment in 1959. Their old depot at Brock Barracks in Reading is still used by the Army Reserve, though the distinctive tall keep has been outside the military compound since 1980 when it became an affordable studio & exhibition space for contemporary artists including at one time Cornelia Parker, OBE, RA.

In Reading, most of the heart of the town has been ripped out and re-modelled with busy roads, office blocks and plastic-fronted shops in pedestrian precincts. There is barely a trace of Sutton's Seeds or of Huntley & Palmers biscuit factory, the businesses that for so long dominated the town. One part that Charles would still easily recognise is Forbury Gardens, *(above)*. Through the trees at the rear right is the red-and-white facade of the old Shire Hall that was built in 1911 for the County Council (though it is now the *'poshest hotel in Reading'*). It was on the steps in front of its columns that the group photographs on p.34 were taken in March 1915. As the men posed for the camera, they would have been looking out at the back of the Maiwand Lion in the centre of the Gardens. One of the biggest

cast iron sculptures in the world, it weighs 16 tons and stands 13 feet (4 metres) tall on top of a 13 feet high plinth. It was dedicated in 1884 to the memory of 11 officers and 318 men of the 66th Regiment (soon to be renamed the 2nd Royal Berkshires) who died fighting in Afghanistan in 1879-1880, with most of them being killed at the disastrous Battle of Maiwand. I wonder if Charles looked through the names on the plinth and spotted 'C Bartlett' listed amongst the Privates. The lion is roaring in anger with its tail raised to very prominently display two parts of its anatomy that are synonymous with courage and I feel sure that Charles could not have resisted a ribald comment. The sculptor, George Blackall Simonds, turned to running his family's brewery in 1910 but came out of retirement to sculpt his village's war memorial after his son was killed in 1914.

The pictures to the right can be directly compared with those on p.28. McIlroy's department store closed in 1955. Some of its facade is still there, *(right, above),* but not the hotel above, and today the outlets below include a tanning salon, a fancy gelataria called Creams, a Tesco Express, and a vape shop. In the other picture, *(below, right)*, you can just about see the McIlroy's sign at the top right, but the White Hart Hotel has been replaced on the left with a Metro Bank and the entrance to the Broad Street Mall. If you turn to the left of this view you are facing down St Mary's Butts where in the Middle Ages the locals practised with their longbows on Sundays (as required by an English law that was only fully repealed in 1863). At the end of the road, you can see St Giles' Church piercing the sky, *(opposite, below)*. From a position of comparative tranquility in the 19th Century the church is now surrounded by the noise of traffic with a busy junction and a flyover close by. Its internal walls are newly plastered, but the external flints remain the same (and provide the atmosphere for pages 118-122 about the memorial service in October 1915).

In France, next to nothing that was in or near Charles's battle zones remains as it was before, during or at the end of the war. If Charles Bartlett were to visit now he'd be hard pushed to recognise any of it except by the overall lay of the land.

Few buildings remain even in places quite a distance behind the lines. One rare exception is what was the Hotel du Commerce in Lillers where Charles had lunch with Frederick Worlock in November 1915 (see p.129). As you can see in **these pictures** the location of the chimney and the configuration of the doors and windows suggests that it is the same building but it has been extensively remodelled (even if the last time it was paid much attention was obviously a long time ago). The house on the left of it has been completely rebuilt but the one on the right still retains the scalloped edge and flat pillar-like decorations. Though they are covered in new paintwork they are one of the few features in these pictures that Charles might have seen, not that I think that he would have paid them much attention.

One thing Charles would recognise from his close day-to-day experience is the quality of the soil and mud in the different areas. Particularly distinctive is the very fine clay on the Somme which forms a slippery surface after initial rain, then a glutinous mass after prolonged soaking, and a thin cracked skin when baked in the sun. I've made use of shots of the ground in the actual areas he was writing to give a feel of the conditions under which he was composing his letters (the exception being the grass background on p.260, which is from Stephen Smith's grave plot in Newbury).

A lot of the chateaus in the rear areas remain but access is not always easy. An exception to that is the Chateau d'Olhain where Charles was sent to convalesce from his lurgi in January 1916 (see p.166, and the pictures on the **following pages**). It is privately owned but opens to visitors on weekend afternoons in the summer. The parts open to the public look like they haven't changed in centuries and you are allowed to wander around poking your nose in dingy basements and up the spiral staircase into the top of the tower looking out over the large moat and the enclosed courtyard. This is one place I could imagine his presence. Despite his befuddled and weakened state I'm sure he couldn't have resisted the temptation to explore, and in the small enclosed spaces I stood where he would have stood looking at the age old graffiti and the amazing construction that gives the skeleton to the conical roof on the tower. I can imagine him having the same curiosity, and can almost hear his voice as he jokes with someone when crossing the narrow drawbridge across the moat.

Lillers — Place de la Gare

The Chateau d'Olhain. ***Above:*** the main keep surrounded by the moat, with the drawbridge to the left. ***Below left:*** the view from the main keep across the drawbridge into the courtyard. ***Below right:*** some of the graffiti covering the walls inside the central tower (which is mostly hidden behind the conical roof at the centre of the above picture, but can be seen on the old postcard on p.166). ***Opposite page:*** the framework inside this nearest conical roof (Charles would have had to stoop in here).

161 HAVERSTOCK HILL N.W.3

When looking for a picture that I could use as background for a section when Charles was on leave, I thought I'd have a look at the area around where he and Margaret used to live at 161 Haverstock Hill. Their house is no longer there (by 1935 it had been knocked down along with the neighbouring houses and the land used to put up a block of luxury flats called 'Havercourt' with a frontage onto Haverstock Hill). There is a 161 Haverstock Hill but the ground floor is an estate agent, *(bottom left)*, and it is in the area where Charles & Margaret's front garden would have been, their house having been set back from the road. In scouting around I could see a few buildings that were from their time including Belsize Park Tube Station just across the road and the old Hampstead Town Hall up the hill, but pretty much everything at ground floor level was covered in modern glass and plastic fittings. Further down the road, I spotted a post box. It had the insignia 'GR' on it so it was from one of the King Georges' eras and without further research I wasn't to know whether it was there during the First World War but I thought,

did I miss a post box nearer their house? So I went back up the road, and there it was: a post box less than 100 yards from their old front door and not only that, it had the 'VR' of Queen Victoria on it, *(left)*. This could have been the very post box in which Margaret posted her letters to Charles when he was in the trenches. It had been repainted many many times (you could see the cross-section of the layers in the places where the paint had been chipped) and with the modern label showing collection times (as well as a ripped sticker saying '*I demand a vote on the final Brexit deal*') it wasn't suitable for a picture for me to put alongside the letters in this book, but I just had to include it somewhere. It's been there for at least 119 years and seen so much change around it. In the picture, *(opposite)*, it is the oldest thing visible – the tarmac and pavement and trees and shopfronts and vehicles (and the bricks and windows of Havercourt you can glimpse through the leaves at top left) have all come in its lifetime. It has remained a constant as thousands of people have passed it by. Maybe some even still post letters in it.

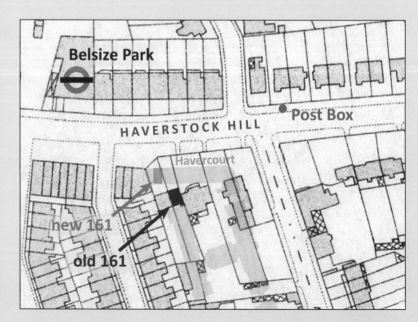

The Badminton Club closed in 1938. The building at 100 Piccadilly was taken over by the Public Schools Club. That too closed in 1972 and the building has now been converted into apartments. The decorations on the arch over the main entrance still remain including the scrolls with 'N° 100' *(above + other stonework gives the background on this page)*. The club's war memorial, *(below)*, is now on the staircase at the East India Club in St James's Square. It includes the names of Douglas Tosetti★, Douglas Hanna★ and Ronald Brakspear★ as well as Alexander Evan Fraser (the brother-in-law of Charles's sister Florrie) and Henry Caversham Simonds, cousin of the sculptor of the Maiwand Lion. Unlike for the Maiwand Lion, there are no names on Reading's civic memorial for the First World War – with the dead numbering in the thousands there were just too many to list.

BADMINTON CLUB

IN MEMORY OF THOSE WHO FELL IN THE GREAT WAR
1914 – 1918
MEMBERS

COL. H. C. SIMONDS
BERKSHIRE YEOMANRY

LT. COL. H. W. COMPTON
ROYAL FUSILIERS

COL. C. H. M. DOUGHTY WYLIE v.c.
ROYAL WELSH FUSILIERS

LT. COL. D. WOOD
RIFLE BRIGADE

MAJOR R. W. BRAKSPEAR
ROYAL BERKSHIRE REGIMENT

MAJOR A. L. GALLIE
DORSET REGIMENT

MAJOR C. W. D. LYNCH
KINGS OWN YORKSHIRE L.I.

MAJOR H. NORFOLK
WORCESTERSHIRE YEOMANRY

MAJOR D. TOSETTI M.C.
ROYAL BERKSHIRE REGIMENT

MAJOR C. O. N. WILLIAMS
K.O.R. LANCASTER REGIMENT

CAPT. A. BARNSLEY
LANCASHIRE FUSILIERS

CAPT. D. H. BRAND M.C.
SCOTS GUARDS

CAPT. W. F. DEW
BEDFORDSHIRE REGIMENT

CAPT. A. E. FRASER
MONMOUTH REGIMENT

CAPT. F. J. HADDEN
REMOUNT SERVICE

CAPT. D. M. HANNA
ROYAL BERKSHIRE REGIMENT

CAPT. G. H. HASTINGS
MIDDLESEX REGIMENT

CAPT. E. K. TAYLOR
DUKE OF WELLINGTON REGT.

LIEUT. P. W. N. FARQUARSON
ROYAL FUSILIERS

LIEUT. W. G. T. HOPE JOHNSTONE
ROYAL FUSILIERS

LIEUT. COLIN K. McGREGOR
ROYAL FIELD ARTILLERY

LIEUT. CECIL W. C. SHELLEY
SCOTS GUARDS

LIEUT. J. G. THORNE-DRURY
THE BUFFS

LIEUT. W. K. TROLLOPE
13TH SQUAD. ROYAL AIR FORCE

LIEUT. F. H. VICAT
IRISH GUARDS

LIEUT. J. N. WARD
IRISH GUARDS

STAFF

H. H. DAVIES
H.A.C.

H. GOODE
FUSILIERS

K. MORRIS
FUSILIERS

G. STRONG
RIFLE BRIGADE

Above: Yes, this really is just one picture, not two joined together. This is the side of the Prince of Wales's Theatre on the road going towards Leicester Square. Looking upwards, very little has changed in over a century but down below it's heading in the direction of *Blade Runner* as people scrabble to relieve passersby of their cash, including cheek by jowl two shops that appear to be on either side of the Brexit spectrum. Many of the theatres from Charles's day are still going strong in the same buildings with original features (including the distressed cherub that I thought was an apt illustration for Charles's leave in October 1916 (see p.342) – it is from above a doorway outside Wyndham's Theatre on Charing Cross Road).

Right: If you look below eye level you can also get a very different view. There are many long-standing features outside Cordings on Piccadilly, where gentlemen & ladies purchase their country clothing. As I tried to get an interesting shot of the name mosaic at the entrance I was treated to a parade of customers in the most unfeasibly shiny shoes.

One day, when wandering just south of Earl's Court, I found myself near Redcliffe Square, *(above)*. Remembering that that was where Charles and Margaret's friend Gracie Leigh lived during the war, I went to have a look. It was very quiet as I walked into the street and even though it was the middle of the day, the shadows from the trees and tall buildings gave it an atmosphere of a winter's evening – and then into my head, completely unbidden, came the feeling of Charles and Margaret walking towards their friend's door. I could almost hear their footsteps and their comfortable quiet chatter as they made their way together along the road. Nearly everywhere-else I've been in the world, there has been silence from the past but here I could really feel it, though frustratingly the truth behind the feeling is still elusive. Gracie lived at N° 22, whose entrance is the second covered porchway along from the left in the picture above.

I went on to have at look at Stanley Mansions where Charles and Margaret lived when they were first married, *(left)*. This was another very smart building in an affluent neighbourhood. I wonder what Charles would have made of the shop opposite that sells men's swim shorts for £135 a pair. He might have also had a wry grin at the fact that a bridalwear boutique now adjoins his old home.

These places of comfort and fine living were all a world away from the discomfort Charles had to bear during the war, firstly under canvas at Boyton Camp and then in the corrugated iron huts at Sandhill Camp (both of those camps have left no trace and are now just fields in the Wiltshire countryside).

Certainly the Grand Hôtel du Cap Martin where he was headed in his last letter (as shown on p.376) would have been more to his liking. It is still there despite having suffered a fire in 1932 and bombardment by the Italians in 1940. It closed as a hotel, though, in 1959 and is now split into apartments and even if it seems unlikely that you'd see a flagpole displaying the Union Jack anywhere in the area, the approach to it now bears the name 'Avenue Winston Churchill'.

Above: the same view as in the picture on p.376 where Margaret and Charles and the other officers are walking in line abreast on the Promenade des Anglais in Nice. The hills at the back have slightly changed shape due to the growth of trees on the top but the biggest difference (other than the use of smartphones) is the complete absence of the structure in the sea on the right of the original photo. That structure was the Palais de la Jetée, *(below)*.

Inspired by Brighton Pier, it had troubled beginnings with a fire all but destroying the original version in 1883 only 3 days after opening. Struggles to finance the rebuilding meant that it was only re-opened in 1891 but it was soon a key draw for visitors to the Côte d'Azur. It had a sad end with the German occupiers starting to strip it of useful metals in 1943 and then completely dismantling it for scrap in 1944. The little that remains is hidden beneath the waves.

Above: 23, Ruvigny Gardens (left hand door), his bolthole in Putney in the 1930s. Though it looks tiny, it is said to have 4 bedrooms and be worth £1.3 million. His final home with his second wife at 41A Putney Hill has been replaced by a block of flats.

Below: Peverel Court, where Charles Bartlett came into the world and where his ashes were scattered.

Closing Thoughts

I am still pinching myself about coming across these letters. That they should have survived through all this time when so much else has been thrown away or lost is incredible. Of course just because something exists for a long time doesn't mean that it is interesting (there are some early 19th Century letters that have been dutifully passed down through the generations of my family that are unspeakably dull), so for these letters to be so readable, so unique and so evocative of their time has been truly wonderful. On first reading I knew they were interesting but it was really only when I came to research the people Charles Bartlett knew, the places he had been and the times in which he lived that I came to fully appreciate what a portal to the past these letters are. When I've been working on the lay-out it's been like building a time machine and I hope that the result has transported you in your imagination to get a feel of what it was like living these lives in those times.

This is also, of course, a book about war. Most people living in this country today have not experienced war at first hand, and many are profoundly ignorant about its realities – that in the long-term both victors and losers experience loss that passes on through the generations, that loud words and a lack of care for humanity can quickly turn into a world war, and that world wars are no respecters of wealth or privilege. At times you may have thought that I have concentrated too much on the maiming and death and loss but in doing so I have been motivated in particular by a need to respond to what I consider to be some 'bad history'.

A few years ago I was about to give a presentation at a public school and was having a chat with one of the history masters when he said that he had recently seen something on TV where it was said that the odds of being killed in the First World War

were 'only' one in ten, which 'doesn't seem too bad'. I was stunned. As you have seen, in some cases the dead could be counted as the lucky ones – those who continued to live with mental and physical scars and with loss were the vast majority. Pure statistics applied without imagination is not a basis for learning about history (or anything else in life for that matter).

Another source of inspiration was in one of the many books that came out for the Centenary of the First World War. It talked about the rarity of men actually having to go over the top and the fact that they rotated between the front, support and reserve lines, with the implication that there was less risk if you were out of the front line. As you have read in Charles's letters, everywhere in the battle zone was in range of shell fire, and in fact those in

the support and reserve lines could often be under just as much risk as those in the front line because they had to move about doing fatigues outside the safety of their dugouts, albeit at night. The average number of British soldiers killed on the Western Front per day throughout the 1,561 days of the war was over 400, and even allowing for big spikes during the major battles, that is still a hell of a loss from everyday events in the trenches (as a comparison, during the whole time in Iraq from 2003 to 2011, there were 179 British service personnel killed). The book also bemoaned the fixation with the Western Front at the expense of other theatres and aspects of the war, but it's no wonder that the descent of civilised people into this primeval quagmire of death and horror should hold such fascination, especially with it being right on our own doorstep, as close as only 60 miles from Dover. It's not healthy to dwell on it, but we do need to remember it as a spur to do what we can to stop it happening again.

The scope of this book is wider than the battle zone but even with all the effort I've put into the research, I still feel that I have only scratched the surface of the people whose life stories are told here. Charles Bartlett has unwittingly left more of himself than most but even so there is so much that I still don't know about him – and for many people, just a few minutes of their existence could have contained more thoughts and memories than have been passed down to history from the whole of their time on Earth. There are people who are only remembered as names and dates, people who are known for just one thing (and that one thing might be the manner of their death), people who did extraordinary things against the odds, people who created beauty and life. What sort of person are you going to be? Someone who

445

has life done to them or someone who does something with life? How are you going to make your difference? I hope there is inspiration in these stories – a kick from seeing so many who have missed using the opportunities and gifts given to them, or the draw of seeing the amazing things that some people have done. No matter what your stage of life, you can do something extraordinary. The news likes to dwell on conflict and what is wrong with the world but every day human beings are doing extraordinary things to make this world a better place. You are unique. Humanity needs you. Make your unique mark.

History has a way of disappearing, or at least of staying hidden. It's amazing though what turns up when you start asking questions and go out looking – and some things can be hiding in plain sight. A classic example of this is what happened when I contacted the family of Cyril Ruff. On the face of it my reason for getting in touch was not a deep one – I'd found some photographs that the husband of Cyril's grand-daughter had posted online and hoped to get better quality versions suitable for printing, as

well as permission to use them in this book. Well, once you get two enthusiasts together, things happen and it was through Dennis and I sharing the material each of us had about Cyril and then looking through it in detail that I spotted the ancient kitchen sinks in the back of the picture on p.408 and realised their significance to Cyril and his family. And it wasn't just that. Dennis's sister-in-law, Cyril's other grand-daughter, had three of the sinks in her garden, still filled with alpine plants (as **below**). She had inherited them from her Dad and just saw them as garden ornaments. It was only when I shared the interview with Cyril I'd found in the newspaper that she realised the deeper significance, that these were things that her grandfather had loved and even though he died before she was born, there was something of him with her she saw every day without even realising.

The familiar often holds hidden depths because it has always been around us – we assume we know all about it and that it will always be there and so often the questions don't get asked and the deeper truths go unfound. That not only applies to objects but also to people and long-held beliefs. It

is only by asking questions and listening to the answers that we can get closer to the truth and make progress as human beings.

The red rose at the *centre of the previous page* is growing next to the grave of Clive Radford, in a war cemetery just behind the Loos battlefield at Vermelles. When the next Centenary of the First World War comes will there still be flowers on these graves? Or will there have been another conflict to swamp our memories? Maybe this generation could even be remembered for a change in the direction for humankind. Most people in every country are good people who want an easy life in the face of the difficulties and mysteries of existence. As George Eliot put it so well, *'What do we live for, if it is not to make life less difficult for each other?'* Charles Bartlett was certainly no saint and there is much from his life not to follow as an example but when I think of that quote I can't help but think of his kindnesses even in the midst of his own worries and difficulties in late 1915: buying fish for the nursing sisters in the hospital, and sending money to my grandmother in the hour of her despair.

Index of People

This index, as well as being a way of looking up individual names, is also a place for further details about some people. These notes give an idea of how it all works:

- I've tried to include every person mentioned in this book, even if I haven't been able to fully identify them.

- The birth and death dates are given for all where known.

- People have been grouped together in families (except for some major characters, like relations of Charles and Margaret, who have separate entries). In the main text this has enabled me to refer to someone just by their relationship (e.g. father) without breaking the flow with their name. You can also relate the details of different members of the family together in one place.

- Not all children or siblings in families are included, usually just those mentioned in the text.

- If someone is referred to in a letter by only their first name or nickname, that name is listed here with a reference to be able to find their surname in the index (if known).

- Bracketed first names implies that those names were not used (e.g. (Douglas) Eric Foot was known as Eric).

- If you'd like further information or sources about anyone mentioned here please email andrew@groupphoto.co.uk.

ABBREVIATIONS AND CODES:

c = precedes a date that is within a year either side of that given (i.e. the date is worked out from a census or an index where it is certain that it is them and I have decided not to spend the money on a certificate to get an exact date)

b = there is some biographical information about that person in a note on that page number

p = there is a picture of that person on that page number

☒ = I have not been able to fully identify that person

surname = a surname (e.g. a maiden name) which is listed under the main person to whom it is related (these surnames also appear in the index with a pointer to the main person under whose entry they appear)

details = further bits of information about individuals that I thought deserved to be included even though there was not space in the main text of the book

★ = the man is in my original Group Photograph and further details about them can be found in my first book or via www.groupphoto.co.uk/background, with their family tree drawing being accessible via:
www.groupphoto.co.uk/extra

COUNTY CRICKETERS.

MR. G. G. NAPIER.
MIDDLESEX.

Index of Subjects and Events

This index is not exhaustive for every mention of every subject and event. Most locations & army units are not included as I thought that would only be of interest to a small percentage of readers and the resulting index would have added too many pages to an already big book. Instead it concentrates on particularly significant items, and then in most cases points to where that item is discussed in some detail or appears in a picture ('p' then follows the page number).

Thanks

Before I thank anyone-else, my huge gratitude goes to the Bartlett family. Firstly to Charles Bartlett's wife ★Margaret for keeping all the letters and passing them down to her daughter ★Paula who in turn kept them and passed them down to her daughter. After all the bitterness of the divorce, they could have been forgiven for throwing away every reminder of him. I'm glad they recognised the value of the letters and kept them for posterity. Charles's grand-daughter ★Gay was incredibly generous in sharing what she had with me and I am grateful for her trust in letting me take the letters away to study them in detail and her support without which this book would have been impossible. Charles's grandsons ★Iain and ★Hugh likewise shared their parts of the family archive and showed themselves to be 'damn fine hosts' in the Bartlett tradition, as did their cousins ★Tony and ★Julian who along with their mother ★Margaret and aunt ★Kit helped me find Charles's descendants. Other important information came from cousin ★Margaret and Charles's second wife's niece ★Joan.

The long list of people I thanked in my first book are of course responsible for so much that has made this book possible. My heartfelt thanks to them all again. Certain of them deserve special repeat mentions for how they have helped with this book and I shall name them again. My parents ★Ben and ★Sue Tatham have enabled me to work full-time on this through their incredible generosity. In addition my parents have supported me utterly in my work and my mother has been a valuable sounding board on Skype as well as being one of my first readers. My cousin ★Val Barr's generosity has also played a huge part in making this book. ★Paul Ebdon has been with me every step of the way, always asking me how it is going and sharing the joy with each extraordinary new discovery as well as providing solace and some obscure film to watch when the going was treacly. He was also brave enough to tell me, with the encouragement and equally perceptive eye of ★Alan Schmidt, that I was making a grave mistake in my initial plan to produce the book in black-and-white. That was being done for what I thought were sound economic reasons but in the end I realised that the result would have been poor by comparison with the richness that full colour brings. Everyone needs friends who are not afraid to tell you the truth even in the face of someone as stubborn as me. ★Jan Campbell picked up the pieces after that discussion and helped me back to equilibrium so that I was able to recognise the truth of what I was being told and carry on anew. ★Tess Berlein has been a lovely true friend and a constant source of boost and perspective even though so many miles away. ★Patrick Miles has been a force of nature, pushing to bring my work to wider notice and being consistently persistent in his encouragement despite all that has been going on with his own book *'George Calderon: Edwardian Genius'*, www.patrickmileswriter.co.uk. In the last year and a half of editing and development I have been sustained by the memory of his response to reading this book – he asked to confirm whether he was the first person to read it in its entirety because he thought his descendants would be proud as he felt sure it would become a classic – and I can say that, yes, he was the first, and I couldn't have wished for a better response from a first reader.

★William Boyd went out of his way to pick my first book as one of his Best Books of 2016 in *The Guardian*. Episodes in his writing still remind me that anything is possible, and that he should agree to write the Foreword to this book is further proof of that.

★Ian Beckett replied when I made an enquiry via the website of the ◆Buckinghamshire Military Museum, www.bmmt.co.uk, and, as well as expert advice, pointed me to a militia photograph album with pictures of Charles Bartlett and his brother that I missed in my initial project research. That would have been enough for my huge gratitude but he then took things to another level by agreeing to pass his expert eye over the whole thing and gave me such a short list of suggested corrections as to really boost my confidence.

★Peter Parker, ★Ian Hislop, and ★John Carey took the time to respond and give me encouragement. ★Richard Van Emden gave me feedback that led to improvements in the final product.

★Sir Michael Morpurgo surprised me by not only finding time to read the book but by giving me three words that showed how much it had meant to him and could mean to other people and which I have put on the front cover.

★Helen Tovey, Editor of *Family Tree* Magazine, read and fed me with her infectious energy and enthusiasm.

Friends who have given particular cheerleading and the right words when I've needed encouragement are: ★Tony Ball, ★Claire Berlein, ★Jacob Carr, ★Laura Carroll, ★David Farmer, ★Tania Holland Williams, ★Mandy Huntridge, ★Jillian Lemmond, ★Fi Maccallum, ★Alison Miles, ★Steve Morriss, ★Anne Müller, ★Vanessa Watkins, ★Sally Webster, ★Alison Wood, and my sister ★Jenny James.

The success of my exhibition and first book have been the springboard to my work on this one. Good ideas are nothing without people who can help turn them into reality and bring them to wider notice: ★Piet Chielens at the ◆In Flanders Fields Museum in Ypres could teach a lot of other gallery and museum heads the value of being open to new ideas and outside contributors. Without his interest and backing I would still be at Square One. ★Manu Veracx's lay-out of my first book has rightly attracted plaudits and I'm grateful for the learning on the job first time around that has helped me now in the design of this book (though I doubt I have reached his high standards!). ★Melvyn Bragg, despite his busyness in all walks of cultural life, gave me my first magnificent review when I was at a very low ebb and sparked all that followed. My friend ★Helen Mitchell introduced me to ★Jeremy Vine, and he and his researcher ★Tom Bigwood believed in me enough to invite me onto his show and start the avalanche. I will forever be grateful to them and for the generosity of Jeremy's listeners. ★Jane Kinnear saw my eyes like saucers as the avalanche bore down on me. Being considerably more business-like than me, and with the right contacts, she stepped in to get a grip and enable me to ride it out successfully.

There are some people who were instrumental at the beginning of the research that went into this book and who I haven't publicly thanked before: my sixth cousin ★Susan Pyne-James picked me up at the airport in Johannesburg and handed me the phone book that led me to Charles's family, as well as providing a base for my research in South Africa. ★Martin and ★Kate Cox allowed me time off from my baby-sitting duties and gave me use of their photocopier for the three days it took me to make my first copies of the letters. ★Mary Douglas, ★Richard Mayo, and ★John Reynolds put me up during the Ontario leg of my research into Peter McGibbon.

To document all the sources for every bit of information in this book would probably require as many pages again, and given that most people wouldn't read that and I want to keep the book affordable, I'm going to limit what I write here to naming general sources and say that I'm open to sharing what I've got if you email me via andrew@groupphoto.co.uk. Major sources have been:

◈The Wardrobe, the Regimental Museum of the Royal Berkshire Regiment in Salisbury, www.thewardrobe.org.uk, in particular ★Simon Cook, ★Mac McIntyre, ★Michael Cornwell, ★Alistair Riggs, ★Bethany Joyce and all the volunteers who have worked so hard to digitise their collection. Not only are there the Royal Berkshire battalions' war diaries but also a database of pictures and objects fully searchable by names that has enabled me to find so many of the pictures for this book, including nine pictures of Charles Bartlett from his pre-war regular service that I missed during my initial project research. This book would have been hugely poorer but for their efforts and assistance.

◈The National Archives in Kew, still my favourite archive and again it has provided me with access to essential material. ★William Spencer was a great help in answering my queries about courts martial and finding records of discharge from the Army.

◈Ancestry, www.ancestry.co.uk, as well as giving access to many digitised sources also has the most used online facility for hosting people's family trees, enabling me to see if my research fitted with theirs or find items not easily found through normal searching (e.g. they may have found a way round a transcription error) or to contact them to ask questions.

◈FindMyPast, www.findmypast.co.uk, as well as having other digitised sources (often easier to search and with more accurate transcriptions than Ancestry) also included access to the British Newspaper Archive in my subscription. Making old newspapers searchable and readable has been the single greatest advance in family history research in recent times, giving clues about things invisible in the official records as well as telling stories that bring people alive (though one has got to be careful, given the lax fact-checking of a lot of journalists throughout history).

◈Norfolk Library Service gave me access to ◈The Times online archive, the Oxford Dictionary of National Biography, etc, etc.

◈www.longlongtrail.co.uk: ★Chris Baker has dedicated himself to making available information on every aspect of the First World War & his was the go-to site when I wanted to find an explanation or some arcane detail related to the British Army in the war.

◈Wikipedia, ◈Internet Archive, ◈National Library of Scotland.

I have made use of much material from the families contacted in my initial project research but there are some individuals who have helped me in connection with the biographical research for this book who deserve special mention: ★John Cloake gave me permission to quote from the memoirs of his grandfather Cecil Cloake★ and use his photographs and memorabilia, including many of the maps that are in this book. ★Brian Berlein let me photograph the entire contents of the two trunks of his late great uncles' belongings and use some of those images as illustrations. Eric Foot★'s family, ★Donald, ★Pamela, ★Simon and ★Sascha, invited me to accompany them on their Centenary pilgrimage to the site of Eric's disappearance and allowed me to take photographs. ★Inez Ross made a generous contribution (and not only of her trademark enthusiasm) in order to help me remember her beloved aunt and uncle, Mabel and Peter McGibbon.

★Dennis Goodman posted lots of material online about his wife's grandfather Cyril Ruff and then bent over backwards to enable me to tell one of the more heart-warming stories in the book, including allowing me to use his picture of the sink full of flowers on p.446, and sourcing the picture of Cyril's shop with the help of ★Alan Warr and ★Tony, son of Smethwick photographer ★Joe Russell.

It is not always easy contacting new people about the painful past but ★Michael & ★Flic Kingerlee welcomed me & made it possible for me to tell the most poignantly uplifting story in this book.

Other helpers with research into individual biographies have been: ★Michael Anstey, ★Matthew Armstrong-Harris, ★Anne Boyd-Skinner, ★Bob Boyer, ★Irva Caldwell, ★Pauline Carpenter, ★Alex Conyers, ★Charles Cook, ★Felicity & ★Kate Fenner, ★Ruth Gavin, ★Tony Girdler, ★James Horn, ★Bernard Ince, ★Stephanie Jenkins, ★Pierre Lecocq, ★David Lyall, ★Jenny Moon, ★Naomi Moris, ★Hilary Munro, ★Peter Newdick, ★Cathy Nicholson, ★Neill Patterson, ★Morton Peto, ★James Pitt, ★Ann Rexe, ★Ken Rhoades, ★Lindsey Scaife, ★Debbie Scott, ★Pat Sheehan, ★Liz Tait, ★Julie-Ann Vickers, ★Debby Was, ★Robert & ★Elizabeth Webber.

A lot of people got in touch with me about my first book. I'm grateful to them all but I'm going to pick out a few who have given particularly appreciated encouragement recently: ★Ann Crichton-Harris, ★Betsy Langford, ★Barbara Picknell.

Assistance with researching the Bartlett family in Buckinghamshire: ★Edward Grimsdale and ★Warren Whyte of the ◈Buckingham Society. ★Carole Fryer and ★George C Lamb in Stone. The staff at ◈Bartlett's Residential Care Home. The staff at ◈University of Buckingham who let me photograph the Bartlett tombs from an upper storey window.

Researching Bethell Robinson: ★Michael Barrett (I can recommend his graphic novel 'Preston North End – The Rise Of The Invincibles' in which Bethell features), ★Ian Rigby (◈Preston North End Football Club historian), ★Peter Holme (◈National Football Museum), and ★Simon Marland (◈Bolton Wanderers Football Club).

Others connected with particular organisations or websites who helped me with my research: ★Julie Somay at the ◈Commonwealth War Graves Commission. ★Valerie Harris at ◈St Giles' Church in Reading. ★Steven John of the ◈West Wales War Memorial Project www.wwwmp.co.uk. ★Fiona at the library of

◆The Institute of Chartered Accountants in England and Wales (ICAEW). ★Rusty MacLean at ◆Rugby School Archive. ★Colin Green of ◆oxfordandbucks.co.uk for the photo of Charles's brother Alfred on p.386. ★Will Bosworth at ◆*The Ringing World*, www.ringingworld.co.uk. ★Roddy Hay, ★Robert Jack & ★Gerry McArdle at the ◆Ministry of Defence. ★Gilles Payen at ◆Musée Alexandre Villedieu in Loos-en-Gohelle. ★Alison Child, www.behindthelines.info, shared from her extensive research into Basil Hallam and gave advice and encouragement. ★Mark Brockway was a contact via ◆www.greatwarforum.org and he very kindly shared with me his extensive research into Gerald Dalby including the photograph on p.136. ★Richard Ritchie of the ◆Old Stagers in Canterbury, www.oldstagers.com. ★Ian Castle's website about the Zeppelin raids was a mine of information www.iancastlezeppelin.co.uk. ★Safina Valiji at ◆Greene's Estate Agents, at 161, Haverstock Hill.

A huge contribution to this book has been made by so many people who have shared their information online, whether posting their family trees on Ancestry, or discussing their interests on message boards or in their personal websites and giving me ideas of sources for information. I'm sorry not to list you all but I am enormously grateful & in the original spirit of the Internet I will freely share any information I am asked for in relation to my research for this book.

Assistance with the process of book production has come from: ◆Dropbox giving me peace of mind by backing up all my work and enabling me to recover old versions of files, ★David Blatner sharing online InDesign advice, and ★Mat Canham and ★Rob Gutteridge at ◆Healeys Printers steering me through all the options and turning my dreams into the reality of what you hold in your hands.

PICTURE CREDITS:

Copyright is an absolute nightmare to sort out, especially when working on my own on such a big project. I do not claim any rights by publishing pictures in this book and my overriding motive is to help people learn from the past (believe me, if I was out to make vast profits I would not have chosen this line of work!). As far as possible I have aimed to use photographs that are out of copyright, making particular use of old publications like *'The War Illustrated'*, *'Berkshire & The War'* and *'The Play Pictorial'* as well as a lot of my own pictures and vintage postcards that I have bought. Permissions for more recent photographs of particular individuals have come from the relevant families. Please get in touch with me via andrew@groupphoto.co.uk if you have any copyright queries relating to material in this book.

Certain pictures require special mention, grouped by each particular source but listed by the page number of the first item from that source:

p.15: Peverel Court – ◆Peverel Court Care (owners of Bartlett's Residential Care Home) (thanks to ★Sophie Lamont).

p.17: two close-ups of Charles Bartlett. *p.62:* Edward Bartlett. *p.404:* officers group for Rose Family – were all in a Royal Bucks (King's Own) Militia album from the ◆Centre for Buckinghamshire Studies collection (thanks to ★Chris Low & ★Katherine Gwyn).

p.28: The White Hart Hotel – ◆Reading Central Library (thanks to ★Katie Amos)

p.72: Portrait of General Holland. *p.296:* Portrait of General Pulteney – drawings by Francis Dodd *(1874-1949)*, from *'Generals of the British Army'* published in three parts in 1917-18 by *Country Life* magazine.

p.80-81: Bayonet – ★Jon at Jaybe Militaria, www.jaybe-militaria.co.uk.

p.82: A particularly unique photo taken by an unknown soldier of the London Rifle Brigade on the first day of the Battle of Loos.

p.90: The Vickers machinegunner depicted is Pte Jackie Lynn who during the 2nd Battle of Ypres kept firing despite having no respirator – he died from gas inhalation the next day and was posthumously awarded the Victoria Cross (from *The War Illustrated*).

p.140: General Crutchley. *p.183:* Generals Rycroft and Perceval – photographed by Walter Stoneman *(1876-1958)*. *p.267:* General Strickland photographed by Bassano Studio – © National Portrait Gallery, London.

p.146: Ten shilling note – ★Jeff at A.D. Hamilton and Co, www.adhamilton.co.uk.

p.187: Mills bomb – ★Jean-Louis Dubois via Creative Commons CC-BY-SA-3.0.

p.208: Loos Church ruins; *p.220:* Double Crassier; *p.229:* Tower Bridge – ★Paul Reed, battlefields1418.50megs.com/loos_photos.htm.

p.211: The French Croix de Guerre pictured here is actually that of Gerald Robinson ★ from the Group Photograph.

p.225: Portrait of Henry Lewin by Philip de László *(1869-1937)*.

p.239: 'Birth of the Irish Republic' painting by Walter Stanley Paget *(1862-1935)* (he was said to be the model for the original drawings of Sherlock Holmes by his brother).

p.259: Aerial photo of Cité Calonne. *p.306-7:* Aerial photo of Bazentin-le-Petit. – © IWM.

p.304: Colonel Collison – from ◆Royal Regiment of Fusiliers Museum (Royal Warwickshire), www.warwickfusiliers.co.uk (thanks to ★Stephanie Bennett).

p.352: Nissen huts by John Lord *(1896-1951)*, via Museums Victoria, collections.museumvictoria.com.au/items/1706363.

p.369: portrait of Lady Michelham by Giovanni Boldini *(1842-1931)*.

p.404: Preston North End team photograph – ◆National Football Museum/Ian Rigby.

FINALLY:

Thank you to Charles Bartlett. He may be in the afterlife but he has been my constant companion for much of the last three years. I shall miss him, though I have a feeling he shall be in my life for a while yet.

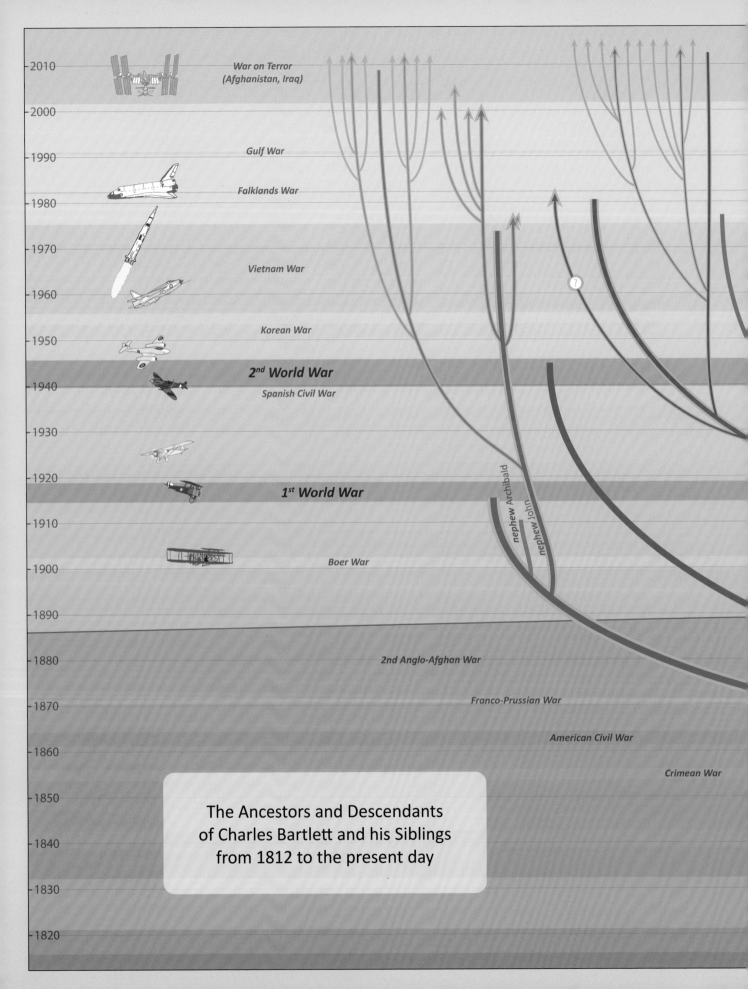

The Ancestors and Descendants
of Charles Bartlett and his Siblings
from 1812 to the present day

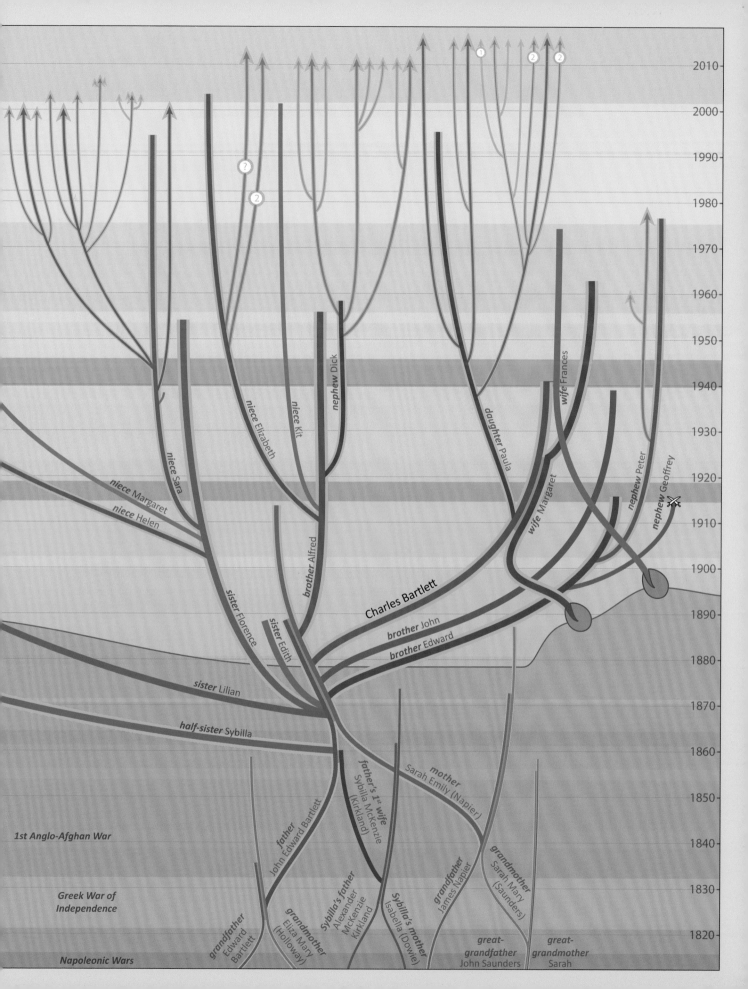

niece Margaret

niece Helen

niece Sara

niece Elizabeth

niece Kit

nephew Dick

sister Florence

sister Edith

brother Alfred

Charles Bartlett

brother John

brother Edward

sister Lilian

half-sister Sybilla

daughter Paula

wife Frances

wife Margaret

nephew Peter

nephew Geoffrey

mother
Sarah Emily (Napier)

father's 1st wife
Sybilla McKenzie
(Kirkland)

father
John Edward Bartlett

grandfather
Edward
Bartlett

grandmother
Eliza Mary
(Holloway)

Sybilla's father
Alexander
McKenzie
Kirkland

Sybilla's mother
Isabella (Dowie)

grandfather
James Napier

grandmother
Sarah Mary
(Saunders)

great-
grandfather
John Saunders

great-
grandmother
Sarah

1st Anglo-Afghan War

Greek War of
Independence

Napoleonic Wars

2010

2000

1990

1980

1970

1960

1950

1940

1930

1920

1910

1900

1890

1880

1870

1860

1850

1840

1830

1820

'A Group Photograph, Before, Now & In-Between'

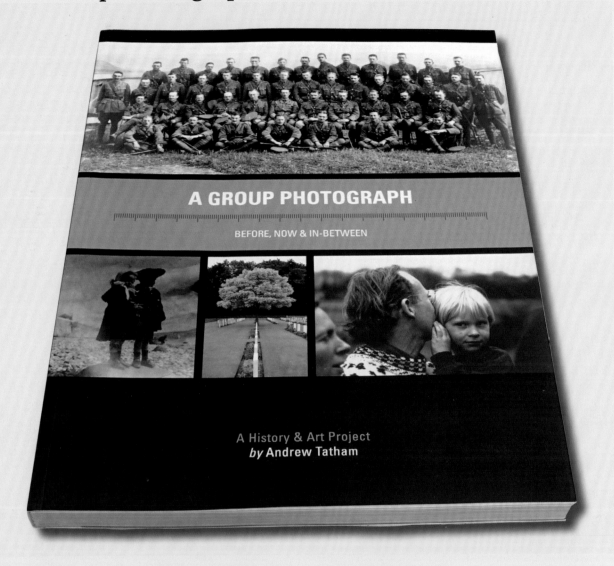

Available from www.groupphoto.co.uk
or by order from your local bookshop